Arkansas Gazette: *The Early Years 1819-1866*

Artist's conception of William E. Woodruff
on the last lap of his trip to
Arkansas Post in 1819.

Arkansas Gazette

The Early Years 1819-1866

A History

by MARGARET ROSS

ARKANSAS GAZETTE FOUNDATION

LITTLE ROCK : 1969

Designed, printed and bound in the United States of America by
The Lakeside Press, R. R. Donnelley & Sons Company
Chicago, Illinois, and Crawfordsville, Indiana

Foreword

THE PAGES of this history tell the story of a newspaper and the related story of a Territory and a State. One could not be told without the other, because the newspaper wrote a continuous record of events, and discussed through the changing years the issues that filled chapters in the annals of Arkansas.

The fierce politics of the times brought hours of tension and sometimes of actual danger. Duels, which William E. Woodruff had the moral courage to decline to have part in, robbed the state of men of prominence, ability and capacity for usefulness.

In writing this book Margaret Ross has done an invaluable service to Arkansas history. Neither time nor labor has been spared in effort to obtain essential information from authoritative sources. She has examined, page by page, the files of the *Arkansas Gazette* and of other Arkansas newspapers; has consulted books, read letters and other documents, searched courthouse records, and always been on guard against errors that have infiltrated Arkansas history.

This volume brings the story of the *Gazette* into the year 1866, when the paper came under the able and progressive management of William E. Woodruff, Jr., who might indeed be called its second founder.

J. N. HEISKELL,
Editor, *Arkansas Gazette*

v

Preface

TO THE MANY PEOPLE who have said that if I should write a good history of the *Arkansas Gazette,* it would be the equivalent of a history of Arkansas, I have always replied, "Not if I stick to my subject."

The skeleton of the *Gazette's* story is a record of the changes in proprietors, staff, mechanical equipment, and format. To tell this and no more would make it possible to have a history of the *Gazette's* entire career in one volume in time for its 150th anniversary. But the development of the *Gazette* has been contingent upon the development of the state it has served, and politics and the *Gazette* have been important to each other. To exclude these subjects would be to rob the story of all meaning, and to deny the *Gazette* its unique niche in Arkansas history. Therefore, the story is somewhere between that superficial skeleton and the definitive history of the state that some readers might expect.

The *Gazette* is the undisputed heroine of this book, and I do not pretend to have given thorough treatment to any other subject. If I have written an acceptable history of the *Gazette,* I shall be more than satisfied, and whatever value the book may have in other areas is lagniappe. To readers who are disappointed by my failure to include some event of importance, I can only say that I had to consider its influence on the *Gazette* rather than its impact on the state as a whole.

A remark I have heard too often is, "A complete history of Arkansas could be written from the *Gazette* files alone." The fact is that a history of the *Gazette* itself cannot be written from its files alone, much less a history of the state, but certainly there are few subjects in Arkansas history that can be written satisfactorily without reference to the *Gazette's* files.

This volume ends with the end of an era, both in politics and in journalism. Just as the people of the South laid aside their old way of life in the aftermath of the Civil War, so also did American newspapers make drastic changes in the conduct of their business. The next volume will trace the evolution of the *Gazette* from a small but powerful country weekly to a metropolitan daily.

So far as journalistic excellance is concerned, the *Gazette* has led the field in Arkansas during most of her long career. This is partly because no other paper could equal her coverage of Arkansas news unless it was published at the capital city. There have been other newspapers that could outshine her briefly, but none that could both outshine and outlive her.

Her durability is not necessarily attributable to her excellence, for many a paper of equal merit did not survive. Certainly it is not because the people loved her, for there have been many times when she also led the field in unpopularity. Nor is it a matter of able business management, for some of her proprietors took her so far downhill financially that only the tireless exertions of a new owner miraculously saved her from oblivion.

The thesis that virtue invariably triumphs is for the story books. Fictional characters may be all good or all bad, but flesh-and-blood people are found to be a little of both, when the veneer of a century of eulogies is peeled away. It goes without saying that the men who guided the destiny of the *Gazette* and the politicians who figured in her story were not exceptions. Since the *Gazette* has been dependent upon fallible mortals, she also was sometimes good and sometimes bad and sometimes a strange mixture of both. She has been often on the "right" side, but she also has been on what time proved to be the wrong side.

My thanks are due to J. N. Heiskell, senior editor of the *Gazette* since 1902, whose collection of Arkansas historical material has supplied most of my source material, and whose continued interest in this book has sustained me throughout the long project. His advice was frequently sought and freely given, and was invariably worth heeding, but never once did he fail to leave me free to make my own interpretations.

The same is true of Hugh B. Patterson, Jr., publisher of the *Gazette,* who not only solved many of the problems connected with writing this book, but also took care of the details of its publication. To his brother, Ralph Patterson, art director of *Nation's Business* and an authority on typography, go my thanks and appreciation for many valuable suggestions pertaining to the design of the book.

Jack Graham and A. L. Scruggs, veteran employees in the *Gazette's* composing room, cheerfully took time from their work to measure type and column widths and to answer numerous questions about the mechanical department of the paper. Most of the photographic work was done by Larry Obsitnik, the *Gazette's* chief of photography, and others of his staff.

Dr. John L. Ferguson, executive secretary of the Arkansas History Commission, went out of his way to make material in his custody easily available and to supply microfilm files of other Arkansas newspapers. Ernie Deane, a member of the *Gazette's* staff for ten years and now a member of the journalism faculty at the University of Arkansas, read a part of the manuscript and made some helpful suggestions.

To David W. Bizzell, a deputy county clerk of Pulaski County, go my heartfelt thanks for assistance far beyond the call of duty. No other person is as thoroughly familiar with the old records of Pulaski County as he, and he not only quickly located every record I called for, but dug out other obscure records I did not dream existed.

I am also indebted to the efficient staffs of the Arkansas History Commission, the Tennessee State Library and Archives at Nashville, the Louisiana State Library at New Orleans, the Arkansas County Court House at DeWitt, the Pulaski County Court House at Little Rock, and the Williamson County Court House at Franklin, Tennessee.

MARGARET ROSS

Contents

FOREWORD   v

PREFACE   vii

CHAPTER

1. FROM PRINTER'S DEVIL TO EDITOR   3

2. THE PRESS IN THE WILDERNESS   19
   Arkansas Post, 1819-1821

3. THE CALM BEFORE THE STORM   43
   Little Rock, 1821-1826

4. THE TURNING POINT   69
   1827

5. COMPETITION AND CONTROVERSY   87
   1828-1832

6. LAST DAYS OF THE TERRITORY   105
   1833-1836

7. THOMAS JEFFERSON PEW   135
   1836-1838

8. EDWARD COLE   161
   1838-1840

9. GEORGE H. BURNETT   175
   1840-1841

10. WOODRUFF AND WELLER   181
    1841-1843

11. BENJAMIN J. BORDEN   195
    1843-1845

12. BENJAMIN J. BORDEN   215
    1845-1848

13. GEORGE B. HAYDEN 245
    1848-1850

14. WILLIAM E. WOODRUFF 271
    1850-1853

15. KNOW NOTHINGISM 299
    1853-1859

16. THE ROAD TO SECESSION 337
    1859-1861

17. THE CIVIL WAR 357
    1861-1865

18. DANLEY AND HOLTZMAN 395
    1865-1866

    BIBLIOGRAPHY 403

    INDEX 411

Arkansas Gazette: *The Early Years 1819-1866*

1

FROM PRINTER'S DEVIL TO EDITOR

TWO YOUNG MEN trudged wearily down the dusty road. Behind them lay the
bustling city of Louisville, which they had found dirty, unhealthful, and unfriendly. Ahead was Nashville, where they hoped to find opportunities worthy
of their talents. In knapsacks slung over their shoulders they carried a few articles of clothing and enough food to sustain them on the long, lonesome
stretches between the log cabins that received strangers hospitably. In their
pockets were their apprenticeship indentures, written long ago, and but recently endorsed by their masters to proclaim to the world that they were full-
fledged journeyman printers.

William E. Woodruff was sure he would never possess a more valuable
document. He had invested six years in it, but it was worth it. It would get him
a job in any printing office in the country that could afford to hire him, and
the training it represented would allow him to realize the ambition he had
long cherished.

It was a modest, practical ambition, involving neither wealth nor fame.
All he wanted was a small printing office of his own, where a combination of
newspaper publication and job printing could provide him a comfortable
living. Given the right location, the dream could begin to materialize with
the purchase of a second-hand press and a set of used type, perhaps for as
little as $100 in this depression year of 1818.

His companion, Henry Van Pelt, had a similar background and the same
dream of the future. Realizing that more newspapers founded in this period
had ephemeral existence than permanent prosperity, they dared to hope that
theirs would survive the rigors of the current financial panic and live to support the families they would have some day. They would have walked more
briskly down this dusty road to success if they could have known that both
would establish great newspapers that would prosper long after they had gone
to their graves.

Woodruff's first step towards journalistic immortality, the founding of the

3

Arkansas Gazette, was only a year away. He would live to a ripe old age, widely acclaimed by his brother printers as "the father of Arkansas journalism." Van Pelt would see 23 years and two failures pass before he would found the Memphis *Appeal,* now the *Commercial Appeal.* He would be honored as "the father of Memphis journalism," but he would not live to hear it.[1]

* * * * *

On a small farm at Fire Place, Suffolk County, Long Island, New York, on December 24, 1795, Hannah Clarke Woodruff gave birth to the first of her five sons, William Edward Woodruff. After pneumonia swept her husband, Nathaniel Woodruff, to a premature grave on June 12, 1808, Hannah took her five little boys to live with her mother at nearby Brookhaven.[2]

Upon the advice of Dr. Isaac Miller, an influential friend and neighbor,[3] William was bound as an apprentice on October 18, 1810 to Alden Spooner, a Sag Harbor printer who published the *Suffolk Gazette.*[4] The apprenticeship was interrupted on February 23, 1811 when the *Suffolk Gazette* suspended publication, but was resumed on June 5, 1811 when Spooner became the proprietor of the *Long-Island Star* at Brooklyn.[5] Among his boyhood friends at Brooklyn were John and James Harper, who were then serving apprenticeships and who later founded the famous publishing firm of Harper and Brothers,[6] and B. L. E. Bonneville, whom he would meet again in Arkansas, and whose military career he followed with interest.[7]

1. Several other newspapers preceded the *Appeal* at Memphis, but were short lived. See "Address of Judge Q. K. Underwood, Before the Old Folks, April 2, 1872," *Old Folks' Historical Record,* I, (Memphis: R. C. Hite, 1875), 531–536. Van Pelt lived at Franklin, Tennessee from 1818 or 1819 until at least as late as 1836. (Williamson County, Tennessee Deed Book J, 221; K, 163, 569; M, 492; N, 228, 432.) Besides the Franklin *Monitor* of his first year's residence there, he was the editor and proprietor of the *Western Balance,* published at Franklin for several years, beginning in the spring of 1825. According to Van Pelt's obituary in the *Appeal* of April 24, 1851, he was born in Kentucky about 1797, began his newspaper career in Kentucky, founded the *Appeal* on April 21, 1841, and died at Memphis on April 23, 1851. See *Arkansas Gazette,* May 2, 1851; *Republican Banner and Nashville* (Tenn.) *Whig,* Apr. 28, 1851. Henry Lewis Bullen, "The First Printing Outfit of the Arkansas Gazette," *Arkansas Gazette Supplement Commemorating the Founding of Arkansas' First Newspaper 1819–1919* (Little Rock, Nov. 20, 1919), 38, says Van Pelt was from New York.
2. The four brothers were Matthew Edmund, George Brown, Nathaniel Milton, and Jehiel Hildreth. See Family Bible of Hannah Clarke Woodruff, Arkansas History Commission, Little Rock; Jane Georgine Woodruff, "William E. Woodruff as Remembered by His Three Daughters," *Gazette Supplement,* Nov. 20, 1919, 28.
3. *Gazette,* June 20, 1885.
4. The original apprenticeship indenture is in the William E. Woodruff Papers, Arkansas History Commission, and is quoted in Dallas T. Herndon, "History of the Arkansas Gazette," *Gazette Supplement,* Nov. 20, 1919, 5.
5. Clarence S. Brigham, *History and Bibliography of American Newspapers 1690–1820* (Worcester, Mass.: American Antiquarian Society, 1947), I, 555–556, 731.
6. *Gazette,* Apr. 25, 1875; June 20, 1885.
7. *Ibid.,* Sept. 22, 1868; Mar. 11, 1877; June 20, 1885.

THIS INDENTURE made the *eighteenth*
day of *October* in the year of our LORD *one thousand eight*
hundred and ten WITNESSETH, that *William E. Woodruff*
aged *fourteen years nine months and twenty four days*
by and with the consent of *Hannah Woodruff* his *Mother*
of *Brookhaven* hath, of his own free and voluntary will,
placed and bound himself apprentice unto *Alden Spooner*
of *Sag Harbor* to learn the trade, mystery or occupation of a *Printer* which he the said
Alden Spooner now useth ; and with him as an apprentice to
dwell, continue and serve from the day of the date hereof, unto the full end and term of *six*
years, two months & six days from thence next ensuing, and
fully to be complete and ended ; during all which term of *six years two months*
and six days the said apprentice his said master well and faithfully
shall serve, his secrets keep, his lawful commands gladly do and obey ; hurt to his said master he
shall not do, nor wilfully suffer it to be done by others, but of the same, to the utmost of his
power, shall forthwith give notice to his said master ; the goods of his said master he shall not
embezzle or waste, nor them lend, without his consent, to any ; at cards, dice, or any other un-
lawful games, he shall not play, taverns or ale-houses he shall not frequent ; fornication he shall
not commit, matrimony he shall not contract ; from the service of his said master he shall not at
any time depart or absent himself, without his said master's leave ; but in all things, as a good
and faithful apprentice, shall and will demean and behave himself towards his said master, and
all his, during the said term. And the said master, in consideration of *the faithful*
service of the said Apprentice
in the said trade, mystery, or occupation of a *Printer,*
which he now useth, with all things thereunto belonging, shall and will teach, instruct, or cause
to be well and sufficiently taught and instructed, after the best way and manner he can—and
shall and will to find and allow unto his said apprentice, meat, drink, washing, lodging, *and*
twenty Dollars per annum during the abovementioned
term, and also two quarters schooling at an Evening
School & the mending of his clothes. The above
sum in two half yearly payments
In Witness whereof, we have hereunto set our and seals, this *eighteenth*
day of *October,* in the year of our Lord, one thousand eight hundred
and *ten.*
Signed, Sealed, and delivered }
in presence of }

Hannah Woodruff

Alden Spooner

Betty Latham

Mary Flores *William E. Woodruff*

William E. Woodruff's apprenticeship indenture,
now owned by the Arkansas History Commission.

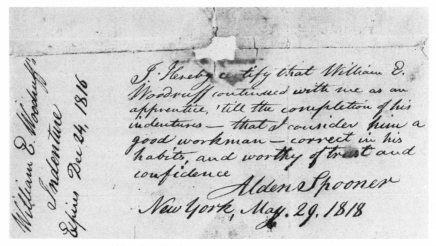

Alden Spooner's endorsement on the back of
Woodruff's apprenticeship indenture.

The War of 1812 did not take Woodruff out of the printing office, for although he enlisted in Captain Brower's heavy artillery company in defense of the city in 1814, he was not called to active duty.[8]

During Spooner's protracted absence of this period, management of the *Star* office was entrusted to the 19-year-old Woodruff.[9] It was a rare opportunity for him to gain valuable experience, for it was not often that anyone other than the proprietor-editor was privileged to conduct the business of a newspaper office outside the mechanical department.

His indenture ended with his 21st birthday on Christmas Eve, 1816,[10] and he worked as a journeyman for T. & J. Swords and for George Bruce in New York until the spring of 1818.[11] Then he was ready to begin the traditional "grand tour," and on May 29, Spooner endorsed the apprenticeship

8. For this service, he later received a pension. *Ibid.,* June 20, 1885; Jane Georgine Woodruff, "William E. Woodruff as Remembered by His Three Daughters;" *The National Cyclopaedia of American Biography* (New York: James T. White & Co., 1893), VIII, 463–464.

9. *Gazette,* June 20, 1885.

10. Herndon, "History of the Arkansas Gazette," 5.

11. *Gazette,* Nov. 20, 1877. T. & J. Swords and George Bruce were book publishers, but George Bruce made his fame as a type foundryman, in partnership with his brother, David. He later pioneered stereotyping in this country, and with his nephew invented the only truly successful type-casting machine. See Allen Johnson (ed.), *Dictionary of American Biography* (New York, 1943), III, 181. According to Jane Georgine Woodruff, "William E. Woodruff as Remembered by His Three Daughters," 29, Woodruff set the type for the first volume of Thomas Moore's poems printed in America.

agreement, attesting that Woodruff had fulfilled the obligations of the contract and was a qualified printer.[12]

In company with another young printer, probably Henry Van Pelt,[13]
Woodruff traveled overland to Pittsburgh, and by skiff down the Ohio River
to Louisville. They took jobs in one of Louisville's three newspaper offices,
and Woodruff briefly considered buying an interest in the paper. About the
middle of September, he received a letter from his old friend, Henry C.
Sleight,[14] who had been Spooner's partner in the publication of the *Star* for
about six months in 1812 and 1813, and who had since published newspapers
at Lexington and Russellville, Kentucky.[15] Sleight relayed an offer of employment from Thomas G. Bradford, proprietor of *The Clarion, and Tennessee State Gazette* at Nashville. Bradford was willing to pay six dollars a
week, board, and laundry, and promised that if all went well, Woodruff would
be given the management of the office. Woodruff sent his acceptance and set
out for Nashville on September 14,[16] with Henry Van Pelt.[17]

Steamboat navigation of the Cumberland River had not yet begun—
Woodruff would witness the arrival of the first steamboat at Nashville during
the coming year [18]—and he had had all he wanted of the discomforts of the
more primitive means of river travel. Stagecoaches did not run on this route,
and neither of the young men owned a horse. They decided to ship their
trunks by keelboat and walk the 140 miles to Nashville, with a rest stop at
Russellville,[19] the only town of any consequence on the way.

To all outward appearances, the *Clarion* was a bright oasis of prosperity,
and was weathering the Great Panic of 1818 in fine style. Soon after Woodruff's arrival its page was increased from five to six columns, a complete set
of new type was ordered, and a new policy was announced that provided for
publication of "extras" between regular weekly issues whenever the importance of the news justified it.[20]

This show of opulence was misleading, for Bradford was heavily in debt,
and his financial distress was destined to increase until he would be compelled
eventually to relinquish the *Clarion* to his creditors.[21] Woodruff must have

12. Herndon, "History of the Arkansas Gazette," 5.

13. Van Pelt is not clearly identified as the printer who left New York with Woodruff, but he is known to have been with him at Louisville and Nashville. *Gazette,*
June 20, 1885; Bullen, "The First Printing Outfit of the Arkansas Gazette," 38.

14. "W. E. Woodruff's Trip from Pittsburg to Louisville," *Gazette Supplement,*
Nov. 20, 1919, 46–47. This is a letter from Woodruff to his mother, Louisville, Kentucky, Sept. 22, 1818.

15. Brigham, *American Newspapers,* I, 161, 168, 177, 555–556.

16. "W. E. Woodruff's Trip," 46–47.

17. Bullen, "The First Printing Outfit," 38.

18. *Gazette,* June 16, 1876. The steamboat was the General Jackson. Woodruff also
saw the first steamboat arrivals at Arkansas Post and Little Rock.

19. "W. E. Woodruff's Trip."

20. *The Clarion, and Tennessee State Gazette,* (Nashville, Tenn.), Nov. 10, 1818.

21. Davidson County, Tennessee Deed Book O, 50; P, 53; Brigham, *American Newspapers,* II, 1063.

The first office of the *Arkansas Gazette* at Arkansas Post, 1819.
Drawn by a Little Rock artist in 1877, under William E. Woodruff's direction.

realized very soon that the *Clarion* could not offer him long-range opportunities.

During his year at Nashville, Woodruff gained a better understanding of the western way of life, which would serve him well in the years ahead. Bradford continued to act as editor and business manager, but Woodruff was made foreman of the paper's mechanical department,[22] and the *Clarion's* typographical perfection was proof that he had mastered his craft.

The long anticipated act of Congress creating Arkansas Territory was approved on March 3, 1819, and the news reached Nashville in less than three weeks.[23] Bradford pointed out the potentialities the new territory held for an industrious young printer.[24] No newspaper had ever been published there,[25]

22. *Gazette,* June 16, 1876.
23. *Clarion,* Mar. 23, 1819.
24. William E. Woodruff's answers to 63 questions, c1876, question No. 5, Ms. in Robert Wilson Trimble Papers, Arkansas History Commission.
25. That the *Arkansas Gazette* was the first paper published in Arkansas stands unchallenged. The claim that it is the oldest newspaper west of the Mississippi is equally indisputable today, but has been made in the past when it was indefensible. In a historical sketch in the Gazette on Nov. 20, 1869, William E. Woodruff, Jr. wrote, "Comparatively few papers in the country can boast so long an existence—perhaps not more than twenty—and ours is certainly the oldest west of the Mississippi, which has been published continuously by the same name." Later writers often ignored the qualifications of continuous publication and title, which at that time made the claim inaccurate.
Earlier newspapers published in Missouri were: The *Missouri Gazette,* established at St. Louis on July 12, 1808 by Joseph Charless, had several changes in title, the last

and the first printer on the ground could take for granted his appointment as public printer, and the other printing incidental to the administration of the new government would automatically fall to him. This was no small item, and might well mean the difference between success and failure. There would be a few lean years before the newspaper's circulation and advertising custom grew and the job printing business developed, but Woodruff was no stranger to poverty. Bradford painted a glowing picture of the prospects, but the summer was almost gone before Woodruff made up his mind to take his chances in Arkansas.

The probable cause of his indecision was an item in the *Illinois Intelligencer,* reprinted in the *Clarion* on July 6, announcing another printer's plans to establish a paper in Arkansas: "Mr. John M'Arthur, of St. Genevieve, has issued proposals for printing a newspaper at the seat of government for the territory of Arkansas, to be entitled the *Arkansas Herald*. From Mr. M'Arthur's known republican principles, it is expected that his establishment will redound much to the benefit and convenience of the territory. We understand that he will be patronized very liberally."

being the *Republic,* and suspended with its sale to the *Globe-Democrat* on Dec. 4, 1919; the *Western Journal,* established at St. Louis in the spring of 1815 by Joshua Norvell, succeeded early in 1817 by the *Emigrant and General Advertiser,* started at St. Louis on May 17, 1817 by Sergeant Hall and discontinued in August, 1818; succeeded by the *Enquirer* without change in volume numbering, established by Isaac N. Henry and Evarist Maury, discontinued in 1829; The *Missouri Intelligencer, and Boon's Lick Advertiser,* established Apr. 23, 1819 at Franklin by Nathaniel Patten and Benjamin Holliday, moved to Fayette in 1826 and to Columbia in 1830, had several changes in title and one merger and suspended publication as the *Herald-Statesman* on June 20, 1938, being correctly called the oldest paper west of the Mississippi at that time; *The Missouri Herald,* established at Jackson on June 25, 1819 by Tubal E. Strange, became the *Independent Patriot* with its sale to Stephen Remington in 1820, and may have continued under other titles until about 1835.

Little is known of the four papers published earlier than the *Gazette* in that part of Louisiana lying west of the Mississippi. *El Mexicano* is credited to both Natchitoches, Louisiana and Nacogdoches, Texas, and its only known extant issue is dated June 19, 1813. The *Louisiana Planter* was established April 17, 1810 by Benjamin M. Stokes at Alexandria. The *Red-River Herald* was published at Alexandria by Thomas Eastin, and the only issue located is Vol. I, new series, No. 4, dated Sept. 10, 1813. The *Louisiana Herald* was established about October, 1818 by George F. Tennery at Alexandria.

Three newspapers earlier than the *Gazette* were published in Texas, not then a part of the United States. They were: *Gaceta de Texas,* the organ of the Gutiérrez-Magee Expedition, edited by William Shaler and José Alvarez de Toledo, printed in Spanish in May, 1813, probably published no more than one or two numbers; *El Mejicano,* by the same men and for the same purpose, also published only one or two numbers; *Texas Republican,* started at Nacogdoches on Aug. 14, 1819 by Gen. James Long as the organ of his expedition to establish a Texas republic, and suspended in Oct., 1819 with the defeat of Long's forces. See James Melvin Lee, "Early Journalism West of the Mississippi," *Gazette Supplement,* Nov. 20, 1919, 46; Brigham, *American Newspapers,* I, 182, 183, 431–434; Walter Prescott Webb (ed.), *The Handbook of Texas* (Austin: The Texas State Historical Assn., 1952), II, 276; William H. Taft (comp.), *Missouri Newspapers: When and Where 1803–1963* (Columbia, Mo.: The State Historical Society of Missouri, 1964), 35, 48, 51, 71, 72, 151–152, 159–160, 165, 170.

Painting of
William Edward Woodruff
as a young man.

McArthur was a former printer and had owned a newspaper at Staunton, Virginia long before he was old enough to vote, but in recent years he had been a somewhat unreliable mail contractor in Missouri. He had visited Arkansas Post, announced his intention of starting a paper there no later than November, and rented a house for use as a printing office. Back at St. Genevieve on June 25, he made formal application to Secretary of State John Quincy Adams for the appointment as public printer for Arkansas Territory. As late as October 1, the people of Arkansas Post expected him to bring his press there before the month ended, but he never returned to Arkansas and no public explanation was ever made for his abrupt abandonment of the project.[26]

26. Brigham, *American Newspapers,* II, 1156; Clarence Edwin Carter (ed.) *Territorial Papers of the United States,* Vol. XV, *The Territory of Louisiana-Missouri, 1815–1821* (Washington: Government Printing Office, 1951), 3, 16, 93, 94, 224, 282, 365, 522; Vol. XIX, *The Territory of Arkansas, 1819–1825* (Washington, 1953), 80, 81, 93–94, 111–112; Jessie Ryon Lucke, "Correspondence Concerning the Establishment of the First Arkansas Press," *Arkansas Historical Quarterly,* XIV, (1955), 161. McArthur's wife was the sister of Dr. Lewis F. Linn, who later became a United States senator. In 1816, while a candidate for the territorial legislature, McArthur challenged his opponent, Auguste DeMun, to a duel for having made remarks about his coining counterfeit money. DeMun declined on the ground that McArthur was not a gentleman, and McArthur later killed DeMun on the court house steps at Cape Girardeau. McArthur was not injured, and was never prosecuted. See Louis Houck, *A History of Missouri from the Earliest Explorations and Settlements until the Admission of the*

The news must have reached Nashville long before this, however, for by the middle of September Woodruff had gathered his materials and was on his way to Arkansas. He would hardly have done this if he had not known McArthur would offer him no competition, for the thinly populated new territory would do well to support one printer, and two would never succeed.

Woodruff bought a second-hand wooden Ramage press at nearby Franklin.[27] It is likely that he purchased it and his other materials from Henry Van Pelt, who had started a weekly paper called the *Monitor* at Franklin late in 1818 or early in 1819. Its publication is presumed to have suspended about the time of his marriage on August 17, 1819.[28] Woodruff bought his press and materials on credit.[29] He later said that Tennessee's first newspaper had been printed on this press,[30] but there is strong reason to believe he was mistaken.[31]

Whatever its background, it had seen better days but was by no means obsolete. Production was begun that year of America's first iron press, but it is not known to have come this far westward yet, and the old wooden Ramage was still the one in general use.[32] Its operation was simple but slow.

State into the Union (Chicago: R. R. Donnelley & Sons Co., 1908), I, 366; C. F. M. Noland, "Early Times in Arkansas, No. 4," *Gazette*, Dec. 19, 1857.

27. *Gazette*, Nov. 20, 1877; Oct. 12, 1879; Bullen, "The First Printing Outfit."

28. Brigham, *American Newspapers*, II, 1057; *Clarion*, Aug. 24, 1819. The only other newspaper known to have been published at Franklin during this period, Carey Allen Harris' *Independent Gazette*, continued regular publication long after Woodruff bought his press.

29. *Gazette*, Dec. 12, 1838; Mar. 18, 1853. This is Woodruff's own statement, but no mortgage executed by him was filed for record at the Williamson County court house at Franklin or the Davidson County court house at Nashville.

30. *Ibid.*, Nov. 20, 1877; Oct. 12, 1879.

31. Tennessee's first newspaper was *The Knoxville Gazette*, by George Roulstone and Robert Ferguson, which began publication at Rogersville on Nov. 5, 1791 and moved to Knoxville with the issue of Oct. 6, 1792. It is believed that its press had been used previously to print the *North Carolina Chronicle, or Fayetteville Gazette,* at Fayetteville, North Carolina from 1789 until 1791. The date of Adam Ramage's arrival at Philadelphia from Scotland accepted by the Franklin Institute of Philadelphia is 1790, but some other sources state it as 1795. In either case, he could not have been building presses in this country in time to provide one for a newspaper publishing as early as 1789. Woodruff's misconception of the history of his press may have stemmed from confusing the *Knoxville Gazette* with the *Tennessee Gazette*, founded in January, 1800 by Benjamin J. Bradford, who also founded the Nashville *Clarion*, which ultimately became *The Clarion, and Tennessee State Gazette.* The *Tennessee Gazette* has often been identified as Nashville's first newspaper, although there was an earlier one called *Rights of Man, or, Nashville Intelligencer,* established on Feb. 11, 1799 and suspended before the end of the summer of 1799. If Van Pelt had purchased a press from one of the Bradfords at Nashville, Woodruff may have known that it had been used to print the first issue of the *Tennessee Gazette,* and may have erroneously assumed that this was the state's first paper. See Brigham, *American Newspapers*, II, 1058–1059, 1063; Samuel C. Williams, "George Roulstone: Father of the Tennessee Press," *The East Tennessee Historical Society's Publications,* No. 17 (Knoxville, 1945), 51–52; Douglas C. McMurtrie, *Early Printing in Tennessee* (Chicago, 1933), 25–27.

32. Bullen, "The First Printing Outfit."

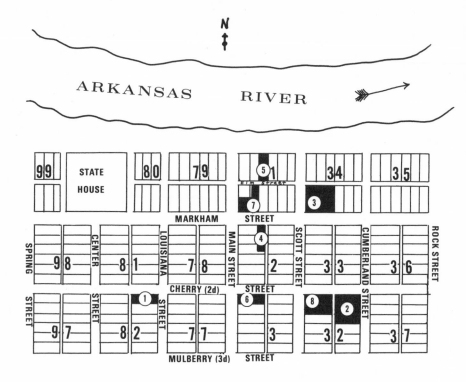

Map showing locations of *Gazette* offices at Little Rock, 1819-1866.

1. Southwest corner Cherry and Louisiana, 1821-1824.
2. Southwest corner Cherry and Cumberland, 1824-1827.
3. Northeast corner Markham and Scott, 1827-1840.
4. South side of Markham between Main and Scott, 1840-1845.
5. North side of Elm between Main and Scott, 1845-1848.
6. Southeast corner Cherry and Main, 1848-1850.
7. Northeast corner Markham and Main, upstairs, 1850-1854.
8. Southeast corner Cherry and Scott, 1854-1866.

Inking rollers had not yet been invented, and the form was inked with a stuffed sheepskin ball, a task requiring little skill and performed by a "ball boy," usually the lowliest apprentice. The form was of two pages, but the platen covered only one page, so the lever that operated the torsion screw had to be pulled twice to print one form.

Woodruff's type, which had not been used long enough to show signs of wear, included several sizes of "Series No. 1," the earliest cut and cast in this country. It was the product of the Binney & Ronaldson type foundry at Philadelphia. The main body type was listed in the type specimen books as Small

Pica Roman and Italic until it was discarded about 1834. It was revived in 1908 as 11-point Oxford.[33]

Woodruff left Nashville about the middle of September on a keelboat. Besides the trunk containing his clothing and personal effects, he had the press, the cumbersome type cases and type, four bundles of paper, a supply of printers ink, a stack of newspapers that would provide most of the contents of his first few issues, and incidentals such as glue pot, ink wells, and scissors.

After 14 days he reached the mouth of the Cumberland at Smithland, then proceeded down the Ohio to the site of Cairo, and thence down the Mississippi to Montgomery's Point at the mouth of White River. Here he and his belongings were deposited on the bank, and the keelboat continued its voyage to New Orleans with its load of flour.[34]

The last lap of the journey was made in a pirogue, a large dugout canoe fashioned by hollowing out the trunk of a tremendous cottonwood tree. Two boatmen were engaged to pole the craft up White River, through the "cut-off" into the muddy Arkansas, and upstream to the village of Arkansas, seat of government of the Territory of Arkansas.[35] Woodruff later recalled that he had to convince a frightened raftsman somewhere along the way that the press was not a machine for spewing bullets.[36]

Within a few miles of his destination on October 31,[37] he saw the first signs of civilization since Montgomery's Point. The quaint French-built plantation houses along the north bank were remnants of a settlement that had once clustered around the military post of French and Spanish dominion. The fort was now in ruins, and only its palisades stood to remind the curious visitor of a bygone era.

The town of Arkansas stood on a high plateau on a broad curve of the river. A bayou on the east separated it from the old fort, and another on the west marked the beginning of the great marshy prairie that stretched along the river for nearly 100 miles, where cities of crawfish castles testified to its unfitness for human cities.

There was more to this town than met the eye. The old village on the river bank was commonly called Arkansas Post or the Post of Arkansas, having grown up adjacent to the fort and appropriated its name without the formality of a recorded town plat. Adjoining it on the north was the town called Arkansas, and north of that was the town called Rome, both laid out in 1818, with streets that looked like a continuation of those in the old village.

33. *Ibid.*

34. *Gazette,* Nov. 20, 1877; Woodruff's answers to 63 questions, Nos. 23 and 26.

35. *Gazette,* Nov. 20, 1877, and many others. In all statements about the trip that emanated directly from Woodruff, only one pirogue is mentioned and later statements by others that he had two dugouts lashed together must be inaccurate.

36. Opie Read, *I Remember* (New York: Richard R. Smith, Inc., 1930), 121.

37. *Gazette,* Nov. 20, 1869; June 20, 1885. The date October 30 is given for Woodruff's arrival at Arkansas Post in William F. Pope, *Early Days in Arkansas* (Little Rock: Frederick W. Allsopp, 1895), 112–113.

—Photo by Larry Obsitnik

Restored *Gazette* office of 1824-1827,
in the Arkansas Territorial Capital Restoration.

The settlement actually consisted of two towns, one village that defies legal description, an abandoned military fort, and an outlying agricultural community. But the people who lived there could not be bothered with such hair-splitting distinctions, and so far as they were concerned there was only one town, and a pretty small one at that, with its 30-odd houses.[38] They did not trouble themselves with the profusion of names either, but referred to the entire settlement as Arkansas Post, except when it was necessary to be more precise, as in the case of deeds and other legal documents. The name of the post office was Arkansas,[39] and Woodruff invariably used that name as long as he lived there.

The people fell into three general categories. There were the indolent,

38. *Gazette,* Nov. 20, 1819; Dec. 2, 1820; Timothy Flint, *Recollections of the Last Ten Years, Passed in Occasional Residences and Journeyings in the Valley of the Mississippi, from Pittsburg and the Missouri to the Gulf of Mexico, and from Florida to the Spanish Frontier; in a Series of Letters to the Rev. James Flint, of Salem, Massachusetts* (Boston: Cummings, Hilliard, and Co., 1826), 264–265; Thomas Nuttall, *A Journal of Travels into the Arkansa Territory, During the Year 1819, With Occasional Observations on the Manners of the Aborigines* (Philadelphia: Thos. H. Palmer, 1821), 72–73, 75, 77–78; Map of Post of Arkansas, Territory of Arkansas, 1829, compiled by F. M. Quertermous (Little Rock: Arkansas Publicity and Parks Commission, undated.)

39. The name of the post office did not become Arkansas Post until 1832. *Gazette,* Apr. 18, 1832.

pleasure loving French people, most of whom owed their residence here to their ancestors. There were the Americans who were known as "old settlers," having arrived before the creation of Arkansas Territory was assured. And there were those who had come within the past year or so, anticipating that the creation of the territory would open a new field of opportunity.

Most of the conflict in the community was between the two groups of Americans, for the French cared little for the turmoil of politics. The American old settlers regarded the newcomers as opportunists who hoped to cash in on the advantages attached to territorial status, especially the appointments to public offices. They believed it was but simple justice to distribute the appointments among men of ability who had cast their lot with this country when it had no such rewards to offer, in preference to outsiders who had only a selfish interest in Arkansas.

Thus far it had not been so, for not one of the president's appointments had gone to an Arkansas man. Most of the new officials appreciated their appointments so little that they were not to be found in Arkansas Territory, although they were already four months overdue. Only one had been on hand when the territorial government was scheduled to go into operation on July 4. He was wiry little Andrew Scott of Missouri, a judge of the Superior Court, whose 130-pound frame housed a quick, violent temper that only a man twice his size could afford. He had shown his good faith by moving his family to Arkansas Post, and even the resentful old-timers did not classify him with the power-mad newcomers.

Brig. Gen. James Miller of New Hampshire, still gathering the fruits of his heroism at Lundy's Lane during the War of 1812, was the new governor, and he left his family at home and delayed his arrival until the day after Christmas. Haughty, aristocratic young Robert Crittenden of Kentucky had left the political nest feathered by his older brother to try his wings as secretary of the new territory. The other two Superior Court judges, Robert P. Letcher of Kentucky and Charles Jouett of Kentucky and Michigan, did not disguise their distaste for Arkansas and the positions they had not sought. Crittenden, Letcher, and Jouett had arrived near the end of July and had joined with Scott in holding a short legislative session, after which Letcher and Jouett had departed for Kentucky, never to return to Arkansas but slow to resign their offices.[40]

Crittenden was only 22 and was intrigued with the almost unlimited power he enjoyed as acting governor, unrestrained by other officials. He built the beginnings of a political machine by passing out the appointments within the gift of the governor with a free hand, leaving no positions of any importance to be filled by Miller.[41]

Ten days before Woodruff's arrival, Crittenden rashly advanced the ter-

40. Carter, *Territorial Papers*, XIX, 51–55, 100, 101, 119, 138–139, 144–145, 180; *Gazette*, Jan. 1, 1820.
41. Ted R. Worley (ed.), "A Letter of Governor Miller to His Wife," *Arkansas Historical Quarterly*, XIII (1954), 388.

A Ramage press.
Courtesy of The Franklin Institute, Philadelphia, Pa.

ritory to the second grade of government and ordered the election of a General Assembly and a delegate to Congress. He gave only 30 days notice of the election,[42] not enough time for fairness in a large, sparsely settled territory where communication facilities were virtually nonexistent. The campaign was in progress when Woodruff reached Arkansas, and since he was determined not to permit his paper to become enmeshed in ruinous political controversy, it was just as well that he could not publish his first issue sooner than election day.

The two-room log cabin Woodruff rented from Richmond Peeler was in the old part of town, on a lot facing Front Street and extending to the river in the rear.[43] Outside the door two barrels were sunk in the ground and filled with drinking water from the river. The larger room was 18 or 20 feet square, and served as an editorial office, composing room, and sleeping quarters for Woodruff, who took his meals at the home of a French lady. The type cases were set on a counter-height shelf, and there was an "editor's table" where Woodruff wrote the original material and clipped articles to be reprinted from exchange papers. There was a bed in one corner, a stove, and probably several chairs for visitors. The smaller room was the press room, and contained the press, the paper and ink, and possibly a table or two and a wash basin.[44]

The long trip had given Woodruff time to ponder the problems of editorial policy and to choose a name for his paper. It would be the voice of the entire territory, so the territory's name must be a part of the paper's name. It was a fortunate coincidence that the town's name was the same, for it was good business for a paper's name to indicate its specific location. Whether "Arkansas" should end with "s" or "w" was a warmly debated subject among the educated people of the territory,[45] but "Arkansas" seemed to predominate locally,[46] and Woodruff accepted this spelling. His choice is thought to have had great influence on the final orthography of the name, since his paper kept it constantly before the people.

The most popular newspaper name of the period was easily *Gazette,* and some journals bearing this name had made outstanding contributions to

42. *Ibid.;* Lonnie J. White, *Politics on the Southwestern Frontier: Arkansas Territory, 1819–1836* (Memphis: Memphis State University Press, 1964), 21.

43. *Gazette,* Dec. 11, 1819; July 15, 1820. Some accounts written much later, as for example Woodruff's obituary in *Gazette,* June 20, 1885, have it that no house was available for rent and that he built or otherwise "extemporized" a cabin.

44. Evalina Woodruff Vaughan and Frances Woodruff Martin, "William E. Woodruff as Remembered by His Three Daughters," *Gazette Supplement,* Nov. 20, 1919, 29, 30; "Old Settler" [Daniel T. Witter] in *Gazette,* Sept. 14, 1873. Witter's is the only detailed eyewitness description found. A pencil sketch of the exterior, first published in the *Gazette,* Nov. 20, 1877, was made under Woodruff's direction and pronounced by him a good representation of the *Gazette's* first building.

45. "Philalaos," in *Gazette,* Dec. 2, 1820.

46. In the earliest deed record books and other county records of Arkansas County, and in other manuscripts of the period, spellings other than "Arkansas" by actual residents rarely are found.

American journalism. It had been often used by first newspapers in the various states,[47] and Woodruff may have felt it would suggest that his had been the pioneer newspaper of Arkansas, after the inevitable appearance of competition. It may also have had personal significance, since he had begun his apprenticeship at the *Suffolk Gazette* and had ended his career as a hired printer at *The Clarion, and Tennessee State Gazette.*

No handbill prospectus for the *Arkansas Gazette* has been found, and none was published in the paper, so it is assumed that Woodruff did not use this time-honored method of getting advance subscriptions.

47. " 'Gazette' as a Name for a Newspaper," *Gazette Supplement,* Nov. 20, 1919, 43.

2

THE PRESS IN THE WILDERNESS

Arkansas Post

1819-1821 ARKANSAS TERRITORY'S first election accounted for only a small part of Woodruff's excitement as he went about his chores on Saturday, November 20, 1819. On the table in the press room was a stack of newspapers, neatly printed on one side several days since.[1] The type for the inside pages was in the form, except for a space left on page three for the election returns for Arkansas Township. Late in the day, Woodruff set the local returns and a news item gleaned from a letter received by a friend, and printed the inside pages of his first issue.

The average reader would marvel that a newspaper comparable with those of the eastern cities had come out of an isolated settlement in Arkansas. The more discerning eye of another printer would find much to admire in it, for it contained such rarities as two-column advertisements and a promise of home delivery to local subscribers.

Only the editor was dissatisfied. In his salutatory Woodruff said, "The present size and complexion of our paper does not exactly suit us; but this we intend to remedy as soon as our patronage will justify our procuring new materials, and enlarging its size." The four pages each measured 18½ inches long and 11¼ inches wide, with four 14½-pica columns to the page.[2]

1. Since the Ramage press and other contemporary models could print only one side of the sheet at a time, it was customary to print the outside pages early in the week, leaving the inside pages for last minute production. Page one was regarded more as a front cover than a front page, a wrapper to protect the inside pages from bad weather and rough handling by mail riders, so it was not considered the proper place for the latest and most important news items. See John E. Allen, *Newspaper Designing* (New York and London: Harper and Brothers, 1947), 221.

2. A pica is a unit of linear measurement for type, approximately one-sixth of an inch. The words "em" and "pica" are sometimes used interchangeably, although their meaning is not precisely the same. Changes in column widths frequently were as little as half a pica, and rarely more than one or two picas. The difference was insignificant to readers, but was tremendously important to printers. In Woodruff's day, printers usually computed column widths and depths in agates rather than in picas or inches. *Ibid.*, 24.

The logotype nameplate was to be an innovation of the near future,[3] and the title was set in 42-point type,[4] all capitals, *THE ARKANSAS GA-ZETTE*. The statement of proprietorship, "By Wm. E. Woodruff," occupied the left end of the front page dateline, with "Arkansas, (Arkansas Ter.) Saturday, November 20, 1819" in the middle, and "Vol. I—No. 1" on the right.

The subscription and advertising rates were at the head of the first column on the front page, and would be left standing indefinitely. The rest of the page was filled with reprinted news articles from St. Louis, Newcastle, New Orleans, Washington, and London, bearing dates from July 3 to September 3.

Page four was filled with reprinted articles, with two poems in the first column under a standing head, "Selected Poetry." In future issues, most advertisements would be moved to this page after their first publication. All the local items were on pages two and three, but even here there were a few reprinted articles. In the future, page two would be filled with material from the exchanges most of the time, and page three would be reserved for local news and new advertisements, with reprinted articles filling whatever space was left over.

The salutatory editorial introduced the paper to the public and declared it Republican in politics, Republican being the current name of the party that ultimately evolved into the modern Democratic party. There were three short items pertaining to the circulation of the paper, the stale announcement that James Miller had accepted the appointment as governor and probably was on his way to Arkansas, an incomplete list of candidates for the offices to be filled at the election that day, a St. Louis obituary almost two months old, and five local marriage notices ranging in date from August 28 to November 16.

Two lengthy contributions from local men were in this issue. One was a description of the village, written by Samuel Calhoun Roane[5] under the pseudonym "A Citizen." The other, signed "A Citizen of the Territory," protested a proposal to move the Cherokees in Tennessee to the Arkansas River.

Advertisements of 15 lines or less cost $1 for the first insertion and 50 cents for each subsequent insertion. The first advertising patronage was impressive, filling three columns on page three, with one ad in the other column. Half of the dozen ads had come from Eli J. Lewis, in his various capacities as merchant, planter, circuit clerk, postmaster, and executor of estates. The largest one, two columns wide and 11½ inches deep, had been inserted by

3. A logotype is a type having more than one letter or other character on its printing surface, cast this way to save time for the compositor. In the case of a nameplate, all of a newspaper's title is cast on a single base.

4. A point is a unit of measurement for type, approximately 1/72 (.0138+) of an inch in the United States system. This system was not adopted as standard until 1886, (Allen, *Newspaper Designing,* 24.) and Woodruff and his contemporaries used names rather than numbers for the various type sizes.

5. *Gazette,* Nov. 20, 1869.

the general merchandise firm of Lewis and Thomas, located across Front Street from the printing office.[6]

Newspaper proprietors were reluctant to accept two-column ads, because the brass column rules came only in full column lengths and it was expensive to break them for use under the ad, and because wide areas of type without the support of column rules had a tendency to "roll" in the old hand presses.[7] Lewis's advertisement as clerk of the Circuit Court was also two columns wide, and the two together filled most of the length of the page. The short space left to be ruled separately was just the right size for a cutoff rule turned vertically. Occasional "work-ups" can be detected in these ads in the weeks that followed.

Two of the remaining six ads were "house ads," one calling for an apprentice and the other offering to do job printing; one was a legal notice pertaining to a divorce suit; and the other three were cards by a doctor, a lawyer, and a tailor. Most of the ads began with two-line initials, and all were set off by cutoff rules (rules running the full width of the column.)

Subscription rates were $3 a year if paid in advance, or $4 at the end of the year. A number of men who were circulating subscription lists had not had time to return them, so Woodruff did not know how many subscribers he had. The most reliable statement of the first subscribers was made in an editorial at the beginning of the paper's twentieth year and repeated later, when Woodruff said he started with fewer than 40 subscribers.[8] In later years, he sometimes said he started without a single subscriber,[9] and sometimes he said there were 100.[10] Perhaps these three statements were not in conflict, for when he printed the first issue no subscribers had been entered on the books in his office, and about 40 must have been the number on the first subscription lists returned to him. Possibly the first press run was 100 copies, but a year passed before he had that many subscribers.[11]

Woodruff often said he started the *Gazette* entirely without assistance, and was its publisher, editor, foreman, compositor, pressman, ball boy, carrier, and mail clerk. But after a few weeks Samuel Calhoun Roane, who was no busier than any other lawyer in a new country where the courts were not yet functioning fully, helped operate the press and did other work around the office.[12] Almost half a century later, it was recalled that Samuel Morton Rutherford's "friendly assistance enabled the first number of the *Gazette* to see the light," but the nature of his help was not stated.[13]

6. *Ibid.,* Apr. 1, 1820.
7. Allen, *Newspaper Designing,* 222.
8. *Gazette,* Dec. 12, 1838; Mar. 18, 1853.
9. *Ibid.,* Nov. 20, 1869; Nov. 20, 1877; Oct. 12, 1879. These are not statements by Woodruff, but he apparently supplied the information.
10. William E. Woodruff's answers to 63 questions, c1876, question number 26, Ms. in Robert Wilson Trimble Papers, Arkansas History Commission.
11. *Gazette,* Dec. 12, 1838; Mar. 18, 1853.
12. *Ibid.,* Sept. 14, 1873. This writer was Daniel T. Witter.
13. *Ibid.,* Apr. 16, 1867 (weekly edition.)

Shortly after the *Gazette* began publication, two young lawyers arrived at Arkansas Post. One was James H. Lucas, who worked as a printer for the *Gazette* for a time, and later became by inheritance the wealthiest man in St. Louis, with an annual income of nearly half a million dollars. The other was Chester Ashley,[14] in whom Woodruff and the *Gazette* found a friend for life. His talent for land speculation would soon make him rich, and his uncanny shrewdness in politics would bring him great power, most of which would be exerted behind the scenes. He was on his way to Little Rock, a town in the first stages of development.

Since all unsigned material originating in the office of publication was automatically attributed to the editor, there was no separation of news from what we now call editorials. If the editor was moved to express his opinion, he did it in the news story. The opinion might constitute the main part of the article, or it might be contained in a paragraph, a sentence, a single word, or the subtle use of italics or small capitals to color the meaning of an otherwise insignificant word.

Woodruff used all these methods sparingly during his early career. He avoided even objective reporting of anything controversial, to the point of complete suppression of some of the most important news concerning the territorial government. Week after week passed with no editorial comment of any kind except a mild complaint about the irregularity of the mails, remarks on the president's message to Congress, and a few words on a proposed post road, all of which echoed the prevailing opinions in the community.

The subscriber-contributors were difficult to handle, and almost destroyed the tranquillity of the *Gazette* at the outset. Nothing caused their ink to flow like politics, and they dealt in personalities as much as in issues. Having side-stepped the campaign bickering by beginning publication after the polls closed, Woodruff had to contend with people who were bent on rehashing the campaign.

It was about this time or soon afterwards that Woodruff had his first clash with Secretary Crittenden, explained only as the result of his refusal to allow Crittenden to dictate his editorial course.[15]

Control of Arkansas politics and government rested on a three-part foundation: the delegate to Congress, to influence appointments and appropriations made in Washington; the governor, to control appointments and administrative functions in Arkansas; and a sympathetic press, to keep the grass-roots element satisfied. These three combined to maintain control of the legislature, though this was likely to fluctuate. By the stroke of fortune that delayed Governor Miller's arrival, Robert Crittenden had five months to establish control of the executive office and to build his own strength by dispensing appointments. To establish control of the delegate was a trifle riskier, for ordinary discretion dictated that this election should be deferred until Miller's arrival. But Crittenden did order the election, and made the

14. *Ibid.,* Nov. 16, 1873.
15. *Ibid.,* Oct. 19, 1831; May 9, 1832.

Robert Crittenden.

campaign period so brief that he had his own man elected and on his way to Washington before Miller reached Arkansas. Crittenden never achieved control of Woodruff's *Gazette,* but had to settle for a press that would neither defend nor condemn him. We cannot know what efforts Crittenden put forth to make the *Gazette* his organ. The public printing usually was the bait dangled before an editor's eyes, but Woodruff knew it could not be taken away from him as long as the territory had no other press. On the other hand, he also knew that Crittenden had the power to make the public printing more or less profitable.

The election made Crittenden vulnerable to criticism on several counts, and this may have caused the first discord between the secretary and the editor. Woodruff published no direct criticism of Crittenden or any other specific person, but neither did he defend him against the mutterings of the community.

Crittenden had been in Arkansas only a few days when he appointed James Woodson Bates judge of the First Judicial Circuit,[16] and when Bates became a candidate for delegate to Congress, some thought Crittenden took an undue interest in his election.[17] Bates was a polished, well educated newcomer from Virginia by way of Missouri, whose brother, Frederick Bates,

16. Clarence Edwin Carter (ed.), *Territorial Papers of the United States,* Vol. XIX, *The Territory of Arkansas 1819–1825* (Washington: Government Printing Office, 1953), 789; Ms. Record of Commissions, 1819–1836, n.p., original in office of secretary of state, photocopy in *Arkansas Gazette* Foundation Library.

17. *Gazette,* July 17, 1827.

was then secretary of Missouri Territory. He walked away with the election in Arkansas Township, receiving 84 of the 102 votes cast, although opposed by four old settlers who had held offices in Arkansas under Missouri Territory.[18] The outlying townships went for old settler Henry Cassidy, and out of a total of 283 votes cast in Arkansas County, Cassidy received 113 and Bates 115.[19] The *Gazette* gave no hint of local dissension, but a race so close and so important could hardly have been free of it, particularly with the acting governor promoting the candidacy of a newcomer against respected old settlers.

When returns from the other four counties were unofficially tabulated, Cassidy dropped to fourth place and Stephen F. Austin moved into second place, with 343 votes to Bates' 401. Austin was a newcomer from Missouri, who had spent most of the summer in southwest Arkansas, where he was developing a townsite at Fulton on Red River. He was also interested in the new town of Little Rock, and was making a desperate effort to have it made the territorial seat of government. He had entered the race only 13 days before the election, and his candidacy was not known in Arkansas County or in two townships of Lawrence County. [20] Otherwise, he might have been the winner.

When Crittenden certified the official returns, he threw out the entire vote of Clark County because there had been an error in making up the returns, and also Austin's 11 votes in Pulaski County, along with a few others. Austin could not have won with these votes anyhow, as the official tabulation gave Bates 403 votes to Austin's 266, with 452 cast for the other four candidates combined. This made a total of 1,120 votes cast, according to the official count,[21] and the Clark County vote would have raised it to 1,263.

Evidence of unpleasantness was more direct in the race for Arkansas County's two seats in the House of Representatives, in which William O. Allen and William B. R. Horner were elected over six other aspirants. In the second issue of the *Gazette* on November 27, before the results of the election were known, a writer who signed himself "Silence" and was said to be a candidate who correctly anticipated defeat, satirized the campaign tactics employed by some of the candidates and their leading supporters. Fragmentary information and allegorical names make the letter unintelligible to modern readers, but the inference of keen rivalry and participation of a political boss is unmistakable. A longer letter written by the same person and in the same vein appeared in the issue of December 4. In the same issue, one who signed "Inquirer" discussed at length whether the election had been held in conformity with the law.

By that time Woodruff had received a reply to the first letter of "Silence," but he did not publish it because the writer had not identified himself, sign-

18. *Ibid.,* Nov. 20, 1819.
19. *Ibid.,* Nov. 27, Dec. 4, 1819.
20. *Ibid.,* Dec. 11, 1819.
21. *Ibid.,* Dec. 25, 1819.

ing only the pseudonym "Tantamount." Woodruff and all subsequent *Gazette* editors insisted upon knowing the identity of pseudonymous writers, for otherwise they might have to stand responsible for the letters. By December 11, "Tantamount" had given Woodruff his real name and had written an answer to the second letter of "Silence," and Woodruff published both his letters and brought the discussion to an abrupt end. "Tantamount" shed no further light on the subject of the election, but delivered a sharp rebuke to "Silence," and indicated that the *Gazette* would do well to steer clear of political controversy. No letters on any subject were published for several weeks after this unsettling experience.

On March 4, 1820 Robert Briggs, a 24-year-old native of Massachusetts and a printer by trade, became Woodruff's partner and junior editor of the *Gazette*. The firm of Woodruff & Briggs reaffirmed the paper's Republicanism, and called for contributions from the readers "on any subject that will impart information or amusement," to fill the space in the absence of news. Lest the contributors abuse the privilege, they were warned, "We shall sedulously endeavor to exclude from our columns all matter that may tend to excite local jealousy, or in the least degree wound private character." The next five weeks passed with no response to the appeal.

Meanwhile, a duel was fought on March 10 by Robert C. Oden and William O. Allen, in which Allen was the challenger. Both were seriously wounded, and Allen died on March 21. Woodruff deplored the practice of settling personal difficulties by duelling, and apparently nobody disagreed.[22]

Many years later, John R. Homer Scott (who was a child of six at the time of the duel) made the only explanation ever offered for this affair of honor. He said Oden was boyishly fascinated by Allen's sword-cane, and on one occasion playfully refused to return it to its owner and made Allen chase him to retrieve it. Allen was annoyed, and the harsh words that followed the incident led to the duel.[23] Although this explanation taxes credibility, it has never been challenged, probably because no other explanation has been found. The correspondence in the *Gazette* about the election in which Allen was one of the winners suggests another possible cause, and one that is much less frivolous. Oden was Crittenden's friend, and Crittenden had appointed him clerk of Pulaski County on October 1, 1819, but because Oden was a minor, he had had to resign the office on November 11. Allen also had been favored by Crittenden at one time, but had recently fallen from his good graces, as evidenced by the fact that Bates had tried to secure his appointment as a judge of the Superior Court but withdrew his support on April 13, not knowing Allen was dead.[24]

A special election was held to fill the vacancy in the House created by Allen's death, and Elijah Morton announced his candidacy on April 15.

22. *Ibid.,* Mar. 25, 1820.
23. *Ibid.,* Sept. 6, 1885; William F. Pope, *Early Days in Arkansas* (Little Rock: Frederick W. Allsopp, 1895), 34–36.
24. *Gazette,* Aug. 11, 1830; Carter, *Territorial Papers,* XIX, 793, 160.

s not capital, was thirty.
as very clear that " re-
hirty-nine stripes—and
· gave Mr. P. such a
gnificant look, as if he
hat the deuce can you
, ?"—However, in this
like Goldsmith's school-

d, he could argue still,"
ew his argument, when,
and gown of my lord
led upon our worthy Jus-
such awful *gravity* " as
· tell," and at the same
a portentous frown on
P. as clearly satisfied
he relinquished his an-
ry would be charged to
also " to be reprimand-
" It was certainly out-
il in Mr. P. to attempt
argument of the Chief
t must be allowed was

THE GAZETTE.

ARKANSAS.

SATURDAY, APRIL 29, 1820.

We are authorized to announce that
JOSEPH STILLWELL, Esq. will serve, if
elected, to fill the vacancy in the House
of Representatives of this Territory, occasioned by the decease of Gen. Allen.

[COMMUNICATED.]

Nous sommes autorisé à annoncer que
Monsieur le Judge JOSEPH STILLWELL
veut servir, s'il est élu, comme membre à
la Chambre Représentative de ce Territoire,
au lieu et place du Gén. Wm. O. Allen,
décédé.

GOOD NEWS!
We learn by a gentleman who left
Nashville, (Ten.) on the 4th inst. that
Congress had authorized the President

COMMUNICA

To the Editors of the A

It gives me much plea
an impartial discussion
place with regard to the
may be brought forwar
cancy in the House of
from this county.

As I have some scrup
about me, and wishing t
impartially, and honor
hope you will excuse t
explanation of the fo
from the Organic Law
in full force and virtue
the gentleman who wa
candidate in the Gazet
April, inst.

" *Sec. 6.* No person
or qualified to be a rep
shall not have attained t
ty-one years, and who
sided in the Territory

Political announcement of Joseph Stillwell,
the *Gazette's* only French-English publication.

Morton was a Kentuckian, owned property in partnership with Crittenden,
and had acted as Oden's second in the duel. His candidacy brought forth
several carefully worded letters, suggesting that he had been persuaded to
run by influential friends, and might not be eligible. The editors said they
knew they would be "censured by some for admitting anything relative to
the election," but they felt that their own impartiality would excuse them.
Morton withdrew from the race in May, saying his candidacy threatened to
introduce a party spirit, and Woodruff refused to print subsequent letters
on the subject. It may be significant that Morton's withdrawal closely followed Crittenden's return to Arkansas after a long trip.[25]

When the surviving principal, Oden, and both seconds, Morton and
George W. Scott, were indicted for participation in the duel, brought to
trial, and acquitted because of some rather far-fetched technicalities, another
dispute was touched off between a letter writer who protested the verdict
and one who interpreted his remarks as a slander against the jury. Woodruff
also halted this discussion before it could get out of hand.[26]

Joseph Stillwell was elected to Allen's seat in the House. His announcement of his candidacy was published on April 29, 1820 both in English and

25. *Gazette,* Apr. 22, 29, May 6, 13, 20, 1820.
26. *Ibid.,* June 24, July 1, 8, 15, 1820. Oden was found not guilty of accepting a
challenge because the correspondence was not produced in court. Morton was acquitted
because the scene of the duel was stated as Arkansas Post when actually it was an island
a mile and a half above the village.

in French, for the benefit of old settlers who knew only French. The French version was labeled "Communicated," to show that it was not written by the editor. Although some writers have said that the *Gazette's* early news columns were printed in both languages, like the New Orleans newspapers of the period, this paragraph is the only one in the entire history of the paper that was printed in French. Woodruff could not have published the *Gazette* in both languages if he had been so inclined, because he did not know French, and because his type did not include the necessary diacriticals. He used a makeshift for the acute and grave marks in this paragraph, and every letter so marked was set noticeably below the line. On another occasion, a "5" was used as a cedilla in a French proper name. The only other foreign language publication in the *Gazette* was a treaty published in 1825 in English and Spanish, by order of the Department of State.

On July 7, 1820, Henry Wharton Conway arrived at Arkansas Post from St. Louis, having been appointed receiver of public monies for the Arkansas Land District.[27] He was a member of a large and clannish family of Conways, Seviers, and Rectors, some of whom had acquired powerful political positions, and had taken care of their relatives by means of a sort of spoils system. Henry Conway had seen the system in his boyhood home in Tennessee, where the Seviers and the Conways had long enjoyed tremendous prestige. He had been a beneficiary of a similar system in Missouri, where he and his relatives had received lucrative contracts for surveying public lands from his uncle, William Rector, surveyor-general of Missouri, Illinois, and Arkansas.[28] It was a safe bet that the ambitious young Conway would not long be content with his job as receiver. A younger cousin, Ambrose Hundley Sevier, came with him or joined him soon afterwards, and near the end of the October, 1820 session of the legislature was appointed temporary clerk of the House.[29] They formed the nucleus of a colony of relatives who would eventually fill many public offices in Arkansas, and would control Arkansas politics for many years.

By a treaty concluded on October 18, 1820, the United States ceded to the Choctaw Indians a large strip of land in southwest Arkansas, lying between the Arkansas and Red rivers. Arkansas would lose two counties and parts of two others, out of a total of seven counties in the territory, and an estimated 5,000 settlers would lose their homes. Besides the personal disaster to approximately one-third of the population of Arkansas, it was a staggering blow to the territory's prospects for rapid settlement and early statehood. The only hope was that the treaty would not be ratified in its original form.

When Congress assembled on November 13, Delegate Bates' most important job was to present the case against the treaty and to prevent its ratification. The House had nothing to do with it, and territorial delegates did not

27. *Ibid.*, July 8, 1820.
28. Carter, *Territorial Papers*, XIX, 636.
29. *Gazette*, Oct. 28, 1820.

have the privilege of the Senate floor, so he could inform the senators only in private conversation. It does not appear that he did this, but decided the proper channel was the Department of War, which administered Indian affairs. He wrote one letter to the secretary of war on November 28, describing the damage the treaty threatened to Arkansas and its people. He expected that the information would be sent to the president, and that he would refuse to submit the treaty to the Senate.[30] To his surprise and chagrin, it was presented and speedily ratified, and was signed by the president on January 8, 1821.[31] Official protests written in Arkansas had not had time to reach Washington.[32]

The people most affected were disillusioned by what they considered the hostility of their government towards them. One person wrote an eloquent attack on Andrew Jackson, one of the commissioners who had negotiated the treaty. It was published over the signature "Helvidius" in the *Gazette* of January 27, 1821, before the treaty's ratification was known in Arkansas. Woodruff's editorial introduction echoed agreement, and another writer, "Veritas," responded with a sketch of Jackson's part in the Seminole War, published on February 10.

Early in May, Woodruff received a letter from Tennessee, demanding the name of "Helvidius." Woodruff declined to give it, saying that only Jackson had a right to call for it, and that even he would be refused unless he could show that his personal character and not his public character had been assailed. In the same issue, a letter signed "Brasidas" took Jackson to task for attempting to stifle public criticism, taking for granted that someone acting for Jackson had asked for the writer's name.[33]

Robert Crittenden may have instigated this unpleasantness, for 23 years later one of his friends said, "Mr. Crittenden quarreled with Mr. *Wm. E. Woodruff,* and never interchanged civilities with him afterwards, because Mr. W. would not give him the name of the author of certain articles that appeared in his paper, ABUSIVE OF GEN. JACKSON!!"[34] The permanence of their estrangement was exaggerated, but certainly this was the situation for months after this incident.

In the *Gazette* of June 2, Woodruff reprinted with editorial agreement part of a Missouri editor's salutatory commenting that numerous enmities were the printer's inevitable lot in life, "but happily those enemies are generally found only among demagogues and the illiterate and meanest of society; contracted in their ideas, vicious in their dispositions, and envious, they hate what they cannot imitate or affect, and seek, by circulating falsehoods to destroy or injure." Eventually the *Gazette's* readers would become familiar with this trick of allowing correspondents or reprinted articles to make points or deliver barbs for which the editor preferred not to stand responsible.

30. *Ibid.,* Oct. 15, 1822; Carter, *Territorial Papers,* XIX, 237–239.
31. *Gazette,* Mar. 31, 1821.
32. *Ibid.,* May 23, 1822; Carter, *Territorial Papers,* XIX, 244–248.
33. *Gazette,* May 12, 1821.
34. *Ibid.,* May 8, 1844.

Immediately after this incident, Crittenden's behavior began to indicate a decided hostility towards Woodruff and his paper. He began to withhold printing jobs, and tried to arrange for a rival press to come to Arkansas, obviously intending to give Woodruff as little business as possible.

As acting governor, Crittenden had made the apportionment of the House of Representatives, and was expected to announce it by proclamation. He had not given the *Gazette* the proclamation for publication, and with the election only seven weeks away and the people uninformed as to how many representatives each county could elect, Woodruff replied to an inquiring correspondent on June 23 that he had no information on the subject. He probably could publish the apportionment if Crittenden were not absent, he said. This gave the impression that it was nothing more serious than an oversight on the part of the acting governor. But the apportionment was never published in the *Gazette,* and Crittenden found another way to announce it, probably by posting it at conspicuous places at each county seat.[35]

The territory's second election, held on August 6, 1821, found the incumbent James Woodson Bates opposed by the venerable Matthew Lyon in the race for Congress. Lyon had represented two states in Congress, and had had considerable experience as a politician and as a newspaper editor, but his fame rested principally on his dramatic battle against the Alien and Sedition Law. Major William Bradford of Fort Smith was a last minute candidate, but his campaign was too short to affect the outcome, and the official tabulation of votes gave Bates the office by a slender margin over Lyon.

Woodruff's restraining hand kept the campaign quiet, so far as the *Gazette* was concerned, but there are more indications than the close vote that it was a hard fought contest attended by strong feelings. Lyon contested the election, charging that Bates and his friends had led unqualified voters to the polls and that Crittenden had manipulated the returns in Bates' favor. He was unable to prove these accusations, and was not seated.[36]

Arkansas's first libel suit grew out of the election for the General Assembly, held at the same time. On the day before the election, William Russell sent a letter to a township in Pulaski County, accusing candidate Edmund Hogan of several varieties of misconduct. Hogan was defeated, and sued Russell for libel. The Superior Court found Russell guilty in April of 1822, and awarded damages of $2,400. The *Gazette* was not involved.[37]

During the period of the Woodruff-Briggs partnership, the *Gazette* published a meteorological journal once a month, beginning March 4, 1820 and ending April 14, 1821. It gave a day-by-day summary of the weather for the preceding month. Another feature was the New Orleans Prices Current,

35. Auditor's Register of Warrants A, 1820–1838, n.p., Ms. in *Arkansas Gazette* Foundation Library. By a warrant drawn on October 25, 1821, $20 was paid "To R. Crittenden for Epence [sic] of announcing the apportionment of Representatives."

36. Lonnie J. White, *Politics on the Southwestern Frontier: Arkansas Territory, 1819–1836* (Memphis, Tenn.: Memphis State University Press, 1964), 33–36.

37. *Gazette,* Apr. 23, 1822.

ARKANSAS, A. T.

SATURDAY, MARCH 4, 1820.

... E. Woodruff and Robert Briggs ... ng formed a connexion in business, Gazette will hereafter be conducted r the firm of WOODRUFF & BRIGGS. e would ... re express our warmest ... s for the generous support already ... ded this establishment, the first ever e in the Territory, and we feel as ... d that the public are perfectly aware ... st encounter many difficulties for e length of time, and, considering the ncy of the country, its final success rest in a great measure upon public ... ality; while we shall, by a firm, p ... dent and impartial course of con ... endeavor to merit their approba ... and confidence.

... e have no hesitation in declaring, that principles are those of Republican ... s and the objects we shall steadily ... in view, are the d...ffusion of cor ... political information—the support ... epublicanism, of the Constitution, ... of the constituted authorities of the on—the advancement of the interests griculture, of manufactures, of arts sciences in general, and the im ... rement of morals. Still, after mak ... this statement, we shall depend in a ... degree on an enlightened and lib ... public for its advancement. In the ... ent dearth of news, we should be ... y happy to receive the productions

METEOROLOGICAL JOURNAL.
NO. 1. FEBRUARY, 1820.

Days of the month	Days of the week	Thermometer			Point of the Wind	Remarks on the Weather
		Sun rise	2 o'clock P.M.	3 o'clock P.M.		
1	T	53	58	50	NW3 SW3	Fair, A. M. cloudy, wind high, P. M.
2	W	51	65	56	SW3 W4 NW3	Continued rain with thunder.
3	Th	27	50	55	NW3 N2	Flying clouds, A. M. fine and clear, P. M.
4	F	30	55	45	NW2 SW2 S3	Weather clear, wind high.
5	S	39	61	58	S2 SW3 W	Flying clouds, wind high.
6	Sa	58	70	66	S1 S2 SW3	Cloudy, A. M. rain & rain, in the night.
6	M	58	60	50	S NW1	Weather fair.
8	T	50	71	68	W1 SW3	Cloudy, A. M. fair, P. M.
9	W	56	75	66	SW W	Fair, A. M. rain and thun. in the night.
10	Th	55	56	42	NW3 NW1	Flying clouds, A. M. clear, P. M.
11	F	34	64	52	SW1 SW3	Fine and clear.
12	S	56	60	65	SW2	Cloudy.
13	Su	43	71	50	SW1	Clear.
14	M	65	79	71	SW3 SW3	Clear, wind high.
15	T	68	83	76	SW3 SW3	Cloudy, rain and thunder in the night
16	W	65	68	53	SW3 SW2	Cloudy, A. M. clear, P. M.
17	Th	53	66	52	SW1 W	Fine and clear.
18	F	43	70	52	W	Fair.
19	S	60	73	70	SW3 S2	Cloudy towards the South.
20	Su	43	53	48	NW3	Clear.
21	M	31	50	50	NW3 W1 SW3	Frosty, A. M. clear and fine.
22	T	50	68	60	SW3 S3	Flying clouds, wind high.
23	W	63	79	70	S3 SW2 S	Cloudy, A. M. Fair, P. M.
24	Th	68	80	70	SW2 SW3	Flying clouds, wind high. [rough.
25	F	70	80	70	SW3 S3 S4	Cloudy, A. M. rain & thun. P. M. wind very
26	S	50	56	49	NW1 NW2	Fine and clear.
27	Su	40	66	56	NW1 W2	Do.
28	M	55	68	56	NW W1	Do.
29	T	50	79	80	W2 W1	Do.

From the above table it will appear that the lowest point of the Thermometer was on the 3d, at sunrise, when the mercury was at 27°, and the highest point on the 15th, at 2 o'clock in the afternoon, when it reached 83°. The different degrees of the wind will be found thus noted, S, scarcely any wind, the vane merely pointing to the South; S1, a gentle breeze; S2, a brisk wind; S3, a gale; S4 ...

soul without restriction. No m ... was however, made on the subject ... the bill for the admission of Maine ... ed the House of Representatives.

When the bill was brought ... Senate it was referred to a comm ... who reported it with an amendm ... which embraced provisions for aut ... zing the formation of a constitution ... state government for Missouri, with ... restriction. Mr. Roberts, of Penn ... vania, moved a re-commitment to ... committee, with instructions to re ... out the amendment. This motion ... advocated by Messrs. Roberts, King ... Burril, Morrill, Otis and Dana, ... opposed by Messrs. Smith, Lloyd, T ... con, Barbour and Logan, and was ... nally decided in the negative by a ... jority of seven. The Senate have ... virtually decided that they will set ... a law for the admission of Maine ... with restriction. The National Intel ... gencer observes "that the question ... sorbs so much attention, that until it ... definitely settled, it may almost be sa ... no other business will be done in Co ... gress." Every Senator voted on t ... subject except Mr. King who has b ... recently re-elected from New York, ... had not arrived. 43 votes were p ... on the subject.

From the present appearances the f ... of the application for admission will ... the same as last year. [Ma. Ga

There are printed in London ab ... three different newspapers, one hund ... and twenty in the several countie ... England and Wales, exclusive of M ... dlesex, and twenty-eight in Scotla ... making together a total of two hund ... and eleven public journals publishe ... England. In Ireland they have al ... one third of the number.

The first Meteorological Journal.

The first Extra.

THE ARKANSAS GAZETTE—EXTRA.

ARKANSAS, (A. T.), TUESDAY EVENING, FEBRUARY 22, 1820.

Washington City, Dec. 7.

... committee appointed yesterday to ... the President reported that they had ... d with the order of the house, and ... sident returned for answer that he ... ake a communication at 12 o'clock. ... age from the President of the United ... as delivered by his Secretary, which ... d by the clerk, as follows:—

MESSAGE.

Citizens of the Senate. *of the House of Representatives:*

... public buildings being advanced to ... to afford accommodation for con ... I offer you my sincere congratulations ... commencement of your duties in ... bled.

... inging to view the incidents most ... ng attention, which have occurred ... our last session, I regret to have to ... that several of our principal cities ... fered by sickness; that an unusual ... that prevailed in the middle and west ... es; and that a derangement has been ... ome of our monied institutions, which ... portionately effected their credit. I ... t, however, to have it in my power ... re you that the health of our cities is ... mpletely restored; that the produce ... ear, though less abundant than usu ... is not only be amply sufficient for home ...

ritory by Spain. It was surrounded by the territories of the United States, on every side, except on that of the ocean. Spain had lost her authority over it, and, falling into the hands of adventurers connected with the savages, it was made the means of unceasing annoyance and injury to our Union, in many of its essential interests. By this cession, then, Spain ceded a territory, in reality, of no value to her, and obtained concessions of the highest importance, by the settlement of long standing differences with the United States, affecting their respective claims and limits, and likewise relieved herself from the obligation of a treaty, relating to it, which she had failed to fulfil, and also from the responsibility incident to the most flagrant and pernicious abuses of her rights, where she could not support her authority.

It being known that the treaty was formed under these circumstances, not a doubt was entertained that his Catholic Majesty would have ratified it without delay. I regret to have to state that this reasonable expectation has been disappointed; that the treaty was not ratified, within the time stipulated, and has not since been ratified. As it is important that the nature and character of this unexpected occurrence should be distinctly understood, I think it my duty to communicate to you all the facts and circumstances, in my possession, relating to it.

his Catholic Majesty, in Florida, which, it was understood had conveyed all the lands, which till then had been ungranted. It was the intention of the parties to annul these latter grants, and that clause was drawn for that express purpose, and for none other.

The date of these grants was unknown, but it was understood to be posterior to that inserted in the article: indeed, it must be obvious to all, that, if that provision in the treaty had not the effect of annulling these grants, it would be altogether nugatory.— Immediately after the treaty was concluded and ratified by this government, an intimation was received that these grants were of anterior date to that fixed on by the treaty; and that they would not, of course, be affected by it. The mere possibility of such a case so inconsistent with the intention of the parties, and the meaning of the article, induced this government to demand an explanation on the subject, which was immediately granted, and which corresponds with this statement. With respect to the other act alleged, that this government had tolerated, or protected, an expedition against Texas, it is utterly without foundation.— Every discountenance has invariably been given to every such attempt from within the limits of the United States, as is fully evinced by the acts of the government, and the proceedings of the courts.

There being cause, however, to appre ... d in the course of the last summer,

other nations, even those most friendly ... her: while, by confining ourselves wit ... that limit, we cannot fail to obtain t ... well merited approbation. We must h ... peace on a frontier where we have bee ... long disturbed, our citizens must be ind ... nified for losses so long since sustained ... for which indemnity has been so long ... justly withheld from them. Accompli ... these great objects we obtain all that i ... sirable.

But his Catholic Majesty has twice ... clared his determination to send a min ... to the United States, to ask explanat ... on certain points, and to give them ... pecting his delay to ratify the treaty. ... we act, by taking the ceded territory, ... proceeding to execute the other condit ... of the treaty, before his minister ar ... and is heard? This is a case which-f ... a strong appeal to the justice, the mag ... nimity and honor of this people. Muc ... due to courtesy between nations. B ... short delay, we shall lose nothing; ... resting on the ground of immutable tr ... and justice, we cannot be diverted fro ... purpose. It ought to be presumed tha ... explanations which may be given to ... minister of Spain, will be satisfactory ... produce the desired result. Is any e ... the delay, for the purpose mentioned, ... a further manifestation of the sincer ... dre to terminate in the most friendly ... ner all differences with Spain, cannot ...

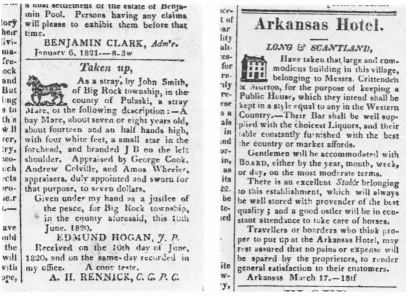

Advertising woodcuts used in 1821.

forerunner of the modern markets reports, which first appeared on January 27, 1821, and was copied from the *Louisiana Advertiser* as often as that paper came to hand.

Type foundries sold an assortment of small woodcuts to be used in advertisements. The *Gazette's* ads had only variations in type to call attention to them until a cut of a running horse was used in the corner of an estray ad on January 6, 1821. A cut of a steamboat appeared in the steamboat Comet's ad on January 27, and a cut of a three-story tavern adorned the Long and Scantland hotel ad on March 17. No more were used until March of 1822, and it was several years before they were used profusely.

Complete news coverage was not attempted by the *Gazette* or any of its contemporaries. Local news was greatly neglected. In the editor's judgment, the most important news pertained to the administration of the national government, and he had done his duty if he gave his readers a summary of Washington events. The most important single item was always the president's message at the opening of each session of Congress, because it was a "state of the union" address. It was always reprinted from the first newspaper that arrived containing it. The first president's message after the establishment of the *Gazette* was delivered on December 5, 1819. Woodruff received it in a package of New Orleans papers brought by a friend on February 18, 1820, and there was not time enough to set it for the next day's *Gazette*. Although the message was already two and a half months old, and Woodruff's paper supply was dangerously low, he distributed the message in his first "extra" on February 22, a four-column half-sheet containing also part of the Congressional Journal and one ad.

Since exchange papers were the main source of news from outside Arkansas, the mail was extremely important to the *Gazette*. Most western towns where newspapers were published were blessed with at least weekly mail service, but Arkansas Post received mail only once in four weeks when the mail rider was on schedule. To fill the space when the mail was late, Woodruff fell back on papers and letters brought to the village by travelers, and apologized when more local news than usual had to fill the space.

Officially there was a fortnightly mail in 1820, but it was far less than that in reality. Often the mail riders were overloaded and brought only the letters, leaving the newspapers to accumulate until they were too old to be useful. Woodruff never gave up complaining about the mail service, both in the columns of the Gazette and in letters to Washington, but he never licked the problem.

The repeated failures of the mails, leaving him without enough material to fill his columns, and the failure of a new supply of paper to arrive forced him to publish five issues on half-sheets, from February 12 through March 11, 1820. He had ordered paper before he left Nashville, but its transportation to Arkansas was delayed by an unusually low stage of the rivers that lasted several months.

Woodruff had to send cash with his orders for paper, ink, and other supplies, and his employees had to be paid in cash at the end of each week.

One of many appeals
for payment of accounts.

List of agents,
November 11, 1820.

THE GAZETTE.

ARKANSAS:

SATURDAY, NOVEMBER 10, 1821.

END OF VOLUME II.

The present paper completes the second year of the ARKANSAS GAZETTE—and we now feel fairly entitled to call on our subscribers for a settlement. To those who have heretofore paid us in advance, or agreeably to the terms of our paper, we tender our sincere and heartfelt thanks, and solicit a continuance of their patronage and punctuality. With those who are in arrears, we earnestly request a speedy settlement. Too frequent dunning through the paper, is not only unpleasant to us, but it becomes disagreeable (perhaps disgusting) to punctual subscribers, who do not wish to pay for that which does not concern them —we therefore hope those who have hitherto been negligent, will relieve us from this unpleasant task hereafter, by a strict compliance with the terms of the Gazette.

⁂ Persons indebted to this office for Printing, Advertising, &c. will please make payment without delay.

AGENTS FOR THE GAZETTE.

The following gentlemen are authorised to receive, and receipt for, any monies due to this office:

Capt. *Amos Wheeler*, p. m.   Little Rock.
R. P. *P. tman*, p. m.   Fourche de Thomas.
Richard Searcy, p. m.   Davidsonville.
Peyton Tucker, p. m.   White Run P. O.
Col. *Daniel Mooney*,   St. Francis.
Benjamin Fooy,   Hopefield.
James M. Stuart,   Hempstead Co'y.
John English, p. m.   do.
Jacob Barkman, p. m.   Clark County.
Thomas H. Tindall, p. m.   Cadron.
James S. Petty,   Mississippi.
Col. *Edmund Hogan*, p. m.   Chrystal Hill.
Peter H. Bennett,   Point Chico.

Extract of a letter from a gentleman in St. Louis. Mo. dated the 15th ult. to his

He much preferred that his subscribers should pay in advance, and made it attractive by offering a 25 per cent discount. The subscribers understood advance payment to mean any time during the subscription year, but Woodruff considered it to mean payment at the time of subscribing. As the end of the year drew near, he modified his terms as a compromise. In the future, subscribers would pay $3 at the beginning of the year, $3.50 at any time within the first six months, or $4 thereafter.[38]

Woodruff handled the collections in the village, and the *Gazette's* agents took care of the rest. All the bills were adjusted to make them due at the end of the volume, regardless of when the subscriptions began.[39] The discouraging response to repeated requests for payment revealed soon after the end of the first year that about half the subscribers had never intended to pay, but had signed up for the *Gazette* only to encourage a project they considered worthwhile. The *Gazette's* expenses far exceeded its receipts during its first 18 months. At the end of that time, Woodruff sent out more than 200 bills, and received in return less than $10 during the next three months.[40]

Polite requests, appeals to the subscribers' sense of justice and honesty, explanations of his need for money, and suggestions that prompt payment would make improvements in the paper possible, all fell on deaf ears. Threats that he would accept only subscriptions paid in advance, or that he would discontinue delinquent subscriptions, or that he would sue the delinquents were largely ignored and Woodruff carried them out only to a limited extent. A threat to advertise the names and new addresses of those who had moved away without paying was not even partially executed.

It was a rare editor who did not accept produce, peltry, and other home products in payment for subscriptions. Woodruff had to do a certain amount of this too,[41] but never once did he mention this type of payment in the paper.

Agents were authorized to accept subscriptions and collect and issue receipts for all debts due the *Gazette,* receiving a small commission for their services. The first list of agents appeared in the second issue on December 4, 1819, and consisted of only two names—Richard Searcy of Davidsonville and Peter H. Bennett of Point Chicot. By the end of the first year there were 13 agents, eight of whom were postmasters.

In the first issue Woodruff advertised, "A lad from 14 to 16 years of age, of respectable connexions, and of studious and industrious habits, is wanted immediately at this office, as an Apprentice to the Printing business." Evidently nobody took advantage of this opportunity right away, for the advertisement continued for several months.

The partnership with Briggs lasted a little more than a year. In the issue of

38. *Ibid.,* Oct. 14, 1820.
39. *Ibid.,* Nov. 11, 1820.
40. *Ibid.,* May 19, Sept. 1, 1821.
41. *Ibid.,* Feb. 26, 1867 (weekly edition).

May 12, 1821, the announcement was made that it had been dissolved by mutual consent, and that Woodruff would attend to the settlement of accounts. There is evidence that the agreement was not made until about the time it was announced, but was made retroactive to March 15, the end of a fiscal quarter, probably to simplify bookkeeping.

When Woodruff rented the little log cabin on Front Street from Richmond Peeler, several lawsuits were pending or threatened against the landlord by his creditors. Joseph Stillwell, father of Peeler's divorced wife, obtained a court order directing a sale of the property occupied by the *Gazette* office. The sale was advertised in the *Gazette's* third issue, on December 11, 1819, to take place on January 11, 1820, but apparently Peeler did not then lose title to the property. The *Gazette* was still occupying the building as late as April 1, 1820, but Peeler made no reference to the *Gazette* as a tenant when he advertised it for sale on July 15, 1820.

A new location for the printing office was not announced in the *Gazette,* but Woodruff and Briggs acquired a lot shown on the plat of the town of Arkansas as lot 14, with a 45-foot front on Poindexter Street. On May 14, 1821, Briggs deeded his undivided half interest in the lot to Woodruff, for a stated consideration of $100.[42] Briggs left Arkansas soon afterwards and worked as a printer at New Orleans, where he died in a yellow fever epidemic on September 19, 1824, at the age of 28.[43]

Joint ownership by the two men suggests that lot 14 was intended as the site of the *Gazette* office, but no proof of the *Gazette's* occupancy of it is found. However, a brick building was pointed out to William F. Pope in 1832 as the former *Gazette* office.[44] If the *Gazette* ever occupied a brick building at Arkansas Post, it must have been located on lot 14.

Woodruff and Briggs were a long time getting the appointment as public printer for the federal government. Woodruff left the matter entirely in the hands of James Woodson Bates, who neglected it until shortly before the end of his first session. Since Bates was a protégé of Crittenden, and since there was a coolness between Crittenden and Woodruff, Bates' negligence may have been significant. In the meantime the secretary of state, taking for granted that John McArthur had established his paper and unaware of the *Gazette's* existence, issued the appointment to McArthur. Woodruff and Briggs had reason to believe this had been done, but assumed that the appointment would be transferred to them when the facts were known in Washington. They could not wait for their appointment to reach them if they were to publish the acts passed at that session within the time prescribed by law, so they began publication of the Laws of the United States on April 8, 1820, without the proper authority. The matter was prolonged for months by their dependence on Bates, their ignorance of the customary procedure,

42. Arkansas County Deed Book C, 669–670.

43. *Gazette,* Nov. 9, 1824; *Courrier de la Louisiane* (New Orleans, La.), Sept. 21, 28, Oct. 4, 1824.

44. Pope, *Early Days in Arkansas,* 67.

and the erratic mail service. For at least the first year and a half of the *Gazette's* existence, the proprietors did not collect a penny from the Department of State.[45]

Woodruff received a small commission for taking subscriptions for a few other publications, and he sold printed blanks to be used by public officials, lawyers, and merchants. Almanacs published elsewhere were offered for sale, but in this field the printing office had competition. Elijah Morton advertised his new store in the same issue in which Woodruff advertised his 1821 almanacs, and included an almanac in the list of his merchandise. Although the usual spot for new ads was on page three with the local news, Woodruff put Morton's ad on page four with the old ads and poetry, where it was likely to be overlooked.[46]

More formidable competition was threatened a few months later. On September 23, 1821, Woodruff published the prospectus of a weekly newspaper to be published at Davidsonville in Lawrence County by John H. Wilkins and Company. Its name was to be the *Arkansas Herald,* and like McArthur's paper of the same name, it never materialized. If Woodruff was not acquainted with Wilkins, he at least knew him by reputation. A few months after he left Nashville, his old boss, Thomas G. Bradford, had surrendered the *Clarion* to his creditors, and Wilkins and Thomas H. Mc-Keen had conducted it for almost a year. Late in August, 1821, it was returned to Bradford's control,[47] and during the same week the prospectus for the *Arkansas Herald* was sent to Woodruff for publication.

This was the rival press with which Crittenden hoped either to bring Woodruff to his knees or eliminate him altogether. Ten years later, Woodruff said Crittenden had tried to effect a proscription of the *Gazette* about this time,[48] which would have been impractical without another press to which the business could be transferred. With Crittenden's help, the proposed *Arkansas Herald* might have succeeded if its proprietors had not set its subscription rates at the high figure of $5 a year, and declined to begin publication unless 300 subscribers paid half a year in advance before November 1.

The legislature's most important problem in the October, 1820 session was one it had wrestled with in the previous session, the selection of a new territorial capital. Little Rock's fight for the seat of government had been complicated by conflicting claims to the land on which the town was platted. Title was still in the United States, and two sets of claimants hoped to get the patent. James Bryan and William M. O'Hara had laid claim to the site in 1819 by virtue of the location of New Madrid certificates. Amos Wheeler of St. Louis had come to Little Rock in December, 1819 to make the surveys and act as their agent.

45. Carter, *Territorial Papers,* XIX, 218, 228–230, 237, 240, 277–278, 287, 296.

46. *Gazette,* Dec. 9, 1820.

47. Nashville *Clarion,* Aug. 22, 29, 1821; Clarence S. Brigham, *History and Bibliography of American Newspapers 1690–1820* (Worcester, Mass.: American Antiquarian Society, 1947), II, 1063.

48. *Gazette,* Oct. 26, 1831.

Soon after his arrival, William Russell, the famous St. Louis land speculator, informed him that he held a pre-emption claim covering the choicest
part of the same land. Pre-emption claims took precedence over all others,
being based on actual settlement of the specific tract involved. Russell as
yet had only a verbal agreement with the supposed owners of the claim, but
he offered a compromise and demanded $25,000, which the New Madrid
proprietors refused to pay. Their investigations convinced them that Russell's claim was worthless, and when he returned on January 1, 1820, they
unceremoniously threw him out. Six days later he had his title to the pre-
emption claim in writing. He then sued out from two justices of the peace a
warrant of forcible entry and detainer, and the jury in the justices' court
returned a verdict in his favor. Chester Ashley had arrived by that time, and
was acting as attorney for the New Madrid proprietors. He brought the case
before the Pulaski Court of Common Pleas on a writ of *certiorari,* and the
proceedings of the justices' court were set aside. Russell appealed to the
Superior Court.[49]

Meanwhile, Wheeler had submitted a written proposition to the legislature
on February 21, 1820, pledging to give the territory a public square and a
building for use as a capitol building and court room, and to give lots for a
county public square if needed, and for markets, schools, churches, and a
cemetery. He also bound the New Madrid proprietors to prepare before
August 1 accommodations for at least 100 people who might be present at
the next session of the legislature.[50] But the legislature could not decide
between Little Rock and Cadron at the February session, and postponed consideration of the matter until October. Wheeler was confident of ultimate
success, and in a burst of exaggerated self importance, wrote his family in
May that he was preparing houses for the legislature's next session, and that
Woodruff and Briggs would bring their printing office to Little Rock early
in June.[51] Probably the most Woodruff and Briggs had promised was that
the *Gazette* would go wherever the seat of government went.

All this time, one Benjamin Murphy held a regular chain of title to the
same pre-emption right Russell claimed, and the pre-emption certificate

49. Amos Wheeler, Jr. to Amos Wheeler, Sr., Wheelersville [Little Rock], Decem-
ber 30, 1819, in Wheeler Family Papers, owned in 1959 by George H. Stone, North
Stonington, Conn.; William Russell vs. Amos Wheeler et al., June Term, 1821, in
Samuel H. Hempstead, *Reports of Cases Argued and Determined in the United States
Superior Court for the Territory of Arkansas, from 1820 to 1836; and in the United
States District Court for the District of Arkansas, from 1836 to 1849; and in the United
States Circuit Court for the District of Arkansas, in the Ninth Circuit, from 1839 to
1856* (Boston: Little, Brown and Co., 1856), 3–8; Pulaski County Deed Book B, 24–31.

50. Amos Wheeler for himself and for William M. O'Hara and James Bryan to the
Legislature of the Territory of Arkansas, Post of Arkansas, February 21, 1820, Ms. in
office of Arkansas secretary of state, photocopy in *Arkansas Gazette* Foundation library.

51. Amos Wheeler, Jr. to Amos Wheeler, Sr., Little Rock, May 21, 1820, Ms. in
Wheeler Family Papers.

THE PRESS IN THE WILDERNESS

was issued to him by the land office at Batesville. This gave him the first right to purchase the land whenever it should be offered for sale by the government, and Russell had no alternative but to abandon his claim. But during the session of the legislature in October, 1820, Russell bought a half interest in Murphy's claim,[52] and the other half went to men of political influence. Subsequent transfers in the spring and summer divided the pre-emption claim among Crittenden and his friends, Henry Conway, Joseph Hardin, Robert C. Oden, William Trimble, and Townsend Dickinson, with Russell still owning half. The New Madridites had also let in a few others, including Chester Ashley, but Bryan remained the principal owner, and Governor Miller was the only high public official on this side.

The act relocating the seat of government at Little Rock was passed on October 11 and was approved by Governor Miller on October 18, to take effect on June 1, 1821. Wheeler's proposals of the previous February were accepted, and he entered into a bond for performance in the penal sum of $20,000.[53] The *Gazette* announced on October 28 that it would move to Little Rock as soon as a suitable building could be erected for its office. Woodruff probably expected to move no later than June 1, but 14 months passed before the first issue of the paper was published at the new capital.

Two keelboats transporting settlers from Tennessee and Kentucky to Little Rock stopped at Arkansas Post on February 18 and 19, 1821, and reached their destination on March 11. Among the passengers were Isaac Watkins and his family, a niece of whom would later become Woodruff's wife. Another passenger was Joseph Thornhill, a young British immigrant and a carpenter by trade.[54] He built and owned the *Gazette's* first Little Rock office.

Thornhill had been at Little Rock only 17 days on March 28, 1821, when he paid $10 for lot 12 in block 82, Original City of Little Rock, and took a deed from Elias Austin Elliott as agent for Henry Elliott, one of the New Madrid proprietors.[55] On this lot, located at the southwest corner of Cherry (now Second) and Louisiana streets, he built a small log cabin.

The first function of the territorial government at Little Rock was a session of the Superior Court held in June, 1821 by Judge Andrew Scott and Judge Benjamin Johnson. Judge Scott was currently the owner of a small part of the pre-emption claim, and he left it to Judge Johnson, who had just begun his service on the bench, to write the decision in the forcible entry

52. Pulaski County Deed Book B, 18–24.
53. Amos Wheeler's bond, Post of Arkansas, Oct. 23, 1820, Ms. in office of secretary of state, photocopy in *Arkansas Gazette* Foundation library.
54. *Gazette,* Feb. 24, 1821; Ms. diary of Maria Toncray Watkins, 1821–1829, at Arkansas History Commission; Deposition of Robert A. Watkins, Sept. 24, 1841, in Ms. transcript of trial of M. Cunningham vs. Chester Ashley and Roswell Beebe in the Pulaski Circuit Court in Chancery, certified Sept. 29, 1848 by Gordon N. Peay, clerk, in Arkansas Supreme Court library.
55. Unrecorded Ms. deed, Elias Austin Elliott to Joseph Thornhill, Mar. 28, 1821, in John E. Knight Collection, Arkansas History Commission.

and detainer case. The decision was in Russell's favor, and the case was re-manded to the lower court for a new trial. The New Madridites were not finally defeated, because the court ruled only on the errors of the lower court, not touching on the relative merits of the two land claims, which would have to be decided by the General Land Office. But Russell now had to be given access to the land he claimed.[56]

Most of the few buildings had been erected by or for the New Madrid proprietors, and they had no intention of surrendering them to Russell. Forti-fied with whisky and disguised with paint and masks, the men of the town and its vicinity used ropes and chains to set the cabins on logs and pull them eastward to the adjoining Quapaw land, which was nearer than their own undisputed land. At least one house could not be moved, and was burned or blown up. By nightfall, the disputed tract was cleared.[57]

There was no need to move the cabins from the land the pre-emptioners did not claim. The pre-emption claim, now covering the full amount of land the law allowed, was an L-shaped tract that took two long, narrow strips out of the nearly square New Madrid claim. The New Madridites had laid out the territorial public square on parts of four blocks. The exact center of the square, where presumably the small frame capitol building stood, was in the middle of Orange Street, (now Capitol Avenue), 75 feet east of its intersection with Main Street. The building and more than two thirds of the square were on land claimed only by the New Madridites, and the part of the square that lay on the disputed tract was in excess of the amount of land promised to the legislature. Thus the New Madridites had the seat of gov-ernment, but the pre-emptioners had the river landing and most of the land fronting on the river.[58]

Even if the New Madridites could have found a good landing on their small strip of undisputed waterfront, they could not have established a new landing because swamps and Russell's ownership of pre-emption claims on the opposite bank cut off the approaches to it. A town without river frontage and a good landing was as good as dead, and could not hope to remain the territorial capital. The pre-emptioners' townsite could not hope to become the seat of government, for it was narrow and oddly shaped, and offered no chance for future expansion. Moreover, both claims were on land that had been owned by the Quapaw Nation at the time of the passage of the laws authorizing their respective types of claims to be established on public lands. This might well be the fatal flaw that would prevent either group from getting

56. Hempstead, *Reports*, 3–8; Depositions of Judge Benjamin Johnson, Sept. 20 and 23, 1841, in Ms. transcript, Cunningham vs. Ashley and Beebe, twice state that this term of court was held at Little Rock.

57. Walter B. Douglas (ed.), *Three Years Among the Indians and Mexicans, by General Thomas James* (St. Louis: Missouri Historical Society, 1916), 100–102.

58. See A Map of the Town of Little Rock by William Russell and Associates, filed February, 1822 and Dec. 24, 1844, Pulaski County Deed Book Q, 84–85; Roswell Beebe's maps of Little Rock, filed Dec. 26, 1839 and Feb. 29, 1840, Deed Book L, 330–331, 490–491.

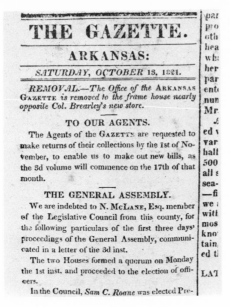

Title page of the first book
printed in Arkansas.

a patent. Clearly, both sets of claimants stood to lose everything unless they combined their holdings.

A compromise was in the making when the legislature convened at Little Rock on October 1, 1821, in the cabin the New Madridites had built. Woodruff had expected to move to Little Rock long before this time. He must have agreed to relinquish his building at Arkansas Post to its next tenant, for the *Gazette* of October 13 announced that its office had been moved to the frame house nearly opposite Colonel Brearley's new store.

The previous legislature had ordered pamphlet publication of the laws currently in force in Arkansas, consisting of the organic laws of the territories of Missouri and Arkansas with all amendments and supplements, the acts passed by the Missouri legislature in 1818, and those passed by the Arkansas legislature in 1819 and 1820. Woodruff had submitted his proposals for printing this pamphlet, and Crittenden had authorized him to do the work in the summer of 1821. The book was finished about the time the legislature assembled at Little Rock, and the extra copies were offered for sale for $1 a copy on October 2, 1821. It was the first book printed in Arkansas.[59]

59. *Gazette,* Sept. 29, 1821; Albert H. Allen (ed.), *Arkansas Imprints 1821–1876* (New York: Published for The Bibliographical Society of America by R. R. Bowker Company, 1947), 1.

Woodruff made his first visit to Little Rock while the legislature was in session in October. He may have traveled with Chester Ashley, who was returning from Missouri with his bride of three months, Mary W. W. Elliott. He visited in Dr. Matthew Cunningham's home,[60] made arrangements to board there, and undoubtedly made the final arrangements for the future *Gazette* office.

His most important business at Little Rock was the delivery of the law books ordered by the legislature. He found Crittenden still angry and uncooperative. As secretary, he refused to allow Woodruff access to the legislature's journals for publication. As acting governor, he refused to give him a copy of his message to the legislature.[61] When Woodruff presented his bill for $5 for publishing Crittenden's proclamation relative to the election of the delegate to Congress, Crittenden refused to certify it, saying Woodruff would have to submit it to Governor Miller for approval. These acts of hostility may have followed the argument over Woodruff's bill for publishing the law book, or they may have preceded it.

Woodruff's rates were in line with those established by the St. Louis printing offices, and he did not adjust his figures to allow for the difference in value between current money and territorial scrip, which he was required to accept at par for public printing, although merchants were then taking it at a discount of about 25 per cent. His system of figuring his charges was the same he had learned in New York, by which the rates were broken down into minute details. He made separate charges for the composition ($1 for 1,000 ems of text and index, plus $2 for 1,000 ems of side notes, plus 1¼ cents for the average of the small type in the body of the pages, such as titles and signatures), for the press work ($3 for the first token worked on each form, plus $1 for each additional token worked on the same form, this having to do with the number of copies printed), for the paper, and for the labor of folding, stitching, and other bindery work. Having no experience in such matters, Crittenden evidently did not realize how high a bill of this kind could mount. Woodruff did a large part of the work himself, but had to hire an extra journeyman to help, and paid him approximately $150 for this work alone.

The bill came to $336.89½. Crittenden considered it much too high, and gave Woodruff an order on the auditor for only $250. Woodruff accepted the warrant for $250 drawn in his favor on October 23, but had no intention of writing off the $86.89½ still due him. Two months later, he asked Governor Miller to compare his bill with his proposals and issue an order for the balance due him. It remained unpaid, and in October of 1823, he petitioned the legislature for an appropriation to cover the bill with interest since the date it was audited, filing a detailed explanation of his charges with the sec-

60. Depositions of William E. Woodruff, Sept. 15, 1841, and Samuel Hinkson, Sept. 29, 1841, in Ms. transcript, Cunningham vs. Ashley and Beebe, 599, 646.
61. *Gazette,* Feb. 26, 1822.

retary of the Legislative Council. The legislature appropriated $86.89 to pay the account, but did not pay the interest requested.[62]

While Woodruff was at Little Rock in October of 1821, the *Gazette* did not indicate that he was absent from Arkansas Post. Upon his return, he did not strike back at Crittenden editorially, but through a correspondent who signed "Arkansas Farmer" in the issue of November 17, he again showed Crittenden that the *Gazette* could be a powerful weapon even when its editor remained silent. This writer complained that Arkansas was afflicted with an acting governor who was a practicing lawyer, and who held the loyalty of an ever widening circle of supporters by patronage and protection. The letter was prompted by an act passed by the legislature and urged by Crittenden in his message, authorizing the governor to borrow as much as $10,000 on the faith of the territory.

The writer, who claimed that some of the legislators who had done Crittenden's bidding had been irregularly elected, took a dim view of individuals and governments who lived on credit, and comforted himself with the thought that Governor Miller would soon return to Arkansas, and surely would refuse to contract this debt.

When the legislature adjourned on October 24, it had not relocated the seat of government, and it had appointed commissioners to select a permanent county seat for Pulaski County, who five months later reported Little Rock as their choice. A compromise agreement that made the rival claimants joint owners of the townsite was signed at Batesville on November 22, 1821 by Chester Ashley, acting for the New Madrid claimants, and William Russell, acting for the pre-emptioners.[63] All these things gave hope that Little Rock would continue as the capital, which in turn gave Woodruff assurance that it would be the permanent home of the *Gazette*.

Two days after the compromise agreement was signed, Woodruff published the last issue of the *Gazette* at the town of Arkansas, and announced that the move to Little Rock was at hand. The first snow of the season fell during the night of November 23, and the weather was bitterly cold for the next few weeks. A trip across the uninhabited prairie in this kind of weather was unpleasant, but it is not likely that Woodruff had any choice but to make the overland trip. The weather did not moderate until long after his arrival at Little Rock, and at one point the river was frozen. Probably there was enough ice in the river when he began the trip to make travel by keelboat dangerous, if not impossible.

There is some question as to when he started the trip. On January 8, 1822

---

62. William E. Woodruff to Governor Miller, Little Rock, Dec. 31, 1821; Woodruff to T. W. Newton, Little Rock, Oct. 16, 1823; Woodruff to the General Assembly, Little Rock, Oct. 16, 1823, Mss. in the L. C. Gulley Collection, Arkansas History Commission; Auditor's Register of Warrants A, n.p.; *Acts Passed by the General Assembly of the Territory of Arkansas, at the Session in October, 1823. Published by Authority.* (Little Rock: Printed by William E. Woodruff, Printer to the Territory, 1824), 54.

63. Pulaski County Deed Book B, 140–145.

he said he had been at Little Rock four or five weeks,[64] which places his arrival between December 4 and 11 and indicates that he left soon after he published his last issue at Arkansas Post. However, he signed deeds at Arkansas Post on December 13, 1821, by which he conveyed to William Russell, Daniel Mooney, and Eli J. Lewis several Spanish land grants and six town lots,[65] the first real estate he had ever owned. This business, together with the hope of a change in the weather and his need for a shipment of paper that was already long overdue could have delayed his departure.

64. Eugene C. Barker (ed.), *The Austin Papers,* Vol. II of *Annual Report of the American Historical Association for the Year 1919* (Washington: Government Printing Office, 1924), Part 1, 461.
65. Arkansas County Deed Book C, 744, 748, 750.

3

THE CALM BEFORE THE STORM

Little Rock

1821-1826 WHEN WOODRUFF PUBLISHED his first issue at Little Rock on December 29, 1821, nothing about the embryonic town merited description. It had only a few crude cabins and perhaps half a dozen families, and the best of the broad streets shown on the plat were nothing more than paths through the woods.

The one-room log printing office was no showplace, but it was sturdy enough to stand another 66 years, in almost constant use. Woodruff slept at the office, and according to custom, was expected to provide quarters for his apprentices and unmarried employees. During the first year at Little Rock, he advertised for an apprentice for almost five months and for a journeyman printer for almost four months. Presumably both positions were filled about the time the ads were withdrawn.[1] He took his meals at the nearby home of Dr. Matthew Cunningham and his wife, Eliza, near the southwest corner of what is now Third and Main streets. Chester and Mary Ashley also boarded there for most of 1822, and later made a place for Woodruff at their own table.[2]

His paper supply was his greatest problem during the first two years at Little Rock. He had expected to receive a new supply in October, but the low stage of the rivers had made it impossible for the manufacturers to ship it, and he had moved to Little Rock with only enough paper to print two is-

1. *Gazette,* Mar. 26 through Aug. 13, May 28 through Sept. 10, 1822.
2. Deposition of William E. Woodruff, Sept. 15, 1841, in Ms. Transcript, M. Cunningham vs. Ashley and Beebe, Pulaski Circuit Court in Chancery, certified Sept. 29, 1848 by Gordon N. Peay, clerk, 594. The Cunninghams may also have fed Woodruff's apprentices and employees during this period, as they advertised for four or five gentleman boarders in *Gazette,* Jan. 7, 1822. The first home of the Ashleys, where Woodruff was a boarder, was a one-room log cabin at Cherry (now Second) and Cumberland. See Jane Georgine Woodruff, "William E. Woodruff," *Arkansas Pioneers* (Little Rock: Arkansas Pioneers Assn., Oct., 1913), 3.

sues.[3] He had stretched it to cover four issues by printing them on half-sheets, partially compensating for the reduced size by using his smallest type. He then had to suspend publication for two weeks, but received a small quantity of paper in time to resume full-sheet publication on February 9, 1822.

The steamboat Eagle, the first to ascend the Arkansas River as far as Little Rock, arrived on March 16.[4] Evidently it brought the paper Woodruff had waited for since October, as well as a few stock woodcuts used to illustrate advertisements.

The next paper order was not filled correctly, and a sheet half an inch shorter and perhaps a quarter of an inch narrower than the regular size was sent. Woodruff had to use it or suspend, but by narrowing his margins he gave his subscribers the usual quantity of reading matter.[5] The next order was delayed by a yellow fever quarantine of the steamboat that transported it from St. Louis,[6] and after that another low water period cut off shipments for almost six months.[7]

3. *Gazette,* Dec. 29, 1821. In later years, Woodruff forgot about the two weeks suspension caused by the lack of paper, and he and his successors boasted that the continuity of the *Gazette's* publication was broken only by the issues missed during the move.

4. *Ibid.,* Mar. 19, 1822.

5. *Ibid.,* June 25, 1822.

6. *Ibid.,* Nov. 5, 1822.

7. *Ibid.,* July 8, 29, 1823.

In the 104 weeks between December 29, 1821 and December 16, 1823 inclusive, two issues were not published, 16 were printed on half-sheets, 30 were printed on the slightly smaller full sheets, 11 were printed on expensive stationery or book stock of approximately half-sheet size but folded into four pages, and six were printed on bright blue full sheets probably intended for job printing. Thus Woodruff had some kind of paper problem for 65 regular issues out of 104.

The editor made a valiant effort to maintain a proper balance between news and advertising during this period, but advertising was the paper's main support, and the law required publication of long legal ads from each county every fall. In the fall of 1823, with the threat of suspension for want of paper hanging over him, Woodruff published at least one supplement and two "extras" on quarter-sheets, to help fulfill his advertising obligations.

The long run of bad luck ended with the issue of December 23, 1823, as the fourth volume was about to close. Woodruff now had a six-months supply of paper, and made arrangements with a paper manufacturer for annual shipments, so that this disaster would not be likely to strike him again. Feeling that the subscribers had not had their money's worth, he gave them a bonus of the next two issues free.[8]

Saturday publication was no longer practical after the move to Little Rock, because the news that arrived in two important mails on Sundays would age another week before Woodruff could lay it before his readers. The first Little Rock issue was published on a Saturday, the next four on Mondays, and thereafter on Tuesday evenings, to allow time for more copious extracts from exchanges received on Sundays.

The irregularities of the mails became increasingly annoying. On one occasion the accumulated eastern mail brought 200 exchange papers, too old to be used, and 24 letters and packets of newspapers sent from Washington by Delegate Bates.[9] The *National Intelligencer* at Washington complained that communication with Arkansas was slower, more difficult, and more uncertain than with almost any other part of the globe.[10] The truth of this statement was dramatically illustrated when copies of the *Gazette* and a Liverpool newspaper arrived on the same day at the Baltimore *Federal Gazette* office, each containing an announcement of the election of John Quincy Adams as president. The *Gazette's* article was based on a rumor and was not entirely accurate, while the Liverpool paper, having later information, reported the election as a definite fact and gave all details correctly.[11]

There was one bright spot for Woodruff in the mail situation. When the fortnightly route between Little Rock and Crawford Court House began in the spring of 1823, the post rider offered home delivery to subscribers living directly on his route, eliminating the inconvenience of calling for the papers

8. *Ibid.,* Dec. 9, 1823.
9. *Ibid.,* June 17, 1823.
10. *Ibid.,* June 24, 1823.
11. *Ibid.,* May 24, 1825.

at the nearest post office.[12] A carrier had delivered the *Gazette* to local subscribers almost from the beginning, but this was the first home delivery outside the town where the paper was published that was mentioned in the *Gazette*. Papers were sent by private conveyance to areas not served by post offices, and it is possible that these may also have had home delivery from the beginning.

The *Gazette* was more than three years old before it had 300 subscribers,[13] and the same old problems of collections continued to plague its proprietor. He had 12 agents when he came to Little Rock, and handled the local business himself. Some of the lawsuits he periodically threatened were filed, and some of the delinquent subscriptions were discontinued, but many people far in arrears still received the *Gazette* regularly. Those who got it by mail were expected to pay the postage each time they took their papers from the post office, but occasionally an indulgent postmaster could be persuaded to put the postage on the cuff. Eventually this was bound to cause trouble, because postmasters were required to turn in their receipts quarterly. Chicot County subscribers who got their mail at Arkansas Post imposed on the postmaster to such an extent that early in 1825 he refused to give them their papers unless they paid their debts for back postage within the current quarter.[14]

Advertising patronage changed with the move to Little Rock, for the merchants and professional men of Arkansas Post rarely advertised after the *Gazette* left their village, and the Little Rock patronage was a new, undeveloped field.

No new special features were introduced during these first years at Little Rock, but some old ones were retained or revived. The New Orleans Prices Current continued as usual most of the time, and at the end of every year a calendar for the coming year was printed. The weather record was resumed on February 9, 1822 under the heading "Journal of the Weather," and continued until June 3, 1823. Another weather feature began on July 12, 1825, when a Little Rock man offered to furnish daily thermometer readings for weekly publication, but he gave it up after seven weeks.

The poetry column was crowded out of the first few Little Rock issues, but returned on January 21, 1822 with a new caption, "The Recess." Up to this time, Woodruff had published only one poem written especially for the *Gazette,* an untitled poem signed "T—m," in the third issue, on December 4, 1819. Late in 1825, the editor received "The Bachelor's Prayer" and "New-Year's Gift for 1826" from a poet using the pseudonym "Coelebs." Woodruff at first planned to circulate the New Year's poem on January 1, possibly as a "carrier's address," but he found it necessary to print both poems in the regular issue for December 27, 1825. He gave them unusual prominence by

12. *Ibid.,* May 6, 1823.
13. *Ibid.,* Dec. 12, 1838; Mar. 18, 1853.
14. *Ibid.,* Jan. 24, 1825.

lag,	stead.			
rce				
tesy	**JOURNAL OF THE WEATHER,** For February, 1822.			

Day of mo.	sun-rise	2 P.M.	Night.	Point of the Wind.	REMARKS ON THE WEATHER.
1	7	46	26	S, NW,	Clear.
2	11	46	25	S, E,	do.
3	27	42	30	W, NW,	Flying clouds.
4	16	44	24	NW, SE,	Clear.
5	17	54	32	SE, SW,	do. high wind at night.
6	16	31	18	NW, NE, NW,	do.
7	8	44	23	NW, SW, S,	do.
8	23	51	34	SW,	Cloudy a. m. clear p. m.
9	23	29	26	NW, N,	Clear, cloudy, snow.
10	11	30	31	SW,	Clear.
11	15	51	39	do.	do. high wind all day and
12	23	62	45	do.	do. [night.
13	31	67	34	SW, W,	Cloudy, fine and clear.
14	26	67	42	NW,	Clear. [p. m. and night.
15	37	55	34	S, SW,	Cloudy, high wind & rain
16	50	66	44	SW, NW,	Cloudy, thunder and high
17	35	50	29	NW,	Cloudy all day. [wind.
18	14	46	28	SE,	Clear.
19	21	43	36	SE, SW, SE,	do. rainy at night.
20	42	57	43	S, SW,	do. very high wind p. m.
21	31	41	28	SW, W,	Cloudy and windy. [& n't.
22	24	46	26	SW, NW,	Clear.
23	20	54	30	NW, W,	do.
24	34	49	30	NW, N,	do.
25	18	55	26	NW, SE,	do.
26	19	61	13	S, SW,	do. with high wind.
27	34	64	54	SW, SE,	do. do. cloudy night.
28	53	55	51	S, SW,	Cloudy, rain p. m. and n't.

Family Medicines

James Miller.

putting them on page three instead of the customary place on page four, with a heading "Original Poetry," and calling attention to them in the news columns. This was the first time original poetry received editorial comment, but according to a study by Howard Cresap Key, the *Gazette* published 65 unquestionably original poems between 1819 and 1843.[15]

The appointment as public printer was renewed in Washington each year as a matter of course, since there was no other printer in Arkansas Territory. For the same reason the office of public printer for the territory, filled by appointment by the legislature, also went to Woodruff automatically. It was the more remunerative of the two, since it involved a greater volume and variety of work, and occasionally offered the possibility of extra money for job printing.

The journals of each session of the legislature were published in the *Gazette*, except that of 1821. No appropriation was made for their publication in pamphlet form until the 1825 session, but Woodruff printed the acts of each session both in the *Gazette* and as pamphlets. By setting the type in slightly wider columns than the *Gazette* usually used, the same type could

15. Howard Cresap Key, "The Arkansas Gazette, 1819–1843: Its Literary Trends," unpublished M.A. thesis, University of Texas, 1935, 113–116.

be used for both newspaper and pamphlet publication, with the addition of the signatures at the end of each act and the topical outlines in the outside margins of the pamphlet version. The territory paid for a specified number of copies to be distributed free to certain public officials, and Woodruff always printed extra copies to be sold from the *Gazette* office to the general public.

The only other books known to have emanated from the *Gazette's* press during these years were two pamphlet editions of the minutes of the Little Rock Association of Regular Baptists in 1824 and 1825, and a pamphlet containing the militia laws in 1826.[16]

After the move to Little Rock, Woodruff no longer studiously avoided every hint of political controversy, but neither did he court it. He neither invited further animosity from Crittenden nor sacrificed his integrity by accepting dictation. Crittenden was the acknowledged political boss, by virtue of Governor Miller's long absences from the territory and his apathy towards most administrative functions except Indian affairs. Most of Crittenden's court of ardent supporters were initially attracted by the political favors he dispensed, but were held at his side by his magnetic personality. His friends loved him wholeheartedly and without reservations, and his enemies silently despised him with the same fervor. Whatever Woodruff's personal feelings may have been, he was not yet ready to throw the *Gazette* into political disputes as an active participant, but more and more he allowed it to be the vehicle for those who cared to discuss political issues. So long as the editor himself remained a silent spectator, he considered that the *Gazette* was in a neutral position.

The *Gazette* had indirectly offered the public a scapegoat to blame for the Choctaw treaty in its issue of May 5, 1821, with publication of part of a letter from a United States senator to a friend in Kentucky, in response to the friend's letter about the treaty. The friend had enclosed a letter from his brother on the same subject, and sent the senator's reply to his brother, who lived at Arkansas Post and gave the letter to Woodruff for publication. One suspects that the Arkansas man was Robert Crittenden, who wrote to his brother, John Jordan Crittenden in Kentucky, who sent the letter to Senator Richard Mentor Johnson of Kentucky, whose brother, Benjamin Johnson, was appointed a judge of the Arkansas Superior Court about that time. Later, Robert Crittenden wrote directly to Senator Johnson about the treaty.[17] The senator's letter to his friend expressed astonishment at the reaction in Arkansas to the treaty, and said the Senate had not had "the remotest intimation from any quarter" that the people of Arkansas had the slightest objection, much less that the consequences of the treaty would be disastrous to them.

16. Albert H. Allen (ed.), *Arkansas Imprints 1821–1876* (New York: Published for The Bibliographical Society of America by R. R. Bowker Co., 1947), 1–4.
17. Clarence Edwin Carter (ed.), *The Territorial Papers of the United States*, Vol. XIX, *The Territory of Arkansas, 1819–1825* (Washington: Government Printing Office, 1953), 694.

No blame was mentioned, but any reader with his wits about him would naturally wonder why Delegate Bates had not seen to it that the senators were fully informed.

Strangely enough, the *Gazette's* correspondents did not pursue this line of reasoning immediately, and if Crittenden had been inclined at first to use it against Bates, he must have changed his mind, for Bates had won his second term as delegate that summer with Crittenden's blessing. Bates attempted to redeem himself in the 1821–1822 session by working to secure a modification of the treaty, and although ultimate success seemed likely, it was not yet achieved.

When Bates returned to Arkansas late in July of 1822,[18] he had other things on his mind. He had been courting a young lady in Maryland, and they were planning to be married as soon as he returned to Washington in the fall for the next session of Congress.[19] The thought of retiring from political life and settling down to a quieter life with his bride was attractive, but he promised his friends at Batesville that he would be a candidate for a third term the next summer.

A letter signed "Westward" in the *Gazette* of October 15 attacked Bates for not exerting himself to prevent ratification of the treaty, and said he did not deserve re-election. Another writer protested the treaty in an open letter to the president, published in the *Gazette* two weeks later. The only reply to "Westward" was signed "Vindex," and was not published until November 19, and "Westward's" letter in reply did not appear until January 7, 1823. The long periods between these letters indicates that they came from some distance, and suggests that "Westward" was Major William Bradford or one of his friends at Fort Smith, and that "Vindex" was Bates himself.

When this exchange began, Crittenden was in Kentucky, where he married Ann Innis Morris on October 1.[20] He did not return to Arkansas until the middle of November. Bates set out for Washington in the meantime, and about the first of November at Greenville, Missouri, he met Henry W. Conway, who was on his way home after a visit in Kentucky and Missouri. The conversation turned to the next campaign. Bates said he had consented to run again but would rather not, and would gladly step aside and support Conway if he wanted to run. Conway replied that he had not yet made a decision and that spring would be soon enough for them to come to an agreement. He promised to notify Bates by mail if he should decide sooner to become a candidate. Both men later had the same basic recollection of the conversation, except that each thought the deal hinged on his own decision. Conway talked to Bates' friends at Batesville, and they said they would not

18. *Gazette,* Aug. 6, 1822.
19. *Ibid.,* Dec. 19, 1857. This writer, C. F. M. Noland, did not date this incident or give it political significance, both of which are arrived at by strong circumstantial evidence.
20. *Ibid.,* Nov. 26, 1822.

hold Bates to his promise to run against his will. Conway then decided to run, and left it to Bates' friends to notify him.[21]

How Conway managed to get Robert Crittenden's support is a secret the two men and those in whom they confided carried to their graves, but it was accomplished very quickly. The alacrity with which Crittenden took Con-way's word that Bates did not want to return to Congress suggests that it was welcome news, for otherwise he surely would have waited for some word directly from Bates on the subject. It has been said that he had become dis-enchanted with Bates because Bates refused to do his bidding in certain mat-ters, but "neglected" may be a better word than "refused." Crittenden had clutched Bates to his bosom without knowing much about him, at a time when the choice was limited, and he may simply have perceived that Conway would be a stronger candidate. Also, there was a friendship between their families, as Conway's brother, William, studied law in the Kentucky office of Crittenden's brother, John.[22] But the most logical supposition is that Conway was determined to run, with or without Crittenden's help, and so great were his potentialities that Crittenden thought it imprudent to risk opposing him, lest he start a new political faction that would draw much of its strength from Crittenden's followers.

Whatever the reason, Crittenden was solidly behind Conway, and even engineered his candidacy to some extent. He called a conference during the December term of Superior Court, when some of his key people accepted Conway as their candidate. Some evidently had misgivings, fearing that he might develop a new party, but he overcame their reluctance by assuring them that he would not be the cause of a schism, but rather would step aside for another candidate if his friends thought the interest of the territory re-quired it in a future election. According to Samuel C. Roane, Crittenden "ar-ranged the difficulties on the subject of the candidates for the next Congres-sional election" at this meeting. William Trimble apparently had expected

21. *Ibid.,* July 8, Aug. 5, 1823.
22. *Ibid.,* Mar. 25, 1874.

to run with the backing of Crittenden and his friends, but he was persuaded to decline to run, and it was agreed that all would support Conway.[23]

Meanwhile, Bates had reached Washington late in November, and learned that his fiancée had died while he was in Arkansas. It was a devastating blow, and many years passed before he was able to put his sorrow behind him.[24] If Bates wrote promptly and the mails were reasonably regular, his friends should have known about it within a month or six weeks. But mail service was considerably deranged about this time, and even more so in the spring, and there is a possibility that Bates' misfortune was not known in Arkansas for some time. Bates certainly thought his friends knew it some time prior to February,[25] and it seems significant that Conway never said he did not know that the circumstances that caused Bates to want to retire no longer existed. It seems likely that Conway, Crittenden, and their friends were informed of it no later than the last week in January, if not by Bates, by some of their other acquaintances in Washington. This could be the reason Conway's candidacy was announced in the *Gazette* of January 28, more than six months before the election. Since Bates' marriage would not take place, it was predictable that he would want to return to Congress after all. The unusually early beginning of Conway's campaign may have been intended to head off Bates' candidacy.

Thomas P. Eskridge and William Trimble also announced their candidacies for the office of delegate in the same issue of the *Gazette*. Trimble was obligated to Crittenden for an appointment as prosecuting attorney of the First Judicial Circuit in the summer of 1819, immediately after their arrival in Arkansas. Eskridge was indebted to him for an appointment as judge of the Second Judicial Circuit shortly after his arrival in the fall of 1820. Both were currently serving as circuit judges, and had ambitions for higher offices.[26] Both were more or less obliged to do whatever it took to retain Crittenden's friendship, for they would need his help in the future. Since the agreement to support Conway was made several weeks before the three candidates announced, it is presumed that Crittenden not only persuaded Trimble and Eskridge to withdraw, but also persuaded them to run in the first place, on the premise that a formal candidate who withdrew in favor of another could throw far more votes to him than one who was merely rumored to be considering running.

Eskridge dutifully followed this plan, and announced his withdrawal in the *Gazette* of February 4, having been in the race only a week. Trimble, however, seems to have reasoned correctly that this was the best chance he would ever have to go to Congress, and he stayed in the race. At Conway's

23. *Ibid.,* Feb. 4, 1823.
24. *Ibid.,* Dec. 19, 1857.
25. *Ibid.,* July 8, Aug. 19, 1823.
26. *Ibid.,* Aug. 11, 1830; Carter, *Territorial Papers,* XIX, 217–218, 789; Register of Commissions, 1819–1836, Ms. record in office of Secretary of State, photocopy in *Arkansas Gazette* Foundation Library, n.p.

request, Woodruff published in the *Gazette* of February 4 a statement by Sam Roane about the conference that had been held during the December term of Superior Court, as Crittenden had told it to him. Ostensibly this was done to counteract a rumor that Conway had promised not to seek a second term under any circumstances. This could hardly have been the real reason, for Roane's statement indicated even more political bargaining than this, and the most important thing it proved in Conway's favor was that Trimble was not sticking to his promise. Even this public reminder did not cause Trimble to withdraw, and his card continued to appear with Conway's.

For some reason, Woodruff took all the political cards out of the *Gazette* in the first three issues in April. When they reappeared on April 22, William Bradford's name was among those asking for the office of delegate. His announcement made it imperative that either Trimble or Conway should get out of the race, for the division of their support might well give the office to Bradford. This probably required expert persuasion, but Trimble's withdrawal was announced in the *Gazette* on May 6.

In the meantime, Bates had pulled himself together sufficiently by February to decide to run for a third term. He remembered the deal he had offered Conway, but did not feel bound by it because Conway had not taken him up on it at the time. He wrote a friend at Batesville that "all the reasons on which that proposition was founded have ceased to exist," and he now wanted another term in Congress.[27] He did not write to Conway on the subject until March 21, when he said, "The motives and the views that led to my disposition at that time to retire, were founded on considerations, that I persuade myself, were as well understood by you as myself. The contemplated event that would have authorized, perhaps required such a course, has been most miserably frustrated. All this you know. I feel a disposition once more to be a candidate."[28]

All during the spring of 1823, the eastern mails were so badly managed that only a small part of Bates' correspondence from Washington reached the addressees within the usual period of time, and we cannot know when the letters pertaining to his candidacy were received. He was not receiving his mail regularly either, and did not know until he reached Arkansas in June that Conway was running in his place, and that all his most influential friends were committed to Conway's support. There was nothing Bates could do but announce that he would not run.[29] He blamed Conway for his plight, and extended his bitter feelings also to Crittenden.

The *Gazette's* contributors had never been squeamish about stating their opinions, but previously Woodruff had made them modify their remarks to remove every trace of insult. With this campaign, he gave them a freer hand, but appealed to them to practice voluntary restraint. He reminded them that communications "of a personal nature, or acrimonious cast" would

27. *Gazette,* July 8, 1823.
28. *Ibid.,* Aug. 19, 1823.
29. *Ibid.,* June 17, 1823.

West side of 1824-1827 *Gazette* office at southwest corner of
Cherry (Second) and Cumberland, as it was in 1892.

disturb or destroy peace and harmony, and might even subject the innocent
printer to disagreeable consequences. Therefore, letters of this kind would
be published only if the writer paid the usual advertising rates. Not even for
money would he publish letters "of a slanderous or scurrilous nature," but
he did not say how he would draw the fine line of distinction between the
degrees of abuse. The *Gazette's* job printing department was available to all
for campaign circulars. Those printed as leaflets to be distributed by the candidates were entitled to one free insertion in the *Gazette*. If only newspaper
publication was desired, the usual advertising rates were charged.[30]

The campaign was fairly brisk, and might have been more so if Bradford
had had aggressive supporters at Little Rock to keep up his end of a fast
moving newspaper exchange, and if the *Gazette* had not had to publish on
half-sheets the last four weeks before the election. Conway won by a vote
of 1,300 to 921.[31]

Settlement and improvement of Little Rock progressed slowly. The first
brickyard was established in the spring of 1821, but was not ready for business until the next winter, and never attracted any customers of any importance.[32] The second one was opened in the spring of 1823 by Christian Brum-

30. *Ibid.,* Jan. 28, 1823.
31. *Ibid.,* Sept. 16, 1823.
32. Lewis Rouse and Allen Mars contracted on April 24, 1821 to operate a brick-
yard for three years at a site 40 or 50 yards east of the townsite. (Ms. lease, Francis
Imbeau to Lewis Rouse and Allen Mars, Apr. 24, 1821, in John E. Knight Collection,

—Courtesy Arkansas Territorial Capitol Restoration Commission.

East side of 1824-1827 *Gazette* office at southwest corner of Cherry (Second) and Cumberland, as it was about 1939. Only the two-story brick part in the extreme right of the picture was standing when the *Gazette* office was located here.

back and Benjamin Clemens.[33] It is believed that they built the second *Gazette* office at Little Rock late in 1823.[34]

The new building stood on the southwest corner of Cherry (now Second) and Cumberland streets, facing Cherry Street. With grounds large enough for expansion, it occupied lots 10, 11, and 12 in block 32, Original City of Little Rock. Chester Ashley and his wife conveyed the lots to Woodruff on January 9, 1824,[35] but the *Gazette* had moved into the building two days

Arkansas History Commission.) Rouse died late in August, (*Gazette,* Sept. 22, 1821), and Mars announced in the *Gazette* of February 19, 1822 that he was preparing a brick-yard and would do bricklaying, stone masonry, and plastering. He may have built a few fireplaces, chimneys, and foundations, but is not known to have built any brick houses.

33. *Memorial of Roswell Beebe, addressed to the General Assembly of the State of Arkansas: With an Appendix* (Little Rock: Printed by G. H. Burnett, 1840), 59. The partnership was dissolved in 1824, and Brumback continued in the business alone. (*Gazette,* Oct. 26, 1824.)

34. William E. Woodruff, Jr., "A Chronicle of Little Rock," *Gazette,* Nov. 7, 1931. The founder's son had no knowledge of earlier brickmakers, and admittedly guessed that Brumback built this building. It seems significant that the brief Brumback-Clemens partnership included the period during which the building was erected. Strangely, Wood-ruff sold the property to Brumback six months after he moved in, and gave him a bond for title dated June 17, 1824, (Pulaski County Deed Book Q, 236) but did not surrender possession to him until 1827. Brumback apparently never perfected his title, which probably means he did not pay all the agreed price.

35. Woodruff, "A Chronicle of Litte Rock;" Pulaski County Deed Book D, 21.

earlier. Woodruff said it was a "new two-story brick house, a few rods west of the tan-yard."[36] There was a long room on the second floor,[37] which Woodruff used as a printing office. Further contemporary descriptions are not found.[38] The old log building at Cherry and Louisiana was returned to its owner, Joseph Thornhill, who made it his home.[39]

About the time the *Gazette* moved into the new building or soon after-

36. *Gazette,* Jan. 6, 1824.

37. William Field, who owned the property many years, first occupied it from his arrival in May, 1830 (*Gazette*, June 29, 1830) until he moved to a farm in the winter of 1831. During this period, a long room in the second story of his home was used as a banquet room, and two public balls were held there. (*Ibid.,* Nov. 10, 1830; Jan. 12, 1831.) Brumback's bond for title was assigned to Field on Sept. 26, 1831. (Deed Book Q, 236.)

38. A two-story frame addition to the two-story brick building was built by a later owner, probably William Field. The *Gazette* of March 17, 1870 reported the sale of these three lots by a commissioner in chancery, and described the improvements thereon as "a large two-story building and outhouses," identifying the two-story brick as one of the city's oldest houses and originally the *Gazette* office. The *Gazette* of Nov. 17, 1881 reported a fire on the previous evening that destroyed the frame addition. The brick portion was again identified as an early office of the *Gazette* and the second brick house erected at Little Rock, but the extent of its damage was not stated. It must have been repaired and the frame addition repaired or rebuilt, for an old building answering its description was standing on this corner when the Arkansas Territorial Capitol Restoration Commission was created in 1939. (See photograph.) Lacking information about the building of the territorial period, the Commission based its decisions entirely on an examination of the existing structures. The result was that the original two-story brick *Gazette* office was torn down, and a small outbuilding of two rooms at its rear (date of construction and original use unknown) was "restored" as the printing office. Parts of the lower stories of the frame addition and of a two-story brick building adjoining on the south, connected by a one-story frame addition, were "restored" under one roof and called the home of Woodruff and his family. Apparently the first members of the Commission were unaware that Woodruff was a bachelor when he lived in this location, and had his living quarters in the *Gazette* building. See Richard and Louise McCue, "Historic Capitol is Built Again," *Gazette* magazine, Feb. 25, Mar. 3, 1940.

39. After the compromise between the rival land claimants, Thornhill's claim to lot 12, block 82 was confirmed by a deed from Ashley and wife on June 8, 1822. (Pulaski County Deed Book B, 311.) On September 13, 1825, Thornhill married Mrs. Catherine E. Pankey Bates, widow of William Bates of Herculaneum, Mo., and a sister of Mrs. Ashley's mother. (*Gazette,* Sept. 20, 1825; Mar. 29, 1850.) On Sept. 25, 1825, he bought from Ashley the two lots adjoining this one on the south, lots 10 and 11, (Deed Book E, 160) but he died on Oct. 29, 1825 (*Gazette,* Nov. 1, 1825) without carrying out whatever plans he had for the lots. His bride of six weeks and her daughter, Mary Clarissa Bates, continued to live in the former *Gazette* building. (*Ibid.,* Sept. 18, 1827.) Mrs. Thornhill married David G. Eller on Jan. 10, 1828. (*Ibid.,* Jan. 15, 1828). Eller put this building and another log building of similar proportions that stood nearby under a common roof and weatherboarded it, giving it the appearance of a frame house. (Woodruff, Jr., "A Chronicle of Little Rock.") We have an occasional glimpse of it in later years as the Eller residence and as the home of Grandison D. Royston, who married Mary Clarissa Bates. It was occupied at one time by Roswell Beebe, (*Gazette,* Oct. 6, 1841), who had married Clarissa Elliott, a cousin of Mrs. Ashley. It was torn down on April 19, 1888 to clear the site for the two-story brick Turner and Gans building, and was the city's oldest house at that time. (*Ibid.,* Apr. 20, 1888.)

Henry Wharton Conway.   Hiram Abiff Whittington.

wards, Charles P. Bertrand left the home of his stepfather, Dr. Cunningham,[40] to live with Woodruff and become an apprentice.

There were other apprentices and journeymen who lived at the *Gazette*
office during the three years it occupied this building. On December 20,
1825 Woodruff again advertised for a journeyman printer, and this time he
wanted one capable of taking complete charge of the mechanical department. Early the next summer, a penniless, poorly clad tramp printer named
William H. Dyer came to the *Gazette* office. Woodruff gave him clothing and
a job, and he stayed five months before he slipped away in the night, having
consistently drawn his pay in advance and contracted debts of about $40 in
Woodruff's name.[41]

Another journeyman was then en route to Little Rock, and Woodruff knew
he could place complete confidence in him. He was Hiram Abiff Whittington, who arrived on Christmas Eve, 1826, Woodruff's 31st birthday, and
observed his own 22d birthday 19 days later. Whittington had come via New
Orleans from New York, where he had worked for a year and a half for the
man who had trained Woodruff, Alden Spooner. He had learned his trade
in a four-year apprenticeship at the Nantucket *Enquirer* office. He was to remain as Woodruff's foreman and loyal friend until the summer of 1832.[42]

40. Deposition of Charles P. Bertrand, in Ms. Transcript, M. Cunningham vs Ashley and Beebe, 469.
41. *Gazette,* Dec. 5, 1826.
42. William S. Speer and John Henry Brown (eds.), *The Encyclopedia of the New
West* (Marshall, Texas: The United States Biographical Publishing Co., 1881), 224;
Margaret Smith Ross (ed.), *Letters of Hiram Abiff Whittington 1827–1834* (Little
Rock: Pulaski County Historical Society, 1956), 1, 31.

Woodruff had begun a new business venture shortly before he moved into the new building, and it was given office space in the *Gazette's* counting room. The territorial scrip he had to accept in payment for the public printing was receivable at par for taxes, but business men took it only at a substantial discount. Woodruff's most advantageous way of disposing of it in the fall of 1822 was to offer it to other taxpayers at a reasonable discount, but when the legislature put hundreds of non-residents on the tax books in the fall of 1823 by making military bounty lands subject to taxation, he was quick to seize the opportunity it offered. On November 11, 1823 he published the act authorizing collection of taxes on military bounty lands, and gave notice of his availability as an agent for non-resident owners. He charged no fee, but required his clients to send specie to pay their taxes and the clerk's fee for recording their deeds. He then paid these expenses in scrip, and his profit was the 25 per cent difference between the value of specie and of discounted scrip. He said his purpose was merely to dispose of the scrip he had on hand, but at the same time he announced that he would accept scrip at a 25 per cent discount for all debts due the *Gazette*. This soon got out of hand, because some of the *Gazette's* agents accepted payment in both scrip and specie, but sent their collections to Woodruff altogether in scrip. Woodruff quit taking scrip for *Gazette* bills in February of 1824, only to resume it in June, when the response to his land agency became heavy. Later in the summer, he even had to purchase extra scrip.

By August 10, 1824, business was so good that he made the agency permanent, and named it the Arkansas Military Land Agency. This business eventually brought him far more wealth than the *Gazette,* and with fewer problems. He acquired title to a great many tracts of land, some by purchase from clients and some by purchase at the tax sales. Later he extended his services to management of all kinds of property.

In the spring of 1825, he began accepting scrip for debts due the *Gazette* only if paid at the Little Rock office, and purchased enough more to fill his needs. That summer, as the time approached to redeem the bounty lands sold at the first tax sale, he was the agent for nearly a third of them. By that time, he was charging a modest fee for his services.[43]

About the time the land agency was started, he also began handling other business matters for non-residents, for a fee. Accounts were left in his hands for collection, and occasionally he was appointed administrator of estates of intestates.

All kinds of ledgers and printed forms were always available at the *Gazette* office, and from time to time the editor offered for sale a variety of other merchandise, including stationery, playing cards, patent medicines, almanacs, maps, Bibles, hymn books, school books, classroom supplies, and clocks. On September 14, 1824 he advertised a long list of books just received from New York, and offered to make special orders for books to be sold at Little Rock for New York retail prices, setting minimum orders at $20. On Novem-

43. *Gazette,* July 12, 1825.

ber 7, 1826 he announced that he would begin an experimental circulating library, which would become a regular service if well received. He started with about 150 volumes, mostly novels and plays. He based his rental fees on the size of the books, charging 12½ cents for the average volume, but he set no definite time for the books to be returned. The experiment must not have succeeded, for it was not until 1843 that Woodruff's circulating library was permanently established.

Andrew Scott and Joseph Selden, judges of the Superior Court, fought a duel on May 26, 1824, in which Judge Selden was killed at the first fire. The duel had been a long time in its development and there had been several postponements. Woodruff made an unfortunate choice of words in reporting it as "the long talked of and much ridiculed duel," and said that "contrary to our expectations" it had resulted in Selden's death. James Woodson Bates and Robert C. Oden, Selden's close friends, took him to task for implying that the judges were objects of ridicule and that their duel had been regarded as a farce that would never come to pass. Bates even professed to doubt that Woodruff had written the article, and suggested that "some wretched paragraphist" had taken shelter under the editorial head to spew forth his insinuations. Woodruff replied indignantly, "Such may be the practice of some editors, but we assure our readers that it has never been ours. We never admit any article into our columns as *editorial,* unless it is such—unless it is written by the person whose name is affixed to the head of our paper as editor, viz. William E. Woodruff." [44]

The vacancy on the Superior Court bench after Selden's death gave Henry Conway an opportunity to reward William Trimble for his cooperation in the campaign of the previous year. Less than a month after Selden's death, Conway recommended Trimble for the position, and President James Monroe gave him a recess appointment immediately, and a regular appointment followed six months later. [45] An attempt was made to create another vacancy by calling for Judge Scott's removal from office for participating in a duel, but nothing came of it at this time, and the subsequent disappearance of the papers filed in Washington makes identification of the instigator impossible. When Scott finally lost the post in 1827, Thomas P. Eskridge received the appointment, having been recommended by Conway and the Virginia Congressmen. [46] These specific rewards could hardly have been promised when Conway's 1823 campaign was planned, because there was then no reason to expect these vacancies.

Everybody intimately involved later insisted that party politics did not exist in Arkansas prior to 1827. Actually, party politics as it is understood today did not begin until 1836, for there were no organized parties at any time during the territorial period. The situation referred to as "a party spirit" is more aptly described as factionalism, for it did not have the elements of a

44. *Ibid.,* June 1, 15, 1824.
45. Carter, *Territorial Papers,* XIX, 679, 681, 735.
46. *Ibid.,* XX, 366, 412, 391–392, 400–401.

regular political party system but rather involved rallying the friends of opposing individuals. From the beginning of the territorial government, it was Crittenden and his satellites who made the greatest effort to prevent the development of a party spirit. Since they had all the power, they stood to lose the most by the rise of an opposing faction. There had been opposition to Crittenden's machine in every election, but never had there been any effort to bring together in a cohesive organization the men who sought to gain their own political goals independently of Crittenden. Those who were unwilling or reluctant to accept his leadership were merely an undetermined number of resentful people, nebulous and leaderless, fighting their battles on an individual basis.

The political explosion of 1827 was the result of the development of two distinct factions. Crittenden was the undisputed head of the previously dominant faction, and his most prominent friends included Robert C. Oden, Thomas W. Newton, Andrew and George W. Scott, William Trimble, and others. Leadership of the opposing faction appears to have been divided among Chester Ashley, Henry Conway, and William Woodruff, with George Izard and Ambrose Sevier as important supporters who might also be considered leaders. One of these had to be the master mind who plotted the overthrow of the Crittenden clique. It seems almost certain that that person was Chester Ashley, but he cannot be given full credit without a shadow of doubt.

Woodruff's position as editor of the *Gazette* placed him in the foreground, and sporadic attempts were later made to explain why he parted company with Crittenden, but it is not likely that his animosity was the key to the 1827

George Izard.

schism. Woodruff said only that the origin of their differences was Crittenden's attempt to dictate the course of the *Gazette* during the first weeks of its existence.[47] Another person who claimed first-hand knowledge said they fell out when Woodruff refused to tell Crittenden who wrote a letter to the *Gazette* criticizing Andrew Jackson.[48] These were indeed two incidents in a series of unpleasant encounters between 1819 and 1821, but they leave unexplained the period of overt friendship between 1823 and 1827, and cannot be the reason for the all-out effort to put Crittenden down in 1827.

The election of Conway in 1823 had a unifying effect, and the undercurrent of discord disappeared, so that these people had the appearance of one big happy political family. However, the memory of previous unpleasantness may have lingered and kept them constantly wary, and we find occasional vague hints that one person in the group did not fully trust another. Crittenden and Ashley formed a law partnership, as did Sevier and Oden, but one suspects that even during this peaceful period, the divisions of loyalty that later became well defined were predictable in most cases, some friendships in the group being on firmer foundations than others. The old animosities were dormant, but not dead.

All these people were engaged in land speculation in varying degrees, and their interests often overlapped. It was a cut-throat business, in which ethics were often cast aside, leaving much room for mutual distrust. Woodruff more or less confined himself to military bounty lands, second-rate lands for which there was little competition. The others went in for more valuable land claims for which there was keen rivalry. An act of Congress in 1824 extending preemption rights to actual settlers prior to that date was applicable to the site of Little Rock and adjoining lands, title to which was still in the United States. The scramble for possession of these lands may have been a factor in the political breach that developed later, as it affected nearly all the people involved.

It is likely that the cautious friendship Ashley, Woodruff, and possibly Conway and Sevier maintained with Crittenden and his old friends was mostly a matter of expedience, and that they were biding their time, waiting for circumstances to favor the success of a coup against the Crittenden machine. This could not happen as long as James Miller was governor and Crittenden was secretary.

When Conway came home from Washington in the summer of 1824, the secretary of war asked him to take $7,000 of Quapaw funds to Crittenden, who was then acting governor and charged with executing a Quapaw treaty. Conway's personal funds ran short on the way home, and he spent $200 or $300 of the Quapaw money. When he reached Little Rock, he told Crittenden he needed more money, and he kept enough to make his debt to the Quapaw fund total $600, turning over the rest to Crittenden. Conway later said Crittenden gave him permission to borrow the $600, but Crittenden de-

47. *Gazette,* Oct. 19, 1831.
48. *Ibid.,* May 8, 1844.

nied it, and contended that he was responsible only for the money that passed through his hands and considered Conway's retention of the $600 a matter between him and the official who had trusted him to deliver it.[49] Both were fully aware that it was illegal to borrow or loan public money, and did not tell anybody about it. If Crittenden did not consent to Conway's keeping the $600, he at least did not insist that he hand it over. He did, however, protect himself by entering in his accounts the receipt of only $6,400, the amount that had actually come to him.

Governor Miller had been absent from Arkansas Territory 18 months when he submitted his resignation on December 27, 1824, to be effective on December 31, and recommended David Brearley, the former Cherokee agent, to succeed him.[50] Crittenden had more or less dominated his administration even when Miller was at his post, and had served three long periods as acting governor while Miller visited his family. Although he had the full responsibility of both offices much of the time, his salary was always the lesser one of secretary, and his friends thought it was time he had the title and salary of governor. Congressman John T. Johnson of Kentucky, a brother of Judge Benjamin Johnson, wrote a recommendation for Crittenden a week before Miller turned in his resignation, and got nine of his colleagues to sign it. Conway submitted it to President Monroe on January 8, 1825, adding his own recommendation and saying he believed Crittenden was the people's choice.[51]

On that same day, Conway was jolted by a note from Thomas L. McKenney of the Bureau of Indian Affairs, who had discovered in auditing Crittenden's accounts that he had received only $6,400 of the money that had been sent to him by Conway. McKenney called upon Conway for an explanation,[52] which must have been made verbally, leaving us no record of it. Conway probably had not anticipated that Crittenden's records would reflect his retention of the $600, and he may have been none too happy at being asked to account for the discrepancy. He later said he had paid the $600 to the secretary of war upon his arrival at Washington, and had explained the situation.[53] Crittenden, however, said Conway had borrowed money from him to make the trip to Washington,[54] which leaves some doubt about his ability to pay the debt upon his arrival.

If Conway made any further effort to influence the selection of the next governor, it was by personal contacts of which no record is found. Monroe left the appointment to the next president, John Quincy Adams, who appointed the man of Monroe's choice, Maj. Gen. George Izard. His commission was dated March 4, 1825, but he did not receive it at Philadelphia

49. *Ibid.,* May 22, June 5, 19, 26, 1827.
50. Carter, *Territorial Papers,* XIX, 737–739.
51. *Ibid.,* 736, 742.
52. *Ibid.,* 742.
53. *Gazette,* June 22, 1827.
54. *Ibid.,* July 24, 1827.

until the end of the month. Izard had hoped for an appointment as a foreign minister, and had shown no interest in the governorship of Arkansas, but he accepted.[55]

Official word of Izard's appointment reached Little Rock about the middle of April. Crittenden was not disposed to relinquish the reins gracefully, and departed immediately for a long visit to Kentucky. Conway apparently had made friendly overtures to the new governor, and it was reported that they would meet at Louisville and travel the rest of the way to Arkansas together,[56] but Conway arrived at Little Rock alone on April 28, and said he had not heard from Izard since he left Washington.[57]

Conway's campaign for re-election had opened with his announcement in the *Gazette* of April 5 and his circular in the issue of April 26, while he was en route to Little Rock. James Woodson Bates had entered the race on April 12, and was Conway's only opponent. Conway's circular listed the things the government had done for Arkansas during his term of office. In the *Gazette* of May 31, one "Thrasybulas" belittled the accomplishments Conway claimed, and two weeks later one who signed "A Voter" replied that Conway could properly claim credit for all the laws referred to in his circular, while Bates could claim only four. Bates' answer was that they had encountered different situations in Washington, for he had had to pioneer the cause of a little known territory and had, in effect, laid the groundwork for Conway's success.[58]

The most damaging accusation against Conway came from a writer who signed "A Citizen of Pulaski County," in the *Gazette* of June 14. He said Conway had withheld from his constituents information about public surveying authorized for Arkansas, so that contracts had gone to his Missouri relatives that might otherwise have been given to Arkansas applicants. This was refuted on June 21 by two of his uncles, Stephen and W. Rector, and an unrelated surveyor named Jonathan L. Bean, who testified that Conway had nothing to do with the contracts. The Rectors and Conway's brother, James Sevier Conway, were his only relatives who had received contracts.

As the election drew near, Woodruff requested postmasters and county clerks to send him local returns as soon as possible, so he could give his readers unofficial returns long before the official returns were available.[59] This method of reporting unofficial returns became standard for the *Gazette* and other Arkansas newspapers that came later. Conway had become so popular that Bates was no match for him, and he won the election on August 1 by a vote of 2,105 to 519.[60] The negligible vote cast for Bates must have embodied whatever protest there was against the Crittenden machine, so it

55. Carter, *Territorial Papers,* XX, 57–60.
56. *Gazette,* Apr. 19, 1825.
57. *Ibid.,* May 3, 1825.
58. *Ibid.,* June 21, 1825.
59. *Ibid.,* July 26, 1825.
60. *Ibid.,* Oct. 4, 1825.

is reasonable to suppose that whatever division of political sentiments had once existed had all but vanished.

After waiting more than six months for delivery of materials, the *Gazette* appeared in a new dress on July 19, 1825, with a complete set of new type and its first logotype nameplate. The new title was in hand crafted Old English letters, and the word *"The"* was dropped.

Woodruff planned to enlarge the *Gazette* to a super-royal sheet with the beginning of Volume VII in January, 1826, but another low-water period delayed the arrival of the paper, and the enlargement did not take place until February 7. The new page measured 13 by 20½ inches, and had five columns to the page, the column width being reduced from 14½ to 13½ picas. The super-royal sheet increased the *Gazette's* reading matter about one third, and involved more labor and expense, but Woodruff decided against raising subscription rates, hoping to have adequate compensation through increased patronage and prompt payment.[61]

In the fall of 1825, with prosperity in his grasp, Woodruff began to think of marriage. Eliza Ann Elliott, Mrs. Ashley's younger sister, had moved to Little Rock, and by October her friends and relatives in Missouri had been informed of her approaching marriage to Woodruff. However, for some reason their plans fell through, and two years later each of them married somebody else.[62]

While public attention was focused on the Conway-Bates campaign, a rift was developing between Izard and Crittenden that would soon reactivate the hostilities that had been latent since 1823. This was not the first time Crittenden had left the territory when the governor was also absent, and there had never been any repurcussions, so he probably expected no trouble on that score. If he had expected that the papers of the executive office left in the care of a friend would be enough to keep Izard busy until his return, he reckoned without the meticulous habits of a man whose forte was systematic, efficient organization. Without wasting much time on the formalities of getting acquainted with local people, he moved into the task of acquainting himself with the responsibilities of his office immediately after his arrival on May 31. He had little tolerance for incompetence and none for deliberate neglect of duty. The negative impression he had of Crittenden for his absence at a critical time increased as he delved into the executive papers and found that Crittenden had handled the office in a slipshod manner. His work was delayed because instructions and correspondence needed for understanding of certain Indian affairs were missing from the files, $10,500 in drafts made payable to Crittenden as acting governor could not be negotiated without his endorsement, and $3,000 in specie had been left at the mouth of White

61. *Ibid.,* July 19, Sept. 27, 1825; Jan. 3, 1826.

62. Eugene C. Barker (ed.), *The Austin Papers,* Vol. II of *Annual Report of the American Historical Association for the Year 1919* (Washington: Government Printing Office, 1924), 1222. Eliza Elliott married Joseph Henderson on June 14, 1827. (Tombstone of Eliza A. Henderson, Mount Holly Cemetery, Little Rock.)

River for several months. Moreover, the proper organization of the militia had been woefully neglected.[63]

Patience was not one of Izard's outstanding virtues, and he fumed because of the inconvenience Crittenden's absence caused him and the haphazard way Crittenden had discharged his duties. It was obvious to all that, unlike his predecessor, he did not intend to take a back seat to a subordinate officer. Some of Crittenden's friends, being none too enthusiastic about the new governor anyhow, kept their distance without being openly impolite, and there was an aloofness about Izard that did not improve the situation. Conway, Sevier, Ashley, and Woodruff did not allow their loyalty to Crittenden to inhibit them, and they promptly became Izard's fast friends and staunch supporters. Conway and Sevier were appointed his aids-de-camp on June 10, with the militia rank of lieutenant colonel,[64] and both wore the title of colonel the rest of their lives.

By the time Crittenden returned late in June or early in July, Izard had found another source of annoyance. Public funds were sent to Arkansas in drafts for large amounts, and Little Rock's few merchants were not prosperous enough to cash them. Izard requested that the money be sent in the future in drafts no larger than $500 each, and decided to send a confidential messenger to New Orleans to cash the $10,500 worth of drafts on hand. The messenger he chose was Thomas W. Newton, Little Rock's postmaster, clerk of the Pulaski Circuit Court, and a close friend and confidential agent of Crittenden, in whose home he lived. Newton did not begin his trip until sometime in October. The round trip was expected to take 50 days, but Newton was detained by lack of steamboat transportation, and upon his return, Izard found that he had "misapplied a portion of the amount" with which he had been entrusted. Izard waited several months for Newton to return the money, and was finally obliged to file a lawsuit to recover it. The money still had not been collected in the fall of 1826.[65]

Chester Ashley became an aid-de-camp to the governor on December 26, 1825, about the time Newton's shortage became known to Izard. He too gained the militia rank of lieutenant colonel with this appointment,[66] and was called Colonel Ashley to the end of his days. He was Izard's personal legal adviser, and undoubtedly advised him in the suit against Newton, and may also have prosecuted it. Since Newton and Crittenden were intimate friends, and since Izard made this one of his reasons for regarding Newton as trustworthy, this lawsuit must have generated more tension between Izard and Crittenden, and ultimately their respective friends were drawn into it. Crittenden's friends thought Ashley promoted much of the factional strife that

63. "Official Correspondence of Governor Izard 1825–1826," in John Hugh Reynolds (ed.), *Publications of the Arkansas Historical Association,* Vol. I (Fayetteville, 1906), 423–426.

64. Carter, *Territorial Papers,* XX, 68; *Gazette,* June 14, 1825. Conway had this militia rank in 1823. (*Ibid.,* June 10, 1823).

65. "Official Correspondence of Governor Izard," 426, 434, 437, 443.

66. *Gazette,* Dec. 27, 1825.

came later, an impression they may have had first while the lawsuit against Newton was threatened. It was sometime during this period that Ashley dissolved his law partnership with Crittenden in the lower courts, though their practice in Superior Court could not easily be separated immediately. No explanation was ever given for the dissolution, but it may well have been the result of a disagreement over this lawsuit. The strained relationship between Crittenden and Izard and the close friendship between Crittenden and Newton leads to the conclusion that Crittenden wanted no part of such a suit except on Newton's side, and would not appreciate his partner's acting on the other side. It was later said that the dissolution was Ashley's idea.[67]

It was not difficult for Newton's friends to defend him, in conversation if not in court. He was not the first of Crittenden's friends to borrow from the public funds and be slow to repay the money. The popular Conway had done the same thing and nobody had made anything of it. This may have been the basis for threats and counter-threats, in view of Conway's friendship with the governor and his associates. Only Crittenden and Conway had known about his default until now, and since Crittenden was still Conway's friend, he probably did not tell the story to harm him, but only to try to help Newton. Conway was not present to defend himself, as he had left for Washington before Newton went to New Orleans, and he did not come home at all in 1826.

By the middle of 1826, the rumblings preceding the forthcoming political season were ominous. Harsh words passed between the two factions constantly, and Crittenden's friends laid a large part of the blame for the turmoil on Izard. It was generally understood that Conway, Oden, Richard Searcy, and William Bradford would be the candidates for Congress, and Oden believed the contest would be entirely between him and Conway. He privately predicted, "The next 12 mths will present a scene of trouble, & confusion hitherto unknown—parties will be more distinct, separate, & violent." [68]

None of this was reflected in the *Gazette,* and distant readers having no other source of information could not have suspected the trouble the future held. If the public was unaware that all-out war between the two factions loomed ahead, Crittenden certainly anticipated it and made frantic preparations to protect himself. He was acutely conscious that his greatest vulnerability was in his records of the public funds he had disbursed as acting governor and superintendent of Indian affairs. In unfriendly hands, these accounts could be a powerful weapon against him, capable not only of bringing him public disgrace, but also of blocking his reappointment as territorial secretary at the expiration of his second term the next March. He could spike this weapon if he could have his accounts audited and approved in Washington. If the bare records had to speak for themselves, or if they were made subject to hostile interpretations, the risk to Crittenden in submitting them would be

67. *Ibid.,* Sept. 1, 1830.
68. Robert C. Oden to James Miller, July 19, 1826, Ms. in Robert W. Trimble Collection, Arkansas History Commission.

great. But if he could appear in person to explain and defend them, he was confident he could invalidate any serious criticism of them.

Crittenden considered his position so precarious that he had to go to Washington at any cost. On August 17, he asked Secretary of State Henry Clay for permission to be absent from the territory for 60 days, beginning November 15. The only obstacle was Izard's plan to leave Arkansas on November 1 for a long visit to his family in Philadelphia, which meant that the territory would have no executive if Crittenden should be absent during the same period. Crittenden and Izard had an unpleasant discussion of this situation late in August or early in September, and about that time they stopped speaking to each other. Crittenden then laid his problem before Clay in more detail, and asked his advice.

Clay's first letter to Crittenden, written on September 25, gave him permission to go to Washington, provided he and Izard could reach an agreement whereby the public service would not be inconvenienced by the total absence of executive authority. Crittenden may have received this letter before Izard left Little Rock on November 1, but by that time there was no hope for such an agreement. He could only cancel his own plans to leave two weeks later, and assume the duties of governor.

Whether well founded or not, it was Crittenden's earnest belief that a scheme was afoot to block his reappointment by exposure in Washington of irregularities in his handling of public funds without mention of the extenuating circumstances. It is obvious that his apprehensions were based on something more tangible than suspicion, and that he expected Izard to be the one who would present the case against him in Washington.[69]

If direct threats had been made, they apparently were withdrawn before Izard left Arkansas. This is evidenced by the fact that Izard went directly to Philadelphia without visiting Washington, and had no plans to go there before his return to Little Rock,[70] and by the fact that Conway put himself out to befriend Crittenden at least twice, early in this session of Congress. Conway's role in the movement against Crittenden at this point is uncertain, for he had spent the summer in Virginia and the autumn in Washington.[71] He could hardly have had a hand in its direction, since he was not in Arkansas from the fall of 1825 until the spring of 1827. There can be little doubt that he was kept informed by mail, and that his sympathies and interests were wholly on the side of Izard and Ashley.

On December 13, Conway attempted to head off opposition to Crittenden's reappointment by asking the secretary of state to influence the president to send his renomination to the Senate in time for the new commission to reach him before the old one expired, saying this would prevent a possible

69. Carter, *Territorial Papers,* XX, 285–286, 287–288, 290, 298–299; James Scull to James Miller, Arkansas, Aug. 18, 1827, and Little Rock, Oct. 28, 1827, Ms. in Robert W. Trimble Collection, Arkansas History Commission.

70. *Gazette,* Mar. 20, 1827.

71. *Ibid.,* Oct. 31, 1826.

interruption of the territorial government during Izard's absence.[72] And on December 19, Conway vigorously defended on the floor of the House the manner in which Crittenden had negotiated the Quapaw treaty of 1824, although the best he could say for it was the rather weak argument that it had been approved in Washington later.[73]

As for Crittenden, he apparently reconciled himself to remaining at his post until Izard's return. This situation smacks of a compromise, or at least a temporary cessation of hostilities, but it was a tense, uneasy truce unaccompanied by the return of friendship. Possibly it was brought about by the death on October 15 of Crittenden's infant son, Morris, his only other child, John, having died at the age of nine months in August of 1824.[74] This misfortune would naturally make him reluctant to leave his young wife immediately, particularly if she were also very ill, and might make his enemies feel that it would be indelicate to attack him publicly at this time.

It was customary for the acting governor also to discharge the duties of superintendent of Indian affairs when the governor was absent, but Izard left the disbursement of Indian funds and other responsibilities of this office in the hands of Bernard Smith, his private secretary and Indian sub-agent. Crittenden took exception to this as evidence of Izard's distrust of him, which he felt was not justified.[75]

On the day Izard left for Philadelphia, Crittenden and Ashley dissolved what remained of their law partnership, the Superior Court practice.[76] This final dissolution could have been made merely because disposition had been made of all the cases in which they had a mutual interest, but the timing seems to rule out the likelihood that the separation was friendly.

Secretary of State Clay's answer to Crittenden's second letter was written on October 24, and shattered all hope of a leave of absence. Realizing that an agreement between Izard and Crittenden was now out of the question, Clay informed Crittenden that he must remain at his post in Arkansas and send his accounts and records by a trustworthy messenger. Clay knew of no opposition to his reappointment, and did not consider either his office or his honor in jeopardy.[77] Crittenden was unconvinced, and did not send the records.

There was another little flurry of activity early in December. On the 6th, Crittenden and Ashley drew up a formal public announcement of the dissolution of their law partnership.[78] On the 12th, Woodruff threw out a broad hint to the public that the political honeymoon was over, with an editorial threatening to publish a catalog of sinners "in high life" and "high in au-

72. Carter, *Territorial Papers,* XX, 324–325.
73. *Gazette,* Jan. 23, 1827.
74. *Ibid.,* Oct. 17, 1826; Aug. 10, 1824.
75. Carter, *Territorial Papers,* XX, 324–325.
76. *Gazette,* Jan. 2, 1827.
77. Carter, *Territorial Papers,* XX, 298–299.
78. *Gazette,* Jan. 2, 1827.

thority" at Little Rock, if the guilty ones did not mend their ways in the matter of gambling and other vices. Vague as it was, everybody at Little Rock knew who they were.

Thus it is seen that as the year 1826 drew to a close, opposition to Crittenden had shaped up enough to place him in a defensive position. Although Woodruff was known to be personally in sympathy with Crittenden's antagonists, it still was unthinkable that the *Gazette's* editorial neutrality would be abandoned, since there was no other paper to see that justice was done the other side.

4

THE TURNING POINT

1827 "AS THIS IS A PROPER season for settling off all old scores, and commencing a-new. . . ." Thus Woodruff prefaced his request for payment of debts due the *Gazette* as the eighth volume began on January 2, 1827. The remark could have been applied with equal force to the political situation, for in that area, some "old scores" were about to come up for settlement, and the *Gazette* was on the verge of "commencing a-new."

The month-old card announcing the two-month-old dissolution of the Crittenden-Ashley law partnership was published as an advertisement in the same issue. The delayed announcement served to inform the public that the last vestige of their association was removed, and to relieve Ashley of whatever odium might later attach to Crittenden.

Tempers flared again during the week that followed. No clue is found to the nature of the quarrel, but it was serious enough to send both factions into immediate, drastic, aggressive action.

The *Gazette's* readers were startled on January 9 to find the heretofore phlegmatic editor bursting forth with a complaint that Crittenden had committed the unspeakable outrage of erasing Woodruff's imprint from the commissions for civil and military officers, so prominently placed as to detract from the dignity of the document. Woodruff protested in a paragraph that oozed sarcasm from every syllable, accentuated by the liberal use of italics, yet deftly conveyed an air of injured innocence. He took the position that the egotistical acting governor surely could not reasonably begrudge the humble printer an imprint in the smallest type, when his own name and title appeared in all the glory of "flaming AMERICAN CANNON characters." Woodruff had printed many a commission without an imprint in his time, including some for Crittenden as acting governor, the remainder supply of which he now tauntingly offered to give him.[1] He well knew that the pre-

1. Apparently Crittenden took the leftover commissions Woodruff offered, for a com-

vailing custom was to place the imprint in an inconspicuous position, usually at the bottom of the sheet, yet he had put it on these forms almost squarely in the center. At the top of the sheet was an American eagle, and the imprint was immediately under the eagle and above the words "Robert Crittenden, Acting Governor of the Territory of Arkansaw." Unless this incident triggered the quarrel of the week, it was of no consequence in itself. The most significant thing about it was that Woodruff had never before used such harsh language in his paper.

Crittenden threw caution to the winds and struck out for Washington on the evening of January 9. Woodruff did not know about the trip in time to mention it in the *Gazette* of January 9, but made the announcement on the 16th, and on the 23d published a note from a friend of Crittenden's saying the secretary had passed beyond the territorial boundaries on the 16th. On January 30, he published Crittenden's terse explanation to the people of Arkansas Territory, written at the mouth of White River on January 14.

James Woodson Bates, still nursing his old grudge, responded with a letter protesting the acting governor's disregard for his responsibilities, and said his motive was his desire to have it known in Washington that Crittenden's desertion of his post was detrimental to the public service. Although he wrote under a pseudonym and stifled his characteristic eloquence, Crittenden's friends instantly guessed his identity. Three of them came to Crittenden's defense, writing also under pen names, and led the discussion off on a tangent by attacking Bates for his incompetence as judge of the Second Judicial Circuit. Bates switched pseudonyms to make a third person defense of himself, but would not be diverted from his complaint against Crittenden.[2]

Meanwhile, letters written about the time of Crittenden's departure reached Conway in Washington on February 21. It was too late to block Crittenden's reappointment, for President John Quincy Adams had acted promptly on Conway's recommendation of December 13 and had sent the nomination to the Senate on December 26, where it had been approved on January 12. But it was not too late to undermine his image as a conscientious public servant, and on the same day Conway received the letters, he introduced a resolution for pre-legislative work looking towards providing for executive authority in Arkansas Territory when both the governor and the secretary were absent. The speech that accompanied it was slyly damaging to Crittenden, and exaggerated the dangers involved in his leaving the territory to the point of attributing the murder of a party of hunters by Indians some 180 miles west of Fort Smith to his leaving while Governor Miller was absent in the fall of 1823.[3] The abruptness of Conway's change of attitude shows that he was already allied with the anti-Crittenden clique, and that the

mission issued by him on January 8, 1827 to Nathan D. Smith as a justice of the peace in Ozan Township, Hempstead County, has neither the eagle nor the imprint. It is now owned by Mrs. Frank E. Wait of Little Rock.

2. *Gazette*, Feb. 6, 13, 20, 27, Mar. 6, 13, 1827.
3. *Ibid.*, Feb. 27, July 17, 1827.

letters did not proselyte him but merely informed him of the change in the situation.

Crittenden reached Washington soon after this speech, took care of his business, and hastened back to Little Rock, arriving on the evening of March 20. He brought the news that on December 26 the Senate had refused to confirm Andrew Scott's reappointment to the Superior Court, and had refused to reconsider it later. Papers filed against him in 1824, after his duel with Judge Selden, were withdrawn from the Department of State by Senator Martin Van Buren, to be studied by the Committee on the Judiciary before it reported adversely to Scott's reappointment. Evidently they were never returned,[4] so we are left with nothing more substantial than a suspicion as to who attempted to effect Scott's removal in 1824, and who called the committee's attention to the existence of the papers in 1827 and engineered his dismissal.

Woodruff saw a letter written by Conway on January 13, in which he told of Crittenden's reappointment, and he must have also mentioned that Judge Scott's commission had not been renewed. Woodruff published the news of Crittenden's reappointment,[5] but withheld the report on Judge Scott, allowing Crittenden to break the news locally almost a month later. It caused a considerable uproar, because Judge Scott was generally regarded as a dedicated and competent public servant, with only the unfortunate duel to blot his record.

Woodruff had not editorially entered the quarrel about Crittenden's unauthorized absence as yet, but his sentiments were known, and his publication of Bates' letters was resented. A month after Crittenden's return the *Gazette's* foreman, Hiram Whittington, wrote to his brother, "Mr. Woodruff, my employer, being an honest and sober man, the majority of the people are his bitter enemies, and he has frequently been threatened. About a month ago, three worthies got into such a fury, owing to a piece published in the *Gazette* criticising the conduct of the Secretary, that they threatened to annihilate all the printers; and one of the judges of the Supreme Court swore that he would pulverize every printer in the Territory in less than a month." [6]

By the time Crittenden returned from Washington, most of the men who were active in public life, and many who were not, had declared themselves on one side or the other. Among the old friends who parted company were Ambrose H. Sevier and Robert C. Oden. In the *Gazette* of February 6, Sevier announced that his law partnership with Oden had been dissolved. Undoubtedly this was because of Oden's plans to run for Congress against Conway. Oden surely understood that Sevier's loyalty to his cousin would place him on

4. *Ibid.*, Mar. 27, 1827; Clarence E. Carter (ed.), *The Territorial Papers of the United States,* Vol. XX, *The Territory of Arkansas 1825–1829* (Washington: Government Printing Office, 1954), 366.

5. *Gazette,* Feb. 27, 1827.

6. Margaret Smith Ross (ed.), *Letters of Hiram Abiff Whittington 1827–1834* (Little Rock: Pulaski County Historical Society, 1956), 2.

Conway's side, and Sevier must have known that Oden would follow Critten-den without hesitation in any controversy. But at this point, nobody was aware of any friction between Conway and Crittenden, and both Sevier and Conway seemed inclined not to participate publicly in the anti-Crittenden movement. Crittenden may have known by this time that he had good reason to hope that Conway would be defeated, but he tried to persuade Oden not to run. Probably he realized that Oden could not hope to win, and feared that the unequal contest would bring grief to everybody concerned.

Conway had not returned from Washington when the *Gazette* announced his candidacy for re-election to Congress on April 10. Oden entered the race a week later and began a vigorous campaign, but until Conway's return about the middle of May, the controversy between Bates and Crittenden continued to occupy more of the attention of the letter writers. It branched out to in-clude many other issues, and a number of other writers became involved. Most of them wrote long letters, and before long Woodruff had to surrender space to them on page two, usually reserved for news from outside Arkansas.

On March 27, Woodruff took time out to move into his new building on the northeast corner of Markham and Scott streets. It was a combination home and printing office with two stories and an attic, was one of the six brick buildings in the town, and was easily the town's best business building. In fact, it was in a class with the mansion Ashley had recently built directly across Markham Street, and the one Crittenden had built on what is now East Seventh Street.

It was built New York style, flush with the brick sidewalks on both Mark-ham and Scott streets. The Markham Street entrance was a narrow stoop of about four feet, with steps on each end. There were four rooms on the ground floor, one of which was quite long and was used as the editorial office and counting room. Here Woodruff also conducted his land agency and his book store, and sold the usual variety of merchandise. There was a long, wide hall with a staircase to the second floor. The largest of the four rooms on the sec-ond floor was the printing office, and the attic was a storage room and lum-ber room. The rooms not occupied by the *Gazette* were living quarters for Woodruff and his employees and apprentices, and later for his family.[7]

About the first of May, Woodruff heard that Oden was boasting that he had the *Gazette's* property in his power. The three lots on which the new *Gazette* building was located (lots 7, 8, and 9 in block 34, Original City of Little Rock) had come into Oden's possession along with several others after the 1821 compromise, when the townsite was partitioned among the various claimants. There were few potential purchasers at Little Rock, so he had given a power of attorney to his brother-in-law, James W. Byrne of Ken-tucky, authorizing him to sell any or all of his lots. Chester Ashley had

7. *Ibid.*, 1, 18; *Gazette,* Mar. 27, Apr. 3, 1827; William E. Woodruff, Jr., "A Chron-icle of Little Rock," and Jane Georgine Woodruff, "A Pioneer Childhood in Little Rock," *Gazette,* Nov. 7, 1931; William F. Pope, *Early Days in Arkansas* (Little Rock: Frederick W. Allsopp, 1895), 104.

subsequently obtained a judgment against Oden on a debt that Oden represented as unjust. When Oden made a trip to Missouri in 1824, Ashley promised he would wait until his return to execute the judgment, but Oden was afraid he would force a sale of his property in his absence. To prevent this, he deeded the lots to Crittenden, who agreed to resist any attempt by Ashley to execute a judgment against them, and who wanted no part of the matter after Oden's return.

When Oden came back from Missouri, Ashley negotiated a sale of these three lots to Woodruff, and at the same time sold to Crittenden the two blocks on which the Crittenden mansion was built soon afterwards. Everybody concerned in the transaction was fully informed of the circumstances of Oden's conveyance to Crittenden, and Crittenden reminded them that a deed from him would be fraudulent because he had no real claim to the lots, having paid Oden no consideration whatever. But Woodruff accepted a general warranty deed from Crittenden without protest on July 9, 1825.

However, Woodruff did not know about the power of attorney to Byrne, which antedated the deed to Crittenden and had never been cancelled. Oden now said that Byrne had sold some of the lots, and said or implied that Woodruff had no valid title to the property in which he had invested some $4,000 and was still improving. Woodruff hurried to the court house to check the county deed records, and found that neither the power of attorney nor the deed to the rumored purchaser had been filed for record, and therefore could not be considered a threat to his title, the documents of which were properly recorded.[8]

Conway arrived at Little Rock on May 16, issued a circular, and left for a campaign tour in southwest Arkansas. The circular replied to a charge made by Oden that Conway had kept $600 of the $7,000 the secretary of war had sent to Crittenden by him in 1824 for the Quapaws. Conway said he had believed nobody knew about this except him and Crittenden, and he was surprised to find it used against him in the campaign. Conway contended that he had Crittenden's permission to retain the $600 temporarily for his personal use, but Crittenden denied it, and this became one of the most hotly contested issues of the summer.[9]

The letters published in the *Gazette* became increasingly abusive, and several writers took up Crittenden's side of the argument, with direct or indirect benefit to Oden. Their letters made numerous charges against Conway, and it was obvious that he would need a defender at Little Rock to make prompt and effective replies. Woodruff could not write the letters without violating the precarious editorial neutrality he was still attempting to maintain. Chester Ashley for some reason did not choose to assume the responsibility. Ambrose Sevier could ill afford to jeopardize his own political ambi-

8. *Gazette,* June 12, 19, July 17, 24 (Supplement), 1827; Pulaski County Deed Book E, 111.
9. *Gazette,* May 22, 1827.

Ambrose Hundley Sevier.

Charles Pierre Bertrand, left,
with Sterling Hartwell Tucker.

tions, being a candidate for a third term in the House of Representatives from Pulaski County, and hoping to go much higher.

Dr. Matthew Cunningham, whose stepson, Charles P. Bertrand, and son, Robert Cunningham, were apprentices in the *Gazette* office, agreed to write the letters on condition that his name would not be revealed under any circumstances, to protect him from involvement in a lawsuit or other unpleasant consequences. He wrote under the pseudonym "A Voter of Pulaski County," but the task was largely clerical because Woodruff, Ashley, and Sevier supplied all the information. Izard had recently returned to Little Rock, but took no part in producing the letters,[10] or any other part of the campaign.

The first letter, published on June 5, was mildly worded, but a series of numbered letters that began the next week were violently abusive. The first of these was a reply to the pro-Crittenden, anti-Conway letter of "A Citizen of the Territory," published the previous week. Woodruff had been given the name of a man who stood responsible for the letter, but "A Voter of Pulaski County" said it was the joint production of four people, including Crittenden and Oden, with the finishing touches supplied by a fifth. He also named several instances in which Crittenden had misused public funds, alluded to the matter of Woodruff's property to show that Oden was basically dishonest and that Crittenden had willingly participated in the attempted fraud, and challenged Crittenden's pretended neutrality in the Conway-Oden campaign.

10. *Ibid.,* Sept. 5, 1832.

Publication of this letter on June 12 brought exactly the kind of results Dr. Cunningham had anticipated. Crittenden and his friends swooped down on the printing office to demand the writer's name, and threatened retribution in the form of cow-hiding, dirking, ear-cropping, and shooting, to be performed by Crittenden if his antagonist were married or by Thomas W. Newton if he were single. Woodruff gained time by saying he would have to confer with the writer before he could reveal his identity, and two days later he wrote the following letter to Crittenden:

Little Rock, June 15, 1827.

Sir—I have communicated, since my note to you of last evening, with the author of "A Voter of Pulaski County." He requests me to say, that considerations of a peculiar character, render it highly improper for him to avow himself as the writer of that publication, and desires that I will not divulge his name. You will therefore consider me as declining to give up the name of the author of "A Voter of Pulaski County."

But, sir, in declining to give up the name of the writer of that publication, I wish you to understand, distinctly, that I do not debar you the privilege of replying, through the same medium, to the charges, (which, by the bye, relate exclusively to your acts as a public officer, and are therefore proper subjects for public investigation,) made therein against you, and of refuting them, if you have the means of doing so.—The columns of my paper are freely offered you for the purpose of disproving those charges, if you think proper to avail yourself of that privilege.

I conceive it to be the duty of all Editors, in cases, like the present, where they decline giving up the names of authors of communications, to assume the responsibility of such publications themselves. You will therefore consider me (though not the author) responsible for the charges alleged against you in the publication which appeared in my yesterday's paper, over the signature of "A Voter of Pulaski County;" and I now announce to you, that I am prepared to sustain those charges, if you think proper to require me to do so, in a legal manner.

(Signed)   WM. E. WOODRUFF

Robt. Crittenden Esq.
Sec'y Ark's Terr., Little Rock.

In the next issue, Crittenden told his side of the story on all the points that had been made against him, but said he could not disprove the charges immediately because some key witnesses were absent from the territory and would not soon return. Therefore he would put the burden of proof on Woodruff by filing a libel suit against him.

Woodruff promised a personal reply to this letter, but postponed it more than a month. He said he could prove everything "A Voter of Pulaski

County" had said, and the letters under that pseudonym continued to goad Crittenden unmercifully. Crittenden was advised to wait to file the suit, in order to include charges to be made in future letters, and was reminded that proof of the statements in court would further expose him. Crittenden had already begun work on the suit, and "A Voter of Pulaski County" said he had deprived Woodruff of the means of defense by engaging all the competent lawyers on his side except two. One of these had declined to bring the suit and the other had agreed to defend Woodruff, with the result that they had been "proscribed for ever" by Crittenden.[11] Undoubtedly they were Ashley and Sevier, who by rights should assume their share of the fruits of the letters they had helped produce. Probably this was the incident that caused Crittenden to begin to exert his influence against Sevier in his campaign for the House.

With tempers high, letters poured into the printing office, often at the last minute before the paper went to press. Woodruff told the writers on June 19 that they must send their letters two or three days before publication day, and promised he would edit them only for spelling and punctuation, and that the writers would be permitted to proofread their letters, provided it did not delay publication of the paper.

On the evening of June 21, Oden brought part of a long manuscript to the *Gazette* office, and tried to have it printed as a circular. It was not finished, but Oden wanted the first part put in type immediately and said he would bring the rest later. Woodruff refused to begin work on it until he could see the whole thing, and Oden brought him the completed manuscript the next morning.

It assailed Conway, Woodruff, Ashley, and Izard in what Woodruff described as "highly abusive and indecorous language, interspersed with slanderous assertions." Woodruff agreed to print the charges against Conway since he was a public official, and presumably took the same position regarding Izard, but said he could hardly be expected to print the offensive remarks about himself or Ashley. He said Ashley would have grounds for a libel suit if the circular were printed, and would be more likely to look to Woodruff for satisfaction than to the less prosperous Oden. This, of course, was subterfuge, for the last thing Woodruff feared was a libel suit against him by Ashley. Oden argued that the mere act of printing the circular would not make Woodruff liable, since Oden would stand as the publisher and would circulate it himself, but Woodruff contended that the printer would be equally liable. He tried to persuade Oden to omit the few objectionable lines, show the deletions with asterisks, and insert a footnote explaining that Woodruff had refused to print that part. Oden refused to compromise, and withdrew the manuscript.

It was a harsh, violent scene. It was reported in other parts of the territory that a group of Oden's friends congregated in front of the printing office with the avowed intention of giving Woodruff a beating, but retreated when

11. *Ibid.,* June 19, 1827.

they discovered that the *Gazette's* printers were prepared to defend their boss. Woodruff denied that any such thing had happened, and said Oden's friends had done nothing more serious than to make a few empty threats for the purpose of intimidation.[12]

Because of Oden's conduct on this occasion, Woodruff announced on June 26 that he would give open opposition to Oden's candidacy through the columns of the *Gazette,* but would continue to allow him and his friends to be heard through the paper. This was the equivalent of an endorsement of Conway, and was the first definite stand the *Gazette* ever took in any political contest.

Though the editor could now speak freely, "A Voter of Pulaski County" was too useful to be unmasked or retired. Through his letters, it was suggested that Oden had never expected that Woodruff would print his circular, but had deliberately written one he knew would be rejected, so he could say Woodruff was persecuting him by suppressing his side of the campaign.[13]

Oden immediately sent his manuscript to Memphis to be printed. This errand was run by two messengers, one of whom was Dr. William P. Reyburn, who lived in Crittenden's home. On the way back to Little Rock, the two men separated when they disagreed on the route they should take in crossing Grand Prairie. After losing his saddle as he made his way through the tangled briars, one of the men finally found the road and reached Little Rock safely. The other, Dr. Reyburn, was lost in the swamps for four days, subsisting on raw crawfish, a few blackberries, and sassafras leaves. The briars tore most of his clothing from his body, and he lost his horse, saddle, bridle, and hat before he came to a house on the river bank 12 or 15 miles below Little Rock. Only the saddlebags containing the precious circulars came through the ordeal without damage, and the circulars were distributed immediately after they reached Little Rock about the middle of July.

At first Woodruff thought the copy had been changed, and allowed "A Voter of Pulaski County" to say in a handbill that the published circular was much less offensive than the original manuscript, and that all the objectionable statements had been deleted. Oden or his friends brought the manuscript to him for comparison, and when Woodruff reprinted the handbill in the next *Gazette,* he had to admit in a footnote that only a sentence or two about Izard had been omitted.[14]

Meanwhile, Crittenden filed his libel suit early in July, and laid his damages at the then astronomical figure of $25,000. Woodruff admitted that "the charges made against Mr. Crittenden, were of a pretty serious nature, and calculated materially to affect his character as a public officer," but said he would rest his cause on the truth of the charges, which he felt fully competent to sustain.[15]

12. *Ibid.,* June 26, July 3, 1827.
13. *Ibid.,* July 3, 1827.
14. *Ibid.,* July 10, 17, 1827.
15. *Ibid.,* July 10, Dec. 5, 1827.

If Woodruff felt any uneasiness on this point, it was not apparent. The letters signed "A Voter of Pulaski County" continued without modification of tone, and on July 24 Woodruff even admitted he had had a part in their production. This was in an editorial footnote attached to a letter written by a friend of Crittenden, in which it was suggested that the mysterious writer had promised to indemnify Woodruff for any damages he might sustain. Woodruff said, "The publication of the several Nos. over that signature, were commenced at the *suggestion* of the *Editor of this paper,* who, *alone,* is responsible for the charges contained therein against Mr. Crittenden, and who voluntarily assumed that responsibility, without any promise or expectation of *indemnification* from the writer or any other person, for any injury which he might sustain by their publication." Perhaps it was the last part of this statement, already familiar, that caused the Crittendenites to overlook the partial confession in the first part. Woodruff never repeated it, and continued to pass himself off as a martyr who had nobly assumed a burden not rightfully his.

On July 24, Woodruff issued a circular under his own signature, in which he made a long delayed and often promised reply to the letter Crittenden had written for publication in the *Gazette* more than a month earlier. All the issues presented thus far were discussed, but the argument about the title to Woodruff's property is particularly amusing. He was careful not to make a direct statement that his own lots were among those rumored to have been sold by Oden's brother-in-law, but he slyly implied that they were. He also made a strong point of the fact that Crittenden had never had a valid title to the lots (and Crittenden himself had stressed this fact), yet Woodruff's experience as a land agent must have taught him that his own title could be no better than Crittenden's, since it was derived from him.

A ludicrous postscript to this episode would come after Crittenden's death. With three of the territory's ablest lawyers and its leading land agent involved in the sale of the lots, they had neglected to have Mrs. Crittenden relinquish her dower rights. As a widow, she went to court to recover dower rights to the property her husband had publicly declared he had never lawfully owned. The case strung out for several years, and went four times to the Arkansas Supreme Court before it was finally decided in Woodruff's favor.[16]

16. Mrs. Crittenden filed her petition for dower in the Pulaski Circuit Court on October 2, 1838, and dower in the lots was assigned to her by a decree of that court dated April 15, 1839, but no move was made towards its execution. The matter first came before the Arkansas Supreme Court in a related case, The State v. Lemuel D. Evans, Jan. Term 1841, 3 *Ark.* 585–591, in which the right of Evans to sit as circuit judge in this case and one other in which Woodruff was a principal was challenged, and the Supreme Court ruled in Evans' favor. In Crittenden, *Ex Parte,* Jan. Term 1850, 10 *Ark.* 333–377, Mrs. Crittenden sought to force execution of the 1839 decree, which had been set aside on November 29, 1841 on Woodruff's petition. The court held that the decree was not final, inasmuch as certain vital information was not immediately available to the lower court, and until final, it remained in that court's jurisdiction and could be

After the publication of Woodruff's circular on July 24, new violence broke out at Little Rock. Hiram Whittington wrote to his brother on July 26, "The inhabitants of this town have been in a terrible uproar for the last three or four weeks, on account of an election which is to take place in August. Night before last, I saw four pistols presented to as many hearts, within six inches of each other, and had it not been for the interference of bystanders there would have been four or five persons killed. That there will be bloodshed before the election is over, there is not much doubt. Mr. Crittenden, Secretary of the Territory, has threatened to cut Mr. Woodruff's throat for publishing a communication concerning his official conduct, and, what is much worse, has threatened to cut off the nose of every printer in the place and pull down the printing office. Should he attempt either, he would be used up very soon. You have no idea what a set of villains inhabit this place. Mr. Woodruff and one of the young men in the office are sick with the fever; brought on, I believe, by fear." [17]

In the last issue before the election, "A Voter of Pulaski County" said he would write no more about the election, but in the future would tell more about the "official misdeeds" of Crittenden. [18]

The election was held on August 6. The next day was the regular publication day for the *Gazette,* and Woodruff printed a few copies for local distribution, but withheld the rest of the edition until late the next afternoon, in order to include the complete unofficial returns from Pulaski and Conway counties. It was another month before the official returns were available, showing a tremendous victory for Conway, with a vote of 2,427 to Oden's 856. [19]

The trend was apparent long before the official returns were released, and on August 14, "A Voter of Pulaski County" returned to the *Gazette's* columns to crow about the victory and to chide Crittenden about the "blighting effect" of his friendship for Oden, claiming that his support had cost Oden at least 500 votes. Sevier's election to the House over Thomas Mathers was cited as another instance of the adverse effect of Crittenden's friendship, for the writer said that as soon as Crittenden "excommunicated" Sevier, he rose in public esteem and his opponent's popularity diminished by the same ratio.

---

set aside. Mrs. Crittenden's application for reconsideration was refused. In Crittenden v. Woodruff, Jan. Term 1850, 11 *Ark.* 82–93, the Supreme Court ruled that Mrs. Crittenden was entitled to dower, reversing the Circuit Court, to which the case was remanded. One of several points on which this decision was based was that Ashley in his deposition had professed a lapse of memory as to Oden's reason for conveying the property to Crittenden, and the court did not consider the evidence conclusive that Crittenden was not the rightful owner. But the final decision in Crittenden v. Woodruff, Jan. Term 1854, 14 *Ark.* 465–470, was in Woodruff's favor, because Roswell Beebe, to whom the patent for the townsite was issued in 1839, had confirmed Woodruff's title by warranty deed, while Mrs. Crittenden had not even applied to him for confirmation.

17. Ross, *Letters of Hiram Abiff Whittington,* 3.
18. *Gazette,* July 31, 1827.
19. *Ibid.,* Sept. 11, 1827.

It cannot be said that the political contest between Oden and Conway was the cause of the chaos of 1827, for Oden was never a sufficiently formidable candidate against the extremely popular Conway to call forth such strong efforts to put him down. From the beginning, even before Oden's candidacy was announced, Crittenden was the main target. Indeed, Crittenden tried to persuade Oden not to run, and until the campaign was well under way, he seemed inclined to remain neutral. Whether it was genuine neutrality or the duplicity it was interpreted to be is debatable. But the close friends of Crittenden and Oden were largely the same people, and since both were opposed by the *Gazette* and its friends, the antagonism towards them overlapped. Certainly Oden did not receive as much attention as Crittenden.

In the aftermath of the election, a few scores remained to be settled. It had been obvious during the summer that Crittenden and some of his friends were spoiling for a duel, the traditional way Southern gentlemen defended their honor. Crittenden was said to have intimated as much in private conversations. The pro-Crittenden writer who signed himself "A Citizen of the Territory" seemed to be trying to force Woodruff to demand his real name instead of the one given him when the first letter was submitted, evidently hoping the demand would lead to a challenge.

Conway was 200 miles from Little Rock on July 24, when a letter written by Crittenden was published in the *Gazette,* and did not see it until after the election. It was another discussion of the $600 Conway had retained from the Indian funds, and related issues. Conway wrote a short letter on August 17, in which he accused Crittenden of willful misrepresentation for the purpose of injuring his chances for re-election, and the letter was published on August 28. Conway had hinted in an earlier letter that Crittenden had lied about this matter, and Crittenden had smarted from it all summer, wishing desperately that Conway would ask him for an explanation but feeling that to volunteer one would dishonor him. Now Conway's meaning could not be mistaken. He had called Crittenden a liar, and to a Kentucky gentleman, that was the equivalent of throwing down the gauntlet. The same day the letter was published, Crittenden sent Conway a note announcing that he would challenge him to a duel on or before October 20. He said he would do it immediately if he were not restrained by the "peculiar situation" of his family,[20] an allusion to the anticipated birth of his third child.

While this duel was pending, Ambrose Sevier is said to have remarked at a barbecue that he would like to fight one of the anonymous letter writers on the Crittenden side. This was the kind of opportunity "A Citizen of the Territory" had been striving for, and it was generally understood that Thomas W. Newton had written the letters Sevier mentioned. When Newton heard about Sevier's remark, he revealed himself as the author. Newton and Sevier met on the porch of Fisher's tavern and almost came to blows, but the fight was stopped. A challenge was subsequently issued, and they fought a duel within the Cherokee boundaries on the morning of September 4. They ex-

20. Ibid., Nov. 6, 13, 1827.

—Courtesy Charles Elias.

Scene looking west on Markham Street from the corner of Cumberland, about 1864 or early in 1865. The brick building in the approximate center of the picture was the *Gazette* office, 1827-1840.

changed shots without injury to either, and their friends adjusted their difficulty without sacrificing the honor of either. When the *Gazette* reported this duel, the names of all participants were withheld, probably for the protection of Sevier and his political career.[21]

Crittenden and Conway were not so fortunate. The two months delay gave time for attempts at reconciliation, and Crittenden's friends made two clumsy overtures in that direction. They said Crittenden would withdraw the notification of challenge if Conway would withdraw the insult, and Conway refused because this would dishonor him. Conway said they required him to request Crittenden to withdraw the challenge. Crittenden's friends always firmly believed that Ashley promoted the quarrel, and influenced Conway against making his peace with Crittenden.

Mrs. Crittenden was at the point of death for nearly ten days after the birth of her daughter. She was not told about her husband's plans to fight a duel, though she was recuperating when he left Little Rock to meet Conway.[22]

The duel was fought on the morning of October 29, on the east side of the Mississippi River, nearly opposite the mouth of White River. Conway was

21. *Ibid.*, Sept. 11, 1827; May 9, 1832; May 8, 1844; Dec. 5, 1857; *Arkansas Banner,* May 1, 1844. The 1844 articles, written over pseudonyms, name Newton as the challenger, but George W. Jones, who served as Newton's second, said in 1888 that Newton was "the challenged party." See "Eyewitness Account of Newton-Sevier Duel," *Pulaski County Historical Review* (Little Rock: Pulaski County Historical Society), I (June, 1953), 8–9. See also James Scull to James Miller, Little Rock, Oct. 28, 1827, Ms. in Robert W. Trimble Collection, Arkansas History Commission, in which Scull says, "Their dispute has been of long standing." This raises the question as to whether the discussion of 1826 about Newton's default as compared with Conway's might have figured in it.

22. Scull to Miller, Oct. 28, 1827.

wounded at the first fire, and was taken to the home of William Montgomery at the mouth of White River. Conway's preparation for the duel had included obtaining letters from Montgomery and Sylvanus Phillips, telling of remarks Crittenden had made to them during the summer, indicating that he wanted to fight the duel weeks before he sent the note to Conway. These letters and Crittenden's note had been left in Woodruff's keeping, and he appended them to his article reporting the duel, published on November 6, to cast the censure for seeking the duel squarely on Crittenden.

Conway died of his wound on the night of November 9. Woodruff received the news on the evening of November 12, and dressed the *Gazette* in mourning the next day. In this issue also appeared a long address to the public, written by Crittenden before he knew Conway was dead, telling his side of the story and commenting acidly on the letters of Montgomery and Phillips.[23]

The legislature was in special session the first three weeks in October, and Montgomery was in attendance as the representative in the lower house for Arkansas and Chicot counties. An argument that undoubtedly grew out of the Crittenden-Conway difficulty developed between him and Thomas Wyatt Johnston, a Kentuckian who was a close friend of Crittenden and had been mentioned as benefitting from Crittenden's misuse of Indian funds on one occasion. Both Montgomery and Johnston were more given to impromptu free-style brawls than to the orderly process of duels, so they fought it out on a Little Rock street. They started with pistols, missed, and fell back on canes and dirks. Bystanders saved Johnston's life by stopping the fight, but this fight or others of a similar nature cost him one eye and left his face and body permanently disfigured. No details are known of a second street fight about the same time that apparently also originated in the campaign controversies.[24]

Crittenden and his friends strongly suspected that Ashley was the master mind behind much of the discord of the summer, but he shrugged off all their attempts to get satisfaction. He was challenged by Oden and also by Thomas Crittenden, who had come from Kentucky to see his brother through this critical period. Both challengers were bachelors, while Ashley had a wife and children, and the unequal family status gave Ashley grounds to refuse both challenges. It was thought that Robert Crittenden himself might challenge Ashley if he should survive the duel with Conway,[25] but if he ever had such plans, they were cancelled by his remorse at having killed Conway and his sensitivity to the strong public reaction to the untimely death of the popular young delegate.

Izard's brief participation in the campaign was inoffensive, and consisted of merely denying that he was concerned with a plot to defeat Oden, so no

23. For more details on the Crittenden-Conway duel, see Van Buren *Press,* Apr. 21, 1888; *Arkansas Banner,* May 1, 1844; *Gazette,* May 8, 1844; Jan. 18, 1850; Dec. 5, 1857.
24. Ross, *Letters of Hiram Abiff Whittington,* 4, 54. One of Johnston's nearly fatal street brawls is described by John R. Homer Scott in *Gazette,* Sept. 3, 1885.
25. Van Burren *Press,* Apr. 21, 1888; Scull to Miller, Oct. 28, 1827. A veiled reference to Thomas Crittenden's challenge to Ashley was used as a threat to silence Ashley by a pseudonymous writer in *Gazette,* May 8, 1844.

attempt was made at retribution against him. Dr. Cunningham was not suspected of having written the letters signed "A Voter of Pulaski County," and he also escaped retaliation.

Woodruff had taken a public stand against duelling as far back as 1820, and his disdain for the Code of Honor was so well known that a challenge to him would have been ineffectual. Moreover, he had made it clear in June that he would fight his battles only in a legal manner, and that facts and words would be his weapons. This ruled out duels, but the danger of sneak attacks and the pending libel suit kept him in a state of anxiety for several months. Fifty years later he recalled, "In 1827 it was not very good. I found it difficult to avoid personal collision. I cannot say that I was afraid of my life but always went armed in those days. At times I had some apprehensions of being assassinated in my own house. Crittenden usually kept a class of men about his person who were regarded with suspicion for some of them were among the most desperate men of the country. He was not inclined to stand in the front but advanced his satelites [sic] and they were ready to do his bidding."[26]

When the legislature assembled on October 1, Woodruff was a candidate for engrossing and enrolling clerk. After three ballots resulted in a tie, one legislator changed his vote and Allen M. Oakley was elected. Woodruff was again unanimously elected public printer, having no opposition.[27]

One marvels that Woodruff found time to court 17-year-old Jane Eliza Mills during the hectic summer of 1827. She was a niece of Isaac and Maria Watkins, with whom she made her home. They were married on November 14, 1827 at the Watkins home.[28] Less than a month after the wedding, Watkins was murdered in a store on Main Street. This murder had no political background, for on the previous day Watkins had accused his killer, John Smith, of stealing hogs from his farm, and this was believed to be the only reason for the murder.[29] His death was a blow to Woodruff in more ways than one, for the proof of the charges made against Crittenden by "A Voter of Pulaski County" depended on the testimony of Henry Conway and Isaac Watkins, and now both were dead.[30]

John T. Garrett was a close friend of Crittenden, and had a personal grudge against Ashley. Garrett was a deputy sheriff, and had reason to believe that Ashley had preferred charges against him to Governor Izard, presumably in an attempt to have his appointment revoked. For some time he had grumbled about Ashley's opposition, and had told several people that he would eventually cowhide or kill him. He planned to start to his father's home on the afternoon of January 17, 1828, but he postponed the trip

26. William E. Woodruff's answers to 63 questions, question No. 63, Ms. in Robert W. Trimble Collection, Arkansas History Commission.

27. *Gazette,* Oct. 9, 1827.

28. *Ibid.,* Nov. 20, 1827; Nov. 14, 1877; May 5, 1876; Family Bibles of Jane Eliza Woodruff and Hannah Clarke Woodruff, Arkansas History Commission.

29. *Gazette,* Dec. 13, 1827.

30. *Ibid.,* Mar. 7, 1832.

and spent the afternoon in the saloons of Little Rock, muttering sinister threats against Ashley.

Late in the day, he entered the *Gazette* office, brandishing a cowhide in one hand and a pistol in the other. Ashley, Woodruff, and several other men were there. In the argument that ensued, Ashley denied having preferred formal charges against Garrett, but said he had talked with the governor about Garrett's position as deputy sheriff. Garrett warned Ashley to beware of him in the future, for he would surely kill him, and stomped out of the office.

He made another quick tour of the neighboring grog shops, repeating the threat several times. At Nicholas Peay's tavern he met Crittenden, who Woodruff later said "seemed to have had more business with him that day than almost any one else." After a short conversation with Crittenden, Garrett returned to the *Gazette* office. In the half hour that had elapsed since his first visit, everybody had left the office except Woodruff and Ashley.

Drawing his pistol, Garrett announced that he had come to kill Ashley. As he fired both barrels, Woodruff grabbed his coat collar and deflected his aim, and both bullets lodged harmlessly in a box near the fireplace. A second pistol was fired almost simultaneously, wounding Garrett in the abdomen. Ashley had drawn his pistol, but had not fired it immediately for fear of killing Woodruff. Just after Garrett was wounded, Ashley fired one shot. The bullet passed through the fleshy part of Woodruff's upper right arm and lodged in the south wall under a map.

Garrett dropped his pistol and stumbled across the street to the saloon and gambling room of James Lemmon and lay down on a bed, where he died about two o'clock in the morning. Dr. Cunningham held a three-day coroner's inquest on which some 20 or 30 witnesses were examined, but the coroner's jury was unable to decide who had fired the fatal shot and the case was closed without an indictment. All the bullets in Ashley's and Garrett's pistols were otherwise accounted for, and Woodruff's testimony that he had not fired a pistol was not challenged.[31]

When the subject was reopened for public discussion later, Cunningham intimated that Woodruff had shot Garrett. Woodruff vigorously denied it, and reminded Cunningham that in the closing hours of the inquest it had been proved that Garrett had carried two pistols earlier in the day. He theorized that the extra pistol was still concealed under Garrett's cloak, and that Garrett himself must have discharged it accidentally. This argument was strengthened by the testimony of one or two witnesses that Garrett's clothing was on fire when he left the *Gazette* office, and another had said there was no bullet hole in either his cloak or his coat. In 1830 and 1832, Woodruff made it clear that he believed Crittenden was responsible for Garrett's attempt on Ashley's life.[32] At the time of the killing, Woodruff made no public statement, but asked someone who presumably had the objectivity of one completely

31. *Ibid.,* Jan. 23, 1828; Apr. 4, 1832.
32. *Ibid.,* July 21, 1830; April 4, 1832.

uninvolved but who had been present at the inquest to write the story for the *Gazette*.

The time consumed by the inquest delayed the publication of the next issue of the *Gazette* one day, and Woodruff announced that thereafter the paper would appear on Wednesdays instead of Tuesdays, until the mails became more or less regular again.

During the week of Garrett's death, the libel suit was settled out of court by a compromise effected by Ashley, who was represented as acting on his own responsibility without any suggestion from either of the principals. Woodruff was in a bad position, relying on truth of the charges and justification as his defense, but unable to prove the most important charges because of the death of his two key witnesses. Crittenden's legal position was good, but he knew he would do well to subdue further unfavorable publicity until the reaction to Conway's death subsided. So both responded favorably to the suggestion that the suit could be withdrawn without imputing dishonor or lack of veracity to either.

Crittenden and Ashley collaborated on an article to be published in the *Gazette* over Woodruff's signature, in return for which Crittenden would withdraw the suit. Woodruff rejected the article and wrote one himself, which Crittenden accepted after two or three days of negotiation. It was not an apology, and Woodruff did not see it as a retraction, but merely as an explanation. He admitted that the letters by "A Voter of Pulaski County" were derogatory to Crittenden's private and public character, and that proof of the statements depended on information from other people. He now said that the writer was unable to furnish the necessary proof to substantiate his charges, and for that reason Woodruff was withdrawing all the derogatory comment contained in the letters.

The copy for this article was in Woodruff's handwriting, and on the back Crittenden wrote his promise to dismiss the libel suit upon publication of the article. Four years later Woodruff accused Crittenden of a "lawyer's trick" that influenced him to withdraw the objectionable statements. Appended to the six or eight counts of libel in Crittenden's suit was a charge that Woodruff had found $25,000 in gold that Crittenden had lost, and refused to return it to Crittenden. Woodruff said he had found no gold, and did not believe Crittenden had ever owned such a sum in gold, much less lost it. He said he could hardly have pleaded truth and justification on this count, as he intended to do on all the others, for it would have been tantamount to an admission that it also was true.[33]

Crittenden was indicted for sending a challenge to fight a duel, but the Superior Court quashed the indictment in October, 1828 because it stated the date in the alternative "on or about" and did not conclude with "against the peace and dignity of the United States," according to the prescribed form.[34]

33. *Ibid.*, Jan. 23, 1828; Mar. 7, 1832.
34. The United States vs. Robert Crittenden, Oct. 1828, in Samuel H. Hempstead,

Conway's vacancy in Congress was filled by a special election on December 17, in which Ambrose H. Sevier, Richard Searcy, and Andrew Scott were the candidates. It is not true, as the Crittendenites later said, that Sevier's kinship with Conway was the main plank in his platform, but it was the one the voters liked best, and he rode into Congress largely on his dead cousin's popularity. There was a strong feeling that Conway's enemies should not profit by his death, and both Searcy and Scott had been friendlier with Crittenden than with Conway in recent months. Scott also had the insupportable burden of having killed Judge Selden in a duel, and this was not a good year for duellists. Many who otherwise would have voted for him felt he had no chance to win and gave their votes instead to Searcy. Searcy might have won if Scott had not run, for the vote was 939 for Sevier, 883 for Searcy, and 116 for Scott.[35]

There was yet another violent death caused by the 1827 election. On May 31, 1828, Judge Scott and Edmund Hogan became involved in an argument pertaining to the August election in which Hogan had barely defeated Scott and Alexander S. Walker for Pulaski County's seat in the Legislative Council. In effect Scott called Hogan a liar, whereupon Hogan sent Scott sprawling on the floor with one blow. Hogan weighed upwards of 250 pounds, while Scott weighed only about 130 pounds, so a fist fight between them would have been ridiculous. Drawing a spear from his cane, Scott stabbed Hogan four times, and Hogan was dead in less than ten minutes. Since Scott had acted in self defense, no charges were filed against him.[36]

The *Gazette* and its proprietor emerged from the fateful year of 1827 with many sorrows, and with their friendships and enmities sharply defined. If Woodruff regretted the course he had pursued he never gave the slightest indication of it, and always contended that he had acted only in the defensive position. Certainly he anticipated even stormier days in the future, but there could be no turning back now.

Reports of Cases Argued and Determined in the United States Superior Court for the Territory of Arkansas, from 1820 to 1836; and in the United States District Court for the District of Arkansas, from 1836 to 1849; and in the United States Circuit Court for the District of Arkansas, in the Ninth Circuit, from 1839 to 1856 (Boston: Little, Brown and Co., 1856), 61.

35. *Gazette*, Nov. 13, 20, 27, Dec. 4, 11, 18, 25, 1827; Jan. 23, 1828.

36. *Ibid.,* June 4, 1828; Sept. 3, 1885; Pope, *Early Days in Arkansas,* 33, 41–43.

5

COMPETITION AND CONTROVERSY

1828-1832   THROUGHOUT THE 1827 unpleasantness, Woodruff repeatedly said that his columns were open to his friends and enemies alike, but it cannot be denied that the Crittendenites labored under distinct disadvantages in the paper war. As the furor subsided, Crittenden and seven of his friends quietly set out to establish a press that would give them the same advantages the other faction had in the *Gazette*.

In the summer of 1828, acting for himself and as attorney for the other seven, Crittenden entered into a contract with a man named Simpson, who agreed to start a paper at Little Rock in the fall. The eight backers paid Simpson $500, but the plan fell through. The arrangements were supposed to be a closely guarded secret, but the ink was hardly dry on the contract before the word leaked out.[1]

The *Gazette* began its tenth volume on December 30, 1828 with a sheet 21 inches long, a hardly noticeable increase of half an inch. The width of the page remained 13 inches, but the width of the five columns was increased from 13½ to 14 picas. There was a new nameplate, in Old English similar to the old one, and *"The"* returned to the title, making it again *The Arkansas Gazette*. Woodruff said the increase in the subscription list during the previous year justified the extra labor and expense of these improvements.

Governor Izard died at Little Rock on November 22, 1828, and Crittenden was once more the acting governor. Three days after Izard's death, both Crittenden and Andrew Scott applied for the appointment as governor, each relying on the friendship of an older brother with Secretary of State Henry Clay and President John Quincy Adams to gain preferment.[2] Before their letters were delivered in Washington, it was apparent that Andrew Jackson

1. *Gazette,* July 21, Sept. 1, 1830.
2. *Ibid.,* Nov. 22, 1828; Clarence Edwin Carter (ed.), *The Territorial Papers of the United States,* Vol. XX, *The Territory of Arkansas 1825–1829* (Washington: Government Printing Office, 1954), 796, 797.

John Pope.

had won a landslide victory in the presidential election held in November,[3] and those friendships became a liability rather than an asset. This was particularly true in Crittenden's case because his brother, John Jordan Crittenden, had been one of Jackson's most powerful enemies.

Adams bypassed both Crittenden and Scott and nominated an outsider, possibly because Sevier had recommended it, saying there was hardly a qualified man in Arkansas who was not tainted with the intense party spirit that had invaded the territory in 1827, and expressing his own "unconquerable hatred" for Crittenden. But the Senate refused to confirm the nomination, leaving the office to be filled by the man of Jackson's choice.[4]

On March 9, 1829, only a few days after his inauguration, Jackson nominated John Pope of Kentucky, and the Senate confirmed the appointment the same day.[5] Pope's fanatical loathing of Clay had made him an ardent supporter of Jackson, though it had placed him in opposition to his own brother-in-law, John Quincy Adams. The appointment as governor of Arkansas Territory was a poor reward for one who considered his campaign services should have earned him the position as United States attorney general, but Pope accepted it.[6]

3. *Gazette,* Dec. 2, 9, 1828.

4. *Ibid.,* Jan. 27, 1829; Carter, *Territorial Papers,* XX, 822–824, 858.

5. Clarence Edwin Carter (ed.), *The Territorial Papers of the United States,* Vol. XXI, *The Territory of Arkansas 1829–1836* (Washington: Government Printing Office, 1954), 3.

6. *Ibid.,* 14; William F. Pope, *Early Days in Arkansas* (Little Rock: Frederick W. Allsopp, 1895), 29; Peggy Jacoway, *First Ladies of Arkansas* (Kingsport, Tenn.: Southern Publishers, Inc., 1941), 35–38; Orval W. Baylor, *John Pope, Kentuckian, His Life*

Jackson owed his election to a grass-roots movement that left him with more than the usual number of campaign obligations to be discharged by appointments to office. It soon became obvious that he would replace Adams men at every rung of the political ladder with his own friends, even in the most insignificant offices. For a while, he seemed to have overlooked the secretary of Arkansas Territory, for he made no effort to replace Crittenden while Congress was in session. But on April 8, 1829, he removed Crittenden from office and appointed William Savin Fulton of Alabama, a personal friend who had served as his military secretary in 1818. The appointment had to be made on a temporary basis, because it would need confirmation by the Senate at the next session.[7]

Woodruff may have known all about this from Sevier by May 6, when he taunted Crittenden with the likelihood of his removal, but he did not announce it until May 20, the day before Fulton and his family reached Little Rock, which made it something of a bombshell. Crittenden retired to the private practice of law, but remained an important political power. Pope arrived on May 31, but returned to Kentucky a month later to bring back his wife, a distant relative of Mrs. Ashley.[8]

The campaign for Congress was in progress when Fulton and Pope arrived, with Ambrose Sevier again opposed by Richard Searcy. This campaign had its tense moments, but was not in a class with that of 1827. The greatest sins credited to Sevier by his enemies were the devious tricks of the unscrupulous land speculator. In the incident most warmly disputed, it was said that Sevier, Woodruff, and Ashley had schemed in the summer of 1828 to delay publication of a new land law, which by the accidental omission of one important word made a certain class of land claim more valuable than the owners knew. The delay would allow time for speculators to purchase many of these claims for a pittance. Actually, Ashley had suggested such a plan, but Woodruff would have no part of it and published the law immediately. Sevier took the same attitude and promptly took steps to notify the settlers of their rights and to offset the defect in the law through the land office, until it could be corrected by Congress.[9]

Sevier's popularity was developing rapidly, and he won the election with 2,064 votes to Searcy's 1,756.[10] The Crittenden faction once again sharply

and Times 1770–1845 (Cynthiana, Ky.: The Hobson Press, 1943), 87, 329–332. Elizabeth Dorcas Janet Johnson, daughter of Joshua Johnson, was the second of John Pope's three wives and the mother of his only surviving child, and died about 1811. Her sister, Louisa Katherine Johnson, married Adams on July 26, 1797. Another sister was the wife of Adams' nephew, William Steuber Smith.

7. Carter, *Territorial Papers,* XXI, 13, 23.

8. Mrs. Frances (Watkins) Walton, who married John Pope on May 1, 1820, was the daughter of Henry Watkins of St. Patrick's Parish, Prince Edward County, Virginia, and the widow of Gen. Matt Walton. See Baylor, *John Pope, Kentuckian,* 168. Pope identified her as a relative of Mary Watkins Worthington Elliott Ashley, wife of Chester Ashley, in *Gazette,* Aug. 4, 1830.

9. *Gazette,* July 2, Aug. 26, 1828; May 27, June 3, 10, 1829.

10. *Ibid.,* Sept. 16, 23, 1829.

felt the need of a newspaper of its own. After the election, plans were made for a second newspaper at Little Rock, but it was not at first identified as friendly to the Crittendenites.

Charles Pierre Bertrand, stepson of Dr. Cunningham, would complete his apprenticeship at the *Gazette* with his 21st birthday on November 23, 1829. Woodruff had no reason to suspect him of duplicity, and when Bertrand issued a prospectus for the *Arkansas Advocate* on November 3, his boss accepted it as a young man's commendable effort to start his own business. Indeed, it was even rumored that the *Advocate* would be nothing more than a branch of the *Gazette,* but Woodruff disclaimed any connection with it, and said Bertrand had not confided in him until he had made his decision.

Regarding local politics the prospectus said, "Disavowing any connection with parties, whose infuriate zeal has, for years, been a reproach to our country, and has retarded her growth, the *Advocate* shall be open to all parties, and devoted to none." This was approximately the position Woodruff had occupied before he had vacated the role of referee to become an active participant, and he undoubtedly believed that Bertrand's personal feelings were similar to his own, but would not be expressed in his paper. In national politics the *Advocate* was to be Republican, as the *Gazette* was, but the *Gazette* had never supported or opposed any national candidate or administration, and Bertrand pledged his paper to the defense and support of Andrew Jackson.

He promised to devote space to articles describing the advantages Arkansas offered to homeseekers, and said he would accept religious communications from any Christian denomination.[11] Woodruff consistently rejected religious discussions on the ground that a newspaper was not the proper place for that kind of dispute.

When Bertrand was released from his apprenticeship, he went to Cincinnati to purchase his materials. He returned in January, and the first issue

11. *Ibid.,* Nov. 10, 1829.

of the *Advocate* appeared on Wednesday, March 31, 1830, printed on a super-royal sheet, the same size as the *Gazette*. Bertrand declared in his salutatory, "With respect to the Editor of the *Gazette,* I hesitate not to say, that the many favors received from him, during an intimate acquaintance of several years, demand my warmest gratitude—and so far as may be consistent with my duties as Editor of an *independent paper,* I will cultivate his friendship. If collisions unhappily arise between us, it must begin with him." [12]

Having gone on record as a Jackson editor, Bertrand hoped he could take the public printing away from Woodruff, whose personal preference for Adams had been well known. But Governor Pope had gone to Kentucky in December and had visited Washington before his return to Little Rock in the spring, and Bertrand surmised that his influence had helped Woodruff keep his appointment as the Arkansas publisher of the United States laws. Secretary Fulton also continued to give Woodruff the territorial public printing that came under his control.

On May 19, 1830, the *Advocate* published a letter signed "Fourche," written by Dr. William P. Reyburn, reportedly with Crittenden's help, inquiring why two such staunch Jacksonians as Pope and Fulton chose to patronize the *Gazette,* which opposed Jackson. Bertrand's reply was that Pope's reason probably was that "money makes the mare go," and that Fulton merely followed Pope's lead. Fulton retaliated by giving the *Gazette* 158 legal advertisements that otherwise would have been divided between the two papers. "Fourche" came back on June 2 to remark that he hoped Bertrand would not passively submit to a situation that gave the spoils of office to an Adams editor at the expense of a loyal Jackson editor.

This moved Woodruff to enter the discussion and define his position on Jackson. In a long editorial on June 8, he admitted he had privately favored Adams' re-election in 1828, and that he had doubted Jackson's ability as a civil officer, but he had patriotically accepted the will of the majority and had found Jackson's administration highly commendable thus far. This belated approval of Jackson was no "political somerset," because he had kept the *Gazette* neutral in national politics since Arkansas Territory could not participate in national elections. He included a few oblique remarks about Jackson men of recent conversion and questionable stability who were trying to siphon off some of the *Gazette's* patronage.

The dispute was instantly bitterly abusive, and Dr. Cunningham, who sometimes wrote editorials for the *Advocate,* dealt and received as many blows as his stepson. Their previous close association with Woodruff had given Bertrand and Cunningham the means of knowing certain details pertaining to the death of John T. Garrett that had not been made public, and they apparently believed that Woodruff had fired the fatal shot. Cunningham and Bertrand evidently thought that the merest hint that they might reveal the secret would silence Woodruff, but they surely must have realized that once it was told, it could never again be used to threaten him.

12. *Ibid.,* Apr. 6, Sept. 1, 1830.

At first they were almost too cautious, and the threat of exposure was so vaguely worded that Woodruff could not be sure which secret was in danger. Beginning on June 16, Bertrand threatened to publish a mysterious "little book" connected with the 1827 unpleasantness, but Woodruff could not recall any such book.

On June 30, Dr. Cunningham ended a scathing reply to Woodruff's latest attack with, "I will ere long give to the public, a history of a certain transaction on the 18th day of January, 1828, with such comments as the occasion will justify." Now his meaning could not be mistaken. The date mentioned was the day after the shooting, the day of Garrett's death, and the first day of the coroner's inquest. The "little book," then, must be the collection of depositions taken at the inquest, copied for Woodruff by Bertrand. Woodruff now discovered that his own deposition was missing, and decided it must be the document Bertrand referred to as "nursed in the dark." He asked Bertrand to send him a copy of the missing deposition, and Bertrand answered that he did not know where it was.

It was not until July 21 that Woodruff recovered his composure enough to drag the supposed skeleton from his closet, having studiously ignored all the threats and innuendo on the subject for six weeks. He called Bertrand's bluff and demanded that he publish the "little book." He probably felt secure in the knowledge that Bertrand did not have the most damaging deposition, but in case he was mistaken, he presented arguments calculated to silence both Bertrand and Cunningham.

By now it was apparent that Bertrand was a Crittenden proselyte and that Crittenden had the means of controlling his press. Woodruff reminded Bertrand that publication of the depositions would bring out the fact that "a certain gentleman" had planned Garrett's attempted assassination of Ashley that had resulted in Garrett's death. Woodruff offered to publish the depositions himself if Bertrand wanted him to, but warned that it would ruin the popularity of the "certain gentleman." Dr. Cunningham was disposed of with the reminder that he was the coroner who held the inquest and gave public and private approval of Woodruff's actions at the time, implying that if he had then protected Woodruff's sinister "secret," he was himself culpable.

Bertrand replied in his next issue with an article headed "To the Public. Little Book—Chapter 1st," but did not take up the subject of Garrett's death. The "little book" never had a second chapter, and Bertrand did not take Woodruff up on his offer to publish the depositions. The weapon he had hoped would be deadly to his enemy had proved to be a two-edged sword.

The missing deposition turned up late in September. After the inquest, Cunningham had given it to the prosecuting attorney, William H. Parrott, who now had a grievance against Crittenden for removing him from office during his last days as acting governor in the spring of 1829. Parrott sent the deposition to Woodruff, who turned it over to the clerk of the Circuit Court, and again dared Bertrand to copy it and proceed with the publication of the "little book." To be certain that Bertrand would not accept the challenge, he

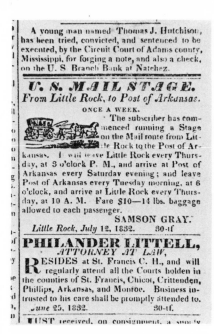

A young man named Thomas J. Hutchison, has been tried, convicted, and sentenced to be executed, by the Circuit Court of Adams county, Mississippi, for forging a note, and also a check, on the U. S Branch Bank at Natchez.

U. S. MAIL STAGE.
From Little Rock, to Post of Arkansas.
ONCE A WEEK.

The subscriber has commenced running a Stage on the Mail route from Little Rock to the Post of Arkansas. I will leave Little Rock every Thursday, at 3 o'clock P. M., and arrive at Post of Arkansas every Saturday evening; and leave Post of Arkansas every Tuesday morning, at 6 o'clock, and arrive at Little Rock every Thursday, at 10 A. M. Fare $10—14 lbs. baggage allowed to each passenger.
SAMSON GRAY.
Little Rock, July 12, 1832.   30-tf.

PHILANDER LITTELL,
ATTORNEY AT LAW,

RESIDES at St. Francis C. H., and will regularly attend all the Courts holden in the counties of St. Francis, Chicot, Crittenden, Phillips, Arkansas, and Monroe. Business intrusted to his care shall be promptly attended to.
June 25, 1832.   30-tf.

JUST received, on consignment, a supply

the necessary Indians to allotted them er, has passed I States by a

reign Affairs natives, have an assistant alary of three m.

e Mechanics' lbany has de/ per cent.— rgest dividend ed States. e first of April six hundred ceived at the

ily paper in ts six hundred country, it is ie for nothing tronage. entatives have luties on Tea, r the 31st of the present

A new novel war has been ntitled "Paul

David E. McKinney, Esq., Clerk of the Superior Court of this Territory.

The Steam-Boat Waverley,
CAPT. PENNYWIT,

Will ply regularly during the ensuing season, between New-Orleans and the several landings on the Arkansas river, and whenever the water will admit, will proceed as far up as Cantonment Gibson and the Western Creek Agency.
She left Little Rock on Monday the 24th ult., for Cantonment Gibson, and is looked for back this evening.
Little Rock, June 1, 1830.   49tf

DRUG STORE.
DOCTORS
WATKINS & FULTON

Have established, in the Town of Little Rock, a DRUG STORE, where they will keep a general assortment of DRUGS and MEDICINES; and also, a supply of the most celebrated PATENT MEDICINES. Their articles are purchased in the City of New-York, which will enable them to sell upon but a very small advance on the New-Orleans prices. They are daily expecting additional supplies. Their Medicines are warranted genuine and fresh. Orders will receive immediate attention.
Little Rock, June 1, 1830.   23tf

NEW GOODS.

again warned that "a cetain gentleman" would be placed in a dilemma from which he could not easily extricate himself with credit.[13]

Simultaneously with this controversy, several others were in progress, some related to it in subject matter and others not. As various writers sought to defend or accuse Pope or Fulton, it was inevitable that comparisons should be made of their performance in office and Robert Crittenden's in the same offices. It was also inevitable that the numerous flashbacks to the 1827 difficulties should again bring Crittenden before the public.

One of Fulton's most articulate defenders and Crittenden's most telling assailants in the *Gazette* used the pseudonym "Jaw-Bone," and probably was Chester Ashley. It was he who first charged that Crittenden had underwritten the *Advocate,* and consequently had control of it. Bertrand denied that Crittenden had any connection with his paper, and proclaimed himself the sole owner. "Jaw-Bone" agreed that the press and materials probably had been purchased in Bertrand's name, but with Crittenden's money or his endorsement as guarantor for the debt. This was neither denied nor confirmed, and appears to be true.[14]

The illustrious Sam Houston, after a brief, ill-fated marriage, turned his back on a distinguished political career in Tennessee and sought oblivion

13. *Ibid.,* Sept. 22, 1830.
14. *Ibid.,* July 21, Sept. 1, 1830.

among the Cherokee friends of his childhood, now living west of Arkansas. A year later he aroused from his besotted lethargy to speak out against the poor treatment the Indians received, in a series of letters to the *Gazette,* signed "Tah-lohn-tus-ky" and "Standing Bear."

The first, published June 22, 1830, was prefaced by this note addressed to the editor: "If at any time the name should be called for, in *person,* by any individual who may feel aggrieved, and say, in writing, that his object is honorable or personal satisfaction, you are requested to give him my name; but not to gratify curiosity, or in answer to any written communication from a distance."

Houston's letters revived an old controversy on the subject of Indians and their agents, but Woodruff was too preoccupied with his own political quarrels to become personally involved in this one. Evidently he forgot he had published Houston's instructions about revealing his identity, for on September 22 he took Bertrand to task for printing almost identical instructions given by a correspondent of the *Advocate* who wrote against Woodruff. This writer had informed Bertrand: "The only condition on which my name must be surrendered is, that the person entitled to it, will leave a note in writing, that it is for PERSONAL SATISFACTION—when that is done, give my name freely."

With verbose indignation, Woodruff pronounced it a blood-thirsty, barefaced attempt to involve him in a duel, and a violation of journalistic ethics by Bertrand. Once again, he went on record as completely scornful of the practice of duelling.

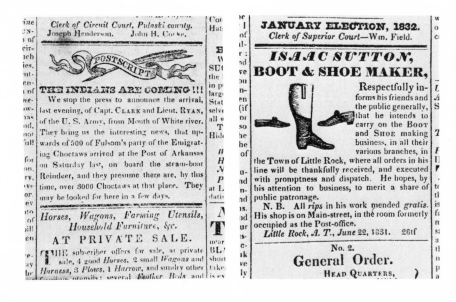

Bertrand replied that Woodruff himself had refused to divulge a writer's name unless the person calling for it pledged in writing that he sought personal satisfaction. Woodruff retorted that this was a base and malicious falsehood, and demanded that the *Advocate's* editors either substantiate the charge or admit they had lied. He recalled that Bertrand had given that answer recently to one who called for a writer's name, and denounced him for this evidence that the object of some of his anonymous correspondents was to promote duels. "This charge I consider of a very serious nature," he said. "It is one which deeply implicates Mr. Bertrand's character, both as an Editor and as a member of society." [15] Strangely enough, Bertrand did not go back three months in his file of the *Gazette* to taunt Woodruff with his own similar sin.

Governor Pope brought his nephew, William Fontaine Pope, from Kentucky in the summer of 1830, and made him his aid-de-camp with the rank of major.[16] Fontaine was hot-blooded, impetuous, and thoroughly saturated with the image of the Southern gentleman as defined by the Code of Honor governing duelling. Being young and able bodied, he considered himself the natural defender of his uncle's honor, for the governor was 60 years old and had lost his right arm as a boy. The governor tried desperately to dissuade Fontaine from taking on his quarrels, but Fontaine plunged headlong into disaster.

Dr. John H. Cocke, a kinsman of the governor's only daughter's husband, was the host at a dinner on July 5. Sevier presided over part of the festivities, and was obliged to read some toasts that were unflattering to Governor Pope, but had no hand in composing them. It was easy to make it appear that he had been a willing participant, despite his protests that circumstances beyond his control had placed him in this uncomfortable position.

Fontaine Pope, writing in the Gazette under the pseudonym "Justice," charged that Cocke and James B. Keatts had arranged the party to promote the rumored rift between Sevier and the governor, and accused Cocke of being two-faced in his relationship with the governor. Cocke obtained the writer's name from Woodruff, and challenged young Pope to a duel. They met on the east side of the Mississippi River opposite the mouth of White River on October 23, and exchanged three shots without injury to either. The *Gazette* reported the duel without mentioning their names.[17] The friendship between Cocke and the Popes was resumed after the duel.

Realizing that his nephew's high temper would lead him into new dangers, the governor decided to take him back to Louisville the next spring, and in the meantime tried to keep him busy outside Little Rock as much as possible.

Charles Fenton Mercer Noland had spent the last few years in the home of James Woodson Bates at Batesville. He had assumed all of Bates' preju-

15. *Ibid.,* Oct. 20, 1830.
16. *Ibid.,* Sept. 1, 1830.
17. *Ibid.,* July 7, 14, 28, Aug. 11, Oct. 27, 1830; Mar. 14, 1832 (Supplement); Pope, *Early Days in Arkansas,* 114–115.

dices against Crittenden, and consequently had been a supporter of Sevier, although he was not quite old enough to vote. But Bates had reconciled his differences with Crittenden, and was living at Crittenden's home while the Superior Court was in session, Bates now being a judge of that court. Noland was also at Little Rock about that time, and his loyalty to Sevier was beginning to falter.

On December 15, the *Advocate* published a letter from Noland signed "Devereaux," accusing Governor Pope of "retailing liquor" to satisfy his greed for money. The governor tried to head off trouble by making his nephew promise to ignore the letter, and obtaining Woodruff's promise that he would not fan the flame of Fontaine's resentment by mentioning the letter in the *Gazette*.

When Fontaine next visited Little Rock, he heard that Noland was "Devereaux" and that he was more interested in making Fontaine challenge him than in insulting the governor. Fontaine resisted the impulse to challenge, but was stung by the knowledge that his failure to respond might be taken as cowardice. He met Noland at a Christmas party and spent the evening in apparent friendship with him. Later he regretted his pleasant conduct, which he thought might be interpreted as an unmanly effort to avoid a fight, and he tried to offset that impression by writing an article attacking Noland.

The governor persuaded him to drop the matter, and Fontaine threw his manuscript in the fire, but wrote another soon afterwards and took it to Woodruff without his uncle's knowledge. When questioned, he told the governor about it, and the governor took the problem to Woodruff, who assured him that he was not willing to print the letter in the *Gazette*. However, a day or two later he published it as a handbill, or *Gazette* "extra" to be circulated with the paper, Fontaine having paid the usual advertising or job printing rates.

The fat was in the fire beyond recall, and after a few more exchanges, Noland challenged young Pope. Attempts at mediation failed, and the duel was fought on February 5, 1831 on the Texas side of Red River in Miller County. Fontaine Pope was wounded and was taken to Washington in Hempstead County. Later he was brought to Little Rock, but the governor went to Kentucky in April, and was not on hand to attend his nephew when death came on June 17.[18]

The campaign of 1831 found Benjamin Desha opposing Sevier in the race for Congress, with the Crittenden faction solidly behind Desha and the other faction still supporting Sevier. The matter of placing blame for the various duels had been discussed at length previously, and was injected into this campaign, but the death of Fontaine Pope a few weeks before the election brought the newspaper discussions of duelling to an abrupt halt. In fact, all

18. *Gazette,* Jan. 5 (Supplement), 12, Feb. 16, June 8, 22, 1831; Mar. 14, 1832 (Supplement); Feb. 2, 1873; Pope, *Early Days in Arkansas,* 119; C. F. M. Noland to William Noland, Apr. 2, 1831, Ms. in Berkeley-Noland Papers, University of Virginia, photostats in *Arkansas Gazette* Foundation Library.

the political discussions were noticeably more subdued in tone after his death.

The campaign had barely opened when it became apparent that Crittenden and his friends were trying to elect men to the General Assembly who would oppose Woodruff. Woodruff correctly surmised that the Crittendenites hoped to bolster the sagging fortunes of the *Advocate* by securing for Bertrand the appointment as public printer to the territory.[19]

During the campaign and later, Woodruff advocated giving the public printing to the lowest bidder, knowing he could afford to underbid Bertrand, even if it meant entering into an unprofitable contract. Sevier defeated Desha by a vote of 2,538 to 2,085, but Crittenden's friends won a majority in the legislature.[20]

Governor Pope returned to Little Rock on October 2, and the legislature convened the next day. The legislature voted to take bids on the public printing, but did not bind itself to give the work to the lowest bidder. Before the appointed committee could begin to function, both houses contracted separately for the printing of the governor's message, and the Legislative Council for its rules. In the Council it was a simple election, and Bertrand won by a vote of 13 to Woodruff's 9. The House voted to give the job to the lowest bidder, and Woodruff was the successful bidder.

The joint committee called on the two printers for sealed bids for the public printing, and Woodruff submitted his bid promptly. Bertrand was ill and was unable to draw up his proposals in time, and Woodruff obligingly requested that "every reasonable indulgence" should be given his rival. It was rumored that Crittenden was lobbying for Bertrand, and that he told some of the legislators they would make a mistake to let any printer set his own price, but should elect one and decide how much they would pay him. Soon the gossip was that Bertrand would not submit a bid, but would agree to match Woodruff's offer if he found he could afford to do the work at Woodruff's price.

Woodruff's bid was opened on October 10, and reported to both houses the next day. It was shown to Bertrand, who wrote a letter offering to "execute the Public Printing for the same that Mr. Woodruff has proffered to do it for." Certainly this was an unconventional bid, but on October 12, Bertrand was elected public printer by a vote of 27 to 19.

Woodruff immediately removed the words "Printer to the Territory" from the *Gazette's* front page dateline, leaving "Publisher of the Laws of the United States, by Authority" as his only advertised claim on the public treasury.

It was a severe blow to his pride, and he did not accept it with good grace. He felt he had not been fairly defeated, and the fact that Crittenden had at last triumphed over him had a sting he could not easily overcome. He told his side of the story in his next issue, and continued to belabor the subject in subsequent issues.

19. *Gazette,* July 20, 1831.
20. *Ibid.,* Sept. 7, 1831.

He thought his support of Sevier entitled him to the votes of legislators whose constituents had voted for Sevier, yet eleven of those had voted for Bertrand. Woodruff published their names, and accused them of voting contrary to the wishes of the people they represented. He said Crittenden had bought this and other favors from the legislature with gifts of "canvass hams." [21]

Congress had granted ten sections of public lands to Arkansas Territory to finance the construction of a capitol building, and this legislature was expected to decide how to dispose of the land to the best advantage. If sold at the minimum price of public lands, the grant would bring only $8,000. William McK. Ball offered $10,000 on 18 months credit, Chester Ashley offered to swap his mansion on Markham Street, and Robert Crittenden offered to trade his home on what is now East Seventh Street, appraised extravagantly at $10,600, and promised besides to locate the ten sections on unimproved lands. On October 11, the House accepted Crittenden's offer by a vote of 15 to 9, and on the 14th the Council accepted it 14 to 7. Crittenden was jubilant, because the ten sections would allow him to free himself from ruinous debts.

The next issue of the *Gazette,* on October 19, announced both of Crittenden's victories of the preceding week, and complained bitterly on both scores. The governor's veto, said Woodruff, was the only hope of saving the territory from the ten-section blunder. And Pope did veto the bill on October 21. Now it was Crittenden's turn to splutter. Only one vote kept the Legislative Council from overriding the veto, and the legislature adjourned on November 7 without settling the disposition of the grant.

The Crittendenites in the legislature were infuriated by Woodruff's remarks on October 19, charging them with selling out for a few "canvass hams," and they met informally to discuss possible methods of retaliation. According to Woodruff, they decided against barring him from copying the journals for his paper only because they feared their constituents would hold it strongly against them. It was finally decided that those who were *Gazette* subscribers would cancel their subscriptions, and that all would use their influence at home to reduce the paper's circulation. The plan failed, probably because the legislators wanted to know what the *Gazette* said about them, even though it made them angry. Only three canceled their subscriptions at the time, and three others followed suit at the end of the session.[22]

In the House on October 21, Dr. Nimrod Menefee read a speech in which Woodruff was referred to in what the editor called "abusive and scurrillous language." In the next issue of the *Gazette,* Woodruff noticed the speech in an article captioned "Mean and Contemptible." He described Menefee as "an obscure individual by the name of Menefee, who possesses more imprudence than sense, and who claims the honor of representing the counties of Conway and Hot Spring," and said his speech was "better suited to the meridian of a brothel, than the grave deliberations of a Legislative body."

21. *Ibid.,* Oct. 12, 19, 1831.
22. *Ibid.,* Oct. 26, Nov. 16, 1831.

This article was published on Wednesday, October 26. On Saturday, while Woodruff was copying the House Journal at the clerk's table, the House took a 30-minute recess and Woodruff was left alone in the room except for the doorkeeper, Maj. Ezra M. Owen. Soon Menefee entered, carrying a heavy cane. After glancing around the room, he moved towards the clerk's table in what Woodruff conceived to be "a threatening manner." When Menefee was five or six feet from the table, Woodruff stood up and told him to keep away.

As Woodruff told the story, "He hesitated a moment, and at the same time raised his cane in a threatening attitude. We then drew a pistol, cocked it, and, carelessly suspending it by our side, waited to see what farther movement he would make.—At this instant he thrust his left hand into his bosom, and seized his dirk. Seeing this movement, and believing his object to be our assassination, we attempted to raise the pistol, and, in doing so, bore too hard on the trigger, and discharged it in the floor. Simultaneously with the discharge of the pistol, we received a blow on the head from his stick, which produced a slight contusion. A clench then ensued, but before either party had received any farther injury, several of the Members interfered and parted us. And thus the affair ended."

Woodruff represented his situation as fraught with danger, and indicated that it was not the leaders of the opposing party that he expected to try to harm him, but their "malapert subalterns" and hired assassins. "They may maim or assassinate us, but they cannot make us swerve from our duty," he declared melodramatically. "That path is plain, and though beset with difficulties and dangers, it shall be steadily and fearlessly pursued." [23]

Absalom Fowler, secretary of the Legislative Council, had exchanged insults with Woodruff several times during the campaign and later. During the entire session, he made it difficult for Woodruff to copy the Council Journal for publication, and on the day after the altercation with Menefee, he served notice that thereafter Woodruff could have access to the journal only in Fowler's law office. His predecessors had allowed Woodruff to take the journals to the *Gazette* office and copy them at his leisure, and Woodruff declined to do the work in Fowler's dark little cabin office, where he could be constantly interrupted and insulted. Fowler was slow to deposit the journal in the territorial secretary's office after adjournment, and Woodruff thought the reason was to prevent his having easy access to it, so the *Gazette* never published the last few days of the Council's journal. [24]

Woodruff had the last laugh in the matter of the public printing. Bertrand had captured the contract at a time when his paper supply was almost exhausted, and he did not have enough for the *Advocate,* much less the acts and journals. He had the temerity to ask Woodruff to sell him paper, and Woodruff refused, knowing he could have no better way to show the people that Bertrand should not have been elected public printer in the first place.

23. *Ibid.,* Nov. 2, 1831.
24. *Ibid.,* Nov. 9, 1831.

Bertrand sent a courier to Memphis, but evidently the newspaper offices there could spare him no paper. Late in October, he started issuing the *Advocate* on half-sheets, suspended for two weeks in the middle of November, and resumed with colored job paper on November 30. It was not until a few days before Christmas that he received a new supply of paper.

Meanwhile, Woodruff took full advantage of the situation by crowing over his rival's misfortune. By permission of the governor and secretary, he began publication of the acts of the legislature in the *Gazette* on November 30. He could no longer label them "By Authority," but printed them under the caption "Pro Bono Publico"—for the public good—and reminded his readers that he received no pay for this public service. Four issues later he printed the last installment, just as Bertrand received his paper and was ready to begin work on them.

Little Rock's municipal government had been conducted since 1828 by a board of trustees, headed by a chairman or president. Woodruff had been a trustee in 1830 and 1831, and had published the town ordinances from the beginning, free of charge at first. The town was incorporated by the 1831 legislature, and Dr. Cunningham was elected its first mayor on January 2, 1832. Woodruff was no longer a member of the governing body, now called the Town Council, and the town's printing was given to Bertrand. On February 1, Woodruff began publishing the Proceedings and Ordinances of the Mayor and Town Council of Little Rock, as a free public service, although Bertrand was paid to do it. He said it was customary in other towns to have the ordinances made known to the people through the local newspaper having the largest circulation, and that many people would never see "the dirty sheet" the Council had selected as its organ.

After Dr. John T. Fulton's resignation as postmaster at Little Rock, Woodruff served as acting postmaster for about four months. The move of the post office to the *Gazette's* counting room was announced on October 19, 1831. In January of 1832, the *Advocate* voiced strenuous disapproval of the manner in which Woodruff handled the office. Bertrand said Woodruff withheld some of the *Advocate's* letters and exchange newspapers, and supported the statement by pointing out that the *Gazette's* Washington news was usually in print a week earlier than the *Advocate's*. Woodruff advised his competitor to extend his exchange list to get the same results, and to improve his paper to make other editors willing to exchange. The *Gazette* exchanged with almost 100 newspapers, and rarely received its earliest Washington news from papers published at Washington. Woodruff estimated the *Advocate's* exchange list at perhaps 12, perhaps 20, or perhaps 25.

At the same time the municipal election was held, Governor Pope's nephew, Maj. William Field, was re-elected clerk of the Superior Court, defeating Henry L. Biscoe, Crittenden's candidate. The *Advocate* said Sevier had connived with Woodruff in franking campaign handbills for Field. Woodruff denied having any knowledge of such a favor to Field. Sevier, however, admitted having franked some circulars because he did not have

time to write personal letters on the subject, but said it was not a fraud against the post office.[25]

On February 15, 1832, the *Gazette* announced Field's appointment as postmaster to replace Fulton, and the plans to move the post office in a day or two from the *Gazette* office to its previous location on the opposite corner. Woodruff often helped Field open the large mails, which brought harsh criticism to the new postmaster.

The parting shot of the 1831 legislature at Pope and Fulton was a memorial to Congress requesting a change in the territory's organic law to allow the people to elect their governor and secretary. Pope did not sign the memorial, but Sevier dutifully and reluctantly presented it to Congress. In spite of it, the president nominated Pope for another term as governor, and the Senate confirmed the appointment on March 23.[26]

25. *Ibid.,* Feb. 1, 22, 1832.
26. *Ibid.,* Feb. 15, Apr. 18, 25, 1832. Richard C. S. Brown, a relative of the Conways and Sevier, a member of the House, and chairman of the committee on enrollments, delivered the memorial to the governor although he knew the House did not intend to

For months, the columns of both papers teemed with the unhappy controversies of the past—the ten section bill, the letters of "A Voter of Pulaski County" against Crittenden, Crittenden's efforts to establish a press friendly to him, his libel suit against Woodruff, the politically inspired duels, the death of John T. Garrett, and many others. Again Crittenden was accused of having had a hand in every duel fought in Arkansas, and he in turn blamed them all on the *Gazette,* saying, "All the blood that has flowed in Arkansas, from political altercations, has been heated in that political furnace."[27] There was a great deal of truth on both sides of this argument. Several others were also blamed for some of the duels, and these charges too were not without merit.

To Woodruff's accusation that its columns were controlled by Crittenden, the *Advocate's* ready answer was that Ashley, Pope, and Fulton controlled the *Gazette.* Of course, Woodruff claimed complete independence, although it was obvious that he was greatly influenced by all three and slanted his paper favorably to them.

Bertrand's election as public printer came up for review on several occasions, particularly in the summer of 1832. Bertrand and his friends contended that the public printer was supposed to do all printing jobs paid for by the territory, while Woodruff and his friends took the position that the legislature could contract only for its own printing, of which the acts and journals were the major part.

Governor Pope left early in May for a visit to Kentucky, and in July Acting Governor Fulton gave Woodruff a proclamation for publication in the *Gazette.* The *Advocate* served notice it would copy all the executive's printing jobs found in the *Gazette,* claiming them as part of the public printing. Woodruff replied that the executive was free to select his own printer for jobs emanating from his office, and that the *Advocate* would not be paid for those copied from the *Gazette.* County officials were similarly free to send their advertisements and other printing jobs to the printer of their choice, and Woodruff got several of these. When Fulton continued to give business to Woodruff, the *Advocate* fulfilled its threat to copy the material, and reprinted these items along with editorials heaping abuse on Fulton and Woodruff.[28] Woodruff answered with perhaps the most venomous editorials of his career.

Pope returned to his post on October 18, 1832, bringing with him another nephew with the same name as the one who had been killed, William F. Pope, who would serve as his private secretary.

submit it for Pope's signature but had appointed a committee to deliver it to Delegate Sevier. Andrew Scott, chairman of the special committee to deliver it to Sevier, attempted to have Brown expelled from the House for this. See *Journals of the Seventh Session of the General Assembly of the Territory of Arkansas, which was begun and held at the town of Little Rock, on Monday, the third day of November, one thousand eight hundred and thirty-one* (Little Rock: Printed by Charles P. Bertrand, Printer to the Territory, 1832), 284–286, 305–307, 313, 316–317, 318.

27. *Gazette,* May 9, 1832.

28. *Ibid.,* Aug. 1, 15, Sept. 12, 1832.

In October, the *Advocate* asserted that Ashley, Fulton, and Sevier controlled the *Gazette,* and even edited the paper. The exchange between Woodruff and Bertrand became dangerously personal. Bertrand left town about the middle of December on a trip to Texas, leaving his stepfather in charge of the *Advocate.*

The sincerity of almost everybody's Jacksonism was challenged by one side or the other. "Jaw-Bone" said that Crittenden and Bertrand had agreed that the *Advocate* would give mild, nominal support to Jackson until the expiration of his term of office, and then would hoist the banner of Henry Clay. Meanwhile, it would give Sevier the same kind of pseudo-support.

Woodruff and some of his correspondents had frequently stated that Bertrand's debt at Cincinnati for his press and materials remained unpaid, and had surmised that Crittenden was anxious to be relieved of his liability as guarantor. On October 3, 1832, Woodruff reported a rumor that Crittenden was dissatisfied with the course of the *Advocate,* and was about to get rid of its editors.

Many other things claimed his attention in the fall of 1832. Migrating Indians brought a cholera epidemic, and early in November the Town Council created a Board of Health to prevent the spread of the disease. Woodruff served on the board with a minister and four doctors, and took care of many of the details of establishing a temporary isolation hospital and other business in connection with the control of the epidemic.

The celebrated Washington Irving spent the night at Little Rock on November 13, on his way to New York after a tour of the Indian country. He was a guest in Woodruff's home, but the *Gazette* did not identify his host.[29]

Fulton was then negotiating with the Bank of Maryland to establish an agency at Little Rock, to deal principally in bills of exchange. He brought his father, David Fulton, to Little Rock to take charge of the agency, and on November 19 and 20, made arrangements for Woodruff and John McLain to act as assistant agents.[30]

In December, Woodruff announced that he had been appointed agent for the *Encyclopaedia Americana.* This was only one of the many assorted items still offered for sale in the *Gazette's* counting room. There was a noticeable increase in horticultural items, including garden seeds, grape vines, and fruit trees. This reflects Woodruff's own interests, for he had extended his garden space and could get his plants cheaper by ordering in quantity.

In 1831, he purchased from Ashley for $300 the lot adjoining the three lots on which his office and home stood, thus extending the grounds eastward. The building stood on the corner, flush with both streets, and the lots

---

29. *Ibid.,* Nov. 14, 21, 1832; Margaret Smith Ross (ed.), *Letters of Hiram Abiff Whittington 1827–1834* (Little Rock: Pulaski County Historical Society, 1956), 31; Robert L. Morris, "Three Arkansas Travelers," *Arkansas Historical Quarterly,* IV (1945), 224.

30. Evan Poultney, *An Appeal to the Creditors of the Bank of Maryland, and the Public Generally* (Baltimore: Printed by John D. Toy, 1835), 20–22.

to the east were used as flower and vegetable gardens and the stable and horse lot, with double gates opening on the Markham Street sidewalk.

The purchase of the fourth lot (lot 10) was a "handshake deal," and the running accounts between the two men were not settled in Ashley's lifetime, including payment for this lot. When Woodruff and Mrs. Ashley settled their accounts on September 25, 1849, he paid $840 for this lot, representing the purchase price and 18 years of accumulated interest. He neglected even then to get a deed, and it remained for the administrator of Mrs. Ashley's estate to get authority from the Pulaski Probate Court to make the deed in July, 1869. Thus for 38 years after the purchase, Woodruff had no written title to the lot.[31]

During the years 1828 through 1832, the *Gazette's* publication day see-sawed back and forth between Tuesday and Wednesday, mostly because of the mail schedules. The mails remained generally unreliable, but service was much better than ever before. On December 30, 1829, Woodruff recalled that he had printed the first president's message after he started the *Gazette* 78 days after its delivery in Congress, while the most recent one had been received in 14 days. He commented that improvements in the postal service had brought Arkansas 64 days nearer the seat of the general government in the past ten years.

The introduction of competition in 1830 proved to be a financial advantage. It was Woodruff's best year so far as an editor, bringing him a subscription increase of more than 20 per cent, and almost as great an increase in advertising and job printing.[32] He always kept his current circulation figures a deep secret, but in later years he said that the *Gazette* had only 500 subscribers in 1829, before competition stimulated his business.[33]

There was little change in the *Gazette's* standing features during these years. Weather observations were not published regularly, but on December 22, 1830, a table kept by Dr. S. Slaughter at Washington, Hempstead County, from June 1 through October 31, 1830 was published. The poetry column, which had been headed "The Recess" since January 21, 1822, became "The Olio" on January 19, 1830, with an ornate woodcut. The heading probably was intended to cover all the reprinted miscellany on page four, although placed directly over the poetry.

An unknown correspondent at Cantonment Gibson who signed himself "X" contributed original fiction, blank verse, essays, and other literary works during the last half of 1830. Woodruff was so pleased with his work that he asked him to send his real name, in order that he might receive a free subscription to the paper.

31. Petition of Thomas R. Welch, administrator *de bonis non* of the estate of Chester Ashley, filed July 7, 1869, in Chester Ashley Estate Papers, Box A-1, Pulaski Probate Files.
32. *Gazette,* Dec. 22, 1830.
33. *Ibid.,* Dec. 12, 1838; Mar. 18, 1853.

6

LAST DAYS OF THE TERRITORY

1833-1836 WITH THE DEMANDS on the *Gazette's* columns steadily increasing, Woodruff had to cram more material into each issue without increasing the size of the sheet. He found a temporary solution in increased use of the smallest body type available, approximately 5½ points by modern measurement. Purchased from the New York type foundry of White, Hager & Company, at a cost of $700 or $800, this machine-cast type admitted approximately 25 per cent more reading matter to the old super-royal sheet.[1] The old type, ordered from O. & H. Wells of Cincinnati in the spring of 1829, included a limited amount of type of the same size, and probably was traded in on the new type at the rate of nine cents a pound.[2]

The *Gazette* appeared in its new dress on March 13, 1833. Like other newspapers of the period, the *Gazette* had never limited itself to a single body type size, and there was enough variety in the new type to allow more leeway than ever before. For instance, the old practice of achieving emphasis by the use of italics or small caps was now supplemented by the use of bolder or slightly larger type.

Hiram Whittington, the *Gazette's* capable foreman, never worked with the new type. Because his doctors advised him that the printing business did not agree with his health, he had left the *Gazette* in the fall of 1832, and moved to Hot Springs early in 1833.[3] George W. Spooner of Brooklyn,

---

1. *Gazette,* Nov. 21, Dec. 26, 1832; Mar. 13, 1833.
2. *Ibid.,* Apr. 29, 1829. In most cases, the companies from which the *Gazette* bought materials and equipment can be identified only by their ads in the *Gazette,* for which they would pay only in merchandise.
3. *Ibid.,* Jan. 21, 1834; Margaret Smith Ross (ed.), *Letters of Hiram Abiff Whittington 1827–1834* (Little Rock: Pulaski County Historical Society, 1956), 30–34. Although Woodruff had long been interested in the phenomenon of the hot water and the geological curiosities abounding at nearby Hot Springs, he never went there until he visited Whittington in the early summer of 1835. See *Gazette,* Apr. 28, Aug. 11, 1835.

probably a relative of Woodruff's first boss, Alden Spooner, may have been Whittington's successor as foreman. When he returned to Brooklyn late in 1833 or early in 1834,[4] another printer trained in the *Long-Island Star* office, Edward Cole, became foreman.[5] James O'Dowd also worked in the *Gazette's* mechanical department about this time for more than a year.[6]

The new type arrived just in time to ease the strain on the *Gazette's* columns occasioned by the 1833 political campaign, which opened early in March. Ambrose Sevier was opposed in the race for Congress by Robert Crittenden. As usual, the platforms and qualifications of the candidates were obscured by mud-slinging reviews of their personal and political sins and those of their associates. Nobody was more maligned than Governor Pope, who was in Kentucky during most of the campaign and for several weeks after it ended.

Because Sevier had obtained the act of Congress that authorized Pope to manage the ten-section grant for the state house and a thousand-acre grant for a court house and jail for Pulaski County, the manner in which Pope had discharged this duty became the biggest issue of the campaign. A related issue was the progress of the construction of the state house. Another hotly disputed subject was the attempted impeachment of Sevier's father-in-law, Judge Benjamin Johnson of the Superior Court, begun in 1832 by William Cummins and foiled by Sevier in Congress in January of 1833. Crittenden was blamed for this attempt, as well as a similar effort by Cummins against Johnson four years earlier. Once again, the political duels of the past were reviewed and responsibility for them fixed, according to the varying bias of the writers.[7]

In May, Woodruff began reprinting the *Gazette's* political articles in handbills for free distribution among non-subscribers outside the Little Rock area. Because these were not circulated at Little Rock, the *Advocate* sneered at them as "secret handbills," but Woodruff explained that everything in them had been read at Little Rock in the *Gazette* of the same week. When Bertrand did the same thing in July, Woodruff hurled the charge of "secret handbills" back at him, but with greater effect, since Bertrand's handbills included material not previously published in the *Advocate*.[8]

The election was held on August 5, and when the official returns were announced more than six weeks later, Sevier had 4,476 votes to Crittenden's

4. *Gazette,* June 2, 1835 notes the marriage at Brooklyn on Apr. 24 of George W. Spooner, "recently of this town," to Miss Charlotte Bedell. William F. Pope, *Early Days in Arkansas* (Little Rock: Frederick W. Allsopp, 1895), 125, erroneously states that Spooner was Edward Cole's partner in the publication of the *Gazette* in 1838, and also says he was later associated with the Hartford (Conn.) *Courant.*

5. *Gazette,* Dec. 12, 1838; May 11, 1855.

6. *Ibid.,* July 5, 1836.

7. For a full discussion of this campaign, see Lonnie J. White, *Politics on the Southwestern Frontier: Arkansas Territory, 1819–1836* (Memphis, Tenn.: Memphis State University Press, 1964), 141–158.

8. *Gazette,* May 29, July 31, 1833.

2,520.[9] Thus the only test before the people of the relative popularity of the nominal leaders of the two political factions showed Sevier almost a two to one favorite.

The viciousness of the political feud that had filled the *Gazette* and the *Advocate* to the exclusion of almost everything else was good for circulation. The *Gazette* received an average of five new subscribers a week during the five months of the campaign, and only one subscription was canceled in protest. This subscriber was a northern Arkansas man who said any decent or moral man would be disgraced by having his name on the subscription list of either paper. Woodruff received his letter two weeks after the election, and apologetically replied that it had been his sacred duty to defend the noble Sevier and save the territory from Crittenden, and pledged that he would allow the political disputes to rest, now that the campaign was over.[10]

True to his promise, he did not permit the post-election reprisals to dominate the *Gazette's* columns, even when the cause of action had originated there. Sevier's address to Congress in behalf of Judge Johnson had been published as a circular, and had appeared in the *Gazette* on July 31, five days before the election. Sevier had concerned himself more with challenging the credibility of the witnesses against Johnson than with refuting their charges, and he had convinced his audience that these men were not worthy of confidence. William Cummins had been dealt with more severely than the others. Four days after the election, Cummins sent Sevier a note, serving notice that within a month he would challenge him to a duel. His explanation for the delay was that he would not be free to risk his life until he had discharged "numerous professional engagements, involving duties to others." Sevier ignored the note and Cummins sent another on September 7, demanding an interview. Sevier borrowed his challenger's language to decline, saying he would consider the duel only after he had discharged his own "numerous professional engagements, involving duties to others," meaning at the end of his term of office or perhaps even the more distant end of his political career.[11]

Crittenden had shown his regret for having killed Conway by vainly trying to stop the duel between Fontaine Pope and C. F. M. Noland in 1831,[12] and another in 1832 between two strangers from Mississippi, Henry S. Foote and S. S. Prentiss,[13] yet once more he considered his honor so violated that he issued a challenge. The offender was Judge Thomas P. Eskridge, whose contributions to the *Gazette* of July 13 and 24 had been written after Crittenden and his friends had given a great deal of provocation. But duelling was against Eskridge's religion, and he declined the challenge.[14]

9. *Ibid.,* Sept. 18, 1833.
10. *Ibid.,* Aug. 21, 1833.
11. *Ibid.,* Sept. 18, 1833.
12. *Ibid.,* Mar. 14, 1832 (Supplement); Feb. 2, 1873.
13. Henry S. Foote, *The Bench and Bar of the South and Southwest* (St. Louis: Soule, Thomas, & Wentworth, 1876), 184–185.
14. White, *Politics on the Southwestern Frontier,* 157–158.

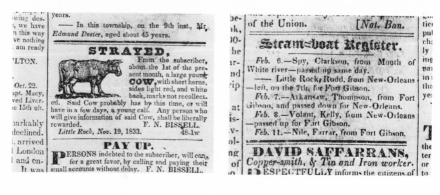

The 1833 legislature took bids for the public printing, but did not bind itself to give the job to the lowest bidder. Because of variations in the forms of the two bids and the difference in the value of scrip and specie, there was room for argument as to which bid was lower. On October 14, Woodruff was elected public printer over Bertrand, 26 to 23. For the first time, the public printer was required to enter into a $2,500 bond to guarantee completion of the work within a reasonable time.[15] "Printer to the Territory" returned to the statement of proprietorship on the *Gazette's* front page dateline on October 23.

Crittenden had met Albert Pike, a poor but brilliant newcomer from Massachusetts, when he visited Pope County during the campaign, and had made arrangements for him to be the *Advocate's* junior editor. The legislature was in session when Pike came to Little Rock, and he served a few days as assistant secretary to the Legislative Council. He began his work at the *Advocate* with an attack upon Woodruff for the manner in which he had regained his position as public printer.[16] Woodruff did not dignify the upstart novice by mentioning his name, but on November 6 awarded him the laurels as the most scurrilous and abusive of all the *Advocate's* writers against him, an honor not easily won. Thereafter he placidly ignored most of Pike's remarks about the prices he charged for the public printing, even when Pike compared the *Gazette's* prices with what was represented as fair prices in parallel columns.

Governor Pope also was under fire for allowing Woodruff to charge exorbitant prices for printing jobs let by the governor. Pope felt that he was the scapegoat who bore the brunt of the criticism while Woodruff reaped all the benefits, and he demanded that Woodruff not only defend him but lower

15. *Gazette,* Oct. 16, 23, 30, Nov. 6, 1833.
16. Robert Lipscomb Duncan, *Reluctant General. The Life and Times of Albert Pike* (New York: E. P. Dutton & Co., Inc., 1961), 64–70; Albert Pike in John Hallum, *Biographical and Pictorial History of Arkansas* (Albany: Weed, Parsons and Company, Printers, 1887), 65.

his prices. Woodruff's refusal began a serious breach between him and the governor.[17] According to Woodruff, Pope's vanity had always made him a difficult friend. He had always expected Woodruff to give him earnest defense against every minor criticism and to keep his name constantly and favorably before the public, to the point of monopolizing the *Gazette's* columns.[18]

Future statehood had been in the back of every politician's mind from the beginning of the territorial government. While Arkansas remained a territory, the federal government would bear the expense of her government and internal improvements, which the small population could not support adequately without oppressive taxation. But residents of a territory could not vote in presidential elections, their one delegate to Congress could cast no vote there, and many people thought the federal government gave funds for internal improvements less generously to Arkansas than to the other territories. Opportunists hoping to derive political or economic advantages from state government agitated the question of statehood often, advocating statehood at that nebulous time when the territory's population and resources should justify it, with the implication that the time was almost at hand. More practical people said substantially the same thing, but implied that the happy day was not immediately forthcoming, and tried to postpone public discussions of statehood to avoid thrusting it upon Arkansas prematurely. It was a subject to be handled delicately, for opposition to immediate statehood could be interpreted as a lack of faith in Arkansas's potentialities.

In the fall of 1830, the *Advocate* took a stand in favor of statehood as soon as the population should reach the required 40,000, but Woodruff pointed.out that this was not yet the case, and that the next Congress probably would raise the required number.[19] Sevier also opposed immediate statehood, and said he would not attempt to gain the admission of Arkansas to the union until he was so instructed by his constituents or the legislature. Woodruff was as much surprised as everybody else when Sevier introduced a resolution in the House on December 17, 1833 calling for committee consideration of authorization of a constitutional convention as the first step towards statehood for Arkansas.

Sevier had to admit that Arkansas was not fully prepared to shoulder the heavy burden of state government. The sheriff's census taken early in 1833 showed her population to be 40,026, not counting one county that had sent no returns, but new settlers were constantly arriving, and statehood would give new impetus to emigration, with a proportionate increase in taxable property. Further hope lay in the possibility that federal grants could finance the more important internal improvements, and that the federal government would give the salines to the state and make a generous turnback arrangement on the sales of public lands.

17. Pope, *Early Days in Arkansas,* 123.
18. *Gazette,* Mar. 17, 1835.
19. *Ibid.,* Oct. 13, 1830.

With Arkansas's ability to support herself contingent on these things yet to be attained and far from assured, and with Sevier's main supporters and advisers at home having no knowledge in advance of his action, it did not take a clairvoyant to guess that something had happened in Washington to cause his sudden about-face. His explanation was that this might be Arkansas's last chance for admission as a slave state for many years. Michigan Territory was asking permission to hold a constitutional convention preparatory to admission as a free state, and would have to be paired with a new slave state to maintain the balance of power in Congress, which then stood at 12 free and 12 slave states. If Florida Territory should be paired with Michigan Territory, the admission of Arkansas probably would be delayed until Wisconsin Territory was ready, which Sevier said might be 25 years.[20]

No more persuasive argument could have been presented, and the people responded with overwhelming approval. Woodruff was slow to take a stand, but finally gave his reluctant approval. The opposing political faction heartily approved Sevier's action, but suggested that his motivation was more personal and less noble than represented. With the trade-outs preliminary to the 1836 presidential election under way and Sevier's wife's uncle, Richard Mentor Johnson of Kentucky, expected to be a candidate for vice president, Sevier's enemies said his real purpose was to get Arkansas's vote for Johnson's ticket. It is altogether likely that they were right. It was also said that Chester Ashley had a hand in Sevier's decision, and that his reason was that statehood would greatly enhance the value of his vast land holdings. The discussion fizzled out temporarily, when Congress adjourned without taking action on the application of either Arkansas or Michigan.[21]

Meanwhile, new developments in the political situation at home foretold the disintegration of the old alliance. Secretary Fulton had smouldered all summer because Pope had turned over the management of the ten-section grant and the construction of the state house to Ashley. Fulton told the 1833 legislature that perhaps Pope had exceeded his authority when he went so far as to plan and build the building and to appropriate the money received for the ten sections, and that further legislation might avoid future trouble. When the legislature sustained Pope, Fulton wrote a long address to the public to explain his viewpoint, and Woodruff published it on November 20, 1833. Woodruff resisted Pope's demands that he should take issue with Fulton editorially in his defense, and this did not set well with Pope, especially since it was about the same time Woodruff was refusing to defend him in the matter of the expense of the public printing.

Late in December, Fulton asked Woodruff to reprint an editorial from the Gallatin, Tennessee *Union* that took Fulton's side and portrayed the legislators as dupes and tools of the governor. Pope and a few of his friends bitterly opposed it, but Woodruff felt obliged to comply because Fulton had been assailed in the *Gazette*. Believing that Fulton had caused the *Union's*

20. *Ibid.,* Jan. 21, 1834; June 19, 1833.
21. White, *Politics on the Southwestern Frontier,* 166–167; *The Times,* May 9, 1835.

article to be written, Pope argued that he should be severely castigated, and warned that Woodruff's friends would regard republication of the article as an act of hostility against them. When this argument failed, Pope threatened, "If you publish it, we will throw you off! we will consider you as no longer belonging to the party!!" For one whose position in the party was as precarious as Pope's to threaten to read Woodruff out of the party was comical. It made Woodruff angry, but he answered mildly that he would do what he conceived to be right, regardless of the consequences.[22]

Some of their mutual friends insisted that Woodruff should at least add an editorial to defend Pope and chastise Fulton. Woodruff reprinted the *Union's* article on January 1, 1834, with editorial comment taking a strong position on Pope's side. Pope later said that some of his friends, especially Samuel M. Rutherford and William Field, were displeased because the editorial was not sufficiently abusive of Fulton, and that this incident led them to bring a new editor to Little Rock.[23]

The individual who took the initiative in importing a new editor was never satisfactorily identified. Woodruff blamed Pope most of the time and Field part of the time, but both consistently denied it. A joint stock company was casually mentioned at one time, but its members were not identified.[24] Nevertheless, it seems significant that when John Steele came to Little Rock late in February to make arrangements to establish a newspaper and a law office, he conferred with Governor Pope before he talked to anybody else.

Steele had been a lawyer about eight years and recently had been editor of the St. Louis *Times*.[25] He had sent a hired editor and two printers to Helena to begin publication of the *Helena Herald* on July 6, 1833, and had assumed the duties of editor upon his arrival in December.[26] Soon afterwards, he was appointed postmaster at Helena.[27] Little was known of his background, and Pope even professed to be unaware that Steele's wife, Mary, was a distant relative of his own brother-in-law.

Pope advised Steele to avoid conflict by forming a partnership with Woodruff, and appealed to Ashley to help bring this about. Pope was not yet inclined to deal Woodruff entirely out of the game, for he conceded that he was a good business man and printer and fully competent to handle those departments of the *Gazette*, but he was not aggressive enough in the defense of Pope and his friends to continue as editor.[28]

Steele called on Woodruff and offered to buy an interest in the *Gazette*, presumably suggesting that he should be the editor and Woodruff the pub-

22. *Gazette,* Jan. 15, Feb. 24, Sept. 30, 1834.
23. *Times,* Mar. 28, 1835.
24. *Gazette,* May 5, 1835.
25. *Ibid.,* Sept. 30, 1834.
26. *Ibid.,* Oct. 3, 1832; July 10, Dec. 25, 1833.
27. *Ibid.,* Apr. 22, 1834.
28. Clarence Edwin Carter (ed.), *Territorial Papers of the United States,* Vol. XXI, *The Territory of Arkansas, 1829–1836* (Washington: United States Government Printing Office, 1954), 982–983.

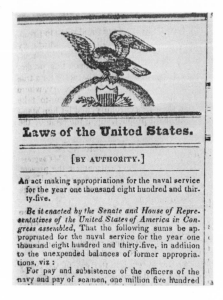

Laws of the United States.

[BY AUTHORITY.]

An act making appropriations for the naval service
for the year one thousand eight hundred and thirty-five.

*Be it enacted by the Senate and House of Repre-
sentatives of the United States of America in Congress assembled,* That the following sums be appropriated for the naval service for the year one
thousand eight hundred and thirty-five, in addition
to the unexpended balances of former appropriations, viz :

For pay and subsistence of the officers of the
navy and pay of seamen, one million five hundred

WM. E. WOODRUFF.
Little Rock, Dec. 8, 1835.

RED RIVER
LANDS & NEGROES
FOR SALE.

THE subscribers will sell
a valuable tract of LAND,
situated in Chickeninny
Prairie, Lafayette county,
Arkansas Territory, containing about

Twelve Hundred Acres,

about four hundred of which is now in cultivation,
and entirely free from inundation, with suitable
buildings thereon.

We would also sell, with said land, if desired,

27 likely NEGROES,

together with a large stock of HORSES, CAT-
TLE, and HOGS, CORN, FODDER, and FARM-
ING UTENSILS.

There are on said farm a good Cotton Gin and
Mill.

For terms, apply to
LEWIS B. FORT, or
FRANCIS E. WHITEFIELD.

Lafayette county, A. T., Nov. 20, 1835.   51–4

To Clerks and Sheriffs.

LL Clerks of the Circuit Court, who have not

lisher. When Woodruff refused, Steele offered to buy the paper outright, and
was again refused.[29] Steele then published a prospectus for a paper of his
own, called the *Political Intelligencer,* to begin weekly publication with all
new materials about May 1. It would be printed on a large imperial sheet at
$5 a year in advance, so it would be larger and more expensive than any
of the territory's three existing newspapers.[30] Steele returned to Helena in
March to prepare for the move, and by the middle of April he had sold the
Herald to Samuel S. Smith, but he did not return to Little Rock with his wife
and three children until June.[31]

Pope's preparations for the uncertainties of the future included looking
for a new circle of political friends. In May, he put out feelers in Crittenden's
direction, proposing a union against Sevier that would send both Pope and
Crittenden to the Senate after statehood, but Crittenden would have no part
of it.[32]

It might be supposed that there was no reason to fear competition from
an unknown editor whose paper would cost almost twice as much as any
other Arkansas paper, but Woodruff was disturbed because the *Intelligencer*
would be much larger than the others, and might well "swallow up all the 7

29. *Gazette,* Sept. 16, 1834.
30. *Ibid.,* Feb. 25, 1834.
31. *Ibid.,* Apr. 15, 1834; Carter, *Territorial Papers,* XXI, 983.
32. White, *Politics on the Southwestern Frontier,* 170; Lonnie J. White (ed.), "A
Letter from Robert Crittenden to John J. Crittenden," *Arkansas Historical Quarterly,*
XXI, (1962) 23.

by 9's in the Territory." [33] The trend in the East was towards larger sheets, and soon the unwieldy mammoth sheets of tablecloth proportions would appear in the West.[34] It would be wise to be prepared to enlarge the *Gazette's* sheet if necessary to meet competition, but the old Ramage press would not accommodate a larger sheet. Already Woodruff's printers were lapping the top and bottom margins of the sheet over the chase. Besides, the Ramage was fast becoming obsolete, and perhaps its operation was too slow to take care of the *Gazette's* expanding subscription list conveniently. The new type had given the subscribers more for their money on the same size sheet, but large bodies of small type were hard on their eyes, and people were more likely to judge a paper by the size of the sheet than by the number of words.

Steele was hardly out of town before Woodruff ordered a new iron Franklin press about April 1, 1834, from the manufacturer, Samuel S. Dickinson of Cincinnati.[35]

Shortly afterwards, news of the failure of the Bank of Maryland reached Little Rock, creating a panic.[36] This was followed by other bank failures, and the *Gazette* began to receive bankruptcy ads from Arkansas people. There could be no doubt that hard times were ahead.

Debts owed the *Gazette* had reached a total of $8,000 to $10,000, in individual amounts of less than $50. Woodruff's debtors were scattered all over the territory, and most of them owed him from one to ten dollars. The signs of the approaching recession indicated that further delay might make collection impossible, some of the accounts being already more than ten years overdue. After giving notice twice in the *Gazette,* Woodruff sent Daniel R. Mills on a collection tour of the counties south of the Arkansas River in May, and planned to send him to the northern counties later,[37] but the trip northward was never made.

Pope said the collections were a front to cover the real purpose of Mills' trip. He said Mills was thinking of establishing an anti-Pope newspaper in south Arkansas, presumably with Woodruff's guidance and financial support

33. *Gazette,* Apr. 28, 1835.
34. *Ibid.,* Oct. 21, 1834 reported enlargement of the *New-York Courier and Enquirer* to an eight-column sheet measuring 45 by 28 inches, "large enough to make a sleeve pattern without piecing." The same paper, according to the *Gazette* of Apr. 7, 1835, increased the size of its sheet to 54 by 48 inches. The *Democrat* of Huntsville, Alabama was mentioned in the *Gazette* of July 17, 1833 as the largest in the Western or Southern country when it changed to a mammoth sheet, and retained its lead even when the St. Louis *Missouri Republican,* a tri-weekly, was enlarged to a mammoth sheet two years later. (*Gazette,* June 16, 1835.)
35. *Ibid.,* Apr. 1, 1834. This is Dickinson's advertisement. The only new iron press he sold was the Franklin, but he also advertised several second-hand Stansbury and Ramage presses, which do not correspond with Woodruff's description of his press as a "new iron press." This ad alone does not necessarily prove that Woodruff ordered the press from Dickinson, but no other firm advertised a stock that included printing presses in time to allow delivery as early as August, when Woodruff's press arrived.
36. *Ibid.,* Apr. 15, 1834.
37. *Ibid.,* Apr. 29, 1834.

and perhaps even his old press, and that Mills' real mission was to get support for this paper and to discourage support of the *Political Intelligencer*. This was accomplished partly by circulating rumors fabricated by Woodruff that the *Intelligencer* would support William Field for Congress in opposition to Sevier, according to Pope.[38]

Steele was at Little Rock a few weeks before the first issue of the *Political Intelligencer* was published on Thursday, July 10, 1834. His charming manner made him a social lion, and he was invited everywhere and often thrust into positions of social leadership, but his new friends were slow to subscribe to his paper or advertise in it.

Sevier arrived from Washington about this time or soon afterwards, and chanced to meet Woodruff on the road to the Sulphur Springs in White County. They spent the night at the same house, and had much to discuss. Certainly they must have talked about Arkansas's bid for statehood and what it would mean to them, and Woodruff's support of statehood had no hint of reluctance thereafter. Looking backward several months later, Governor Pope deduced that they plotted his destruction that night, including his ruin in Arkansas and in Washington.[39]

The first salvo was not fired at Pope, but indirectly at his nephew, William Field, who was suspected of harboring an ambition to replace Sevier in Congress and of helping to bring Steele to Little Rock. Field held the elective office of clerk of the Superior Court and the appointive office of postmaster of Little Rock, but was currently unable to attend to either because of illness. On August 12, Woodruff offered a reward for apprehension of the thieves who had removed $48 in territorial scrip from a letter he had mailed to Helena and $40 in United States bank notes from a letter mailed to him from Cane Hill. He mentioned that he also knew of a letter containing $100 that had been mailed from Chicot County to Little Rock and was never delivered, and that his letter of inquiry to his Cane Hill correspondent had been delivered with its seal broken. Woodruff made no insinuations against Field or his deputy, but asserted that somebody on one of these routes was a thief.

Field did not take exception to it at first, but since the Little Rock post office was the common denominator, he considered it his business to investigate. He soon proved to Woodruff that his letter to Helena had never contained any scrip, and Woodruff had to admit that he must have neglected to enclose it. He also had to admit that he had absent mindedly addressed his Cane Hill friend as the postmaster, forgetting for the moment that another man now held that position. The old postmaster had told his successor to open mail addressed to him in his official capacity, and this explained the broken seal on Woodruff's letter.

Field thought Woodruff should hasten to correct the injustice done him and his post office, but one or more issues of the *Gazette* appeared without Woodruff's acknowledgment that he alone was to blame. When he finally

38. *Ibid.*, Sept. 16, 1834.
39. *Ibid.*, Mar. 17, 1835.

made this statement, he excused his carelessness as an honest mistake, made no apologies, and buried it near the end of a tirade against Pope that ran more than a full newspaper page.[40] A year passed before the public was told by the Cane Hill postmaster in a paid advertisement that the letter mailed to Woodruff from his office had never contained any money, as proved by the records that showed it had been mailed at the single letter rate, which would have been impossible if it had contained an enclosure.[41]

This controversy had barely begun when Woodruff opened fire on Pope.

Efforts to publish a digest of Arkansas laws by subscription had been made at least three times, but all had failed.[42] Plans had been made at Little Rock in the summer of 1833 for Sevier to get a congressional appropriation to pay for a digest, and it had been agreed that the bill would be written so as to give the governor the supervision of the work. Pope in turn had promised that he would appoint as compilers Judge Johnson and William Field. It had either been promised or taken for granted that the printing job would go to Woodruff, as usual. As there was no reason to suppose that either the appropriation or the appointments would be blocked, Johnson began work on the compilation soon after the agreement.[43]

News came in May, 1834 that Sevier had secured an appropriation of $3,000 for the digest.[44] Pope took no steps to begin the work, and the tension between him and his former friends was such that it was imprudent to prod him. Besides, Johnson was still working on the compilation and nothing except the formal appointments could be done until his work was finished, so the matter was allowed to ride.

About the time Steele began publication of his paper, his wife came down with a malignant fever that did not respond to treatment. After five weeks of suffering, she died on the night of August 11.[45] The *Political Intelligencer,* with only five or six issues in print, suspended publication about this time, yet its employees continued to work. It was soon known that the entire staff had been put to work on the digest of laws, and the paper had been suspended to expedite the job. Without public announcement or notification to those expecting the appointments, Governor Pope had given Steele the entire project, both the compilation and the printing. This had been done during Mrs. Steele's illness or at the time of her death, according to Pope, who said he did it out of sympathy and because he considered Steele competent to handle both jobs.[46] One suspects that Steele had the promise of the jobs much earlier than Pope admitted, for otherwise he could not have begun the printing so soon.

Steele apparently did none of the actual work on the digest. He was not a

40. *Ibid.,* Aug. 12, Sept. 16, 30, 1834.
41. *Ibid.,* Aug. 18, 1835.
42. *Ibid.,* Apr. 22, 1823; June 20, July 4, 1832; Sept. 30, 1834.
43. *Ibid.,* Sept. 16, 1834.
44. *Ibid.,* May 27, 1834.
45. *Ibid.,* Aug. 12, 1834.
46. Carter, *Territorial Papers,* XXI, 984.

printer, and must have left supervision of the mechanical work to his fore-man. Johnson's unfinished compilation was not considered, but arrangements were made for James McCampbell of Jackson County "to aid in the compila-tion." McCampbell had completed a digest that included all the laws passed from the beginning of the territorial government through the 1831 session, which he had tried unsuccessfully to publish by subscription in the summer of 1832.[47] Probably he had brought his digest up to date by adding the laws passed at the 1833 session, and it seems likely that his manuscript was used intact, though he had to share the credit with Steele.

Steele began printing the digest within a few days after his wife's death. Johnson brought the news to Woodruff,[48] who was so furious at being done out of this job that the pretense of friendship between him and Pope could be kept up no longer. Whether he had received the word by August 19 is uncertain, but on that day he published as a paid advertisement the proceed-ings of a public meeting in Miller County protesting in strong language one of Pope's recent appointments in that county. Pope complained around town of Woodruff's discourtesy in publishing the ad without first clearing it with him, but said nothing about it to Woodruff.[49]

Open editorial hostility to Pope came on August 26, when Steele's appoint-ment was reported. Woodruff told his readers that a newcomer who was not a practical printer and whose qualifications as a lawyer were unknown had captured the only really good printing job ever offered in Arkansas and an attractive legal job as well, in preference to well qualified old residents. He said these remarks were not intended to disparage Steele either as a law-yer or a printer, and congratulated him on his good fortune in securing "a good fat job." The expression "good fat job" was often used thereafter to refer to lucrative government printing jobs, but rarely by the printer who landed such a job.

In the next issue on September 2, Woodruff needled Pope about the Miller County ad, and said Pope could have space for a reply in the *Gazette* only at the usual advertising rates, since the other side had paid for its space. Pope was itching to reply, not so much to the Miller County people as to Woodruff, but would not humble himself to ask for space in the *Gazette,* free or paid. He apparently prevailed upon Steele to come to his defense, which Steele did in a quarter-sheet "extra" of the *Intelligencer* on September 9, taking the unwarranted position that he also had been attacked.

This was precisely what Woodruff's own experience with Pope had taught him to expect, and there can be little doubt that from the day he published the Miller County ad, he was trying to draw Pope into a paper war with Steele's position as his defender clearly defined. This would give further weight to Woodruff's accusation that Pope had used the digest to buy an editor who would vindicate his conduct, right or wrong, and who would be-

47. *Gazette,* June 20, July 4, 1832.
48. *Ibid.,* Mar. 17, 1835.
49. *Ibid.,* Sept. 2, 1834; Carter, *Territorial Papers,* XXI, 981.

lieve in "the infallibility of the Pope," as the governor often facetiously said his friends must do. It also gave him grounds for waging open warfare against Steele, who now became a villain in his own right, whereas previously he had been merely the beneficiary of Pope's villainy. Woodruff now made stronger his previous suggestions that Pope would cut himself in on the $3,000 for his token superintendence of the work, alluding to the governor's habit of finding legal ways to "finger" the public funds he administered.

Steele minimized his disability as a newcomer by saying that he, as a native of the Mississippi valley, had as much or more right to Arkansas patronage as "a little narrow hearted YANKEE," and said the fact that he was not a printer was offset by the fact that every printer in his office was more skillful than Woodruff.

Woodruff had speculated that Sevier would not be pleased with Pope's handling of the digest. Steele replied that Sevier and his friends, including Woodruff, were more indebted to Pope than to any other man in the territory for their political influence. This was patently ridiculous, for Sevier was easily the territory's most popular man in public life, and had been before Pope ever set foot on Arkansas soil. Woodruff was not personally popular, but he had played a vital part in the creation of Sevier's public image. Pope, on the other hand, had been a liability to Sevier from the beginning, but could not see that he had been the weakest member of the now shattered alliance.

It remained now for Woodruff to await the final fall of Pope, the unmourned victim of his own crippling egotism. This could be expedited by gouging him in the areas of his greatest vulnerability, and nobody understood these better than Woodruff. He pulled out all the stops in an article of more than a page in the *Gazette* of September 16, and threw in a remark that it was generally understood that Pope would not be reappointed as governor, and that the president had been expecting his resignation for some time.

Pope did not rise to the bait immediately, and the next week Woodruff gloated that with the *Intelligencer* suspended, the governor could reply only in the *Gazette* or the *Advocate,* which had long delighted in violent abuse of him. This time he would not be required to pay for *Gazette* space, but would have to send his reply to the *Gazette* before any other paper published it, and would have to allow three or four days for Woodruff's printers to set it, since his communications usually were tediously long.

Woodruff's crowing over having Pope at his mercy had the desired effect of forcing the *Intelligencer* to resume publication three days later, although the digest was only about half finished. Pope's reply to Woodruff, nearly six columns long, appeared in the first issue on September 26. The governor was forever through with Woodruff, but his attitude towards Sevier was uncertain. He suspected that Sevier had been something more than an uninvolved bystander in Woodruff's assaults on him, but he attributed this more to Sevier's false friends than to the delegate himself.[50]

50. Carter, *Territorial Papers,* XXI, 977–991.

Woodruff had to move with embarrassing swiftness from lauding and defending Pope to attacking him, but he accomplished the transition without apologies for either his past or present position. He still regarded some of Pope's past acts as praiseworthy, especially his role in the ten-section matter, but he now decided he had mistakenly interpreted the governor's motivation as patriotism and that mercenary considerations had been his real incentive. Undoubtedly Pope would insist on receiving a commission for disbursing the public funds involved, as he had done on previous occasions.

The digs at Steele were vague, since nothing much was known about him. Woodruff brought out an article from a Missouri newspaper almost four months old, referring to the brief career of the "notorious" John Steele as a Missouri editor, and predicting that he would devote himself at Little Rock to stirring up party and personal strife and to the support of bad men and measures.[51] Later, an anonymous correspondent hinted that there was more to be known about Steele than had been made public, but did not supply the information.[52]

Steele brought out an "extra" on October 14, in which he made much of Woodruff's wealth, which he estimated at $50,000. He arrived at this figure by evaluating Woodruff's real estate and the *Gazette* office at $40,000, and adding $10,000 for the debts due him. Woodruff placed the value of his holdings at much less than half that amount.

Steele then set out to show that not all this fortune had been acquired by honest toil, and that Woodruff could outdo Pope in "fingering" public funds. Steele said Woodruff had acted as territorial auditor in William Pelham's absence and as territorial treasurer in Samuel M. Rutherford's absence, and showed that one person in both offices could certify his own accounts and then pay himself according to his own certification. This accusation fell apart when it was proved that Woodruff never had acted in both capacities simultaneously, and furthermore had never had authority to issue territorial scrip as acting treasurer, only to receive scrip paid into the public treasury. There was good evidence that Steele knew this when he wrote his article.[53]

Sevier had managed to stay out of the Pope-Fulton rift, and remained friendly to both, and evidently he hoped to do the same thing in the controversy between Pope and Woodruff. Pope so far misjudged his own popularity as to suppose he could afford to make an enemy of Sevier if he would not join him in his dispute with Woodruff. Woodruff now slyly began to use the same tactics the *Advocate* had used to promote the mild tension between Pope and Sevier, and said that Pope was only now casting aside the cloak under which he had long hidden his hostility towards Sevier, and that Sevier was well rid of the political burden of Pope.[54]

51. *Gazette,* Sept. 30, 1834.
52. *Ibid.,* Oct. 14, 1834.
53. *Ibid.,* Oct. 28, 1834.
54. *Ibid.,* Sept. 30, 1834.

Sevier said nothing until the evening of November 3, when he called on Pope and told him he had had no part, directly or indirectly, in Woodruff's war against him, and assured him of a continuation of his friendship.[55] The next day, Sevier left his old home on Judge Johnson's plantation six miles below Little Rock to live on the Johnson plantation in Chicot County, expecting to stay there two or three days, and then go to Washington for the next session of Congress.[56] Whatever his reason was for moving his permanent residence, it had the happy effect of making him unavailable for ready participation in the political intrigue constantly brewing at Little Rock. By not declaring his position until the eve of his departure, he could not be maneuvered into entering the public discussion.

There was some indication that Fulton might be planning to open up a new line of attack. The *Advocate* of September 30 reported a rumor that yet another press was at the mouth of White River, waiting to be brought to Little Rock and put into the service of Secretary Fulton, to defend him against "the machinations and intrigues of his old political friends and asso-

55. *Ibid.*, Mar. 10, 1835.
56. *Ibid.*, Nov. 4, 1834.

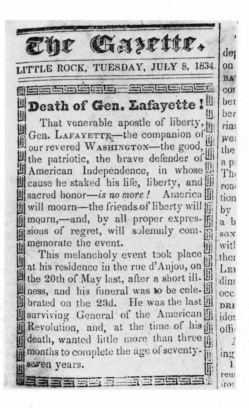

The Gazette.

LITTLE ROCK, TUESDAY, JULY 8, 1834.

Death of Gen. Lafayette!

That venerable apostle of liberty, Gen. LAFAYETTE—the companion of our revered WASHINGTON—the good, the patriotic, the brave defender of American Independence, in whose cause he staked his life, liberty, and sacred honor—*is no more!* America will mourn—the friends of liberty will mourn,—and, by all proper expressions of regret, will solemnly commemorate the event.

This melancholy event took place at his residence in the rue d'Anjou, on the 20th of May last, after a short illness, and his funeral was to be celebrated on the 23d. He was the last surviving General of the American Revolution, and, at the time of his death, wanted little more than three months to complete the age of seventy-seven years.

ciates." Woodruff laughed this off as one of the *Advocate's* weekly fabrications, and threw in another current rumor that Steele was trying to replace Bertrand as editor of the Crittenden organ.[57]

The *Gazette's* new press arrived late in August.[58] During the summer, Woodruff ordered some new type and other materials from his former employer, George Bruce, who now had a type foundry at New York. In the fall, he ordered more materials from S. Ecklin & Company of Philadelphia, and in the spring of 1835 more were purchased from the stereotype foundry of Martin M. Barnet of Cincinnati, operated in connection with the factory from which the press had been purchased.[59]

Vol. XVI opened on December 23, 1834, and with it came the promised enlargement. There were six columns to the page, and the page was the same length, 21 inches, but was two inches wider than before, now 15 inches. The column width remained 14 picas.

The front page format was strikingly different. The new nameplate was in shaded Old English, somewhat smaller than the old one, and the word *"The"* was again absent from the title. The nameplate and dateline were only four columns wide, and were centered over the four middle columns, with the tops of the two outside columns flush with the top of the nameplate.

The heavy expense of the improvements did not cause an advance in subscription rates, which remained $3 in advance or $4 after the first six months. Again Woodruff got rid of unprofitable subscribers by removing from the list all who owed for two or more years.[60]

The political situation with which Woodruff moved into 1835 was as new as the *Gazette's* format. While in the process of parting with his old friend, John Pope, Woodruff was also called upon to part with an old enemy. Robert Crittenden was stricken in a Vicksburg courtroom, and died on December 18, 1834. News of his death reached Little Rock in time for the *Advocate* to publish his obituary on January 2. The *Gazette's* obituary notice, four days later, was written by a friend of Crittenden. It was the custom for newspapers to be draped in mourning at the death of a person of Crittenden's prominence, by reversing the column rules so that the heavy base printed instead of the usual thin line. Woodruff probably felt that such a display would be hypocritical, and he did not so much as box the obituary in the fancy borders sometimes used for this purpose. He never made editorial mention of his worst enemy's death, but published the resolutions of respect adopted by the Superior Court and the Little Rock Debating Society.[61]

Bertrand lost no time getting rid of the *Advocate*. Albert Pike's bride of three months, Mary Ann Hamilton, had inherited a substantial estate, and he was now in a position to pay $2,500 for the *Advocate*. He became its

57. *Ibid.*, Oct. 7, 1834.
58. *Ibid.*, Aug. 26, 1834.
59. *Ibid.*, June 24, Nov. 11, 1834; Apr. 7, 1835.
60. *Ibid.*, Dec. 2, 16, 1834.
61. *Ibid.*, Jan. 13, 27, 1835.

proprietor and editor on January 20, 1835. He had just been admitted to the bar, and would not have to depend on the paper for his full support.[62]

John Steele's press had served his purpose. The 578-page digest was printed and ready to be bound, and the rapid completion of the job and collection of the money were uppermost in Steele's mind. Late in January, he sold the printing office to Andrew Jackson Hunt, a young printer who had come to Little Rock from Zanesville, Ohio about ten months earlier. He changed the name of the paper to *The Times,* and brought out Volume I, Number 1 on January 30, reducing the size to a super-royal sheet of five columns. He soon discovered that he had been sold a padded subscription list, and that only a few of the *Intelligencer's* readers had been paid subscribers.[63]

By the time the *Times* began publication, Steele's bindery machinery and equipment had arrived, and he was busily at work binding the digest, in partnership with Lemuel R. Lincoln, a recent arrival from Cincinnati. Enough copies were finished by the first week in February for distribution to begin.[64] Woodruff could not praise the book, but did not go overboard in criticizing it at the moment, although he later said it was a "miserable affair, a mere catch-penny." By February 10, Steele & Lincoln, book binders and stationers, opened their doors for public business, the first bindery in Arkansas.[65]

The *Times* showed a friendliness to Governor Pope from its first issue, and an anonymous correspondent of the *Gazette* promptly charged that Pope dictated its editorial policy.[66]

The *Gazette* of March 3, 1835 was ready to go to press when the Memphis mail brought a letter from Sevier, written at Washington on January 28. On that day, President Jackson had nominated William S. Fulton for governor of Arkansas, his term to begin on March 5 when Pope's term ended. The president also had nominated Lewis Randolph of Virginia, a grandson of Thomas Jefferson, to replace Fulton as secretary. This was indeed a bombshell, and Woodruff brought out his fancy "Post-script" logotype to give the story prominence.

A letter from Sevier to Pope arrived in the same mail, and gave the governor his first indication from Washington that he would not be reappointed, although he had heard rumors that Woodruff, Ashley, and probably several others had been informed nearly a month earlier that this was likely. He thought Sevier might at least have warned him, and he thought it was significant that Sevier had been the one who had given the president the date March 5 as the expiration of his term, when actually it was March 23. The suspicions that had been allayed by Sevier's profession of friendship in No-

---

62. *Ibid.,* Jan. 27, 1835; Pike in Hallum, *Biographical and Pictorial History of Arkansas,* 216–217.

63. *Gazette,* Jan. 27, 1835; *Times,* Jan. 30, June 6, Sept. 19, Oct. 10, 1835.

64. *Times,* Jan. 30, Feb. 5, 1835.

65. *Gazette,* Feb. 10, Apr. 28, 1835.

66. *Ibid.,* Feb. 3, 1835.

vember now seemed to be valid, and Pope placed most of the blame for his downfall on Sevier, without excusing Woodruff from all responsibility.[67]

Actually, Fulton had played an important part in it. In December, he had written to Jackson and to one of his trusted advisers, undermining Pope as an enemy to the administration and warning of the dangers of reappointing him. Pope had been a political chameleon, and his Jacksonism was considered dubious, and Fulton based his arguments on what Pope might be expected to do in the next presidential campaign.[68]

Pope and his wife left on April 29, in a race with death. They did not reach their Kentucky home in time to see his beloved only daughter before she died on May 1.[69]

The end of Pope's career in Arkansas was no blow to John Steele, for he had never intended to continue his involvement in Arkansas politics longer than it took to get his money for the digest. When the binding job was finished, Luther Chase took over his interest in the bindery, and on April 13, 1835, the firm of Chase & Lincoln announced its move to the room behind the *Advocate* office.[70]

Steele left Arkansas about that time, none too soon for his own safety. Parts of Arkansas had been terrorized for some time by a gang of ruffians later identified as part of the organization of "land pirates" headed by the infamous John A. Murrell. Their operations included a wide variety of crimes, but they rather specialized in stealing slaves, selling them, stealing them again or otherwise recovering them, selling them again, *ad infinitum*. Steele's uncanny success in locating and restoring stolen slaves to their rightful owners for a fee, his acting as attorney for some of the members of the gang, and the escape from jail at Little Rock of several members who were his clients had caused Woodruff and others to suspect that he might be the gang's local "front man," [71] but no accusations were made as long as he remained at Little Rock.

On at least four previous occasions, Woodruff had advocated lynching "by prudent and respectable persons" in cases where inadequate laws or laxity of law enforcement allowed shocking crimes to go unpunished.[72] On March 10, 1835, he suggested that the band of thieves had respected "front men" at various points, including probably Pulaski County, and strongly advised the people to lynch "every suspicious person who cannot give a good account of himself," because it was often difficult to get enough evidence to convict them in court. The jail break came a month later, and Woodruff said it illustrated the futility of legal methods in dealing with criminals. He recommended the secret organization of a company of skilled woodsmen to hunt

67. *Ibid.,* Mar. 10, 1835.
68. White, *Politics on the Southwestern Frontier,* 171.
69. *Gazette,* May 5, 1835; *Times,* May 30, 1835.
70. *Gazette,* Apr. 14, 1835.
71. *Ibid.,* Apr. 28, 1835.
72. *Ibid.,* Apr. 30, Oct. 21, 1828; Aug. 19, Nov. 4, 1834.

down the robbers and murderers infesting the country as they would hunt wild beasts, and to leave their carcasses as "food for the buzzards," leaving the courts and juries to confine themselves to matters they were capable of handling effectively.[73]

Steele left town a few days after this editorial was published, saying he was going to New Orleans to buy goods for a store he planned to open. According to Woodruff, he was next heard from a couple of weeks later "cheek-by-jowl with a band of murderers and thieves on White River, whom it is supposed he has visited with no very honest intentions." [74] In the fall, on the strength of a letter to somebody he knew, Woodruff published a story accusing Steele of helping to steal back a slave that had been stolen from one of his two companions. The story proved to be false and he had to retract it with apologies to Steele's two friends, but none to Steele.[75] Steele was reported to be living with the gang on the east side of the Mississippi just below Helena that autumn. Woodruff again urged their lynching, and did not believe the report in November that Steele had died.[76] Steele apparently never returned to Little Rock. He had left town owing James McCampbell $650, probably for his work on the digest of laws. In the February, 1836 term of Pulaski Circuit Court, McCampbell obtained a writ of attachment and had it served on Dudley D. Mason, who held possession of Steele's belongings at Little Rock. Mason tried to avoid execution because Steele owed him more money than the property was worth. McCampbell took it to court, and the verdict of the Circuit Court was in his favor. The decision was affirmed by the Arkansas Supreme Court in 1840.[77]

Albert Pike was the only Little Rock editor who could see the dangers in lynching in the summer of 1835. After five professional gamblers were hanged without a trial at Vicksburg, the *Times* called for similar action at Little Rock. William Copp, a transient gambler currently living at Little Rock, wrote a letter to the *Advocate* under the pseudonym "Sportsman," in which he deplored the Vicksburg lynching, took the *Times* to task for its editorial, and complained that the *Gazette* was as virulent against the local gamblers as the *Times*. He said the gamblers had behaved well and abided by the laws, and would leave any time the people refused to encourage them with profitable patronage. Pike published the letter as a paid advertisement at double the usual rates, $15 in advance.[78]

Editor Hunt obtained the writer's name, and wrote a long editorial denouncing him and heaping acid criticism on Pike for publishing the letter. He had favored allowing the gamblers to leave town alive, but now he said he would support any measures the people decided to take against them.

73. *Ibid.,* Apr. 7, 1835.
74. *Ibid.,* Apr. 28, 1835.
75. *Ibid.,* Sept. 1, Nov. 17, 1835.
76. *Ibid.,* Oct. 27, Nov. 24, 1835; *Times,* Nov. 23, 1835.
77. *Times,* Mar. 14, 1836; Dudley D. Mason v. James McCampbell, Jan. Term, 1840, 2 *Ark.* 506.
78. *Arkansas Advocate,* July 24, 31, 1835.

Portrait of Albert Pike, about 1844,
by Charles Loring Elliott.

Woodruff heartily endorsed Hunt's statements. A public meeting was called, in which all the editors participated, and the Anti-Gaming Association was organized on July 26, with a constitution providing for handling the gambling problem "in a legal manner."

Pike injected a note of sanity into the newspaper discussion, but was shouted down. He said he would join any movement providing legal means of getting rid of the gamblers, but could not support anarchy, mob law, Lynch's law, or despotism. Five days after the public meeting, the *Times* reported that the gamblers had been routed, some having left town and those remaining being "quiet as doves," a happy situation that lasted about a month. Again Pike came forward with a practical suggestion, that the territory needed a penitentiary, the county jails being inadequate for detention of all prisoners.[79]

At the request of the Anti-Gaming Association, the Town Council on August 9 authorized the organization of the Little Rock Guards, a company that would carry out the Association's pledge to help the civil authorities punish "all persons coming within the purview of the statute against vagrancy." [80]

Shortly before Pope and Steele left, Woodruff had another argument with William Field. Both Field and Sevier had been sensitive to demands for bet-

79. *Ibid.,* July 31, 1835; *Times,* July 25, Aug. 1, Sept. 5, 1835; *Gazette,* July 28, Aug. 18, 1835.
80. *Gazette,* Sept. 15, 1835.

ter postal service, when complaints were sufficiently specific to suggest a course of action. When departure time for the western mail from Little Rock delayed delivery in the spring of 1834, Field changed the schedule. Soon afterwards, at Woodruff's suggestion, Sevier persuaded the postmaster general to allow this mail to go twice a week instead of weekly.[81] Early in January, 1835, in response to complaints voiced at a public meeting about the irregularity of the mail from Memphis, Field exceeded his authority to discharge the contractor and employ another, but the situation only became worse. About the same time, Woodruff and others complained of the irregularity of the mail between Little Rock and Hot Springs, and Sevier arranged for a separate mail on this route.[82]

After many complaints that the *Gazette* was not delivered by mail regularly, Woodruff asked the territory's postmasters on March 3, 1835 to help him determine which post office was detaining his papers. He put their answers together and concluded that most of the trouble was at Little Rock. He reminded Field that there was no acceptable excuse for leaving part of the mail behind, and warned that in the future he would make his complaints to the postmaster general.

The *Advocate* was delivered fairly regularly, and Woodruff thought Field was showing partiality. Field indignantly denied it, and said the trouble was not in his office but in others whose irregularity worked a hardship on him. Field said Woodruff probably wanted the postmaster's job for himself or one of his friends. The argument was bitter but brief, because Field declined to continue it though Woodruff tried to keep it alive. Woodruff left little doubt that the main thing he held against Field was the part he was believed to have played in bringing John Steele to Little Rock. Field's resignation as postmaster in June, 1835 ended the dispute. Dr. John T. Fulton was appointed a month later.[83]

Woodruff undertook a new business responsibility in the fall of 1835, when he and Daniel R. Mills purchased David Rorer's horse-propelled ferry across the Arkansas River, which landed at the "lower landing" on the Little Rock side. A stable and tavern were established at the north bank landing, and Mills took charge of the entire operation.[84]

The ornate caption "The Olio" disappeared from the miscellaneous selections on the *Gazette's* back page with the issue of July 1, 1834, and no heading was used until December 30, 1834, when the unimaginative title, "Poetry," was placed at the head of the first column.

Every newspaper in the country published a small calendar at the end of every year. Usually the *Gazette* published it in December, rarely later than the first issue of the new year, and often repeated it in several subsequent

81. *Ibid.,* Mar. 4, 11, Apr. 22, 1834.
82. *Ibid.,* Jan. 13, 20, Feb. 3, 17, Mar. 3, 1835.
83. *Ibid.,* Mar. 17, Apr. 21, 28, May 5, June 30, Aug. 25, 1835; *Advocate,* Apr. 24, 1835; *Times,* Apr. 25, May 2, 1835.
84. *Gazette,* Oct. 20, 27, 1835.

issues. In 1836, however, nobody on the staff had time to prepare it at the proper time, and it was issued as an "extra" on March 15.

The statehood movement absorbed much of Woodruff's time and attention in 1835. The sheriff's census taken early in the year showed a population of 52,240, a number in excess of the minimum requirement. Because Congress had failed to act in the matter, the Michigan legislature had assumed the authority to order a constitutional convention, and planned to submit a constitution for the consideration of the next Congress in December. Sevier urged Arkansas to do the same thing, arguing that after this session it might be impossible for her to gain admission as a slave state. His circular, published in the *Gazette* on March 31, had Woodruff's enthusiastic endorsement.

Woodruff warned the people of the growing strength of the abolition movement that now looked forward to abolition of slavery in the District of Columbia and the territories. He kept his readers aware of the danger of emancipation of their slaves by publishing occasional articles about the evils of free Negroes, such as amalgamation of the races by intermarriage. In July, he briefly advocated sending all free Negroes under 60 to Liberia. In the fall, he was so incensed by abolition tracts received in the mail that he said if the postmaster general did not put a stop to it, the people of the South would have to seize and destroy the tracts, as the people of Charleston had done recently. Strangely enough, the postmaster general agreed on this point. He advised the Charleston postmaster that he had no authority to exclude newspapers from the mail or prohibit their delivery, but he considered it patriotic for the postmaster to disregard the laws to detain papers aimed at the destruction of the community.[85]

Woodruff suggested in March that Governor Fulton should call a special session of the legislature to authorize a constitutional convention, but Fulton was at Fort Gibson and his return was delayed by the serious illness of his wife and the death of his infant daughter. After his return, he was still pursued by domestic afflictions, as another daughter died on May 5.[86] Explaining that it was now too late for a special session to expedite the matter appreciably, Woodruff suggested instead on May 26 that the people should vote for or against statehood at the August election, which of course would not give them a constitution to present to Congress.

The *Times* continued its opposition to statehood, even after Jefferson Smith, who had served his apprenticeship at the *Gazette* office, bought a half interest in the paper and took charge of its mechanical department in June.[87] When the *Helena Herald* resumed publication in June after a long suspension, it joined the *Gazette* and *Advocate* in support of statehood.[88]

The 1835 political campaign was the quietest in many years. Woodruff served notice on prospective candidates on April 21 that those who were

85. *Ibid.*, Mar. 31, July 7, Sept. 1, 8, 1835.
86. *Times*, Feb. 28, May 23, 1835.
87. *Ibid.*, June 20, 1835; *Gazette*, June 23, 1835.
88. *Times*, June 13, 1835; *Gazette*, June 16, 1835.

not *Gazette* subscribers could not expect free announcements. The price of the announcement was one year's subscription, paid in advance, and the candidate could have the paper sent to him or not, as he chose.

Sevier was unopposed, and Woodruff was left free to concentrate on defeating his old enemy, Absalom Fowler, who was again a candidate for the territorial House of Representatives from Pulaski County. But the influence of the old Crittenden party was stronger than the *Gazette's* in Pulaski County, and both Fowler and William Cummins were elected by such large majorities that Woodruff called it "a Waterloo defeat," and accepted it philosophically and in amazingly good humor.[89]

Governor Fulton issued a circular on August 4, declining to call a special session because he believed the territory did not have a right to frame a constitution without an enabling act of Congress. When the legislature convened on October 5, Fulton ceased his opposition to statehood, but still could not be classified as a supporter of the movement. The act of the legislature authorizing a constitutional convention became a law without his signature.

In the meantime, A. J. Hunt had died and John H. Reed had become editor of the *Times,* as Jefferson Smith's new partner. He had changed the *Times'* position on statehood, making the Arkansas press unanimously in favor of it.[90]

As the election of the public printer approached in October, 1835, Woodruff and Pike agreed that the work should bring a reasonable profit. If all the candidates submitted identical bids, their advantages in the election would be equal, except in the matter of personal or political popularity. They drew up a bid based on Woodruff's 1831 bid, and both Woodruff and Pike submitted this bid.

Smith and Reed refused to submit the same bid, because they had not had time to get a following in the legislature, and their only hope was to underbid their competitors. Their bid was 32 per cent lower than Pike's and Woodruff's, and Pike withdrew from the race in disgust. Woodruff did not know it in time to withdraw, but he should have suspected something of the sort when he encountered unusual difficulty in finding a legislator who was willing to nominate him. Smith's and Reed's friends circulated rumors that Pike's and Woodruff's identical bids proved they had wiped out all their old differences to make a united effort against the *Times.* Smith and Reed received 56 votes to Woodruff's humiliating 4.[91]

Woodruff accepted his defeat with more dignity than Smith and Reed accepted their victory. Thereafter, when both the *Gazette* and the *Advocate* disagreed with the *Times* on unrelated questions, the *Times* said the real reason was that Pike and Woodruff were peeved because the *Times* office got the public printing, and were jealous of the *Times'* rapidly increasing

89. *Gazette,* Aug. 4, 1835.

90. *Ibid.,* Sept. 22, Oct. 6, 1835; *Advocate,* Sept. 18, 1835; *Times,* Sept. 19, Oct. 3, 10, 1835.

91. *Gazette,* Oct. 13, Nov. 24, 1835; *Advocate,* Oct. 16, 1835; *Times,* Oct. 19, 1835.

circulation.[92] The *Gazette* published the acts of this session *"Pro Bono Publico."* The journals did not receive pamphlet publication, and were printed only in the newspapers.[93]

While the *Times'* low bid made the public printing unprofitable, it had compensating advantages in building the paper's subscription list. The *Times* began to boast of its increasing circulation just before the election of the public printer, and went so far as to give actual figures, a thing no Arkansas newspaper had ever done. By the middle of December, the *Times* had 800 subscribers. The *Advocate* said its list was also growing, but the tone of the article was not convincing. The *Gazette* made no comment until the end of the volume in December, when the editor said that 1835 had brought him an increase of 300 subscribers and a proportionate increase in advertising and other patronage, but left the total number of subscribers to the imagination of the readers.[94]

At the organization of the Constitutional Convention in January, 1836, only Pike and Woodruff were nominated for printer to the Convention. Pike won, by a vote of 27 to 23,[95] with the predictable result that the *Gazette* and the *Advocate* waged a running battle during the next few weeks over the fairness of the price for this "good fat job."

Woodruff had other battles to fight during the session of the Convention, for as usual, it was considered expedient to take advantage of the presence of Democrats from all parts of the state to prepare for the next campaign. Previously party politics had been a game to be played openly only when politicians alone were involved, behind the scenes in the legislature or in county caucuses. Extreme subtlety had been necessary when the voters were involved, because of the prevailing opinion that party politics was machine politics, fostering all manner of undesirable things. As Robert Crittenden had once epitomized it, "The *political parties* in Arkansas—a nick-name for a few private and personal feuds, as dishonorable to the *parties* as disgraceful to Arkansas . . ." [96]

As Woodruff analyzed his party's prospects in the forthcoming election, he concluded that the Democrats could not hope to win unless they boldly appealed for support of party rather than of individual candidates. He tried to convince leading Democrats, but their advice was unanimously against it, because they thought it would bring certain defeat. Woodruff knew only too well that the blame for defeat would be laid at his door, as editor of the party's organ, although he could not expect the credit for victory. And so he decided to conduct the campaign according to his own judgment, and make it a party question. It was a more drastic decision than modern readers can realize, and was based on the fact that both the national and state

92. *Times,* Dec. 14, 1835.
93. *Gazette,* Sept. 9, 1840.
94. *Ibid.,* Dec. 15, 1835; *Times,* Oct. 10, Dec. 14, 1835; *Advocate,* Oct. 16, 1835.
95. *Gazette,* Jan. 12, 1836.
96. *Ibid.,* July 6, 1831.

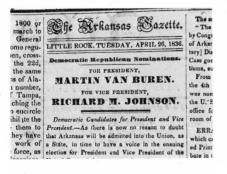

tickets had weaknesses that would prove fatal unless the necessity of voting a straight Democratic ticket were stressed.

Martin Van Buren, who was to be the Democratic candidate for president, had little to recommend him to Arkansas voters except the ardent support of the ever popular Andrew Jackson, and Woodruff feared that would not be enough. His running mate, Richard Mentor Johnson, was a liability to the ticket nationally, but in Arkansas the support of Sevier and other influential relatives would give him strength. Van Buren's leading opponent, Hugh Lawson White of Tennessee, took a position on the slavery question that was far more pleasing to Southerners than Van Buren's, and would have strong appeal for the substantial number of Arkansas voters of both parties who had come from Tennessee and Alabama.

In later years, Woodruff mentioned only the weakness of the national slate when he explained why he decided to conduct the *Gazette's* part of the campaign along strict party lines,[97] but there can be little doubt that the weakness of the state ticket was an even more compelling reason.

Although it was occasionally alluded to by the Whigs, most Arkansas voters did not realize how extensively nepotism had infiltrated their government. Since 1823, the only major office filled by popular vote, the delegate in Congress, had been held by only two men, Henry Conway and Ambrose Sevier, who were first cousins. The colony of relatives had been reinforced as other relatives moved into Arkansas or married into families having members who wanted to be on the public payroll. Sevier's marriage in 1827 to a daughter of Judge Benjamin Johnson had been the most important marital alliance in the clan, extending its influence into the powerful Johnson family of Kentucky. As Arkansas Territory's only representative in Congress and a relative of the Johnsons, Sevier had found it easy to control appointments originating in Washington. Control of appointments made by the governor had been nip and tuck, but a large part of the time Arkansas had had governors who acted with Sevier and his friends. Offices within the gift of the legis-

97. *Arkansas Banner,* Mar. 11, 1846.

lature were more difficult to influence, but proof that it could be done was found in the election of William Pelham, who had married Conway's sister, to the office of auditor in 1833, and of Elias N. Conway, the youngest of the brothers, to the same office in 1835. Lesser jobs, involving neither elections nor appointments, had been found for other relatives and friends in various government offices from time to time.

Regarding the manipulation of Arkansas politics, a *Times* correspondent had once commented, "Arkansaw has long been ruled by a press [the *Gazette*], and the man that dictates its course [Ashley], with Sevier to act under their direction." Another had based his objections to statehood on the supposition that the new government would be controlled by the few men then dominating Arkansas politics, saying, "We would have all our offices, state and federal, saddled upon us by one family: we would, in truth, be governed by a dynasty east of the Mississippi." [98] This implied that Richard Mentor Johnson would be heavily involved, even to the point of domination.

True to the Whig predictions, Sevier and his friends viewed the increased number of elective offices opened by statehood as so many opportunities to strengthen their control, giving some to relatives and using others to reward friends or divert men who might otherwise lead a large portion of the party into revolt.

It was already understood that the first state legislature would send Sevier and Fulton to the United States Senate, this to be Fulton's reward for relaxing his opposition to statehood and for not taking his followers into new channels. The greatest fly in the ointment was Archibald Yell, who stubbornly clung to his burning ambition to be the state's first governor, even after he knew it was decreed that this honor would go to James Sevier Conway, brother of Henry and Elias Conway, who had previously been taken care of with the appointive office of surveyor general. Conway would not be as strong a candidate as Yell, who was a master campaigner and extremely popular. Persuasion failing, Yell's candidacy was headed off in the Constitutional Convention by making four years residence one of the qualifications for the office of governor. Yell had come to Arkansas in December, 1831, but had returned to Tennessee the next summer and had not re-established his residence in Arkansas until late in 1834, and was therefore ineligible to run for governor. He probably was correct in his belief that this clause had been inserted in the Constitution for the sole purpose of keeping him out of the race.[99]

Still Yell gave the party leaders some uneasy moments. He suggested C. F. M. Noland as a possible Democratic candidate for Congress, without Noland's knowledge. Noland had always been identified with the Whigs, but he admired Andrew Jackson, and had been writing articles for the Florence,

98. *Times,* May 9, 30, 1835.
99. Melinda Meek, "The Life of Archibald Yell," *Arkansas Historical Quarterly,* XXVI (1967), 17–20, 163–164; Hallum, *Biographical and Pictorial History of Arkansas,* 114.

Alabama *Gazette* promoting Van Buren's candidacy.[100] The message the Democratic leaders got from Yell's suggestion was that he could conceivably organize a third party that would make a strong bid for both Democratic and Whig votes. In a move that smacks of strategy aimed at avoiding this, Yell was offered the consolation prize of the Democratic party's nomination for Congress, and probably also the promise that he could be the state's second governor. His acceptance was reluctant enough to remind the old party leaders that he would bear watching, for he was too independent to allow others to control his fate forever. In the flurry of covert opposition to his candidacy within the party's leadership, the Whig press said the *Gazette* was his secret enemy, and that the party bosses were afraid he would not divide the spoils of office according to their wishes. The preference shown Sevier's relative moved the *Times* to challenge, "Are the people of Arkansas willing to say, that the offices of the State shall be filled by one blood kin, and be hereditary?" [101]

Sevier was aware that the large number of his relatives holding public offices might begin to operate against him, and probably also that this might make Johnson's candidacy for vice president a liability to the state ticket.

The formal nominations of Democratic candidates for state offices were made at half a dozen county meetings,[102] but obviously had been previously decided in a caucus at Little Rock. As the friends of this period became enemies a decade later, Woodruff referred either to the caucus or the Pulaski County meeting when he said: "The first Convention assembled in 1836. It was a small secret affair, composed of six or eight individuals, who very modestly appointed themselves; and who very modestly claimed all the principal offices of the General and State Governments; and the most of them succeeded in obtaining the offices, which they had in Convention apportioned out among themselves. This meeting was called a 'Convention,' but it was a sort of oyster-party, in which the movers devoured most voraciously the fish, while the shells were distributed with a liberal hand to the People!" In another reference to the subject he said, "Every Convention that has heretofore been held in this State, has been used for the benefit of a family Clique at this place, which has very modestly claimed all the important offices of the General and State Governments, for its members and their strikers. Look at the secret Convention in 1836, and it will be seen at once how well the members of the family Clique provided for themselves. Not a single office of any magnitude escaped their voracity . . ." [103]

What he neglected to mention was that he was himself a member of that clique in 1836, as was Ashley, and both undoubtedly had a voice in the

100. *Arkansas State Democrat,* June 12, 1846.
101. *Times,* June 27, 1836.
102. For a discussion of contemporary reports of the county meetings, see D. A. Stokes, Jr., "The First State Elections in 1836," *Arkansas Historical Quarterly,* XX (1961), 130–133.
103. *Arkansas State Democrat,* Sept. 10, 17, 1847.

so-called nominating convention. Indeed, it is likely that the office of state treasurer was formally promised to Woodruff at that time, and that it had been informally promised him by Sevier to secure his support for statehood during their roadside conference at which they were said to have plotted John Pope's destruction.

When the Constitutional Convention was winding up the last few details of its business, delegate Nimrod Menefee submitted a resolution calling for a committee to find out how much it would cost and how long it would take for the various printing offices to print the pamphlet copies of the Constitution. No action was taken on it, presumably because this was a part of the job of the Convention's official printer. The next day a resolution was adopted directing the secretary of the Convention to make a copy of the Constitution on parchment to be sent to Congress, and another copy on paper to be placed in the state archives, after which the Convention elected a messenger to take the parchment copy to Washington. After six men had been nominated, John F. King, a pragmatic delegate representing Carroll County, nominated the United States mail. He kept his nominee in the race through all seven ballots, and voted alone for it on five of them, but C. F. M. Noland of Batesville was elected. This was on Friday afternoon, January 29, and the Convention adjourned the next day.[104]

On the following Thursday, February 4, Woodruff brought out a half-sheet "extra," containing the text of the new Constitution. It was delivered to Little Rock subscribers that evening and mailed to those at a distance the next morning.[105] In his haste to be the first to present the Constitution to the public, Woodruff left a few typographical errors uncorrected and omitted the signatures of the delegates and the important ordinance containing the twelve points or propositions by which Arkansas Territory offered herself for statehood. The *Advocate* of February 5 contained the Constitution with the signatures but minus the ordinance, as did the *Times* of February 8. It is likely that the ordinance, which should have been printed at the head of the Constitution, was not available during the first few days because the secretary was using the only official copy to prepare the manuscript for Noland.

Woodruff reprinted the Constitution in his regular issue of February 9, with the typographical errors corrected and the ordinance and signatures added. It took Pike about six weeks to finish the 5,000 pamphlet copies, but on March 18, he announced that they were ready for distribution. In the intervening weeks, he and Woodruff sniped at each other about the exorbitance of their respective fees, and Woodruff made much of the fact that Pike had

104. *Journal of the Proceedings of the Convention met to form a Constitution and System of State Government for the People of Arkansas at the session of the said convention held at Little Rock, in the Territory of Arkansas, which commenced on the fourth day of January, and ended on the thirtieth day of January, one thousand eight hundred and thirty-six.* Published by Authority. (Little Rock, Ark.: Printed by Albert Pike, 1836), 48, 50–52; *Gazette,* Feb. 2, 1836.
105. *Gazette,* Feb. 9, 1836.

received $850 for the pamphlets in advance, and therefore had no particular reason to hurry the job.[106]

Noland left for Washington on the morning of February 5 on the steamboat Neosho,[107] with the certified copy of the Constitution prepared by the secretary of the Convention. A copy of the *Gazette* "extra" addressed to Sevier went out in the mail of the same day.[108] Noland took what he considered the quickest route in the winter season, going by boat to Mobile and then overland to Washington by way of Richmond. But snows had made the roads virtually impassable, and he did not reach Washington until shortly before noon on March 8.[109]

The *Gazette* "extra" had arrived eight days earlier and had been submitted to the House on March 1, since time was growing short and Sevier thought it unwise to wait for the certified copy. Woodruff presumed that the *Gazette's* complete copy of the Constitution reached Sevier on March 4 and was referred to the same select committee that was studying the "extra", but no direct statement by Sevier to that effect is found. There was no reason to doubt the accuracy of the *Gazette's* copy and it would do for the committee to study, but because it was not certified or even published by authority of the Convention, it could only be regarded as an unofficial copy, and consequently the final action of Congress could not be based on it.[110]

When Noland arrived, the commitee had just finished its deliberations and voted to report a bill for the admission of Arkansas. Sevier was irked to learn that Noland had brought only one copy of the Constitution, and that it was addressed to the secretary of state, who could not be expected to take the same personal interest in it as the territory's delegate. He interpreted this to mean that the Convention possibly did not want him to engineer statehood for Arkansas, although certainly he had already done enough to entitle him to most of the credit. He also implied that he had not seen the ordinance

106. *Ibid.,* Mar. 22, 1836.
107. *Times,* Feb. 8, 1836.
108. *Gazette,* Mar. 29, 1836.
109. *Ibid.,* Apr. 5, 1836; *Advocate,* Apr. 22, 1836.
110. *Gazette,* Mar. 29, 1836.

The Gazette.

Little Rock, Thursday, Feb. 4, 1836.

CONSTITUTION
OF THE
STATE OF ARKANSAS.

Knowing the anxiety of our patrons to get a sight of the CONSTITUTION OF THE STATE OF ARKANSAS, we have been at considerable extra labor and expense to lay it before them in an extra sheet, in anticipation of our regular publication. Although not *smart* enough to secure the *fat jobs* of the Legislature and Convention, our readers shall ever find us, as usual, not behind our competitors in *industry*, in laying before them, at the earliest period, the result of the labors of those bodies.

until Noland's arrival, which suggests that Woodruff was mistaken in supposing that the *Gazette's* complete copy was in the hands of the committee.[111]

The bill for the admission of Arkansas passed the Senate early in April, and the news reached Little Rock by mail on the evening of April 20. Woodruff gave his readers the news in an "extra" on the morning of April 22. In his regular issue four days later, he hoisted the banner of the Democratic Republican nominees, Martin Van Buren for president and Richard M. Johnson for vice president.[112] The next issue of the *Advocate* endorsed the People's Anti-Caucus candidates, Hugh Lawson White and John Tyler.[113]

The House did not pass the bill until June 14, and the president signed it the next day. But Woodruff was confident when it passed the Senate that statehood was assured, and he had plans of his own that did not include the arduous duties of a newspaper editor. On May 10, he announced that he had sold an interest in the *Gazette* to Thomas J. Pew, who would be the sole editor, while Woodruff would continue as the business manager.

John H. Reed became sole proprietor of the *Times* by his purchase of Jefferson Smith's interest late in May, and gave his support to the White and Tyler presidential ticket.[114]

Little Rock had not grown in proportion to the territory's increase in population. The sheriff's census of 1835 showed the town's population to be 726, a gain of only 60 in two years.[115] Woodruff continued to take an active part in municipal government. In 1833, he was again elected to the Town Council, while his wife's uncle by marriage, Rev. William W. Stevenson, was mayor. He was not a candidate for the Council in 1834, but the Council elected him town treasurer.[116]

When Richard C. Hawkins' new frame home was destroyed by fire on January 28, 1834, Woodruff editorially urged the people to raise money to buy a fire engine, and to organize and train a company to man it. As town treasurer, he spoke with authority when he said the corporation was too poor to afford one.[117] The Town Council authorized the purchase of a fire engine in July, provided its cost did not exceed the funds available in the treasury and the amount that could be raised by subscription, but the people showed little interest in it, and Little Rock continued without so much as a fire bell or a bucket with which to fight fires.[118]

As Woodruff vacated the editor's chair in the spring of 1836, he expected to be more or less free of the political strife that had been his lot for more than 16 years. He was soon to learn that this would not be possible as long as he was connected with a newspaper in any capacity.

111. *Ibid.,* Apr. 5, 1836.
112. *Ibid.,* Apr. 26, 1836.
113. *Advocate,* Apr. 29, 1836.
114. *Times,* May 23, 1836; *Gazette,* May 24, 1836.
115. *Gazette,* Mar. 27, 1833; May 8, 1835.
116. *Ibid.,* Jan. 9, 1833; Jan. 8, July 29, 1834.
117. *Ibid.,* Jan. 28, 1834.
118. *Ibid.,* July 29, 1834; Dec. 29, 1835; *Times,* Aug. 1, 1835.

7

THOMAS JEFFERSON PEW

1836-1838 THOMAS JEFFERSON PEW became editor of the *Arkansas Gazette* just as the newspapers of the prospective state were announcing their preferences for the forthcoming presidential election. In his first editorial on May 10, 1836, he reaffirmed the *Gazette's* support of Martin Van Buren and Richard M. Johnson, whose names had been at the head of the editorial columns for two weeks. At the same time, Woodruff said he would confine himself to the paper's business management, leaving to Pew "the labor and perplexity incident to the life of an Editor." Pew's editorial autonomy was emphasized the next week when "Thomas J. Pew, Editor" was placed under the editorial head.

His stormy journalistic career had begun at Versailles, Kentucky, and he had published a paper at Alexandria, Louisiana before he was 20 years old. He had become the editor of a daily paper at New Orleans in the fall of 1827, and had been elected public printer of Louisiana four years later. His last position as editor of the old and influential *Kentucky Gazette* at Lexington had vastly enhanced his reputation as an outspoken Democratic editor. He had served as a delegate from Kentucky to the Baltimore convention that had nominated Van Buren and Johnson, and had represented Illinois and Indiana by proxy. As a part of the effort to discredit the nominations, the Whig press was currently making an issue of his representation of "several states and territories" that had never been his home.[1]

He had previously run afoul of George D. Prentice, the brilliant Whig editor of the Louisville *Journal,* whose caustic pen brought forth the skeletons from Pew's closet, with embellishments to suit his fancy. The Randolph, Tennessee *Recorder* charged that the Baltimore convention leaders had sent Pew to Little Rock, and the Arkansas Whig editors took it up, first Albert

1. *Advocate,* June 5, 1835; June 10, 24, 1836; *Gazette,* July 25, Oct. 4, Nov. 29, 1836; *Times,* June 13, 1836.

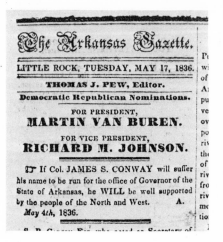

Pike of the *Advocate*,[2] and then John H. Reed, who became sole proprietor of the *Times* on May 23.[3]

A newcomer who attempted to influence Arkansas voters before he was acclimated could expect to be considered a presumptuous upstart, and a salaried political writer could expect to be branded a journalistic prostitute who would stoop to write the convictions of others for money. Nobody was ever able to prove that Pew was only an employee, but this did not keep the opposing press from charging repeatedly that Woodruff had been persuaded by the promise of rich rewards not clearly delineated to relinquish the editor's chair to Pew, for the purpose of promoting Van Buren's candidacy in Arkansas. The *Times* soon dubbed Woodruff "the retired editor," and then "the pensioned editor," and referred to Pew as "the hireling editor."

Since the admission of Arkansas might come at the eleventh hour, and since the Constitution did not prescribe the precise manner of taking the votes in the presidential election, Pew expressed an opinion that the legislature might have to cast the state's first vote in a national election. This highly unpopular suggestion was cast aside on the evening of June 27, when Elias N. Conway arrived from Helena with an article copied from the *National Intelligencer,* announcing that the bill for the admission of Arkansas had passed the House without amendment on June 13. It needed only the signature of the president, who was known to be friendly to it, so it was safe to assume that it was already a law. About half of the *Gazette's* edition of June 28 had already been printed, but the "Postscript" logotype was brought out for inclusion of this item in the other half, and the *Gazette* scooped both the *Times* and the *Advocate* on the big story of Arkansas's admission to the

2. *Advocate*, May 27, June 10, 1836.
3. *Times*, June 13, 1836.

union.[4] To accommodate the subscribers who received the copies that did not contain the story, an "extra" was issued the next day.[5] It was not until July 12, two issues later, that the editor remembered to change "A. T." (for Arkansas Territory) to "Ark's." on the front page dateline.

The political factions of territorial days had been informally identified by the names of their respective leaders, but now that Arkansas could participate in national elections, they adopted the names of the national parties to which they adhered. The old Sevier party became the Democratic Republican party, and labeled its state ticket "Jackson Republican." The old Crittenden party was essentially Whig, but adopted the People's Anti-Caucus label for the 1836 campaign because its presidential candidate was not the Whig nominee but the anti-Jackson candidate whose supporters were gathered from both parties.

The Democratic slate for state offices was announced in the same issue of the *Gazette* that gave the news of the admission of Arkansas to the union. The opposing slate had been announced during the previous week. James Sevier Conway was opposed for governor by Absalom Fowler, and William Cummins ran against Archibald Yell for Congress. Both parties had a full slate of candidates for county offices.[6]

Pew's job as editor of the *Gazette* made him the principal spokesman for the Democratic party. He was in the uncomfortable position of having to prime a gun he could not shoot, for he was not eligible to vote. Six months residence in Arkansas was required, and he would have only three months residence before the August election for state officers, and would either barely qualify or fall a few days short by the time of the November presidential election.

One of his most articulate enemies was Allen M. Scott, a Washington County schoolmaster and part-time preacher, son of a Tennessee minister, who aspired to a newspaper career. He had been a contributor to the *Gazette's* columns since his arrival in Arkansas in 1832, but he had quarrelled with Woodruff about the time he moved to Little Rock late in 1835 or early in 1836, and had transferred his talents to the *Times*. He wanted to learn the printer's trade so he could establish a paper at Fayetteville, so he became a journeyman and clerk in the *Times* office, and wrote articles for the paper and taught school on the side. A series of political satires, captioned "Chronicles," began in the *Times* in June, with a deliberately exaggerated Biblical style that lent itself to presentation of behind-the-scenes events strongly suspected but not subject to proof. Rumor credited these satires to Scott, but the *Times* denied that he wrote any of its political articles.[7]

4. The *Advocate* had the story on July 1, the *Times* on July 4, 1836.
5. *Gazette,* July 5, 1836.
6. *Advocate,* June 24, July 1, 1836; *Times,* June 27, 1836.
7. *Times,* July 25, 1836. A similar series with the same title, probably also written by Scott, had previously appeared in the *Gazette.* Scott was still using the Biblical style as an outlet for his political opinions almost 30 years later. A series of articles in a Memphis daily paper about the Civil War was so popular that it resulted in a 344-page

The second and third chapters of the "Chronicles" told the story of the supposed decision at the Baltimore convention of a group of Democrats headed by Silas Wright to send Pew to Arkansas. Woodruff was represented as standing to lose nothing if Van Buren should not be elected, for he could take his paper back and blame the fiasco on Pew.[8]

This opened a full scale war between the two papers, and a personal war between Scott and Pew. In the course of the controversy, Scott said Pew had once edited an anti-Jackson paper and had discreetly switched sides after Jackson's election. He threatened to use a better weapon than the pen, and said it would remind Pew of the cowhiding he had taken "like a cringing slave" at the hands of one Holman on a Frankfort street. Scott called Pew a fool, coward, and liar, in an obvious attempt to provoke him into challenging him to a duel.[9] Pew would not oblige him, but said he had had no difficulty with Holman and denounced both the writer and the paper that allowed "such a vagabond as A. M. Scott to reiterate his contradicted falsehoods against its contemporaries." He said he had stricken the *Times* from the *Gazette's* exchange list, and declared he would wash his hands of both the *Times* and Scott.[10]

This further infuriated Scott and Reed, both of whom wrote angry replies. Reed said the *Gazette's* vile course in this matter had increased the circulation of the *Times,* which was now printing 960 papers a week, and was distributing 80 copies in Little Rock, 30 more than the *Gazette.* Indeed, the *Times'* prosperity was such that Reed had purchased the materials to enlarge the paper to a mammoth sheet, which would make it the largest in the state. The only thing that delayed it was prevention by his enemies of his obtaining additional employees, but he sent to the nearest printing centers for journeymen,[11] and made the promised enlargement on August 8.[12]

Reed was even more enraged by an article headed "The Fruits of Illicit Love" in the *Gazette* of July 19, the same issue that announced the removal of the *Times* from the exchange list. It was a whimsical essay about Albert Pike's secret visits to Reed's home, which after nine months brought forth an "abortion" in the form of an "extra" pertaining to the presidential campaign. It also hinted that the *Times* and the *Advocate* might soon merge. The article

---

hardback book. See Rev. Allen M. Scott, *Chronicles of the Great Rebellion from the Beginning of the Same until the Fall of Vicksburg* (Cincinnati: C. F. Vent & Co., 1863.) Scott was also the author of a textbook, *The New Southern Grammar,* published at Memphis in 1862. (*Arkansas True Democrat,* Feb. 13, 20, 1862.) He was editor of the *Sage of Monticello* for several months in 1858. (*Gazette,* Apr. 24, 1858.)

8. *Times,* June 27, July 4, 1836. Senator Silas Wright, Jr. of New York was regarded as the manager of Van Buren's political interests. The *Gazette* never gave any clue as to how the arrangements were made for Pew to become its editor. It is possible that Sevier may have recommended him to Woodruff, and that Sevier may have been influenced by Wright or others at the convention.

9. *Ibid.,* July 11, 18, 1836.

10. *Gazette,* July 12, 19, 1836.

11. *Times,* July 25, 1836.

12. *Ibid.,* Aug. 1, 1836; *Gazette,* Aug. 9, 1836.

was unsigned, and the word "Communicated" indicated it had been contributed by somebody not editorially connected with the *Gazette*. Reed called the article obscene, and believed Woodruff had written it. Because it wounded him "in a tender point," Reed tried to make it a personal matter between Woodruff and himself,[13] but Woodruff ignored his remarks. Pew said Woodruff had not written a political article for the paper since the change of editors, and that Reed had brought his name into it as a diversionary move to keep from having to prove or retract his remarks about the Holman affair.[14]

On the evening of July 19, Governor Fulton received a letter from Maj. Gen. Edmund P. Gaines, who was charged with the defense of the southwestern frontier of the United States. Gaines informed Fulton that the Mexican army had been substantially reinforced and was advancing on the Texas army with the avowed intention of taking everything as far as the Sabine. He asked Fulton to send him a regiment of ten companies of mounted gunmen to serve six months, and Fulton immediately issued a proclamation calling for volunteers. It was too late to include this in the *Gazette* of that day, so an "extra" was issued the next day, containing Gaines' requisition and Fulton's proclamation.

While this "extra" was on the press, a letter arrived from the northern part of the state, with payment for 500 unsigned copies of it in handbill form. The letter censured Absalom Fowler for his record on the subject of the basis of legislative apportionment. Since the *Gazette* had taken an editorial stand against agitation of this question, the letter could not be admitted to the regular edition. It was put in type and added to the last part of the press run of the "extra," and was circulated a day later than the first part of the same publication. This was an important last-minute gubernatorial campaign document on Conway's side. Because the second version of the "extra" was not circulated in all parts of the state, the *Advocate* took the *Gazette* to task for a back-stabbing "secret *Gazette* extra," taking for granted that the letter had been written in the *Gazette* office.[15]

The Democrats won the state election in August, with Conway and Yell polling handsome majorities and a predominance of Democrats elected to the legislature. Conway received 4,855 votes to Fowler's 3,024, and 28 were cast for Alexander S. Walker, a last minute independent candidate. Yell's victory was a landslide, with 6,094 votes to Cummins' 2,379.[16]

Shortly before the legislature convened, the *Advocate* began publication of a series of letters signed "Casca," written by Albert Pike, which made penetrating analyses of some of the Democratic leaders. He spoke of a "Triumvirate" that ruled the party, and represented Ashley as the most power-

13. *Times,* July 25, 1836.
14. *Gazette,* July 26, 1836.
15. *Ibid.,* July 26, Aug. 2, 1836; *Advocate,* July 29, 1836.
16. D. A. Stokes, Jr., "The First State Elections in Arkansas," *Arkansas Historical Quarterly,* XX (1961), 140.

ARKANSAS ADMITTED!!!

After our paper of this day had gone to press, we received, by express from Helena, the gratifying intelligence that Arkansas is now a SOVEREIGN STATE OF THE AMERICAN UNION! The bill passed its third reading in the House on the evening of the 13th June, as will be seen from the following extract from the National Intelligencer, of the 14th inst. :

Yesterday, the bills which have passed the Senate, for the admission of the States of Michigan and Arkansas into the Union, being again the special order of the day in the House of Representatives, occupied the whole day.. The former of these bills was ordered to a third reading about four o'clock; and the latter about six o'clock. After which, the bills were read a third time and passed. Both bills having passed without amendment, have no need of being returned to the Senate, and, being known to be acceptable to the President, they may be already considered as laws of the land.

Steam-boat Register.

June 23.—Arrived Steamer, Arkansaw, Hal-derman. 8 days from New-Orleans.

Announcement of the admission of Arkansas to the union, in the *Gazette* of June 28, 1836.

ful, Sevier as the tool of Ashley but able to control the legislature, and the third member (Woodruff) left unidentified. Ashley was portrayed as vastly superior to all others of his clique in intellect, ability, power, and wealth, but uninhibited by integrity either in business or in politics. Sevier was represented as weak and shallow, bound by a feeling of obligation to accept the dictation of the other two, devoid of statesmanship, yet retaining a spark of decency that must cause him to be disgusted with some of the things he was called upon to do, and which could eventually cause him to cast aside his masters though it would surely ruin him. Yell was represented as an incompetent, unlettered opportunist who had parlayed himself into Congress by devious means. Fulton was represented as so hopelessly naive as to attach himself to this clique, but too honorable to be associated with it permanently.

Sevier's election to the Senate was a foregone conclusion, and "Casca" considered his control of the legislature absolute, enabling him to choose the other senator. "Casca" was confident that Sevier wanted a colleague who would be subservient to him, which Fulton was not likely to be. Thanks to the "indiscreet volubility" of one of Sevier's friends, "Casca" heard a few days before the Senate election that Ashley wanted to go to the Senate, and that Fulton probably would be doublecrossed to allow Ashley's election. "Casca" appealed to Sevier to block this.

Another pseudonymous correspondent simultaneously revealed that the grand jury of Pulaski, White, and Saline counties had charged Ashley with subornation of perjury, and that Ashley had filed a $10,000 libel suit against the grand jury, which then had offered to prove his guilt in three instances. Ashley had demurred to the form of the pleas without touching upon the issue at stake, and when the demurrer was overruled, he had quietly allowed the judgment to go against him.[17] "Casca" later referred to this incident as Ashley's reason for seeking a high public office from the legislature, as an endorsement of his character, and said he had first wanted the Senate seat, and when that was blocked, he had sought election to the Supreme Court, but had finally had to settle for a position as a director of the State Bank.[18]

"Casca's" information probably was basically correct, but it seems likely that it was obsolete by the time it came to him, and that the matter had been decided much earlier than he supposed. Ashley might have discussed it with Sevier as early as 1834, and public office could have been the inducement Sevier offered in exchange for Ashley's support of statehood. If so, Ashley had to step aside when it became necessary to persuade Fulton not to veto the bill for the Constitutional Convention. It could have happened at the small gathering Woodruff later called the first state convention, which must have been prior to the appearance in the *Gazette* of communications endorsing Conway for governor and Yell for Congress early in May, while Sevier was still at Washington. If so, it lends weight to the statement made eight years later by an anonymous Whig writer at Batesville, probably C. F. M. Noland, that it was Wharton Rector who had thwarted Ashley's early ambition for a political career. "Casca" may have been correct in supposing that only Sevier could influence the legislature to that extent, but Rector's influence in the small circle of the party's leadership may have been great enough to hold Ashley in check. The Batesville writer said, "Wharton Rector cherished a deadly hatred for Ashley, which neither time nor circumstance could abate; and Wharton Rector was a man who concealed nothing. . . . Ashley was afraid of him." [19]

By the time the legislature elected the senators on September 19, it was cut and dried. Only Sevier, Fulton, and H. F. Walworth were nominated. With eight legislators absent, Sevier received all of the 60 votes cast, and Fulton received 56, losing only four to Walworth.[20] The election of judges of the Supreme Court on October 1 was similarly uneventful, with only six men nominated, and Townsend Dickinson, Daniel Ringo, and Thomas J. Lacy elected on the first ballot. Ashley was not among those nominated.[21]

It now became apparent that Woodruff wanted to be state treasurer, and had spent the campaign period lining up his support in the legislature. He

17. *Advocate,* Aug. 26, Sept. 2, 16, 1836.
18. *Ibid.,* Dec. 9, 1836.
19. *Gazette,* Nov. 27, 1844.
20. *Ibid.,* Sept. 20, 1836; *Advocate,* Sept. 23, 1836.
21. *Gazette,* Oct. 4, 1836; *Advocate,* Oct. 7, 1836.

also wanted to get the public printing for the *Gazette* office, which made it necessary for him to ask for two public offices on the same day. Some of his friends in the legislature vowed they would not vote for him for both offices, a pledge they did not keep.[22]

There was a minority movement early in the session to give the printing to the lowest bidder, but it was scotched when a bill was passed making the public printer a regular state officer to be elected for two years, with compensation fixed by law.[23] Woodruff's friends overlooked the constitutional provision that no holder or collector of public monies would be eligible to hold any office of trust or profit, which made Woodruff ineligible for one of the offices he sought.

The election was held in joint session on October 1. Woodruff was elected state treasurer on the first ballot, defeating David Fulton by a vote of 40 to 30. The election of the public printer followed immediately. Woodruff and Pew of the *Gazette,* John H. Reed of the *Times,* and William E. Woodruff were nominated. Presumably the separate nomination of Woodruff indicated an undercurrent of sentiment against Pew, and it placed Woodruff in the awkward position of running against himself. This election also was decided on the first ballot, with 50 votes for Woodruff and Pew, 14 for Reed, and 5 for Woodruff alone.[24]

Pike promptly raised the question of Woodruff's eligibility to hold both offices, but nothing came of it. He also complained because the legislators had agreed to establish the prices for the public printing before electing the printer, but this had bogged down in committees and red tape.[25]

The State Bank and the Real Estate Bank were created by this legislature, each having a parent bank at Little Rock and branch banks in other towns. The officers of the State Bank were elected in a joint session on November 2. The Whigs charged that Chester Ashley manipulated the whole election, using reprehensible tactics, but nobody had a harder time getting elected than Ashley. Of the twelve directors of the principal bank, all elected on the first ballot, only Ashley barely got the 32 votes necessary for election. The next day, it was discovered that the clerk had made a mistake in entering the votes, and Ashley lacked one vote having enough. This made a second election for this position necessary. Ashley and William Cummins tied on the first ballot, but Ashley rounded up four more votes and won on the second ballot.[26]

In later presidential campaigns, the candidates for electors took the lead and canvassed the state thoroughly, but in 1836 they were not selected in time to take an active part in the campaign except in the vicinity of their homes. On September 17, five days before the legislature convened, the

22. *Advocate,* Oct. 14, 1836.
23. *Ibid.,* Sept. 16, Oct. 7, 1836.
24. *Gazette,* Oct. 4, 1836.
25. *Advocate,* Oct. 7, 14, 1836.
26. *Ibid.,* Nov. 4, 11, 1836; Jan. 20, 1837.

A typical group of marriage and
obituary notices, from the *Gazette*
of June 21, 1836.

Democrats then at Little Rock met and chose three candidates. Only one was
present to accept the nomination, and a change was made soon afterwards
when it was learned that one nominee had volunteered for military service.[27]

The election was held in November, just as the legislature was adjourn-
ing, and most of the legislators voted at Little Rock, as did a military company from Lawrence County that was en route to its rendezvous point at
Washington. The Whigs said Little Rock people gave a majority for White,
but the votes of the legislators and soldiers made the Little Rock vote 220
for Van Buren and 175 for White.[28] The official tabulation for the state
gave 2,557 votes to Van Buren and 1,363 to White.[29] Van Buren was the
national winner, and his running mate, Johnson, was elected vice president
by the Senate on February 8, not having received a sufficient majority in the
popular election.[30]

Several improvements were made in the *Gazette* late in 1836. On June 14,
the editor announced that arrangements were being made to enlarge the paper, or at least to increase its reading matter. This decision was made in response to a steady increase in subscriptions at the rate of 12 to 15 a week,
amounting to 400 since the adjournment of the 1835 legislature. New type
was ordered late in the summer from the New York foundries of Conner &

27. *Gazette,* Sept. 20, 27, Oct. 4, 1836.
28. *Advocate,* Nov. 11, 1836.
29. *Gazette,* Dec. 20, 1836.
30. *Ibid.,* Feb. 28, 1837.

Cooke and E. White & Hagar.[31] A year later, 500 pounds of old type metal was offered for sale to gin builders.[32]

A new nameplate on October 11, 1836 reflected Woodruff's pride in Arkansas's statehood, for the paper's title was now *Arkansas State Gazette.* It was in Old English, similar to the one discarded, but it used the full width of the page, whereas the old one had been only four columns wide. The statement of proprietorship was on a separate line directly under the nameplate, "By William E. Woodruff and Thomas J. Pew, (Printers to the State, and Publishers of the Laws of the United States), at Four Dollars per annum, or Three Dollars in Advance." This left the dateline immediately below uncluttered, having only the place, date, and volume number.

The enlargement did not come until the beginning of Volume XVIII on December 20, 1836. There still were only four pages of six columns each, but the columns were now 15 picas wide, and the sheet was 24 inches long and 17¾ inches wide, which gave the promised two or three additional columns of reading matter. This left an unusually wide margin, but instead of dividing the extra white space between the two margins, the one on the inside edge was about half an inch, while the outside margin was a whopping 1¾ inches. The main body type was still about 5½ points.

The first local market report, listing prices currently paid at Little Rock for farm produce, appeared on November 22, 1836. This was done to encourage farmers to bring their produce to the Little Rock market, since many erroneously supposed they could get better prices elsewhere. The *Advocate* began a similar feature about the same time.

Pew began the practice of law in August of 1836.[33] Perhaps his most sensational case was his unsuccessful defense in association with two other lawyers of William F. McKee for the murder of Beauford P. Scott, tried on April 13, 1837.[34] Pew also was an occasional speaker before the Pulaski Lyceum in the winter of 1837.[35]

A series of original poems in the *Gazette* in the spring and summer of 1837 gave insight into Pew's social life, representing him as a "ladies' man" who was given to flirtations with a multitude of women, particularly a certain widow and a maiden who had a keen sense of rivalry.[36] The poetry column was not often in its usual place on page four while Pew was editor, and finally was discontinued altogether, but poetry was frequently used in the news columns.

The departure of Allen M. Scott soon after his quarrel with Pew [37] did not leave the editor without antagonists. His name was a natural for unflatter-

31. *Ibid.,* Aug. 2, Sept. 13, 1836.
32. *Ibid.,* Sept. 5, 1837.
33. *Ibid.,* Sept. 6, 1836.
34. *Ibid.,* Apr. 27, 1837.
35. *Ibid.,* Jan. 31, Feb. 7, 1837.
36. *Ibid.,* Apr. 25, May 2, 9, Aug. 15, 1837.
37. *Ibid.,* Aug. 16, 1836.

ing puns, and his enemies made the most of it. Scott claimed that Postmaster General Amos Kendall had habitually called him "Pewk-e" at one period.[38] Albert Pike's *Advocate* argued with Pew on every conceivable point, but rarely if ever dignified him by mentioning his name, beginning article after article with "The *Gazette* says . . . ." Some 30-odd years later, Pike spelled the name "Piew" in a reminiscent article,[39] revealing that the bitterness had survived the man. Charles P. Bertrand delivered the subtle insult of "thomas j. pew."[40] George D. Prentice of the *Louisville Journal,* the adversary who most annoyed Pew, consistently spelled his name "Pooh."[41]

Long before Pew came to Arkansas, he incurred Prentice's enduring enmity by reprinting in the *Kentucky Gazette* an anonymous letter signed "Tincartiana," which Prentice said was a "scurrilous and filthy" article against him.[42] Prentice never forgave Pew for this, and never ceased to try to get even. He was the master of barbed ridicule, and made his comments sufficiently brief and pointed to be reprinted by Whig papers all over the country.

Pew ignored Prentice's articles charging him with representing "several states and territories" at the Baltimore convention without the proper authority, until other papers began to base articles on Prentice's information. Pew then made a satisfactory explanation on July 26, 1836 of how he happened to hold the proxy for Illinois, in addition to representing his own state of Kentucky.

Pew found no sting in political accusations, but it was a different story when his personal integrity and dignity were assailed. The *Times* copied an article by Prentice that accused Pew of sneaking away from Alexandria, Louisiana and leaving his security to pay his debt of $1,000, and later pleading minority to evade payment. Pew declared he would compel Prentice to retract this story,[43] but he was never able to wring a contradiction from him. Pew sent Prentice a detailed explanation of the incident, clearing up the half truths of the *Journal's* version, and demanded that Prentice publish it. Prentice declined to do justice to Pew unless Pew would withdraw his endorsement of the "Tincartiana" article or say he had no agency in its republication. Pew refused, and Prentice continued to taunt him with his failure to get a retraction.[44] Pew steadfastly ignored these articles, although the local competitors reprinted them. Finally on August 22, 1837, he threatened to silence Prentice by recalling "Tincartiana" to tell of two episodes in Prentice's career in which he had been chastised for unfounded abuse of others. Prentice retaliated with a paragraph stating that Pew often had been kicked at Versailles, Kentucky. Pew denied having had any such difficulties in that town,

38. *Times,* July 11, 1836.
39. *Gazette,* Nov. 20, 1869.
40. *Advocate,* Aug. 12, 1836.
41. *Ibid.,* June 24, 1836; *Gazette,* Oct. 4, 1836.
42. *Gazette,* Nov. 29, 1836.
43. *Ibid.,* Sept. 6, 1836.
44. *Ibid.,* Oct. 4, Nov. 29, 1836; *Advocate,* Mar. 3, 10, 24, 1837.

although he had once knocked down a friend of Prentice's named Woolley for attempting to shoot him.[45]

Among the petty annoyances of this period was a wag at Pine Bluff who mailed advertisements to the *Gazette* for places of business that did not exist, signing the names of Pine Bluff residents. The unsuspecting editor published them, only to learn that they were hoaxes for which he would receive no payment. The first was for a hotel called Front Street House, and was published in August of 1837 over the signature of Redditt and Pullen. The second was the announcement of the opening of the Pine Bluff Academy by Dr. and Mrs. Samuel H. Webb, published in December of 1837. The indignant Dr. Webb offered a reward for the pranksters, and a month later the editor said he had identified the culprits and threatened public exposure and possible lawsuits unless they sent $7 for each of the ads.[46] One suspects that this threat was sheer bravado, and that neither Woodruff nor Pew had any idea who had taken advantage of them, for they became extremely wary of all communications from Pine Bluff unless they knew the senders. An ad for the Pine Bluff Female Academy, conducted by newcomers from Kentucky, was delayed one week in February of 1838, until the advertisers convinced the editor that their ad was genuine, probably by paying for it in advance. An unsigned obituary postmarked at Pine Bluff was denied publication in May of 1838 for the same reason.[47]

The timing of Arkansas's admission to the union in the middle of a congressional term of office threw her first election off schedule. The people elected Archibald Yell to the House in August of 1836, and the legislature elected Ambrose H. Sevier and William Savin Fulton to the Senate in October. These elections were for the remainder of the current term, but they were held about the time when elections for the ensuing term should have been held. Fulton drew the long term in the Senate, which would not expire until March 3, 1841, but Sevier's and Yell's offices would be vacant when their terms ended on March 3, 1837, since no election had been held for the next term.

The situation was unique in the history of the American Congress, and nobody was sure what was the proper procedure for filling the vacancies, since a full term of office was involved. If only the usual two sessions of Congress had been held, it would have made no practical difference, but when an extra session was called for September, it became important for the vacancies to be filled.

Governor Conway already had taken care of the difficulty in the Senate by appointing Sevier,[48] and the legislature made his position secure by re-electing him at its next session. On June 5, the governor called a special

45. *Gazette,* Nov. 21, 1837.
46. *Ibid.,* Dec. 19, 1837; Jan. 17, 1838.
47. *Ibid.,* Feb. 7, 14, May 23, 1838.
48. *Extra Session [216]. In the Senate of the United States. Report of Mr. Grundy of the Committee on the Judiciary, to whom were referred the credentials of the honorable Ambrose H. Sevier,* March 7, 1837; *Journals of the Special Session of the Gen-*

James Sevier Conway.

election to fill the vacancy in the House.[49] It was held on July 3, and the Whigs were unable to put a candidate in the race on such short notice. Yell was re-elected without opposition, except for a Whig candidate that appeared on election day and was known only locally.[50]

The situation had not been made clear to the people, and many supposed that this election was only for the extra session, and that the regular election would be held in October for the full term ahead. Actually, the extra session was a part of the next full term, and the *Gazette* argued that Yell had just been elected to that term and did not have to run again. Yell ended the dispute when he decided to submit his candidacy to the people again, even though it was legally unnecessary.[51] The Whig candidate, John Ringgold, entered the race too late to pose a serious threat, and Yell defeated him by a large margin.[52]

eral Assembly of the State of Arkansas, which was begun and held at the capitol, in the City of Little Rock on Monday, the sixth day of November, one thousand eight hundred and thirty-seven, and ended on Monday, the fifth day of March, one thousand eight hundred and thirty-eight, in accordance with a proclamation of the Governor, dated July 18, 1837 [Little Rock, 1838], 177–178.

49. *Gazette*, June 6, 1837.
50. *Ibid.*, July 4, 18, Aug. 15, 1837.
51. *Ibid.*, Aug. 22, Sept. 5, 1837.
52. *Ibid.*, Sept. 19, Oct. 3, 1837.

THOMAS C. SCARBOROUGH, *Sheriff*
of the parish of Ouachita, La.
Monroe, Parish of Ouachita. Sept. 8, 1838. 41–3w

SPLENDID CIRCUS.

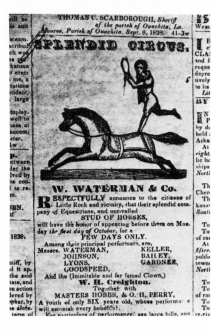

W. WATERMAN & Co.

RESPECTFULLY announce to the citizens of
Little Rock and vicinity, that their splendid company of Equestrians, and unrivalled
STUD OF HORSES,
will have the honor of appearing before them on Monday *the first day of October,* for a
FEW DAYS ONLY.
Among their principal performers, are,
Messrs. WATERMAN,   KELLER,
    JOHNSON,   BAILEY,
    LYONS,   GARDNER,
    GOODSPEED,
And the (inimitable and far famed Clown,)
W. H. Creighton.
    Together with
MASTERS HOBBS, & O. H. PERRY,
A youth of only SIX years old, whose performances
will astonish every beholder.

kansas has been withheld from sale, on account of the location of a donation claim thereon; And whereas, said location has been removed therefrom:—
Now, therefore, be it known, that I shall be prepared to receive applications for the same, at my office in the town of Washington, on the eighteenth day of August next, at ten o'clock of that day.
GEORGE CONWAY, *Register.*
REGISTER'S OFFICE,
Washington, Ark's, July 9, 1838. 31–2w

TOWN OF D'CANTILLON.

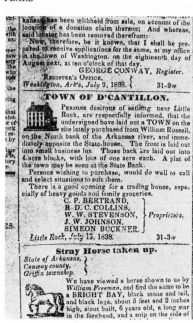

PERSONS desirous of settling near Little
Rock, are respectfully informed, that the undersigned have laid out a TOWN on the site lately purchased from William Russell, on the North bank of the Arkansas river, and immediately opposite the State-house. The front is laid out into small business lots. Those back are laid out into 4 acre blocks, with lots of one acre each. A plat of the town may be seen at the State Bank.
Persons wishing to purchase, would do well to call and select situations to suit them.
There is a good opening for a trading house, especially of heavy goods and family groceries.
C. P. BERTRAND,
R. D. C. COLLINS,
W. W. STEVENSON,   } *Proprietors.*
J. W. JOHNSON,
SIMEON BUCKNER.
Little Rock, July 13, 1838.   31–3w

Stray Horse taken up.

State of Arkansas, }
Conway county, }
Griffin township. }

We have viewed a horse shown to us by *William Freeman,* and find the same to be a BRIGHT BAY, black mane and tail, and black legs, about 5 feet and 2 inches high, stout built, 6 years old, a long star in the forehead, and a snip on the side of

SALE OF LOTS
IN THE
TOWN OF SEARCY.

ON the three first days of May next, (it being the three first days of the Circuit Court of White county), there will be offered at Public Auction, on the premises, a number of choice Lots in the above Town; which is situate at the White Sulphur Springs, in White county, about two miles south of Little Red river, and about fifty-five miles north-east of Little Rock.
Terms of Sale.—Six and twelve months' credit, purchasers giving bond with approved security.
JAMES WALKER, }
JOHN HOWERTON, } *Proprietors.*
JOHN COOK. }
April 11, 1837.   18–2w

TOWN LOTS FOR SALE.

THE Commissioners of the county of Johnson, will expose to sale, on Monday, the 5th day of June next, to the highest bidders, on twelve months' credit, (with bond and approved security); fifty of the lots in the town of CLARKSVILLE; sale to commence on Monday, the 5th day of June next, and continue from day to day, until fifty lots be sold.
The town of Clarksville is situated in the well watered valley of the Big Spadre Creek, about three miles from Spadre Bluffs, surrounded by an immense quantity of fertile barren lands; a soil well adapted to the cultivation of corn, cotton, wheat, and oats; and is now settling rapidly with emigrants from the different States of the Union; and, no doubt, in a few years, will be densely populated. It is chosen for the permanent Seat of Justice of the county of Johnson.
Persons wishing to own town property, will do well to examine for themselves, and attend the days of sale, where due attendance will be given by us.
JOSEPH STEWART,
ABRAHAM LASETER, } *Commissioners*
JOHN THOMAS, } *of the county*
L. N CLARKE, } *of Johnson.*

NEW STAGES.

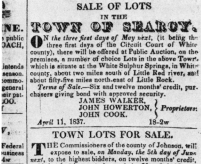

THE subscriber begs leave to inform the citizens of Little Rock, and the public generally, that he has just purchased and brought to this place, for their accommodation, a NEW and SUBSTANTIAL NINE PASSENGER COACH, with four superior Horses; and, also, one handsome and easy running CARRIAGE, for four persons, of superior workmanship and to be drawn by two substantial Horses, purchased expressly for the purpose, and which are equal to any that could be had in Louisville, Ky.
He will run his Coaches to any point in the Territory where the roads will permit, when desired. It is his intention, when the Arkansas is at a low stage, to run at least one of his coaches between the *Hot Springs by way of Little Rock,* to the mouth of Arkansas and back.
He has good drivers, and every accommodation possible will be extended to passengers while performing trips.
☞ Those wishing to hire in my absence, will apply to Maj. Peay.
WILLIAM BARKELOO.
May 23, 1836.   24–tf

Prices had been mounting steadily for a year or two, and Woodruff decided it was time to raise advertising rates to cover increasing production costs, leaving subscription rates as they were. A simultaneous increase by the leading competitor was desirable, and Woodruff and Pike had never permitted their political differences to block business agreements of mutual advantage. They drew up a new scale of rates, based largely on those charged by Nashville and Huntsville printers, and the two papers announced identical advertising rates and policies, the *Gazette* on March 14 and the *Advocate* on March 17, 1837.

The 1819 base price of $1 per square for the first insertion and 50 cents for subsequent insertions was still in effect, but the square was now figured at ten lines instead of the original 15. Accounts running between $50 and $100 in one year were entitled to a 25 per cent discount, and those of $100 or more to a 50 per cent discount. Discounts did not apply to overdue accounts or to legal advertising required by law to be published. There was an additional advantage to the advertiser in signing a contract at the time of insertion, for a definite term of the ad. Contracts by the year, renewable at pleasure, now cost $20 a year for ten lines or less, $30 for 30 lines, and $50 for 60 lines, with the same discount arrangement. Standing ads could be had for $6 for the first square for three months, and $4 for each additional square; $10 for six months, and $8 for each additional square; and $15 for 12 months, and $12 for each additional square.

Still hoping to discourage the airing of personal altercations, and feeling that the printer was entitled to extra pay for whatever unpleasantness might come to him because of such things, double rates were charged for this kind of ad. Only seven weeks earlier, Pew had tried to shame into silence two men from Clark and Pike counties, John Speer and Jacob Brindley, who were carrying on a protracted personal dispute in the *Gazette's* advertising columns.[53]

By this time, the *Gazette's* list of agents had grown to 66, covering all sections of the state, with one in Missouri, one in Louisiana, and three in the Indian country west of Arkansas.[54]

The long rumored consolidation of the *Gazette's* local rivals was accomplished on April 27, 1837, and the paper that came of it was called the *Arkansas Times and Advocate*. Pike was the senior editor and Reed the junior editor and business manager, but Pike soon withdrew to devote all his time to his law practice, and Reed's next partner was John J. Budd. In the summer of 1838, the *Times and Advocate* was sold to two newcomers, Eli Colby and Michael J. Steck.[55]

Pew was deprived of Woodruff's guiding hand most of the time in the spring and summer of 1837, while Woodruff was learning that "the labor and perplexity incident to the life of an Editor" could also plague a state trea-

53. *Ibid.*, Jan. 24, 1837.
54. *Ibid.*, Feb. 28, 1837.
55. *Ibid.*, May 2, 1837; May 9, July 4, 1838; *Times and Advocate,* July 11, 1838.

surer. He was elected on October 1, 1836, and two days later the legislature fixed his salary at $700 a year. Woodruff took for granted that he would receive the additional compensation of ten per cent commission on the redemption of lands sold for taxes, which had been allowed the treasurer since 1827. Indeed, it was these fees that made the job attractive. After posting the required $300,000 bond, he began his duties on October 27.

Two days later, the legislature made it his duty to receive from the Secretary of the Treasury the share of the surplus federal revenue allotted to Arkansas, a total of $286,757.49, to be paid in three installments. The money was to be the major part of the State Bank's initial operating capital, but Woodruff had the responsibility of its safety until the bank was ready to receive it.

Each installment was paid with two drafts on two federal deposit banks at Natchez. When the first installment arrived in February, Woodruff cashed one draft for specie in the hands of the receiver of public monies at the Little Rock land office. The second installment arrived on April 1, and Woodruff left for Natchez two weeks later to cash the three drafts. A widespread financial crisis was developing, and banks all over the country were failing. A disastrous run on Mississippi and Louisiana banks had just begun, and the two Natchez banks declined to cash his large drafts immediately, in specie. However they made arrangements for him to get specie for one of the drafts in New Orleans, and promised to send him specie for the other two by July 1.

He returned to Little Rock from New Orleans on May 8. The news came three or four days later that the Natchez banks had suspended specie payment, and Woodruff took the next steamboat to Natchez. The cashier was obliged to withdraw his promise to deliver the remaining $100,000 in specie by the specified date, so Woodruff had the two drafts protested and headed for Washington. The secretary of the treasury canceled the old drafts and issued new ones on banks at Cincinnati, Louisville, and New Orleans. Woodruff stopped at Cincinnati and Louisville on his way home and collected the drafts in the notes of those two banks, which were almost equal in value to specie at Little Rock.

Returning home on July 4, he found that the State Bank had opened in his absence, and he deposited all the state's money that was in his hands. He also found that the third installment of the surplus revenue had arrived, drawn as before on the two Natchez banks. The State Bank's officers declined to receive the three uncollected drafts, so Woodruff sent an agent to Natchez and New Orleans to cash them. The agent collected part of the New Orleans draft in notes issued by that bank and part in a credit with authority to draw, but the Natchez banks would pay only in their own notes, so the agent returned with these two drafts still not collected, following Woodruff's instructions. Soon afterwards, the State Bank undertook their collection, and accepted payment in the notes of the Natchez banks.[56]

---

56. *Gazette,* May 9, July 11, 18, 1837; Nov. 30, 1842; Report of William E. Woodruff, State Treasurer, to Governor James S. Conway, Nov. 1, 1837, in *Journals of the Special Session 1837–1838,* 196–200, and Abstract C following, unpaged.

Thus the full amount of the surplus revenue was collected, and the state had more of it in specie than could be reasonably expected. Nevertheless, the Whigs were highly critical of the manner in which Woodruff handled this business. In his absence, they circulated rumors that he had added $10,000 to his personal fortune by making loans to planters at ten per cent interest from the $90,000 in specie that was in his custody before the State Bank opened,[57] and also that he had permitted Chester Ashley to use some of the money to clear his accounts with the land offices.[58] The Whig press in Arkansas, Kentucky, and Ohio accused him of negligence and wailed that Arkansas probably would lose her share of the surplus revenue because of her treasurer's ineptitude.[59]

Woodruff had made three trips to Natchez, one of which was extended to New Orleans and one to Washington, and his agent had made a trip to New Orleans with a stop at Natchez. Woodruff had paid the expenses of these trips and the incidental expenses of the collection of the drafts, since no appropriation had been made to cover them. Naturally, he expected to be reimbursed, and when he submitted his accounts for settlement at the end of his first year in office, he charged the state with $595 for collection and transportation of the surplus revenue, including traveling expenses. He also retained $2,100.43 as his commission on redemptions of lands sold for taxes.[60]

Auditor Elias N. Conway referred these matters to the legislature, which met in special session soon afterwards. He had no authority to rule on the travel expenses, and he was not sure the treasurer was entitled to a commission on the entire amount received for land redemptions, since $290.86 of the $21,004.15 received was interest on script.[61]

This special session convened on November 6, 1837, took a six-weeks recess between December 19 and February 5, and adjourned on March 5, 1838. It is best remembered for the murder on the floor of the House of J. J. Anthony, a representative from Randolph County, by Speaker John Wilson on December 5, but Woodruff had good cause to remember it for many other reasons, for he was almost constantly under fire.

The *Gazette* office had been slow to deliver the pamphlet edition of the acts of the 1836 legislature, partly because the legislature had swamped the office with other printing orders, and partly because the paper supply ran out and the extra paper ordered was delayed more than three months by ice in the Ohio River. All the acts of general interest were published promptly in the *Gazette,* but the legislature's 500 copies of the pamphlet edition of the acts were not delivered until April of 1837, and the copies offered for sale

57. *Gazette,* June 6, 1837.
58. *Ibid.,* June 27, 1837.
59. *Ibid.,* July 11, 18, 1837.
60. *Ibid.,* Nov. 30, 1842.
61. Report of Elias N. Conway, State Auditor, in *Journals of the Special Session 1837–1838,* 193.

to the public were not ready until August.[62] It was said that Woodruff and Pew refused to print the 200 pamphlet copies of the journals ordered because the price fixed by law was too low,[63] but some adjustment must have been made, for they were issued in 1837 under the imprint of Woodruff and Pew.[64]

When the special session convened, the Whigs were out to get Woodruff, under the leadership of his old enemy, Absalom Fowler of the House, and the Democrats were none too friendly. The House's committee on ways and means investigated the execution of the public printing by Woodruff and Pew, and decided to allow the account. But on the committee's recommendation, the House voted 41 to 2 to declare the office of public printer vacant because Woodruff and Pew had not entered into the required bond.[65] Apparently this resolution died in the Senate.

The main business of this session was the consideration, point by point, of the voluminous codification of the state's laws, authorized by an act of the legislature in 1836. It had been prepared by Samuel Calhoun Roane, president of the Senate, and William McK. Ball, a member of the Senate, under appointments by the governor with the advice and consent of the Senate. This code of laws would replace the old digest by Steele and McCampbell, which was highly defective. Instead of merely making a systematic arrangement of the laws passed by the Arkansas General Assembly, Roane and Ball drew on the laws of other states as well, so that action by the legislature was necessary to put the laws in force in Arkansas. Some of the Whigs, especially Fowler and C. F. M. Noland, had strong and well founded objections to the content of the new code of laws.

Since the code of laws would represent the basic laws of the new state, it was an extremely important work. The legislators were anxious to make it available to the public as soon as possible, and they wanted the book to compare favorably with similar works of other states.

The session had barely begun when Woodruff and Pew were asked how soon an edition of 2,000 copies, estimated to contain 600 royal octavo pages each, could be printed and bound and ready for delivery in a style equal to the *Revised Statues of New-York,* a copy of which was presented for their inspection. They replied that they could not match the elegance of this book immediately or at the prices allowed by law for public printing. They would have to buy a new press, new type and other materials, and a supply of fine paper, possibly at Cincinnati but probably at New York. This would delay the beginning of the work about three months, and the book could not be ready for the bindery sooner than six months after that. Having no experience in binding, they could only guess how long that part of the work would take, but they supposed 50 copies could be bound within a week after the printing

62. *Gazette,* Feb. 14, 28, Apr. 4, 11, Aug. 22, 1837.

63. *Advocate,* Apr. 27, 1837.

64. Albert H. Allen (ed.), *Arkansas Imprints 1819–1876* (New York: Published for The Bibliographical Society of America, by R. R. Bowker Company, 1947), 13.

65. *Journals of the Special Session 1837–1838,* 308–309, 315–316.

was finished, and the work completed at the rate of 30 to 50 copies a week. The expense to the printers would be about $4,000, and the equipment they would have to purchase would be of little or no use to them for other jobs for several years.[66]

The proprietors of the *Times and Advocate* surprised Woodruff and Pew by saying they would do the printing the *Gazette* office could not do, for the same prices currently paid for public printing, and would charge their usual rates for types of work where the prices were not fixed by law.[67] Actually, the *Times and Advocate* office was no better equipped to publish such a book than the *Gazette* office was, and it was decided to have the printing done elsewhere. On the last day of the session, March 5, Albert Pike was elected to superintend the printing of the revised statutes.[68] He took the manuscript to Boston to be printed, using the North Carolina statutes as a pattern. Realizing that there would be a delay in the publication of the book, the legislature instructed the governor to put these laws into operation by proclamation whenever the book could be made generally available. As it turned out, Pike took so many liberties in editing the manuscript that he was later obliged to ask the legislature to declare the laws in force *as printed*.[69]

Meanwhile, the laws passed at the special session that were not intended for inclusion in the revised code, being of a local or private nature, were published in pamphlet form at the *Gazette* office.[70]

Some of the legislators were dissatisfied with the new code of laws, and Fowler led an effort in the special session to block an appropriation compensating Roane and Ball for their work, but a bill passed both houses allowing them $3,600. The next day, a large majority of the House refused to pass a Senate bill designating the appropriation as specific, which would authorize immediate payment. Fowler pushed an amendment through the House that withheld payment to Roane and Ball until their accounts were approved in detail by the legislature, and instructed the auditor and treasurer to draw no warrant or pay no sum to them for such services by virtue of any appropriation made by the General Assembly.[71] This was on the last day before the six-weeks recess, and learning that the Senate would not act on this amendment before the recess, the House passed a resolution that said the same thing as the amendment. A resolution does not have the force of law, but it was intended that this expression of the House's sentiment would keep Roane and Ball from collecting the money during the recess under authority of the appropriation law, and the clerk of the House was ordered to deliver a copy of the resolution to the auditor and one to the treasurer.

66. *Ibid.,* 17–18.
67. *Ibid.,* 36, 37.
68. *Ibid.,* 170–171, 471–472.
69. *Ibid.,* 307; *Revised Statutes of the State of Arkansas, Adopted at the October Session of the General Assembly of Said State, A.D. 1837. . . .* Revised by William McK. Ball and Sam. C. Roane; notes and index by Albert Pike (Boston: Weeks, Jordan and Company, Publishers, 1838), iii–x.
70. *Gazette,* May 30, June 6, 1838.
71. *Journals of the Special Session, 1837–1838,* 355, 356–357.

Roane and Ball hastened to the auditor's office when the Senate adjourned on December 19, but the clerk of the House arrived soon afterwards and told them about the House resolution, and Conway refused to issue the warrant. The next morning, Roane and Ball sent the auditor a note, informing him that their appropriation was specific, neglecting to mention that the House had not concurred in the Senate bill making it specific. The auditor drew the warrant and the treasurer subsequently paid them the $3,600. Woodruff had not received a copy of the House resolution and said he had not been informed of it, though Fowler contended that he knew about it.[72]

When the legislature reassembled in February, Fowler called for an investigation of the conduct of Roane, Ball, Woodruff, and Conway. Fowler was chairman of the investigating committee, and reported on February 17 that Roane and Ball had drawn the money "in the absence of any law authorizing the same." The friends of the people involved managed to delay consideration of the report until the afternoon of February 19, when it was adopted by a vote of 26 to 20. The next day, the House passed a resolution stating that it had not intended "to impute improper motives to the Auditor, Treasurer, or Clerk of this House," but on Fowler's motion, a part of it was stricken out that would have made these people free of censure for granting and paying the warrant.[73]

Fowler's report made Woodruff spluttering mad. He had not been called before the committee to explain his part in the matter, as the others involved had been, and he printed a circular reproducing the report, with the parts he found objectionable set in small capitals, and a letter telling his side of the story. He intended to distribute it among the members of the House, and sent it in an envelope addressed to the clerk of the House, instructing the messenger to deliver it to the doorkeeper. But Speaker Grandison D. Royston ordered the doorkeeper not to allow any communication from Woodruff to be brought into the House, so the doorkeeper did not give the envelope to the clerk. Royston refused to spread Woodruff's letter on the journals because he said it was "not in language respectful to the House." Woodruff published the entire circular in the next issue of the *Gazette*. He defended himself well, saying the appropriations act passed by both houses and approved by the governor gave Roane and Ball the right to draw the money, and he could not legally refuse to pay it on their demand simply because a House resolution to the contrary had been passed.[74]

Even before this appeared in the *Gazette,* Fowler tried to get the House to adopt a resolution directing Roane and Ball to return the $3,600 to the state treasury, and asking the governor to remove them from office and appoint two others. When this failed, another resolution was introduced that simply

72. *Ibid.,* 390–392; *Gazette,* Feb. 21, 1838.
73. *Journals of the Special Session, 1837–1838,* 366–367, 390–392, 397–398, 405–406.
74. *Gazette,* Feb. 28, 1838.

required them to return the money, and instructed the auditor to sue them for it if they failed to return it. This resolution was also tabled.[75]

The legislature decided that the 1836 act fixing the treasurer's salary at $700 a year had repealed the 1827 act allowing him the additional compensation of ten per cent commission on land redemptions, and that the $2,-100.43 Woodruff had retained on this account properly belonged in the state treasury. Moreover, the legislature did not propose to pay for the trips he had made to New Orleans and Washington, believing he had tried to protect the Van Buren banks at Natchez, and said he was entitled to "nothing more than what would appear just and reasonable for the expenses that might be incurred in cashing the drafts at Natchez." Only $300.25 of his $595 expense account was allowed, and he was ordered to return the remaining $294.75. The person who had performed the duties of treasurer in his absence had been paid $134.25 of Woodruff's salary, so the return of the rejected part of his expense account would make his total salary for a year's work only $271.[76]

A committee was appointed to enter an order on the treasurer's books requiring Woodruff to pay into the treasury the $2,395.18 representing the commission and the disallowed travel expenses, and the committee reported on March 2 that he had declared he would not relinquish the money "until the judicial tribunals of the State shall decide that he is not legally entitled to the same." The next day, Fowler introduced legislation requiring Woodruff to pay five per cent per month interest on the retained money, and an additional five per cent on all other state funds that remained in his hands longer than ten days, but this was modified to require him to pay interest only on the money he had retained, at the rate of 25 per cent per annum. Also on March 3, Fowler attempted to begin impeachment proceedings against Woodruff for "malversation and misconduct in office," citing only his refusal to return the $2,395.18, but the House rejected this proposal by a vote of 29 to 12.[77]

The subscription book for the capital stock of the Real Estate Bank for central Arkansas was kept open for 40 days in the *Gazette's* counting room, beginning March 6, 1837, and the bonds to be sold to provide capital for both the State and Real Estate Banks were printed at the *Gazette* office. As the State Bank opened for business in the summer of 1837, the *Gazette's* job department turned out blank checks and sold them in quires or bound books.[78]

Woodruff was one of seven elected as directors of the principal Real Estate Bank, located at Little Rock, in October of 1837. He was one of three

75. *Journals of the Special Session, 1837–1838,* 425–426, 440–441.
76. *Ibid.,* 86–88, 400–402; *Gazette,* Feb. 28, 1838; Nov. 30, 1842.
77. *Journals of the Special Session, 1837–1838,* 432, 454–455, 159–160, 462, 467–468; *Gazette,* Nov. 30, 1842.
78. *Gazette,* Mar. 7, Aug. 8, 1837.

chosen by the directors to represent the principal bank on the Central Board that would direct the entire Real Estate Bank system.[79]

When the commissioners returned from the East coast in the spring of 1838 and reported they had been unable to sell the bank bonds, the *Times and Advocate* blamed Woodruff in his capacity as state treasurer for "a material error" in the printing, making the bonds payable in 29 years instead of 30 years. The *Gazette* replied that the copy had been prepared according to instructions from the bank officials, and that Woodruff had had nothing to do with the bonds except to countersign them. The Eastern capitalists had refused to buy them because they were letter-press printed instead of engraved, and lacked the usual detachable coupons for semi-annual interest payments. The commissioners had plates engraved and brought them back to Little Rock to be printed at the *Gazette* office, signed by the governor, and countersigned by the treasurer, the old printed bonds being canceled by the governor.[80]

On May 16, 1838, without public explanation, Pew relinquished his interest in the *Gazette* to Woodruff, who again became sole proprietor and editor. There is no indication that Pew continued his newspaper career. Probably he practiced law, at least part of the time at New Orleans, his former home. He was at Little Rock much of the time during the last four months of 1839,[81] and came again to Little Rock from New Orleans in 1842 for a brief visit.[82] His fortunes descended, and in 1848 he was described as "a loafer on the levee at New Orleans." [83] For all his ability, he was a man of unsteady habits, and his talents were completely dissipated. When at last alcoholism had robbed him of the last vestige of his pride, he appeared one day at the Louisville *Journal* office to beg a dollar from his greatest enemy, George D. Prentice. Prentice was so overcome by compassion for the now ragged and repulsive Pew that he gave him $25, and pleaded with him to reform.[84] Pew died unmourned several years before the Civil War.[85]

Offensively personal letters to the editor were again a problem in the summer of 1838. After the trial at Benton of John Wilson for the murder of J. J. Anthony, a writer who used the pseudonym "Saline" submitted a letter complaining of the manner in which the trial was conducted. Because it was highly personal, Woodruff refused to publish it in the *Gazette,* and the writer paid for publication of 200 copies as a *Gazette* "extra," to be distributed with the paper of June 20 to subscribers in Pulaski and Saline counties. One of the lawyers severely criticized was the venomous, eccentric John Taylor, who demanded that Woodruff make an immediate disavowal of concurrence in

79. *Ibid.,* Oct. 17, 1837.
80. *Ibid.,* June 13, 1838.
81. *Ibid.,* Dec. 18, 1839.
82. *Ibid.,* Feb. 2, 1842.
83. *Ibid.,* June 22, 1848.
84. Junius Henri Browne, "George D. Prentice," *Harper's New Monthly Magazine,* Vol. L (1874–1875), 200.
85. *Gazette,* Nov. 20, 1869.

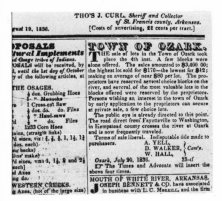

the remarks about him. Woodruff meekly complied, saying his only partici-pation in the matter was the mechanical work of printing.[86]

Woodruff made up his mind to reject all highly personal communica-tions,[87] but reluctantly yielded when his old friend, William Strong, fell out with William D. Ferguson and wanted to discuss the matter in the *Gazette*. Possibly because the two men lived some distance from Little Rock and the mails were slow, it took from July 25 until October 3 to get three of these communications in print.

The congressional election absorbed much of Woodruff's attention in the summer and early fall of 1838. Early in June, the *Gazette* announced that candidacies would be announced free for paid-up subscribers, but others would have to pay $3 in advance.

It had been known for some time that Yell would not seek re-election, and Democrats present for the special session had chosen as their candidate Judge Edward Cross of Hempstead County, brother-in-law of Chester Ash-ley's wife. The *Gazette* announced his candidacy on June 13, and the Whigs put William Cummins in the race. To the delight of the Whigs and the dis-may of the Democratic leaders, Judge Lewis B. Tully of Carroll County also insisted upon running as a Democrat. Woodruff added his name to the list of candidates at the head of the editorial columns on June 27, but made it clear that the *Gazette* would support Cross and that Tully should withdraw, in justice to himself and his party. Obviously the Whigs hoped Tully would split the Democratic vote and insure Cummins' victory, and Woodruff sur-mised that they also hoped to capture the office of judge that Tully would be expected to resign as the campaign progressed.

Tully stayed in the race about two months, and withdrew in a manner that suggests strong persuasion from party leaders. His name disappeared from the *Gazette's* list of candidates on August 22 without editorial comment, and

86. *Ibid.,* July 4, 1838.
87. *Ibid.,* July 11, Aug. 1, 1838.

the next week Woodruff said the last mail had brought news from friends in the northern counties that Tully had withdrawn because of ill health and an honest desire to preserve party harmony. Tully himself never made a public statement concerning his withdrawal.

At the election on October 1, Cross defeated Cummins by a vote of 6,722 to 4,156. The *Gazette* said the vote in its home county of Pulaski, 337 for Cummins and 196 for Cross, was not an indication of the relative local strength of the two parties, but might even be considered a Democratic victory, since Cummins had a much wider acquaintance here than Cross. There still was confusion about the term of office, and the *Gazette* explained that Yell's term would not end until March 4, 1839, when Cross would take office.[88]

The Democrats again claimed a large majority of the members of the legislature, elected at the same time. Even so, this legislature showed marked hostility towards Woodruff. The session began on November 5, and three days later the House ordered Woodruff to make a detailed report of the public printing ordered since 1836, the time it was supposed to have taken to complete it and the time it had actually taken, how and when the journals had been distributed, and the payment authorized. Such a report could not be quickly prepared, and its Whig sponsor, Dr. Lorenzo Gibson, soon became impatient. On the fifth day after it was ordered, the House resolved on Gibson's motion to cite Woodruff for contempt of the House if his report had not been submitted by the following morning, but did not carry out its threat. The report was presented to the House on November 17, the ninth day after it was requested. It was tediously long and detailed, and as the clerk droned through it, some of the members were thoroughly bored.

Woodruff's staff was not at its full strength, and preparation of the long report had consumed much of his own time. The legislature, particularly the House, had called for a great mass of extra printing early in the session, including reports of various state officials and bills under consideration. Woodruff failed to deliver these printing orders within a reasonable time, and the legislators were irked because it delayed their work. The House gave him a gentle nudge on the day his report was read. It did not bring the desired results, and two days later, Nimrod Menefee tried to get the House to demand delivery by the next morning or require an explanation from Woodruff. The other members refused to pass this resolution, probably because they did not care to be treated to another long report. Later the same day, the House rejected a sarcastic suggestion to recess until the next November, to give the public printer time to do his work. The Senate showed less irritation, but authorized having its printing done elsewhere if Woodruff could not deliver it within a specified time.[89]

88. *Ibid.,* Oct. 3, Nov. 14, 21, 1838.
89. *Journals of the Second Session of the General Assembly of the State of Arkansas, which was begun and held at the Capitol, in the City of Little Rock, on Monday, the fifth day of November, one thousand eight hundred and thirty-eight, and ended on*

THOMAS JEFFERSON PEW   159

This was the attitude of the legislature when bids were solicited for the public printing for the next two years. Woodruff declined to submit a bid on November 17, saying he did not have enough printers to do the work. But the *Gazette's* foreman, Edward Cole, subsequently turned in a bid and was elected on November 20, by a vote of 48 to 20 over the proprietors of the *Times and Advocate*. The next day, Woodruff explained to the public that he had not been a candidate because he intended to retire soon from the printing business.[90]

Woodruff also had had all he wanted of the unprofitable office of state treasurer, and was not a candidate for re-election. His successor, John Hutt, was elected at the same time as the public printer. The salary was increased, the duties were decreased, the official bond was cut in half, and part of the commission for land redemptions was restored.

Discovering that Woodruff had not returned the $2,395.18 he had retained, the legislature passed an act near the end of the session requiring the prosecuting attorney of the Fifth Judicial Circuit to bring suit against him on his official bond to recover the money, with damages.[91] This was the beginning of protracted litigation that cost Woodruff and the state much more than the amount involved, to say nothing of work and worry. The case was before the Arkansas Supreme Court at least four times between 1839 and 1847,[92] and the United States Supreme Court ruled on it in the spring of 1851,[93] but Woodruff finally had to pay the claim of the state against him, with interest and costs.[94] The state Supreme Court declared the law requiring him to pay 25 per cent per annum interest unconstitutional in 1841, and several times Woodruff unsuccessfully tried to end the litigation by appealing to the legislature for relief.[95] After he had paid the claim, he tried again in March of 1852 to get the legislature to do justice to him,[96] but again he failed.

While Woodruff wasted his time in the service of the state, his other business interests continued to expand, and had to be entrusted to others. The ferry had a new horse boat in the summer of 1836,[97] but the partnership of Woodruff and Mills was dissolved on September 9, 1837, and Woodruff became sole owner. Mills remained in charge of the ferry for several

---

Monday, the seventeenth day of December, one thousand eight hundred and thirty-eight [Little Rock, 1839], 173, 187, 198, 199, 202, 204, 37.

90. *Ibid.*, 30–31, 39, 206; *Gazette*, Nov. 21, 1838.

91. *1838 Journals*, 79; *Gazette*, Nov. 30, 1842.

92. Auditor, for use of the State, v. Woodruff and others, July Term 1839, 2 *Ark.* 73; Wm. E. Woodruff et al. v. the State, January Term 1841, 3 *Ark.* 285; Woodruff et al. v. the State, January Term Adjourned to April 1846, 7 *Ark.* 334; Woodruff v. Attorney General Pro Tem, July Term 1847, 8 *Ark.* 236.

93. *Gazette*, Apr. 18, 1851.

94. *Ibid.*, Mar. 5, 1852.

95. *Ibid.*, Nov. 30, 1842.

96. *Ibid.*, Mar. 5, 1852.

97. *Ibid.*, July 26, 1836.

months,[98] and then moved to Jefferson County. Possibly its management was then assumed by Woodruff's brother, Nathaniel, who had moved here in the fall of 1836 and established a blacksmith shop at the ferry landing on the north side of the river.[99] He also moved to Jefferson County in the early 1840's.

During the first week of August, 1838, a small steamboat called the Little Rock, built for Woodruff that spring at Cincinnati, replaced the horse boat. Its design and equipment far exceeded the needs of a ferry boat, and it soon began making trips to the mouth of the river to bring up supplies.[100] Undoubtedly Woodruff had this in mind from the beginning, for he had suggested two years earlier that the people of Little Rock should own a small steamboat that could bring them supplies during the low water seasons when large boats could not navigate the Arkansas as far up as Little Rock.[101] Soon the steamboat Little Rock was regularly in the trade, and the next fall it was put into the Ouachita River trade, as the property of Woodruff and Simeon Buckner. Buckner was its sole owner by the spring of 1840, when it sank in the Boeuf River.[102]

Edward Cole, who had been the *Gazette's* foreman since about 1834,[103] handled much of the business of Woodruff's land agency during his long absence on state business in 1837, and established himself as an independent land agent. Woodruff announced on July 17, 1838 that he had turned over his agency's correspondence to Cole, although Cole's agency did not supplant Woodruff's.[104]

Cole was ambitious and capable, and when Woodruff made up his mind to get out of the newspaper business altogether, his foreman decided to buy the *Gazette.* He had everything it took except money, and Woodruff made him such attractive terms that he could not afford to let the opportunity pass. The deal was made between November 17 and 20, 1838, and on December 12 as the nineteenth volume ended, the announcement was made that Cole would be the editor and sole proprietor of the *Gazette,* beginning with the next issue.

98. *Ibid.,* Sept. 12, 1837.
99. *Ibid.,* Nov. 15, 1836.
100. *Ibid.,* July 4, Aug. 8, Oct. 17, Nov. 21, 28, 1838.
101. *Ibid.,* Oct. 11, 1836.
102. *Ibid.,* Apr. 17, Oct. 2, 1839; May 6, 1840.
103. *Ibid.,* Dec. 12, 1838.
104. *Ibid.,* July 18, 1838.

8

EDWARD COLE

1838-1840 NOSTALGIA WAS TEMPERED with relief as William E. Woodruff bade farewell to the paper he had founded. He had seen Arkansas change from a sparsely populated wilderness to a flourishing new state, and he noted with pride that the *Gazette* had enjoyed a parallel prosperity. "I DETERMINED TO SUCCEED in my undertaking," he said. "I persevered under the most unfavorable and discouraging circumstances— and I have succeeded, far, very far beyond the most sanguine expectations I had formed at the outset."

Proof of his success was found in the *Gazette's* subscription list, now in excess of 1,800, more than three times the 500 subscribers of 1829. He attributed the increase in patronage to the introduction of competition, but the rapid influx of new settlers also had some bearing on it.

Now, at the end of the nineteenth volume, and with a total of 1,417 weekly issues behind him, Woodruff said the *Gazette* had "afforded me the means of retiring, while yet in the prime of life, to employments better suited to my taste and disposition." He could not put the business affairs of the *Gazette* behind him immediately, however, for its patrons still owed him more than $30,000, in individual sums less than $100.[1] Ten months passed before he had most of his bills prepared and in the hands of agents for collection,[2] and many were never collected.

Edward Cole took over as proprietor and editor at the beginning of Volume XX, on December 19, 1838, pledging to continue the *Gazette's* support of the Democratic party. Only two political issues excited sufficiently strong feelings to be mentioned in his salutatory editorial, and he saw them as closely related. One was the Northern movement for abolition of Negro slavery, which until recently had been considered the project of a few fanatics, but which now had to be recognized as a serious threat to the South. Cole

1. *Gazette,* Dec. 12, 1838.
2. *Ibid.,* Oct. 9, 23, 1839.

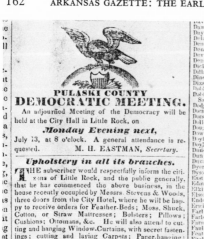

PULASKI COUNTY DEMOCRATIC MEETING.

An adjourned Meeting of the Democracy will be held at the City Hall in Little Rock, on

Monday Evening next,

July 13, at 8 o'clock. A general attendance is requested.   M. H. EASTMAN, *Secretary.*

Upholstery in all its branches.

THE subscriber would respectfully inform the citizens of Little Rock, and the public generally, that he has commenced the above business, in the house recently occupied by Messrs. Stevens & Woods, three doors from the City Hotel, where he will be happy to receive orders for Feather-Beds; Moss, Shuck, Cotton, or Straw Mattresses; Bolsters; Pillows; Cushions; Ottomans, &c. He will also attend to cutting and hanging Window-Curtains, with secret fastenings; cutting and laying Carpets; Paper-hanging; Drapery, &c.

All orders (from the country or in the city,) will be punctually attended to, and neatly and quickly executed. "Small favors thankfully received, and larger ones in proportion."   J. L. HANCOCK.

Little Rock, July 1st, 1840.   30–3w

JUST received, and for sale at the Gazette office, "A new Map of the State of Arkansas, constructed principally from the United States surveys, exhibiting counties, townships, and sections, by H. S. Tanner, 1839."—Price, handsomely mounted on rollers, and varnished, $3; neatly done up in morocco, $1 50.

JOHN MILLER, of Independence Co.
JOHN McCLELLAND, of Washington Co.
SAMUEL M. RUTHERFORD, of Saline Co.

PULASKI COUNTY DEMOCRATIC TICKET.

For Representatives,
THOMAS THORN,   ROBERT W. JOHNSON,
SAMUEL H. HEMPSTEAD.

"I must go into the Presidential chair the inflexible and uncompromising opponent of every attempt to abolish slavery in the District of Columbia, against the wishes of the slave-holding States, and also with a determination equally decided, to resist the slightest interference with it in the States where it exists."
MARTIN VAN BUREN.

"Should I be asked if there is no way by which the General Government can aid the cause of emancipation, I answer, that it has long been an object near my heart to see the whole of surplus revenue appropriated to that object."
WILLIAM HENRY HARRISON.

☞ MONEY. ☜

☞ All persons indebted for subscription to the Gazette, advertising, job-work, &c., are requested to remit the amount they owe us, either by mail, through our Agents, or any ready means which may offer.— Those living in and near Little Rock, would do us a favor by calling at the office. We cannot carry on the war without the sinews of war, and the money must come. We hope our friends will not neglect us at the present juncture. Owing to our duties, we have but little time to attend to money matters, yet we cannot get along without it. They will see the necessity of the case.

☞ Agents are requested to be prompt in remitting all funds which may be paid them on our account.

---

stand all attacks of the weather; they may also be washed without injuring the cloth or colors in the slightest degree.

Rooms and Halls painted in rich Morocco, or in Landscapes in oil or distemper as best may suit.

Military or Masonic Banners, also Fire Screens painted from any pattern or Engraving.

Marbling, &c. of all kinds executed with neatness and despatch.

All Orders, whether in town or country, will be punctually attended to, and neatly executed, on the shortest notice, and the most reasonable terms.

Little Rock, Aug. 19, 1839.   36–tf

SALOON.

THE subscribers respectfully inform their friends, and the public generally, that they have rented the Saloon, (which has been newly fitted up) and are now prepared to supply their customers with the best Wines and Liquors that can be purchased in the Northern markets. They hope by strict attention to business, to merit a liberal share of patronage.

PETER JOHNSON & CO.

Little Rock, Aug. 21, 1839.

N. B. A Lunch will be prepared every day at 11 o'clock.   36–4w

VALUABLE COTTON LAND AT AUCTION.

State of Arkansas, }
County of Chicot. }

BY virtue of an order of the Probate Court of Chicot county, at the July term thereof, A. D. 1839,

---

for nothing, I am willing he shall now stay on.

Respectfully,   E. M. OWEN.

Benton, Ark. Sept. 26, 1840.

MARRIED,

In Hempstead county, on the 24 Sept., by R. L. Phillips, Esq., Ca t. *Chambers Etter,* one of the editors of the Washington *Telegraph,* to Miss *Judah C. Blevins.*

[The Telegraph must be prospering beyond all other papers in the country. This is the first marriage of an editor we have heard of for a twelvemonth.]

DIED,

Of bilious inflammatory fever, on the 31st of August, at the house of Rev. C. Byington, near Eagletown, Choctaw Nation, Mrs. *Nancy Woodbury Barnes,* a highly useful member of the Choctaw Mission.

At the same place, of bilious fever, on the 10th of September, *Edward H. Byington,* son of Rev. Mr. Byington, aged eleven years.

MACKEREL

OF the latest and best quality, Nova Scotia cured, for family use, and warranted good, on retail, 3 doors east of the City Baths, on Elm-street. Also, sundries of domestic GROCERIES, by

JAMES KELLEY.

Little Rock, Sept. 26, 1840.   42*3w

promised that the *Gazette* would advocate "the surest and most prompt means of stopping any encroachments which may be attempted by the favorers of this fanaticism—whatever means the exigency may require." The other was the establishment of a national bank, which he opposed largely because it would tend to consolidate the union, destroying the independence of the states and giving the free states the balance of power, thus resulting in the destruction of the South and its institution of slavery.

Cole had been born within a stone's throw of the famous Brooklyn Heights, in the western part of Brooklyn, New York. Like Woodruff, he had learned the printer's trade in an apprenticeship of seven years in the office of the *Long-Island Star*.[3] He lacked editorial experience, but he had been the *Gazette's* foreman for nearly five years, and had conducted his land agency for more than a year.

With his purchase of the *Gazette,* Cole plunged recklessly into debt, and this ultimately proved to be his ruin. The sale included all the equipment belonging to the printing office—the subscription list, advertising custom, and good will of the *Arkansas State Gazette,* two printing presses (presumably the old Ramage and the iron Franklin press bought in 1834), one standing press (a device used to clamp pamphlets or pads while the spines were being glued, the simplest type of binding), all the type, stands, racks, chases, galleys, composing sticks, and other printing materials, and all the office furniture. The price was $5,000, to be paid in five installments of $1,000 each, with interest of six per cent per annum, for which Cole executed five notes to Woodruff. No part of the purchase price had to be paid immediately, since the first note was not due for one year.[4]

The *Gazette* office was still in Woodruff's home, and undoubtedly neither Woodruff nor Cole wanted it to remain there. On December 1, Cole purchased from Major Jacob Brown a piece of ground that was less than the equivalent of one city lot. It had a frontage of 40 feet on the south side of Markham Street in the block immediately east of Main Street, and a depth of 130 feet running along the alley next to Peay's and Pope's hotel. The lots in this block front on Main and Scott streets, and in order to get Markham Street frontage, it was necessary for Cole to buy the east or rear 40 feet of lots 1, 2, and 3 in Block 2, excepting the 20 by 40 feet in the southeast corner of lot 3 at the rear of the tract purchased.

This was probably the best business location in town, but even so, the purchase price of $4,000 was high for the times, and the eight per cent interest brought the total price to $5,460. Cole gave Brown three notes for the principal, one for $1,000 payable in three years, another for the same amount payable in four years, and another for $2,000 payable in five years. He also executed five other notes to cover the accruing interest, payable every year on December 1, beginning in 1839. The first three of these were for $320, the fourth for $240, and the fifth for $260. Woodruff signed all eight notes as

3. *Ibid.,* May 29, July 31, 1839; May 11, 1855.
4. Pulaski County Deed Book K, 352; M, 144.

Cole's security, and Brown gave Cole a bond for title, pledging to make him a deed when the entire purchase price had been paid. These notes were made payable at the Real Estate Bank.[5]

To save Woodruff from possible loss as his security on these notes, and to provide security for his notes to Woodruff for the purchase of the *Gazette,* Cole mortgaged the land to Woodruff on December 13, 1838.[6] Some time in 1839, Cole made arrangements for a new *Gazette* office to be built on this property, thus contracting additional heavy indebtedness he could never discharge.

Cole was a bachelor,[7] and probably would have boarded in a hotel or private residence if he had not had to provide living quarters for his unmarried employees and apprentices. During the period before the new building was ready for occupancy, he established a home in a house rented from Thomas Thorn, built on two lots on the corner of Mulberry (now Third) and Scott streets.[8] In July, 1839, Cole was appointed temporary adjutant of the Pulaski County regiment of Arkansas Militia by his landlord, who was the commanding colonel.[9]

Thorn was a brick mason who had come to Little Rock to work on the state house. He did some of the brick work on the new *Gazette* building,[10] but John Robins, a brick mason who had recently moved to Little Rock from Pennsylvania, was the principal contractor.[11] Brick masons of this period also did plastering. Others known to have worked on the building were William Morison and C. L. Sullivan, painters and glaziers, and Darwin Lindsley, a carpenter.[12]

The *Gazette* office was moved into the new building during the week preceding April 22, 1840. The main building was a three-story brick, 40 feet wide and 60 feet deep, built flush with the property lines on the north, west, and east sides. The ground floor was divided into two large rooms, each having a cellar underneath, and separated by a staircase leading to the upper floors. The *Gazette's* counting room, Cole's land agency, and his book and stationery store occupied the east room, next to the alley. The west room and its cellar were rented to other businesses. The rooms in the second and third stories and garret served as living quarters for Cole, his bachelor employees, and his slaves, and some may have been rented out as sleeping rooms.

At the rear of this building was a two-story brick building or wing. The printing office occupied the entire ground floor, and the second story was

5. Deed Book K, 348.
6. *Ibid.,* 352.
7. *Gazette,* Nov. 27, 1839.
8. *Ibid.,* June 19, 1839; Apr. 22, 1840.
9. *Ibid.,* July 24, 1839.
10. Thorn and Robins v. Woodruff and Rutherford, as Administrator, Jan. Term 1843, *5 Ark. 55.*
11. *Gazette,* Nov. 8, 1843.
12. Brown v. Morison and Sullivan, July Term 1843, *5 Ark.* 217; *Gazette,* Nov. 24, 1841.

The south side of Markham Street,
looking east from Main Street, about 1864.
The three-story building nearest the camera
was the *Gazette* office, 1840-1845.

used as a drying room and storage room. The basement was used as a kitchen
and for other domestic work. A stable and other outbuildings were at the
rear, and there was a fence that separated the property from its neighbor on
the south side.[13]

The new building would have at least partial fire protection, for Little
Rock had at last acquired a fire engine and a volunteer fire company. The
engine arrived in September of 1839. It had no hooks and ladders, and the
company of volunteer firemen lost interest after the first few drills, and was
not prepared to cope with the next big fire. This was on April 26, 1840, only
a few days after the *Gazette* moved into its new building. It destroyed all
the buildings on the west half of the block fronting on Markham between
Main and Scott, directly across Markham Street from the *Gazette*.[14]

The credit system was firmly entrenched in the newspaper business, although it had ruined many a struggling newspaper. The *Gazette,* along with
most other papers, had always preferred advance payment for both subscriptions and advertising, and had encouraged it with liberal discounts, but

13. *Gazette,* Aug. 5, 1840; Sept. 21, 1875; William E. Woodruff as agent for Jacob
Brown's heirs to Q. A. and A. J. Gilkey, Jan. 1, 1858, and to Leonard M. Filkins, Jan. 1,
1860, Ms. lease in William E. Woodruff Papers, Arkansas History Commission; William
E. Woodruff to George H. Burnett, Oct. 3, 1840, Ms. lease in L. C. Gulley Collection,
Arkansas History Commission.

14. *Gazette,* Aug. 28, Sept. 18, 1839; Apr. 29, 1840.

could not require it without a serious loss of business. The same problem existed in most other businesses, and there was little any individual could do to fight a system so well established. A few American publishers had successfully adopted the system used in England, where publishers had solved the problem of subscription collections by selling their papers to street vendors,[15] but it was not practical in this country except in densely populated areas.

The currency situation was the greatest stumbling block. Only paper money could be transmitted by mail with reasonable safety, and $5 bills were the smallest denomination in general circulation. Many merchants and some municipal corporations issued "change tickets," by which customers could be given change for purchases of less than $5, redeemable for cash in lots of $5. This was fairly satisfactory in the town where they were issued and the people had current knowledge of the solvency of the underwriters, but in other towns people did not like to accept them.

The *Gazette* charged only $3 for subscriptions paid in advance, and $4 at the end of the year. Either way, the subscriber was due change from a $5 bill. If he paid through a *Gazette* agent, he could receive change in some form or make up the difference in postage, since most *Gazette* agents were postmasters. If he paid by mail, he was likely to be reluctant to send more money than he owed. Cole did not offer *Gazette* change tickets, but suggested that his subscribers send $5 to pay for the past year and one-third of the next.[16]

Cole's business office sent bills for advertising to the agents within a week or two after the first insertion, and for subscriptions at the end of the year, and depended on local advertisers and subscribers to come to the office to pay. Aggressive agents had pretty good records of collections, and were able to get advance payment in many cases, but far too many accounts were delinquent for several years.

A movement among newspaper proprietors to switch to the cash system, requiring advance payment without exception for both subscriptions and advertising, had been gathering momentum for several years, but no practical means of overcoming the obstacles had been found. Cole frequently noted the progress of the movement in 1839, but could not bring himself to risk disaster by adopting a strict cash system for the *Gazette*. In July, the decision of Mississippi publishers to move to the cash system caused Cole to debate its merits and demerits. A month later, with proprietors of Eastern dailies contemplating it, he seemed to be giving serious consideration to adopting it if his customers and fellow publishers were receptive to the idea. In September, a convention of Tennessee printers was proposed to consider a mass change, and about the same time one lone Arkansas publisher adopted it without waiting for the support of his rivals. This was J. M. Martin, whose previous failure at Helena may have had something to do with his insistence upon advance payment when he started the Napoleon *Journal*.[17]

15. *Ibid.*, Aug. 21, 1839.
16. *Ibid.*, Dec. 11, 1839.
17. *Ibid.*, July 24, Aug. 21, Sept. 11, 1839.

Cole ended his first year with a considerable amount of red ink on his books, and began giving local advertisers an occasional free editorial plug, a thing the *Gazette* had done previously only for traveling theatrical companies. It worked so well that it became a general rule, and eventually was a great nuisance, since advertisers came to expect free editorial notices as a bonus.

Not all the *Gazette's* debts could be deferred. The employees expected to paid every Saturday, and Cole did not always have the cash on hand to pay them. One Saturday in March of 1840, he had to go out and make enough collections to meet the payroll, and was able to raise only $75. He said he did not intend to do it again, and notified all those indebted to him that they must bring the money to him.[18]

Vice President Richard Mentor Johnson arrived at Little Rock on the evening of October 29, 1839, just as the *Gazette* of the next day was going to press. Cole stopped the press to insert a brief announcement of the arrival of the distinguished visitor, who had come on personal business with the State Bank. It probably was no coincidence that the names of Martin Van Buren for president, Richard M. Johnson for vice president, and Archibald Yell for governor appeared at the head of the editorial columns in this issue, although the election was almost a year away.

18. *Ibid.,* Mar. 4, 1840.

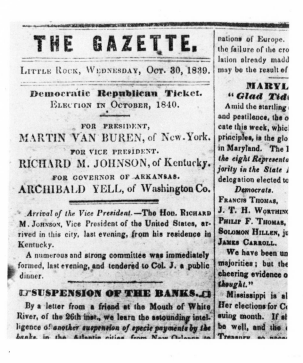

It was generally understood that Van Buren and Johnson would seek second terms, and that the Democratic party would hold no national convention to make nominations, so Cole did not risk bolting the party with this premature endorsement of Van Buren. There might be some question in Johnson's case, for there was a movement under way to nominate Govenor James K. Polk of Tennessee for vice president in his place. Cole would have no part of this, and gave his support wholeheartedly to Johnson.

Thus the *Gazette* opened its 1840 campaign far ahead of the usual time, as did most other newspapers. The gubernatorial campaign was quiet, since there was no contest. The incumbent, James Sevier Conway, had wanted to resign his office since the fall of 1838 because of ill health. His friends had persuaded him to complete his term, but it was certain that he would not seek re-election. Archibald Yell became the Democratic candidate and was unopposed.[19] Edward Cross was again the Democratic candidate for Congress.

Cole had little taste for newspaper wars—a novelty among Arkansas editors—but his attempt to remain aloof from the controversies of the day was not altogether successful. In his first issue, he declined to publish the report of a trial at Fayetteville sent by a friend, with the explanation that "crime begets crime," and that many heinous crimes never would have been committed if the criminals had not read about similar crimes in newspapers. He consistently refused to print communications of a personal nature, and took great pride in the fact that his paper did not contribute to hard feelings in this way.

A paid advertisement in the *Gazette* of August 28, 1839 resulted in a libel suit brought by John Finn against James H. Obaugh, but the *Gazette* was not made a party to it. The advertisement warned the public against trusting Finn, a plasterer who Obaugh said had left Little Rock without paying his numerous debts, swindling him out of $55 paid him for work promised but left undone. The jury in the lower court found Obaugh guilty and assessed damages at $200 and costs. Obaugh appealed to the Supreme Court, and the judgment was reversed because the lower court had refused to discharge the jury on the plaintiff's motion.[20]

The many farmers who subscribed to the *Gazette* were pleased to find the agricultural articles they had enjoyed during Woodruff's more peaceful years back among the miscellaneous selections on the back page. The poetry column, discontinued by Pew and not revived during the few months of Woodruff's management after Pew left, was occasionally back in its place on page four, but was not a regular weekly feature.

Eli Colby was a newcomer to Little Rock when he became editor and part owner of the *Times and Advocate* in the summer of 1838, and while he was a staunch Whig, he did not seem to be inclined to bear the brunt of ancient animosities harbored by local party leaders. Pressed to reveal the identity of

19. *Ibid.,* Sept. 18, 1839.
20. Obaugh v. Finn, Jan. Term 1842, 4 *Ark.* 110.

the writer of a venomous letter in his columns, he gave William Cummins' name. It was said that this caused Cummins a great deal of trouble, and that he narrowly escaped personal violence in retribution. Chagrined at the means he had to resort to in order to save himself, and further disenchanted by Colby's refusal to print some of the abusive communications offered, Cummins decided the party needed a more aggressive editor. His friends agreed, and a group of Little Rock Whigs quietly raised money and made arrangements to bring another newspaper to town.[21]

David Lambert, a lawyer who had previously been connected with a New York newspaper, arrived at Little Rock on April 1, and within the next two weeks hung out his shingle as a lawyer and issued a prospectus for a weekly newspaper to be called the *Arkansas Star,* to begin publication as soon as it had enough subscribers. The prospectus did not indicate that it was to be a Whig journal, or that it was to be politically aggressive, but Absalom Fowler, who busied himself writing letters to gain support for the new paper, assured his friends that it would be "Whig to the Core," and emphatically not in the conservative class.[22]

While the groundwork for the *Star* was being laid, a spirited controversy was in progress concerning the management of the Real Estate Bank, involving the annual election of directors for the principal bank that had been held by the stockholders in January. Under Cummins' leadership, the Whigs challenged the legal status of the directors, and in the course of the hearing, the Supreme Court insisted upon an examination of the constitutionality of the bank's charter. The case was argued by Cummins as prosecutor *pro tem,* and by Chester Ashley, one of the new directors and obviously the main target of the Whigs. Ashley was represented by the Whigs as hostile to the bank and trying to bring about the destruction of its charter, which he denied. The Supreme Court recessed before the conclusion of the case, leaving the public discussions to run wild.

Cole said newspaper discussions were improper until the court handed down its decision, but the *Times and Advocate* and the Batesville *News* commented on it freely, and Cole finally allowed space in the *Gazette* for Ashley to defend himself. Cummins responded with a series of letters, published under a pseudonym in the *Times and Advocate,* and included Cole in his abusive remarks. Cole mildly rebuked the editor of the *Times and Advocate* for admitting such letters to his columns. Cummins then accused Cole of slander, vindictiveness, urging the unconstitutionality of the bank in the *Gazette,* being the tool of Ashley and Woodruff, and other similar charges. Cole denied all these accusations, keeping his remarks in a more or less good humored, bantering tone.[23]

21. *Gazette,* July 1, 1840.

22. *Ibid.,* Apr. 10, 17, 1839; Apr. 15, 1840; Absalom Fowler to Jesse Turner, Little Rock, June 26, 1839, Ms. inside circular prospectus of the *Arkansas Star, Arkansas Gazette* Foundation Library.

23. *Gazette,* Mar. 13, May 1, 29, June 5, 1839; The State v. Chester Ashley and others, Jan. Term 1839, 1 *Ark.* 179.

At about this point, the first issue of the *Arkansas Star* appeared, on July 25, 1839. It was printed on a large imperial sheet, and Cole said he could find no fault with it except its Whiggery, although he would have been better pleased if its editor had been a printer. "We do not like the notion of lawyers reaping the profits of a profession at which we served seven long years as an apprentice," he said, "but they will wring in, and we must admire their taste and judgment in changing their occupation." [24]

This brought defensive comments from Lambert, to the effect that printers usually lacked the mental and moral qualifications editors should have. Cole replied that lawyers could not often understand all the duties of an editor, but would learn by experience that editing a paper involved more than merely writing scurrilous political articles. [25]

Colby took up the defense of his craft, and Cole virtually retired from the argument, although he reported its progress from time to time. Colby brought out the role played by Cummins in the establishment of the *Star*, and soon the dispute blossomed into a street fight between Colby and Lambert, with guns and knives as the weapons. Cole chided them for resorting to violence, being careful to keep his remarks in a light vein, [26] and did not see fit to mention in his paper his own fight with Lambert, which must have occurred soon after this.

The real beginning of the 1840 campaign came in May, when each party selected its three candidates for presidential electors. The Whigs held a celebration at Little Rock on May 13 to kick off the campaign. In honor of their candidates, William Henry Harrison and John Tyler, "Tippecanoe and Tyler too," they raised a log cabin and a liberty pole on a vacant lot at Second and Scott, and hard cider was much in evidence. [27]

About two o'clock on the morning of June 6, 1840, Little Rock was struck by a devastating tornado, and the *Star* office was one of its casualties. The building was badly damaged, the press was broken, and the type pied. The wind also snatched the Whig flag from the liberty pole and deposited it some distance away, which the *Gazette* said was emblematical of the fate of the Harrison cause. [28] The announcement was made that the *Star* would reappear as soon as its materials could be repaired and paper procured, and that it would hereafter be published by Cornelius Stone and Samuel McCurdy. Lambert was expected to continue as editor, and he started for Louisville, Kentucky to buy paper, with money supplied by his backers. Instead he stopped at Lexington, opened a law office, and notified his backers at Little Rock that he would have nothing more to do with them. [29]

The *Star's* new editors were at least as abusive as Lambert but less tal-

24. *Gazette*, July 31, 1839.
25. *Ibid.*, Aug. 7, 1839.
26. *Ibid.*, Aug. 14, 21, 1839.
27. *Ibid.*, May 6, 13, 20, 27, July 1, 1840.
28. *Ibid.*, June 10, 1840.
29. *Ibid.*, June 17, July 1, 1840.

ented, and Cole noticed their first issue with unflattering remarks about all three, which were not softened by his usual touch of genial humor. The *Star* then alluded to Cole's fight with Lambert, giving what Cole said was a highly distorted account. Cole had whipped Lambert with a cowhide in a public place. The *Star* cited two witnesses who said Cole had crept up behind Lambert and struck him with a cowhide, and said that one had sent word to Cole that he had made the assertion that he had seen this happen, and that Cole had threatened to whip anybody who said such a thing. Cole denied every part of this statement, and said one of the *Star's* witnesses was a notorious liar and the other was "in such a position that he could not see straight." Their testimony, he said, could be refuted by any of the others present.[30]

As part of the Fourth of July political activities, the Democrats brought out the first issue of a campaign newspaper called *The Tornado*. It was a four-page paper, three columns to the page, each page measuring 9 by 11½ inches. Issued every Saturday, it was not intended to endure beyond the election, and was given no volume number, although each issue was numbered. The only copy known to be extant is Number 13, dated September 26, 1840. It had no advertising, and presumably was paid for by members of the Democratic party. Its editors and printers are not mentioned, but apparently it was produced at the *Gazette* office.

Having lost the patronage of the most influential Whigs at Little Rock, the *Times and Advocate* was compelled to reduce its size to a half sheet in August. Cole was sympathetic, and appealed to those indebted to Colby to pay their bills.[31]

Cole tired of the long, tedious political communications he received from his subscribers. On September 30, 1840, the last issue he published, he said illness among his employees made it impossible for him to publish all these letters, particularly since some were so badly written that only an experienced compositor could decipher them. Also, he did not care to impose on his other subscribers by publishing those of purely local interest.

The election for state and county officials was held on Monday, October 5, but Cole was not present to give the results. One year and ten months after he bought the *Gazette,* he gave it up and left Little Rock, never to return. William F. Pope recalled many years later that Cole, "getting into bad odor in Little Rock, was compelled to leave." [32] It seems unlikely that this is true, for nothing is found in contemporary sources to indicate that he was generally unpopular or that he was driven out of town.

However, his debts had multiplied until he could not step outside his office or even into his backshop without meeting one or more of his creditors, and there seemed to be little hope that he could ever satisfy all the claims against

30. *Ibid.,* July 15, 1840.
31. *Ibid.,* Aug. 26, 1840.
32. William F. Pope, *Early Days in Arkansas* (Little Rock: Frederick W. Allsopp, 1895), 125.

him. He may have left town rather suddenly, but he did not leave without making arrangments for others to assume his liabilities.

At first it looked as if Woodruff would have no choice but to take the *Gazette* back, and assume the part of Cole's debts for which he stood as security. An "extra" was distributed on October 2 to announce that Cole had turned the paper over to its founder again, but the next day an agreement was made with George H. Burnett that relieved Woodruff of the responsibility of the paper and allowed Cole to make an honorable exit without leaving his creditors holding the bag. Burnett had been employed as the *Gazette's* business manager since shortly after Cole bought the paper, and was fully acquainted with all details of Cole's financial predicament.

Cole had never paid any part of the purchase price for the lot he had bought from Jacob Brown, the first of the notes covering the principal not being due for another year and two months. One note for $320 interest had fallen due the previous December, and Woodruff had had to pay it. Another for the same amount would be due in another two months, and Woodruff would also have to pay it.[33]

Cole also had failed to pay Woodruff any part of the purchase price for the *Gazette,*[34] and was further indebted to him in the amount of $3,000 on a settlement of book accounts. Possibly a part of this money had been used to pay for new type he had ordered in the fall and winter of 1839 from the New York foundries of George Bruce and Company and Conner and Cook.[35] On June 13, 1840, Cole had given Woodruff his note for $3,000 to cover this debt. Moreover, Woodruff was Cole's security for a debt of $950 to the State Bank, due in October of 1840. To give Woodruff further protection against loss occasioned by these debts, Cole had executed another mortgage on the *Gazette* and its real estate on June 13, 1840. As he prepared to leave Little Rock on October 3, he signed another instrument whereby he assigned to Woodruff the bond for title to the lot occupied by the *Gazette* office. The understanding, expressed in another instrument executed the same day, was that Woodruff would rent the building and use the income to remove the encumbrances on the title to the property.[36]

Thus Cole's equitable interest in the real estate was transferred to Woodruff, and the men who had built the building could look only to Woodruff for payment. Several took the matter to court without success. Robins, Thorn, Lindsley, Morison, and Sullivan obtained judgments against Cole's estate, and all except Lindsley attempted to enforce mechanics' liens against the *Gazette* property, but the Supreme Court ruled that Woodruff's lien by virtue of his prior mortgage took precedence over all others, and that a mechanic could not acquire a lien on land unless legal title to it was vested in the person

33. *Gazette,* Nov. 8, 1843.
34. 5 *Ark.* 217.
35. *Gazette,* Oct. 9, Dec. 18, 1839.
36. Pulaski County Deed Book M, 144, 279.

who employed him.[37] Woodruff never paid any of the purchase price or any of the interest after the first two notes, and in 1846 title to the lot reverted to Jacob Brown after a commissioner's sale authorized by a decree in chancery.[38]

On May 16, 1840, Cole and Burnett in partnership had purchased for $1,400 from James Madison Liggin and wife a 200-acre tract a few miles southwest of Little Rock. They had borrowed $1,000 from Lemuel H. Goodrich and Norman Boardman, Little Rock merchants, agreeing to repay it with interest of nine per cent per annum, and had applied the borrowed money to the debt to the Liggins, the rest of which was paid by other means. As Cole settled his affairs at Little Rock, he conveyed his undivided half of this tract to Burnett on October 3, 1840, and Burnett agreed to pay Cole's part of the debt to Goodrich and Boardman and release him from all liability in the matter. The debt was still unpaid at the time of Burnett's death, and Goodrich and Boardman began foreclosure proceedings against the property early in 1844, recognizing the judgments against Cole's estate held by the men who had built the *Gazette* building.[39]

In August of 1840, Cole had borrowed $1,900 from the State Bank to pay for a slave woman and her three small children he had bought from Peter T. Crutchfield. Crutchfield and Roswell Beebe had signed his note to the bank as his securities, and Cole had in turn mortgaged the slaves to them.[40] He made no written provision for this debt when he left Little Rock, and presumably turned the slaves over to his securities and allowed them to foreclose their mortgage.

Among the debts Burnett agreed to pay were the $3,000 owed to Woodruff, an additional $433.37 since borrowed from Woodruff, the $950 note to the State Bank, an estimated $30 for real estate taxes, $963 owed to Lafflin, Stevens and Company of New Orleans for paper, $47.93 owed to Dudley and Nelson of New Orleans, the *Gazette's* postage bill of about $30, another $385.73 borrowed from Goodrich and Boardman, and the overdue salaries of the *Gazette's* employees. These included his own salary of $675, and those of three journeymen, $300 to William Peach, $196 to John W. Farley, and $75 to Francis M. Van Horne. By Cole's and Burnett's arithmetic these obligations came to a total of $7,178.03.

Cole itemized 19 other debts he owed to Little Rock people, most of whom were merchants or lawyers, and mentioned debts to several correspondents of his land agency, which he figured came to a total of $2,787.93. Burnett did not assume these debts, but agreed to apply to their payment whatever money might be left over from the collection of accounts due Cole, after the other debts were paid.[41]

37. 5 *Ark.* 55; *Gazette,* Nov. 24, 1841; Nov. 8, 1843.
38. *Gazette,* Mar. 23, 1846.
39. *Ibid.,* Feb. 28, 1844; Pulaski County Deed Book M, 91, 282.
40. Deed Book M, 238.
41. *Ibid.,* 283.

Also on October 3, Woodruff leased the *Gazette* buildings to Burnett, reserving only the west store and cellar on the ground floor of the three-story building, which was occupied by other tenants. Burnett agreed to pay $1,050 a year for the use of the property, payable quarterly on January 2, April 2, July 2, and October 2. He executed four notes for $262.50 each to cover the rent, with the interest rate set at ten per cent per annum.[42]

Thus Cole left his problems for others to untangle and departed, considerably disillusioned by his fiasco. He spent some time with a surveying party on the isthmus of Panama, and eventually returned to New York, where his brothers, Samuel and James Cole, still lived. He got a job as a printer in New York. At 3:15 on the morning of April 23, 1855, a night watchman near Pier 15 on the New York side of East River, adjoining the Wall Street ferry, heard a splash that sounded like a person falling into the water. He hurried to the spot and soon drew out the lifeless body of the 55-year-old Edward Cole.[43]

42. Woodruff to Burnett, lease, Oct. 3, 1840.
43. *Gazette,* May 11, 1855.

9

GEORGE H. BURNETT

1840-1841 "THE *Gazette's* halcyon day of peace and rest" was the founder's son's apt description of the 14 months of George H. Burnett's proprietorship.[1] This happy situation was brought about in part by Burnett's amiable disposition and his commendable conception of ethical behavior, but it must also be partially attributed to the fact that his tenure at the *Gazette* was between political campaigns, beginning near the end of an unusually tranquil campaign that had no unpleasant aftermath, and ending before the next campaign opened.

In his salutatory editorial on October 7, 1840, Burnett said all the things that had come to be typical of such essays. He had been active during the summer in the meetings of the Pulaski County Democrats, serving as secretary,[2] so his announcement that the *Gazette* would continue to support the Democratic party came as no surprise. He made the usual pledge, threadbare from constant repetition by editors who found themselves unable to keep the lofty promise, that he would exclude from his columns all discussions of the private affairs of men in public life, although he considered their public acts a fit subject for the scrutiny of the press.

The difference between Burnett and other editors who made this solemn promise was that he spoke from a sincere conviction that personal abuse in a newspaper was altogether indefensible. He had an opportunity in the eighth week of his proprietorship to prove that he could not be stampeded into an exchange of insults, even when his own reputation was at stake. Someone had attacked him through the columns of another newspaper, making remarks of a personal nature. Charitably leaving his assailant and the newspaper that published the article unidentified, and without alluding to the subject matter involved, Burnett stated his position regarding public airings of private matters. He had no intention of allowing his paper to become the

1. *Gazette,* Nov. 20, 1869.
2. *Ibid.,* July 22, 1840.

vehicle of personal slander and detraction, and he did not consider his private affairs to be of sufficient interest to the public to justify filling the *Gazette* with whatever quarrels others might have with him, and he suggested that they should use one of the many other means of communication to settle their arguments. "Every candid, reasoning man will, we are assured, approve our course," he said, "and think with us, that the conductor of a public press who indulges in coarse personalities, is indecent, ungentlemanlike, and vulgar. . . . There creeps not on earth, a more contemptible reptile than a man whose sole pleasure consists in defaming his neighbors. Such a thing cannot reflect the image of its maker, or the light of heaven." [3] And that was that, so far as he was concerned.

The election for state and county officials was held two days before Burnett's first issue, and he had only to report the returns. He was himself a successful candidate for justice of the peace,[4] and since June had held the appointive position of brigade inspector of the Second Brigade of Arkansas Militia, with the rank of major.[5]

Unofficial returns dribbled in, and not until November 11 were the official returns available. Archibald Yell received 10,554 votes for governor, and B. H. Smithson, who had offered only token opposition, received 392 votes. In the race for Congress, illness had prevented the incumbent, Edward Cross, from making a campaign. His Whig opponent, Absalom Fowler, had canvassed the state for six months, and although he received a majority of Pulaski County's votes, he lost the election by a vote of 7,876 to 5,788.[6]

The presidential election in November gave Arkansas's three electoral votes to Martin Van Buren by a vote of 6,048 to 4,663.[7] One of the three Democratic electors was Samuel M. Rutherford, whose wife, Eloise Maria Beall, was the sister of Burnett's wife, Susan W. Beall. The sisters were the daughters of Asa Beall, Sr., of Saline County, and Burnett had married Susan on June 27, 1839.[8]

By December 2, there was no doubt remaining that Arkansas had voted with the minority, and that the Whig candidates, William Henry Harrison and John Tyler, had won the election. Burnett decided not to publish the long tables of figures showing the trend of the election, and said he would wait for a complete official table of returns from other states.

Burnett was elected public printer by the legislature in December, without regular opposition.[9] He continued to get his share of the job printing, and sold patent medicines and office supplies from the *Gazette* office, but collection of the *Gazette's* overdue accounts for subscriptions and advertising seemed virtually impossible.

3. *Ibid.*, Nov. 25, 1840.
4. *Ibid.*, Oct. 7, 1840.
5. *Ibid.*, June 24, 1840.
6. *Ibid.*, Oct. 14, Nov. 11, 1840.
7. *Ibid.*, Nov. 25, Dec. 9, 1840.
8. *Ibid.*, July 3, 1839.
9. *Ibid.*, Dec. 30, 1840.

He began with the usual polite requests that his predecessors had found in-effectual, then reminded his delinquent friends that postal regulations per-mitted postmasters to frank letters containing payment for newspaper sub-scriptions.[10] On November 25, 1840, he offered to accept wood, pork, corn, and other produce at market prices in payment for subscriptions, if delivered before the next March 20.

Apparently Burnett had been sold on the cash system during the two years he had been the *Gazette's* business manager, and perhaps it was he who had urged it upon Cole. As the new volume began on December 16, he put the cash system partially in effect by withdrawing credit from out-of-state sub-scribers and from advertisers living outside Little Rock. Most of the out-of-state subscribers would owe $10 for two and a half years on June 9, a sum that could be sent by mail easily. They were billed far in advance, and noti-fied that they would be stricken from the subscription list if they had not paid by June 9. Furthermore, no new subscriptions from outside Arkansas would be accepted unless the cash was sent in advance. A new rule for figur-ing advertising rates, counting 100 words as a square, was adopted to make it easy for advertisers to send the money with their ads.

This was only the beginning. Burnett had determined to put the *Gazette* entirely on the cash system, and he served notice to that effect on January 13, 1841, hoping to get the support of other publishers, but intending to do it whether or not the other Arkansas newspapers went along with him. A week later he announced that the cash system was in effect, and that no new sub-scribers would be accepted without cash in advance, regardless of residence, and old subscribers would be dropped on June 9 unless they had paid all arrearages and paid in advance for the coming year. No advertisements would be published unless accompanied by cash, or payment assumed by "some person of known responsibility." Said Burnett, "We are aware that a strict adherence to this rule will considerably reduce our subscription list, but we are also aware that 1000 punctual paying subscribers are more profitable than 2000, of whom one-half never pay."

By the next week, Eli Colby, now the sole proprietor of the *Times and Advocate,* had joined Burnett in the cash system, and Burnett showed the people it was no idle threat by refusing to publish several advertisements that had been sent without money.[11] During the second week, Cornelius Stone and Samuel McCurdy, proprietors of the *Arkansas Star,* added their names to the list.[12] As the stack of unpublishable ads mounted, Burnett sent collectors on the road. In February, M. H. Eastman made a collection tour of Conway, Pope, and Scott counties, and at the end of March, J. O. Higbee began a collection tour of 13 counties south of the Arkansas River.[13]

It was a bold step bravely taken, but the rewards were something less

10. *Ibid.,* Oct. 21, Nov. 4, 1840.
11. *Ibid.,* Jan. 27, 1841.
12. *Ibid.,* Feb. 3, 1841.
13. *Ibid.,* Feb. 10, 17, Mar. 31, 1841.

than spectacular. Stone withdrew from the *Star* two weeks after adopting the cash system,[14] leaving McCurdy to suspend publication soon afterwards. The *Times and Advocate,* already in financial difficulty because of the rift in the Whig party, was saved by a mysterious friend from execution of a judgment against its press in September.[15] The *Gazette* fared little better, suffering a serious loss of patronage but managing to continue publication without interruption. The Napoleon *Journal,* since called the *Messenger,* the first Arkansas paper to adopt the cash system, gave up the struggle in December of 1840, about the time Burnett made the initial effort towards the cash system. Its proprietor simply disappeared, leaving his press and materials behind to be attached for debts.[16]

Subscribers could hardly be blamed for their slowness to pay in some instances, because the inefficient postal service made it impossible to guarantee regular delivery. One subscriber complained in February of 1841 that six mails had arrived without delivery of the paper, and about the same time the mail service in western Arkansas was so bad that the *Gazette* usually was four weeks old before it reached Van Buren.[17] These were not isolated cases, but rather were typical of the complaints received by the publisher.

President Harrison died on April 4, 1841, exactly a month after his inauguration. The *Gazette* had been extremely critical of him throughout the campaign and during his brief term of office, but showed respect for his high office by reversing the column rules on the two inside pages on April 21, to drape the paper in mourning. The office of president descended to Vice President John Tyler. Undoubtedly Burnett did not expect to retain his appointment as publisher of the laws of the United States very long after the Whig administration began. The blow fell in June, and with the issue of June 23, this distinction was removed from the *Gazette's* flag without editorial comment.

It was a minor catastrophe, compared with another misfortune that came simultaneously. Burnett had been ill for several months. He had referred to his ailment only once in the *Gazette,* leaving the impression that he was suffering from the recurring fevers and chills of the ague.[18] Actually, he was slowly dying of consumption,[19] and as his condition grew steadily worse, he eventually had to take to his bed.

Stephen S. Tucker, a 29-year-old lawyer from Orange County, Vermont,[20] who evidently was a recent arrival at Little Rock, took charge of the business and editorial departments of the *Gazette* as an employee, with the issue of June 23, 1841.

Shortly before this, the low stage of the river had delayed a shipment of

14. *Ibid.,* Feb. 17, 1841.
15. *Ibid.,* Sept. 22, 1841.
16. *Ibid.,* Dec. 23, 1840.
17. *Ibid.,* Feb. 10, Mar. 24, 1841.
18. *Ibid.,* Mar. 10, 1841.
19. *Ibid.,* Nov. 20, 1869.
20. *Ibid.,* Dec. 21, 1842.

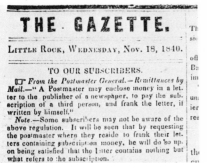

THE GAZETTE.

LITTLE ROCK, WEDNESDAY, Nov. 18, 1840.

TO OUR SUBSCRIBERS.

☞ *From the Postmaster General.—Remittances by Mail.*—" A Postmaster may enclose money in a letter to the publisher of a newspaper, to pay the subscription of a third person, and frank the letter, if written by himself."

Note.—Some subscribers may not be aware of the above regulation. It will be seen that by requesting the postmaster where they reside to frank their letters containing subscription money, he will do so upon being satisfied that the letter contains nothing but what refers to the subscription.

THE undersigned beg leave to inform their friends and the traveling community, that they have purchased the tri-weekly line of stages running from Little Rock to Washington, Hempstead county, (formerly owned by Beall and Richmond.) The stages are undergoing a thorough repair, and great pains have been taken by our agent to select careful and experienced drivers. The line is now in full operation, and every exertion will be used on our part to make those who travel with us agreeable.

THORN & WILSON.

January 20, 1841. 6-tf

paper, and the *Gazette* of June 9 had been issued on a smaller sheet than usual, having only five columns to the page. The next week it had returned to its usual size of four six-column pages.

Tucker was merely "holding the fort" at the *Gazette,* in the hope that Burnett could soon return to duty, and he showed even less inclination to indulge in controversy than Burnett. From the beginning of his proprietorship, Burnett had published frequent articles on agriculture clipped from his exchanges, and had encouraged Arkansas farmers to contribute original articles on the agricultural methods they had found profitable.[21] He had attended a meeting proposed by the *Times and Advocate* to organize a state agricultural society in November, 1840, but only two or three others appeared, which he attributed partly to inclement weather and partly to the widespread resistance to "book farming." He had tried to arouse interest in the projected organization, and had offered the *Gazette* office for another meeting,[22] but Arkansas was not quite ready for this kind of thing.

Tucker continued publication of the agricultural articles, and an occasional original contribution was received and published. A growing interest in the undeveloped natural resources of Arkansas brought a number of original geological and topographical descriptions, and the *Gazette* seemed to be fulfilling the promise most new editors made and broke to provide a steady flow of useful, informative articles aimed at improving the country.

Arkansas was making rapid strides towards advancement. The 1840 census gave the state a population of 97,574, a dramatic increase of 221.1 per cent since the 1830 census. The national rate of increase was only 32.7 per cent, and Arkansas was second only to Michigan, which had an increase of 590 per cent.[23]

21. *Ibid.,* Nov. 4, 1840.
22. *Ibid.,* Nov. 25, 1840.
23. *Ibid.,* June 2, 1841; *Thirteenth Census of the United States Taken in the Year 1910, Statistics for Arkansas* (Washington; Government Printing Office, 1914), 568. The *Gazette's* article, reprinted from the Newburyport *Herald,* gives the Arkansas rate of increase as 220 per cent.

Little Rock also was booming, with a cosmopolitan population representing almost every state in the union and several foreign countries, large and impressive buildings, and such imported delicacies as oysters, bananas, pineapples, and citrus fruits being brought in fairly regularly by improved transportation facilities.[24] Yet by the summer of 1841, there were an estimated 50 vacant houses in the town, which a *Gazette* correspondent attributed to a variety of bad situations, including jealousy of country folk of the advancement of the city, the habit of Little Rock merchants of cheating country people, the banks, and the credit system.[25] On May 19, 1841, the *Gazette* published its first advertisement of a local fire insurance agency, inserted by Jonas Levy as agent for the Protection Insurance Company of Hartford, Connecticut, one more proof that the town was no longer in the backwoods class.

Burnett died on December 17, 1841, at the age of 27, and Woodruff resumed control of the *Gazette* with the next issue.[26] Three appraisers set the value of the *Gazette* and its materials at $5,062.57 on December 30, which was partially offset by the $3,000 mortgage Woodruff held, plus $444.25 in accrued interest. Woodruff gave his note for the remaining $1,618.32, with George C. Watkins and John J. Clendenin as securities, and Samuel M. Rutherford, as executor of Burnett's estate, conveyed the *Gazette* to Woodruff on January 6, 1842, making the transfer retroactive to December 9, the end of the 22d volume.[27]

Relieved of his editorial chores, Stephen Tucker accepted an appointment as prosecuting attorney of the Third Judicial Circuit, and opened a law office at Pocahontas.[28] He returned to Little Rock in July, and in the fall opened a race track called the Far West Course.[29] He was the principal clerk of the House of Representatives in 1842 and 1844, and acted as secretary of the Democratic convention at Little Rock in January of 1846.[30] When ten new United States regiments were authorized at the beginning of the Mexican War, he was appointed a captain in the Third Regiment of Dragoons, his commission dating from May 27, 1846. He was the only officer appointed from Arkansas under the initial operation of the "Ten Regiment law," and distinguished himself in the battle of Chapultepec. He remained in the army until 1851,[31] and never lived in Arkansas again.

24. *Gazette,* Dec. 9, 1840.
25. *Ibid.,* June 16, 1841.
26. *Ibid.,* Dec. 22, 1841.
27. Samuel M. Rutherford, as executor of George H. Burnett, to William E. Woodruff, Little Rock, Jan. 6, 1842, Ms. in William E. Woodruff Papers, Arkansas History Commission.
28. *Gazette,* Jan. 26, Feb. 2, 1842.
29. *Ibid.,* July 27, Sept. 28, 1842.
30. *Ibid.,* Dec. 21, 1842; Nov. 6, 1844; Jan. 12, 1846.
31. *Ibid.,* June 15, 1846; May 10, 1849; Francis B. Heitman, *Historical Register and Dictionary of the United States Army, from its organization, September 29, 1789, to March 2, 1903* (Washington: Government Printing Office, 1903; Urbana: University of Illinois Press, 1965), I, 873.

10

WOODRUFF AND WELLER

1841-1843 WOODRUFF WAS NOT EAGER to resume the responsibilities of the *Gazette,* but he tackled the job with his usual vigor, and immediately made two improvements in the paper. He began a brief listing of all the cases before the Arkansas Supreme Court, giving the names of the parties and the decisions rendered. Previously only an occasional case of general interest had been reported, and the new feature was well received by the legal profession. In response to several requests, Woodruff announced on February 16, 1842 that the feature would be expanded to include a synopsis of each case as often as space limitations permitted. The current term of court was almost over and the next term was the first to receive full coverage.[1]

Standing advertisements that had been published at least once and moved to the back page were fitted into the page at random until January 26, 1842 when Woodruff began classifying them under such heads as "Legal Advertisements," "Cards," and "Rents, &c." A month later, he applied the same system to the standing ads on page one,[2] but the new ads on the inside remained a hodge-podge, there being too few in each category to justify classification.

Arkansas bank notes were dropping rapidly in value, and were quoted at New Orleans at a discount of 50 to 55 per cent. After almost three months notice, Woodruff stopped taking them at face value on May 1, and subscribers who did not observe the deadline found their accounts credited with only half payment.[3] At the half-year mark on June 8, almost 400 subscribers were stricken from the list for delinquencies of one to ten years, and 500 were dropped before the end of the volume in December.[4]

1. *Gazette,* July 27, 1842.
2. *Ibid.,* Feb. 23, 1842.
3. *Ibid.,* Feb. 16, Mar. 16, Apr. 27, May 4, 1842.
4. *Ibid.,* Mar. 16, May 11, June 1, 8, Dec. 7, 1842.

The rumor that Edward Cross wanted to retire brought out several other possible Democratic candidates, and got the campaign for Congress off to an early start. Without authority from Cross, Woodruff placed his name at the head of the *Gazette's* editorial columns on February 9, 1842, explaining that Cross was virtually certain to run again, in response to "the wish of a large majority of his constituents." Lemuel D. Evans entered the race and based his campaign largely upon a protest against the tactics of Woodruff, Yell, and others of the "Little Rock junto," who seemed bent on re-electing Cross whether he wanted the office or not. Evans accused Woodruff of violating a promise that the *Gazette* would announce his candidacy simultaneously with Cross' announcement. Dr. Daniel J. Chapman wrote to Woodruff on May 31 that he would run, and Woodruff promised him fair and courteous treatment but not the support or neutrality of the *Gazette,* which would exert its influence for Cross.[5] Euclid L. Johnson became the fourth Democratic candidate.

Too many Democratic candidates could mean a Whig victory, and some of the Democratic leaders thought a state nomination convention should be called to concentrate the entire strength of the party on one candidate. Woodruff told them there would be little chance of getting delegates from half the counties, and besides, he doubted that any of the other candidates posed a serious threat to Cross. The Whigs were then trying to put a candidate into the race, but were having trouble finding one. If they should succeed, Woodruff's advice was for the Democrats to unite behind Cross, without a convention.[6] William Cummins finally consented to run again on the Whig ticket.

After six years, the State and Real Estate banks had exhausted their means and acknowledged their insolvency. During the same period, the state government's expenses had quadrupled and a debt of nearly $300,000 had accumulated, but there was little to show for it. The treasury was empty, and the revenue was so diminished that it would not cover current expenses. There was a corresponding financial distress among the people, who now called for the elimination of extravagance and corruption from the state government, with particular reference to the flagrant mismanagement of the banks. This had long been the battle cry of the Whigs, and now many rank-and-file Democrats were thinking along the same lines. It became the principal factor in the election of members of the legislature.

Eli Colby, who aspired to represent Pulaski County in the lower house, was the principal promoter of a meeting of farmers and mechanics of both parties held on June 18 to nominate a "union" ticket of working men as candidates for the legislature, without regard to their party affiliations, so long as they were not stockholders or directors of either bank. Believing that Whigs would control the meeting, and fearing that a new party might be founded on the bank question, Woodruff sabotaged the meeting by arranging a Democratic meeting for June 30 to make nominations along strict

5. *Ibid.,* Apr. 6, June 8, 1842.
6. William E. Woodruff to Thomas S. Drew, Little Rock, July 8, 1842, Ms. in *Arkansas Gazette* Foundation Library.

party lines. It was announced by handbills and in the *Gazette* a week before the union meeting was held, and reduced the participation of Democrats in the union meeting to almost nothing. Rain caused a further drain on the crowd, and the union meeting was a dismal failure, with no nominations made. Colby said the Democratic meeting would be controlled by "the bank men of both parties for the purpose of seducing the unwary into a support of Bank candidates." Woodruff denied that any Whigs were involved, and agreed that honest, trustworthy farmers would be better legislators than men subject to the influence or dictation of the banks.[7] The people felt the same way, and the movement for this kind of nominations spread to all parts of the state.

The campaign preliminaries failed to bring a purchaser for the *Gazette,* so Woodruff hired Cyrus W. Weller as editor. Weller was an ardent Democrat who had lived in Arkansas three years, and came to Little Rock from Columbia, Chicot County, to assume his duties on July 13, 1842. His former residence in Sevier's home county and his zealous support of Sevier suggest the possibility that Sevier might have arranged his employment at the *Gazette.* He was a lawyer, and continued his practice at Little Rock and in the Chicot Circuit Court even in the busiest part of the campaign, and offered besides to make collections in any part of the state.[8]

Weller was 23 years old, nine months older than the *Gazette*. He had the enthusiasm of youth, but did not allow it to sweep him into the bickering that often accompanied a difference of political opinions. The quarrelsome Colby promptly tried to engage him in a war of words, and other Whig editors also attacked and ridiculed him, but he met them all with silence.[9]

A month after he became editor of the *Gazette,* he published a list of qualifications he thought a responsible editor should have, arranged in the orderly fashion of an outline. His first point was that an editor should be temperate in all things. This idea was expanded with three sub-topics, total abstinence from intoxicating drinks to keep the head clear and the heart pure, temperate language, and respect for a differing opinion. (Weller campaigned for temperance as long as he was editor of the *Gazette,* was active in the Arkansas State Temperance Society, and advocated legislation to control the retail sale of whiskey.) The second point was the quality of truth, and in three sub-topics he defined what was *not* truth—distortion, the defense in every particular of a favored candidate or party, and the denunciation of every act of an opposing candidate or party. Here Weller touched on a shortcoming of editors in all periods, many of whom could see only good in their political friends and only bad in their political enemies. His third major point was circumspect behavior, which he defined as a studious endeavor to avoid personal quarrels, refusal to publish offensive or insulting material unless the public interest demanded it, and avoidance of slander. His fourth and last

7. *Gazette,* June 15, 22, 1842.
8. *Ibid.,* July 13, 20, Aug. 24, 1842.
9. *Ibid.,* July 27, Aug. 10, 1842.

point was integrity, which ruled out lying, gambling, allowing adverse public opinion to silence an editor when he was convinced he was right, praising a man for pay, and allowing anonymous correspondents too many liberties.[10]

The redundance was on points worthy of emphasis by repetition, and the outline and the accompanying editorial were so aptly phrased that editors who habitually violated these rules squirmed. Out-of-state editors praised Weller's code of ethics, but the Whig press of Arkansas twisted his words and used them as ammunition against him. When some editors protested his sharp replies, he mildly reminded them that they were the aggressors, and that some had trespassed beyond the point where forbearance ceases to be a virtue.[11]

In the spring, Woodruff had reported a panic caused by a transient white man who had hidden in the home of a free Negro while attempting to persuade several slaves to run away. This incident had prompted Woodruff to expound the dangers of allowing free Negroes to live in a slave community, and to suggest that the legislature should follow the example set in most of the other slave states and pass a law excluding free Negroes from Arkansas.[12] Weller made the same suggestion in the autumn, after noting a recent act of the Louisiana legislature imposing heavy penalties on people who brought free Negroes into that state.[13]

The *Gazette's* first front page editorial was also its first signed editorial of a political nature, and appeared on August 3, 1842. It was about the unconstitutionality of a national bank, and explained the conflicting positions of the Whig and Democratic parties. It was on the front page only because it was three columns long and there was not room for it in the usual place on the inside. It was signed "By the Editor of the *Gazette*" only because otherwise readers would take for granted that it had been reprinted from another paper, since its subject was of national interest and it was on a page usually reserved for reprinted material.

Weller always referred to the opposing party as the "federo-whig" party. His enemies made fun of his coinage of the word "federo" as a pompous, meaningless affectation. He said he could take no credit for originating it, and directed his critics to the writings of Thomas Jefferson, where they would find his pet word "standing out in bold relief." [14] He never explained its meaning, but obviously used it to direct attention to the Federalist tendencies of the Whigs.

Edward Cross' name stood alone at the head of the *Gazette's* editorial columns until Weller's second issue, when he added "For President and Vice President, The Candidates Who May Be Nominated by a Democratic National Convention," although the next presidential campaign was two years

10. *Ibid.,* Aug. 10, 1842.
11. *Ibid.,* Aug. 17, 24, 31, 1842.
12. *Ibid.,* Mar. 16, 1842.
13. *Ibid.,* Sept. 28, 1842.
14. *Ibid.,* Aug. 24, 1842.

THE GAZETTE.

CYRUS W. WELLER, EDITOR.

LITTLE ROCK:

WEDNESDAY MORNING, NOV. 30, 1842.

FOR PRESIDENT AND VICE PRESIDENT,
THE CANDIDATES WHO MAY BE NOMINATED BY A

DEMOCRATIC NATIONAL CONVENTION.

ARKANSAS MONEY.

AGENTS and PATRONS of the GAZETTE, are again reminded, that we *do not* receive the Notes of the banks of Arkansas (except the State Bank, *payable at Little Rock,*) *at par,* for subscriptions or other dues to this office. Our terms of subscription, advertising, &c., are predicated on *specie prices,* and all payments MUST be made in *specie* or its equivalent.

For the accommodation of those who cannot procure better funds, we receive Arkansas money at 50 per cent. discount, and will continue to do so until we give notice to the contrary, under this head.

TO THE PATRONS OF THE GAZETTE.

Our next paper will complete the 23d volume (or year) of the "*Arkansas State Gazette.*" Such of our patrons as have not paid in advance, are earnestly desired to pay up immediately; and those who wish to continue subscribers for the ensuing year, will do well to pay *in advance,* on or before the receipt of the first No. of the next volume, otherwise they will be charged $4 for the year.

Those indebted for Advertising, Job Printing, &c., are requested to pay up forthwith.

Our expenses are very heavy, and have to be paid in

away, and "For U.S. Senator, Ambrose H. Sevier." The list of candidates for state offices soon grew long, and Weller said, "There are other candidates for some of the above offices—but we only announce those who pay us for it." [15]

As Woodruff had privately predicted, Chapman and Johnson withdrew from the race for Congress early in September, but Evans remained to the end. When he advocated federal regulation of the currency, which he chose not to label as a national bank although it was in essence the same thing, Weller accused him of deserting his party, this being a Whig doctrine. [16] In reporting the early election returns in October, the *Gazette* listed Evans as "of doubtful politics." [17] Official returns gave Cross the victory with 9,413 votes, Cummins receiving 5,315, and Evans running a poor third with 1,686. [18]

15. *Ibid.,* July 20, Aug. 10, 1842.
16. *Ibid.,* Sept. 14, 1842.
17. *Ibid.,* Oct. 12, 1842.
18. *Ibid.,* Oct. 26, 1842.

The excitement of the election was eclipsed by the arrest on the previous day of some of the members of a band of ingenious burglars and counterfeiters. The people could talk of nothing else for months, and for many years it remained Little Rock's most sensational criminal case. The master mind of the gang was Samuel G. Trowbridge, who had been elected mayor of Little Rock in a special election in May.[19] This gang was blamed for most of the crimes committed at Little Rock during the past four or five years, and its guilt was proved in two lucrative burglaries so cleverly executed that the community had suspected the victims of faking the robberies.[20] For about three years, the gang had specialized in making and passing counterfeit money, including gold and silver coins of the United States, bank notes of other states, and corporation notes of the town of Little Rock.

The offices of the *Gazette* and the *Times and Advocate* were indirectly involved in the production of the spurious corporation notes. Ira B. Whitmore, an expert engraver, was hired by the Town Council to engrave part of the plates used in issuing the genuine notes, and he made duplicate plates for the Trowbridge gang. He also made the small hand press used to print the counterfeit notes, and a few pieces of type that could not be stolen from either printing office.

The work was so skillfully done that few people could detect the counterfeits until their defects were pointed out and compared with the genuine notes. Most of the printing was done by Francis M. Van Horne, who had come to Little Rock in 1839 after an apprenticeship in a Philadelphia printing office. He had worked for the *Gazette* for about four months during one session of the legislature, while Edward Cole was the proprietor. George H. Burnett, then the business manager, had fired him without explanation, probably because the need for strict economy at the *Gazette* at that time made it necessary to reduce expenses after the legislature's printing was finished. Van Horne's salary was $28 a week, but Cole still owed him $75 when the *Gazette* was sold to Burnett in October of 1840. After a peddling excursion with J. M. Martin, who had recently abandoned the publication of the Napoleon *Journal,* Van Horne had returned in February of 1841 and found a job as foreman in the *Times and Advocate* office. His salary was $19 a week, but Colby owed him $400 when he left in January of 1842, and could pay him only $100. He became a member of the Trowbridge gang while he worked for the *Times and Advocate.* He stole a few pieces of the type needed from the *Times and Advocate* office, and got a few other pieces from the *Gazette* office through Burrell Leadbetter, a boy who worked for the *Gazette* and was represented as a member of the gang.

Van Horne printed two batches of counterfeit notes, then bought a printing press that had been confiscated by the sheriff—probably that of the defunct *Arkansas Star*—and moved to Van Buren, where he started the *Arkansas Intelligencer* late in January, 1842, in partnership with Thomas Sterne.

19. *Ibid.,* May 11, 25, Oct. 5, 1842.
20. *Ibid.,* Oct. 31, 1841; Aug. 31, Oct. 5, 1842.

One other batch was printed after he left Little Rock, and some members of the gang said Leadbetter did the printing.

The trials in this case were the big story of 1843. Several members of the gang were found guilty and sentenced to the penitentiary, Van Horne's sentence of six years and six months being the lightest of all. Leadbetter was not indicted, probably because he was little more than a child.[21]

The session of the fourth legislature was another long one, beginning on November 7, 1842 and ending on February 4, 1843. The people had responded to the suggestion that men dominated by the banks should not be chosen to make their laws, and there were many new faces in this legislature. The devious tricks of politicians were foreign to them, and they had little inclination to allow party affiliations to influence their decisions, for they were more interested in finding out what had gone wrong and correcting it than in being re-elected. A large majority were Democrats, but the new ones ("tender-footed Democrats," as Sevier called them) were closer in their thinking to the Whigs than to the veterans of their own party, when it came to weeding out men and measures depending on political favors. There were enough holdovers of both parties to keep old animosities alive, but not enough to rule the session. This situation placed the old string-pullers in a quandary, for they did not know how to appeal to a legislative body that recognized no political heroes as uncensurable, that had no reason to legislate by the time-honored method of "trading out," and that did not place party loyalty above good government.

Both houses authorized representatives of the newspapers to come within the bar to take notes on the proceedings, but the *Gazette* had no reporter to send and the editor did not attempt to cover the session himself. Stephen S. Tucker, former editor of the *Gazette,* was clerk of the House, and provided the *Gazette* with an abstract of the journal every day. If he sent the usual skeleton of the official journal, it did not appear in print that way, for considerable editorializing was injected. The Senate refused to give the editors access to the journals, and Weller gave the senators to understand that it was a matter of complete indifference to him whether their proceedings were published, and that he only offered to report their work as a courtesy to them.[22] Later he complained that he could learn what was going on in the Senate only by conversations with the members, and gave the House credit for outdoing the Senate in the work of the session.[23]

Sevier was one of many who found himself in a precarious position. Irregularities in his conduct as commissioner for the sale of the bonds for the banks had come to light, and a joint committee was appointed to make a thorough investigation. It was the first serious blemish on his record that the Whigs had been able to discover, and they took full advantage of it.

21. *Ibid.,* June 21, 1843; Feb. 2, 1842; Martin and Van Horne v. Webb, Jan. Term 1843, 5 *Ark.* 72; Van Horne v. the State, Jan. Term 1844, 5 *Ark.* 349.
22. *Gazette,* Nov. 9, 16, 1842.
23. *Ibid.,* Dec. 28, 1842.

He was a candidate for re-election to the Senate, and his friends managed to get the election scheduled early in the session, long before the committee's report was ready. Lorenzo Gibson, who had long fought Sevier and his party with every weapon that came to hand, was an influential member of the committee although not its chairman, and he made a strong effort to block Sevier's re-election, basing his attack on the bank scandal. Weller believed in Sevier's honesty and gave him his wholehearted support, making an editorial counter-attack against Gibson.[24] Sevier was re-elected on November 22, with 71 votes cast for him, 10 for Albert Pike, and 3 for Col. John Miller.[25] It had the appearance of an overwhelming vote of confidence, and Sevier departed for Washington with no uneasiness about the outcome of the investigation.

But the committee's report on December 17 was very damaging. It censured Sevier and his fellow commissioner, Gen. T. T. Williamson, for converting the $500,000 in gold or its equivalent that they had received for the bonds into discounted Southern and Western bank paper, for loaning a total of $9,050 to four Arkansans in New York, for retaining for their own use more than $14,000 each, for paying themselves $5,000 for their services as commissioners, and for paying an agent $5,000 to handle the sale of the bonds, all without legal authority. Albert Rust and A. G. Mayers filed a minority report that sought to excuse the irregularities and told the legislators that their almost unanimous re-election of Sevier would be interpreted as condoning whatever misconduct they now charged him with, and action on the report was delayed until later in the session.[26]

Woodruff had been so sure of getting the public printing contracts that he had bought extra paper and had arranged for extra printers. There were two reasons for his self confidence, and he used them as arguments in lobbying: first, he thought the Democrats in the legislature owed him this much for his part in making the last campaign a rousing success; and second, the only other printing office in town, the *Times and Advocate* office, was on the brink of bankruptcy and could not do the work promptly and competently. Colby had been printing his newspaper for more than six months on paper purchased from Woodruff, and had rarely been able to raise the price of more than one week's supply.

To Woodruff's dismay, the Whigs convinced a majority of the legislators that the public printing should be given to the lowest bidder. The *Gazette* office printed the bills, resolutions, reports, and other work needed for the daily use of the legislature early in the session, and when bids were called for, Woodruff decided not to cut his prices to meet possible competition from Colby. He submitted a bid he said gave him a reasonable profit, and Colby

24. *Ibid.,* Dec. 13, 1842.
25. *Ibid.,* Nov. 23, 1842.
26. *Journal of the House of Representatives for the Fourth Session of the General Assembly of the State of Arkansas, 1842–1843.* . . . (Little Rock: Printed by Eli Colby, 1843), 168–173, 240–246.

RACES.

Far West Course, Little Rock.

THE FALL RACES over the Far West Course, will commence at Little Rock, *on the 22d day of November next.*

PURSES VERY LIBERAL.

This late day has been appointed with the intention of accommodating all parties, if possible, anticipating a *visit* from several *tall* Stables from a distance. Gen. A. J. Davie, from Tennessee, with *his* Imperial high-bred stud; Col. A. L. Shotwell, who is "*always there,*" on a race course; whose nags, like himself, are *not slow* in the *budget of sport*; Moore, with his never-tiring Medoc; Col. W. S. Denton, with several fine horses, and, neither last nor least in the legitimate sport of the *Turf*, Capt. T. T. Tunstall, with his gallant *menage* of Arkansas breeding, covered with the laurels of many a well contested field: all—all will be there. The Legislature will be in full session. We shall anticipate an overflow of ripe sport, for, if their is no fun in the Arkansaws, there is no salt in *old briney.*

S. S. TUCKER, *Proprietor.*

Little Rock, September 24, 1842.   42—4w

THE ARKANSAS FORM BOOK.

JUST published, and for sale at the Gazette office, price $3, (par funds), the ARKANSAS FORM BOOK, containing all the necessary forms of process, proceedings, and docket entries, for Justices of the Peace, with forms for Constables, Coroners and Sheriffs, and a copious collection of forms of Deeds, Convey-ances, &c., with an Appendix containing a summary of the principles of law most likely to be useful to Justices of the Peace, by ALBERT PIKE, Esq., Coun-

Thomas Willoughby Newton.

submitted one 33 per cent lower. With such a great difference, the Demo-crats did not dare vote for Woodruff, knowing that the Whigs would loudly protest, and that the public would not accept political patronage as an excuse for this seeming extravagance in a legislature pledged against it. They tried to persuade Woodruff to do the work at Colby's unprofitable price, but he refused, and Colby's bid was accepted on December 6. Apparently the legis-lators thought that requiring Colby to enter into a bond for performance with three good securities would give ample protection against the patent inability of his office to do the work. It took him almost two weeks to make his bond, and he began his work by keeping the Senate waiting for two important bills, probably because he had no paper and Woodruff would not sell him any.[27]

Woodruff was considerably peeved at losing the job, and the *Gazette* said the state had lost $4,000 by giving it to Colby. This figure was arrived at by estimating past and future delays at seven days, counting the cost of the legislature's meetings at $400 for every day lost in waiting for the work, and assuming that Colby would charge about $2,000, which was $660 less than Woodruff would have charged.[28]

27. *Ibid.,* 129, 136, 184, 209; *Arkansas Banner,* Mar. 18, 1846.
28. *Gazette,* Dec. 28, 1842.

It was Albert Pike's responsibility as Supreme Court reporter to let the printing contracts for the court's reports. Late in November, Colby took him to task for not giving the *Times and Advocate* office a chance to bid on the job, and Pike replied with a brief history of the printing of the first four volumes. He had given the first to John H. Reed, then proprietor of the *Advocate,* because his bid of $2.75 a page was the lowest. The office had changed hands twice while the long delayed work was being done, the volume had been badly printed, and the full number of copies promised had not been delivered. The other three volumes had been printed at the *Gazette* office, the second by Cole at $2.70 a page, the third by Burnett at $3 a page, and the fourth by Woodruff at $2.70 a page in par funds.[29] Although still a staunch Whig, Pike did not hesitate to patronize a Democratic printer to get the best work possible. A book of his own, the *Arkansas Form Book,* was printed at the *Gazette* office during the summer of 1842.[30]

When Weller made a trip to Memphis during the first two weeks of December, 1842, John D. Logan was editor of two issues of the *Gazette.*[31] He was no stranger to the *Gazette* office, but he had never expected to occupy the editor's tripod. His father had bound him to Woodruff as an apprentice on November 4, 1834, and his indenture was supposed to end with his 21st birthday on September 11, 1839, but he had run away on January 14, 1838 with another apprentice, Jefferson C. Smith. Woodruff had offered rewards for their apprehension without success. Logan had been working as a printer at Louisville, Kentucky when his wife, Sarah, died on December 7, 1841, and soon afterwards he had returned to Little Rock, where he had conducted a singing school devoted to sacred music, in the spring of 1842. His temporary job as editor may have raised some eyebrows, for he was now a Whig, although he injected no Whig doctrines into the *Gazette.* His employment suggests that Woodruff was friendly to him, but he was not willing to forgive the breach of the apprenticeship contract, and in the November, 1843 term of the Pulaski Circuit Court, Woodruff brought an action of covenant on the apprenticeship indenture. The court ruled in Logan's favor because he was a minor when the contract was made and there was not enough evidence that he had affirmed it after he arrived at lawful age. Woodruff appealed to the Supreme Court, which in 1845 reversed the decision because the indenture was made for Logan's benefit and his minority therefore did not annul it.[32]

Upon Weller's return, he noted a rumor that a number of Whigs and disaffected Democrats had agreed to unite to establish a newspaper "to advocate a politico-educational spirit throughout the State," with the ulterior motive of splitting the Democratic party, and with the *Gazette* and the governor as the main targets.[33]

29. *Ibid.,* Dec. 7, 1842.
30. *Ibid.,* Sept. 28, 1842.
31. *Ibid.,* Dec. 7, 21, 1842.
32. *Ibid.,* Jan. 17, 1838; Dec. 29, 1841; Feb. 2, 16, 1842; Woodruff v. Logan, July Term adjourned to October 1845, 6 *Ark.* 276.
33. *Gazette,* Dec. 21, 1842.

Woodruff had yet another favor to ask of this legislature, and he could predict that it would be denied. He had petitioned the legislature again to relieve him of his debt to the state incurred by his withholding the money he considered due him in connection with his services as state treasurer in 1837. It was not a simple question of which side of the dispute was legally right, for the law was on the side of the state. Woodruff felt that it was an unfair law, and asked for legislation to invalidate a law passed especially to keep him from retaining money he thought was rightfully his. The House took no action on his petition, and the Senate's committee on claims devoted little time to its report on the matter, presented and adopted on December 22. Woodruff's petition was not granted, and the reasons given were that a similar request had been thoroughly investigated and rejected in a previous session, and that the case was then before a court that had full power to hear and determine all matters pertaining to it. This, of course, ignored the fact that the court did not have the power to change the law.

Woodruff already was burning with anger over the loss of the public printing, and the legislature's refusal to relieve him of the charge of defalcation was the last straw. He had anticipated this, and had let it be known that he would sell the *Gazette* unless his party gave it full support, because he could not afford to continue it otherwise. A few people wanted to help him, but did not have the means. Only Elias Conway offered practical assistance. He proposed to raise by subscription the amount for which the state was suing Woodruff, but Woodruff said, "My pride would not permit me to accept it. I was not a beggar. I considered it degrading to accept as a *gratuity* what I claimed as a *right*." [34]

Woodruff was his own worst enemy, in regard both to the public printing and the default. He should have had the public printing because he was the only local printer equipped to do the work satisfactorily, assuming that his price, although higher than Colby's, was as reasonable as he said it was. He should have had the legislature's support in the matter of the 1837 default if it was true that the law that barred him from justice was a spiteful law designed to harm him unfairly. Instead of pressing these points exclusively, he also reminded the legislators that they owed him a favor, and favoritism in government was the very thing they were crusading against. Certainly Woodruff's contention that the Democratic legislators should reward him with public funds for services to the party was indefensible. The debt to him for campaign services was properly the party's and not the state's, and he had no right to expect, much less demand, that it be paid in this way. On the other hand, if his requests had been judged on their own merits without regard to personalities or extraneous issues and found to be fair, they should have been granted.

Woodruff represented his financial condition as dire. He was heavily in debt, and his creditors were pressing for payment. He had expected the income from the daily printing of the session to cover the debts that had to

34. *Senate Journal 1842–1843,* 118; *Banner,* Mar. 18, 1846.

be paid immediately, and he pessimistically predicted that before the next session he would have to sacrifice his property to settle the state's claim against him for the 1837 default. At least part of his distress was attributed to the sale of the *Gazette* in a flourishing condition in 1838 and its repossession in such a depreciated condition that it was worth little more than the materials in the office. Other Democrats thought he exaggerated his predicament, and said there had never been a time in recent years when he could not raise from $1,000 to $3,000 on short notice. It may have been true that his general financial situation was not as bleak as he painted it, for he always "talked poor," but it is also likely that the *Gazette* was a drain on his other resources unless it had the public printing to sustain it. At any rate, he decided that he was compelled to sell the *Gazette* to save himself from financial ruin.

The price he asked was $6,000, with $1,000 to be paid to him in cash, and $5,000 worth of his notes to the Real Estate Bank to be assumed by the purchaser. A few days after he made known his decision to sell, he had an offer that met his price and terms, but he was asked not to reveal the names of the purchaser and others involved for three days, at which time the deal would be closed. Apparently this agreement was reached on December 27. It was a political time bomb, for the purchaser was Benjamin J. Borden, a lifelong Whig who undoubtedly would make the *Gazette* a Whig organ.

Some details of the negotiations will never be known, for it was three years before the showdown came when Woodruff told his side of the story, and as opposing Democrats drew additional information from him, several discrepancies developed. As nearly as it can now be reconstructed, it happened this way:

Albert Pike was much involved in the negotiations, and was the main person who made it possible for Borden to buy the *Gazette*. It seems likely that the first conferences were between Pike and Woodruff, and that it was Woodruff who approached Pike. Apparently Pike was interested in acquiring the *Gazette* for the Whig party, but had no desire to return to the newspaper business himself. Logan's two weeks as editor may have been a "trial run," for at one point Woodruff implied that he put the paper up for sale before the final action on his petition was taken, because all signs were against its being granted. Borden was willing to take the *Gazette,* but did not have the necessary cash and wanted assurance that the paper would pay for itself. Pike and other prominent Whigs were in a position to supply both. Thomas W. Newton was considerably involved. The Democrats said he acted as the agent to negotiate the sale, but it is more plausible that he and Pike worked together to make arrangements for Borden to finance the purchase. Some ten or twelve Whigs loaned Borden the $1,000 in cash, among them Pike and probably Newton and William H. Gaines, and the officers of the bank were persuaded to make concessions concerning the notes.

As the bank's attorney, Pike had control of its legal advertising and some of its other printing. It was agreed that Borden would get all these printing jobs, and that his account would be credited with the amount charged for the printing. The entire amount of the principal and interest of the notes were to be paid in this manner, with the approval of the bank's trustees, who further agreed that no suit would be brought on the notes as long as the entire amount of the bank's printing bill was credited to their payment. Pike agreed in addition to give Borden all other printing and advertising possible, and other Whig leaders undoubtedly made the same promise.

Borden gave the bank two notes of $2,500 each, payable on January 1, 1844, with eight per cent interest from date, and with the interest paid in advance to maturity. His securities were William B. Borden, James Lawson, Luther Chase, and Philip L. Anthony. It was understood that the debt was entirely Borden's, but the bank required Chase to be the principal in one of the notes, probably because he was the only security who was not related to Borden by blood or by marriage.[35]

In 1846, Woodruff first said that the three-day delay between the offer and the final sale was at his request, so that he might have time to decide whether to accept or reject the offer, and to give the Democrats one last chance to buy the *Gazette* at the same price and on the same terms. He went to Governor Yell's office to tell him the news, but finding that Yell was surrounded by visitors, he sent the message by Rev. William W. Stevenson, who brought the reply that Yell could not help it, as he did not have the means to buy the paper. Indeed, Woodruff said, no responsible Democrat made any effort to buy it.[36]

Then he was reminded that Elias Conway, Robert Ward Johnson, and Samuel H. Hempstead had offered him the same price and terms the Whigs offered, and he had refused to sell to them. Conway and Johnson called at his office to present the offer, with Conway agreeing to furnish the $1,000 in cash and Johnson and Hempstead agreeing to assume the notes to the bank. Woodruff told them he was bound by his previous agreement to sell to others if they could meet his terms within three days, and that the delay was made at their request, to give them time to raise the money and make arrangements for assumption of the notes. On December 30, the money was delivered to Woodruff by D. J. Baldwin, and the bill of sale was drawn up and signed.[37]

Actual delivery of the *Gazette* to the new owner did not take place until January 4, 1843, and was announced to the public on the same day. In his valedictory editorial, Woodruff did not delve into the differences with his party that had caused him to sell the paper. "Suffice it to say," he wrote, "that the pressure of the times, which is causing pecuniary distress and embarrassment throughout the land, admonishes me of the propriety as well as necessity of curtailing my business, as the surest means of satisfying my credi-

---

35. *Banner*, Apr. 24, June 19, 1844; Mar. 18, 1846; Borden et al. v. Peay, Receiver, etc., May Term 1859, 20 *Ark.* 293.

36. *Banner*, Mar. 18, 1846.

37. *Arkansas Democrat*, May 21, 29, June 19, 1846.

tors and saving sufficient from the hard earnings of more than 23 years' incessant toil, to support my family and rear and educate my children."

Whig control of the *Gazette* came at a crucial point in the career of Ambrose Sevier, when his enemies had knowledge of a scandal that had the power to blight his political future, and place his party in a precarious position. It also came at an inopportune time for Elias Conway and Robert Ward Johnson, who were poised to move up to high offices. Weller, who still had unbounded faith in Sevier and the party, used his last issue of the *Gazette* to strike one last blow for the Democrats. He filled the paper with warnings of devious Whig tricks that could be expected before the next election, and persuasions for the Democrats to stand fast.

The new owner's political affiliation was not mentioned, but everybody knew he was a Whig. Weller's valedictory left no doubt that the unexpected sale left him disillusioned and a bit suspicious of Woodruff's motives, and he showed this as subtly as his injured pride would permit. Since he had never owned any interest in the *Gazette* but was a mere hired hand, he disclaimed any responsibility for its future editorial conduct, and in fact, did not even have knowledge of its political future, "not having been honored by an initiation into the objects of the transfer." The implication was strong that he regarded the sale as an indication of Woodruff's lack of fidelity to his party. This was the gossip on every street corner in town, for the Democrats were convinced he had sold the paper to the Whigs to spite them. One of the few who defended him was his old friend, Chester Ashley, who was heard to say that he did not blame Woodruff for selling the *Gazette,* that he would have done the same thing, "and let the Democrats go to the devil!!" [38]

The circumstances preceding this sale were so similar to those before the 1838 sale to Edward Cole that the inescapable conclusion is that it also was an attempt to show the Democrats that Woodruff would not support the entire burden of the party's organ unless he got something in return. That sale also had been negotiated during a stormy legislative session in which matters important to Woodruff had not been decided in his favor.

As Weller left the *Gazette,* he assured his readers that he would remain a loyal Democrat as he went about his business as a Little Rock lawyer. Nobody could have made him believe that he would shortly become as disenchanted with Sevier as he was with Woodruff, and that he would have similar feelings toward other revered party leaders.

38. *Banner,* Mar. 18, 1846.

11

BENJAMIN J. BORDEN

1843-1845 "THE CONSTITUTION AND THE LAWS" appeared under the editorial head in Benjamin J. Borden's first issue of the *Gazette* on January 11, 1843, and remained the paper's motto as long as it had a Whig proprietor. It epitomized Borden's editorial policy of insistence that public servants should rigidly adhere to the organic and statutory laws, and his salutatory promised impartial exposure of those who betrayed their trusts.

The announcement of the *Gazette's* switch to the Whig party was withheld, because the party would be better served if this declaration were reserved for the opening of the campaign. Some Democrats may have held to the slender hope that the paper would be neutral, or at least not aggressive in its Whiggery, for the new proprietor-editor was a quiet, scholarly man, not much given to controversy.

Born in Duplin County, North Carolina on October 23, 1812, he was one of ten children of Dr. Levi and Charlotte (Beck) Borden. After his father's death, his mother had married James Lawson, Sr., and had moved to Little Rock in 1836 with her husband and some of her children. A graduate of the University of North Carolina and the law school at Georgetown, District of Columbia, Benjamin had followed his relatives to Little Rock, where he had begun the practice of law in June of 1839.[1]

His purchase of the *Gazette* deprived the Democrats of their only newspaper having statewide circulation. The party rose to the emergency with several well attended meetings where plans were made to establish another newspaper under the auspices of the Democratic party. A Democratic Central Committee was appointed to get the paper started. Its ten members included two former editors of the *Gazette,* (Stephen S. Tucker and Cyrus

1. John Hugh Reynolds and David Yancey Thomas, *History of the University of Arkansas* (Fayetteville: University of Arkansas, 1910), 441–442; *Gazette,* June 2, 1854; Sept. 18, 1887; June 12, 1839.

W. Weller), and four who were in some way related to Sevier, (Samuel H. Hempstead, Robert W. Johnson, Elias N. Conway, and Euclid L. Johnson). The other members were Samuel M. Weaver, Jared C. Martin, John McQuaid, and Charles Fisher.[2]

Woodruff discreetly stayed away from the meetings, where several long-winded orators denounced him as a traitor to his party. Borden came to his defense in the next issue of the *Gazette,* but otherwise watched the proceedings with detached amusement, predicting that the proposed newspaper would meet with disaster as the factions within the Democratic party struggled for its control.

Borden could see no good in either faction, and he and his correspondents fired with impunity the ammunition abundantly provided against both by the legislature. The main complaint against Yell at the moment was his refusal to appoint a state geologist to implement an act of the legislature authorizing a geological survey of Arkansas, the first step towards development of the state's rich natural resources. The legislature had intended that he should appoint the brilliant but eccentric Dr. William Byrd Powell of Little Rock, and many people, including Borden, believed that Yell's refusal was based on a personal prejudice against Powell. Yell said he could not put the law into operation because the state could not finance the project.[3]

The complaint against Sevier was far more serious, and threatened to take many of his friends with him to political ruin. As soon as Borden had control of the *Gazette,* he threw himself into the discussions of the bank scandals, publishing numerous editorials and communications from correspondents condemning Sevier, and throwing in his relatives for good measure. The Batesville *News,* a Whig paper, also denounced him. The legislature applied the finishing touch with its adoption of the investigating committee's report, thus placing Sevier officially under censure.

Sevier was faced with the greatest crisis of his career, with only the mercy of a hostile press to allow his side of the story to be heard. He wrote long letters to the editors of the *Gazette* and the *News,* and his brother-in-law, Robert Ward Johnson, asked Borden to publish them. Borden granted the request, but made a blistering reply in the same issue.[4] The controversy continued week after week, and the more explanations Sevier offered, the worse he made his situation. He admitted every material charge against him, and the extenuations he mentioned not only were highly unsatisfactory to his critics, but were ruled legally unsound by the Supreme Court.[5]

The scandal so excited public interest that new *Gazette* subscriptions came in every mail, and the supply of back issues was insufficient to meet the demand. In May, Borden reported a letter-writing campaign by the "little junto" at Little Rock to persuade the *Gazette's* old patrons to cancel their

2. *Gazette,* Jan. 18, 1843; *Arkansas Banner,* Sept. 16, 1843.
3. *Gazette,* Feb. 8, Mar. 15, 22, 29, Apr. 19, May 10, 1843.
4. *Ibid.,* Feb. 15, 1843.
5. *Ibid.,* Jan. 17, 1844.

subscriptions. Borden professed not to comprehend the displeasure of Sevier's and Yell's friends, but declared he would continue his relentless exposure of the misdeeds of public servants. The contest, he said, was no longer between two political parties, but between "a suffering people and those who have so long misruled and oppressed them." [6]

Then came the news that President John Tyler had removed Thomas W. Newton from the office of United States marshal for the District of Arkansas, and had appointed Henry M. Rector in his place. Borden blamed Sevier and James S. Conway,[7] and his correspondents echoed and expanded the accusation. One who used the pseudonym "Big Rock" pointed out on May 31 that Sevier, Rector, and Conway were cousins, and referred to the clan as "the reigning dynasty," a nickname that caught on quickly. The Batesville *News* said the change had been made partly because of Sevier's old grudge against Newton that had its genesis in their 1827 duel, partly to avenge the legislature's censure of Sevier, and partly to get a good government job for yet another member of their family. This writer listed 18 relatives who held public offices, most of them by appointment.[8] Newton's part in the sale of the *Gazette* may also have figured in his removal, for he had been an officer of the Real Estate Bank from its beginning, and his assistance in arranging extremely liberal terms for payment of Borden's notes had been invaluable.

As the plans for the new Democratic paper slowly matured, there was considerable speculation among the Whigs as to whether it would support Yell or Sevier. The Democrats maintained there was no rift between them, and that support of one would not be incompatible with equal support of the other. At one point, it was said that the paper would support Sevier in preference to all other Democrats, and that Yell was considering starting a paper of his own.[9] The preponderance of Sevier's relatives on the Central Committee gave weight to this theory, but Yell took a hand in obtaining the press and materials and employing the editor. He looked to Woodruff for guidance,[10] and even gave serious consideration to Borden's recommendation of a potential editor, who unfortunately proved to be a Whig.[11]

The final decision was to import an editor from outside Arkansas, presumably on the theory that an uninvolved outsider could deal impartially with the rivalry within the party. The man chosen was Dr. Solon Borland, who had been given a share of the credit for James K. Polk's victory in the Tennessee gubernatorial election in 1839.[12] Since Polk was expected to be

6. *Ibid.,* May 17, 24, 1843.
7. *Ibid.,* May 24, 31, 1843.
8. *Ibid.,* June 7, 1843.
9. *Ibid.,* July 5, 1843.
10. *Ibid.,* Oct. 2, 1844.
11. *Ibid.,* June 12, 19, 1844.
12. *Banner,* Dec. 2, 1843; June 19, 1844. Solon Borland was born at or near Suffolk, Nansemond County, Virginia, the son of Dr. Thomas Borland and the former Miss Godwin. The date usually given for his birth is Sept. 21, 1808, and one biographi-

the next Democratic nominee for president, Borland's experience in success-ful promotion of his candidacy was a decided asset.

When the Democrats of Arkansas called him to their service, he was liv-ing at Louisville, Kentucky,[13] and was not immediately available. The first issue of the *Arkansas Banner* made its appearance without him on Septem-ber 16, 1843, a seven-column folio having a slightly larger page than its competitors but slightly less reading matter because it used larger type.[14] It had 1,000 subscribers before its fourth issue, and 300 more before its twelfth.[15] For eleven weeks the public was not told who conducted the paper or who its absent editor was, and its tone was so mild that the Whigs scoffed at its "softness" and the Democrats began to show impatience. There was talk that Woodruff might take it over, for even his harshest critics conceded that he was a born fighter.[16]

Eleven issues of the *Banner* passed into history before Borland mounted the tripod on December 2, having arrived on November 23.[17] He issued a

---

cal sketch gives the date Aug. 11, 1811, which agrees with the age, 39, listed for him in the 1850 census. Borland said in a letter to his wife that his birthday was August 8. His father, a physician and a member of the Virginia legislature, instilled in his sons a hearty respect for the Democratic party. The family moved to North Carolina in 1823, where Solon lived for 12 years and received his education at prep schools and/or the University of North Carolina. He married Mrs. Huldah Wright and became the father of two boys, Harold and Thomas. After his wife's death, he moved to Memphis in 1836, where he married Mrs. Eliza Hart on July 26, 1839. She died without issue a few months later.

Both Solon and his brother, Euclid, were physicians. Solon had practiced medicine during most of his six-year residence at Memphis, and had practiced law for a while. But he found politics more fascinating than pills, and this was the second time he had strayed into the newspaper business. On the ruins of the *Memphis Gazette,* he had founded the *Western World and Memphis Banner of the Constitution* in January of 1839, with which he had promoted Polk's candidacy for governor. He had sold the paper to Woodruff's old friend, Henry Van Pelt, who used the materials to start *The Memphis Appeal* on April 21, 1841. We are not told what he was doing at Louisville, but his frequent "puffing" of the Louisville Medical Institute in 1844 suggests that he might have been on its faculty.

See: *Gazette,* Jan. 23, 1839; Dec. 27, 1843; May 2, 1851; Dec. 24, 1852; *Banner,* Dec. 2, 16, 1843; Jan. 30, July 24, 1844; *Arkansas Democrat,* Oct. 22, 1847; J. Willis Stovall in Memphis *Commercial Appeal,* Aug. 7, 1927; 1850 U.S. Census, Hot Springs, Hot Spring County, Arkansas, Dwelling 441; Robert Talley, *One Hundred Years of the Commercial Appeal* (Memphis: The Commercial Appeal, 1940), 6; *The National Cy-clopaedia of American Biography* (New York: James T. White & Co., 1893), IV, 386; Ansel Wold (comp.), *Biographical Directory of the American Congress 1774–1927,* 69th Cong., 2d Sess., House Doc. No. 783 (Washington: Government Printing Office, 1928), 717; Fay Hempstead, *A Pictorial History of Arkansas* (St. Louis and New York: N.D. Thompson Publishing Co., 1890), 789; Allen Johnson (ed.), *Dictionary of American Biography* (New York: Published under the auspices of American Coun-cil of Learned Societies by Charles Scribner's Sons, 1943), II, 464.

13. *Banner,* Dec. 9, 1843.
14. *Ibid.,* Sept. 23, 1843.
15. *Ibid.,* Oct. 7, Dec. 2, 1843.
16. *Gazette,* Nov. 22, 1843.
17. *Banner,* Nov. 27, 1844.

belated prospectus, changed the front page format, and adopted a motto, "No Bank—No Protective Tariff—No Monopolies of Any Kind—But Equal Rights, Equal Taxes, and Free Trade," which summarized the national policies of the Democratic party. He made it clear that there would be no interference with his editorial policies, and the Central Committee, now reduced to seven members, implied that its job had been completed with the relinquishment of the *Banner* to Borland.[18]

His first issue was published on the eve of a Democratic state convention, held early in December. It was the first state nominating convention, for the 1836 gathering was nothing more than a self-constituted caucus. There can be little doubt that the 1843 convention was as "rigged" as the 1836 meeting, and for similar reasons. It was time to advance one more member of "the reigning dynasty," and still another was waiting his turn and would eventually inherit the leadership of this wing of the party.

Elias Nelson Conway's desire to be governor and Robert Ward Johnson's desire to go to Congress probably had motivated their effort to buy the *Gazette* while Woodruff's deal with Borden was pending. The minimum age for both offices was 30, which Conway had reached on May 17, 1842, and which Johnson would attain on July 21, 1844, so the 1844 election was their earliest opportunity to put their plans into operation. Conway's chance would come first, probably because Johnson's birthday was uncomfortably close to election day, and he would have to wage most of his campaign before he was legally eligible for the office. The multiplicity of independent Democratic candidates in the last congressional campaign had taught them the advisability of getting some semblance of an official nomination by the party, so that a plea for party loyalty would be on their side and Democratic opponents could be branded as disorganizers. A convention was the logical way to accomplish this, but it could get out of hand unless carefully controlled.

Gen. Richard C. Byrd wanted to be governor, and realizing that the odds were against his getting the support of the entire party, he laid the foundation for an independent campaign. During the summer a newspaper called the *Independent Democrat* had been started at Little Rock by one W. D. Chapman, advocating Byrd's prospective candidacy and believed to be financed by him. It was printed as job work in a Whig printing office, possibly the *Gazette*. Chapman was a stranger in town, but he soon was spirited away by someone using blackmail tactics, and Byrd's friends suspected the Dynasty. His departure had ended the *Independent Democrat's* short career.[19]

Despite this setback and the certain knowledge that Conway had the advantage with the party's leadership, Byrd's determination to run did not falter. One of his most articulate supporters was Cyrus Weller, who had lost all faith in the Dynasty after Sevier's explanations of his conduct as bank commissioner, and who had retired from the Democratic Central Committee. The convention was far from a full representation of the party, having

18. *Ibid.,* Dec. 2, 1843.
19. *Ibid.,* June 12, 1844; *Democrat,* Oct. 16, 1846.

only about 30 delegates from 16 of the 42 counties. Weller fought fiercely for Byrd, but the convention nominated Conway for governor and Dr. Daniel J. Chapman of Independence County for Congress, with only two dissenting votes. Borland refused to publish Weller's long, indignant explanation of his negative vote, saying the party's organ could not give space to renegades working against the regular nominees. Weller said the real reason was that the *Banner* was owned by a few friends of the Dynasty, and made no effort to work for the whole party. He turned to the *Gazette,* and Borden obligingly published his letter.

Not all of Weller's reasons for refusing to accept Conway's nomination would bear investigation. He said Conway was too young, too inexperienced, and too incompetent to be governor, but he did not back up these statements with convincing arguments. Clearly his main objection, and the only one likely to carry much weight with the voters, was that abler men had been bypassed to launch the career of yet another member of the Dynasty.[20]

Lest publication of Weller's letter be mistaken as evidence that the *Gazette* was allied with the discordant Democrats, Borden on the same day, December 13, raised the standard of Henry Clay for president, subject to the decision of the forthcoming Whig National Convention. Previously the abuses of power in state government had claimed most of Borden's attention, and he had not fought that battle under the Whig banner. In occasional discussions of national issues, such as the tariff and a national bank, he had advocated Whig doctrines but had avoided using the name of his party. Now the *Gazette* was altogether in the Whig ranks, and to the disgust of the Democrats, Borden referred to his party as the Democratic Whig party.

Borland claimed that his references to the *Gazette* had forced Borden to define his position, after a full year without showing his colors. He shrugged off Borden's pride in the *Gazette's* advanced age with the comment that the *Gazette,* as the people had always known and respected it, had ceased to exist with the sale to Borden. In the same issue, Borland sniped at Borden with half a dozen short articles that were somewhat more personal than the usual editorial bickering.[21] Borden kept his dignity as he explained that his tardiness in bringing party politics into the *Gazette's* columns was because the campaign was the proper time for it, and because he had been more concerned earlier with government than with politics.[22]

The next issue of the *Banner,* on December 23, replied to various *Gazette* articles with numerous short paragraphs, in which the tone sharpened and became more personal. Then Borden also injected a personal remark, alluding to the many fragments of Borland's background that had been mentioned in the *Banner's* editorials or its reprinted notices of the new paper, implying that Borland's egotism was showing. He facetiously toyed with

20. *Gazette,* Dec. 13, 1843.
21. *Banner,* Dec. 16, 1843.
22. *Gazette,* Dec. 20, 1843.

the idea of writing Borland's biography from these scraps of information, and said the only missing fact was his birth date.[23]

The *Gazette* was published on Wednesdays and the *Banner* on Saturdays, giving each editor ample time to prepare replies to the other's editorials. As the new year began, Borland changed the *Banner's* publication day to Tuesday. The mail schedules and his convenience were his stated reasons, but he also gained the valuable advantage of putting his paper in his rival's hands after most of the next issue of the *Gazette* was in type.

The first Tuesday issue of the *Banner,* on January 2, 1844, was liberally laced with short, biting insults. Borland pondered whether Weller was the principal editor of the *Gazette* or only an assistant. Twice he suggested that Borden's vacillation on the subject of the annexation of Texas was because he dared not take a stand until he was sure what position Henry Clay, the Louisville *Journal,* and others of his party would take. Borden had thanked a friend for a gift of turnips, saying this was "the most flatulent diet in the world." Borland ridiculed this unfortunate choice of words, saying the *Gazette* was already entirely too windy, and now that its editor was fed on turnips, he would surely burst. He requested that Borden's biography of him should stick to the truth and leave out the Latin and Logic. In other paragraphs he called Borden unscrupulous, illogical, envious, insincere, and lachrymose, each with cutting embellishments. He topped it off with, "The logical Editor of the *Gazette,* in one paragraph, calls us, first 'pugnacious' and then 'lamb-like.' His readers need no such bleating nonsense to prove that he is a *goat.*"

In spite of the shortness of time, Borden replied the next day with short, caustic paragraphs sprinkled between the news stories and editorials, using for the first time precisely the same form and tone that had characterized Borland's paper for three issues. He remarked that the last *Banner* "looks very much like a half-worn, dirty coverlet, composed, as it is, of patches of flimsy, vulgar witticisms. We would suggest that its name be changed to the 'Family Quilt.'" Another item said, "If the editor of the *Banner* continues the blackguard strain adopted in his last number, he will soon write himself out of all claims to have his paper admitted into the family circle, or himself to enter genteel society." In other paragraphs he ridiculed Borland's literary pretensions, with particular reference to his superficial knowledge and use of Latin; replied to the accusation that the *Gazette* was windy with comment that the *Banner* was engaged weekly in puffing such ciphers as Conway, Chapman, and its editor; and chided Borland for his overestimation of himself with a quotation from Hudibras, "Many a monkey's thought himself a man, And many a goose had thought herself a swan."

Any of these paragraphs might have moved Borland to violence, but it took two others to turn the trick, both of which charged him with faintheartedness. Because Borland had called him a goat, Borden said, "We do

23. *Ibid.,* Dec. 27, 1843.

not wish to confine our comparison of the editor to any single animal; for he certainly has the qualities of several. In view of his effrontery, however, and tameness of spirit, we will content ourselves at present with saying that he is 'A dog in forehead, in heart a deer.' " Borland had pointed out Borden's inconsistency in calling him both pugnacious and lamb-like in the same paragraph. Borden answered, "We did no such thing; we never suspected that the editor could, under any circumstances of insult, 'start a spirit' which would entitle him to be called pugnacious. We only spoke of his *style,* the war-tone of which only proved how natural it is for one to prate loudest of that virtue to which he has the least claims."

Before the day ended, Borden learned—the hard way—that he was mistaken in supposing that Borland's courage on paper was not matched by his physical courage. The intimation of cowardice was too much for Borland to accept calmly, and he sallied forth and gave his antagonist the beating of his life. Two days later, William E. Woodruff wrote this account of the fight to William S. Fulton:

"We have nothing new here that I recollect, except that the editors of the *Banner* and the *Gazette* had a 'set-to' on Wednesday last, which made some stir among the respective friends of the contestants. The attack was made by Doctor Borland on Mr. Borden, in consequence of his remarks in his paper of that day, in relation to the doctor. It was a fisticuff fight, and I am told that the doctor used Ben. pretty roughly—having beaten his face into a jelly, and bro't the claret with every blow.

"Ben. has not made his appearance since; indeed, I have seen neither since. Some seem to think that the affair is not over, but I think it is. They now *know* each other, and know that a contest is no child's play, and both, I think, will be willing to let the matter drop and treat each other courteously in future. The result of this fight has rather discouraged the whigs, who do not now think the doctor as 'lamb-like' as they did previous to the affray. The result certainly astonished me, as I never suspected him for being pugnacious, but I am told he is a ready, expert fightist, and equally ready with the pistol or knife; but, with that, a very mild and gentlemanly man—as much so as any I know. I think he is quite an acquisition to the democratic cause, and, now that he has got his name up for a fightist, I think his blustering opponents will not attempt to run over him." [24]

For all his experience in sizing up men and situations, Woodruff predicted inaccurately in this instance. Friends of the two editors tried to settle the quarrel peaceably, and drew up a statement that the difficulty had been "honorably and satisfactorily adjusted, by the voluntary intermediation of their friends." It was dated January 17, but was not published in the two newspapers until the end of the month. It was signed by three Whigs, (Frederick W. Trapnall, Charles Rapley, and Thomas W. Newton), who obviously

24. John Hallum, *Biographical and Pictorial History of Arkansas* (Albany: Weed, Parsons and Company, Printers, 1887), 210.

acted for Borden, and by three Democrats, (William Field, Lambert J. Reardon, and Samuel H. Hempstead), friends of Borland.[25]

Nevertheless, Borden challenged Borland, and they fought a duel in the Indian Territory opposite Fort Smith, using regulation duelling pistols at ten paces. Borden's second was James B. Keatts and his surgeon was Dr. James A. Dibrell. Borland's second was Henry M. Rector. When the command to fire was given, Borden accidentally fired his pistol into the ground. Borland took deliberate aim, and the ball entered Borden's right side between the fourth and fifth ribs, and passed out his left side about four inches above his heart. Borland was the first to rush to his fallen opponent, whose wound at first was believed to be fatal. Some 35 years later, Borden recalled that a strong friendship between him and Borland began immediately after the duel and endured as long as Borland lived. He said over and over, "I thank God that it was no worse, and that I was hit in place of Borland." [26] It is a shame to spoil this happy ending, but the files of the two newspapers do not reflect the undying friendship. The editors continued to take pot-shots at each other, and at times their remarks were every bit as offensive as those that led to the duel.

While the duel was in the making, the Whigs made up their slate for the state election. Borden placed the Pulaski County candidates for the legislature under his editorial head on January 3, and two weeks later he added the names of Dr. Lorenzo Gibson for governor, David Walker for Congress, and three candidates for presidential electors.

The trouble in the Democratic party did not subside. Byrd made up his mind to run for governor as an Independent Democrat, and it was obvious that he would wage his campaign more against the regular Democrats than the Whigs. Borland not only refused to publish his communications, but even declined to print a paid announcement of his candidacy without a written request. Byrd turned to the *Gazette,* and Borden published his letters and Weller's reports of his speeches.[27] In February, Lewis B. Tully of Batesville became an Independent Democratic candidate for Congress.[28]

Eli Colby, who had been wasting away with consumption for three years, died on March 15, 1844.[29] A few days later his brother, John Colby, hired Weller to edit the *Times and Advocate.*[30] He turned the paper into an Independent Democratic journal, supporting Van Buren for president and Byrd for governor, and the impositions on the *Gazette's* columns ceased. Two years later, the *Banner's* wing of the party charged that Woodruff and Ashley were underwriters of Weller's paper, saying Woodruff owned the type and press and Ashley subscribed $300 to sustain the paper and otherwise assisted

25. *Ibid.; Banner,* Jan. 30, 1844; *Gazette,* Jan. 31, 1844.
26. *Gazette,* Oct. 15, 1879; Hallum, *History of Arkansas,* 211; William F. Pope, *Early Days in Arkansas* (Little Rock: Frederick W. Allsopp, 1895), 271–272.
27. *Gazette,* Jan. 10, 1844.
28. *Banner,* Feb. 20, 1844.
29. *Ibid.,* Mar. 20, 1844; *Gazette,* Mar. 20, 1844.
30. *Gazette,* Mar. 27, 1844.

Thomas Stevenson Drew.   Mr. and Mrs. Chester Ashley.

it. Woodruff flatly denied both statements, and reminded the writer that both he and Ashley were viciously attacked repeatedly in Weller's columns, although Woodruff had befriended Weller early in the year and had ministered to his family during a protracted illness.[31]

Some of the leading Democrats had recognized Conway's nomination as a serious blunder from the first, and had realized that the party unity so desperately needed could be achieved only with a new ticket that excluded him.[32] The strength of the Whig ticket and the grass-roots protests against Conway's candidacy further convinced them that a change was necessary, and his friends persuaded him to withdraw.[33]

Another convention held late in April, with only 35 delegates from 20 counties, completely revamped the ticket. It almost unanimously nominated Dr. Chapman for governor, Archibald Yell for Congress, and Mark W. Izard, Chester Ashley, and Williamson S. Oldham for electors. Ashley's nomination for elector had been expected of the first convention. A few days later, Yell resigned the office of governor to canvass for Congress, and Samuel Adams served the rest of the term as acting governor.[34] In July the ticket changed again when Chapman withdrew, pleading ill health, and the Democrats turned to Thomas Stevenson Drew as their gubernatorial candidate.

31. *Democrat,* Aug. 7, 1846.
32. Hallum, *History of Arkansas,* 210.
33. *Gazette,* July 24, 1844.
34. *Ibid.,* Apr. 24, 1844; Apr. 5, 1856. *Banner,* Apr. 24, 1844.

He was not well known, his main qualification being that he was from the northern part of the state, and it was thought that this section deserved the governorship.[35] As Drew saw it, he was merely the instrument by which his party sought to save itself from disaster.[36]

Yell and his highly respected opponent, David Walker, stumped the state together at least part of the time, and Walker good naturedly admitted he had no antidote for Yell's tendency to vary his policies and personality to suit the attitudes of the communities they visited.

Because the candidates for electors were the principal spokesmen for their respective presidential condidates and for their parties as a whole, they were frequently attacked. Alfred W. Arrington on the Whig ticket and Chester Ashley on the Democratic ticket bore the brunt of it, both on matters unrelated to politics and government. Borland dragged out a well documented eleven-year-old scandal about Arrington's having given up the Methodist ministry in Missouri after exposure of his attempt to abandon his wife and elope with his married paramour. The *Gazette* tried to minimize it, but Borland relentlessly pursued it and denounced Arrington in sanctimonious terms, although Borland himself was at that moment involved in a clandestine love affair that soon became a great scandal. Shortly before the election Arrington withdrew from the Whig ticket, but Borland continued to attack his character.[37]

Ashley was accused of misconduct as a land speculator, but Borden was reluctant to publish letters on this subject because he thought Ashley's private business was not the public's business. An anonymous Whig from Batesville, probably C. F. M. Noland, undertook a few months later to explain Ashley's belated entry into active politics, after 25 years of manipulations from the sidelines. He said Ashley had been afraid of Wharton Rector, a cousin of Sevier and the Conways, who had cordially despised him and would not have hesitated to use his tremendous influence against him. Rector's death on February 8, 1842 had been regarded by those in the know as a signal for Ashley's political career to begin.[38] Actually, he had been nominated for the Senate in 1840, when William Savin Fulton was elected to his second term, but had received only seven votes.[39]

Ashley's candidacy for elector gave him a good excuse to canvass the state for other candidates and build his own strength for a later candidacy. He was at first an indifferent campaigner, and made only four speeches before the unexpected death of Fulton on August 15, after a ten-day illness attributed to sleeping in a freshly painted room. It was common knowledge that Yell intended to run for the Senate at the end of Fulton's term in 1846, and

35. *Gazette*, July 24, 1844; *Banner*, July 17, 1844.
36. Thomas S. Drew to William Black, Little Rock, Oct. 1, 1846, Ms. in Robert W. Trimble Papers, Arkansas History Commission.
37. *Banner*, June 12, 19, July 31, Oct. 16, 23, 1844.
38. *Gazette*, Nov. 27, 1844.
39. *Banner*, Nov. 19, 1845.

there was speculation that he might now contend with Ashley to finish Fulton's unexpired term. If there was any doubt that Ashley had Senate ambitions, it was dispelled after Fulton's death, for he took the stump in earnest and visited 40 counties in 40 days. Ostensibly he was campaigning for the entire ticket, but privately he was campaigning for himself with legislators and prospective legislators. He concentrated on the northern and western counties, where Yell had the strongest following.

Sevier's opinion was that if Ashley should win the election for the remainder of Fulton's term, even the popular Yell could not unseat him two years later, and Yell was said to have realized that this was true. Some of the Whigs held the same opinion, and admitted that Ashley's talents were so great that his colleagues in Washington would marvel that such a man had been kept in the background so long.[40]

Ashley told Yell's friends that he wanted to be elected to the Senate only because the dignity of the office would counteract the slurs against his character that had long injured the standing and feelings of his family. Presumably he referred to the accusations regarding his business methods, and late in the summer he had the *Banner* publish his explanations of some of these charges. He was 53 years old, and his snow white hair made him look older. He told Yell's friends that, considering his age and unpopularity and Yell's popularity, he would not stand in Yell's way at the end of the three sessions left in Fulton's term. To some, he remarked that by that time he would be old enough to retire. Yell's friends took this as a pledge that he would not run against Yell in 1846, but Woodruff later said it was not a promise, only an opinion. It appears to have been a crafty evasion, whereby Yell's friends were seemingly assured that Ashley would not oppose him, while Ashley's conscience was salved by the knowledge that his careful choice of words had left him a loophole.[41]

Woodruff had a larger correspondence than any other man in the state, and he wrote many letters to advance the Democratic candidates. He was particularly helpful to Drew,[42] but undoubtedly Ashley was his main interest. He had a personal interest in the campaign for the legislature too, for he planned to try again at the next session to be relieved of his 1837 default.

The bank scandals were again an issue in the legislative campaign, as there was a deftly managed movement afoot to elect legislators who would expunge the record of all action taken against Sevier in the previous session. The Democrats offset the imputations of dishonesty against their heroes by casting doubt on the behavior of the Whigs connected with the banks. This directed attention to the circumstances under which Borden had bought the *Gazette,* and the printing he had done for the bank was freely discussed. The *Banner* and its correspondent, "Pulaski," repeatedly said Borden was completely under the control of Albert Pike and Thomas W. Newton. "Pulaski"

40. *Ibid.,* Oct. 29, 1845; Apr. 8, 1846; *Gazette,* Nov. 27, 1844.
41. *Banner,* Apr. 16, Dec. 31, 1845; Jan. 21, 1846.
42. *Ibid.,* Apr. 8, 1846.

maintained that not all of the legal advertising incidental to the liquidation of the banks had been necessary, and that Borden had made enough from the bank's printing to cover the full $6,000 purchase price of the *Gazette.* This was far from true, for on May 1, 1844, Borden had submitted his first bill for printing and advertising done for the bank since his purchase of the *Gazette,* and it came to only $888. Indeed, the bill for the next four years was only $1,715.29.[43]

The committee appointed to prepare the Whig party's address to the voters decided to use Pike's speech to the convention in January. It was printed in February and again in March as a 29-page pamphlet, and circulated as a *Gazette* "extra." The *Banner* said it was handled this way to save postage, since newspapers got cheaper postal rates than pamphlets. Andrew Hammond, postmaster at Jackson in Lawrence County, got a ruling from the postmaster general's office that it was "a pamphlet, not periodical, of two sheets octavo," and could not be sent through the mails at newspaper rates. Hammond sent a copy of the ruling to the *Gazette,* but Borden would not publish it, so Borland did.[44]

Illness and short pleasure trips often took Borland away from his post. Borden was out of town during the last week in May and the first week in June, and two issues of the *Gazette* were edited by an unidentified young man who worried about discrepancies in the *Gazette's* political opinions, since he and Borden disagreed on a few minor points.[45]

As the summer ended, Borden hired a young man whose name was never announced to assist with the editorials. Borland interpreted his employment as evidence that Borden was incapable of conducting the campaign alone, and attached significance to the fact that the man was hired about the same time Newton got sick and Pike was about to leave the state for several weeks. He wondered whether the high salary of $50 a month was paid by Borden or by Newton and Pike, and did not soften his derisive tone when he learned it was only $40.[46] These and other insinuations of the same period might have developed into another serious difficulty if Borden had not postponed his replies in deference to Borland's illness.[47]

Other Arkansas editors were also preoccupied with personal problems during the closing weeks of the state campaign. Judge J. C. P. Tollison of the Helena *Arkansas Journal* was prosecuted on charges the Democrats said were trumped up by his Whig enemies to discredit him and his paper in the campaign.[48] When John D. Logan of the Van Buren *Western Frontier Whig*

43. *Ibid.,* Mar. 20, Apr. 24, May 15, June 19, 1844; *Gazette,* May 1, 8, 22, June 26, 1844; Borden et al. vs. Peay, Receiver, etc., May Term 1859, 20 *Ark.* 293.

44. *Gazette,* Feb. 14, Mar. 27, 1844; *Banner,* June 26, 1844; Albert H. Allen (ed.), *Arkansas Imprints 1821–1876* (New York: Published for The Bibliographical Society of America, by R. R. Bowker Company, 1947), 35.

45. *Gazette,* May 29, June 5, 1844.

46. *Banner,* Sept. 4, 11, 1844.

47. *Gazette,* Sept. 25, 1844.

48. *Banner,* Aug. 7, Sept. 4, Oct. 23, 1844.

insulted George W. Clarke of the Van Buren *Arkansas Intelligencer* in his paper, Clarke challenged him to a duel. It was fought in the Cherokee Nation near Fort Smith on October 1, without injury to either.[49] True to the predictions, the *Times and Advocate* did not survive the campaign. Its last issue on September 30 announced the termination of Weller's service as editor and his departure from Arkansas. With his wife and son, he moved to Covington, Tennessee, where he died of inflammation of the lungs on December 10, 1844, at the age of 25 years and 10 months.[50] The *Times and Advocate* suspended publication with its office under a heavy mortgage. John Colby and his partner, Jacob Gish, issued first the *Arkansas Farmer* and then the *Spirit of the Age* from this office soon afterwards,[51] but both were short lived.

Many Democratic newspapers used a stock woodcut of a crowing rooster to announce the party's victories. It was satirized in the *Gazette's* first cartoon, published on October 9, 1844, the first issue after the election for state offices. It was a crudely executed one-column political cartoon, in which the usual procedure of cutting away the background was reversed, making the picture predominantly black, with the lettering and outlines of the figures white. It showed a racoon, the Whig symbol, strangling a rooster and saying, "cant you crow," with punctuation omitted. It was used in connection with the Whig victory in Pulaski county, in which the editor's brother, William B. Borden, was one of the winners, being elected sheriff of Pulaski County on the Whig ticket by a substantial majority.

Shortly afterwards the *Gazette* had to acknowledge defeat on the state level. The official tabulation in the governor's race gave Drew 8,797 votes, Gibson 7,066, and Byrd 2,504. In the race for Congress, Yell received 11,-112 votes to Walker's 7,583 and Tully's 112. The Democrats gained 12 seats in the legislature, making 21 of the 25 senators and 63 of the 75 representatives Democrats.[52]

One prominent Whig credited his party's defeat to the emigration of the past four years that had brought in more new Democrats than Whigs.[53] This, of course, was an oversimplification. The importance of Byrd's candidacy cannot be overlooked, for the protest vote he received would have been sufficient to elect Gibson.

On the Saturday before the state election, the Whigs had a celebration at Little Rock to emphasize the forthcoming concentration of attention on the presidential campaign. They raised a tall but rather crooked flag pole and sent a coonskin to the top, only to be embarrassed by the attentions of a passing buzzard. Their candidate for state senator from Pulaski County, Thomas W. Newton, who was also vice president of the state Temperance Society and a deacon in the Presbyterian Church, chose this occasion to fall

49. *Ibid.*, Oct. 23, 1844.
50. *Gazette,* Dec. 30, 1844; *Memphis Appeal,* Dec. 27, 1844.
51. *Banner,* Oct. 2, 1844; *Gazette,* Dec. 16, 1844; Jan. 20, 1845.
52. *Banner,* Nov. 6, 20, 1844; *Gazette,* Nov. 6, 1844.
53. *Gazette,* Oct. 30, 1844.

off the wagon in a somewhat spectacular manner. And the editor of their leading newspaper, Borden, displayed uncharacteristic belligerence by brandishing a large Bowie knife and shouting that he would "wade knee deep in blood" if he could find a worthy person to fight. Needless to say, the *Banner* made much of these incidents. The Democratic celebration the next Saturday was tame by comparison. Borland arose from a sick bed to accept for the party a banner presented by the ladies of Little Rock, and if there was any rowdiness it was not publicized.[54]

Immediately after the state election, Borden announced that he would be gone for a few weeks "on a trip of business to Kentucky." It turned out to be very personal business—his marriage on October 29 at Danville, Kentucky to Sarah Yeiser, daughter of Daniel Yeiser. He missed the rest of the campaign, as he did not return with his bride until the middle of November, when he set up housekeeping in a rented house at the corner of Markham and West Main (now Broadway).[55]

Ratification of the treaty for the annexation of Texas was a big issue in the presidential campaign. Borden saw the annexation as an act of bad faith towards Mexico, a violation of existing treaties, and a threat to the union because it would give new impetus to the slavery question. He also thought this extension of the American frontier would give Texas new settlers at the expense of Arkansas. Self preservation was the only justification he could see for it, and he favored making Texas a part of the United States only if it should become necessary to prevent its becoming a part of the British empire. Consequently he took a locally unpopular stand in opposition to immediate annexation as early as September of 1843, but by the next June he reworded his position to favor eventual annexation, advising against making it a partisan question.[56]

A movement that would soon give the nation a new political party began during this campaign. It had its roots in the slavery question, and aimed at restricting the citizenship rights of immigrants from foreign countries, on the theory that they tended to become abolitionists, and that those who were Catholics remained subjects of the Pope, a foreign power. The *Gazette* was mildly friendly to these doctrines, but Borland taxed his rhetoric to the utmost against them[57]—a position he would eventually reverse, with equal eloquence.

The Democratic candidates, James Knox Polk and George M. Dallas, received Arkansas' three electoral votes at the November election, and before the month ended it was apparent that they had won a substantial majority nationwide, although the popular vote was close. The *Gazette's* explanation was, "If Foreigners, Abolitionists, and Catholics, had not voted *in a body* against us, we should have triumphed."[58]

54. *Banner,* Oct. 2, 9, 1844.
55. *Ibid.,* Nov. 20, 1844; *Gazette,* Oct. 9, Nov. 13, 1844; Apr. 7, Sept. 22, 1845.
56. *Gazette,* Sept. 20, Dec. 27, 1843; May 22, June 26, 1844.
57. *Banner,* Oct. 2, 1844.
58. *Gazette,* Nov. 27, 1844.

Shortly before election day, Borland opened a law office in Ashley's brick row, in partnership with Elbert H. English, and took English into the *Banner* office as junior editor.[59] It was said that he expected his campaign services for Yell and Polk to get him an appointment as United States prosecuting attorney, and thought it would look better if he could be called a practicing lawyer.[60]

The legislature convened in Borden's absence, and bids for the public printing were taken early in the session. Borden had printed the acts and journals of the previous session under a contract let to him as the lowest bidder after the session adjourned, the legislature having left the selection of the printer to the secretary of state.[61] He hoped to get the job for the 1844 session, and his bid was submitted by his foreman, S. F. Logan. Albert Rust, chairman of the public printing committee and a distant relative of Sevier and the Rectors, told Logan he was taking bids only for the daily printing, and would call for bids for the acts and journals later. The *Gazette's* bid was accordingly submitted only for the daily printing, but the *Banner* office and Colby and Gish turned in bids covering both the daily printing and the acts and journals, and the *Banner* office got both jobs. Upon Borden's return, he complained of Rust's deception, and said the Democratic legislature was robbing the people to sustain a Democratic journal, in spite of the fact that three-fourths of the people were Whigs.[62] He was wrong, of course, for the recent elections had proved that the Whigs were in the minority. The usual argument about the justice of the election of the public printer followed, and once again Borland's remarks became dangerously personal.[63]

The Senate election also was held before Borden returned from his honeymoon. Correspondents of the *Banner* advanced Ashley, Yell, and William Field as possible candidates. Undoubtedly Field was the Dynasty's candidate, for some of the hierarchy distrusted Ashley's statements that he would not oppose Yell in 1846, and probably they thought Field would merely hold the office for Yell until then. Elias Conway wrote an argument against Ashley's candidacy, privately circulated in manuscript, in which he said Ashley's office of elector was a constitutional bar to his election as senator, and that his resignation as elector would be detrimental to Polk. But Yell must have decided to accept Ashley's presumed promise not to oppose him in 1846, for he announced that he had not authorized his name to be presented as a candidate and would not run, being satisfied with his seat in the lower house.[64]

Ashley won an easy victory. The *Gazette's* temporary editor was lavish with praise as he reported Ashley's election, Acting Governor Adams' fare-

59. *Banner,* Oct. 23, 30, 1844.
60. *Democrat,* May 29, 1846.
61. *Gazette,* Feb. 15, May 10, 1843.
62. *Ibid.,* Dec. 4, 1844.
63. *Banner,* Nov. 27, Dec. 11, 18, 1844.
64. *Ibid.,* Oct. 30, Nov. 6, 1844.

well speech, and Governor Drew's inaugural address, although Borden had strenuously opposed all three. Borden was back at his desk for the next issue, and explained that his youthful friend was too quick to approve untried public servants, and expressed a confidence in certain men that the regular editor did not share.[65] Five months later, a temporary editor of the Van Buren *Intelligencer* reprinted the editorial lauding Ashley to show the *Gazette's* inconsistency.[66]

Ashley left for Washington soon after his election, and Solon Borland,— now called General Borland, having been appointed adjutant general by the new governor [67]—was elected to perform his duties as presidential elector.[68] To Borden's surprise, Ashley sent as many public documents to the *Gazette* as to the Democratic newspapers.[69]

Sevier departed for Washington in a happy frame of mind too, because the legislature not only removed all censure of his conduct as bank commissioner, but officially declared that he deserved the thanks of the people for his skillful discharge of his duties. The *Gazette* deplored this whitewashing, and supposed that the other commissioner had not been included because the legislature considered a private citizen's reputation less valuable than a senator's.[70]

Woodruff did not fare as well. His memorial praying relief from the 1837 default was supported by a petition signed by many prominent men of both

65. *Gazette,* Nov. 13, 20, 1844.
66. *Ibid.,* Apr. 14, 1845.
67. *Banner,* June 11, 1845.
68. *Ibid.,* Dec. 4, 1844; *Gazette,* Dec. 4, 1844.
69. *Gazette,* Dec. 30, 1844.
70. *Ibid.,* Dec. 16, 1844.

parties and by a *Banner* editorial, and the committee to which it was referred returned a favorable report. But again it was laid on the table, which Woodruff said was "through the scruples of some over-conscientious democratic members, who happened to be a little tender-footed." [71] He was left to continue to plod his way wearily through the courts with it.

Except for a few minor incidents, the controversies of 1845 did not directly involve the *Gazette*. There was a brief unpleasant correspondence between Charles P. Bertrand and Albert Rust,[72] and a more protracted exchange between Williamson S. Oldham and Alfred Wallace that claimed space in both the *Gazette* and the *Banner*.[73] A 26-day revival held in February won 95 converts for the Christian Church, most of them proselytes from other denominations, and caused great dissension in the community. Borden refused to open his columns to writers who wanted to discuss religious doctrines, and suggested to one who accused one of the evangelists of heresy that he should make his arguments in an oral debate.[74]

The *Gazette's* relative tranquillity of 1845 can be attributed in some measure to the fact that Solon Borland was out of town most of the time, and that the unpleasantness late in the year was within the Democratic party. Borden felt no obligation to report news of the opposing party in great detail, much less to become involved in it.

Borland did not enjoy the same peace of mind. A recent episode in his private life caused a scandal so great that his political support in the next campaign might well be a liability. Madame d'Estimauville de Beau Mouchel came to Little Rock six weeks after Borland's arrival and established a fashionable school for girls, which Borland "puffed" at every opportunity.[75] It was later hinted that she had followed him here to continue an illicit romance, which remained a secret throughout 1844.[76] He left for Washington to see the inauguration on February 8, 1845, five days after the third session of her school began.[77] About that time, they apparently knew their secret love affair would soon be exposed. Soon after he left, she made arrangements to move to a recently settled agricultural community in Dallas County, where she would be the superintendent of a young ladies' academy. The announcement was made on March 1, and the academy was to open on April 14. She had so charmed the community leaders who served as trustees of the school that they had even named their town d'Estimauville in her honor.[78]

Sevier and Ashley left Washington soon after the inauguration and ar-

71. *Banner,* Mar. 11, 1846.

72. *Gazette,* Feb. 10, 1845.

73. *Ibid.,* Jan. 27, Feb. 10, 24, Mar. 3, 1845; *Banner,* Jan. 29, Feb. 5, 1845.

74. *Gazette,* Feb. 17, 24, 1845; Pope, *Early Days in Arkansas,* 145–146; John Rogers, *The Autobiography of Elder J. T. Johnson* (Cincinnati, 1861), 225–226.

75. *Banner,* Jan. 9, 16, 23, Feb. 13, May 1, 8, July 10, Aug. 21, Sept. 11, 1844; *Gazette,* Jan. 31, Feb. 14, Aug. 21, 1844.

76. *Arkansas True Democrat,* Dec. 11, 18, 1855.

77. *Gazette,* Jan. 13, 1845; *Banner,* Jan. 15, Feb. 12, 1845.

78. *Gazette,* Mar. 3, 1845; *Banner,* Mar. 5, 1845; *True Democrat,* Dec. 18, 1855.

rived at Little Rock during the first week in April. Sevier had good reason to hurry home, for his wife had been ill for a long time, and died at Little Rock on March 16, while he was on his way home. Also, it was rumored that he would be sent to Mexico as secretary of legation on a mission pertaining to the annexation of Texas.[79]

Borland was in no such hurry, and in fact, seemed eager to prolong his absence. He had stopped to visit old friends at Memphis on his way to Washington, and stopped there again on his way home. He did not return to Little Rock until the first week in May, having been gone almost three months. In the *Banner,* he gloated over his bachelor status and boasted that the ladies had welcomed him home by showering him with gifts of fruit and flowers.[80]

On the evening of May 27, he was married to Mary Isabel Milbourne, the only daughter of George Milbourne, a Little Rock merchant. It must have been a whirlwind courtship, and his old friends at Memphis were astonished at the news.[81] Undoubtedly his friends at Little Rock were even more surprised, for his affair with Madame d'Estimauville was known by that time. In the next issue of the *Gazette* after the announcement of the marriage, there was a sad little unsigned poem of seven stanzas, written especially for the *Gazette* by somebody in Dallas County. It described happy hours with a loved one in the past and the loneliness of the present, and ended:

> "Thy heart is cold, or changed,
> *And we can meet no more!*" [82]

Obviously, Madame d'Estimauville had gotten the message, probably by the marriage notice in the newspapers. Soon afterwards her story was also out in Dallas County, and she left in disgrace. The town's name was changed to Tulip.[83]

On the day before the wedding, John W. Farley, publisher of the *Banner,* withdrew from S. Borland & Co., the firm that published the paper under a contract with the Democratic Central Committe. On July 16, Elbert H. English, junior editor, also withdrew, because the *Banner* could not support more than one editor, though one did double duty as editor and publisher. English opened a law office at the State Bank building, his law partnership with Borland having been dissolved.[84]

Another name-calling episode between Borden and Borland lasted two or three issues late in July. The kind of language that had caused many a duel was used freely. Borden made it understood that he regarded Borland as a man of decidedly low character, and mentioned a rumor that the men controlling the *Banner* were considering getting rid of him. Borland shrugged off

79. *Gazette,* Apr. 7, 1845; *Banner,* Mar. 19, Apr. 9, 1845.
80. *Banner,* Feb. 26, May 7, 14, 28, 1845.
81. *Ibid.,* May 28, June 18, 1845; *Gazette,* June 2, 1845.
82. *Gazette,* June 9, 1845.
83. *Biographical and Historical Memoirs of Southern Arkansas* (Chicago, Nashville and St. Louis: The Goodspeed Publishing Co., 1890), 704.
84. *Banner,* May 28, July 16, 1845; *Gazette,* July 21, 1845.

as renegades the dissatisfied few of his party who were "making love to the *Gazette*." [85] Two weeks later, Borland left the *Banner* in the hands of the foreman and others, and took his family to Hot Springs for a month, saying the entire family was ill. They returned about the middle of September, but the illness of the family continued. [86]

Borden was hard pressed to get out the *Gazette's* issue of June 2, 1845 on time, because during the preceding week, he moved the *Gazette* office half a block north, to the old Recess saloon building on Elm Street. The building he vacated, built by Edward Cole, was rented to others. In 1858 all except the cellar and the two stores on the ground floor were leased to the proprietors of the Anthony House, and connected with the hotel by a bridge over the alley at the second floor level. [87] It was still an annex to the Anthony House when both buildings were destroyed by fire in September, 1875. [88]

Elm Street was not really a street, but had been platted as an alley 20 feet wide without a name, parallel with Markham Street and the river, and between them. Its proximity to the river front made a street more desirable than an alley, and it was used and regarded as such in spite of its narrowness. The Recess building, which now became the *Gazette* office, was on lot 4, block 1, Original City of Little Rock, in the middle of the north half of the block bounded by Main, Markham, and Scott streets and the Arkansas River. The buildings on this half of the block fronted on the alley called Elm Street and had the river at their rear. The three lots on the east end of the south half of the block were vacant, and across this open space could be seen the Anthony House and the Woodruff home on two corners of Markham and Scott. The new office was directly opposite the old one, with a half block intervening.

The Recess building had been built in the mid-1820's. A fire originating in it had destroyed all the buildings on the north side of Elm Street between it and the market house in the next block east, on April 26, 1840. [89] Saloons and billiard parlors had occupied the building since its erection, and next door was another saloon called the Arcade, equally well known as the resort of loafers. [90] When the *Gazette* moved into the building, it was owned by Noah H. Badgett and the heirs of John McLain. [91] On May 16, 1848, William B. Wait bought it [92] and became the *Gazette's* landlord.

85. *Banner,* July 23, 30, 1845; *Gazette,* July 28, 1845.
86. *Banner,* Aug. 13, 20, 27, Sept. 3, 10, Nov. 5, 12, 1845.
87. William E. Woodruff, as agent for Jacob Brown's estate, to Q. A. and A. J. Gilkey, Jan. 1, 1858, and to Leonard M. Filkins, Apr. 1, 1860, Ms. lease in William E. Woodruff Papers, Arkansas History Commission.
88. *Gazette,* Sept. 21, 1875.
89. *Ibid.,* Apr. 29, 1840.
90. William E. Woodruff, Jr., "A Chronicle of Little Rock," *Gazette,* Nov. 7, 1931.
91. Pulaski County Deed Book F, 197.
92. Pulaski County Deed Book T, 381. The building was later the *True Democrat* office, and the *National Democrat* and the *Unconditional Union* were printed there during the Civil War. When it burned on Feb. 3, 1867, it was a job printing office owned by Richard H. Johnson and Calvin C. Bliss, and a German newspaper, the *Staats Zeitung* was being printed there. See *Daily Gazette,* Feb. 5, 1867.

12

BENJAMIN J. BORDEN

1845-1848 CHESTER ASHLEY and Archibald Yell had gone to Washington in 1844 as deadly rivals, each determined to be elected to the Senate seat that would be vacant in 1846. Each had his hardcore support at home, and each tried to expand it by strategic dispensation of favors.

Solon Borland was definitely on Yell's side, and was living in Yell's home at the northeast corner of Second and Louisiana.[1] Ashley blocked Yell's effort to have Borland appointed United States prosecuting attorney, and about that time Borland brought his hostility towards Ashley into the open.[2] In October, 1845, Woodruff was appointed postmaster at Little Rock to replace Barnett Williams, Sevier's uncle-in-law, who was removed from office.[3]

The competition between Ashley and Yell was the main topic of political discussion as the Democratic nomination for Congress loomed ahead. If anybody but Yell were nominated, it would mean Yell definitely would be a candidate for the Senate. Robert Ward Johnson was a candidate for the nomination, and some believed he would take the seat as Yell's protege.[4]

Ashley had decided Sevier was expendable. This may have been simply because Sevier did not exert his influence to draw support away from Yell in Ashley's favor. But the seeds may have been sown as early as 1833, when Sevier began his efforts towards statehood without first clearing it with his supporters at home. This had been the first step towards making Sevier the real leader of the party, and the control Ashley and Woodruff had once enjoyed had slowly diminished. In retrospect, Woodruff may have concluded that Sevier's efforts to help him get out of the newspaper business in 1836

1. *Arkansas Banner,* Oct. 5, Dec. 3, 1845.
2. *Arkansas Democrat,* May 29, 1846.
3. *Gazette,* Nov. 3, 1845; *Banner,* Nov. 5, 1845.
4. *Democrat,* July 24, 1846.

Robert Ward Johnson.

had the ulterior motivation of the chance to control the *Gazette* with a more pliable editor.

In the summer and fall of 1845, Ashley worked to establish a new political machine within the framework of the Democratic party. He made several overtures to Governor Thomas S. Drew, who steadfastly insisted upon remaining neutral in any contest between Democrats. At last, Ashley laid before Drew the proposition that they should use their combined influence and patronage to build a machine, with the help of a new journal that would supersede the *Banner*. Drew's ultimate reward would be the Senate seat that Sevier had held for many years.

Drew was horrified, for he considered Sevier the most distinguished man in the state. He firmly rejected Ashley's proposition, and said Ashley then turned to Daniel J. Chapman, whose influence in northern Arkansas was comparable with Drew's, and who was soon as completely under Ashley's control as Woodruff. According to Drew, Ashley lived in fear that his proposal to Drew would be exposed, and had Chapman write letters to the *Banner* to undermine Drew's influence in his own section.[5]

Ashley had the support of the Van Buren *Intelligencer* in the west and

5. Thomas S. Drew to William Black, Little Rock, Oct. 1, 1846, Ms. in Robert W. Trimble Papers, Arkansas History Commission.

the Helena *Journal* in the east. He could not hope for the support or neutrality of the *Banner* as long as Borland was its editor, and its importance as the only Democratic newspaper with statewide circulation could not be overlooked. But Borland had privately served notice that he wanted to leave the *Banner*, whether as his own decision or in response to the rumored dissatisfaction of some Democrats is not clear.[6] He had returned to the medical profession on a part-time basis early in the fall of 1845, opening an office in Yell's little law office adjoining his home. Before the year ended, he had written and published a 45-page pamphlet entitled *An Essay on "The Milk Sickness" of the Human Subjects, or "The Trembles" of Animals; Embracing Its History, Cause, and Treatment.*[7]

Too late Ashley regretted his refusal to provide one-third of the *Banner's* finances in the beginning,[8] and it was reported that he now tried to buy all or part of the paper, with the condition that Woodruff should be its editor, but the Democratic Central Committee rejected his offer.[9] Borland retired with the issue of December 3, 1845, and announced that he would devote all his time to the practice of medicine and surgery. He was succeeded as editor on December 10 by Archibald Hamilton Rutherford, an indirect relative of the Dynasty and as strong a supporter of Yell as Borland, though hardly as effective.

A letter signed "Jefferson" in Rutherford's second issue told of Ashley's promises in 1844 not to run against Yell in 1846. Ashley left for Washington soon afterwards, without confirming or denying that he had made such promises. The reply was made by one who signed "Old Settler," probably Woodruff, who denied that Ashley had made these promises and quoted directly the ambiguous reply he had made when Yell's friends had tried to exact such a pledge.[10] The *Banner* countered on January 21 with statements by Solon Borland, Acting Governor Samuel Adams, and legislators John S. Houston, Williamson S. Oldham, and Col. J. G. Walker, testifying that Ashley had assured them he would not run against Yell.

Johnson's nomination for Congress by the convention made Yell's candidacy for the Senate a certainty, and many people believed he had swapped his influence in the senatorial campaign for Yell's influence in his own race. Ashley's friends agreed to accept Johnson's nomination only after he promised not to interfere with the senatorial election.[11]

An anonymous writer had said in 1844, "Do you not know that there is a mysterious link—or something stronger than even parental love—binding Woodruff to Ashley—that for him life, fame, or fortune would be deemed a trifling sacrifice."[12] Woodruff proved this so well in 1846 that as he made

6. *Banner*, July 30, Nov. 5, Dec. 3, 1845.
7. *Ibid.*, Oct. 5, Dec. 3, 1845; Jan. 7, 1846; *Gazette*, Dec. 29, 1845.
8. *Gazette*, Oct. 14, 1845; Jan. 5, 1846.
9. *Banner*, Apr. 1, 1846.
10. *Ibid.*, Dec. 17, 31, 1845.
11. *Ibid.*, Jan. 21, 1846.
12. *Gazette*, Oct. 2, 1844.

the preliminary arrangements to take out a $5,000 life insurance policy that fall, the *Gazette* commented that if he was worth that much to his family, he was worth twice as much to Ashley. "He is to the Senator what Boswell was to Johnson," said the *Gazette,* "and no doubt records for future use every wise saying uttered by him." [13]

Ashley already was convinced of his old friend's fidelity, and knew he could trust him to take care of his interests as if his own life depended on it. When Ashley returned to Washington in the spring of 1846 for the last session of his term of office, he stopped sending his offerings for the *Banner* directly to the editor, and sent them to Woodruff instead. Woodruff made copies of the letters, possibly because Ashley's handwriting was difficult to read and possibly because recent changes in the situation at home sometimes made editing desirable, and took the copies with the congressional documents and marked articles in newspapers to the *Banner* office. [14]

Thus Woodruff was prepared to make other arrangements for publication of Ashley's material on short notice. Eventually this would lead to the new paper, but first sufficient justification for starting a rival paper had to be skillfully established.

Ashley's efforts to control appointments became an issue the first week in March, when it became known that the postmaster general was about to take the postmastership away from Woodruff because of Yell's opposition. Yell had told the postmaster general that Woodruff was on record as a defaulter to the state government and was therefore ineligible to hold any state office, and that it was unfair to allow him to hold federal office. [15]

The *Gazette* and its Whig correspondent at Batesville had given strong approval to Woodruff's appointment. When word came of the effort to remove him, Borden expressed surprise that his opposition should come from a high ranking and much obligated member of the party he had served long and well. [16] But so far as the Yell clique was concerned, Woodruff's sale of the *Gazette* to a Whig had canceled all the party's debt to him. The controversy that followed brought out information about the sale of the *Gazette* that otherwise never would have been made public. Borden did not care to be involved in it. He said it was nothing to him how many people the *Banner's* editor read out of the Democratic party, and that Woodruff was fully capable of defending himself. [17]

Woodruff had to defend Ashley as well, for the dispute over his rumored removal opened the subject of Ashley's attitude towards the president's appointments. A *Banner* correspondent said Ashley not only had failed to support Polk's measures, but had worked against his appointments by harassing

13. *Ibid.,* Oct. 26, 1846.
14. *Banner,* Mar. 25, 1846.
15. *Ibid.,* Mar. 4, 1846.
16. *Gazette,* Nov. 3, 17, 1845; Mar. 2, 1846.
17. *Ibid.,* Mar. 9, 1846; *Banner,* Mar. 4, 1846.

him and department heads for appointments for his favorites and refusing to withdraw his objections when others were chosen.[18]

An amusing aspect of this dispute was that neither side cared to say that Polk had made the appointments in question upon Yell's recommendation. This would have made it a simple struggle between Ashley and Yell, with the president only incidentally involved. This would collapse the arguments of Yell's friends that Ashley's failure to support Polk in all things proved he was not a good Democrat. Ashley's friends did not want to emphasize the fact that Yell had more influence with the president than Ashley, and based their argument on the fact that even the most loyal senators should not have to give rubber-stamp approval to all the president's decisions, especially in local situations where the executive could not know all the pertinent facts.

A writer who used the pseudonym "Fair Play," undoubtedly Woodruff, predicted that the *Banner* would support Yell and violently oppose Ashley, and therefore could not claim to be the organ of the entire party. Taking for granted that Rutherford would refuse to print this letter, the writer submitted it to the *Gazette,* and paid for the space. Borden published it on March 9, and said neither faction could expect favors from the *Gazette* without paying, "for they would both unite tomorrow to beat a Whig."

Two days later, Woodruff began a series of signed letters in the *Banner*. Rutherford agreed to give him two columns, but Woodruff found he could not abridge his defense with justice to himself. As the writing progressed, he asked for more and more space, until the first letter became seven columns long, the equivalent of a full page.

First, he discussed the controversy over the postmastership, disclaiming any agency in Williams' removal and proving it was Yell who had attempted his own removal. This he did by reproducing the correspondence on the subject, obviously supplied by Ashley, who had made a strong defense of Woodruff's 1837 default. Then Woodruff explained his role in the 1836 election, to show that Yell was indebted to him for his first election to Congress, and to explain the hatred the Whigs bore him. This was a prologue to his explanation of the default.[19]

The second letter, published a week later, told as much about the sale of the *Gazette* as he cared to make public, although a few other details were subsequently drawn from him. He argued that he had as much right to sell his paper as any other personal property, but said his only other choice was bankruptcy, and that he could have kept the *Gazette* only if the 1842 legislature had given him the public printing and relieved him of the defalcation charge. Woodruff's feelings were very near the surface on this subject, but he showed resentment only towards a few unnamed Democrats who had given him only sympathy when he had needed help.

18. *Banner,* Mar. 4, 1846.
19. *Ibid.,* Mar. 11, 1846.

Rutherford was unmoved by Woodruff's eloquence. He did not believe that Woodruff's financial situation had been so bad as to make the sale of the *Gazette* necessary, and he still said it had been an act of spite against the party. Moreover, Woodruff's letter had again far exceeded the space allotted it, and Rutherford said nobody had a right to monopolize the *Banner,* to the exclusion of other subscribers and his own editorials.[20]

Rutherford was particularly incensed by Woodruff's contention that the *Banner* was the organ only of the Yell clique, and he claimed impartiality towards all good Democrats. But at the same time, he stated his preference for Yell over Ashley, having demonstrated it for weeks by packing the *Banner* with editorials and contributed articles favorable to Yell and admitting none that took the opposite position except Woodruff's two letters. "Fair Play" returned to the *Gazette* the next week to make this point.[21]

On March 23, Woodruff took to the *Banner* office two of his own letters and several letters and clippings sent by Ashley. Two days later Rutherford published one short letter by Woodruff that accused Yell of appointing defaulters to office while he was governor, and two letters and one newspaper article sent by Ashley, telling of recent action in Washington on matters of interest in Arkansas. But Rutherford complained of Ashley's discourtesy in sending these things by Woodruff, and made a thrust at Woodruff with two quotations from Shakespeare intended to imply that Woodruff's greatness was all in the past.

Because Woodruff refused to modify or omit objectionable passages in his second letter, Rutherford declined to publish it in the *Banner,* but on March 28 it was published as an extra half sheet of the *Banner* at Woodruff's expense. It contained his recent appeals to his party and the rejected letter. He ended with this warning: "But, rest assured that I WILL BE HEARD, while I have the strength to wield a pen, or can find a press sufficiently INDEPENDENT to publish for me. And, if even that resource shall fail me, I can still resort to my old trade of 'basket making,' and establish a press myself, which no power on earth can MUZZLE." [22]

In the conversation of March 23, Woodruff offered to buy three columns a week in the *Banner*. He wanted to pay $300 a year for the space, and would pay in addition for whatever number of copies he might desire. He wanted to conduct the three columns as a newspaper within a newspaper, with his name shown as editor. He said his purpose was to give Ashley's friends an equal chance with his enemies. Rutherford required Woodruff to put this proposition in writing, which he did on March 31.[23]

In the *Banner* the next day, Rutherford complained that Woodruff made increasingly unreasonable demands, threatening to seek another medium unless Rutherford would agree to assist in his own defamation. He thought

20. *Ibid.,* Mar. 18, 1846.
21. *Ibid.,* Mar. 23, 1846.
22. *Gazette,* Mar. 30, 1846.
23. *Ibid.,* Apr. 13, 1846.

Woodruff was trying to make him refuse him his columns so he could say he was forced to take his material to the *Gazette* or establish his own press, and that recent use of the *Gazette* by Ashley's friends foretold a possible alliance with the Whigs to produce a split in the Democratic party.[24]

Woodruff's battle over the postmastership was won by this time, for within the next few days the news came that the postmaster general refused to remove him from office, saying his efficiency made it unnecessary to inquire which Democrat was his friend.[25]

One of Ashley's supporters took Rutherford to task for agitating the rivalry between Ashley and Yell, and insisted that Ashley was still the favorite in his locality. Because the writer was influential, Rutherford published the letter,[26] the first pro-Ashley letter except Woodruff's to appear in the *Banner* since he became editor.

The accusations against both Woodruff and Ashley continued, and Woodruff took his replies to the *Gazette*. Borden said he could not care less who won, for the Whigs would not benefit in either case, but he published Woodruff's letters because Woodruff paid for the space, and they were always labeled "PAID FOR" at the end.[27]

Borden was glad to have a cash-in-advance customer, for he had the same collection problems his predecessors had had. He sent out traveling collection agents from time to time, and had begun to insist on cash payment in advance at the end of his first year, with $3,000 on his books in red ink.[28] He had brought on a new problem with his announcement on January 5, 1846 that the *Gazette's* subscription rates were reduced from $3 to $2 a year, provided payment was made within two months after the subscription began. He advertised the *Gazette* as "the cheapest paper in the state." Rutherford resisted all efforts to reduce the *Banner's* rates, saying no newspaper the size of the *Gazette* or the *Banner* could sustain itself with such rates until its circulation was at least 2,000 or 3,000. He predicted that eventually Borden would have to return to his old rates,[29] and Borden undoubtedly was beginning to agree. He excused his publication of Woodruff's communications with, "An editor in Arkansas is doing injustice to himself and friends, if he rejects what is to him a source of profit, merely to save appearances." [30]

However, he was not willing to sell the *Gazette* back to Woodruff, and refused his liberal offer because it would again make the *Gazette* Democratic. Borden's public statement a month later implied that he was too noble to do what Woodruff had done. "And if I had only consulted my pecuniary interest, I should, perhaps, have been induced to sell;" he said, "but there were other

24. *Banner,* Apr. 1, 1846.
25. *Gazette,* Apr. 6, 1846.
26. *Banner,* Apr. 8, 1846.
27. *Gazette,* Apr. 13, 1846.
28. *Ibid.,* Dec. 9, 1844. Among the collection agents mentioned 1844–1847 were Josiah Giles, John W. Farley, John M. Butler, H. Von Seckendorf, and J. C. M. Hicks.
29. *Banner,* Apr. 1, 1846.
30. *Gazette,* Apr. 27, 1846.

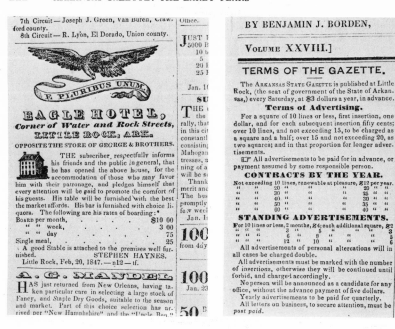

and higher considerations in the way. It bore too much the appearance of betraying the Whig standard, entrusted to my care, to the enemy. My feelings revolted at the idea . . ."[31] More than a year later, the *Banner* alluded to the *Gazette's* comment on Woodruff's political treachery in connection with his sale of the *Gazette* to Borden, but neither Woodruff nor Borden chose to consider this article as touching upon that subject.[32]

Woodruff's first letter was published in the *Gazette* on April 13, and consisted of a copy of his offer to buy space in the *Banner,* with his explanation that Rutherford had not yet given him an answer, though he had prodded him four days after writing the offer. He could see that further attempts to publish his side of the controversy in the *Banner* would be useless.

Rutherford said the words "PAID FOR" at the end of Woodruff's letter indicated an alliance between disorganizing Democrats and Whigs. He said both Ashley and Woodruff had previously shown signs of defection, and reached all the way back to Woodruff's unpublicized preference for John Quincy Adams in territorial days as weak proof. The *Gazette* had never stopped its accusations against Ambrose Sevier, and the *Banner* tried to correlate the attacks on Sevier and those on Yell in the same paper.[33]

31. *Ibid.,* May 25, 1846.
32. *Democrat,* Oct. 15, 1847.
33. *Banner,* Apr. 15, 1846.

From this point, Rutherford and his correspondents bogged down in constant repetition, unable to add new arguments and finding only new ways to word the old ones. Woodruff's "PAID FOR" articles continued in the *Gazette,* but he too could only repeat what he had said before. Borden cautioned the Whigs against identifying themselves with either faction of the opposing party, explaining again that his publication of Woodruff's articles was purely a business transaction.[34]

On April 27, Woodruff announced that he would start his own paper as soon as he could make the necessary arrangements. He admired Borden's independence in selling him *Gazette* space, but some of his friends objected to his patronage of a Whig paper, and he had decided he could fight best with his own weapons. By purchasing a part of the materials of the old *Times and Advocate* office, he could start his paper without waiting for all new materials to be shipped from the Eastern cities. This revived the old charges that he had owned the *Times and Advocate's* press and type when the paper came under Cyrus Weller's control, which he denied.[35] Woodruff continued to fill most of his three columns in the *Gazette* with his own articles and the effective "public sentiment" letters from correspondents through the issue of May 11, when he announced that he would begin publication of the *Arkansas Democrat* the next week.

Solon Borland came back to the *Banner* as its principal editor on May 6, at the request of Rutherford, who remained as junior editor.[36] Borden viewed this as evidence that the Yell clique dared not pit the inexperienced Rutherford against "the Patriarch of the Arkansas press." He expected to enjoy watching the two veteran editors match wits, and hinted that either the *Banner* or the *Democrat* might not survive the battle.[37] The *Banner* withheld the customary welcome to the new paper, and accused Woodruff of detaining its papers in the post office and employing one of Ashley's slaves to handle the mails.[38]

The announcement of the forthcoming newspaper was overshadowed by the arrival on May 9 of news that war with Mexico had begun, and that Gen. Zachary Taylor had sent the governors of Louisiana and Texas a requisition for troops. Anticipating a similar call on Arkansas, Governor Drew alerted the Arkansas State Militia.[39]

Woodruff brought out the first issue of the *Arkansas Democrat* on May 21, using most of the space to repeat his side of the dispute that had led to its establishment. He demanded that the *Banner* prove or retract its recent statement that he had refused in 1842 to sell the *Gazette* to the Democrats a few days before he had sold it to the Whigs. The *Banner* surprised him the next

34. *Gazette,* Apr. 27, 1846.
35. *Democrat,* July 24, 1846.
36. *Banner,* May 6, 1846.
37. *Gazette,* May 11, 1846; *Democrat,* May 21, 1846.
38. *Banner,* May 13, 19, 1846.
39. *Ibid.,* May 13, 1846; *Gazette,* May 11, 1846.

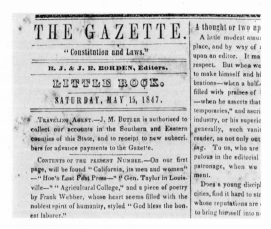

week with Elias Conway's statement telling of the effort he, Johnson, and Hempstead had made to buy the *Gazette*. Woodruff contended that the time element saved both his veracity and Conway's, because Conway said Woodruff told them he was bound by a previous purchase agreement.[40] Johnson then offered a statement corroborating Conway's, which Woodruff said only strengthened his contention that the offer from the Democrats had come too late.[41]

On May 25, Borden announced that his 23-year-old brother, John B. Borden, had joined the *Gazette's* staff as junior editor. Both editors were practicing attorneys, and one would always be on duty at the *Gazette* when the other was out on the circuit. The elder brother was still the *Gazette's* sole proprietor, and denied the rumors that he was about to sell the paper. The *Democrat* was now the only Little Rock newspaper with a single editor, and Woodruff suggested that the doubling of teams foretold a coalition to bring the Whig party to Yell's support.[42]

The news that had been anxiously awaited for more than two weeks arrived on May 27. Congress had authorized the president on May 13 to accept the services of 50,000 volunteers for the invasion of Mexico, and he had directed the secretary of war to call for troops. Arkansas was asked to furnish one cavalry regiment for service in Mexico and one infantry battalion to replace troops withdrawn from the Arkansas frontier. Governor Drew issued a proclamation to implement the call, and designated Adjutant General Borland to receive the cavalry companies and muster them into service.[43]

For several years, Capt. Albert Pike had commanded a military company called the Little Rock Guards. Pike was out of town, and the company de-

40. *Democrat,* May 29, 1846.
41. *Ibid.,* June 19, 1846.
42. *Ibid.,* May 29, 1846.
43. *Gazette,* June 1, 1846.

cided to wait until his return to volunteer. Woodruff's oldest son, 17-year-old Alden Mills Woodruff, had been a member of the Guards about three years. He was so eager to go to war that he rushed forward to enlist in a new company being recruited, but withdrew and returned to the Guards when Pike returned and the Guards volunteered for the war. This was done with his father's approval but without his advice.[44]

Stephen S. Tucker had been elected colonel of the 13th Regiment of Arkansas Militia a few days before the call for troops, and was expected to be elected captain of the new company bound for Mexico. But on May 27, he was commissioned a captain in the new Third Regiment of United States Dragoons, which would not enlist men from Arkansas.[45] Consequently, he withdrew from the new company, and Solon Borland was elected its captain on June 6.[46]

Borland had announced a few days previously that he was retiring from the *Banner* to go to war,[47] and three days after his election he went into camp near Little Rock. Here on June 12, he wrote to Dr. Lewis Shanks of Memphis University to decline an appointment as professor of Materia Medica and Medical Jurisprudence, in the medical department of the University.[48]

John B. Borden's career as junior editor of the *Gazette* was cut short by his enlistment as a private in Pike's company. It was not announced until after the troops had marched off for the rendezvous at Washington,[49] and his name remained in the masthead as junior editor during the entire period of his service in Mexico.

The elder Woodruff was less fired with the spirit of war than his son, and told his readers that the call upon them was unnecessary, and that their services were needed more to check possible Indian hostilities on their home frontier than in Mexico.[50] Nor did the enlistment of his two greatest enemies deter him from attacking them.

When Borland's retirement from the *Banner* was announced, Woodruff said the *Banner* was a sinking ship and the rats were leaving it, and that the pay of a mounted gunman was more than that of a foot soldier in the Yell

---

44. *Democrat,* June 12, July 17, 1846.

45. *Banner,* May 19, 1846; *Gazette,* June 15, 29, 1846; *Democrat,* July 17, 1846; Francis B. Heitman, *Historical Register and Dictionary of the United States Army, from its Organization, September 29, 1789, to March 2, 1903* (Washington: Government Printing Office, 1903; Urbana: University of Illinois Press, 1965), I, 973. Tucker's commission dated from May 27. He commanded Company K in the new regiment and apparently never returned to Arkansas. He was appointed collector of customs at San Francisco in 1849 (*Gazette,* May 10, 1849), and resigned his army commission on June 30, 1851.

46. *Gazette,* June 8, 1846; *Democrat,* June 12, 1846.

47. *Democrat,* June 5, 1846.

48. *Ibid.,* June 19, 1846; Solon Borland to Dr. Lewis Shanks, Camp Catholic near Little Rock, June 12, 1846, Ms. in *Arkansas Gazette* Foundation Library.

49. *Gazette,* June 29, 1846.

50. *Ibid.,* June 1, 1846.

corps.[51] A few days after Borland's camp near Little Rock was established, Woodruff published as a communicated item, "He that has burned General Jackson in effigy, should never aspire to military honors.—D'Estimoville." [52] The sly dig in the misspelled name may have hit home, but it was ignored.

Archibald Yell vacated his seat in Congress, arrived at Little Rock on June 18, and enlisted immediately as a private in Borland's company. Woodruff said Arkansas was not so hard pressed to fill her quota that her Congressman had to desert his post. He surmised that Yell would be a candidate for colonel of the regiment, but he thought Yell intended neither to win the election nor to go to war in the ranks. His enlistment, Woodruff said, was only an excuse to leave Washington and get a head start on Ashley in campaigning.[53]

Borden did not attempt to guess Yell's political strategy. He simply said he was glad Yell had enlisted because he would be useful to his country as a soldier, while if he remained in Congress, he would strike a blow at the nation's best interests with his vote against the tariff.[54]

There was small risk of his losing the election for regimental commander, for President Polk paved the way. On the day Yell left Washington, the secretary of war wrote to inform Governor Drew that Yell hoped to command the regiment, and that this was also the president's wish.[55] Presumably it was left to Drew and other local Democrats to influence the election in Yell's favor.

The election of staff officers was held at Washington on July 4, and Yell was elected colonel, John Selden Roane lieutenant colonel, Solon Borland major, and Gaston Mears adjutant. In the company elections to fill the vacancies occasioned by these promotions, Christopher C. Danley became captain of Borland's old company.[56]

Woodruff kept Yell's desertion of his post in Washington constantly before the people, and with his reports of every important measure that came before Congress, he never failed to point out that Arkansas was without representation in the lower house.

Until the Mexican War started, the *Gazette* was far ahead of other Arkansas newspapers in illustrations. The production of cuts was tedious, expensive, and highly specialized. To have one made for one use only was impractical, and the work could not be done locally if it was to be of professional quality. The use of foundry stock woodcuts in advertisements was standard practice, and cuts made especially for a particular newspaper to use in every issue were not unusual. The *Gazette* introduced one of these under the masthead on May 1, 1844. It was a small but elaborate picture of a group of men

51. *Democrat,* June 5, 1846.
52. *Ibid.,* June 12, 1846.
53. *Ibid.,* June 19, 1846.
54. *Gazette,* June 22, 1846.
55. *Ibid.,* Aug. 3, 1846.
56. *Ibid.,* July 13, 1846; *Democrat,* July 10, 1846.

holding an American flag, a temple of liberty topped by an eagle with "E Pluribus Unum" emblazoned on streamers, and an abridgment of the *Gazette's* motto, "Constitution & Laws" on a massive boulder.

About the time Borden became proprietor of the *Gazette* in January of 1843, Dr. J. P. Norman of Little Rock received a few copies of a new book, *Rambles in Yucatan,* written by B. M. Norman. The doctor obtained seven of the beautifully executed plates used to illustrate the book, and loaned them to Borden, who reprinted in two installments a long review of the book, taken from the *New World.* Three of the plates were used with the first installment in the *Gazette* on February 8, 1843, and the other four appeared with the second installment on March 1.

Later that spring, Dr. William Byrd Powell presented three plans for damming the communication between the Arkansas River and Fourche Bayou, by which the poor drainage in the east end of the city and just below it could be controlled. A simple map showing the course of the two streams and the proposed location of the dam could easily be carved on a block of wood for newspaper reproduction, since it required no intricate details. The one-column map, crudely executed by Dr. Powell, was published with his explanation of the plans for the dam in the *Gazette* of May 31, 1843, and was the *Gazette's* first local illustration.

The Mexican War offered a similar opportunity for the use of locally produced maps, but the *Gazette* came in third in a three-way race among the

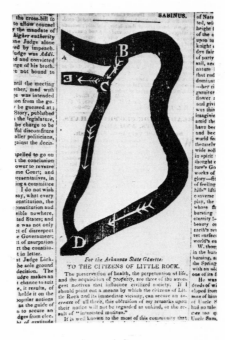

The *Gazette's* first local illustration, a map by William Byrd Powell showing the communication between the Arkansas River and Fourche Bayou, in the *Gazette* of May 31, 1843.

Little Rock papers. The *Banner* was first, with a four-column map of the seat of war copied from the New Orleans *Courier* by editor Borland on May 19, 1846. During the first week in June, the New Orleans *Delta* arrived, containing a detailed account of the battle of Palo Alto. It was written by an army officer stationed at Point Isabel, Texas, who also drew a simple diagram of the battlefield, a cut of which was made at New Orleans for the *Delta*. All three Little Rock newspapers reproduced the map, the *Democrat* on June 5, the *Gazette* June 8, and the *Banner* on either June 2 or 9. Woodruff facetiously said that the *Democrat's* map "was hastily scorched out, upon a pine knot, with the point of our devil's tail." The *Gazette's* two-column cut was made on old type metal by C. J. Garner of Little Rock, and appeared on page one. Only the *Democrat* properly credited the article and the original map to the *Delta*. The *Gazette's* editor patted himself on the back for his enterprise in thus making his paper interesting, and admonished his readers to encourage him with subscriptions and payment. The *Banner's* editor had the audacity to imply that the writer-cartographer was his own correspondent.

The *Delta's* editor's reaction to this piracy was, "We do not know if Little Rock, Ark., is a mean town—we should be sorry to insinuate that it is—but this we do know, it has got two mighty mean editors in it—him of the '*State Gazette*', and his contemporary of the '*Banner*.' They are so mean that we wonder their shadows are not ashamed to keep them company. Each of them copies from the *Delta*, our correspondent T.'s account of the battle of Palo Alto, diagram and all, without mention of the source from which they received it. Nay, they individually glorify themselves in being able to furnish it to their readers." [57]

Ironically, on the same day this comment was published in the *Delta*, June 22, the *Gazette* published another letter from the *Delta's* correspondent, telling of the battle of Resaca de la Palma, with a three-column battle map, and again failed to give the *Delta* credit for first publication. A week later, Borden had seen the *Delta's* complaint, and grudgingly acknowledged the origin of the material, commenting that journals of standing were sometimes annoyed when other papers reprinted their editorials without giving credit, but it took "a small concern, indeed" to have such proprietary feelings about the work of its correspondents.[58]

No more battle maps appeared in the Little Rock papers until October 23, when the *Democrat* had a one-column map copied from the Jefferson *Inquirer*. On June 18, 1847, the *Democrat* published the first battle map drawn especially for an Arkansas paper, a two-column cut showing the topography of Cerro Gordo. It illustrated a letter signed S.S.T., undoubtedly Stephen S. Tucker.

All these maps were produced by carving the details and lettering on a block of wood or type metal, so that the background rather than the map

57. *Democrat*, July 3, 1846.
58. *Gazette*, June 29, 1846.

took the ink. The result was a predominantly black picture, with white letters and details.

The forthcoming senatorial election dominated the 1846 campaign, with the candidates for the legislature having no more decisive planks in their platforms than their pleges to vote for either Ashley or Yell. In spite of Robert Ward Johnson's promise to take no part in the senatorial election, he expressed his preference for Yell as he stumped the state in his campaign for Congress.[59] As evidence of Woodruff's acceptance of his nomination and his effort at party unity, Johnson's name was kept at the head of the *Democrat's* editorial columns from its first issue, but the editor's failure to tout his candidacy passed unnoticed because he had no opponent. At the election on August 3, Johnson received 16,425 votes, with 101 scattering votes for men who were not formal candidates.[60] The legislature elected at the same time was predominantly Democratic, which meant that no Whig could be seriously considered as a candiate for the Senate.

Borden left immediately after the election for a two months visit to Kentucky. He left the *Gazette* in charge of Milton Fowler,[61] Absalom Fowler's 45-year-old brother, who was regularly employed as the deputy of Borden's brother, Sheriff William B. Borden.[62]

Like Borden, Milton Fowler had no favorites among the Democratic leaders, and figured the state woud be the loser no matter which man won the senatorial election. While he opposed both, he gave Ashley more trouble than he gave Yell. After Ashley arranged the appointment of Dr. Ewing H. Roane as surgeon of the Arkansas regiment, Fowler and one of the *Gazette's* correspondents said Roane was not qualified and that the appointment was supposed to get Ashley the votes controlled by the doctor's father and uncle, Samuel C. and John Selden Roane.[63]

Ashley and Sevier came home from Washington on August 26. In the next *Gazette,* Fowler substituted Ashley's name in reprinting an anecdote told of another senator, in which the senator was ridiculed for his vanity. Woodruff had seen the article in an Eastern newspaper, and reprinted the original version and the *Gazette's* version, identical except for the name of the senator. Woodruff accused the temporary editor of literary petty larceny and counterfeiting, and said Borden should hurry home to salvage the *Gazette's* integrity. Fowler twisted the rebuke into a compliment for the *Gazette's* usual high standards under its regular editor, and declined to return the compliment.[64]

Late in September, Lambert Reardon became postmaster at Little Rock, Woodruff having resigned. Reardon was of the Yell wing, and a month later

59. *Democrat,* Sept. 10, Oct. 8, 1847.
60. *Ibid.,* Sept. 25, 1846.
61. *Gazette,* July 26, Aug. 3, 1846.
62. *Ibid.,* Mar. 27, 1847; Feb. 8, 1849.
63. *Ibid.,* Aug. 24, Sept. 7, 1846.
64. *Ibid.,* Aug. 31, Sept. 14, 1846; *Democrat,* Sept. 4, 1846.

his son, Lambert Jeffrey Reardon, replaced Rutherford as editor of the *Banner*.[65]

According to Governor Drew, the *Democrat* had waged an insidious warfare against him almost from its beginning. He was accused of interfering in the senatorial election, and Woodruff's tone was gentle sorrow that Drew was misguided by bad advice. Drew said he had remained neutral, but now he wrote to at least one personal friend of long standing, the state senator from Randolph County, to explain why he could not support Ashley, no matter which Democrat was his opponent. Yell was not his first choice, but Drew would support him if he should be the strongest candidate the Democrats could field against Ashley. He regarded Ashley as "the most unsafe man in the state," and speculated that Ashley's willingness to sacrifice Sevier, his warm friend, indicated that he would be equally willing to "sacrifice the whole state at the shrine of his individual promotion and self aggrandizement." Said the governor, "It must be acknowledged that he has talents, although not of the high order of which he has credit, and they have been prostituted so long to the low groveling occupation of acquisition, acting on the principle that all which is not crime is righteousness, that really his exorbitant conceptions of self and his puny views of others, totally disqualify him to represent a free people, who recognize the principle of equality as paramount." [66]

Woodruff and Ashley were playing a cat-and-mouse game with the *Banner* about that time. The *Banner's* press had been bought in 1843 from John C. Rives of Washington by the members of the congressional delegation, Sevier, Fulton, and Cross, at the request of the Democratic Central Committee. No part of the $150 purchase price had ever been paid, and no note had been given for the debt. Undoubtedly Ashley had pulled the strings that placed in Woodruff's hands an order signed by Rives, directing the editors of the *Banner* to deliver the press to Woodruff. The order was dated August 10, 1846, but Woodruff did not present it to the *Banner's* business manager until early in October. The necessary money, plus $25, was speedily gathered from three members of the Yell faction and the debt to Rives was paid. This probably was the expected outcome, for neither Woodruff nor Ashley had paid Rives any money and this was probably one of Woodruff's services as a collection agent, but it served to make the opposition nervous in the last days before the senatorial election. Even now, Woodruff reminded them that they still owed for the rest of the materials and for $350 worth of paper on which the *Banner* had been printed the first year.[67]

Yell's supporters had other last minute worries. With the election a month away, the letters received from soldiers told of a quarrel between Borland

65. *Democrat,* Sept. 25, Oct. 30, 1846; *Gazette,* Nov. 2, 1846.
66. Drew to William Black, Oct. 1, 1846, in Trimble Papers. See also Drew to E. H. Fletcher, Little Rock, Aug. 22, 1846, Ms. in Elliot H. Fletcher Papers, Arkansas History Commission.
67. *Democrat,* Oct. 9, 16, 1846; *Gazette,* Oct. 19, 1846.

and Yell at San Antonio de Bexar late in August. As it was understood in camp, the cause was trivial—Yell refused to allow Borland to leave camp without the consent of the officer of the day, carrying a step further an order of Gen. John Wool forbidding any officer to be absent from camp without his commanding officer's written permission. After a violent quarrel, Borland submitted his resignation, which Wool did not accept. Wool's attempt to effect a reconciliation was not successful, and a permanent breach developed between the two old friends. Yell got the worst of it, for the majority of the officers and men sided with Borland,[68] who was soon reported to be the most popular field officer in the regiment. Yell's popularity correspondingly declined, and it was said that he had become an object of ridicule.[69]

A few days before the senatorial election, a letter from Borland arrived, telling his side of the dispute and heaping harsh criticism on Yell. Borland asked the man to whom he wrote to have the letter published in the *Banner*,[70] which indicates that he considered the estrangement permanent, was so angry that he was willing to give the election to Ashley in retaliation, and wanted to find out if the *Banner* would side with him. The *Banner* did not publish the letter, and the public remained ignorant of the cause of the disagreement. The sophomoric quarrel over the pass was a satisfactory explanation for the other soldiers, but was more likely effect than cause. Borland's subsequent behavior seems to indicate that he had learned something that not only reversed his opinion of Yell, but would cause the same drastic change in his relationship with his political friends at home, especially Sevier.

On October 30, Woodruff brought out his paper in a complete new dress and changed its title to *Arkansas State Democrat,* signifying his determination to make it the organ of the entire Democratic party in Arkansas. The *Democrat's* printing office had been moved during the week to the second story of the building on the southeast corner of Main and Elm, with an entrance on Elm Street, not far from the *Gazette's* front door across the street. The business office was at the old office in Woodruff's home, on the northeast corner of Markham and Scott. John E. Knight, a lawyer from Newburyport, Massachusetts who had come to Little Rock in 1843, had recently become junior editor of the *Democrat*,[71] refusing the title of editor because Woodruff would not allow him complete control.

When the legislature met early in November, Yell's friends tried to postpone the election, hoping to proselyte enough members to win, but it was held in joint session at noon on November 9. Ashey won a landslide victory on the first ballot, receiving 57 votes to Yell's 19. William K. Sebastian, a

68. Maurice Garland Fulton (ed.), *Diary & Letters of Josiah Gregg, Southwestern Enterprises, 1840–1847* (Norman: University of Oklahoma Press, 1941), 218–219, 226.

69. *Gazette,* Oct. 12, 19, 1846.

70. *Democrat,* Nov. 6, 1846.

71. *Gazette,* Oct. 19, 1846; Hannah Donnell Knight, "Hospitality of Early Days," *The Arkansas Pioneers* (Little Rock: Arkansas Pioneers Association, September, 1912), 11–12.

Democrat, received 12 votes, and C. F. M. Noland, a Whig, received 3. Davis Thompson and Abaslom Fowler each received one vote, though they were not in nomination.[72]

From his camp near Parras, Mexico, Yell wrote to Governor Drew on December 13 to explain why he had not resigned his seat in Congress. He said he had expected the war to end by November or December, and that he would be back in his seat for the session beginning on December 7. A temporary armistice after the battle of Monterey in October had strengthened his opinion, and he thought the middle of December would be the latest date he would reach Washington. When word came on November 17 that the war was not yet in its last stages, he mailed his resignation to Drew. He suggested that possibly it had gone astray in the mails.[73]

Actually, his seat in Congress was lost before he wrote his resignation. The steadily rising complaints that Arkansas was without representation in the House had led to a movement to get the governor to declare the seat vacant and order an election to fill the vacancy. Drew resisted these demands until November 12, when the state Senate decided that Capt. J. S. Ficklin, senator from Lawrence County, had in effect vacated his seat by his recent enlistment as a 12-months volunteer for military service on the western frontier. The parallel with Yell's case was quickly drawn, and the governor at last declared his seat vacant and issued a proclamation for a special election.

Neither party nominated a candidate, but the race attracted three Democrats (George W. Paschal, Albert Rust, and Herndon Haralson), and two Whigs (Thomas W. Newton and C. F. M. Noland.) The brief canvass was conducted mostly by circulars and the newspapers. Noland exhibited refreshing candor in his circular, assuring the voters, "If you should elect me, it would only be for a period of about six weeks—too short, in which to do either much good or harm." [74]

The election was held December 13, and the result was doubtful for almost six weeks. The official tabulation gave Newton 1,745 votes, Paschal 1,722, Rust 1,654, Noland 854, and Haralson 138. With only a 23 vote majority, Newton was commissioned and left for Washington on January 21. Paschal was confident that Newton owed his victory to an erroneous decision of the secretary of state regarding some of the excluded votes, but decided it was not worth contesting for a term of only a few days. Newton served only 25 days,[75] but had the distinction of being the only Whig ever elected to Congress from Arkansas.

It was a period of general depression, and the state was heavily in debt. The 1846 legislature followed the example set by Congress and other legislatures to reduce the expenses of government, with considerable wrangling

72. *Gazette,* Nov. 9, 1846; *Democrat,* Nov. 6, 13, 1846.
73. *Democrat,* Feb. 5, 1847.
74. *Ibid.,* Nov. 13, 20, 27, 1846.
75. *Ibid.,* Jan. 22, Feb. 26, 1847; *Gazette,* Jan. 16, 23, 1847.

over proposed salary reductions and other economy measures.[76] At this inopportune time, Woodruff again memorialized the legislature for relief from his 1837 default,[77] and again was unsuccessful.

Governor Drew vetoed a resolution passed early in the session to give all categories of the public printing to the lowest competent bidder, because it included the executive printing and he wanted to select his own printer. The legislature then modified the resolution to cover only its own daily printing, took sealed bids, and gave the job to the *Gazette* at an unusually low price.[78] The work was unprofitable and annoying, as rush jobs took so much time that one issue of the *Gazette* was delayed, and another did not receive the editor's usual attention.[79]

Later in the session, a general retrenchment and economy bill was passed almost unanimously, and included a provision that all categories of the executive printing should be done under contracts let to the lowest bidder. Drew gave the bill the "pocket veto" by holding it until it was automatically lost. Woodruff said he did not want to state his objections and give the legislature a chance to make compromises.[80]

Secretary of State D. B. Greer incurred some displeasure by awarding contracts without calling for bids. The laws of the session were to be published in at least one newspaper, in addition to the pamphlet edition, and the $500 appropriation presumably was intended as the maximum cost. When the *Banner* began publication of the laws without competitive bidding a week after the session ended, Woodruff sent Greer a written offer to publish the laws and send copies to every county clerk for $100. Greer could only reply that the *Banner* already had the contract. Whigs and Ashley-wing Democrats alike saw this as catering to the governor.[81]

Estray ads for every county were now to be published in a single newspaper, an economical but impractical arrangement. Again without calling for bids, Greer let the contract to Quincy K. Underwood of the Whig *Southern Shield* at Helena.[82]

The *Gazette* office turned out the 216-page pamphlet edition of the laws with unprecedented speed, delivering 2,100 copies to the secretary of state on February 26, 1847, having previously sent 500 or 600 copies to the western counties for distribution. The job was finished 65 days after the legislature adjourned, six weeks earlier than usual. Borden was uncomfortably aware that the book needed more editing than it received, but he was authorized to correct only spelling and punctuation.[83]

Borden sent a free copy to the *Democrat* office, and the editor was pleas-

76. *Gazette,* Jan. 16, 1847; *Democrat,* Dec. 18, 1846.
77. *Democrat,* Nov. 20, 1846.
78. *Ibid.,* Jan. 1, 1847; *Gazette,* Jan. 16, 1847.
79. *Gazette,* Nov. 9, 23, 1846.
80. *Democrat,* Jan. 1, 1847.
81. *Ibid.,* Jan. 8, 1847; *Gazette,* Feb. 6, 1847.
82. *Gazette,* Jan. 9, 1847.
83. *Ibid.,* Feb. 20, 27, 1847.

antly surprised. He commented, "Our surprise arose from our knowledge of his [Borden's] parsimonious disposition; and our gratification, from our needing the work and not liking to pay the extravagant price ($1.50) he asks for it. But we suppose he had a *'selfish'* object in view in presenting it to us, and that was the expectation of a *compliment* for the manner in which it was executed." This the *Democrat's* editor could not give with a clear conscience, and he gave wholehearted admiration only to the speed with which it was done. However, he was unable to point out a specific fault. He grudgingly conceded that the head notes and table of contents were prepared competently, and that the paper and printing were pretty good, considering the low remuneration.[84]

The *Gazette* office also printed the current volume of Supreme Court reports, the first prepared by Elbert H. English. Binding was done by John W. Bayly at Lemuel R. Lincoln's bindery. Coincidentally, the binding was finished on the same day Borden delivered the pamphlet laws to the secretary of state,[85] so two books from the *Gazette's* press made their appearance in one day.

Publication of news sent by correspondents still had its problems, and Jefferson County was still a trouble spot. A letter received on July 1, 1847 gave information of the murder of a Jefferson County resident who in fact had not even been injured. Fortunately, the letter arrived on the *Gazette's* publication day and the story was ascertained to be false before the next issue was published. It never made the paper, but the unknown perpetrator of the hoax received a scolding in the next issue.[86]

Newspaper carriers always presented subscription accounts for payment at the beginning of each year, and the publishers usually supplied them with a "carrier's address" to give their customers, who were expected to respond with a small tip. Usually the carrier's address was a long poem written especially for this purpose, reviewing the highlights of the recent news. It is not known when the *Gazette* took up this tradition, but the first poem published in the paper that was unquestionably identified as a carrier's address was in the issue of January 5, 1846. It was an unsigned poem of 26 quatrains, covering foreign affairs, national and state politics, and one or two items of non-political local interest. Others may have been published earlier only in the form in which they were given to subscribers, and not repeated in the paper. In 1848, the carrier's address took space on the front page that had been devoted to agricultural articles for four months.

News of the Arkansas men in the Mexican War took precedence over local politics during much of 1847, and was usually about two months old by the time it got in print. It was a story of the hardships of the march, widespread illness, and bickering among the officers. Soldiers writing to the anti-Yell newspapers spoke of the continuing decline of Yell's popularity and the

84. *Democrat,* Mar. 5, 1847.
85. *Gazette,* Feb. 27, 1847.
86. *Ibid.,* July 8, 1847.

corresponding rise of Borland's, and one officer said their quarrel had made Borland extremely apathetic. They made a show of standing together in an incident on December 1, 1846, when Yell's rejection of the regiment's assigned campsite, with Roane's and Borland's suppor�, resulted in the arrest and court martial of all three. They were honorably restored to their commands on December 6.[87]

The next big story was the capture at the hacienda Encarnacion on January 23 of some 72 American soldiers, half Kentuckians commanded by Maj. John P. Gaines and half Arkansans commanded by Borland. Capt. C. C. Danley, who had recently returned to duty after a dangerous illness of four months, was the only Arkansas officer who shared Borland's captivity.[88]

On the heels of this story came the news about the first of April of a terrible battle at the hacienda Buena Vista on February 22 and 23, in which Yell was killed by a Mexican lancer on the second day. After the battle, John Selden Roane became commander of the Arkansas regiment.[89]

As the *Democrat* began its second volume in May, its editor boasted that it was the state's best paper, gave all the news, and was cheap. Borden pronounced his remarks disgusting, and Knight replied that Borden was chagrined at seeing the *Gazette* so quickly outstripped, and said the *Gazette's* limited circulation made its occasional mention of the *Democrat* a small favor indeed. Borden mentioned several articles in the *Democrat* of the previous day that had appeared in the *Gazette* from six days to two weeks earlier, and said the *Gazette* had given Arkansas readers their first news of the American victories at Palo Alto, Resaca de la Palma, Monterey, Buena Vista, and Cerro Gordo.[90] In the spasmodic recurrences of this subject, Borden was always willing to argue about the completeness of his news coverage, but he never challenged the *Democrat's* remarks about the *Gazette's* small circulation. Seven months later, on December 10, 1847, the *Democrat's* editor claimed that his paper had almost as many subscribers as the *Gazette* and the *Banner* combined.

Borden recognized the wisdom of Woodruff's policy of excluding contributions that would lead to arguments between religious denominations, but his own growing interest caused him to print occasional religious discussions that he thought contained no seeds of controversy. In March of 1846, he printed an article by Rev. James Wilson Moore that assured the readers that the translation of the Bible in current use contained "the revealed will of God." Borden explained that he could see nothing of a denominational nature in the article. A week later, he published a letter from a layman about the Catholic Church and the situation in Germany, with the result that another reader accused him of attacking Catholicism without knowing much

87. *Ibid.,* Jan. 16, 23, 1847; *Democrat,* Jan. 15, Feb. 12, 1847.

88. *Democrat,* Dec. 18, 1846; Jan. 1, 22, Mar. 19, Apr. 9, 1847; *Gazette,* Mar. 20, 1847.

89. *Ibid.,* Apr. 2, 16, 23, 30, 1847; *Gazette,* Apr. 17, 1847.

90. *Democrat,* May 14, 21, 28, 1847; *Gazette,* May 22, 1847.

about it. Borden was not a Catholic, but he had attended a Jesuit college, and was better informed than his irate subscriber suspected. He replied that it was his duty to inform his readers in areas other than politics, but he still insisted upon avoiding sectarian controversies.[91]

Another Campellite evangelist from Kentucky, Rev. W. P. Clarke, visited Little Rock early in 1847, and took up where the Johnson-Ricketts revival of 1845 had left off. There was talk of a debate between Clarke and a local Methodist minister, Rev. J. F. Truslow, each defending his denomination's doctrines on baptism. When Truslow expressed a willingness to debate but said he would not be free until after Clarke's return to Kentucky, Borden offered to give either minister one column in brevier type on the outside pages of the *Gazette* if the *Banner* would give the other the same amount of space. This would allow the community to be enlightened on a matter of current interest by a dignified, temperate discussion conducted by well qualified clergymen. The *Democrat* volunteered the opinion that such a discussion would be dull and uninteresting, and would stir up unpleasantness of a type that had no place in a political newspaper. Borden reproached the *Democrat* for ridiculing religion, and said the preachers' articles would be more interesting and more worthwhile than the dry, pointness political letters from Chester Ashley that appeared regularly in the *Democrat*. The proposed newspaper debate did not come to pass, but Borden received two well written religious articles from laymen. He declined to publish them because the writers were not ministers, and if he accepted them he would have to accept others from laymen who might allow the calm discussion to get out of hand.[92]

On November 11, he added a feature headed "Moral and Religious," that consisted of articles on religious subjects reprinted from well known periodicals. It appeared from time to time as long as Borden owned the *Gazette,* and was continued on the same irregular basis by his successor.

The enlistment of the Arkansas volunteers expired the first week in June, 1847, and they arrived at Little Rock on four steamboats early in July. John B. Borden came home with his comrades, but his name was dropped from the *Gazette's* masthead on August 5, without explanation. He soon moved to Lewisville, county seat of Lafayette County, where he opened a law office before the next February, and where he died on September 10, 1851, at the age of 27.[93]

The homecoming was marred by dissension that began in Mexico. It started with a letter written by Capt. Albert Pike on February 14 and published in the *Gazette* on March 27 and copied by the *Banner* and the *Democrat*. Pike deplored the behavior of some members of Capt. Edward Hunter's and Capt. C. C. Danley's companies, who had killed some Mexican peons to avenge the murder of a private in Danley's company, and he wrote his letter

91. *Gazette,* Mar. 9, 16, 23, 1846.
92. *Ibid.,* Feb. 6, 13, 20, 1847.
93. *Ibid.,* Feb. 10, 1848; Sept. 19, 1851; 1850 U. S. Census for LaGrange Township, Lafayette County, Arkansas, Dwelling 79.

to make it clear that his company was not involved.[94] His account was based on camp gossip, and the facts suffered the distortions that might be expected from such sources.

Pike's company and one other were detached from the Arkansas regiment and attached to Col. John May's regular army command for the battle of Buena Vista. A retrograde movement executed with some disorder by the rest of the regiment was described as an "inglorious retreat" first by a pseudonymous writer in the New Orleans *Tropic,* and later in more detail by an officer of Pike's company in a letter to the *Gazette.* Pike almost certainly wrote the letter to the *Gazette,* and possibly wrote or influenced the one to the *Tropic.* Both were interpreted as imputations of cowardice against the Arkansans, but the *Gazette's* correspondent clearly blamed the disorder on the incompetence of the officers, who had not given the men adequate drill and discipline.[95]

By voicing this opinion freely, Pike thoroughly antagonized most of the Arkansas officers except those in his own company. Pike's company had been held in reserve except for two or three brief periods in the battle, but he gave it more glory than rightfully belonged to it. Some of the other officers implied that Pike's company's comparatively safe position was cowardly, and Lt. Col. John Selden Roane went so far as to say that the two detached companies were not in the battle at all.[96] In a letter to the *Democrat,* written on May 16, Roane offered proof that the regiment had behaved honorably at Buena Vista, and deplored its defamation by one of its own, aiming his most caustic remarks at Pike without mentioning his name.[97]

As the relationship between Pike and Roane became more and more strained, Pike requested a court of inquiry, hinting that it might avert a duel. The court of inquiry convened on May 26 at Buena Vista, and the matter was settled by making a written statement by Pike a part of the record. It amounted to a retraction, for it explained the disorder in the regiment's battlefield movements without dishonor to the men. Pike admitted the imperfections of his information, but excused himself because his sources were supposed to be reliable. The court's opinion was "that the difficulty between Captain Pike and the officers of the Arkansas regiment, grew out of a misunderstanding, and that neither party are at all to blame in the matter." Pike took the irrational position that this settlement was altogether favorable to him.

That Pike's transgressions were neither forgiven nor forgotten was evident

94. *Gazette,* Mar. 27, 1847; *Democrat,* Apr. 2, July 30, 1847; *Banner,* Mar. 31, 1847; Maurice Garland Fulton (ed.), *Diary & Letters of Josiah Gregg. Excursions in Mexico & California 1847–1850* (Norman: University of Oklahoma Press, 1944), 36–37, 40.

95. *Gazette,* Apr. 10, 24, May 1, 1847; *Democrat,* Apr. 16, 1847.

96. *Gazette,* Apr. 24, 1847; *Democrat,* July 30, 1847; Fulton, *Diary & Letters of Josiah Gregg, 1847–1850,* 48, 58.

97. *Democrat,* June 25, 1847.

in Roane's last general order, issued on June 18 near Camargo, Mexico. In general, it was the complimentary effusion typical of farewell addresses, but it included this barb for Pike: "None will detract from the living—much less the gallant dead—who are not cravens, and who did not basely falter, and cowardly skulk from danger themselves.—The poisoned shafts of defamation from this polluted source have been attempted to be fastened on the escutcheon of this Regiment, but have fallen far short of the mark; and he who vilely hurled them is destined to wear the mantle of shame, and be the scoff of all honest and honorable men." In his commendation of officers, Roane mentioned nearly every officer still on duty except those of Pike's company, and did not soften it by saying that this company was on detached service at Buena Vista. The order was first published in the New Orleans *Delta* on July 12, as the regiment was en route home, and it and other documents pertaining to the conflict between Pike and the rest of the regiment appeared in the Arkansas papers within a few days after the troops reached Little Rock.[98]

Out of these circumstances grew two personal altercations. The first was a street fight between John E. Knight, junior editor of the *Democrat,* and Lambert J. Reardon, editor of the *Banner*. In attacking Knight's editorial position on the subject, Reardon took the word of some of Pike's soldiers that he could not be "placed in a false position by the printed misrepresentations of a mercenary Yankee, or the street assertions of a cast-off political hack." Knight was from Newburyport, Massachusetts, Pike's home town, and in the next issue of the *Democrat* he informed Reardon, "We have never yet had cause to blush for our *extraction*." All he meant to say or imply was that he did not feel apologetic about being a Yankee, but Reardon's father interpreted the remark genealogically instead of geographically, and convinced his son that it was a slur against his family. The two editors met on the open space in front of the *Gazette* office on the evening of July 17, and young Reardon began beating Knight with a hickory stick, Knight defending himself with a similar weapon. They were parted before either was badly hurt, and it was not until later that the bewildered Knight learned why he had been attacked. He hastened to assure Reardon's father that he had not intended to insult him.[99]

The second altercation was a duel between Pike and Roane, in which Pike was the challenger. It was fought in the Cherokee Nation, immediately opposite Fort Smith, on the morning of July 29. After two ineffectual shots were exchanged, the surgeons intervened and the seconds and friends arranged a settlement based on an agreement that there would be no further discussion of the cause of the duel. The state's newspapers heartily agreed, and there the matter ended.[100]

The Encarnacion prisoners came home about the middle of October without Borland and Danley. After a delay caused by Danley's serious illness, they had escaped from prison on August 1, and were smuggled out of Mexico

98. *Ibid.,* July 30, 1847.
99. *Ibid.,* July 23, 1847; *Gazette,* July 22, 1847.
100. *Democrat,* Aug. 6, 13, 1847.

City on August 8, Borland's birthday. With Danley almost at the point of death, they were hidden by friends near Mexico City until he was able to travel. They made their way to the American lines on the morning of August 20, and found a battle in progress at Contreras. Borland got a musket and fell into the ranks, by chance placing himself in the company commanded by his old friend, Capt. Stephen S. Tucker.

Borland was made an aid to General Worth, and Danley was given the same position on General Quitman's staff. They served with distinction in the storming of the Tacabaya gate of Mexico City on October 13, and entered the city of their captivity as part of the conquering army. At Tacabaya, Tucker was slightly wounded, Borland was struck by three spent balls but was uninjured, and Danley received a wound in his left knee that made him a cripple for life. After serving briefly as acting surgeon of Worth's division, Borland returned to Little Rock on December 1, leaving Danley in a critical condition in a military hospital in Mexico City.[101]

Zachary Taylor's military victories early in the war had caused the Whigs to urge him to be a candidate for president in 1848. He was willing to serve if drafted, but refused to be the candidate of a party, saying he would administer the government unhampered by party schemes. This attitude and the possibility that Henry Clay would seek the nomination caused many Whigs to withdraw support from Taylor.

But not Benjamin Borden. On August 12, 1847, this endorsement appeared under the *Gazette's* editorial head: "For President of the U. S. in 1848, GEN'L ZACHARY TAYLOR, Subject only to a ratification by the People at the ballot-box." Thus the *Gazette* was committed to Taylor's support whether he won the Whig nomination or not. The accompanying editorial stoutly proclaimed, "We admire him the more for his refusal to sink the patriot in the partizan."

This raised a few Whig eyebrows, and pleased the Democrats immensely. The *Democrat's* editor saw it as a repudiation of party organization, and said that if it did not make the Whig party in Arkansas a thing of the past, it at least eliminated the party's organ at the capital.[102]

Yell's death had by no means dissolved his wing of the Democratic party, which was largely in the hands of Robert W. Johnson and did not relax its opposition to Ashley. In August of 1847, as a prelude to the Democratic nominations for the 1848 campaign, a controversy over the receivership of the Lawrence Land District at Batesville was aired. On the recommendation of Sevier and Cross, the president had made an interim appointment of Col. John Miller in the fall of 1846. Miller was a former Whig, now a Yell-wing Democrat. Ashley had recommended Henry Neill, and with the help of a protest letter signed by several members of the legislature and Woodruff, he had persuaded the president to submit Neill's nomination for confirmation at the next session of the Senate instead of Miller's. Since Miller had already begun

101. *Ibid.,* Oct. 15, 22, Nov. 12, Dec. 3, 1847; *Gazette,* Oct. 14, 1847; Jan. 13, 1848.
102. *Democrat,* Aug. 20, 1847.

his duties, it amounted to his removal from office in favor of Neill. Johnson obtained the documents in the case from Washington, which showed that Ashley was altogether responsible and had misrepresented some aspects of the matter to the president. Johnson made an issue of it and published the documents in the *Banner,* and sent a counter petition to the president.[103]

During the last four months of 1847, the public was treated to a rare sample of what happens when politicians fall out. When the Johnson faction began making arrangements for a Democratic state convention, Woodruff correctly surmised that it would be a stacked convention with the nomination of Johnson for Congress and Drew for governor cut and dried. Woodruff appealed to the rank and file to prevent this by sending full delegations, chosen without manipulation by the Johnson clique. He told the sordid history of the conventions held by his party since statehood, representing them as corruptly managed by the Dynasty. While revealing a number of ancient political secrets, he did not go so far as to take the story of the Dynasty's rise to power back to its beginning, or to suggest that he and Ashley had been implicated in any part of it.

Woodruff now made an issue of the Dynasty, that collection of relatives that had long dominated Arkansas politics. For the time being, he was reluctant to wage war against his old friend and ally, Ambrose H. Sevier, who was the common denominator of the Dynasty's tangled interrelationships. Instead he labeled Johnson as the viper who was leading the Dynasty's current corruption, and named as his fellow conspirators the Conway brothers, Henry M. Rector, Samuel H. Hempstead, and assorted other relatives in comparatively minor positions, as well as a few such men as Drew who were not relatives but tools of the Dynasty.

When Johnson called attention to Woodruff's tendency to avoid any allusions to Sevier that could be given an invidious or hostile interpretation, Woodruff replied that Sevier's name, like the lamented Yell's, was unnecessarily brought into every argument, and that Sevier's great misfortune was the

103. *Ibid.,* Aug. 27, 1847.

greedy horde of office seekers who clung to his coat tails. The *Banner* implied that Sevier was with Johnson all the way. Unconvinced, Woodruff gave his old friend one last warning: If Johnson's bid for monopoly of all the high offices should succeed, it would be at Sevier's expense, and would sound the death knell for his prospects for re-election.[104] Sevier would understand his meaning better than anybody else. Unquestionably, it was an ultimatum.

There had been one earlier indication that the friendship between Sevier and Woodruff was faltering. In May of 1846, Woodruff had said that the 1844 legislature, in rejecting his request for relief from his default but relieving Sevier of the aspersions cast upon his character in the previous session, had "strained at a gnat and swallowed a camel." On that occasion, the Johnson clique had accused Woodruff of introducing Sevier's name into an unrelated discussion.[105]

Johnson left on October 30 for Washington by way of his Mississippi plantation, leaving the bubbling political pot in the care of Elias Conway and others. Ashley departed for Washington on November 20, depending on Woodruff to guide the destiny of his faction.

Woodruff was hampered by the dearth of strong candidates to oppose Drew and Johnson. The *Democrat* gave blanket approval to several others who were campaigning for the nominations, but did not concentrate its efforts on a specific candidate.

A movement started early in November that foretold a strange new alliance that would ultimately give Woodruff the candidate he needed, but it did not develop fast enough to be effective in this campaign. An unsigned letter in the *Democrat* of November 5 suggested that Solon Borland would be a good candidate for Congress, and C. C. Danley would be equally acceptable for governor. Neither had ever run for office, but a running account of their experiences as prisoners of war had been told so dramatically that they qualified as military martyrs, if not heroes.

With remarkably good timing, the *Democrat* published the news of their service at the storming of the gates of Mexico City a week after their candidacy was suggested, and Borland returned to Little Rock on December 1, the same day the official reports of the battles near Mexico City arrived, in which he and Danley were favorably mentioned. Danley remained in the hospital in Mexico, and could not be considered as a candidate. Borland might have been a formidable candidate if he had come home earlier, but not even the deft hand of Woodruff could work this miracle in one month.

Borland's differences with Yell had remained unreconciled at the time of Yell's death. His alienation from the faction he had helped to build was not yet apparent to the public, but he had begun to send letters and other offerings to the *Democrat* instead of the *Banner*. He left Little Rock on December 2 for Hot Springs, where his family was living with his wife's parents,[106]

104. *Ibid.,* Sept. 3, 10, 17, Oct. 1, 8, 1847.
105. *Banner,* May 19, 1846.
106. *Democrat,* Nov. 12, Dec. 3, 1847; *Gazette,* Dec. 2, 1847.

but he evidently reached an understanding with Woodruff before he left or upon his return.

The *Democrat* of December 17 endorsed his candidacy for the nomination for Congress, giving him its preference without withdrawing its approval of some of the other candidates. It also reported that White County's convention delegates had been instructed to vote for him, and that he was viewed favorably by some of the southern counties. His image as a self-sacrificing officer bent on fatherly care of his men at all hazards to himself was bolstered by the testimony of several returned Encarnacion prisoners, published in the same issue of the *Democrat*. Nobody had the temerity to edit these documents, and an astute observer might have noticed that Borland's habitual misspelling of one of his favorite words, "intirely," gave him away as the writer of these high compliments to which his former soldiers had affixed their signatures. Borland had made the switch to the Ashley wing, but some of the leaders of the other wing had not gotten the message yet.

The Whigs did not nominate for state offices, leaving the contest between the two Democratic factions, and offering the possibility that either faction might use the non-partisan attitude of Zachary Taylor to unite with the Whigs. There was a persistent rumor that Ashley and Woodruff were trying to build a new party that would take in the Whigs, using as bait a prominent position on their slate for a Whig. That Whig was said to be Thomas W. Newton, but he vigorously denied it, and pointed out that Woodruff and Ashley had used their influence against him in the election that had sent him briefly to Congress.[107] The fact was that Woodruff was unwilling to ask Democrats to vote for a Whig,[108] and Newton was not likely to run on anything but a Whig ticket. Nevertheless, there was a grain of truth in the rumors that Ashley would have Whig support of a sort.

At the Democratic convention on January 3, 1848, Johnson won the nomination for Congress on the first ballot with 34 votes, his three opponents receiving a total of 21 votes. Borland was barely in the running with only the one vote of White County. It took two ballots to nominate Drew for governor, and Borland was a candidate on the second ballot, receiving seven votes. He was one of 14 men appointed as delegates to the Democratic national convention.

Several obvious irregularities gave grounds for resisting the nominations, and the slate was almost unanimously hostile to the Ashley wing, the sole exception being one of the three candidates for electors. But Woodruff accepted the nominations with a show of good grace, promptly placed the slate at the head of the *Democrat's* editorial columns, and prepared to give the candidates his full cooperation. It was rumored that he was bullied into acquiescence by the threat of a resolution that would expel him from the party, but nobody who knew his background as a fighter believed he could be

107. *Gazette,* Nov. 11, 1847.
108. *Democrat,* Feb. 18, 1848.

so easily intimidated.[109] Judging by subsequent events, it is more likely that Borland had arranged a trade-out with Drew.

The events of this period would affect the *Gazette* later, but it was completely out of the important political maneuvering, because the Whig party was on its last legs. Nobody was more aware of this than Borden, who had the proof in his dwindling subscription list. For some time he had wanted to sell the *Gazette* and turn to one of the more profitable fields in which he was well qualified.[110]

He had received the promised printing jobs in connection with the liquidation of the Real Estate Bank, but only twice did he submit his accounts for settlement, on May 1, 1844, some 14 months after he bought the *Gazette,* and his final accounting on September 15, 1848, covering the period between June 5, 1844 and February 3, 1848.

This last bill was for $1,715.29 in Arkansas paper money, valued at about 30 cents on the dollar. The four-year lapse between settlements made the payments on his notes delinquent, but according to the agreement at the time of his purchase of the *Gazette,* no suit was to be brought against him on the notes as long as the proceeds from the bank's printing were applied only to payment of the notes.[111]

He also got the contract for printing the reports of the Arkansas Supreme Court in 1843, 1845, 1846, and 1847, all that were published during his proprietorship.[112]

Pike had fulfilled his promise to give Borden as much private job printing as possible, including a 200-page book of his own, *The Evil and the Remedy,* published in January, 1844 under the pseudonym "Sabinus." He got the Whig party's printing as a matter of course, and printed two of the pamphlet proceedings of the Masonic Grand Lodge.[113] In December of 1847, he published the first almanac calculated for the meridian of Little Rock, *The Arkansas Planters' and Merchants' Almanac for 1848,* compiled by Philip Lee Anthony.[114]

To enable him to hold his own in job printing competition, Borden bought a large assortment of fancy job type from the Cincinnati Type Foundry, which he said was as good as any available in the Eastern cities and almost as cheap. It arrived during the first week in February, 1844, along with enough other new type to print all the *Gazette,* with the possible exception of the advertisements.[115] His next type purchase in February of 1846 came from

109. *Ibid.,* Jan. 7, 1848; *Gazette,* Jan. 13, 1848.

110. *Gazette,* Feb. 10, 1848.

111. Borden et al. v. Peay, Receiver, etc., May Term 1859, 20 *Ark.* 293.

112. Albert H. Allen (ed.), *Arkansas Imprints 1821–1876* (New York: Published for The Bibliographical Society of America by R. R. Bowker Company, 1947), 30, 37, 41.

113. *Ibid.,* 35, 38, 42.

114. *Gazette,* Oct. 14, Dec. 9, 1847; *Democrat,* Oct. 29, Dec. 31, 1847.

115. *Gazette,* Feb. 7, 14, 1844.

the New York foundry of Cockcroft and Overend, specializing in type hand-cast in new moulds from new matrixes.[116]

The next purchase of type allowed Borden to present the *Gazette* in a complete new dress on January 27, 1848, including a new four-column name-plate. Standing in the left "ear" was the table of advertising terms, and in the right "ear" a house ad for job printing. Borden credited this show of affluence to the daily increase in the *Gazette's* subscription list, and said the *Gazette* was read in every section of Arkansas and in almost every state in the union.

A new postal regulation in the spring of 1847 required prepaid postage of three cents for newspapers except those mailed by the publishers to sub-scribers, in which case the addressees could still pay the postage upon de-livery. The postage in this case was only one cent within the state or 100 miles outside the state, and a cent and a half for greater distances.[117] This may have caused a slight increase in the subscription list, but the total num-ber of the *Gazette's* subscribers probably was every bit as low as Woodruff implied.

The sale of the *Gazette* to George B. Hayden was announced in the issue of February 10, 1848, the deal having been closed on February 4. Borden soon moved to Dallas County, where he became prominently identified with the educational movement that gave the village of Tulip an enviable reputa-tion as a pioneer cultural center. He was a trustee and professor in the Alex-ander Military Institute when it opened in the fall of 1850,[118] and later added to his duties the jobs of principal and professor in the Tulip Female Seminary and minister in the Methodist Episcopal Church.[119] By 1858, he was super-intendent of the male academy at Washington, Hempstead County,[120] but was teaching again in Dallas County in 1860.[121] He moved to Kentucky in 1867, and was principal of schools at Stanford, Somerset, and Perryville be-fore returning to Arkansas in the fall of 1875 to take charge of the high schools at Washington. He was mentioned for the presidency of the Arkansas Industrial University, now the University of Arkansas, but instead was elected to the University's faculty as professor of mental and moral philosophy. Re-turning to Kentucky in 1877, he was principal of a school at La Grange until 1879, and at Somerset from 1880 until his death on September 15, 1887 at Somerset.[122]

116. *Ibid.*, Feb. 16, 1846.
117. *Ibid.*, Apr. 10, 1847.
118. *Ibid.*, Aug. 9, 30, Nov. 8, 1850.
119. *Ibid.*, May 14, June 13, July 11, Dec. 17, 1851; Aug. 27, 1852; Sept. 18, 1887.
120. *Ibid.*, Apr. 3, 1858.
121. 1860 U. S. Census for Smith Township, Dallas County, Arkansas, Dwelling 304.
122. John Hugh Reynolds and David Yancey Thomas, *History of the University of Arkansas* (Fayetteville: University of Arkansas, 1910), 441–442; *Gazette,* Aug. 6, 1875; June 27, July 20, Sept. 2, 1876; Aug. 11, Nov. 1, 1877; Sept. 16, 1887.

13

GEORGE B. HAYDEN

1848-1850 GEORGE B. HAYDEN was one of a long line of lawyers whose interest in politics and government led him to the *Gazette's* tripod. A zealous Whig, he had worked for the election of William Henry Harrison in 1840 as editor of an Alabama newspaper, and now was equally enthusiastic in the cause of Zachary Taylor's candidacy. He brought to the editorial chair a wide range of knowledge, acquired partly in college and partly by copious reading.[1]

Upon his arrival at Little Rock, he had opened a law office in Ashley's Brick Row on Markham Street, his professional card first appearing in the *Gazette* on February 28, 1844. By the summer of 1845, he had formed a law partnership with Ebenezer Cummins,[2] the younger brother of the late William Cummins.

His negotiations for the purchase of the *Gazette* had begun more than a month before the date of the sale. Like all the previous purchasers, he did not have the money. He borrowed a total of $2,595, all of which was applied to the purchase, and probably was the amount demanded in cash. On January 1, 1848, he executed a note for $1,000, with Albert Pike and Dr. Shepherd Laurie as securities. A second note for $500 with the same securities probably was made the same day, but was dated August 1, 1848, presumably to make payments more convenient. He got the rest of the money on February 1, when he executed two more notes, one for $250 and the other for $845, with Pike and Dr. Albert W. Webb as securities. All were payable

1. *Gazette*, Feb. 10, 1848; May 31, 1849. Hayden's family consisted of his wife, Louisa, and two children, Ella Corinne and James. They lived in a rented two-story frame house on the southeast corner of Cherry (now Second) and Center streets, just west of the *Gazette's* first Little Rock office. Hayden had gained respect as an attorney and recognition as an orator, and had served as orderly sergeant in Capt. William Annear's militia company. 1850 U.S. Census, Little Rock, Pulaski County, Arkansas, Dwelling 679; *Gazette*, June 16, 23, 1845; July 17, 1844; Dec. 10, 1847.

2. *Ibid.*, August 11, 1845.

in 12 months from date except the one for $845, which was due January 1, 1850. The notes were later secured by a mortgage on the *Gazette* office, dated August 31, 1848.[3]

Hayden did not formally assume Borden's notes to the Real Estate Bank, but it was agreed that the entire proceeds of the bank's printing would continue to be applied to their retirement, and that Hayden would be responsible for the unpaid balance after Borden's account was brought up to the date of the sale.[4] The transfer became effective on February 4, making the accounts due Borden extend through the issue of the previous day.[5]

As Hayden began his duties with the issue of February 10, he made no changes in the *Gazette's* format or policies. As was the case during most of Borden's proprietorship, the *Gazette* was in no position to exert much political influence, because the Whig party was not strong enough to make the important political news in Arkansas. The effect of the political events of this period on the *Gazette* at the moment was mostly a drain on its patronage, but they were of more significance in the picture of the paper's past and future.

By this time, Woodruff was fully satisfied that although Ambrose H. Sevier had remained in the background, he had been hand in glove with the younger members of the Dynasty in their hostility to Woodruff and opposition to Ashley. He was determined that one by one they would all pay for this with their coveted political offices, beginning at the top with Sevier. Whether the plan originated with Woodruff or Borland is debatable, but Woodruff received much of the credit for its success. He could devote all his energy to it, now that Ashley no longer required his constant attention. Indeed, Ashley was now so secure that he discontinued the almost daily letters from Washington, and sent only the printed proceedings of the Senate.[6]

Woodruff set out to create for Borland in a few short weeks the same kind of public image he had built for Sevier over a period of more than two decades. In this, he had Borland's full cooperation, and also that of George W. Clarke, editor of the *Arkansas Intelligencer* at Van Buren. Exactly how much time he had to produce the desired image was a thing he could not know, for it depended in part upon the end of the war with Mexico.

Committed to the support of the regular party nominees and intent upon working entirely within the framework of the party, he publicized but resisted a suggestion from White County that the Drew-Johnson ticket could be defeated by a third party involving a union with the Whigs, and running Borland for governor and Thomas W. Newton for Congress. Woodruff said the time for opposing Drew and Johnson had passed with their nomination, and that he hoped no Democrat would vote for Newton, a Whig.[7]

3. Pulaski County Deed Book T, 434.
4. 20 *Ark.* 293.
5. *Gazette,* Feb. 10, 1848.
6. *Democrat,* Feb. 11, 1848.
7. *Ibid.,* Feb. 18, 1848.

Borland was not to be wasted in the defeat of Drew, when he had the potentiality of stalking bigger game, and when it was not even necessarily desirable that Drew should be defeated. Borland wrote a long reply to his White County friends, spurning personal advancement at the expense of the Democratic party, and professing surprise at the movement to pull him into active politics as a candidate for public office. Newton was showing signs of abandoning the Whig party, but he had not actually done it, and Borland declared he would not join him on any ticket except a regular Democratic one.[8]

Meanwhile, Borland was attempting to obtain pay and allowances for the Encarnacion prisoners covering the period of their captivity, which had been withheld on the grounds that they had been subsisted by the Mexicans. In a long letter to the *Democrat,* he said he had sent all the details to Johnson and had asked him to inform Ashley and Sevier, to whom he had written only short notes, asking them to work for congressional action in the matter. He painted a graphic picture of the horrors the prisoners had endured, pleading altogether for his men but making his own involvement clear. His letter was published with a petition for pay and allowances signed by Joseph Jester, one of the prisoners, but the telltale trademark "intirely" identifies the petition as having been written by Borland. This petition also told the heart-rending story of suffering and mistreatment.[9] The story was kept alive in all the Little Rock newspapers by Borland's discussions of the laws covering the situation, with frequent letters from Danley telling of his slow and unsatisfactory recuperation in Mexico City, and with the testimony of other prisoners telling of Borland's unselfish sacrifices for his men.

The project of building up Borland was gathering momentum nicely when the magic moment for positive action came. It had been generally expected for a long time that Sevier, chairman of the Senate's committee on foreign relations, would be appointed by the president to handle peace negotiations with Mexico. Because of the prestige and money (variously stated between $18,000 and $22,500) it would bring him, he wanted to accept the appointment. On the other hand, a trip to a notoriously unhealthful country during the "sickly season" would further jeopardize his already failing health, and the necessity of resigning from the Senate might bring on a crisis in his political career.

These considerations were carefully weighed by Sevier and his friends and by Borland and his friends, and each took steps to offset whatever the other might do. It was in these advance maneuvers that Sevier lost a great part of his battle.

Borland's two most important advantages were an arrangement whereby big news from Washington could reach Little Rock in a fantastically short time, and a mysterious agreement with Governor Drew relative to the appointment of Sevier's successor in the Senate.

News that Gen. Winfield Scott and Nicholas P. Trist had made a treaty

8. *Ibid.,* Feb. 25, 1848.
9. *Ibid.,* Feb. 18, 1848; *Gazette,* March 2, 1848.

with the Mexican government ending the war reached Little Rock in time for the *Democrat* to announce it on March 3, 1848. This was the starting gun in the campaign against Sevier, and in the same issue, there was an opportunity to undermine him for causing delay in consideration of a Senate bill of Ashley's to divide the federal judicial district of Arkansas.

The Senate modified the peace treaty before ratifying it on March 10, and the president on the same day appointed Sevier as commissioner to Mexico to negotiate the execution of its terms after its final ratification by the Mexican government. The Senate confirmed the appointment on March 14, and Sevier's resignation from the Senate was laid before his colleagues the next day.

Woodruff announced Sevier's resignation in the *Democrat* only nine days later, a feat he said was accomplished "by the combined efforts of the lightning Telegraph, steam, horse flesh and humanity." Governor Drew would have to appoint a man to serve in Sevier's place in the Senate until the next meeting of the legislature in November, when the legislature would elect someone to finish the three unexpired months of his current term and also someone to fill the position for the next full term of six years. Drew was out of town on personal business at the moment, but Woodruff said his decision was already made, and that the appointee was one that would please the entire state.[10]

Sevier hoped his resignation would be regarded as a mere formality, the equivalent of a leave of absence, for he expected to complete his mission and return long before the legislature's next session. He hoped that whoever assumed his Senate duties would simply keep the seat warm for him and surrender it quietly upon his return. Samuel Hutchinson Hempstead, who was in the Dynasty's inner circle by virtue of his wife's kinship with the Rectors,[11] would do this. Manifestations of Borland's personal ambition clearly indicated that he would not.

Sevier attempted to sidetrack Borland by working on both the appointor and the appointee. With Robert Johnson's help, he persuaded President Polk to offer Borland an appointment as secretary of legation to the court of Spain, which Borland thought was accomplished by misrepresentation of his desires and his situation in life. Sevier also wrote Drew of his wish that Hempstead should be appointed to his Senate post, sent Reardon notification that he wanted to be re-elected to the Senate, and sent an address to the people of Arkansas explaining why he was temporarily vacating his Senate seat. His apprehensions were apparent in this address, as he spoke of his heavy-hearted reluctance to accept the mission to Mexico and the hazard to his health that

10. *Democrat,* March 24, 1848.

11. On August 10, 1841 at Little Rock, Hempstead married Elizabeth Rebecca Beall, daughter of Samuel T. and Sally (Rector) Beall, and granddaughter of Frederick and Elizabeth (Conner) Rector. The political power of the Rectors in Missouri that branched out into Arkansas had begun with the sons of Frederick and Elizabeth Rector, and was now being continued in Arkansas by their grandsons and other relatives.

prompted him to say, "It may be the order of Providence that we may never meet again." In all these things, Sevier depended upon the mails, and they did not reach Little Rock in time to be effective.

All the letters from Washington arrived in the night mail on March 29. Among them was a letter written by Johnson to Borland, notifying him of his appointment to the Spanish legation. Borland immediately declined the appointment,[12] and wrote Johnson a scathing reply that he exhibited freely but never mailed. It was said that he told Johnson to let Hempstead have this post.[13]

Drew's secretary, John D. Adams, sent word to him of the arrival of Sevier's letter, and also showed it to Elias Conway, who began gathering support for Hempstead's appointment. When the governor returned to Little Rock, Sevier's and Hempstead's friends tried to persuade him to honor Sevier's request, but on the morning of March 30, the appointment of Borland was made and accepted.[14]

The New York *Herald's* Washington correspondent, who Woodruff said seemed to know the administration's secrets, had speculated that the United States would need a resident minister in Mexico, and that Sevier would be a logical choice. As Woodruff announced Borland's appointment, he reprinted this suggestion,[15] to plant doubt as to whether Sevier wanted his Senate seat back. The *Banner* then published Sevier's letter to Reardon saying he wanted to be re-elected.

Because illness made it impossible for Sevier to leave immediately for Mexico, Attorney General Nathan Clifford was appointed associate commissioner and started for Mexico with the revised treaty on March 18.[16] Sevier followed six days later, accompanied by his physician and his private secretary, James Johnson.[17]

When Borland departed for Washington on April 6, he left behind him a lengthy circular addressed to his constituents, in which he outlined the main things he hoped to accomplish in the Senate. He placed himself squarely before the public as Sevier's opponent by announcing that he would be a candidate before the legislature in November not only for the unexpired part of the current term, but also for the next full term beginning March 4, 1849. He did not seek the office at the expense of another's removal, he said, for Sevier had voluntarily relinquished it. Woodruff gave the circular wild approval, but Hayden was willing to publish it only as a paid advertisement, and withheld editorial comment.[18]

12. *Democrat,* March 31, 1848.
13. *Ibid.,* July 14, 1848; *Gazette,* Jan. 25, 1849.
14. *Gazette,* March 30, 1848; *Democrat,* March 31, 1848; July 14, 1848. Drew later said his letter was addressed to Hempstead, and a Dynasty conference was held over it before it was sent to him. See *Gazette,* Mar. 15, 1856.
15. *Democrat,* March 31, 1848.
16. *Ibid.; Gazette,* March 30, 1848.
17. *Democrat,* April 7, 14, Oct. 20, 1848.
18. *Ibid.,* April 7, 1848; *Gazette,* April 13, 1848.

As Borland passed through Louisville en route to Washington, he said that Cassius M. Clay of Kentucky, who had been captured with him at Encarnacion, had made an ignominious effort to save himself by informing his captors of his relationship with Henry Clay. This started a dispute between Borland and Clay that lasted several months, with Borland charging Clay with cowardice and Clay making a variety of counter charges relative to Borland's behavior at Encarnacion and in prison.[19]

While Woodruff waited for Borland's letters from Washington to begin, he filled the *Democrat* with reprinted editorials, letters, and reports of meetings praising Borland and promising to support his forthcoming candidacy against Sevier.[20]

Borland arrived at Washington on April 23, and the next morning Senator Ashley presented his credentials to the Senate, and he was seated. Soon afterwards, Ashley left the Senate chamber and went to his lodgings at Blackwell's Hotel to go to bed, saying he felt chilly and slightly ill. He was soon delirious with a raging fever, but his wife was not alarmed because this had always been his reaction even to the most minor indisposition. Three days later, Mrs. Ashley summoned a doctor, who called in another for consultation, and Borland joined them in constant attendance until the afternoon of April 29, when the patient died. His disease was diagnosed as quinsy, and a liver ailment was also mentioned. There was a state funeral in Washington on May 2, after which his family started for Little Rock, with Ashley's remains following in the care of the Senate's assistant doorkeeper.

The news of Ashley's death reached Little Rock by the night mail on May 10. Hayden had only time enough to insert a brief notice in the *Gazette* of the next day, which he set off with slightly heavier end rules at top and bottom. Woodruff had lost his dearest and oldest friend, and he wrote the *Democrat's* obituary himself, and reversed the column rules on the two inside pages, the outside pages probably having been printed earlier.[21]

As soon as Governor Drew knew Ashley was dead, he appointed William King Sebastian of Phillips County to the vacancy in the Senate, thus postponing the inevitable scramble for the office. The second vacancy meant that the legislature would have to elect two senators in November, and Samuel H. Hempstead, William Field, and Williamson S. Oldham lost no time in announcing their candidacies for Ashley's seat. While professing great admiration for Hempstead and Field, Woodruff favored Oldham, saying the western and northwestern parts of the state deserved the position. Field withdrew from the race on May 27, stating that the united west was solidly behind Oldham.[22]

The steamboat Cotton Plant docked at Little Rock on the morning of May 27, with Chester Ashley's coffin aboard. It was greeted by an artillery

19. *Democrat,* May 12, 1848; *Gazette,* May 25, 1848.
20. *Democrat,* April 14, 21, 28, 1848.
21. *Ibid.,* May 5, 12, 19, June 2, 1848; *Gazette,* May 11, 1848.
22. *Gazette,* May 11, 1848; *Democrat,* May 12, 19, 26, June 5, 1848.

salute provided by a detachment from the United States arsenal, intended not as a tribute to the dead senator but to Capt. Christopher Columbus Danley, who hobbled ashore on crutches. The town turned out to pay its last respects to Ashley and to welcome Danley home as a war hero.[23] Danley wrote a rebuttal to Cassius Clay's statements against Borland, branding them all as malicious lies,[24] and then went to Hot Springs for further recuperation from his wound.[25]

Sevier's friends saw the second vacancy in the Senate as an opportunity to effect a compromise that would heal the breach in the party, allowing the election of both Sevier and Borland. When news of Ashley's death reached Little Rock, Thompson B. Flournoy of Desha County was in the city with his family, en route to Hot Springs. That evening he wrote a letter to Borland, promising that if he would switch his candidacy from Sevier's to Ashley's seat, he would give him his warm support in spite of Hempstead's decision to run for Ashley's office. If Borland would publish a conciliatory letter, "disclaiming a wish to run against Colonel Sevier particularly, paying a just tribute to his claims," and become a candidate for Ashley's seat instead, then both he and Sevier could be assured of election, and the party's schism would be forever ended.[26] Flournoy was a candidate for the legislature, and if elected, could put the weight of the Dynasty behind Borland on election day.

Borland would have no part of such a deal. He wrote to Flournoy, courteously refusing to withdraw from the race against Sevier, but not indicating that he considered the suggestion offensive.[27] He saved his indignation for a letter written on June 4, about the same time he wrote to Flournoy, addressed to George W. Clarke, editor of the Van Buren *Intelligencer*. He told Clarke that a friend of Sevier's had approached him with "an insulting proposal . . . to close a corrupt bargain."[28]

Sevier's friends were so confident that Borland would accept the proposition that the *Banner* delayed its campaign against him, and word was circulated in western Arkansas that he had decided to try for either of the vacant seats and cease his opposition to Sevier. After the Clarksville *Standard* alluded to this several times, Woodruff took it upon himself to deny it, although he had not heard from Borland on the subject and did not know about Flournoy's letter.[29] A week later, he published an anonymous letter analyzing the suggested compromise, and arguing that Sevier's friends were trying to cut Borland entirely out, for they would surely support Hempstead for Ashley's seat.[30] During the next week, the *Intelligencer* came to hand with an

23. *Democrat,* May 26, June 2, 1848.
24. *Ibid.,* June 2, 1848.
25. *Ibid.,* July 7, 1848.
26. *Ibid.,* Nov. 10, 1848.
27. *Ibid.,* Nov. 3, 1848.
28. *Ibid.,* June 30, 1848.
29. *Ibid.,* June 16, 1848.
30. *Ibid.,* June 23, 1848.

excerpt from Borland's letter to Clarke, in which he denounced the unnamed friend of Sevier for insulting his integrity by offering to bargain for an office that only the people had a right to control. Clarke also was eloquently scornful, and it was not necessary for Woodruff to add his own comment when he reprinted the article on June 30.

There could no longer be any doubt that Borland's ambition was not simply to serve in the Senate, but also to keep Sevier from resuming his old post. This at last moved the *Banner* to come out openly for Sevier and against Borland.[31] Whatever doubts may have been generated concerning Sevier's intentions were dispelled early in July, with the publication of another letter from him to Reardon, in which he said he was a candidate for the unexpired term for which he had been elected in 1842 and for the full term following it, and that he would not consider running for the seat left vacant by Ashley's death.[32]

Woodruff often had found it effective to allow his correspondents or a reprinted editorial from another newspaper to introduce a subject or to make an important point instead of doing it with his own editorials. In this manner, he allowed the *Intelligencer* to bring up the subject of Sevier's nepotism,[33] and the Batesville *Eagle* to indicate that Governor Drew was now against Sevier and Hempstead.[34]

Drew was unopposed in his bid for a second term as governor. In the election on August 7, he received 15,962 votes, with 635 cast for others who were not formal candidates.[35] Thomas W. Newton ran for Congress against Robert W. Johnson, not as a Whig, but as an "independent freeman." The *Gazette* endorsed his candidacy,[36] but the *Democrat* offered him only personal and not political friendship.[37] Johnson won the election easily, but Newton polled 381 votes to Johnson's 325 in Pulaski County.[38]

With the state election out of the way, the presidential campaign and the campaign for offices to be filled by the legislature gathered momentum. After the Whig national convention nominated Zachary Taylor of Louisiana and Millard Fillmore of New York for president and vice president, the *Gazette* placed their names and the names of three Whig candidates for electors at the head of the editorial columns on June 15. The Whigs did not hold a state convention, and the candidates for electors were selected by the Whig Central Committee.

Democratic candidates for electors had been selected in January, and their names announced long before the *Democrat* on June 16 raised the

31. *Ibid.*, June 29, 1848.
32. *Ibid.*, July 7, 1848.
33. *Ibid.*, June 23, 1848.
34. *Ibid.*, July 14, 1848.
35. *Ibid.*, Nov. 10, 1848.
36. *Gazette*, June 22, 1848.
37. *Democrat*, July 7, 1848.
38. *Ibid.*, Aug. 11, 1848.

banner of Lewis Cass of Michigan for president and William O. Butler of Kentucky for vice president. At the election on November 7, Arkansas gave her three electoral votes to Cass and Butler by a vote of 9,257 to 7,582. There was no celebration of the victory, for by the time the official vote of Arkansas was available, it was apparent that Taylor and Fillmore had won the election nationally.[39]

Sevier had returned to Washington from Mexico on July 13,[40] and both he and Borland were back in Arkansas by the end of August. Sevier's health remained in a wretched condition, and the struggle to regain his office looked like a greater physical burden than he could bear. He and Borland met at the mouth of the Arkansas River as they traveled homeward, and Borland agreed to Sevier's proposal that neither should canvass the state or make public appearances unless accompanied by the other. With this settled, Sevier went to his plantation in Jefferson County, and Borland to his home at Hot Springs. As the invitations to speak at meetings poured in, Sevier often refused because of his illness, and Borland, bound by his promise, had to refuse also.[41]

Because its own party was not involved, the *Gazette* was slow to take a stand. Hayden said in midsummer that he had a preference and hinted that it was for Sevier,[42] but he took it no further until a month after the legislators had been elected. When the *Intelligencer* represented the *Gazette* and the Batesville *Eagle,* the two leading Whig journals, as allies of the *Banner* in support of Sevier, Hayden at last explained that he was not for Sevier so much as he was against Borland. He had no great zeal for either, since both were Democrats. Sevier was a talented man with a good record, whose interests were all in Arkansas, and who had never wronged Hayden. Moreover, said Hayden, "he has never wronged or injured our city, our society, or our State. He has never insulted the wives or the daughters of the citizens of Little Rock—and we respect him, in that, so far as we know, he has done none of us any wrong."

Borland, on the other hand, was a disgrace to the state, and had "taken occasion to travel out of his legitimate sphere to attack, abuse, and vilify us, and so to constitute himself our personal adversary," and consequently Hayden opposed him as a politician and detested him as a man.[43]

So far as their records in the Senate were concerned, Sevier had the advantage of long service, while Borland had the advantage of having accomplished a great deal in a short time. He had initiated congressional action on such important things as the western branch of the federal court, the reclaiming of swamp lands, and pay for the prisoners of war. All these had been well publicized, and evidence had been presented that Sevier had impeded action

39. *Ibid.,* Dec. 1, 1848.
40. *Ibid.,* July 28, 1848.
41. *Ibid.,* Sept. 1, Nov. 10, 1848.
42. *Gazette,* June 29, 1848.
43. *Ibid.,* Sept. 7, 1848.

on the bill for the court, and that Johnson had delayed the bill for relief of the prisoners of war.[44]

Woodruff used the length of Sevier's service against him, calling it a monopoly of the office and saying Sevier had lost interest and effectiveness. He had accomplished a great deal during his first ten years as a senator, but Woodruff could think of nothing important he had done for Arkansas in the last ten years, and he said that was the reason he could no longer support his old friend.[45] The *Banner* was hard pressed to list four major things Sevier had done for Arkansas in the Senate, but three had been earlier than the last ten years, and the fourth had been nine years in the past.[46]

Sevier had similarly neglected his public relations at home. He no longer kept the people informed by sending letters and documents to the newspapers, and only once in the past 12 years had he canvassed the state.[47] Considering the influx of new settlers during that period, he probably was justified in his fears that he had "outlived the affections" of his constituents.[48]

Neglect of duty and nepotism proved to be the most effective weapons against him. A clever correspondent of the *Intelligencer* began the complaint against the Dynasty's monopoly of public offices in the spring, and the *Democrat* took it up in the fall.[49] It was a delicate subject for Woodruff, for he had done as much as anybody to build the Dynasty's strength, but neither side cared to mention that.

Neither candidate profited by a comparison of their service in Mexico. Borland's newspaper controversy with Cassius Clay lasted all summer, and brought out many points that damaged Borland's image as an able, conscientious military commander.[50] Sevier's mission to Mexico might have helped him tremendously because of its importance, but his illness had made him vulnerable to the charge that Clifford and others had done all the work, and that his main interest in it was the high salary.[51]

Borland's supporters were strangely silent on the subject of the bank scandals, which had hurt Sevier more than anything else in the past. Not one word did the *Democrat* or the *Intelligencer* print about this, even when the *Banner* tried to goad them into it by accusing them of "resurrecting whig charges against Col. Sevier." [52] Possibly this was because they did not believe Sevier had been guilty of mishandling the bank's funds, but more likely it was because the charges had originated with the Whigs, and because some of the legislators who had voted to absolve Sevier of all censure were still in the legislature and might take agitation of the subject as personal criticism.

44. *Democrat,* Apr. 7, June 30, Aug. 18, 1848.
45. *Ibid.,* Sept. 29, 1848.
46. *Ibid.,* Oct. 6, 1848.
47. C. F. M. Noland in New York *Spirit of the Times,* Dec. 22, 1849.
48. *Democrat,* July 7, 1848.
49. *Ibid.,* June 23, Sept. 22, Oct. 20, 1848.
50. *Ibid.,* May 12, 26, Aug. 11, 18, 1848; *Gazette,* May 25, Aug. 10, 1848.
51. *Democrat,* April 7, July 14, 28, Oct. 20, 1848.
52. *Ibid.,* Sept. 15, 1848.

Late in October, a correspondent of the *Intelligencer* accused Sevier of withholding from William Brand of Fort Smith and later from his heirs about $3,000 he had collected for him on a claim against the federal government. The *Democrat* reprinted all the *Intelligencer's* articles on this subject, but made no charges of its own.[53]

Woodruff brought up the subject of the *Banner's* ownership, in an attempt to show why Reardon supported the Dynasty. He said the original owners were Ambrose Sevier, William S. Fulton, and Edward Cross, and that Sevier still owned his part, but that Johnson had bought Cross' share and Conway now had Fulton's interest. Reardon admitted that Sevier had been one of the first owners, but was evasive about the current ownership. This discussion gave Reardon a chance to delve again into the story of the sale of the *Gazette* to the Whigs, and to say that Borland had once conducted the *Banner* under an arrangement identical to his.[54]

This reminded Reardon that Borland had gathered evidence to support a contemplated accusation that Woodruff was guilty of subornation of perjury in connection with the purchase of certain state treasury warrants. Borland had left these and other papers in the *Banner* office when he went to Mexico, but had reclaimed them upon his return, and Reardon said he had used them to blackmail Woodruff into working for his election. Borland and Woodruff vigorously denied the whole thing. Woodruff saw it as an effort to cause a rift between him and Borland, and he challenged Reardon to produce the records that supported the allegation of subornation of perjury, pointing out that Borland's papers had to be copies of an official record still in its proper place. Reardon said the records were in Jared C. Martin's possession when Borland copied them, but he postponed producing them, and the subject was allowed to die.[55]

At one place in Prairie County, a vote had been taken on the senatorial election at the August general election, for the guidance of the legislators elected at that time.[56] It was contended that certain candidates were elected or defeated because of their pledges to vote for one or the other. Notable among these was Henry Massie Rector, a member of the Dynasty, who was elected to the Senate from the Saline and Perry district. He made no pledges early in his campaign in spite of his preference for Sevier, but he finally promised to vote for Borland because he said he found it to be the wish of the people of his district.[57] As the time for the legislature to convene approached, Borland's supporters began circulating petitions to make a show of popular preference for Borland, as "instructions" for legislative delegations, much to the horror of the editors of the *Banner* and the *Gazette,* who said it amounted to "packing" the legislature. The *Democrat* denied having a hand in these

53. *Ibid.,* Oct. 27, Nov. 3, 10, 1848.
54. *Ibid.,* Sept. 22, 29, Oct. 6, 13, 1848.
55. *Ibid.,* Oct. 13, 20, 27, 1848.
56. *Ibid.,* Nov. 10, 1848.
57. *Ibid.,* Sept. 15, 29, 1848; *Gazette,* Sept. 28, 1848.

petitions, and said the rank and file of the Whig party had started the movement.[58]

Woodruff was confined to his bed with pneumonia, his first illness in the 29 years he had lived in Arkansas,[59] when Thompson D. Flournoy challenged Borland to a duel on October 28, but he was back at his desk in time to write the editorials for the *Democrat's* next issue on November 3. The controversy grew out of Borland's letter to the *Intelligencer* in which he told of the attempt of "a peculiar friend" of Sevier to persuade him to run for Ashley's seat instead of Sevier's. Flournoy knew the allusion was to him, and he resented Borland's representing his suggestion as a dishonorable deal. Flournoy called on Borland at Hot Springs a few days after his return from Washington, and assured him that the suggestion had not been intended as bargaining for the office. He seemed to be satisfied with Borland's reply that in that case he had misinterpreted the letter, and his remarks in the *Intelligencer* could not apply to Flournoy. They parted on friendly terms.

Flournoy wrote to Borland on October 26 to ask him to publish the statement made to him in this conversation, because he had discovered that many people knew it was he who had been accused of attempting to make a corrupt bargain. Both men were at Little Rock, and Flournoy sent his letter by Frederick W. Trapnall. They met that evening by accident, and Flournoy assured Borland that he still felt friendly towards him.

In his written reply the next day, Borland stressed the fact that the conversation at Hot Springs had been one of mutual explanation, and refused to publish a statement concerning it unless Flournoy would authorize publication of his letter that had started the trouble, which was essential to a clear understanding of the situation. Flournoy would not consent to this, and denied that he had had any explanations to make at Hot Springs, much less that Borland's explanation was based on his. Again he demanded that Borland should publish a statement that he had misconstrued the letter, and again Borland refused unless he could also publish the letter. Borland thought Flournoy was acting under the guidance of Sevier or his close friends, and he said he preferred to deal directly with "the head of the house."

Considering this last reply unsatisfactory and incensed by its insinuations, Flournoy sent his challenge, designating Trapnall to act as his friend. Borland sent his emphatic refusal the next day, saying he had too much at stake to throw it all away with a senseless duel, and that no such controversy could be forced upon him except with Sevier, who alone held an equal stake with him. Flournoy published all the correspondence in the *Banner* the next day, introducing it with a card denouncing Borland as "a liar, a paltroon, and a coward, and beneath the contempt and unworthy of the notice of any honorable man." The *Gazette* copied the correspondence from the *Banner,* and the *Democrat* also reprinted it, with the addition of a long address to the people of Arkansas in which Borland belabored his side of the dispute. Wood-

58. *Democrat,* Sept. 22, Oct. 27, 1848.
59. *Ibid.,* Oct. 27, 1848.

ruff commented editorially that Sevier had once refused a challenge under similar circumstances, and that it had only increased his constituents' admiration for him.[60]

Flournoy now called upon Borland to publish the letter that had caused the quarrel. Borland published it in the next issue of the *Democrat,* but gave some passages emphasis the writer had not intended by marking them to be set in italics or all capitals. Borland obviously had capitalized on a triviality, for without this subtle distortion, there was no suggestion of a corrupt deal. The worst that could be said of it was that it was a routine trade-out in which one politician stated the terms on which he was willing to support another.

Sevier also had written to the *Banner* to object to Borland's innuendo to the effect that he had directed Flournoy to stir up the argument, and to remind him that he had been in Mexico when Flournoy's first letter was written. He also defended himself on other points that had rankled him since his return from Mexico, such as Borland's accusation that he had tried to put him out of the way with an appointment to the court of Spain.[61]

For several weeks the *Democrat* and the *Banner* added up the legislators committed to vote for their respective candidates, and each predicted a landslide victory for his favorite. There were 77 Democrats and 23 Whigs in the legislature, and both editors charged that the Whigs were supporting the other candidate.[62] Actually, the Democrats were about equally divided. Three Whigs were under instructions from their constituents to vote for Sevier and one to vote for Borland, and the remaining 18 were unpledged and were simply determined to vote for neither.

As Danley later told the story, Borland tried to persuade Sevier's friends to put the whole weight of the party behind a candidate chosen in caucus. When this proposition was rejected, Borland proposed that the one receiving the most Democratic votes on the legislature's first ballot should be considered the party's choice, and the other should be withdrawn. This also was rejected. Sevier's friends took steps to delay the election in the hope of proselyting some of Borland's supporters, while at the same time cutting off Borland's hope of recruiting support from the Whigs. They made a bargain with the 18 unpledged Whigs, whereby the Whigs nominated their own candidate, C. F. M. Noland, and stuck to him tenaciously throughout the balloting. There was no hope that he could be elected, but neither could Borland or Sevier as long as he remained in the race. The reward for the Whigs was the election of David Walker to a seat on the Supreme Court.

The General Assembly convened on November 6, and began balloting for the unexpired three months of Sevier's term the following Monday, November 13. Borland had a slight lead in the five ballots taken on the first day, with 41 votes to Sevier's 36 and Noland's 18, with one lone Democrat voting for John Miller. Henry Rector, who had made much of his pledge to

60. *Ibid.,* Nov. 3, 1848; *Gazette,* Nov. 2, 1848; May 19, 1860.
61. *Democrat,* Nov. 10, 1848.
62. *Ibid.,* Sept. 1, 8, 15, 29, 1848.

his constituents to vote for Borland, ignored his instructions after the second ballot and switched to Sevier, but it was offset by another legislator's switch from Sevier to Borland. Sevier gained the vote cast for John Miller on the second day, but Borland also gained one from an absentee of the previous day, and the three ballots of that day gave Borland 42, Sevier 37, and Noland 18. There was no balloting on the third day, and the two ballots taken on the fourth day indicated that nobody had changed his mind or was likely to do so—Borland 41, Sevier 37, Noland 18.[63] Clearly the Whigs had no intention of withdrawing Noland, and clearly Borland would not yield to Sevier.

At last Sevier's supporters decided in caucus to withdraw him from the competition for the unexpired term, giving his illness as the excuse, on the theory that it would strengthen his chances to be elected to the full six-year term following.[64] When the eleventh ballot was taken on November 17, Sevier was not in nomination and Borland received 74 votes and Noland 19. Five legislators were absent or not voting, and Richard C. Byrd and Thompson B. Flournoy showed their contempt for Borland by voting for Grandison D. Royston, who had not been nominated.[65]

The election for Ashley's unexpired term followed, and William King Sebastian was elected on the sixth ballot, his leading opponent being Williamson S. Oldham.[66] Sebastian and Johnson left for Washington on November 21, and Borland left two days later, against the advice of some of his friends. He left behind a circular addressed to the General Assembly, explaining that he could not put his personal interests ahead of his duty to the people, which required him to be present when Congress convened.[67]

Actually, Borland probably felt that he could well afford to leave before the election. It was obvious that Sevier was losing ground, and that his withdrawal from the race for the unexpired term had been detrimental to his candidacy for the full term. Moreover, his health was so bad that he could not mix much with the legislators to try to regain what he had lost.[68] The deal with the Whigs was still in force, but was operating more in Borland's favor than Sevier's.

When the legislature met on November 28 to ballot for the full term, Sevier was nominated first, then Borland, then Lorenzo Gibson. Gibson's nomination foretold another impasse, for the Whigs undoubtedly would cleave to him as they had to Noland. Sevier's nomination was immediately withdrawn, but Flournoy still was reluctant to give the election to Borland. He nominated Governor Drew, who a few days earlier had announced his intention of resigning as governor. Drew had not authorized his nomination, and indeed, had given written promises not to run to the friends of both Sevier and Bor-

63. *Ibid.*, Nov. 17, 1848; Apr. 22, 1853; *Senate Journal 1848–1849*, 41–42, 43–44, 52–53.
64. Noland, *Spirit of the Times*, Dec. 22, 1849.
65. *Senate Journal*, 57; *Democrat*, Nov. 24, 1848.
66. *Senate Journal*, 57–60.
67. *Democrat*, Nov. 24, 1848.
68. Noland, *Spirit of the Times*, Dec. 22, 1849.

land. At his insistence, Flournoy tried to withdraw his nomination after the balloting began, but it was ruled out of order. Borland won an easy victory on the first ballot with 71 votes, Gibson receiving 15 and Drew 9.[69]

Borland's friends celebrated the victory with a champagne party at the Anthony House, inviting the public without party distinctions to come and "bury the hatchet." It was a joyless victory for Woodruff, for it had severed his last ties with an old and valued friend whom he still liked and respected. He could not bring himself to gloat, but merely reported the results in a matter-of-fact way, being careful to refer to it as Borland's victory rather than Sevier's defeat, and declining to analyze its causes.[70] If it was any consolation, it had been Woodruff's most dignified, most restrained campaign, with personal invective studiously avoided. Sevier was a pathetic figure as he departed for his father-in-law's plantation, his health broken though apparently slightly improved for the moment,[71] his distinguished public career abruptly ended, and feeling rejected and friendless.

Woodruff had an interest in one more legislative election in this session, for the benefit of another pathetic figure. Christopher C. Danley had come home from Mexico crippled for life in the service of his country. Some had visualized that he and Borland could be a team that would outdo the Dynasty, with one in the Senate and the other in the governor's office. But Danley had no such ambitions for himself, although he was willing to pour all his strength into the promotion of the career of his idol, Borland. What he required at the moment was the means of supporting himself, and his physical disabilities placed a limit on the possibilities for steady employment. And so he became the instrument whereby the second step in the downfall of the Dynasty was accomplished—he was chosen to supersede Elias N. Conway as state auditor.

At 30, Danley had no particular trade or occupation, and had never been in the limelight until his military service in Mexico.[72] Shortly after his return

69. *Ibid; Senate Journal,* 97, 350; *Democrat,* Dec. 1, 1848; *Gazette,* Mar. 15, 1856; July 10, 1858.

70. *Democrat,* Dec. 1, 1848.

71. Noland, *Spirit of the Times,* Dec. 22, 1849.

72. Christopher Columbus Danley was born in Missouri on June 5, 1818, the eldest of six sons and two daughters of Eleanor and Col. James Danley. The family had moved to a farm near Little Rock in December, 1832. He was mostly self-educated, having attended Rev. James Wilson Moore's school at Little Rock for three months and various three-month country schools from time to time, all of which added up to less than two years. He grew up working on the family farm, and in 1834 he and his brother, James M., alternated in carrying a semi-weekly mail between Little Rock and Crawford Court House, under a contract held by his father. His mother died on November 15, 1840, and in the spring of 1842, he went to Texas in search of adventure. He joined the army of the Republic of Texas, and served under the gallant Ewen Cameron on the Mier Expedition, the last and most disastrous of the raids into Mexico. When he returned home in March of 1844 he learned that his uncle, who lived in Texas, had informed his family that he had been killed. His father, who had married Mrs. Mary Ann Fenton, widow of E. J. Fenton, on January 22, 1843, died on March 16, 1844, about the time Columbus came home from Texas. Col. Danley's creditors had

from Mexico, an anonymous call had been made upon him to run for the House of Representatives,[73] but he had made no response. After the election in August, C. F. M. Noland commented in the Batesville *Eagle* that Elias Conway had been auditor too long, and that it was time to pass the job on to somebody outside "the family." A correspondent of the *Democrat* approved this and suggested Danley for the post.[74] The *Intelligencer* then endorsed Danley, and Woodruff announced his candidacy with flattering editorial comment.[75]

The thought of replacing Conway with the likes of Danley was shocking to the *Banner's* editor, Reardon, who said Woodruff opposed Conway only because of the position he had taken regarding the sale of the *Gazette* to the Whigs and because he gave his printing business to the *Banner*. Woodruff replied that he had committed no act of opposition, unless his simple announcement of Danley's candidacy could be so construed. When Reardon continued to express disapproval of Danley's attempt to take Conway's job, Woodruff said Reardon himself had wanted to run against Conway in 1846, and that he had been made editor of the *Banner* to prevent this. Reardon, of course, stoutly denied it.[76]

Woodruff did not conduct an overt campaign for Danley in the columns of his paper, for he undoubtedly was aware that it would do more harm than good. He had little to say against Conway, and he never once tried to belittle Conway's competence in the job he had held 14 years, and he did not try to show Danley as better qualified, since he had had no comparable experience. But he kept his military service constantly before his readers and made a continuous appeal for sympathy that bordered on pity,[77] and rendered his most valuable assistance in his private contacts with legislators. It was also helpful that Danley's brother-in-law, Dr. Stephen H. Chism, represented Scott and Franklin counties in the Senate.[78] Hayden liked Danley, in spite of his intimate friendship with Borland, but he thought Conway was an efficient auditor and was not eager to have him replaced, so the *Gazette* took no stand on the subject.[79]

At the election on January 2, only Conway and Danley were nominated,

---

long since resorted to legal measures to collect his long overdue debts, and two months after his death, his slaves were sold at public auction to satisfy a judgment issued against him on the day of his death. Among them was the slave Henry, who had been given verbally to Columbus as payment in full for his services as mail rider, and who was sold to Henry M. Rector. Columbus had worked for a while as bartender at the Anthony House before his enlistment for the Mexican War in the spring of 1846. *Gazette,* May 27, 1853; July 5, Sept. 13, 1856; Jan. 15, 1859; Oct. 5, 1865; 10 *Ark.* 211; 22 *Ark.* 263.

73. *Democrat,* June 30, 1848.
74. *Ibid.,* Aug. 18, 1848.
75. *Ibid.,* Sept. 1, 1848.
76. *Ibid.,* Sept. 8, Oct. 6, 13, 1848.
77. *Ibid.,* Dec. 22, 1848.
78. *Ibid.,* Dec. 29, 1848.
79. *Gazette,* Aug. 10, 1848; Jan. 4, 1849.

and Danley won on the first ballot, by the narrow margin of two votes. He received 42 votes to Conway's 40, with one vote cast for John M. Ross, and with 17 legislators absent or not voting.[80] A few days later, Conway opened a law office and land agency.[81]

The legislative session was nearing its end when the steamboat Medium brought the corpse of Ambrose Sevier to Little Rock. He had died on December 31 at the home of his father-in-law, Benjamin Johnson. The cause of death was not mentioned in his obituaries, but it was generally known that he had been ill for a long time, and that he had suffered a relapse or had contracted a new ailment in Mexico from which he had never fully recovered.[82] A cryptic remark in a *Gazette* editorial several weeks later remains unexplained. Hayden said that if the *Banner* had given Sevier as bold and vigorous support as the *Gazette* had from the beginning of his contest with Borland, "he might have still adorned the Senate Chamber of the Union, instead of slumbering in the eternal silence of the cemetery." [83]

Woodruff was particularly affected by Sevier's death, and wrote a touching obituary in which he said that the recollections of the days when he and Sevier had worked side by side had crowded into his mind "to the exclusion of every thought or feeling of coldness or estrangement, and we grieved because our ancient friend was no more." The column rules on all four pages of the *Democrat* were reversed.

It is uncertain which set of Drew's friends had promised to get the governor's salary raised, but it had not been accomplished by the day of his second inauguration, and could not be done thereafter. Undoubtedly Drew felt that he had been duped into running, and he made up his mind to resign forthwith. He notified the legislature on November 23 that his resignation would be submitted on the last day of the session. He said his reasons were personal, and not of public interest.[84]

Because there would be little time before the special election to fill Drew's vacancy, the Democratic members of the legislature undertook to select the party's candidate, although some thought they were presumptuous to act for the entire party. The leading contenders were John Selden Roane and Bryan H. Smithson. Roane had Dynasty support, but was not a popular candidate. One of the principal arguments against him was that the law precluded a duellist from holding public office, and his duel with Pike had made him ineligible. Nevertheless, he received the Democratic nomination at the second caucus on December 8.[85]

A few days later, Smithson entered the race as an Independent Democrat,[86] and in January, James A. Moon of Desha County became the third Demo-

80. *Ibid.*, Jan. 4, 1849; *Democrat,* Jan. 5, 1849; *Senate Journal,* 276.
81. *Democrat,* Jan. 12, 1849.
82. *Ibid.; Gazette,* Jan. 11, 1849; Noland, *Spirit of the Times,* Dec. 22, 1849.
83. *Gazette,* Feb. 8, 1849.
84. *Democrat,* Nov. 24, Dec. 1, 1848; *Gazette,* Dec. 14, 1848.
85. *Democrat,* Dec. 1, 15, 1848; Feb. 9, 1849; *Gazette,* Dec. 14, 1848.
86. *Democrat,* Jan. 26, 1849; *Gazette,* Jan. 25, 1849.

cratic candidate. Moon was not well known, and announced his candidacy as a protest against the method used to nominate the party's candidate.[87] An attempt was made in the Senate shortly before adjournment to repeal the law placing the duelling clause in the governor's oath of office, but the House did not concur,[88] and the Democrats were left with only the weak argument that Roane could not have honorably refused Pike's challenge.[89]

When Drew resigned on January 10, he stated his reason to be the failure of his friends to arrange the increase in salary and his inability to live at Little Rock on the present salary, and had his statement spread upon the journals.[90] Richard C. Byrd, as president of the Senate, became acting governor.[91]

It was not anticipated that the Whigs would have a candidate for governor, but the weakness of the Democratic choice gave them hope, and they soon had two men in the race. Haley S. Edington of Desha County wrote to Hayden on January 17, requesting him to announce his candidacy. But about that time the Whig leaders at Little Rock decided to nominate Rev. Cyrus W. Wilson, a Cumberland Presbyterian minister and a state senator from Pulaski and Prairie Counties, who was not known outside his district. Thinking this would discourage Edington, Hayden withheld his announcement and announced Wilson as the party's official candidate, notifying Edington that he would delay his announcement until he heard from him again. But Edington insisted upon running, and his candidacy was announced late in January.[92]

While the *Gazette* pleaded with the Whigs to unite behind Wilson and the *Democrat* and the *Banner* took the same position regarding Roane, the wire-workers of both parties set out to persuade the independent candidates to withdraw. Smithson obliged, with the election less than three weeks away, explaining that he had expected the contest to be between him and Roane, and that Whig opposition had caused him to drop out. Moon also was induced to withdraw a week later, but Edington stayed in the race until the last minute.[93]

The election was held on March 14, and a month passed before the acting governor announced the official returns. In the meantime, the unofficial returns showed it to be a nip-and-tuck race, with the result uncertain until the last county had reported. Roane won by the skin of his teeth, with 3,486 votes to Wilson's 3,323. The oath of office was administered on April 19 by Chief Justice Thomas Johnson, who did not see fit to make an issue of that part of the oath pertaining to duels.[94] The Whigs could console themselves

87. *Democrat,* Feb. 1, 9, 16, 1849.
88. *Gazette,* Feb. 15, 1849.
89. *Democrat,* Feb. 9, 1849.
90. *Senate Journal,* 349–351.
91. *Ibid.; Gazette,* Jan. 11, 1849; *Democrat,* Jan. 12, 1849.
92. *Gazette,* Jan. 25, Feb. 1, Sept. 27, 1849; *Democrat,* Jan. 26, March 9, 1849.
93. *Gazette,* Feb. 22, 1849; *Democrat,* Feb. 2, 9, 16, 23, March 21, 1849.
94. *Gazette,* April 5, 12, 19, 26, 1849; *Democrat,* March 23, April 6, 13, 20, 1849.

with the fact that Wilson had lost by only 163 votes, but his good show-ing was not a sign of renewed Whig strength but merely a protest against the Democratic choice of a candidate. Wilson could have held the office only five months, for he died on September 22, 1849.[95]

As brief as the campaign was, it brought Hayden a challenge to a duel from Lambert A. Whiteley, a cousin of Lambert J. Reardon who had worked at the *Banner* office throughout the 1848 campaign, although he was not announced as its publisher and associate editor until November of 1849. With the rashness of youth, he had so thrown himself into Sevier's ranks as to become involved in some serious personal conflicts, and he was still touchy on the subject of his dead hero.[96]

In a campaign editorial early in February of 1849, the *Banner* predicted that Wilson would run "very far behind." The *Gazette* classified this with the *Banner's* earlier prediction that Sevier would have a majority of 20 over Borland, and said both could be laid on the shelf. The *Banner* took Hayden to task for his bad taste in bringing Sevier's name into it so soon after his death, and said, "We could find even the scrupulous editor of the *Gazette* sometimes at fault, were we to look over his files, but we would not disturb the ashes of the dead to convict him of it." Hayden defended himself well, chided the *Banner* for the delay in its all-out support of Sevier, and went so far as to imply that Sevier might still be alive if he had won the election.[97]

The *Banner's* reply on February 3 was, "If the editor of the *Gazette* has suddenly contracted a fondness for opening old sores, we refer him to a post-script published not long since, in the *Banner*. His memory seems familiar with our files. How did you feel, neighbor? Didn't you want to bite?" Obvi-ously, this was intended to remind Hayden of some sort of skeleton in his closet.

Hayden's reply on February 22 was better understood by Whiteley and the men who had served with him in Pike's company in the Mexican War than by most of the other readers of the *Gazette:*

"As we happen not to be a dog, we did not feel at all like 'biting.'

"We felt only as if a very dirty and cowardly dog, had employed a still more dirty, and more cowardly dog to vomit his filth upon a gentleman. Does the *Banner* or its strikers know anything of a certain 'Brandy stealing' story, from the pen of the author of the aforesaid Post Script.

"Is 'the ground wet' any where in your neighborhood? Got any Beans?

"What about the Louisville Journal—the 'sot habit'—the 'liar profession' —the 'breeches-mender trade'!

"We are 'familiar' with other files, besides those of the *Banner*."

These remarks were unintelligible to anyone who did not already know the whole story, but Whiteley knew Hayden could offer explanations that would give them meaning. Hayden's reference was to a letter published under

95. *Gazette,* Sept. 27, 1849.
96. *Ibid.,* July 22, 1869; *Democrat,* Nov. 30, 1849.
97. *Gazette,* Feb. 8, 1849.

a pseudonym in the *Democrat* of October 20, 1848, and left unanswered. It was common knowledge that Borland had written it. It sought to discredit an anonymous correspondent of the *Banner* by alluding to his pilfering of brandy and food and his fear of going unarmed into San Antonio while serving in the Arkansas regiment during the Mexican War. The thefts apparently were nothing more serious than "soldiering" for the luxuries of camp fare, but Whiteley seems to have been more proficient in this ancient art than most of his comrades, and for political reasons his offenses had been magnified. Whiteley was in a difficult position, for while his offenses had been trivial, they certainly were not admirable or easily defensible. Neither Borland nor Hayden had mentioned his name or told the whole story, but there were a great many people who could identify him as the man who had done the things mentioned.

Whiteley promptly challenged Hayden to a duel, and Hayden as promptly declined; whereupon Whiteley inserted this card in the *Banner:*

TO THE PUBLIC.

George B. Hayden, the Editor of the *Arkansas State Gazette,* having published, editorially, in his paper, a base and malicious slander, for which he has not rendered satisfaction, but seeks, by paltry and contemptible artifices, to avoid the consequences of his villainy; I hereby pronounce him a paltroon, a liar, and a scoundrel, and beneath the notice of any honorable man.

L. A. WHITELEY.

Hayden responded in the *Gazette* of March 1 with republication of the letter Borland had written for the *Democrat* four months earlier, and a brief explanation of the situation. "We don't fight duels under any circumstances," said Hayden. "They are out of fashion, especially between single men, and fathers of families." He also published statements by three former members of Pike's company, two of whom testified that a widespread rumor that Whiteley had stolen and consumed Pike's brandy had been generally believed, and one of whom said he knew it to be true. "I can't afford to 'render satisfaction' to such an 'honorable man,'" Hayden said. Having received and declined a challenge, he said he was now duly qualified for the United States Senate and all intermediate offices.

The *Gazette* ended the year 1848 in a new office. The move was scheduled for the last week in October,[98] but for some reason was postponed until the second week in December, possibly because there had been unusual illness among the employees.[99] The move prevented publication of the issue of December 7, but that issue could not have been delivered to out-of-town subscribers on time anyhow, because heavy rains had brought on a flood that had washed out bridges and temporarily stopped Little Rock's mail service.

98. *Ibid.,* Oct. 26, 1848.
99. *Ibid.,* Oct. 12, 1848.

Hayden did not expect his subscribers to pay for an issue that was never published, and he extended the subscription year one week to give them the full 52 issues.[100]

The new office was a single long, narrow room on the south side of the ground floor of a two-story brick house on the southeast corner of Cherry (now Second) and Main streets, facing Main Street. It occupied lot 1, block 3, Original City of Little Rock, next door to the old frame building that had been the first permanent home of the Presbyterian Church. The building had been built in 1839 for the home and office of Dr. Alden Sprague. He had died in 1847, and Hayden rented the office from his estate. The two rooms on the ground floor were occasionally advertised as "large and commodious" quarters for merchants, but they could not have been more than 20 feet wide. They were separated by a hall with a staircase leading to the upper floors. On the second floor were six or eight rooms and a hall, part of which were still occupied by the Sprague family. The attic was a large hall, leased to Western Star Lodge No. 2, Free and Accepted Masons, of which Hayden was currently the worshipful master. It was also used for the meetings of the Arkansas Grand Lodge, of which Hayden was deputy grand master, Union Chapter of the Masonic Lodge, and the local chapter of the Independent Order of Odd Fellows. A two-story brick kitchen, other outbuildings, and a well were on the back side of the lot.[101]

The cheap rent was the main advantage of this small office. Its location was not as good as any of the last three buildings the *Gazette* had occupied, and the necessity of confining the entire production of the paper to one room presented problems. There was no longer space for such things as the reading room Hayden had opened in February of 1848 in a front room of the building on Elm Street, where the exchange papers had been made available to the public.[102] About the middle of May, Hayden arranged to have a private editorial office, separate from the printing office.[103] Probably this was done by partitioning the room, but it could have been done by renting one of the upstairs rooms.

Woodruff lost no time in taking possession of the *Gazette's* old Elm Street office, and moved the *Democrat's* printing office into it the week after the *Gazette* vacated.[104]

The Town Branch crossed Main Street in front of the new *Gazette* office, and the spring rains in 1849 caused it to overflow into the street, doing considerable damage to Cherry Street. Hayden complained bitterly of the dangerous condition of the board crossing, but it was not properly repaired. In July, the editor was injured in an accident that apparently involved the Town

100. *Ibid.,* Dec. 14, 1848.
101. *Ibid.,* Dec. 14, 1848; Feb. 15, 1850; Apr. 25, 1851; Oct. 7, 1853; Jan. 23, 1858; Francis J. Scully, "The High-Lights of the Early Days of Western Star Lodge No. 2," *Arkansas Research Lodge No. 739* [Little Rock, 1947] Vol. I, No. 1, 77–78, 87, 97.
102. *Gazette,* Feb. 17, 1848.
103. *Ibid.,* May 17, 1849.
104. *Democrat,* Dec. 22, 1848.

Branch and its crossing, and again poured out an ineffectual complaint of the negligence of the City Council.[105]

Hayden had become the proprietor of the *Gazette* at a time when the Whig party was rapidly declining, and he had the additional burden of the unwise reduction in subscription rates made by his predecessor. With his first issue on February 10, 1848, he announced that the $2 rate would continue only until April 10, after which time it would be $2.50 in advance or $3 for deferred payment. A newspaper struggling to survive against great odds could ill afford to raise its rates.

While Hayden prayed he could keep the subscribers he had inherited from Borden and collect what they owed him, Woodruff boasted of the *Democrat's* steadily increasing patronage, promised to build a telegraph line across Arkansas and publish a daily paper as soon as he had 40,000 subscribers, and viewed the territory acquired from Mexico as an addition to his circulation area. He gave no clue to the current size of the *Democrat's* subscription list, but said it was by far the largest in the state.[106] Thus he made a subscription to the *Democrat* a vote for progress, although his figure of 40,000 future subscribers was unrealistic. Hayden ridiculed it by saying that only the fear of being accused of stealing the *Democrat's* thunder kept him from offering to build a wire suspension bridge from New York to Liverpool or a submarine railway to Canton if he could get 100,000 subscribers.[107]

The public did not consider Woodruff's promises far-fetched, and he got good response. Telegraph wires were then being strung east of the Mississippi, and Memphis was connected with the great Eastern line a few months later.[108] Arkansas was the only state in the union that had no daily newspaper,[109] and many veteran printers considered it an impractical project until telegraphic communication could be established to provide a steady flow of news from the outside world.

Both the *Gazette* and the *Banner* argued with the *Democrat's* boast of having the largest circulation in the state. Hayden said the *Gazette's* circulation was at least equal to any other newspaper's in the state, and that furthermore it had no "free list," but sent the paper only to actual subscribers.[110]

The *Gazette* had no agents at that time, either general or local. While the move to new quarters was being planned in October of 1848, Hayden asked his delinquent subscribers to send their remittances by their legislators, who were about to start to Little Rock. In November, he made arrangements with T. H. Kimber, the *Democrat's* traveling agent who had also been retained to collect the accounts due Borden, to make collections for the *Gazette*.[111]

105. *Gazette,* May 24, July 26, 1849.
106. *Democrat,* Feb. 11, March 3, 24, 1848.
107. *Gazette,* Feb. 17, 1848.
108. *Ibid.,* Sept. 14, 1848.
109. *Ibid.,* Feb. 11, 1848.
110. *Ibid.,* March 16, 23, 1848.
111. *Ibid.,* Oct. 26, Nov. 2, 1848.

The legislature's election of Hayden as public printer [112] offered some relief from his immediate financial problems, but he would not be paid until the printing was finished, and he had to borrow $2,300 to allow him to carry out the contract. He borrowed the money from Abner E. Thornton, and on January 26, 1849 executed a mortgage in Thornton's favor on the *Gazette* and all its equipment, furniture, and supplies. Thornton was further protected by orders on the state treasurer for the money that would be due Hayden, and by an agreement embraced in the mortgage that if Hayden should be prevented by death or other contingency from completing the public printing, Thornton could take possession of the *Gazette* office, cause the job to be finished, and draw the pay. The debt was to be paid in state scrip or treasury warrants at the rate of 80 cents on the dollar.[113]

Hayden went to Louisville and Cincinnati in March to purchase paper and materials, leaving the *Gazette* in charge of John J. Budd, who was probably the foreman.[114] The public printing was completed about the middle of the summer, and on September 3, 1849, Thornton acknowledged full satisfaction of the mortgage.[115]

Meanwhile, Hayden had made repeated appeals for payment of overdue accounts, and on April 12 had adopted a strict cash system in all departments. In July, he revived the county agent system, but he started with only two agents and was able to get only one more. Postmasters were required by postal regulations to do a certain amount of a newspaper agent's work anyhow, and on August 23, Hayden asked them to act as collection agents for the *Gazette,* giving them a choice between 10 per cent commission and a free one-year subscription as remuneration.

Advertising took a step forward during this period, as occasional cuts appeared that were not stock foundry cuts, but had been made especially for products having widespread distribution. Most of them were one column wide or less, as ads wider than one column were still out of the ordinary. For this reason, the two-column cut illustrating Colver's Rotary Concave Beater Churn and offering "Butter in 5 minutes" on April 12, 1849 was one to attract attention.

The Carrier's Address for 1849 was as bad a piece of poetry as the *Gazette* ever published, but its heavy use of local names and events made it interesting. Hayden must have liked it, in spite of its lack of literary merit, for the next week he published a long supplement to it, in equally bad poetry, covering the legislature that had just adjourned. The calendar for this year was headed "Counting-House Almanac, For 1849." [116]

The California gold rush was the big news in 1849, as the prospects of getting rich quickly and easily lured many Americans westward. Throughout

112. *Ibid.,* Jan. 11, 1849.
113. Pulaski County Deed Book U, 172.
114. *Gazette,* May 10, 1849.
115. Deed Book U, 172.
116. *Gazette,* Jan. 4, 11, 1849.

the year, all Arkansas newspapers published letters from local men telling of their activities in California. One of the first to sign up in the Little Rock and California Association was young Alden M. Woodruff,[117] whose thirst for adventure had not been satiated by two tours of military duty in Mexico, and whose journey to the gold fields would postpone his more prosaic duties in his father's printing office.

Political excitement was not much in evidence in Arkansas in 1849, but there were a few flurries in Washington that were of interest at home. Early in January, Robert Ward Johnson accosted Solon Borland on Pennsylvania Avenue on the subject of the letter Borland had written him about the appointment to the legation of Spain. Johnson had never seen the letter, but Borland had shown it to many others, who had told Johnson about its severity. This was only a battle of words, in which Johnson was the aggressor and the victor, but it caused almost as much comment as if it had been a fist fight or a duel.[118]

Borland's health was never robust, and he seems to have taken minor ailments far too seriously. One such illness in February of 1849 even caused him to ponder the untimely deaths of the three men who had represented Arkansas in the Senate before him, and to meditate uneasily upon the possibility that the office was a jinx. On February 9, he wrote to John E. Knight, "I have been very unwell, for two days—cold, headache, and, as the French doctor says, a feeling of General Malaise." Two days later he wrote to Knight, "My indisposition of which I spoke in my last, though not now so severe, continues to an uncomfortable degree. I have, almost constantly, sore throat, pain in my heart, etc.—what if I, too, were in a little while to follow into the grave, 'the footsteps of my illustrious predecessors?' What a commentary upon ambition, and the struggle it induces us to engage in! And yet it is not an unlikely fate." [119] On June 15, after his return to his home at Hot Springs, he told Knight he had spent most of the previous week in bed with a fever, and that his wife, baby, and mother-in-law were also ill. "Under these circumstances," he added, "you may well suppose I am not in the best spirits in the world—nor able to do much in the way of business as a Congressman." [120]

Hayden viewed with alarm the steadily rising tension caused by the slavery issue, and deplored the rise of the national Free Soil party. "We may be in error as to the time," he said on October 11, 1849, "but it is certainly manifest that, if not to-day, still very soon the south must stand for her liberty and her life." He did not think it was yet time for the inevitable war, but he did believe it was time to take steps to "dismiss from amongst us those who are calculated by conduct, example, or situation, to excite dissatisfaction

117. *Democrat*, Feb. 2, 1849.
118. *Gazette*, Jan. 25, 1849.
119. Dallas T. Herndon (ed.), *The Arkansas History Commission Bulletin of Information No. 6* (Little Rock, June, 1913) 279–280.
120. *Ibid.*, 282.

amongst our slave population." This was a pitch for legislation to expel free Negroes from the state, a measure Woodruff had long advocated.

Twice in June, minor illness caused Hayden to give little or no attention to the *Gazette's* editorial columns. It happened again in September, and drew complaints from some of the readers. Hayden refused to allow this to disturb him. "Just look at your last receipt (if you have one,) and see for how many years you are indebted for subscription," he said. "If you will all pay us the small pittance you owe us, you shall have no ground of complaint—if you will not, you have no right to complain." [121]

For all his brave words intended to give the impression that the *Gazette* was holding its own, its fortunes had descended to rock bottom. The *Democrat* of January 18, 1850 announced that the *Gazette* had been sold to Dr. Albert H. Webb during the preceding week, and it was not known whether its publication would continue. Hayden's last issue probably was published on January 10, 1850. [122]

Evidently the transfer to Webb involved a foreclosure on the four notes Hayden had executed at the time of his purchase of the *Gazette*. They were payable on January 1, February 1, and August 1, 1849, and on January 1, 1850. An extension of time was ruled out in the mortgage he had executed on August 31, 1848 to his securities, Albert Pike, Dr. Shepherd Laurie, and Dr. Webb. Furthermore it authorized the securities, individually or collectively, to force the sale of the *Gazette* if the notes were not met punctually. [123]

It seems likely that Webb was only the nominal owner at this point, and was acting as agent for the others to negotiate a sale to William E. Woodruff. Probably the reason was that the others who had an equitable interest had been such prominent Whigs that they preferred not to be publicly identified as selling the paper back to the Democrats. Webb was a physician who had lived in Chicot County before statehood, and had moved to Little Rock in the summer of 1845. [124] He had no journalistic or political background or ambition, and the *Gazette's* publication was suspended for three issues while the sale was being negotiated.

The deal was closed on January 30, 1850 and Woodruff again became the *Gazette's* owner. Borden's account with the Real Estate Bank on the debt of Woodruff that he had assumed as a part of his own purchase agreement had been credited with a payment of $350 on January 1, representing the price of the printing Hayden had done for the bank's trustees during his proprietorship. On January 30, Borden made a cash payment of $1,000, which he undoubtedly had received from Webb's sale of the *Gazette*. This was the last payment he made, and on July 9, 1851, the bank's trustees started legal pro-

---

121. *Gazette,* June 14, 28, Sept. 13, 20, 1849.
122. The last issue in available files is Vol. 31, No. 4, dated December 20, 1849. The file resumes as the *Arkansas State Gazette and Democrat* with the volume numbering for the *Gazette* Vol. 31, No. 8, dated February 8, 1850.
123. Pulaski County Deed Book T, 434.
124. *Gazette,* Aug. 23, 1836; June 23, 1845.

ceedings against Borden and his securities to collect the unpaid balance and the accrued interest. The case dragged out for several years, and apparently the debt was never paid in full.[125]

In the Democrat of February 1, 1850 Woodruff announced that he had bought everything except the *Gazette's* political principles, and would merge his two papers under the title *Arkansas State Gazette and Democrat,* beginning the next week. The *Gazette's* old subscribers would receive the new paper free for one month, to give them time to notify Woodruff if they wanted to continue as subscribers.

125. 20 *Ark.* 293.

14

WILLIAM E. WOODRUFF

1850-1853 WILLIAM E. WOODRUFF acquired little by his purchase that he cared to keep except the *Gazette's* name and its prestige as the state's oldest newspaper. After he had set aside the best materials from both offices for his own use, he had enough left over to equip an office as large as any in the state, or two or three small country offices. He advertised the surplus materials for sale on February 22, 1850, including one iron double medium printing press, one iron super-royal printing press, one wooden frame super-royal printing press, one large standing press, and a variety of type and other materials.

The new title, *Arkansas State Gazette and Democrat,* was cumbersome, but there were advantages in retaining the titles of both papers. To drop either would be to see a competitor take it up and have a name that suggested long term stability in the case of the *Gazette,* or one that implied it was the state's leading Democratic journal in the case of the *Democrat.* By leaving *Gazette* in the title, Woodruff also reduced the effectiveness of those who were wont to harp on his sale of the paper to the Whigs. He ascribed to sentiment his decision to give the *Gazette* precedence over the *Democrat* in the title,[1] but when the title was abbreviated editorially, it was always either the *Gazette and Democrat* or the *Democrat,* and never the *Gazette.* The new title line was Roman type, all capitals, and extended the full width of the page.

By the union, the *Gazette* gained one column per page, as Hayden's *Gazette* had been a six-column folio, while Woodruff's *Democrat* had been a seven-column folio since May 19, 1848. At the left of the line under the title was the statement of proprietorship, (By Wm. E. Woodruff); in the center was the motto carried over from the *Democrat,* ("TRUTH is in no danger from ERROR, so long as REASON is left free to combat it."—Jefferson.); and the subscription rates at the right, (At $4 per annum, or $3 in advance.)

1. *Gazette,* Feb. 8, 1850.

The dateline immediately below had the place and date in the center, the volume numbers of both the *Gazette* (Vol. XXXI) and the *Democrat* (Vol. IV) at the left, and the issue numbers of both at the right. From the beginning of the *Gazette's* second volume on November 18, 1820, Woodruff had added the "whole number" to the volume numbering, and subsequent proprietors had continued its use, so that each issue showed how many numbers had been published since 1819. But now that the paper had an unusually long title and a double volume numbering, the whole number was discontinued.

The fiscal year ran with the *Democrat's* volume numbering, with payment of accounts due at the beginning of its new volume, while the *Gazette's* changes in volume numbering passed without notice.[2]

The type title line was used only four months. On June 14, 1850, the paper appeared with the most ornate nameplate it would ever have, so fancy as to be downright gaudy. A well known Philadelphia artist named Spittal had designed it, using three pictures of local scenes sketched by an unidentified transient artist. It extended the full width of the page. In the center was a picture of the Little Rock river front as seen from the opposite bank. At the top of the picture were the words *"Arkansas State"* in small block letters. At the bottom was another fragment of the title, the word *"and."* On each side of this picture was a ribbon-like scroll. On the scroll at the left was the word *"Gazette,"* and on the one at the right the word *"Democrat,"* in shaded Old English letters. Only these two words had prominence, and the rest of the title was virtually lost, as was the sequence of the words. In the bottom or inside curve of the left scroll was an Arkansas River scene, with a steamboat in the foreground and the Maumelle Mountains in the background. In the corresponding position on the right was a plantation scene, showing a force of slaves at work in a cotton field.

The *Democrat's* office had moved during the week of October 26, 1849 to the second floor of a two-story brick building that had entrances on both Markham and Elm streets in the block between Main and Scott streets. It occupied an L-shaped plot on parts of lots 7 and 8, block 1, Original City of Little Rock, with a frontage of 77 feet and 9 inches on Markham and 25 feet and 9 inches on Elm.[3]

2. *Ibid.,* Apr. 18, May 9, 1851; Apr. 6, May 7, 1852.

3. This building was sometimes called the Byrd building, because Richard C. Byrd had built the main part of it, completely covering a plot fronting 52 feet and 9 inches on Markham and 80 feet on Main Street, which he had purchased in 1833. (Pulaski County Deed Book G, 325.) It was also called the Alhambra building, the name of a general merchandise firm that had once occupied it. It was currently called the DeBaun building, Byrd having sold it to James DeBaun and Thomas Thorn in January, 1836. (Deed Book I, 115.) In November, 1836 they had bought an adjoining plot from Ashley, part of lot 8, fronting 25 feet on Markham and running the entire 140-foot length of the lot from Markham to Elm. (*Ibid.,* 421.) They had built an addition to the Byrd building, giving it a front of square sandstone columns on Markham Street, and also a front on Elm Street. (William E. Woodruff, Jr., "A Chronicle of Little Rock," *Gazette,* Nov. 7, 1931.) DeBaun later became the sole owner, and on Nov. 2, 1839, he bought

With the death of Ashley and Sevier, Woodruff had lost his motivation for running a newspaper. Still, he was unwilling to give absolute control to John Elliot Knight, the young lawyer who had assisted with the editorial chores almost from the *Democrat's* beginning.[4] Under those circumstances, Knight had refused to be the nominal editor of the *Democrat* when Woodruff wanted to devote most of his time to his other interests, and preferred to be known only as "an *attache* of the Press." For some time he had done most of the editor's work, but at the beginning of the *Democrat's* fourth volume on May 18, 1849, he had made it clear to the public that Woodruff was still calling the shots and that he considered his own position temporary. This was the situation when the *Gazette* and *Democrat* united, and Knight was at the same time conducting a law practice and pension agency on the side.[5]

For three decades a nervous peace between the slave states and the free states had been maintained by means of the Missouri Compromise of 1820, but the vast new territory acquired by the Mexican War threatened to tear the nation apart in 1850. Much of this territory lay south of the 36° 30″ line established by the Missouri Compromise and the South hoped to claim its share of it as slave territory, while the North hoped to block any further extension of slavery. The discovery of gold had brought about an abnormal

---

from Ashley a strip of land 60 feet long and 9 inches wide, running along the western boundary of the north end of the part on lot 8. (Deed Book L, 278.) This indicates that the building had been built flush with what DeBaun thought was the property line, but actually was nine inches beyond it. During the *Gazette's* occupancy, title to the property was disputed by Roswell Beebe, who had sheriff's deeds to it, and tenants of A. Beirne, Jr. and J. Burnside of New Orleans, who held an unsatisfied mortgage from DeBaun. (Fitzgerald, *et al.* v. Beebe, Jan. Term 1847, 7 *Ark.* 305; Beebe v. De-Baun, Jan. Term 1848, 8 *Ark.* 510.)

The entire building had been occupied by William B. Wait's store for five years prior to 1849. (*Democrat,* Mar. 9, 1849.) A week before the *Democrat* moved into the upper story, the general merchandise firm of D. Bender & Co. moved into the ground floor. (*Ibid.,* Oct. 19, 1849.) A crew was then at work widening the alley called Elm Street at the north front and removing obstructions. (*Ibid.,* Oct. 12, 1849.) A donation of land by property owners along Elm Street in the three blocks east of Main Street made an eight-foot increase in width possible, bringing it to 28 feet. The City Council then declared these three blocks a street, and no longer an alley. (*Ibid.,* Dec. 7, 1849.) The main entrance to the newspaper office was the door on the north side of Markham Street just east of Bender's store. (*Gazette,* Feb. 8, 1850.)

4. John Elliot Knight was born at Newburyport, Massachusetts on Sept. 20, 1816. In 1843 he married Hannah Donnell, who was born at Newburyport on Dec. 15, 1822, and soon afterwards they came west to seek a new home in a mild climate. Eli Colby was then in very bad health, and had sent for his brother, John, to take charge of the *Arkansas Times and Advocate.* John Colby persuaded Knight to move to Little Rock, and he and his wife arrived on Nov. 3, 1843. Knight found employment with Roswell Beebe, as overseer of the old Richard C. Byrd plantation. The job involved the supervision of 30 slaves, and Knight did not enjoy it. Beebe took him to Woodruff, who made him assistant editor of the *Democrat,* which had recently begun publication. See Mrs. Hannah Donnell Knight, "Hospitality of Early Days," *The Arkansas Pioneers* (Little Rock: Arkansas Pioneers Assn., Sept., 1912), Vol. I, No. 1, 11–12; Tombstone of John Elliot Knight, Mount Holly Cemetery, Little Rock.

5. *Gazette,* Feb. 8, 1850.

westward migration and hastened California's application for admission to the union as a free state. This revived the old controversy, and kept Congress in session from December 3, 1849 until September 30, 1850. Early in the session the situation was so grim that many observers proclaimed it the beginning of the end of the union. Old party distinctions lost their power, and sectional bias became the determining factor in the positions taken on the issue.

The *Gazette's* stand was at first in the hands of John Knight. He was a transplanted Yankee who had partially accepted slavery because, as his wife expressed it, "If we live in a slave state we must do as the rest do." [6] He had lived in Arkansas a little more than six years, and had come a long way towards adopting the typical Southern attitudes, but he still had a long way to go before his opinions would be compatible with those of most of his neighbors.

Knight considered the national crisis too serious for either party politics or sectional bias to rule, and could not accept the views of Southern extremists who wanted to solve the problem by breaking up the union and forming two separate nations. Some readers complained to Woodruff in March of 1850 that this attitude was a violation of "the spirit of Democratic principles." Knight replied that no party question was involved, and that he alone was responsible for the offensive editorials.[7]

In the early stages of the controversy, both Solon Borland and Robert Ward Johnson showed an inclination to go along with John C. Calhoun's recommendations, smacking of disunion. Borland and Senator Henry S. Foote of Mississippi, a strong unionist, met in front of the *National Intelligencer's* office in Washington on March 14, 1850, and Borland lost his temper when Foote made a remark about Calhoun's "servile followers." Bystanders were treated to the spectacle of two middle-aged United States senators scuffling like schoolboys. They were soon parted, with Foote's bloody nose and damaged pride the most serious injuries. Foote challenged Borland to a duel, but the demands of honor were fully satisfied with the exchange of about half a dozen letters, and publication of the correspondence brought the matter to an end.[8]

The correspondence was not copied into the *Gazette,* and there was no hint of a threatened duel in the *Gazette's* columns. Instead, the long standing

6. Hannah Donnell Knight to Mrs. Mary Boston, Little Rock, Aug. 25, 1851, Ms. in *Arkansas Gazette* Foundation Library. Hannah had taken pride in doing all her household chores, but they had hired a servant after the birth of their daughter, Lizzie, on Dec. 20, 1844. Hannah wrote, "I sometimes say that I will do my work myself but John says he will have a servant as long as he can get the money to pay for one." In fact, Hannah rather sheepishly confessed that they had lost their aversion to owning a slave, partly because they could have bought one for what slave hire had cost them, and partly because they had come to understand that slavery was not exactly as they had been led to believe.

7. *Gazette,* Mar. 22, 1850.

8. T. N. Parmelee, "Recollections of an Old Stager," *Harper's New Monthly Magazine,* XLVI, Jan., 1873, 274–275.

friendship between Borland and Foote was played up, and the incident was represented as the result of impulse. Borland denied reports that he had apologized contritely on the spot, but said both had expressed regret and insisted that they harbored no hard feelings.[9]

A compromise plan for the newly acquired territory was offered by a congressional committee, and was stoutly resisted by the South on the ground that all its advantages were for the North. A small minority still talked of secession if Congress should adopt the plan without modifying it to give the slave states equal rights with the free states. But as public opinion solidified, it became apparent that most responsible Southerners wanted their congressional delegations to fight for modification of the compromise, but favored accepting it as the law of the land even if it should pass Congress in its original form. This was Woodruff's thinking on the subject.[10]

Knight, on the other hand, thought the original plan was reasonable, and was wholeheartedly in favor of its adoption without modification. In an editorial on June 21, he analyzed the support both sides had in the Senate. They were numerically equal, but Knight thought the side favoring the plan far outweighed the opposition in intellect, statesmanship, and experience. Arkansas's two senators were in the opposition ranks, but Knight could not believe they would actually vote against the plan. His remarks undoubtedy did not set well with Woodruff and others of like mind.

To the dismay of his constituents, Borland came home at the end of June, while the controversy was at its peak, giving serious illness in his family at Hot Springs as his excuse.[11] He made a long speech at Little Rock on July 19 on the slavery question and the proposed compromise, which was the subject of two editorials in the next issue of the *Gazette* on July 26.

The first, probably written by Woodruff, said that the audience had assembled with the predominating opinion that the compromise should be accepted even if it could not be modified, and also that the fire-eating opponents of the plan wanted to dissolve the union unless the desired changes were made. But Borland convinced them that it was best to oppose the plan unless it was modified and to defer the final decision until the next session. He emphatically denied that he or any other Southerners in Congress favored dissolving the union under any circumstances.

Knight's editorial, identified as his work by the initial "K" at the end, took a directly opposite position. Clearly, he liked the compromise plan exactly as it stood. He closed his editorial with these remarks: "If the reasons and views we have offered, and the opinions we have expressed, are acceptable, it is well—if not, it is no worse. Like all the editorials on these 'great questions' and other smaller matters, which have appeared in our columns, the suggestions are not intended to commit this paper to their support. They have been thrown out by the writer for the adoption of those who choose to take them,

9. *Gazette,* Apr. 5, 1840.
10. *Ibid.,* Aug. 23, 1850.
11. *Ibid.,* July 5, Aug. 30, 1850.

and to be disapproved of by any who may feel prompted to such a course."

In the next issue of the *Gazette* on August 2, this announcement appeared: "In consequence of a difference of opinion in reference to the course to be pursued by this journal, Mr. Knight's connection with the editorial department terminated with the number of last week."

The *Banner* accused Woodruff of trying to force Knight to change his opinion to conform to his own, but Woodruff said he had only insisted that it was his right and duty to decide his paper's policies, and that Knight's retirement had been altogether amicable.[12]

Robert Ward Johnson was identified with the most extreme Southern element from the beginning. He wrote an open letter to the Arkansas press approving Calhoun's claim that Southerners almost unanimously endorsed his thesis that the Southern states could not remain in the union without dishonor. Knight published it, with editorial comment that there was still hope that the union could be preserved in a way that would be satisfactory to both North and South. The *National Intelligencer* reprinted part of this editorial, along with similar excerpts from other Southern newspapers, in an effort to discredit Calhoun's claim of almost universal Southern support. Johnson informed the *Intelligencer's* editors that the *Gazette* could not be relied upon at the moment on this question, but popular opinion would soon force it to become "as strongly Southern" as any other newspaper in the South. Knight replied that the *Gazette's* large and rapidly increasing subscription list established its reliability as an index to the opinion of the people of all classes in Arkansas. Johnson shot back a long tirade denouncing as traitors his constituents who did not endorse his viewpoint.[13]

As the tension mounted, Johnson grew increasingly rabid and wrote rash, impulsive letters that calm observers could excuse only because they assumed he would be more rational when the excitement abated. In one of these letters he directed the publication in the *Banner* of a letter written by an obscure Ohio abolitionist of the most fanatical type, probably thinking it would shock the people into recognizing their peril.

William H. Sutton of Little Rock considered such letters incendiary whether circulated by abolitionists themselves or by the Southern press. He wrote a long letter to the *Banner,* protesting its publication and pointing out that the writer's opinions were not representative of the majority in Ohio. Sutton appealed to the people not to allow their fears of what might happen to cause them to lose their heads, but to wait for "some overt act, something

---

· 12. *Ibid.,* Aug. 23, 1850. Knight devoted his time to his law practice and pension agency after he left the *Gazette.* On Jan. 6, 1851, he was elected mayor of Little Rock. (*Ibid.,* Jan. 10, 1851). He was a candidate for county and probate judge a month later, but ran a poor fourth in a field of four. (*Ibid.,* Feb. 7, 1851.) He was an alderman in 1853. (*Ibid.,* Jan. 7, 1853.) He was editor and one of the proprietors of the *Chronicle,* which published ten issues between Oct. 11 and Dec. 13, 1855. (*Ibid.,* Sept. 15, Dec. 28, 1855.) He lived quietly at Little Rock until his death on Oct. 28, 1901. (Tombstone, Mount Holly Cemetery.)

13. *Gazette,* Apr. 19, May 17, 1850.

tangible and incontrovertible." He expressed respect for Johnson and faith in the purity and sincerity of his motives, but said that "no man is under obligation to adopt his opinions or reject the dictates of his own judgment."

Lambert J. Reardon, senior editor of the *Banner,* rejected this letter because he did not agree with it and because it would be distasteful to Johnson. At Sutton's suggestion, the letter was submitted to a man of Reardon's selection whose loyalty to Johnson was unchallengeable. This man also thought the letter should be rejected, and Sutton then took it to the *Gazette,* where it was published on May 31.

Johnson learned of Sutton's letter and the *Gazette's* editorial references to him through letters from his friends. Although unflattering remarks about him had been meticulously avoided, he was beyond toleration of a difference of opinion, and the expressions of disagreement sent him into a towering rage. In a letter to the *Banner,* he complained of these "bitter attacks" on him, and made a point of the fact that the issues of the *Gazette* containing them had not been sent to him.

The reason he had not received the recent numbers of the *Gazette* was that he had not heeded the warnings made repeatedly to delinquent subscribers that all who were in arrears for two or more years on May 10 would be stricken from the subscription list "without respect to persons." Johnson had been a subscriber to the *Democrat* for almost four years, and had paid for only the first year, and had been dropped from the list along with two or three hundred others.[14]

Woodruff had been driven to this measure by the fact that nearly one fourth of the *Democrat's* original subscribers had never paid for any part of their subscriptions, and many others owed for one to three years. Most of them owed from $8 to $16, and the total debt to Woodruff was approximately $12,000. He adopted a strict cash system, and declared he would never again permit any subscriber to owe him more than $5.[15]

The family emergency that had brought Solon Borland home during a national crisis did not confine him to Hot Springs long. He spent enough time at Little Rock and had enough influence over the *Gazette's* editorial policies to give rise to a rumor that he was editing the paper.[16] The dangerous illness of his wife in September and of their child late in October caused two postponements of his return to Washington, but he finally left on November 9,[17] too late for the session that had adjourned on September 30 after adoption of the compromise, but in time for the one that would begin on December 2.

Borland's friends considered his tribulations sufficient justification for his protracted absence from the Senate, but his enemies criticized him for it throughout the summer and fall. In January of 1851, as the state House of Representatives was considering a resolution commending the congres-

14. *Ibid.,* Aug. 16, 1850.
15. *Ibid.,* Mar. 1, May 10, 17, 1850.
16. *Ibid.,* Sept. 6, 1850.
17. *Ibid.,* Sept. 20, 27, Nov. 8, 15, 22, 1850.

Elias Nelson Conway.   Leonidas Trousdale.

sional delegation for its conduct during the session, an amendment was offered to withhold the commendation from Borland. It was introduced by Valentine Sevier, and was supported by a long, theatrical speech by Thompson B. Flournoy, but it was defeated.[18]

One measure Woodruff had advocated for years was a law forbidding the residence of free Negroes in Arkansas. He usually said merely that they were a bad influence on the slave population, and left unspoken the well understood fear that they could be the instruments by which the abolitionists could spread their propaganda urging slave insurrections and runaways. A bill for the removal of free Negroes was introduced in the House in November of 1850,[19] but failed to pass.

Elias N. Conway tried to reclaim his old job as state auditor during this session, but again C. C. Danley defeated him by a majority of one.[20]

Legislators wishing to send newspapers to their constituents were offered the special rate of 50 cents for each set of the *Gazette* covering the session, each sealed in a strong wrapper ready for mailing.[21]

Woodruff had come to consider even the routine editorial chores a bur-

18. *Ibid.,* Jan. 10, 1851.
19. *Ibid.,* Nov. 8, 1850.
20. *Ibid.,* Jan. 3, 1851; *House Journal* 1850–1851, 368–369; *Senate Journal* 1850–1851, 353–354.
21. *Gazette,* Nov. 8, 1850.

den, and a legislative session made extra work, so he hired an editor for the *Gazette*. No announcement was made, but a sharp difference in the paper's editorial policies might have tipped off discerning readers.

The new editor was Leonidas Trousdale, who preferred to be known as Leon. He was 28 years old, and had lived in Tennessee and Mississippi all his life except for the time he had served in the Mexican War. Newspapers had held a fascination for him since childhood, and since the war he had been editor of two Democratic journals. His older brother, Cincinnatus Trousdale, had lived in Arkansas since about 1842, and was currently practicing law at Dover in Pope County.[22]

Trousdale's opinions on the slavery issue and the compromise were as much at variance with Woodruff's as Knight's had been, but he went to the other extreme and took about the same position as Robert Ward Johnson. In an editorial on December 13, 1850, he spoke of the dissatisfaction of both sides, and predicted that Northern abolitionists would not rest until the fugitive slave bill was repealed. Trousdale said he hoped the slave states would unite to work out a plan for their protection and independence within the union, but he said the events of the past year had destroyed part of the South's natural patriotism and her respect for a Constitution that no longer gave her equal protection. "She wants equality in the Union, or no Union at all," he declared.

As evidence that these were not the sentiments of a substantial number of Southerners, there was a movement to demonstrate the willingness of the people to accept the compromise terms by affirming their unionism in public meetings. Trousdale condemned these meetings in an editorial on January 21, 1851. Four prominent Clarksville men canceled their subscriptions in pro-

22. Leonidas Trousdale, son of Bryson Blackburn and Susan (Hicks) Harrington Trousdale, was born in Robertson County, Tenn. on Feb. 12, 1823. The family moved to Jackson, Madison County, Tenn. when Leon was in his fourth year. Here he received an elementary education. At the age of 12 he was sent to Liberty Academy in Robertson County, where he edited a manuscript weekly newspaper and circulated it among the students. He enrolled at the University of Nashville in 1837 at the age of 14, and two years later produced another manuscript periodical for distribution among the students. After his graduation in 1841, he taught school in Carroll County, Miss., and in 1843 was appointed deputy clerk of the Chancery Court there. He served in the Mexican War at the mouth of the Rio Grande, in the storming of Monterey, and in the battle of Buena Vista, after which he became second lieutenant of his company. Returning to Carrollton after he was mustered out of the service, he was editor of the *Weekly Democrat* until 1850, when he was elected assistant clerk of the Mississippi Senate. He next lived briefly at Gallatin, Tenn., where he was editor of the *Tenth Legion*, and then moved to Little Rock. His brother, Cincinnatus, was about two years his senior, and had practiced law in Arkansas since about 1842, except while serving in the Mexican War in Company A of the Arkansas regiment, emerging as a first lieutenant. Cincinnatus later lived at Helena, where he died on Feb. 3, 1853, at the age of 32. See *The National Cyclopaedia of American Biography* (New York: James T. White and Co., 1893–1916), VIII, 310–311; Karl Truesdell, *Descendants of John Trousdale of Orange County, North Carolina* (Chevy Chase, Md., 1952), 28–29, 48–49; Dallas T. Herndon (ed.), *Arkansas History Commission Bulletin of Information No. 6* (Little Rock, 1913), 186; *Gazette*, Feb. 18, 1853.

test, and deplored the *Gazette's* tendency to defend principles that made continuance of the union a matter of secondary importance. Trousdale branded this as a trumped-up excuse to discontinue their subscriptions, as he had not expressed or implied anything against the union itself, but only the union meetings. There was a difference, he said, but did not explain what it was.[23]

In the next issue, on February 28, 1851, Woodruff announced that Trousdale was the *Gazette's* new editor, and said he had been in charge of its editorial conduct for several weeks. His name and title were placed under the editorial head, so that in the future Woodruff would not be responsible for opinions conflicting with those he had previously expressed.

Woodruff and Trousdale also differed on the subject of Robert Ward Johnson. Immediately after adoption of the compromise in the fall of 1850, Johnson had announced that he would not seek re-election to Congress in 1851. Woodruff had applauded his decision as one of the wisest and most admirable things he had ever done, and made no pretense of ever having been more friendly to him than party loyalty required. Said Woodruff, "Such are the irresistible and ungovernable passions and prejudices of his nature, that it is impossible for him to divest himself of their influences." Furthermore, he carried his private animosities into the halls of Congress, as proved by his opposition to important legislation favorable to Arkansas simply because it had originated with Ashley and Borland.[24]

By the time the congressional delegation returned to Arkansas late in March, there was a movement afoot to nominate Johnson for re-election, and Johnson went along with it if he did not actually instigate it. The *Gazette* gave no opposition to his candidacy, and when the *Banner* said the *Gazette* made every effort to put him down, Trousdale replied that he did no such thing—first, because he had not considered Johnson a candidate since his voluntary withdrawal, and second, because Trousdale admired and approved Johnson's course on "the great question of the day," and therefore had no grounds for opposition.[25]

Woodruff and Danley, however, were quietly working to get the Democratic nomination for George W. Clarke. At the convention on April 28, Woodruff held the proxy for Polk County with instructions to vote for Clarke, and Danley held proxies for Carroll, Washington, Franklin, and Mississippi counties by which he cast eight votes for Clarke.[26]

Danley made a determined effort to persuade the convention to adopt a platform and require all aspirants to pledge support of both platform and nominee before they could be considered candidates for the nomination. He thought the convention rejected his suggestion because the Johnson faction was unwilling to support Clarke or to lose control of the platform.[27] Trous-

23. *Gazette,* Feb. 21, 1851.
24. *Ibid.,* Oct. 4, 1850.
25. *Ibid.,* Apr. 18, 1851.
26. *Ibid.,* Apr. 4, May 2, 1851.
27. *Ibid.,* Sept. 12, 1851.

dale was secretary of the convention, and recorded 34 votes for Johnson, 21 for Clarke, 8 for William Conway B., and one for Richard C. Byrd.[28]

Thus Johnson again won the Democratic nomination, and again Woodruff bowed to the will of the majority and allowed Trousdale to place Johnson's name under the *Gazette's* editorial head as the endorsed candidate. The Whig candidate was John Preston, Jr., who ran on a strong unionism platform, since it was generally believed that Johnson favored disunion.

When Johnson announced his speaking appointments, Borland said he would appear with him, to take advantage of Johnson's crowds to account for his work in the Senate to as many people as possible. The enmity between the two men was well known, and it was whispered that Borland intended to tell the people how Johnson had obstructed his legislation, in the hope of defeating his re-election. Apparently the rumor was true, but Johnson exacted a promise from Borland to postpone discussions of their differences until after the election, and Borland's speeches did Johnson no damage.[29] Johnson was re-elected on August 4 by a majority of 3,099 votes over Preston. His friends called it a victory over Borland, but Trousdale saw it as a triumph of Southern rights over pseudo-unionism.[30]

The campaign was barely under way when a controversy over the public printing developed that was to remain in the news almost a year, and would recur later. Lambert A. Whiteley, junior editor of the *Banner,* had been elected public printer after submitting an extremely low bid. He had presented his account for printing the acts to Secretary of State David B. Greer. The bill was so technical that Greer could not understand it, so he had it checked by two experienced printers, Fred S. Garritt and John J. Budd. They made only one small deduction before pronouncing it accurate on May 19. On the strength of their opinion, Greer certified the account and Whiteley was paid $4,216.20 the next day.

Auditor Danley suspected that Whiteley had overcharged, and since Garritt and Budd worked for the *Banner,* he did not consider their opinion the last word. He asked Woodruff to check the account, and instructed him to interpret the contract liberally so as to give Whiteley the benefit of every doubt. Woodruff found a large error, mostly in the charges for "rule and figure work." He said Whiteley had been paid $1,301.88 too much, a figure that rose to $1,531.62 because he was not paid in specie but in Arkansas treasury warrants at 85 cents on the dollar.

The matter came before the public on July 22, 1851, when Greer published a defensive card in the *Banner.* Without conceding that Whiteley had been overpaid, he said that any overpayment could be deducted from his account for printing the journals. Woodruff defended his figures in the next issue of the *Gazette,* and Danley added a card telling his side of the story.[31]

28. *Ibid.,* May 2, 1851.
29. *Ibid.,* June 13, 27, July 25, Aug. 29, 1851.
30. *Ibid.,* Aug. 29, Sept. 12, 1851.
31. *Ibid.,* July 25, 1851.

The error was established soon afterwards in agreement with Woodruff's figures, and Whiteley agreed to Greer's deduction of the amount from his account of almost $3,500 for printing the journals. This left something less than $2,000 to be paid to Whiteley for the journals, but Danley deducted an additional sum of more than $1,500. This was the amount charged for publication of the appendix to the House Journal, which had been printed by the *Gazette* office during the session as documents appended to the governor's message, and which Danley said had not been authorized by the House for republication as part of its journal.

The auditor had no legal right to withhold his warrant for an account that had been certified by the official authorized by law to examine it, in this case the secretary of state. Whiteley attacked Danley's refusal to issue the warrant in the *Banner* of September 9, and said the underlying reason for Danley's vigilance was his uncompromising hostility to Johnson and his friends, and that he was being made to pay dearly for the *Banner's* support of Johnson in the campaign just ended. In his reply in the *Gazette* of September 12, Danley acknowledged this hostility, but said Whiteley's friendship with Johnson gave him no right to plunder the state treasury. So far as the *Banner's* effectiveness in Johnson's campaign was concerned, Danley asserted that one of its editors was absent from the state and the other bordering on delirium tremens during most of the campaign. He made a flat accusation of attempted fraud, not only in the case of the acts and journals, but also in printing accounts for the Supreme Court and the state land office, both of which he said had been successful swindles. Another such attempt had been thwarted by Acting Governor John R. Hampton, a former practical printer, who had measured the work before ordering payment. As a parting shot, Danley again referred to the touchy subject of Whiteley's reputation in the army.

When Whiteley refused to accept Danley's reduction of his second account, Danley suggested that he should take his grievances to court and compel him with a writ of mandamus to pay whatever the court decided was just.[32] This was extremely irksome, because there would be no court in session to issue the writ of mandamus before December, and the possibility of appeal to the Supreme Court might delay payment further. Whiteley abandoned his editorial anonymity and replied over his own signature in the *Banner* of September 16. He repeated much of what had been said previously, brought in irrelevant disagreements of the past, and charged Danley with ignorance and incompetence, citing several instances in which Danley had caused the state to lose money since he had been auditor. He went so far as to taunt Danley with his physical disabilities, Danley having lost the use of one arm as a boy and of one leg in the war.

As Danley discussed the situation with his intimate friends, they agreed that Whiteley was trying to provoke him into attacking him physically.

32. *Ibid.,* Sept. 19, 26, 1851.

It was agreed that this would be unwise, as Danley thus far had the advantage and a fight would only confuse the issues—and besides, Danley was a cripple, while Whiteley was physically fit. Some of Danley's friends advised him to carry a pistol to protect himself in case Whiteley should attack him, but he decided against it.

Solon Borland and Dr. John W. Pope had a front row seat at the beginning of the fight shortly before noon on September 16. As they sat conversing on the veranda of the Anthony House, they saw Whiteley and Reardon walk down Markham Street and seat themselves at the alley corner of the Anthony House bar room. Whiteley later said he had heard a few minutes earlier that Danley was about to attack him.

Danley and his brother, Sheriff Benjamin F. Danley, soon appeared, walking eastward on Markham Street and headed for the Anthony House, where they had boarded for several years. When they were 30 or 40 feet away, Whiteley and Reardon rose to their feet and stood close together. All four were tense and wary. As the Danleys passed the editors, both Whiteley and Reardon reached into their pockets, and C. C. Danley saw the gleam of Whiteley's pistol, partly drawn. Interpreting this as either a threat or an insult, the auditor struck at Whiteley with his cane, which Whiteley later called a "club" and a "bludgeon." Whiteley warded off the blow with his left arm, leaped backwards out of Danley's reach, and fired his pistol with his right hand. The shot hit nobody, and Danley was later surprised to learn that it was intended for his brother, who had offered no offense.

Whiteley then ran down the alley with the two brothers in pursuit. Borland watched from the hotel porch until he saw Reardon move in behind C. C. Danley and point a pistol at his back. Thinking his friend was about to be shot from the rear, Borland ran to the alley and disarmed Reardon with one hand while he shoved him to his knees with the other. At this point Gordon M. Peay, a bystander, thought Reardon was wounded, and he grasped Borland's hand to release his hold on Reardon. Borland stepped aside and allowed Peay to raise Reardon to his feet. Reardon was promptly knocked down again by William Danley, another brother of the auditor, and Reardon was carried away, unconscious.

William Danley, a steamboat engineer just out of a sick bed, had been about a block away when the fight started. He headed in the direction of the pistol shots, and on the way was told that one or both of his brothers had been killed in a fight with Reardon and Whiteley. His blow at Reardon was his first participation in the fight.

Meanwhile, Whiteley had run down the alley after he fired at Ben Danley, clutching at his bosom in a vain effort to draw his bowie knife. C. C. Danley was unable to overtake him because of his lame leg, but Ben Danley caught up with him and hit him with his cane. Ben had also lost the use of one hand in the Mexican War, and it was an easy matter for Whiteley to take the cane away from him and knock him down. Whiteley was standing over the stunned sheriff, raining blows on him, when the auditor hobbled up to him and made one futile attempt to hit him. Whiteley returned several blows to C. C. Danley's right arm and then backed away up the alley, still trying to draw his bowie knife, and moving faster backwards than the crippled auditor could follow.

The prostrate sheriff, still a little dazed, drew a pistol and fired, the shot striking the retreating Whiteley in the fleshy part of his right breast. The wound was slight, and Whiteley ran faster. When he reached the pavement in front of the Anthony House, he encountered William Danley, who had just knocked Reardon down. William attacked Whiteley with his stick, but was no match for him. Whiteley knocked the stick out of his hand, and then knocked William down. C. C. Danley overtook him about that time and at last delivered one effective blow, which knocked Whiteley off his feet and ended the fight.

In the next *Banner,* the fight was represented as a conspiracy by the three Danley brothers and Borland to assassinate Whiteley and Reardon. The story was told with considerable melodrama, and Danley countered with a similar accusation against the editors.[33] On the second day after the fight, Borland and C. C. Danley were summoned to appear before Justice of the Peace John Hutt for an investigation of the affair. Borland refused, and instead gave bond for his appearance at the next term of Circuit Court, although he knew he would be in Washington by that time. Ben and William Danley left town on business trips the next day.

Hutt's investigation was held in the last week of September. It was nominally a prosecution of Whiteley and Reardon, and was decided in their favor. The Danleys and their friends said it was a farce, and that no effort was made to elicit full testimony. Some of the people involved were placed under recognisance to answer before the Circuit Court in December, among them Ben Danley, who gave bond for his appearance upon his return to Little Rock.[34]

The *Banner* rehashed the fight every week, and the *Gazette* allowed Danley and his friends to tell their side of the story in reply, but declined to try to unscramble the conflicting information or to take sides. From the beginning, each side contended that the other was largely motivated by the ill will between Borland and Johnson.

Leon Trousdale retired from the *Gazette* on October 10 to make room for the proprietor's eldest son, Alden Mills Woodruff, who had returned from the California gold fields several months earlier, wealthier only in experience. His health had not been good since his return, and this had delayed the realization of his father's desire to turn the *Gazette* over to him and eventually also to his younger brother, William E. Woodruff, Jr., who was then away at school.[35] Young Alden evidently did not share the full measure of his

33. *Ibid.,* Sept. 19, 26, 1851; *Banner,* Sept. 30, 1851.
34. *Gazette,* Oct. 10, 1851.
35. Alden Mills Woodruff was born at Little Rock on Aug. 27, 1828. William Edward Woodruff, Jr. was born June 8, 1831. The only other living son, Chester Ashley Woodruff, was born Jan. 12, 1850, and was too young to be considered in connection

father's enthusiasm for this project, but was willing to give it a try. He had not served a regular apprenticeship in his father's office, and was not a practical printer, but had grown up in the printing office and figured he could handle the job.

At no time during almost ten months of Trousdale's editorship had the elder Woodruff shown open displeasure with his management of the paper. The conflict in their political philosophies had been offset by Trousdale's zeal for promoting internal improvements, in which Woodruff heartily concurred, and the *Gazette* under Trousdale's leadership had done much to encourage this important work. They were also in complete agreement on exclusion of denominational religious discussions. When the *Gazette's* job department printed a sermon by Rev. Joshua F. Green, pastor of the Presbyterian Church and a foe of Catholicism, and the *Gazette's* business office sold it, Trousdale refused to allow any part of it to be reprinted or discussed in the paper. He said he was a "thorough Protestant," but did not consider it a political newspaper's business to promote any set of denominational doctrines.[36] As they parted company, Woodruff and Trousdale expressed mutual regard, with a ring of sincerity.[37]

---

with the *Gazette.* One other son, George Watkins Woodruff, was born Nov. 26, 1829, but had died on Aug. 1, 1830. One daughter, Maria Jane, born May 3, 1833, had died on July 11, 1834. Woodruff's other daughters and their birth dates were: Harriet Maria, Jan. 31, 1836; Mary Eliza, Apr. 17, 1838; Evelina Walton, June 21, 1840; Frances Clarke, Apr. 4, 1843; Jane Georgine, Feb. 23, 1845; and Lizzie Ashley, Jan. 9, 1848. All these lived to a ripe old age except Lizzie Ashley, who died Oct. 29, 1854, and Chester Ashley, who died at the age of 49 on Feb. 3, 1899. See Family Bibles of Hannah Clarke Woodruff and Jane Eliza Mills Woodruff at Arkansas History Commission; tombstones on Woodruff lots, Mount Holly Cemetery, Little Rock.

36. *Gazette,* Aug. 8, 29, 1851.

37. Trousdale became one of the editors of the Memphis *Appeal* seven months later, and remained with that paper until 1860, when he went to Nashville as editor of the *Union and American.* The Civil War caused it to suspend publication. Trousdale served during the early part of the Civil War as an aid-de-camp to Governor Isham G. Harris, and later as a brigade adjutant general on Gen. Marcus J. Wright's staff. Because of failing health, he resigned from the army after the Chickamauga campaign of 1863. With Maj. Frank M. Paul, he edited the Chattanooga *Rebel* until its plant was destroyed by Federal troops. After the war, he was briefly editor of the Memphis *Commercial* and then returned to the *Appeal.* He served for four years as secretary of the Memphis Chamber of Commerce and the Agricultural and Mechanical Association, was bookkeeper for the Shelby County trustees, and in 1874 and 1875 was editor of the *Old Folks' Historical Record.* He moved to Nashville to accept an appointment as state superintendent of public instruction, and served six years. In 1883, he became clerk and assistant superintendent of the Bureau of Public Instruction, and editor of the *Southwestern Journal of Education.* President Grover Cleveland appointed him surveyor of customs for the port of Nashville in 1885, and he held this position about two years. He married Virginia Frances Joy, daughter of Levi and Martha Johnson Joy, at Bolivar, Tenn., in December of 1853. They had five children, four of whom lived to maturity. Trousdale died near Nashville on Apr. 21, 1897, and was buried at Mount Olivet Cemetery at Nashville. See *Cyclopaedia of American Biography,* VIII, 310–311; Truesdell, *Descendants of John Trousdale,* 28–29, 48–49; *Gazette,* May 14, 1852; Jan. 27, 1866; Jan. 28, 1870.

While Trousdale was editor, Woodruff as business manager arranged for the *Gazette* to be represented outside Arkansas by professional newspaper agents whose work was similar to that of modern national advertising representatives except that they also took subscriptions and accepted payments of accounts. V. B. Palmer was announced on March 7, 1851 as the *Gazette's* only authorized agent in New York, Philadelphia, and Boston. A week later the Boston agency was given to S. M. Pettengill. S. H. Parvin of Cincinnati was added to the list on June 6, and E. W. Wiley of the Southern Literary and Advertising Agency at New Orleans on January 9, 1852. The work of the *Gazette's* local agents in Arkansas was supplemented by traveling collection agents who worked on a commission basis and had other clients besides the *Gazette*.[38]

A change in postal regulations effective July 1, 1851 made a sharp reduction in postage paid on newspapers. Subscribers within a 50-mile radius of the place of publication now had to pay only 20 cents a year, 300 miles 40 cents, 1,000 miles 60 cents, and 2,000 miles 80 cents, but prepaid postage was demanded for papers sent for less than three months. Prepaid letters could be sent for three cents, but it cost five cents if paid by the recipient, so Woodruff began prepaying postage on all business letters sent from the *Gazette* office in August of 1851, and requested his correspondents to do the same.[39]

There is some evidence of the purchase of new type in May, 1851 from George Bruce's New York Type Foundry, and in July from the Cincinnati Type Foundry.[40] Paper was being purchased during this period from Nixon and Company at Cincinnati, who offered to pay the highest market price for rags or to exchange paper for rags.[41] All American newspapers were still printed on rag stock, and their steadily increasing needs had caused the demand for rags to exceed the easily available supply. Straw paper had been used for some time as wrappers for mailing newspapers, but was not good enough for printing newspapers.

About the time Trousdale came to the *Gazette* office, an advertisement for Roswell Beebe's Little Rock Foundry and Smithery was inserted in the paper, beginning December 6, 1850. It had a small woodcut of a building with "Little Rock Foundry" lettered on its facade. This probably was the first picture of a local building in the *Gazette* except those on the nameplate.

On July 4, 1854 the new style called "the bloomer costume" was described in detail and illustrated with two woodcuts that had appeared in the Louisville *Courier*. On August 8, a two-column cut copied from the London *Punch* showed five variations in the bloomer costume, all having dresses above the knees, and one having bloomers that came only to the knees. To show how daring the fashion was, this model was shown smoking a cigarette. Neverthe-

38. *Gazette,* July 18, 1851; Sept. 24, 1852.
39. *Ibid.,* May 30, Aug. 1, 15, 1851.
40. *Ibid.,* May 23, July 4, 1851.
41. *Ibid.,* Aug. 20, 1852.

less, Little Rock did not reject it, but apparently adopted it mostly for children. On the evening of August 20, a procession of about 25 little girls wearing bloomer costumes paraded past the *Gazette* office.[42]

On November 28, 1851, a few weeks after Trousdale left the *Gazette,* a prize of one year's free subscription to the paper was offered for the best Carrier's Address submitted. A committee of at least three "literary gentlemen" whose names were not announced were to serve as judges. Contest rules limited the length of the address to between 60 and 150 lines, and December 25 was the deadline for entries to be deposited in the Little Rock post office. This was the *Gazette's* first contest, and no effort was made to promote it or to make it a circulation builder. The winner's name was not announced in the paper, and his poem was not published in the *Gazette,* but it was printed as a circular to be distributed by the carriers on New Years Day.

As Alden Woodruff assumed his duties at the *Gazette* on October 10, 1851, both he and his father referred to him as the editor of the paper, and did not indicate that he would share the editorial responsibilities with anybody. But the next issue on October 17 showed William E. Woodruff and A. M. Woodruff as editors, and it became obvious that the father was the senior editor and the son was junior editor. The father was also shown as publisher and proprietor.

The *Gazette's* reluctance to give all-out support to the Danley-Borland side of the current dispute vanished with Alden Woodruff's first issue, although there was still an occasional disavowal of participation in the quarrel. Editorially, by contributions of the Danleys, and by reprinted articles from the Van Buren *Intelligencer,* the street brawl was refought and attention was directed back to the hassle over Whiteley's fees as public printer that had started the trouble.

About the middle of October the *Banner* issued an "extra" pertaining to the fight. The *Gazette* of October 17 branded it as a "secret circular" and said it showed that Whiteley and Reardon were agitating the matter of the street fight only to divert attention from Whiteley's alleged frauds and to crush Borland and all who opposed the Dynasty.

During the following week, the *Banner* office published a pamphlet entitled *Testimony and Proceedings of the Examining Court Relative to the Affray of the 16th Ult.,* with a preface said to have been written by Whiteley, and sent bundles of copies to the various post offices for free distribution. Its main burden was the charge that Borland had been so disturbed by the effectiveness of the *Banner's* opposition to him that he had taken drastic steps to get rid of its editors—first by putting Danley up to accusing Whiteley of fraud, and when that failed, by joining the Danleys in an attempt to assassinate them.[43]

About the time this pamphlet was being distributed, Whiteley retired from

42. *Ibid.,* Aug. 22, 1851.
43. *Ibid.,* Oct. 24, 31, 1851.

the *Banner* and left the state. He was succeeded by Richard Henry Johnson, younger brother of Robert Ward Johnson, not quite 26 years old, but every bit as articulate and as zealous for the Dynasty's success as his brother.[44]

With Danley's help, the *Gazette* was then exposing some other accounts in which Whiteley was said to have padded his printing fees on state contracts, all of which had already been paid.[45] Borland left for Washington on November 7, and with Whiteley also gone, the case pertaining to the fight that was scheduled to be heard by the Circuit Court in December apparently collapsed.

The dispute over the printing contracts did not subside, but rather continued until everybody was thoroughly sick of the subject, and grew more complicated as other issues were brought into it. Danley was now pitted against the secretary of state, and with Woodruff taking a hand in the controversy, it soon became as much his fight as Danley's. His 1837 default was again called up for review by the *Banner,*[46] and the *Banner* began casting about to find instances in which the *Gazette* office had charged extravagant prices for state printing. Although not the public printer, the *Gazette* office had had its share of executive printing and the advertising of the various counties. After Whiteley's departure, Danley had a good excuse to give printing jobs to other offices, for technically there was no public printer. He had given the *Gazette* the advertising of the auditor's list of forfeited lands, and the *Banner* complained that the $90 charged by the *Gazette* was twice the amount it should have been. The *Gazette* replied that it was not bound by Whiteley's contract, not being the public printer, and therefore did not have to deduct the 50 per cent Whiteley had agreed to deduct.[47]

Although Whiteley was absent from the state, the Pulaski Circuit Court issued a writ of mandamus against Danley on his petition, in its December, 1851 term. Danley's response made the clear cut accusation of an elaborate system of frauds against the state, refusing to concede that the overpayments were honest errors. His attorneys, Charles P. Bertrand and Elbert H. English, included in the response a long list of state contracts for which Whiteley had overcharged, whereby it was shown that he owed the state $794.60½.[48] The writ of mandamus was suspended pending appeal, and the case came before the Arkansas Supreme Court in its January term, 1854. Its decision was rendered in Whiteley's favor, because the lawful authority for certification

44. *Ibid.,* Oct. 24, 1851. Richard H. Johnson was born at Little Rock on Feb. 22, 1826.

45. *Ibid.,* Oct. 31, 1851.

46. *Ibid.,* Nov. 28, Dec. 5, 19, 26, 1851. Woodruff had tried to pay the judgment against him in notes of the State Bank, which the state's special attorney had refused to accept. The case had then gone to the United States Supreme Court, which held that the state was bound to receive her own paper in payment of the judgment. Woodruff said the State Bank notes had been sealed up and in safe keeping for more than five years, ready to be paid to the proper state authorities whenever the decision of the United States Supreme Court should be filed with the Arkansas Supreme Court.

47. *Ibid.,* Jan. 2, 1852.

48. *Ibid.,* Jan. 23, 1852.

of the accounts in question was vested in the secretary of state, and the court held that the auditor's issuance of the warrants was purely a ministerial duty and not one in which he had discretionary powers.[49]

Meanwhile, Borland had settled another argument with his fists, this time in the United States Senate chamber. The census enumerators in 1850 had gathered a wide variety of information not previously collected, and Joseph Camp Griffith Kennedy, superintendent of the census bureau, was determined to include in the published abstract of the census certain supplementary material that Borland considered unauthoritative. Borland was a member of the Senate's committee on printing, and argued that Kennedy exceeded his authority in including this material.

Kennedy soon made a pest of himself with his persistent efforts to change Borland's mind, and Borland began to avoid him and to abruptly end conversations with him that he could not avoid. Undaunted, Kennedy continued to seek him out to argue for publication of the sections Borland found objectionable.

The Senate debated the matter at length on February 5, 1852, and after adjournment, Borland was going over some printing estimates with Senator James A. Pearce of Maryland and Lem Towers, a Washington printer, when Kennedy approached him and again tried to explain why he wanted to include the material. Twice Borland told him he did not want to discuss it with him, and attempted to return to his business with Pearce and Towers. Kennedy said, "You are like others, who most need advice, but are least willing to receive it; but I shall take the liberty of giving it to you whenever I think proper." Borland's answer was a swift punch in the face that sent the frail Kennedy reeling, broke the bridge of his nose, and according to some overly dramatic accounts, possibly disfigured him for life.

It was rumored that Kennedy would challenge Borland to a duel, and once again Borland's undisciplined temper brought him a great deal of adverse national publicity. The *Gazette* tried to ignore the incident, but after other newspapers devoted a considerable amount of space to it, defended Borland's blow to Kennedy as the natural reaction to a deliberate insult. Borland wrote a statement of his side of the matter to Kennedy's superior, the secretary of the interior, and appended to it a supporting statement by Towers. But the result was that Borland was soon removed from the Senate's committee on printing.[50]

The *Gazette's* choice for president in 1852 was Stephen A. Douglas of Illinois, and for vice president, Jefferson Davis of Mississippi. Their names were placed under the masthead on March 15, as the endorsed candidates, subject to the decision of the Democratic national convention. But on May 7, in conformity with the preference of the state convention, Davis' name was dropped in favor of Gideon J. Pillow of Tennessee. The national convention nominated Gen. Franklin O. Pierce of New Hampshire for president and Col.

49. Danley, Auditor, etc., v. Whiteley, Jan. Term 1854, *14 Ark.* 687–706.
50. *Gazette,* Feb. 27, Apr. 2, May 7, 1852.

William R. King of Alabama for vice president, and the *Gazette* accordingly raised their banner on June 11.

When it came to a candidate for governor, the Woodruffs were less inclined to go along with their party's convention. John Selden Roane's surprise announcement in December that he would decline a re-election [51] made it almost certain that Elias Nelson Conway would try again to get the nomination. Woodruff's suggestion that each county represented should cast the same number of votes in the convention that it had polled in Democratic votes in the last Congressional election was adopted, but it failed to defeat Conway's nomination. Because the nomination was made by the system Woodruff suggested, he grudgingly placed Conway's name at the head of the *Gazette's* columns on May 7. He promised cordial support of the candidates for presidential electors, but only unenthusiastic performance of duty in Conway's behalf. Even that would be speedily withdrawn, he warned, if Conway should oppose or be lukewarm to internal improvements.

When Conway returned to Little Rock after a visit of five or six weeks to his ailing brother, William, he belatedly wrote his acceptance of the nomination, and had the *Banner* berate Woodruff for offering his party's nominee only passive support. Woodruff shrugged and replied that he could hardly be expected to exert himself for Conway, who had never rebuked the *Banner's* editors for their slanderous comments about him, when the party could have nominated a man of at least equal qualifications who had never been identified with the controversies of the past few years. However, if Conway could convincingly say that he favored repeal of the acts distributing among the counties the proceeds of two federal land grants, and that he would advocate a general system of internal improvements in Arkansas, he would continue to be Woodruff's candidate. Otherwise, Gen. Bryan H. Smithson of Washington County, who was running as an Independent Democrat on an internal improvements platform, would get the *Gazette's* support.[52]

Conway's acceptance of the nomination appeared in the next issue of the *Banner,* and included a platform. After Woodruff indulged in a bit of nitpicking, he announced that Conway's statement was noncommittal and unsatisfactory on the subject of internal improvements. Therefore, the *Gazette* withdrew from him the token support it had previously offered, and raised Smithson's standard with a good show of enthusiasm.[53]

To play up the contrast between Smithson's all-out support of internal improvements and Conway's apathy on the subject, Woodruff planned to keep standing in every issue of the *Gazette* the complete text of Smithson's letter announcing his candidacy and Conway's letter accepting the nomination. After they were crowded out a couple of times, he settled for the shorter and more effective gimmick of keeping standing a quotation from each letter.[54]

51. *Ibid.,* Dec. 19, 1851.
52. *Ibid.,* May 28, 1852.
53. *Ibid.,* June 4, 1852.
54. *Ibid.,* June 11, July 9, 1852.

Political cartoons in *Gazette*
of July 23, 1852.

An anonymous correspondent of the *Gazette* on July 2 referred to Conway as the "Dirt Road" candidate, and Woodruff made it Conway's campaign nickname.

The *Gazette* had two one-column political cartoons on July 23, each with an explanatory cutline. The first showed two men straddling the top two rails of a four-rail fence. The cutline was, "THE FENCE GAME. Our cut represents the fence-game in the Governor's election, which is affording considerable amusement to the lookers-on in these parts. The expectants and those who fear Conway's bull against 'Deserters' are 'holding-on' yet; but there will be some tall straddling before the polls close. If there be not some necks broken among the jumpers, they will be very lucky." The second showed a man digging a two-wheeled ox-drawn cart out of the mud. Its cutline was, "This cut has been got up as an appropriate vignette for the Dirt Road ticket. Orders for any number ornamented with this device, will be promptly filled at the lowest rates, at this office."

At the election on August 2, Smithson won a majority of 19 votes over Conway in Pulaski County, but as usual, the vote of the state ran contrary

A variety of items under the editorial head of September 10, 1852, including the unflattering standing notice of the appropriation of a part of the paper's name by its leading competitor.

One version of the crowing rooster cut used to proclaim political victories, from the *Gazette* of August 6, 1852.

to that of Pulaski County. Conway was elected with 15,442 votes to Smithson's 12,414, with one lone dissenter voting for C. F. M. Noland.[55]

It had long been understood that Bob Johnson planned to attempt to move up from the House to the Senate when Borland came up for re-election, to avenge Sevier and gratify his own ambition simultaneously. But in the spring of 1852 it became known that he had decided not to wait for the expiration of Borland's term, but instead would be a candidate for the seat held by his warm friend, William K. Sebastian. According to the gossip, Sebastian's reward for quietly relinquishing his office to Johnson would be the position of chief justice of the Arkansas Supreme Court, also to be filled by the next legislature.

Borland was not pleased by the news, although it meant he would be spared the rigors of a campaign against Johnson directly. With considerable emphasis he declared, "If *J.* is to go into the Senate, I prefer his doing so

55. *Ibid.,* Aug. 6, 1852; *House Journal 1852–1853,* 53.

over my head. I don't wish to *serve with* him. I had rather be *beaten* by him."

Whoever Johnson's nominal opponent might be, his real opponent would be Borland, and Borland lost no time in getting a counter campaign under way. In a letter to Elbert H. English, which probably was representative of his personal correspondence of this period, he recited some compliments recently paid him by prominent politicians, and with disarming candor, asked English to write some flattering articles for the *Gazette.* He stressed his desire that the articles should be not only a "lick ahead" for him and his friends, but also a "lick back" for Johnson and his faction. Borland was particularly anxious to be given full credit for the act of Congress for reclamation of swamp lands, which he said Johnson and others had sneered at on the grounds that it was impractical and asked for more than Arkansas could reasonably expect to get. When it passed the Senate, to the surprise of most of the seasoned politicians, Johnson realized he had to push it through the House or incur the displeasure of his constituents, and now he seemed inclined to take more than his share of credit for it.[56]

Johnson was optimistic about his chances for election. In mid-summer, his brother, Richard H. Johnson, wrote to a friend, "Bob's election to the Senate is beyond a question . . . He will be elected by about 85 votes out of the 100. The Borland faction cannot get a candidate to take the field openly against him." [57]

His brother's ambition to be a senator probably was the main reason Dick Johnson became publisher and one of the editors of the *Arkansas Banner* on October 21, 1851.[58] Already the *Banner's* managers had made a move to give it more definite identification as the leading organ of the Democratic party by changing its name to the *Arkansas Democratic Banner,* with the issue of March 11, 1851, with a new power press and complete new dress at the same time. Woodruff had refrained from commenting on this change of title, saying only that he did not care to resurrect an old matter of controversy of which he and the public were weary.[59] But when his leading competitor began a new volume on September 7, 1852 with the title *The True Democrat,* it was too much. There was a double volume numbering system that gave the paper both an "old series" and a "new series" volume number, thus giving it the dual advantage of the stability of age and the separation from past associations.[60]

The explanation editors Johnson and Reardon gave for the new title was, "We wish our paper to bear a name that shall indicate its principles. Democrats immigrating to the State, and desirous to take a newspaper of their own

56. Solon Borland to Elbert H. English, Washington, Apr. 1, 1852, Ms. in Samuel W. Williams Collection, Arkansas History Commission.

57. R. H. Johnson to [John M. Ross?], Little Rock, July 6, [1852], Ms. in Samuel W. Williams Collection.

58. *Gazette,* Oct. 24, 1851.

59. *Ibid.,* Mar. 14, 1851.

60. John A. Hudson and Robert L. Peterson, "Arkansas Newspapers in the University of Texas Newspaper Collection," *Arkansas Historical Quarterly,* XIV (1955), 218, 222.

political faith, have been imposed upon by a false beacon." Woodruff was so enraged that he all but foamed at the mouth. The direct slur against his paper as a "false beacon" of his party was nothing more than a new wording of an old accusation, threadbare from constant repetition and no longer capable of getting more than a slight reaction from him. But the appropriation of his paper's name was something else. His paper was the one referred to when the most abbreviated title, the *Democrat,* was used, as a carryover from the days when it had been the *Arkansas State Democrat.* That was his own favorite short name for it, although he and others also often called it the *Gazette and Democrat.* His rival's new title might also be abbreviated as the *Democrat,* but even if it were not, he would be at a disadvantage if his paper were known as the *Democrat* and the other one as the *True Democrat,* with its implication of party superiority.

In his next issue, Woodruff placed under the editorial head a "Caution to Correspondents and Exchanges," which was kept standing as long as he owned the paper. It advised correspondents and exchange papers to address mail intended for this office to the *Gazette and Democrat* or to the editors and proprietor by name. It began with the startling explanation: "As there is a bastard and piratical Newspaper established in this city, under the inappropriate title of '*The True Democrat,*' which is doubtless designed to intercept and appropriate to its own use the correspondence as well as the patronage of the *Gazette and Democrat . . .*"

The Johnsons must have chuckled with satisfaction at the accompanying editorial, which made liberal use of heavy boldface type and multiple exclamation marks to emphasize its most biting remarks. Its chief complaint was that the other paper had stolen its name as a desperate, last-ditch measure to save itself from bankruptcy.[61] Woodruff's wrath did not abate, and he belabored the subject again and again in the weeks that followed.

The congressional delegation came home late in September.[62] The legislature convened on November 1, and on the afternoon of November 10, met in joint session to elect a senator and a chief justice. Apparently the scheme to advance Johnson to the Senate and Sebastian to the court had been abandoned, for only Sebastian was nominated for the Senate, and only George C. Watkins for chief justice. A few legislators demonstrated their opposition to the Johnson clique by voting for others not in nomination, but Sebastian received 85 votes—exactly the number Dick Johnson had predicted his brother would receive.[63]

The *Gazette* office printed the message of the retiring governor and two departmental reports the previous legislature had ordered, but the *True Democrat* office and the *Arkansas Whig* office received the job work of the session. Selection of the printer of the acts and journals was left to the joint committee on printing, and for the first time, the contract was awarded to a

61. *Gazette,* Sept. 10, 1852.
62. *Ibid.,* Sept. 24, Oct. 1, 1852.
63. *House Journal 1852–1853,* 88.

printer outside the capital city, Robert L. Pegues of Arkadelphia. Laws of a general nature and others requiring immediate publication were published in the *Whig*.[64]

The *Arkansas Whig* had begun publication at Little Rock on May 22, 1851, with John M. Butler as publisher and Robert C. Farrelly as editor.[65] At the end of its first quarter, its editor took exception to the *Gazette's* claim of "Circulation larger than any other Paper in the State," a boast kept standing under the editorial head, and challenged Woodruff to make a public comparison of the circulation figures of the two papers. Woodruff refused, and advised the *Whig* to delay bragging about its patronage until those who did not pay for their subscriptions had been removed from the list.[66] Farrelly retired from the *Whig* in November, leaving Butler as its sole proprietor.[67]

As the campaign progressed in the summer of 1852, Woodruff offered a special subscription rate of 50 cents for the months of June, July, and August, ending with the gubernatorial election. Clubs of 15 could have the *Gazette* for these three months for $5. Those who wished to extend their subscriptions through the presidential election in November could have it for $1, or clubs of eight for $5, all making payment in advance.[68]

After the gubernatorial election, when the presidential election was the next hurdle, Woodruff offered a challenge to the supporters of the Whig nominee, Gen. Winfield Scott. Regular subscription rates were still $3 a year in advance or $4 at the end of the year. Woodruff offered to receive subscriptions for $5 a year, payable when the Democratic nominee, Franklin Pierce, should be elected president, and pledged himself to send the paper free for one year to such subscribers if Pierce were defeated. This touched off another brief skirmish with Butler, who offered the same terms in reverse, but required those who wanted to bet with him to gamble only the $3 ordinarily charged for the *Whig*. He boasted in September of several new subscribers received on these terms, and Woodruff smugly replied that only one person had been willing to accept his offer. Two more took up the wager during the next week, and Woodruff made his challenge stronger by offering a premium of 20 per cent to anyone who would get 100 responsible subscribers on those terms, and said he would increase it to 33⅓ per cent for a responsible person who would enter into a written obligation to pay the money within 60 days after Pierce's election.[69]

Early returns indicated an easy victory for Pierce and King. The *Gazette* used a woodcut of a crowing rooster standing over a prostrate coon to announce the apparent Democratic victory in the issue of November 12, 1852,

64. *Ibid.,* 69–70, 78, 135–136, 231, 246, 269, 332.
65. *Gazette,* May 9, 23, 1851; Hudson and Peterson, "Arkansas Newspapers in the University of Texas Newspaper Collection," 220.
66. *Gazette,* Aug. 29, 1851.
67. *Ibid.,* Nov. 14, 1851.
68. *Ibid.,* June 4, 1852.
69. *Ibid.,* Aug. 13, Sept. 3, 10, 1852.

Political cartoons from the *Gazette* of November 19, 1852.

The crowing rooster and prostrate coon cartoon, in the *Gazette* of November 12, 1852.

and facetiously claimed it had been borrowed from the *Whig*. On November 19, two half-column cartoons with the overline "Heads of the People" depicted local reactions to the dispatches giving the news of election results. A grinning man was labeled "Democrat," and a grim visaged man was labeled "Whig." The artist was not identified, but he may have been Edward Payson Washburn, a native artist who had recently opened a studio at Little Rock, hoping to earn enough money to finance a trip to the East for formal instruction in art, and who later acquired regional fame with his painting of "The Arkansas Traveller." Arkansas gave Pierce and King her four electoral votes, by a popular vote of 12,162 to 7,325.[70]

In looking forward to the new administration, some of Borland's friends ventured to suggest that he might be appointed secretary of the interior, and there was some support for it in neighboring states.[71] The *True Democrat* and the *Whig* were not impressed, and in the spring of 1853, they complained that Borland had not participated in passing the bill granting lands in Arkansas for the proposed Cairo and Fulton Railroad. Only a few months earlier, the *Gazette* had accused Johnson of neglecting to call up in the House the Arkansas railroad bill that Borland had pushed through the Senate, and assigned as his motives envy and malice towards Borland. Now the *Banner* and the *Whig* made the same charges against Borland, in connection with Johnson's railroad bill.

70. *Ibid.*, Dec. 3, 1852. There was the usual slight variation in the votes for individual candidates for electors, and the figures quoted are the average of the votes given for each party.
71. *Ibid.*, Dec. 17, 31, 1852.

As Borland told the story, he did not like the Cairo and Fulton bill, but only Sebastian's deception had prevented his voting for it, as the only chance to get a railroad grant for Arkansas. Borland had been ill and wanted to spend a few days in Virginia, but he hesitated to leave Washington because Sebastian had given notice that he would call up the railroad bill for discussion. Sebastian had not called up the bill on the designated day, and four days later he had told Borland he could safely go to Virginia, as he thought nothing affecting Arkansas would come up right away. Borland left Washington on a Thursday evening and returned the following Tuesday to find that Sebastian had called up the Cairo and Fulton bill in his absence, and it had passed the Senate after a short debate.[72]

Borland's illness had begun with a severe cold contracted on the trip to Washington in November of 1852. He wrote to the Woodruffs on February 28, 1853 that the cold still lingered and was different from any he had ever had, affecting his whole system and disabling him for any kind of work, although he had stayed in bed only two days. After the first month of the session, he had given up his habit of sleeping no more than five hours and devoting much of the night to correspondence. His vision was affected by his illness and the long hours of writing by candlelight, but it had improved with rest and the use of colored glasses.[73]

Woodruff laughed off a rumor that he was about to sell the *Gazette* in the fall of 1852,[74] but on March 18, 1853, he announced that he had sold it to Capt. C. C. Danley, who would take charge immediately. His farewell editorial, in which he outlined his career as an editor and the simultaneous growth of his paper and the state it served, was largely a revision of earlier editorials, drawing heavily on his 1838 valedictory and his 1843 salutatory, with long passages lifted from them verbatim. He did not explain the sale, beyond his statement that he was retiring to "employments better suited to my taste and disposition." Certainly the newspaper business had lost much of its fascination. Most of the time, the primary purpose of his political work had been to advance the career of a close personal friend, but he had outlived those whose battles he was eager to fight.

Woodruff, now in his 58th year, considered himself "not yet much beyond the prime of life," but others were already thinking of him as an old man, and would shortly begin to describe him as "venerable." He was to live another 32 years, in the quiet pursuit of his land agency business and other interests. Never again would he show more interest in politics and government than the average uninvolved citizen. He showed more interest in the *Gazette,* especially in his declining years, when he took note of its anniversaries and occasionally demonstrated that he retained his craftsman's skill by setting a stick of type. Several times he submitted to interviews on the subject of the *Gazette's* history, but his written contributions to the paper were

72. *Ibid.,* Sept. 3, 1852; Mar. 11, 1853.
73. *Ibid.,* Mar. 18, 1853.
74. *Ibid.,* Sept. 3, 1852.

conspicuous by their absence. Many times before his death on June 19, 1885,[75] questions pertaining to Arkansas history were in the news, but they never drew response from Woodruff, although it was often suggested that he was among those best qualified to supply the answers.

Alden Mills Woodruff had three separate careers after he left the *Gazette's* tripod, first as a planter, then as a steamboat owner and commander, and finally as the manager of the *Gazette's* job printing office. He died at Little Rock of Bright's disease on September 10, 1893.[76]

75. *Ibid.,* June 20, 1885.

76. *Ibid.,* Sept. 12, 1893. Alden Mills Woodruff married Eliza Sizer on Dec. 17, 1856 at Little Rock, (*Ibid.,* Dec. 20, 1856) and had two children, Janie and George. Early in the Civil War, he served as the Military Board's financial agent, and when state troops were transferred to the Confederate service, he became chief commissary in Gen. William J. Hardee's command, with the rank of major. After the fall of Nashville, he resigned and came home because of the illness of his wife, who died soon afterwards in childbirth, her infant son, William, dying shortly after her death. (*Ibid.,* Nov. 22, 29, 1862.) He served as chief clerk of the House of Representatives in the 1862 session. He married Clementine Clay Sparks in December, 1863, and by her he had one daughter, Willie. He operated a cotton plantation and gin opposite Little Rock. (*Ibid.,* May 7, 1867; Aug. 12, 1869; Jan. 10, 1871.) He had the steamboat Hallie built at Little Rock in 1872–1873, naming it for the daughter of his sister, Harriet Maria, and her husband, John Nicholas Jabine, Captain Jabine being financially interested in it. With Woodruff as captain, the Hallie ran regularly in the Arkansas and Mississippi River trade until she was damaged beyond repair in the Brooks-Baxter War of 1874. (*Ibid.,* Oct. 29, 1872; Apr. 1, 4, 1873; June 13, July 15, 1874.) Woodruff was chief secretary of the Senate in the special session held during the Brooks-Baxter War. His next steamboat was the Maumelle, which he commanded and owned in partnership with Jabine and two others between September, 1874 and December, 1876. (*Ibid.,* Sept. 3, 4, 24, 1874; Dec. 9, 1876.) After that he was captain of the Big Rock and other steamboats in the Arkansas River trade. (*Ibid.,* Feb. 18, 1880.) His son, George, became the manager of the *Gazette* job printing office, and when he died as a young man, the father inherited and continued the business with the intention of selling it, but stayed with it until his own health failed. (*Ibid.,* Sept. 12, 1893.)

15

KNOW NOTHINGISM

C. C. Danley, Solon Borland, William F. Holtzman

1853-1859 AS CHRISTOPHER COLUMBUS DANLEY made his bow to his readers on March 25, 1853, he reaffirmed his loyalty to the Democratic party but vowed he would not allow the *Gazette* to become the organ of any political clique. He scoffed at the stock platitude by which editors frequently promised to support "measures, not men," saying that while principles were all-important, they were useless without men to apply, expound, and defend them.

He favored expansion of the nation by annexation of new territory whenever honorably possible. On the state level, he was particularly eager to promote internal improvements, concentrating first on one good railroad and development of natural resources.

His paper looked much as it had under Woodruff's management, with the same format, ornamental nameplate, motto, and double numbering system for the *Gazette* and the *Democrat*. The claim that its circulation was larger than that of any other Arkansas paper, and the location of the office "upstairs in Beebe's buildings on Markham and Elm Streets" were retained under the editorial head, but Danley dropped the standing notice about the "bastard and piratical" competitor who had stolen part of his paper's name. He also discontinued Woodruff's standing notice listing out-of-state and traveling agents.

Danley had just returned from Memphis, where he had arranged for S. H. Lamb, a bookseller and stationer, to act as the *Gazette's* agent. On May 27, John M. Shaw, a general agent for periodicals at Memphis, was authorized to act for the *Gazette* in east Arkansas, west Tennessee, and north Mississippi.

When Woodruff put two men on the road in the fall to collect accounts due him, Danley also engaged them to collect for him. Isham W. Wyatt's collection tour of 18 counties south of the Arkansas River was announced on September 9, and a tour of 19 counties north of the river by Simon P. Hughes, a future governor of Arkansas, was announced on October 14.

Danley's attachment to Solon Borland, amounting almost to hero worship, was so well known that anybody might have guessed that Borland was the man he intended to promote, and that the measures he would try to popularize would be those advocated by Borland. In a long editorial captioned "Small Potatoes" in his first issue, Danley defended Borland against "one-horse editors and bar-room politicians" who did not comprehend the difference between the railroad land grant bill that Borland had failed to get through Congress and the one Bob Johnson had successfully sponsored. The terminal points specified in Borland's bill were those the people had requested, said Danley, while Johnson's starting point of Cairo, Illinois had never been mentioned by his constituents.

J. C. Claiborne, editor of the Batesville *Commercial Standard,* was not pleased with the editorial and implied that it could not have been written by the same person who wrote Danley's salutatory. "He is mistaken," replied Danley. "We do all of our own writing. The reason that there is a difference in some of our articles, is, that we always choose a gun, with calibre in proportion to the size of the game we are hunting. We never think of such a thing as shooting small game with a big gun. It don't pay." [1]

Danley was not aware when he penned these words that Borland had embarked on a new phase of his career that would require him to bring into service the biggest guns at his command. The word came a week later that President Pierce had appointed Borland governor of New Mexico Territory, and Danley wrote a glowing review of his career, representing him as the greatest statesman Arkansas (and indeed the entire Mississippi Valley) had ever sent to either house of Congress. [2]

By May 6, the news had come that Borland had declined this appointment, and instead had accepted an appointment as minister plenipotentiary to Central America, one of the most important foreign assignments available. Borland had not endeared himself to the Washington press, and had many enemies in Washington and at home. On one occasion, there had been an attempt to burn him in effigy in the streets of Washington. It was not surprising that his enemies should view with alarm his appointment to this position. It was conceded that his background in foreign affairs, particularly his belief in adherence to the Monroe Doctrine, was in his favor, and that his facility with the Spanish language would be helpful. But the memory of the easy belligerence that had led him into several well publicized brawls caused many to question the wisdom of giving the post to one of his temperament.

He arrived at Little Rock on May 15, spent a few weeks with his family at Hot Springs, and began his journey to Central America on July 4. In his farewell address to his constituents, he explained that he had not formally resigned his seat in the Senate, since his acceptance of the ministerial post made

1. *Gazette,* Apr. 15, 1853.
2. *Ibid.,* Apr. 22, 1853.

Solon Borland.

Christopher Columbus Danley.

it automatic. His family remained in Arkansas, and Borland promised that he would return to Arkansas to spend the rest of his days, and would not again seek public office.[3]

Arkansas was now entitled to two congressmen, and nominating conventions were held in both districts early in May. Danley was able to attend the southern district's convention at Hot Springs by arranging for Alden and William E. Woodruff to take charge of the *Gazette,* but they wrote only a few short local items and no editorials for the one issue they put out.[4]

Robert Ward Johnson was not a candidate, and Edward A. Warren was nominated in the southern district and Alfred B. Greenwood in the northern district. The Whigs nominated Frederick W. Trapnall in the southern district and gave Greenwood no opposition. Danley offered a campaign wager similar to those Woodruff had offered, with subscribers agreeing to pay $2.50 for a year's subscription upon Warren's election, and Danley agreeing to send them the *Gazette* free if he were defeated.[5] When word came that Trapnall had become dangerously ill on the campaign trail, Danley deferred discus-

3. *Ibid.,* May 20, 27, July 8, 1853.
4. *Ibid.,* May 6, July 22, 1853.
5. *Ibid.,* June 17, 1853.

sion of his political merits.[6] Trapnall died on July 4, and Danley respectfully reversed the column rules bordering the column containing his obituary on July 8. The Whigs put James M. Curran into the race in Trapnall's place, but the campaign was nearly over and Warren defeated him by a large majority.[7]

During the last two or three weeks of the canvass, there was more interest in the vacancy in the Senate than in the campaign for Congress. Borland's friends realized that he had virtually given the seat to Johnson, for Conway surely would appoint Johnson unless by some miracle he could be persuaded to call a special session of the legislature to fill the vacancy. Many people pressed Conway to call a special session to take care of necessary legislation in connection with the federal railroad grants, but he refused, and appointed Johnson to the Senate on July 6.[8]

To offset the complaints about the perpetuation of the Dynasty that this announcement would bring on, the *True Democrat* deplored the nepotism practiced by the Borland and Danley families and estimated the amount of money they would draw from the public treasury if they all held their present positions as long as the law allowed. Danley was the state auditor, his brother Benjamin had been appointed receiver of public moneys at Little Rock by President Pierce, and his brother James was chief clerk in the surveyor general's office. Borland's only relative on the public payroll, since his two sons no longer had situations, was his father-in-law, George Milbourne, who had been appointed surveyor general by the president.

Danley's job as state auditor especially galled the *True Democrat's* editor. He said that all of Conway's time had been devoted to the office when he was auditor, and charged that the time Danley spent editing the *Gazette* caused the work of the auditor's office to suffer. At the same time, he said an extra clerk had been hired to take care of the neglected chores, and that William E. Woodruff and John E. Knight were helping Danley edit the *Gazette*. Danley denied all these statements,[9] and denied again a month later that Woodruff had any connection with the *Gazette* or any control over any of its contents except his own advertisements.[10]

This was not the first comment on Danley's attempt to be auditor and editor simultaneously. In his second issue of the *Gazette* on April 1, in response to many inquiries, he had said that he had no intention of resigning

6. *Ibid.,* July 1, 1853.

7. *Ibid.,* Sept. 2, 1853.

8. *Journal of the House of Representatives for the Tenth Session of the General Assembly of the State of Arkansas, Which was Begun and Held in the Capitol, in the City of Little Rock, on Monday, the Sixth Day of November, one thousand eight hundred and fifty four, and ended on Monday the twenty-second day of January, one thousand eight hundred and fifty-five.* Published by Authority. (Little Rock: Johnson & Yerkes, State Printers, 1855), 44; *Journal of the Senate for the Tenth Session of the General Assembly of the State of Arkansas . . .* Published by Authority. (Little Rock: Johnson & Yerkes, State Printers, 1855), 42.

9. *Gazette,* July 22, 1853.

10. *Ibid.,* Aug. 19, 1853.

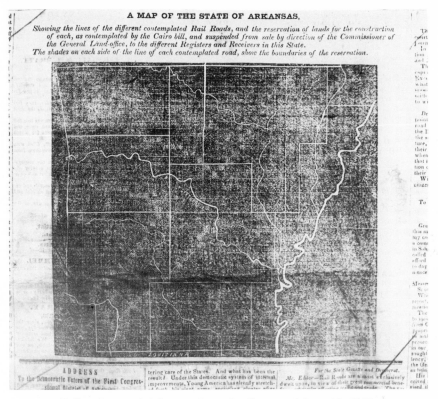

Railroad map of Arkansas, from the *Gazette* of June 10, 1853.

his office as auditor. On both occasions, he seemed to think the discussion had originated with Conway.

When Danley made a trip to Hot Springs and left Knight in charge of the issue of September 23, the *True Democrat* called attention to it. In the next issue, Danley credited Knight with the editorials of the previous week, and said he would never leave the *Gazette* in the hands of an irresponsible man, and implied that he would always state who it was. However, he often failed to do this in his later absences.

On June 10, 1853, Danley published a three-column map of Arkansas, showing the lines of railroads authorized by Johnson's bill, and the lands reserved from sale for their construction. Its details were in white, and the lines and letters were so thinly carved that the map was not easily legible against its heavy black background.

With the issue of July 29, 1853, a feature captioned "Little Rock Prices Current" was added to the market reports copied from out-of-state news-

Local market report from the *Gazette*
of July 29, 1853.

Steamboat Register from the *Gazette*
of June 2, 1854.

papers. It was prepared every week by Sterling H. Tucker, one of the leading merchants of Little Rock.[11] This had been attempted in the 1830's, and one of the drawbacks to its regular publication still existed. The local market depended to a great extent on the navigability of the Arkansas River, and when goods could not be shipped to Little Rock by the river, the local market all but disappeared. The next seasonal low period lasted long enough for the supply of merchandise to be exhausted, and Danley announced on February 3, 1854, "We continue the publication of the Little Rock Prices Current, merely to show what the articles quoted could be sold for, if there were any in the market."

When the *Whig* announced at the end of the year that its 1854 Carrier's Address had been written by the celebrated poetess, Mattie G_____ of Kentucky, and would be delivered by its devil on January 2, Danley said his devil would also deliver a Carrier's Address on that day, but it had been written by an Arkansan. The *Gazette's* devil, being a native "to the manor born," preferred native to foreign genius.[12]

Danley began the year 1854 with a restatement of the principles the *Gazette* would endorse. They were the same as those mentioned in his salutatory, with the addition of a "temperance reformation," to be accomplished by legislative action.[13] In line with his policy of promoting internal improve-

11. *Ibid.,* Aug. 5, 1853.
12. *Ibid.,* Dec. 30, 1853.
13. *Ibid.,* Jan. 6, 1854.

ments, he soon advocated a state fair for the exhibition of Arkansas products, a project first suggested by William Quesenbury of the Fayetteville *South-West Independent,*[14] and contributed to a cash prize made up by a group of Arkansas editors to be given to the best looking native baby.[15]

Danley was well pleased with the increase in subscriptions since his purchase of the paper. A new circulation gimmick just beginning to make the rounds was to group a newspaper with a periodical devoted to fine arts, sports, or some other special field, and to offer both at an attractive price and sometimes with an additional premium. Early in 1854, Danley offered for $4 a year's subscription to the *Gazette* and a year's subscription to the New York *Musical World and Times,* with a bonus from that publication of a fine steel engraved portrait of composer William Vincent Wallas, which Danley said was alone worth the subscription price for both papers.[16]

After a series of fires in which arson was suspected, Danley said on February 10, 1854, "We are, as a general thing, opposed to the execution of Lynch Law; but we would like to see one incendiary hung summarily. The law is too tardy in its operations, and justice is administered with too sparing a hand, to such offenders."

Eleven days later, Danley was one of the victims of the most disastrous fire Little Rock had ever had, which destroyed all the buildings on the three lots at the northeast corner of Markham and Main. The fire started about one o'clock on the morning of February 21 in the wood house at the rear of the *True Democrat* office, a brick building owned by Mrs. Lambert Reardon and occupying a plot that fronted 52 feet on Elm Street and 23½ feet on Main Street.[17] The adjoining brick building on the south, owned by Jacob Reider, stood on a plot of the same dimensions and fronted on Main Street.[18] South of this building was a plot 13 feet wide and 52 feet deep, fronting on Main, that had once been covered by a building that housed the El Dorado Saloon and later the silversmith and jewelry shop of Benjamin and Henry W. Linebaugh.[19] Either this building no longer existed or was thought of as a part of one of the adjacent buildings, as it was not mentioned in accounts of the fire. South of this was the L-shaped Alhambra building, which covered the remaining 80 feet of Main Street frontage and, with its addition, fronted 77 feet and 9 inches on Markham and 25 feet and 9 inches on Elm, a part of the narrow addition adjoining the rear of the three small plots.[20] The *Gazette* office occupied the second floor of this building, and the tenants in the lower story were the fancy and dry goods store of David Bender and Company, the book and stationery store of John E. Reardon, the drug store of Dr. W. W. Adams, and the tin shop of J. Brisbin and Company. Next door to the Alham-

14. *Ibid.,* Jan. 13, 1854.
15. *Ibid.,* Feb. 3, 1854.
16. *Ibid.,* Jan. 27, Feb. 10, 1854.
17. Pulaski County Deed Book I, 429.
18. Deed Book H, 74.
19. *Ibid.,* 30.
20. Deed Book I, 115, 325; Deed Book L, 278.

bra building on the east was the old Rapley building, 77 feet wide and 140 feet long, with fronts on both Markham and Elm streets. Its owner was William B. Wait, who occupied a part of the building and rented a part to Levy's dry goods store. All these buildings dated back at least as far as the 1830's.

The fire spread rapidly, and soon all these buildings were in flames. Little Rock's official fire fighters were self-trained volunteers, whose equipment was provided by the City Council, but a major fire was everybody's business and the fire bell brought the whole town and many visitors to the scene. Many pitched in to help fight the fire and to move property out of burning buildings, but others merely stood and watched, and some spent their time and energy in plundering. All the buildings mentioned burned to the ground, but the fire's progress was arrested before it could ignite the unfinished shell of the Odd Fellows and Masonic Hall on the east end of the block. Danley estimated the cost of the fire at $100,000 or more.

Most of the merchandise in the stores was carried to safety, but nothing in the *Gazette* office was saved except the books and files and a few miscellaneous papers. The two outside pages of the issue of February 24 had been printed, and were rescued by a local doctor named Hummell and a visitor from Maryland named Burke. Henry Brookin, a *Gazette* employee, saved the copy for an unpublished advertisement sent by a state land agent. Everything else was lost, and was not covered by insurance. The *True Democrat* office also was an uninsured total loss.

The next issue of the *Gazette* appeared on time, thanks to the proprietor of the *Arkansas Whig,* who placed the facilities of his office at Danley's disposal. The outside pages were smudged and dirty because of the rough handling they had received in the fire. Except for a few items pertaining to the future of the *Gazette,* the contents of the two inside pages, including the advertisements, had appeared in the *Whig* earlier in the week.

Danley had already sent an experienced printer to New York to buy the materials for a new office, and he said publication of the *Gazette* would be resumed within a few weeks. Meanwhile, he hoped to issue an occasional advertising sheet from the *Whig's* press, the first of which would contain the lengthy land ad that Brookin had saved from the flames. These would be sent free to subscribers, and their subscription year would be extended to make allowance for the lapse in regular publication. Danley said enough money was owed him in small individual debts to pay the entire cost of refitting his office. To hasten the payment of accounts, he offered to reduce the amount due for deferred payment of subscriptions from $4 to $2.50, the price charged for advance payment.

As they viewed the smouldering ruins of one of the best business blocks in town, the citizens muttered about the suspected arsonist, the theft of exposed property, and the town's primitive fire-fighting methods. A meeting was held at the city hall the day after the fire, and another two days later, to try to find a way to prevent similar disasters in the future.[21] The result was the organi-

21. *Gazette,* Feb. 24, 1854.

zation of the Defiance Hook and Ladder Company, a volunteer fire company that gave effective service to the community for many years.[22]

William E. Woodruff and Sterling H. Tucker supplied Danley's agent with letters of credit, by which they stood as guarantors for Danley's debt of $2,501.80 to A. S. Barnes and Company of New York, who underwrote the purchase of the new press, type, and other materials. Woodruff also loaned Danley $500, probably to cover the expenses of his agent's trip to New York. James M. Danley loaned his brother $1,000 to enable him to build a printing office on lots 1 and 2, block 32, Original City of Little Rock. To secure his benefactors from loss, Danley executed a mortgage on May 23, 1854 on the real estate, the building, and all the furniture and equipment of the office.[23]

The new Superior Royal Hoe Washington press and other machinery were purchased from Richard Hoe and Company of New York, and the type and other materials from John T. White's foundry of New York.[24] Additional type or other materials came during the summer and the following spring from George Bruce of New York and L. Johnson and Company of Philadelphia, and probably also from A. H. Joselyn of New York.[25]

Danley's mortgage stated that the money borrowed from his brother was to build a printing office, but the main building had been standing at least as early as 1831, and was new when the *Arkansas Advocate* office occupied it from May, 1831 until October, 1832.[26] Danley's brother, Benjamin, was managing the property as administrator of the estate of William Barkeloo when Henry F. Shaw, who lived in the building, entered into a purchase agreement in the spring of 1852. Shaw asked to be released from the agreement that fall, and on October 19, 1852, C. C. Danley assumed Shaw's part of the bargain. The purchase price was $1,310, for which he gave three notes, the interest to bring the total cost to $1,370.20 At that time the dwelling house, stable, and other improvements stood on these lots. Presumably Shaw continued to occupy the house until his death in the early summer of 1853.[27] Danley eventually completed the contract and his title to the lots was fully recognized, but he never received a deed, possibly because he and his brother neglected to take care of this detail. He was still living at the Anthony House when his office burned, but he moved into the building at Second and Scott when it became the *Gazette* office.

John Robins had paved the sidewalk on the Scott Street side with brick

22. *Ibid.,* Feb. 22, 1874.
23. Deed Book X, 429–430.
24. *Gazette,* May 5, 1854; Little Rock *National Democrat,* Feb. 27, 1864.
25. *Gazette,* July 14, 1854; Mar. 23, Apr. 20, 1855.
26. *Arkansas Advocate,* May 18, 1831; Oct. 10, 1832. The owner of that period, who presumably built the building, apparently never perfected his title to the property and cannot now be identified. The next owners, Darwin Lindsley and his partner Moffett, described it as a "long row of buildings . . . immediately south of the bridge" over the Town Branch, and used it for shops. (*Gazette,* Mar. 6, 1833.) It became a residence when Lindsley sold it to William Barkeloo in 1835. (Deed Book K, 301.)
27. *Gazette,* Mar. 12, 1852; June 3, 1853; Pulaski County Probate Court Records, Book B, 309–310, 321–322, 395; Book C, 60–61.

in 1847.[28] The white frame L-shaped building was flush with the sidewalks on both streets, running the full 100-foot width of the lots on Scott Street and about 60 feet on the Cherry Street side.[29] Dickison Brugman, who began his newspaper career a few years later in this building, gave this description of the editorial office: "Major Danley worked in the front room, the furnishings in which consisted of a deal table, piled high with exchanges, a shelf on which there were several books of reference and a box filled with sawdust, which he used for a spittoon." [30] This room was on the north end of the building, facing Scott Street. The Cherry Street extension must have included the two rooms Danley occupied as living quarters, and possibly also the mechanical department of the paper. At the rear of this property, on the lots adjoining it to the east, stood the two-story brick building that had been the *Gazette's* office from 1824 until 1827.

The *Gazette* resumed publication on Friday morning, May 5, 1854, having missed only nine weekly issues. The new format was a great improvement, mostly because one small blessing found in the tragedy of the fire was the loss of the fancy pictorial nameplate. The new title line was in sedate Roman type, all capitals. Except for a different spacing that gave more white space, the rest of the flag was the same as before, including Danley's name as editor and proprietor, the motto from Jefferson, the subscription rates, and the double volume numbering that took up where it had been interrupted.

The first issue appeared just as the 1854 political season opened, and after preparing the editorials, Danley left for Princeton to attend the Second Congressional District's Democratic convention on May 1. It was his habit to give new advertisements a free plug in the editorial columns, and one ad arrived after he left town and did not receive this attention. The advertiser, who gave a Saratoga Springs, New York address, sent enough money to pay for two insertions, so the ad was published. He offered to inform ambitious young men who would send him $1 of an honorable way to earn $1,000 to $1,500 a year on a capital of no more than $5. When Danley returned, he gave the ad its second publication, but warned his readers not to send the man any money. It was a new kind of swindle, he said, adopted by petty villains whose hearts were "as black, and more corrupt, than most of the public thieves, who are caught, convicted and sent to the Penitentiary." [31]

A new weather feature, giving a weekly report of local weather conditions during the preceding week, was contributed by "a friend," beginning with the issue of July 26, 1854.

The Democratic nominees for Congress were Alfred B. Greenwood in the First District and Albert Rust in the Second District.[32] Greenwood had no

28. *Arkansas State Democrat,* June 15, 1849.
29. *Gazette,* Dec. 25, 1872. The only known picture of the building is in an 1871 panorama of the entire city, "Bird's Eye View of the City of Little Rock."
30. *Gazette,* Nov. 7, 1931.
31. *Ibid.,* May 12, 1854.
32. *Ibid.,* May 12, 19, 1854.

formal opposition, and Rust's Whig opponent, E. G. Walker, was a weak candidate, so there was no need for Democratic editors to exert themselves in this campaign. At the election on August 7, Greenwood received all the votes in his district except 298 cast in two counties for W. C. Myrtle. Rust won an easy victory with 9,378 to Walker's 4,862.

Danley's main interest in this campaign was a proposed constitutional convention, the question having been referred to the people by the previous legislature. Strongly in favor of sweeping changes in the state's organic law, Danley had begun his endorsement of the convention before the fire, and had long editorials on the subject in every issue except one between May 5 and August 4. Among the measures he favored were popular election of all public officers, clarification of jurisdiction and modernization of operations of the courts, an increase in the ratio of representation to reduce the legislature's membership and cost, restriction of the legislature's appropriations to works of general improvement, and discretionary power for the legislature to authorize private banking. In spite of the sound arguments for a new constitution, the people voted against the convention 15,897 to 10,997.

The Whigs on June 5 nominated Charles P. Bertrand and Joseph Stillwell for the House of Representatives from Pulaski County, and Rev. James T. Morris for the Senate from the district composed of Pulaski, Prairie, and Perry counties.[33] Elbert H. English, long a mainstay of the Borland wing of the Democratic party, had agreed to run for the state Senate provided he would have no opposition from his own party. A small convention that Danley branded as another cut and dried convention manipulated by the Johnson wing, made the Democratic nominations on June 10, and chose B. C. Totten of Prairie County as the party's candidate for the Senate. Danley said he was well qualified and had never participated in the factional disputes, and gave him the *Gazette's* endorsement and support. But he refused to accept the two nominees for the House, Henry M. Rector and Jared C. Martin, both of whom had been strong members of the Johnson faction from the beginning, although Rector's mercurial disposition had so often led him to stray into strange paths in recent years that one hardly knows how to classify him at this point. Danley refused to give them any kind of encouragement, and said that unless other Democrats entered the race, its outcome was a matter of complete indifference to him.[34] Totten was elected to the Senate by a narrow margin of six votes, and Rector and Stillwell were elected to the House.[35]

One suspects that the Dynasty's efforts for Rector in this race came as the result of a compromise by which he was placated and returned to the fold after having bolted rather spectacularly. One such memorable occasion had come in 1848, when Rector switched from Sevier to Borland during his canvass for the state Senate, with considerable fanfare, and then quietly switched back to Sevier after the balloting began. The most recent evidence that he had

33. *Ibid.,* June 9, 1854.
34. *Ibid.,* June 16, 23, 1854.
35. *Ibid.,* Aug. 11, 1854.

his differences with the Dynasty was his open letter of October 8, 1853, first published in the Pine Bluff *Republican* of October 22, in which he condemned Conway for refusing to call a special session to accept the railroad grants. Albert Rust, also a "blood relative" member of the Dynasty, had taken a similar stand, and Danley had then praised them both.[36] Now that they had made their peace with the Dynasty again, he washed his hands of them, or at least of Rector.

Theirs had been only a small part of the clamor for a special session in 1853. Ostensibly, the main reason was the feeling that there should be no delay in the state's acceptance of the railroad grants and the legislation necessary for the railroad construction to begin. But the old conflict between the Borland and Johnson wings of the party also figured in it, as a special session at that particular time might not have sent Johnson to the Senate to finish Borland's unexpired term, and Conway's appointment of him was valid only until the next meeting of the legislature. Conway argued that there was no need for a special session, as the next regular session could take care of the railroad matter, and besides, special sessions were expensive.[37]

Conway wanted to show the people that the state could not afford a special session by publishing a report of the condition of the treasury. On September 23 or 28, 1853, he sent Danley a written request for the quarterly reports required of the auditor by law, with detailed instructions on the items to be included. Conway said Danley neither sent the reports nor acknowledged receipt of the letter, but Danley said he did not receive any such letter until the governor sent him a copy of it with a second request for the reports, dated January 30, 1854. Still Danley made no reply and sent no reports, so on June 20, 1854, Conway petitioned the Pulaski Circuit Court for a writ of mandamus to compel him to submit the reports. A writ of alternative mandamus was issued, and Danley's reply to it was that he had not made quarterly reports because he was guided by the precedent set by Conway as auditor, who had compiled them as quarterly statements to be filed every two years shortly before the legislative session. Danley challenged the governor's right to demand the reports, and the court's right to prescribe their form. After the usual legal maneuvers, the court issued a peremptory mandamus against Danley on June 26, and he filed the reports four days later.[38] On August 5, he sent the governor his resignation, to take effect on September 16.[39]

Solon Borland had arrived at Greytown, Nicaragua in September of 1853, and had begun his official tour of the Central American republics a few days later.[40] The following May he completed his tour and started for the seaport

36. *Ibid.*, Oct. 28, Nov. 4, 1853.
37. *Ibid.*, Nov. 4, 1853.
38. *Senate Journal 1854–1855*, 18–19, and *Appendix*, 45–52; *House Journal 1854–1855*, 20–21, and Appendix, 45–52.
39. *Gazette*, Aug. 11, 1854.
40. *Ibid.*, Sept. 30, Nov. 18, 1853.

with the intention of going home. He had been involved in at least one un-pleasant incident, when he had interceded in behalf of one Henry Greer, an American arrested and mistreated for no apparent reason at Virgin Bay, Nicaragua on October 3.[41] He also had negotiated a treaty with Nicaragua whereby the boundaries of Nicaragua as recognized by the United States were extended to cover all the territory claimed by the Mosquito Indians.[42] About the time he started home, American newspapers announced that he had resigned his ministerial post on April 17, but it was not effective until June 30.[43]

After the captain of the American steamboat that brought Borland down the San Juan River shot and killed a belligerent native, Borland refused to permit his arrest by native officials whose authority was not recognized by the United States or Nicaragua, and bluffed a native posse out of boarding the steamboat. There was a confrontation that night at Greytown between Bor-land and a group of armed natives who were bent on arresting him for inter-fering, and someone in the crowd threw a broken bottle and slightly wounded Borland's face. He was not arrested, but was prevented from returning to his steamboat by native sentinels who patrolled the beach all night. This was the night of May 16, and the next day he sailed for New York.

When Borland made his report at Washington, President Pierce sent the ship of war Cyane to Greytown to demand an apology for the indignities to Borland and to demand payment of a damage claim of Cornelius Vanderbilt's Accessory Transit Company. The people of Greytown ignored the demands, and the Cyane's commander, Capt. George N. Hollins, gave them 24 hours notice before he destroyed the town on the morning of July 13. The town's 300 inhabitants had taken to the woods. The Cyane bombarded Greytown at intervals, and then Hollins sent a detachment ashore to burn the buildings the shelling had not completely demolished.[44]

The boldness of the retaliation and the circumstances that led to it were the talk of the nation for weeks. Anti-administration politicians, editors, and citizens filled the newspapers with their opinions of Borland's behavior, as well as all others concerned, and those friendly to the administration were equally vocal in their defense. Needless to say, the Gazette was on Borland's side all the way.[45]

When Borland finished his business in Washington, he returned to Arkan-sas as a private citizen. His home was now a large frame farm house described as a mile south of Little Rock, now included in Wright's addition to the city. He had acquired this property from several owners just before his departure

41. *Ibid.,* Nov. 18, 1853.
42. *Ibid.,* May 12, 1854.
43. *Ibid.,* May 19, July 14, 1853; *The National Cyclopaedia of American Biography* (New York: James T. White and Co., 1893–1916), IV, 386.
44. *Gazette,* June 9, 30, July 14, Aug. 11, 18, 25, Sept. 1, 1854.
45. *Ibid.,* Sept. 8, 15, 22, 29, Oct. 6, 20, Nov. 3, 1854.

for Central America.[46] In partnership with Dr. J. J. McAlmont, he purchased Dr. W. W. Adams' drug store at the corner of Main and Cherry streets, changed its name to Dr. J. J. McAlmont and Company, and left his partner to operate the business while he opened an office a block away in the south end of the *Gazette* building and resumed the practice of medicine.[47] In November, Borland and Dr. Craven Peyton issued a prospectus for a monthly medical journal called the *Medical Reporter,* to be published from the *Arkansas Whig* office at Little Rock beginning the first Monday in January.[48] It never began publication, probably because it did not attract enough advance subscribers.

Danley also was expanding his business interests about this time. In the *Gazette* of October 6, 1854, he announced that he would do business as a land agent and collector, and on November 3, he announced the opening of a new stationery store as an adjunct to the *Gazette* office.

46. Deed Book X, 80, 167, 169, 170. The deeds were dated July 6 and 7, 1853, and Borland had left Little Rock on July 4. Probably his family had lived on this land during his absence. His father-in-law also owned farm land not far from Little Rock.

47. *Gazette,* Sept. 22, Oct. 13, 1854.

48. *Ibid.,* Nov. 24, Dec. 1, 1854.

On November 10, 1854, the legislature unanimously elected Bob Johnson to complete Borland's unexpired term in the Senate, and also to the next full term of six years.[49] In the spring the word came that Borland's father-in-law, George Milbourne, had been removed as surveyor general and Henry M. Rector appointed in his place, indicating that Rector was back in the Dynasty's good graces and that the Johnson-Borland feud was not yet finished.[50]

Two months before the 1854 session of the legislature opened, S. M. Scott, editor of the *Arkansaw Traveler* at Camden, suggested a convention of the state's editors and publishers, to be held at Little Rock on Friday, November 3, just before the legislative session was to begin. Many editors would be coming to Little Rock to observe part of the session, and probably could come a few days early for this convention. The main purpose was to give them a chance to get acquainted and to establish uniform prices for advertising and job printing and perhaps attain some degree of uniformity in other phases of their work. Danley heartily endorsed the suggestion, and wanted to include proprietors of job printing offices that did not publish newspapers. He saw the convention as the first step in the organization of a state press association, with membership confined to those who actually controlled printing offices. Organizations of printers, the forerunners of the modern labor unions, were being effected in other states and would soon spread to Arkansas. Danley saw this as a good reason for their employers to organize, to be ready to deal with the organizations of employees. He also thought it would give the profession greater dignity.

Several editors responded favorably, but when the appointed day came, it still was uncertain whether enough editors were in town to justify holding the meeting. If not, Scott said it could be held during the following week.[51] Probably a meeting was held, though perhaps with disappointing attendance, but the *Gazette* did not report it, and it did not result in a permanent organization.

The *True Democrat* had resumed publication after the fire in the old frame Recess building on the north side of Elm Street, where the *Gazette* had been located in Benjamin Borden's day. Dick Johnson and his partner, Reuben S. Yerkes, bought the building two days after the fire, [52] and Danley made much of the fact that Bob Johnson had said he had provided his brother with the means to put the *True Democrat* back in business. Danley used this to show that the *True Democrat* was the organ of Conway and Johnson not only because its editor was a relative and the governor's private secretary, but because the senator and possibly also the governor had invested money in it. Dick Johnson vigorously denied this,[53] and charged in turn that Woodruff still owned and controlled the *Gazette* and that Borland had great influence

49. *Senate Journal 1854–1855,* 53–54.
50. *Gazette,* Apr. 13, 1855.
51. *Ibid.,* Sept. 15, 29, Oct. 6, Nov. 3, 10, 1854.
52. Deed Book X, 354.
53. *Gazette,* Dec. 29, 1854; Jan. 19, 1855.

over its policies, both of whom were still being regularly assailed in the *True Democrat's* columns. Danley admitted that Woodruff had helped get him elected as auditor, but was silent on the subject of the financial assistance he had given him after the fire. When Danley referred to Dick Johnson as a drunken loafer, the *True Democrat* replied that Danley had once worked as bartender at the Anthony House, and even now kept a jug of whisky under his bed. Danley said he had never been ashamed of the humble occupations of his youth, but he left some doubt as to whether he had kept bar, and occasionally came very close to denying it.[54]

Borland was not one to stay on the political sidelines very long. Late in 1854, some Memphis Democrats who were dissatisfied with the *Appeal* proposed that he should take charge of it. He seemed receptive, and on December 28, 1854, one of the *Appeal's* three proprietors wrote to him offering to sell his interest in the paper. Borland replied on January 8, 1855 that he might be interested if the terms and other circumstances were right. He went to Memphis on other business in May, and the same Democrats again approached him on the subject, and Borland said he would insist on owning at least two-thirds of the paper. Two days later, one of the editors offered to sell him his one-sixth interest, but said that if his partners were willing to sell, the price would be at least $15,000 or $20,000. Borland said it was much too high, and thought no more of moving to Memphis.[55]

Returning to Little Rock, he entered into a partnerhip with Danley, whereby he became senior editor and owner of a half interest in the *Gazette*. He began his duties with the issue of June 22, 1855, while Danley was at Pine Bluff attending a wedding. In his salutatory, Borland disclaimed any ambition to hold public office again, hoping only to render valuable service to Arkansas as an editor and private citizen. The policies of the *Gazette* would remain the same, he promised, for he and Danley were in complete agreement.[56]

A new party had sprung up in 1854, officially called the American party and nicknamed the Know Nothing party. In the beginning, it was generally understood to be a secret order, having its roots in secret fraternal organizations of similar principles.[57] It was solidly committed to nativism, its main thesis being that immigrants and Catholics should not be permitted to take an active part in government.

As early as August 25, 1854, Danley had placed himself on record as Anti-Know Nothing, declaring that the party's principles were in conflict with the spirit of America, being based on political and religious intolerance. On November 3, 1854, he had chided Dick Johnson for not defining the *True Democrat's* position on the subject, and had predicted that if the new party should

54. *Ibid.,* Dec. 8, 15, 1854; Jan. 19, June 8, 1855.
55. *Ibid.,* Nov. 2, 23, 1855.
56. *Ibid.,* June 15, 22, 29, 1855.
57. W. Darrell Overdyke, *The Know-Nothing Party in the South* (Baton Rouge: Louisiana State University, 1950), 14–15.

prove to be in the majority, Johnson would be "the Know Nothingest Know Nothing in the country."

Early in 1855, the *True Democrat* began to take a stand against the party, and in April accused Danley of being affiliated with it, basing this on the fact that some anonymous articles favorable to Know Nothingism had been published in the *Gazette*. Danley replied that he had published them merely to show both sides and not as an endorsement, and was not thereby committed to Know Nothingism any more than Johnson was committed to temperance by his occasional publication of temperance articles.

About the same time, the *South Stamp* of Camden said that Danley had applied for membership in the Know Nothing order and had been rejected. Danley vigorously denied that he had ever held or desired membership in the Know Nothing order or any society having similar principles, and the Camden editor gracefully backed down by saying he had made his remarks "in a vein of pleasantry."[58]

On June 1, Danley took note of a rumor that Northern and Southern Know Nothings had split over the slavery question, and the Northerners had formed another secret organization known as the Sag Nichts, or Say Nothings, to oppose the Know Nothings. Danley took a dim view of all secret political organizations, and called upon the South to unite without party distinctions and stand undivided before the next Congress to secure her rights.

This was the situation when Borland began his work at the *Gazette* on June 22, and apparently he felt precisely as Danley did at the moment, but the reports of the Know Nothing national convention held in June caused him to make a second appraisal of the party and to soften his attitude. The injunction of secrecy no longer existed. The plank in the platform that had caused the withdrawal of most of the free state delegates favored maintaining existing laws on slavery, and declared that Congress had no right to legislate on the subject of slavery in the states, and should not attempt to control it in the territories.

The *Gazette's* long editorial on July 6 was written by Borland, as evidenced by the use of his pet word "intirely." It was difficult for a devoted Southerner to find fault with the party's stand on slavery, and Borland said its position was truer to the Constitution and better for the South than any other party's had ever been. He sought only to give the devil his due, and disclaimed favor or affection for the new party. "We are *democrats,* in principle and in practice," wrote Borland, "and, our faith proved by the works of our lives, we shall ever remain so. But we are not to be hoodwinked by *names,* nor led away from principle, by *professions.*"

Borland was ill when he wrote this editorial, and took to his bed nine days after it was published, with four physicians and his friend Danley in attendance. He was out of the office four weeks, during which time Danley twice denied that the editorial of July 6 had been anything more than an act

58. *Gazette,* Apr. 20, 17, May 4, 1855.

of justice to the Know Nothings, and flatly denied that the *Gazette* had become a Know Nothing organ.[59]

The lingering death of the Whig party was followed by the demise of its organ, the *Arkansas Whig,* in May of 1855. Its founder, John Milton Butler, who had sold the paper in 1853,[60] had become a Know Nothing and was confidential printer for the party's State Council. In partnership with his brother, James D. Butler, he was operating a job printing office and was planning to start a Know Nothing newspaper at Little Rock.[61] But on August 5, 1855, Milton Butler and his brother-in-law, Edward Marcus, shot it out on Markham Street and both were almost instantly killed. They had been quarreling for some time, and some thought their differences were mostly political. The circumstantial evidence that led to this conclusion was that Marcus was a German immigrant and a Democrat, strongly antagonistic to the Know Nothings, while Butler was even more plain spoken and ardent in the cause of Know Nothingism.[62] Whatever the reason, Butler's death deprived the new party of its organ at Little Rock, but the deficiency was supplied by the *Gazette* five days later.

Borland was back at his desk in time to write the editorial for August 10, announcing the *Gazette's* switch to the American party. He used most of the space to explain that he still clung to the principles of the Democratic party, but could no longer support the old party organization because it had abandoned those principles that he considered most important. As he expanded this theme, it became obvious that the slavery question was the root of his dissatisfaction, for he contended that the Democratic party had been abolitionized on the national level and in the Northern states to such an extent that Southerners could no longer feel any enthusiasm for it. Moreover, the Democrats were advocating an increase in the foreign born population, and could see no reason why Catholics should not be equal in all respects to non-Catholics. Borland said he would not withhold the rights and privileges of full citizenship from foreigners or Catholics who were already here, but thought no more should be encouraged to come, mostly because they tended to settle in the free states where they strengthened anti-slavery forces.

His explanation of this point left something to be desired, but the fact was that the Southern wing of the new party considered that foreigners having no background in a country where slavery existed were not likely to be friendly to it, and that Catholics came too much under the influence of the pope—a foreign power—to be defenders of slavery. Slavery did not figure in the attitude of the Northern wing, whose rejection of foreigners and Catholics was based on the premise that foreign powers were using them to weaken the American government.

The *True Democrat* promptly threatened to reprint some of Borland's

59. *Ibid.,* July 20, 27, Aug. 3, 10, 1855.
60. *Ibid.,* May 18, 1855; June 3, 1853.
61. *Ibid.,* Oct. 5, 1855.
62. *Ibid.,* Feb. 14, 15, 1893; *True Democrat,* Aug. 7, 1855.

editorials written for the old *Banner,* in which he had stoutly proclaimed his undying loyalty to the Democratic party. Borland replied that it would make a better newspaper than Johnson could produce, and began to strike at Governor Conway for withdrawing from the Methodist Church to attend the Catholic Church. To the *True Democrat's* comment that Danley's position regarding the Know Nothings was not mentioned in the editorial, the *Gazette* replied that Borland's editorial expressed the opinion of both editors.[63]

The new party attracted many heretofore zealous Democrats and many leaders of the defunct Whig party. Albert Pike threw himself into it wholeheartedly. Even so, the Know Nothings made less progress in Arkansas than in any other Southern state except possibly South Carolina.[64]

Not the least of the indignant reaction to the *Gazette's* apostasy was the demand that it should drop the word "Democrat" from its title, since it had repudiated the party and was now anti-Democratic. Danley and Borland refused to be placed on the defensive, and offered no explanation for keeping "Democrat" in the title, contenting themselves with a withering blast at the individuals who had contested their right to it.[65]

There was a rash of meetings to ratify the platform adopted by the national party in its June convention. Both editors frequently attended and addressed party meetings in other towns, and sometimes both were absent at the same time.[66] Borland's bad health, two deaths in Danley's family, and Danley's election in November as grand master of the Arkansas Grand Lodge of the Independent Order of Odd Fellows also took them out of the *Gazette* office from time to time.[67]

The *Gazette* office undertook the printing for the American State Council, published the party's platform as a handbill, and kept it standing in the paper for several weeks. The *Gazette* was named the official organ of the party at the session of the State Council in October.[68]

Borland was a prime target for the criticism of the Democrats, not only because he was considered more responsible than Danley for the *Gazette's* political policies, but because his career afforded more grounds for complaint. None of his past transgressions, personal or political, escaped Dick Johnson's caustic pen. All phases of his political career, from his contest with Sevier to the Greytown affair, were reviewed. Borland defended himself point by point on the political questions, but when Johnson dragged the skeletons of his personal life out of the closet, Borland would not argue.

On December 11, the *True Democrat's* editorial accused Borland of per-

63. *Gazette,* Aug. 17, 1855.
64. *Ibid.,* Apr. 12, 1856; Overdyke, *The Know-Nothing Party in the South,* 73, 113–114.
65. *Gazette,* Aug. 24, Sept. 14, 1855.
66. *Ibid.,* Sept. 7, 14, 21, 28, Nov. 9, 1855.
67. *Ibid.,* Oct. 19, Nov. 2, 9, 1855; Jan. 26, 1856.
68. *Ibid.,* Sept. 7, 1855; Jan. 5, 1856.

suading the people of Little Rock to accept his mistress as a suitable teacher and companion for their daughters, quoting from the files of the *Banner* his lavish recommendations of Madame d'Estimauville in 1844. Without directly referring to the subject matter of this editorial, Borland replied that it was "notoriously false in fact" and "indecent, alike in language and allusion," and was an unsuitable subject for the columns of a respectable newspaper. In a separate editorial paragraph, he struck a counter-blow by alluding to the gossip about miscegenation in the Kentucky branch of Johnson's family.[69] Johnson shamed him for his denial and added, "Why sir, we have not yet alluded to the grand *denoument* [*sic.*] of your guilt; and the truth of the charge we brought against you is as well known to the citizens of Little Rock, as that there ever was a town in Dallas county called D'ESTEMAUVILLE!" [70]

Apparently Borland thought the less said about the d'Estimauville affair, the better. He made no response in the next *Gazette* except on political issues, and the *True Democrat's* editor professed to be "stupefied with amazement" at his refusal to discuss the matter. Borland replied with a few vague remarks about Johnson's lack of decency.[71] Still Johnson would not drop the subject, although he did not go so far as to tell the whole story. In the *True Democrat* of January 1, 1856, he again referred to Borland's prostitution of the *Banner's* columns in praise of a lewd woman with whom he had been improperly intimate.

Borland decided this was a good time to pay a long visit to his brother, Dr. Euclid Borland, who lived near New Orleans. On January 6, he and his family boarded the steamboat Fox, intending to be gone four or five weeks.[72] In the *Gazette* of January 5, he discussed Johnson's latest political accusations, but remained silent on the subject of the ancient scandal.

This issue also contained a communication signed "Father," undoubtedly written by Borland, telling of the tendency of his seven-year-old daughter, Fanny, to talk in rhyme and meter almost from the time she learned to talk. It included six lines of perhaps the worst poetry his daughter ever composed, with the explanation that this was the way she had told of a dream she had on New Year's morning. She had said, "I wish somebody would put it in a book," and so her first published poem appeared in the *Gazette*.[73]

69. *Ibid.,* Dec. 14, 1855.
70. *True Democrat,* Dec. 18, 1855.
71. *Gazette,* Dec. 28, 1855.
72. *Ibid.,* Jan. 12, 1856.
73. Borland's daughter, who later spelled her name Fannie, was a belle in Little Rock society after the Civil War. (*Ibid.,* Jan. 22, 1867.) She married James C. Moores of Memphis on April 21, 1869, and thereafter lived at Memphis. (*Ibid.,* Apr. 23, 1869.) She wrote many poems that were published in newspapers, but never in book form. The real beginning of her career as a poet came at the age of 14, with publication in the *Gazette* of November 22 and 29, 1862 of two poems inspired by her vigil at the bedside of her dying mother and her gravely ill father. Her favorite subjects for poems pertained to the lost cause of the Confederacy. (*Ibid.,* Jan. 21, 1872.) Albert Pike, who was himself a poet of no mean ability, said she was "the best writer of verse in the southwest." (*Ibid.,* Oct. 23, 1875.) She died at Memphis on August 23, 1879, a victim of the great yellow fever epidemic. (*Ibid.,* Aug. 20, 24, 28, Sept. 5, 1879.)

In this same issue, January 5, 1856, the *Gazette* appeared in a new format. The paper was enlarged from seven to eight columns, making it as large as any other in the state. Since its type was smaller than that of other Arkansas papers of the same size, the proprietors figured it offered about 20 per cent more reading matter.

The nameplate perversely continued the complete old name, *Arkansas State Gazette and Democrat,* in Roman letters. The nameplate was only six columns wide, the tops of the two outside columns being flush with the top of the nameplate, with the masthead and subscription terms occupying the left and the advertising terms the right. The old motto adopted by Woodruff for the *Democrat* in 1843 was reworded to read, "ERROR ceases to be dangerous, when REASON is free to combat it." It had been credited to Thomas Jefferson until after the 1854 fire, and Jefferson had indeed expressed this thought in different words on several occasions. The old construction, "TRUTH is in no danger from ERROR, so long as REASON is left free to combat it," left some doubt as to whether reason was expected to combat truth or error, and presumably that was why it was changed.

Danley had little taste for poetry, and had already advised his correspondents that he would not waste any of the *Gazette's* space on their verses, since he was not publishing a literary journal.[74] However, he had reprinted from the *South-West Independent* of Fayetteville a long poem by its editor, William Quesenbury, about the wedding of John Selden Roane and Mary Kimbrough Smith, at which both editors had been guests. Quesenbury, who gained regional fame as "Bill Cush," was an able poet, writer, and artist, and this poem, like many of his others, was illustrated with a small cartoon.[75]

The annual carrier's addresses were in rhyme, and previous editors had not often published them in the paper, but Danley nearly always did, in spite of their length and his disdain for poetry.[76] Borland must have liked poetry, for the *Banner* had published a lot of it while he was its editor. Now that the *Gazette* had an extra four columns every week, Danley decided he could spare a little space for poetry occasionally, sometimes written by Arkansans and sometimes reprinted from the exchanges. He was reluctant to rely on his own judgment for its selection, and said he would depend on his correspondents and other friends to send suitable poems. For the quality of the first selection, he had the glowing recommendation of no less a person than George D. Prentice, editor of the Louisville *Journal* and a fine poet. The poem was written by a young man of Little Rock, a native of Jefferson, Kentucky, who signed the initials "A. T. H." Like his earlier poems, it had been published first in the Louisville *Journal.*[77] Danley's willingness to gratify the desire for poetry of some of his readers did not last long. Eventually he went back to the arguments that the *Gazette* was not a literary journal, that the

74. *Gazette,* Sept. 21, 1855.
75. *Ibid.,* Mar. 9, 1855.
76. *Ibid.,* Jan. 5, 1856; Jan. 3, 1857; Jan. 2, 1858; Jan. 7, 1860.
77. *Ibid.,* Jan. 12, 1856.

hidden beauties of some verses submitted were so well concealed that he could not find them, and that it was a mistake for correspondents who had not mastered prose to think they could write poetry.[78]

The entire Know Nothing ticket was elected in Little Rock's municipal election on January 7, 1856. The *Gazette* did not fail to point this out, but neglected to mention that except for the new offices of constable and city justices, most of the successful candidates were the incumbents. Danley was one of the new aldermen.[79]

Borland was a single-minded editor, with politics as his only theme. Danley had other interests, especially internal improvements, and did not fill his paper with political discussions to the exclusion of everything else, but he kept the ball rolling in Borland's absence. One of his contributors sent an unsigned letter and poem that had all the earmarks of Quesenbury's work. It was illustrated with an original cartoon that portrayed the famous Democratic crowing rooster as "a miserable foreign stock, having the body of a Shanghai [a breed of chicken], the Pope's head, and a coon's tail." [80]

The meetings of the American National Council and the American national convention, held at Philadelphia in February of 1856, were disastrous. Northern Know Nothings had not visualized nativism as a vehicle to protect slavery, and succeeded in removing from the platform the section that made the Southern viewpoint on this subject the party's official policy. The plank that replaced it was more neutral, unacceptable to the Southern delegates but not strong enough to impress the Northerners. Albert Pike, who was now practicing law in New Orleans and was a member of the National Council, was one of the leaders of a Southern attempt to block modification of the platform, and withdrew in a huff when he failed. The nomination of Millard Fillmore of New York for president and Andrew Jackson Donelson of Tennessee for vice president brought some Southerners back into the convention, but not Pike. He decided instead to aid in an attempt to organize a splinter party called the American Party South, which nominated John C. Fremont for president and William F. Johnston for vice president. Pike argued that the platform was indefensible in the South, and the presidential candidate too much identified with the old Whig party to be acceptable to former Democrats.[81]

The nominations were announced in the *Gazette* on March 8, but Danley did not commit himself to the support of either the candidates or the platform until the next week. He said he wanted time to study the platform,

---

78. *Ibid.,* Oct. 9, 1858; Aug. 25, 1860.
79. *Ibid.,* Jan. 12, 1856; Jan. 5, 1855.
80. *Ibid.,* Jan. 19, 1856.
81. *Ibid.,* April 12, 1856; Robert Lipscomb Duncan, *Reluctant General: The Life and Times of Albert Pike* (New York: E. P. Dutton and Company, Inc., 1961), 142–143; Overdyke, *The Know-Nothing Party in the South,* 127–141; [Albert Pike], *To the American Party South* [1856].

to be sure it gave assurance to Southerners regarding slavery, but he made it clear that preservation of the union was of primary importance.[82]

Borland did not return to Little Rock until March 19.[83] On March 29, he announced that he had sold his half interest in the *Gazette* back to Danley, who would again be sole proprietor and editor. Knowing that some would interpret his withdrawal as a sign that either he or the *Gazette* was wavering in zeal for Know Nothingism, he assured the readers that both were still steadfast in the party's service, but this did not prevent an occasional rumor that he had abandoned the party. Ratification meetings, where Know Nothings approved the national platform and candidates, were just beginning, and both Danley and Borland addressed several of them.[84]

Borland's name was not mentioned in the proceedings of the American state convention at Little Rock on April 28, but Danley was a member of the Central State Committee, the platform committee, and the organization committee, was a convention delegate from Pulaski County, and held proxies for Desha and Greene counties. James Yell of Jefferson County, a nephew of Archibald Yell, was nominated for governor, and two candidates for presidential electors for the state at large were nominated,[85] one for each of the two congressional districts being added to the ticket later. During the next week, a full slate was nominated for Pulaski County offices.

82. *Gazette*, Mar. 15, 1856.
83. *Ibid.*, Mar. 22, 1856.
84. Borland withdrew from the partnership with Dr. McAlmont in the drug store on June 21 (*Gazette*, June 28, 1856), and the next spring began the practice of law at Little Rock. (*Ibid.*, Apr. 25, 1857.) He moved his family to Princeton in Dallas County in February of 1858. (*Ibid.*, Feb. 27, 1858.) One son, Thomas Borland, died at the Anthony House at Little Rock on January 9, 1859, aged about 25. (*Ibid.*, Jan. 15, 1859.) In June, 1859, Borland bought an interest in the Memphis *Enquirer* and became one of its editors, the other being Jere Clemens, also a former United States senator. (*Ibid.*, June 11, 18, 1859.) The family home remained in Dallas County, and Borland's first visit home was extended from the planned one month to about six months because of his illness. (*Ibid.*, Aug. 13, Oct. 22, 29, Nov. 19, 1859; Feb. 11, 1860.) In the spring of 1860 he purchased Clemens' interest in the *Enquirer*, but Clemens remained as senior editor until June. (*Ibid.*, Apr. 28, June 30, 1860.) He sold the *Enquirer* in March of 1861 (*Ibid.*, Mar. 16, 1861) and returned to Little Rock, where he figured prominently in some of the political and military events of the early part of the Civil War. Severe illness caused him to leave the Confederate army and return to Little Rock, where he briefly resumed his medical practice in June of 1862. A son, George Godwin Borland, born March 11, 1846, died at Clarksville, Texas on June 24, 1862, shortly after his discharge from Brig. Gen. Albert Pike's Confederate command because of illness. (*Ibid.*, July 5, 1862.) Borland's wife, Mary, died at Little Rock on October 23, 1862, in her 39th year. (*Ibid.*, Oct. 25, 1862.) Borland refugeed to Texas, and died near Houston. Most of his biographical sketches give his death date as January 31, 1864, but his son, Harold, who administered his estate in Pulaski County, gave the date December 15, 1864, and listed the other heirs as Borland's daughters, Fannie G. and Mary M. Borland. (Solon Borland Estate Papers, Folder No. 66, Box B-1, Pulaski County Probate Files.) The Little Rock *National Democrat* of February 13, 1864 said he died "recently." The correct date probably was December 15, 1863.
85. *Gazette*, May 3, 1856.

The Democratic nominee for governor was the incumbent, Elias Conway, and the Democratic district convention held at Hot Springs on May 12 nominated Albert Rust for Congress from the Second District. The Know Nothing convention at the same place a week later nominated Absalom Fowler to oppose Rust. Danley attended the Democratic convention as a spectator, and was a delegate to the Know Nothing convention. The Know Nothing nominee for Congress in the First District was Hugh F. Thomasson, who was opposed by the Democratic incumbent, A. B. Greenwood. Danley remained at Hot Springs for a two weeks rest before beginning his campaign duties, and was back at Little Rock by the end of May.[86]

As he swung into the campaign, Danley began to refer to the Democrats as Anti-Americans, which made opposition to the American party sound rather subversive. He also began to call them the "Pizerinctums," a word he was later erroneously credited with inventing.[87] He had used it only once before, on December 15, 1854, with the explanation that he had borrowed it from Pennsylvania politicians, and applied it to people whose constantly changing party affiliations made their votes and influence unpredictable, politicians who "like the little speckled pig, frisk about so that they cannot be counted." He began using the word again on April 5, 1856, this time as a synonym for Democrats, although his first definition made it seem more apt for his own party. As the summer wore on and the word came into general use among the Know Nothings, an anonymous correspondent of the *Native American,* a Know Nothing newspaper at Pine Bluff, volunteered an explanation of its derivation from the Hindu words *pizo,* meaning "to squirt," and *rincto,* meaning "backwards," [88] and this also was later credited to Danley.

Borland made a trip to Fayetteville on personal business, and although he said he had not expected to be called upon to speak, he made five-hour speeches for the American party at Dover, Van Buren, and Fayetteville.[89] Danley also made a number of speeches,[90] but rendered his greatest service to the party through the *Gazette.* In the closing days of the campaign, the *True Democrat* complained that the party had subscribed for 1,000 copies of the *Gazette* to be circulated among non-subscribers. Danley replied that 2,000 extra copies had been circulated, but the expense had been borne by individuals and not by the party.[91]

Danley had been having a running battle with the Little Rock post office for several months. The removal of William F. Pope as postmaster and the subsequent appointment of John E. Reardon was part of the Dynasty's spoil system. Shortly after the *Gazette's* switch in politics, Danley had registered a complaint that the Little Rock post office was deliberately obstructing the

86. *Ibid.,* May 10, 31, 1856.
87. *The Clipper* (Little Rock), Feb. 19, 1887.
88. *Gazette,* July 26, 1856.
89. *Ibid.,* June 7, 14, 21, 1856.
90. *Ibid.,* June 28, 1856.
91. *Ibid.,* Aug. 2, 1856.

circulation of the *Gazette* by failing to send it promptly on its way to other offices and failing to give it to subscribers who called for their mail at Little Rock. It was a well established local custom for such subscribers to receive locally published papers through the post office without payment of postage, though this free service was not required by postal regulations until the summer of 1857. Reardon had defended his office on both charges, and had advised the *Gazette's* Pulaski County subscribers to demand their papers at the *Gazette* office, because he said no copies addressed to some who called for them had been deposited in his post office.[92] According to Danley, circulation of the last issue before the election was hindered by the deliberate detention at the Little Rock post office of papers bound for southern Arkansas, and by corrupt postmasters along the route to points in northwest Arkansas. The only cure, as Danley saw it, was a new national administration.[93]

At the election on August 14, Conway defeated Yell easily, with a vote of 27,612 to 15,249. Yell won a small majority in seven of the state's 54 counties, and the vote was a tie in one other county. Yell's home county of Jefferson gave Conway a small majority.[94] Pulaski, Conway's home county, gave the American party a bare victory, and the *Gazette* promptly reported its returns,[95] but never gave official or unofficial figures for the state. The Democratic candidates for Congress also won a substantial victory.

The Gazette was similarly reticent about the results of the presidential election in November. The Democratic candidates, James Buchanan and John C. Breckinridge, easily won Arkansas's four electoral votes and the national election. The Republican party, strongly anti-slavery and composed largely of the remnants of the old Free Soil and other parties, had been organized in 1854 and was gathering momentum steadily, but not in the South. Its presidential nominee was John C. Fremont, whose earlier nomination by the seceding Know Nothings had come to nothing, and his running mate was William L. Dayton of New Jersey. This party had no organization in Arkansas, and consequently was not on the ballot for want of candidates for electors.

Rheumatism in his right hand having plagued him for several months, Danley went to Hot Springs for treatment on August 13. During his absence of two or three weeks, he did not announce that the *Gazette's* editorials were written by somebody else, and the *True Democrat* made an issue of it. Upon his return, Danley said he did not feel obliged to identify the writer unless his subscribers complained. A week later, he reminded Johnson that Hot

92. *Ibid.,* Sept. 14, 21, 1855.
93. *Ibid.,* Aug. 9, 1856.
94. *Journal of the House of Representatives for the Eleventh Session of the General Assembly of the State of Arkansas, which was begun and held in the Capitol, in the city of Little Rock, on Monday, the third day of November, one thousand, eight hundred and fifty-six, and ended on Thursday, the fifteenth day of January, one thousand, eight hundred and fifty-seven* (Little Rock: Johnson & Yerkes, State Printers, 1857), 46–47. The *True Democrat,* Sept. 1, 1860 gave Conway's vote 28,139 and Yell's 15,436.
95. *Gazette,* Aug. 9, 1856.

Springs and Little Rock were less than 60 miles apart, and a tri-weekly mail and private conveyances afforded daily communication between the two towns, implying that he could have written the editorials himself.[96]

To a *True Democrat* correspondent's statement that there had been a serious withdrawal of patronage from the *Gazette* after the August election Danley replied, "The *Gazette and Democrat* is, on this day, in a more prosperous condition than it ever has been—and its business and subscription are increasing every week." [97]

Danley did not like subscription clubs or anything that smacked of a reduced price as a circulation gimmick. To inquiries about the *Gazette's* terms for subscription clubs, he had replied on September 21, 1855 that the *Gazette* had no clubs because "our paper is worth its subscription price, and we can make no deduction from our present terms." However, there was an arrangement that was the equivalent of a club, since the *Gazette* allowed any person who obtained 10 subscribers paying in advance to deduct a 20 per cent commission, and if this were allocated to the 10 subscribers, their individual subscriptions would cost $2 instead of the usual $2.50.

Danley now had a bad opinion of professional newspaper agents and had long since discontinued standing notices of the *Gazette's* agents in other states. When two Eastern newspapers published testimonials commending the agency of S. M. Pettengill and Company of New York, Danley added his unreserved endorsement, and said W. S. Swymmer of St. Louis and S. H. Parvin were equally worthy of praise. But he added, "The names of these gentlemen we mention as honorable exceptions to the rule, which, so far as our experience goes, has taught us, that, as a class, these agents are as very a pack of diddlers, as ever disgraced any honest profession." [98] Many other newspaper proprietors were of like mind, but all seemed to trust Pettengill.[99] But when Danley decided to give the agents another chance in the spring of 1857, he chose James E. Dudderidge of St. Louis, successor to Swymmer, and L. M. Elliott and Company of Baltimore, Maryland.[100]

Little Rock printers had joined other mechanics in sporadic efforts at organized labor since the 1830's, but the first known attempt at an organization specifically for printers was reported in the *Gazette* of September 20, 1856, when the second meeting was announced for September 25. In their first meeting, the journeyman printers of Little Rock had organized the "Little Rock Typographical Union No. —," elected officers, and agreed to adopt a constitution and by-laws, rules of order, and bill of prices. Probably there was hope of affiliation with a national printer's union, since a future number

---

96. *Ibid.*, Aug. 16, Sept. 6, 13, 1856. Probably the writer was C. F. M. Noland. See Ted R. Worley and Eugene A. Nolte (eds.), *Pete Whetstone of Devil's Fork* (Van Buren, Ark.: The Press-Argus, 1957), xxviii.
97. *Gazette,* Sept. 6, 1856.
98. *Ibid.*, Mar. 22, 1856.
99. *Ibid.*, Oct. 16, 1858.
100. *Ibid.*, May 23, 1857.

for the local union was suggested, but this organization does not appear to have accomplished that goal. The only other reference found to this union is its resolutions of respect, dated April 24, 1858, for a member of the Memphis Typographical Union who had died at Little Rock, and whose funeral the union attended in a body that afternoon.[101] A new organization of the mechanical trades was effected that fall, called the Mechanics Institute. Its primary purpose was to resist the use of slaves, free Negroes, and convict labor in competition with the labor of Southern white mechanics, and it seems to have concentrated mostly on the construction business.[102] It is uncertain whether printers participated in this organization.

With the issue of October 4, 1856, Danley had a new partner, William Frederick Holtzman, who had worked as a printer in this office for ten years. No announcement was made, but the statement of proprietorship now had "C. C. Danley, Editor" on the left and "W. F. Holtzman, Publisher" on the right. Holtzman had purchased only a one-third interest in the *Gazette*,[103] and owned no part of the real estate.[104] He was a well qualified printer, and all his interest and experience were in the mechanical department. He had no aspirations to be a writer or editor, and left the editorial department strictly to Danley except when circumstances compelled him to pinch-hit.[105] When he began his proprietorship a shipment of paper from New Orleans was late, and the issues of October 4 and 11 had to be printed on a smaller sheet than usual, having only seven columns and making a temporary change necessary in the front page format.

When the General Assembly convened on November 3, 1856, Danley's observation that the American party was "greatly in the minority"[106] was a masterpiece of understatement. Whatever influence with the legislature he might have once enjoyed, never very great, had been sacrificed at the altar of Know Nothingism. Nathan Ross, a Democratic legislator from Chicot County, told Danley privately that he agreed with him on most public questions and especially on swamp lands legislation, but pleaded with him not to discuss these matters editorially, because his and Dr. Lorenzo Gibson's

101. *Ibid.*, May 8, 1858.
102. *Ibid.*, Sept. 18, 25, Oct. 9, 16, 1858.
103. *National Democrat,* Feb. 27, 1864.
104. Pulaski County Deed Book G–2, 364–365, 365–367.
105. William F. Holtzman was born at Washington, D.C. on July 7, 1824, and lived there during his childhood. He moved to Wheeling, Virginia (which became West Virginia later) and served an apprenticeship in the office of the Wheeling *Times*. He came to Little Rock at the age of 21 in 1846 and went to work for Woodruff in the *Democrat* office, remaining there through the subsequent changes in proprietors and names. He married Jenetta Brookin at Little Rock on January 7, 1850. He had followed Danley and Borland into the American party, and was currently serving as an alderman for the city of Little Rock, having been elected on the American ticket along with Danley in January of 1856. (Tombstone of William F. Holtzman, Mount Holly Cemetery, Little Rock; *Gazette*, Jan. 12, 1856; Aug. 18, 1866; *Democrat,* Jan. 11, 1850; Argenta, Ark. *North Little Rock Times,* Mar. 10, 1906.)
106. *Gazette,* Nov. 15, 1856.

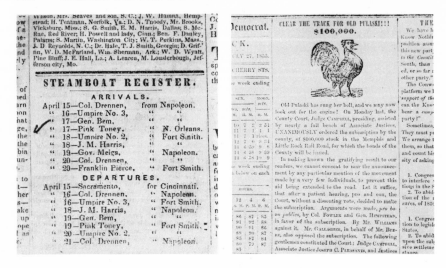

support would surely defeat any measure that came before the House. (Dr. Gibson was a Know Nothing representative from Pulaski County.)[107] After both houses passed the objectionable bill stopping swamp lands reclamation work, Ross and 21 other House members signed a formal protest.[108] Danley was also greatly displeased with the Democrats in the legislature for defeating a bill to force free Negroes to leave Arkansas.[109]

One Democratic legislator asked Danley to be a candidate for public printer, but he said he would not accept office from this General Assembly. Senator William S. Keith nominated him anyhow, but Johnson and Yerkes won by a vote of 81 to 10, with one Democrat voting for William Quesenbury, who was not in nomination.[110] The vote shows the relative strength of the two parties, for Danley said all the Know Nothings voted for him, and all but one of the Democrats voted for Johnson and Yerkes. Danley objected to their election on the ground that two men could not hold the same office, and this could present a problem if either of them should die or resign. Actually, the thinking on this point was in terms of a contract awarded to a business firm, although by law the public printer was an elected official.

This election also gave Danley new material for an old complaint that he had aired periodically since the preceding session, when the legislature had failed to elect a public printer. A resolution to give the printing to the lowest bidder had been passed on the last day, but Governor Conway had

107. *Ibid.,* Dec. 6, 20, 1856.
108. *House Journal 1856–1857,* 290–292.
109. *Gazette,* Dec. 27, 1856.
110. *House Journal 1856–1857,* 266.

vetoed it and had given the printing to Johnson and Yerkes without legal authority. Moreover, he had fattened their contract by ordering publication of numerous reports and other material too limited in interest to justify the expense of printing. Danley called these documents, published as appendices to the journals, "a vast amount of trash, which constituted no part of the history of the proceedings of the General Assembly." [111]

Danley had contended from the beginning that only the legislature could legally authorize publication of the journals, and that acts of a private nature, passed for the benefit of specific individuals, should not be published at all because they were of no use or interest to the public. He had published the acts of a public nature in the *Gazette* as a public service, and he argued that the governor should have called for competitive bids for their publication in pamphlet form. The *True Democrat* denied that the governor had made any formal appointment of a public printer, but Danley showed that he had referred to Johnson and Yerkes as the public printers in his written instructions to the auditor.[112]

Bad health kept Danley out of the *Gazette* office much of the time in 1857. He served as mayor *pro tem* in January,[113] but soon afterwards he began to have serious trouble with his eyes that made it difficult for him to do his usual work. All or most of the editor's work was done by others for every issue between February 14 and June 27, and again between August 8 and September 5.

His illness was diagnosed as "an attack of rheumatism which had settled in his eyes," affecting mostly his right eye, and was so disabling that he feared it would result in blindness. A steamboat trip was recommended, and he took passage on the steamboat Arkansas on February 18 for her trip to Napoleon and back. When he returned two weeks later, his eyes were still so weak that his doctor strongly advised him not to attempt to read or write.[114]

C. F. M. Noland began doing the editor's work sometime in February, but it was not until the issue of March 21 that personal references in the editorials revealed his identity. Danley was able to write a little by May 23, but had decided to return to Hot Springs for more baths, his physician having decided that this treatment might "eradicate the rheumatism entirely from his system." Noland continued as temporary editor while Danley went to Hot Springs, but now Danley was able to send an occasional letter reporting the activities at Hot Springs. The *Gazette* relied heavily on its exchanges to fill its columns, and local news items were few and short.

Noland's health was much worse than Danley's, for he had been slowly wasting away with consumption since about 1833, and the disease was now in its final stages. He was developing his plantation "Fairway," located sev-

111. *Gazette,* Dec. 20, 1856.
112. *Ibid.,* Jan. 26, Feb. 16, 1855; July 26, 1856.
113. *Ibid.,* Jan. 17, 1857.
114. *Ibid.,* Feb. 14, 21, Mar. 7, 21, 1857.

eral miles below Little Rock, and was living with his family at the nearby plantation home of his old friend, James B. Keatts, until a house could be built at Fairway.[115] His frequent contributions to the *Gazette,* in the form of letters to Danley, were datelined Fairway.

Business matters made it necessary for him to spend a great deal of time in Little Rock, and a second residence in the city was desirable, since the state of his health made the daily trip from the Keatts plantation to town difficult. His assumption of Danley's duties at the *Gazette* increased the time he had to spend in the city, though much of the writing could be done at the plantation. The location of his town quarters has not been ascertained, but attention is irresistibly drawn to the small red brick house that stands today as a part of the Arkansas Territorial Capitol Restoration and is represented as his home. It was conveniently close to the *Gazette* office, their back doors being only a few steps apart.[116]

Governor Conway was also seriously ill during this period. His illness had delayed his second inauguration so long that Lorenzo Gibson, fearing it was a trick by which his term of office could be extended, had attempted to force his installation in office.[117] Conway left Little Rock on April 21 to recuperate at White Sulphur Springs, Virginia, and did not return until September 14. John R. Hampton, as president of the Senate, served as acting governor during his absence.[118]

With Conway and Danley absent, and no campaign shaping up, it was a quiet political season. Noland's whimsical approach to politics brought forth a satire on the popular pictorial publications of the day, one of their favorite subjects being illustrated biographies of President Buchanan, with attention to the most inconsequential details. The *Gazette's* takeoff on this, in the issue of May 23, 1857, used a variety of stock woodcuts intended mostly for advertisements. The familiar three-story building often used in hotel ads was represented as Buchanan's home, and there were agricultural implements, livestock, and other items represented as his property. A small duck was shown as the president's "quack" doctor, and the woodcut ordinarily used with runaway slave ads was represented as his faithful servant following him to Washington by forced marches.

Noland and his family left Little Rock on June 17 for a three weeks visit to Memphis and Jacksonport,[119] which proved to be a sad journey because

115. Worley and Nolte, *Pete Whetstone,* xv, xxviii.

116. Noland never owned this house, and no evidence of his residence in it at any time is found, but if he ever lived there, it must have been during this general period. The house certainly was not in existence as late as April of 1840 (*Gazette,* Apr. 22, 1840), and probably was built sometime between 1842 and 1849. It was occupied by its owner or members of his family until the spring of 1850, when it was advertised for sale as a new house that rented for $150 a year. (*Ibid.,* Apr. 12, 1850.) Its owner in 1857 was Dr. Roderick L. Dodge, who had bought it in 1852 (Deed Book W, 245) but did not live in it. Noland may have rented it from him.

117. *House Journal 1856–1857,* 193–196.

118. *Gazette,* Apr. 25, Sept. 19, 1857.

119. *Ibid.,* June 20, 1857.

of the drowning of Mrs. Noland's father, John Ringgold of Batesville, in White River on the same day.[120] Presumably Holtzman and others of the *Gazette's* staff did the editor's work until Danley's return from Hot Springs, in time for the issue of July 4. Danley's eye was better, but still gave him enough discomfort to make heavy dependence on the exchanges necessary.

Several projects that were dear to Danley's heart were afoot that summer, and he used the *Gazette's* columns freely to promote them. Track laying on the Memphis and Little Rock Railroad was started, and the company had enough money to build the railroad from the Mississippi River to the St. Francis, including a bridge across the St. Francis.[121] Danley also promoted a state fair,[122] and there was considerable interest over the state in the project, but not enough for success.

In spite of his general good health and the improvement in his eye, he was soon advised once more against reading or writing, and on August 2, he went back to Hot Springs. Noland's health had taken a turn for the worse and he was unable to leave his room at his lodgings in the city, but he valiantly assumed Danley's duties at the *Gazette* again. A few days later, he was confined to his bed, and by the end of the month he weighed only 104 pounds, but predicted that he would be "good as new" in less than a week.[123] Danley was back in the office for the issue of September 12, and had hopes that his eye would be completely well before winter.

Noland had been an enemy of the Dynasty much longer than Danley, but time, illness, and his inherent good humor had diluted his bitterness and led him to seek the best side of friends and enemies alike. He still was unable to see the good in some of the state's politicians, especially Albert Rust and N. B. Burrow, but he gave Robert W. Johnson, William K. Sebastian, Samuel Hempstead, and others of the clan the kind of praise they had never expected to see in the *Gazette*. As Danley resumed his duties on September 12, he said that he and Noland differed in their opinions of some men and some measures, but he added philosophically, "Where men think they must differ— and we would not leave our paper in charge of anyone who had not a mind of his own, and a will to express his thoughts."

Possibly Noland's editorials had some bearing on a rumor that reached Danley five months later, that the *Gazette* had been sold to the "Rotation wing" of the Democratic party and would be used to influence Hempstead's election to the United States Senate. Danley replied that nobody had tried to buy the *Gazette* for any purpose, that it was profitable and he did not want to sell it, and would not in any case ever consider selling it to either wing of the Democratic party. Both factions, he declared, "seem to exist only for the purpose of misgoverning and disgracing the State . . . We shall continue to

120. *Ibid.,* July 4, 1857.
121. *Ibid.,* July 18, 1857.
122. *Ibid.,* July 25, 1857.
123. *Ibid.,* Aug. 8, 15, 29, Sept. 5, 1857.

kick the one, and cuff the other, whenever inclination shall prompt, or duty require." [124]

A letter from William Strong, an Arkansas pioneer, set Danley to wishing that somebody would write the history of Arkansas. He thought several old settlers were competent to the task, and mentioned Woodruff, Noland, Bertrand, Strong, and Terrence Farrelly as those most knowledgeable on the subject. If no one person would tackle the whole project, he suggested that these and others might at least put their own experiences on record. [125]

Noland already had written a series of five sketches such as Danley visualized, for the New York *Spirit of the Times*. He had not attempted a history of the state, but had written character sketches of some of the most important figures in Arkansas politics of the territorial and early statehood periods. [126] A couple of weeks after Danley made the suggestion, Noland's health improved enough to allow him to leave his city dwelling for his plantation home, [127] where most of his papers were kept, and he soon went to work on more sketches. The first installment appeared on November 28, 1857, and ten were published between that date and March 27, 1858. At first they appeared every week, but as Noland's health became worse, the articles were separated by intervals of four or five weeks. Like the earlier ones, these were mostly character sketches, and were captioned "Early Times in Arkansas, by N." or "Early Settlers of Arkansas, by N." [128]

This was the *Gazette's* first significant venture into local history, though it was not formal historiography but highly entertaining reminiscences, containing much valuable information in spite of Noland's tendency to eulogize. The sketches were well received by the readers and the Arkansas press, and some readers requested republication of them in book form, [129] but this was never done. The Carrier's Address for 1858, almost two columns of unsigned poetry, [130] also smacked loudly of Noland, although he is not known to have written poetry.

In April, Noland made a steamboat trip to New Orleans for treatment, still expecting a medical miracle. [131] The miracle was not to be, and he died at the Keatts home near Little Rock on June 23, 1858. [132]

Soon after Noland's death, a reader called upon other early settlers to continue the sketches of Arkansas pioneers. [133] William Jasper Blackburn, who had grown up in northeast Arkansas and was currently publishing a newspaper at Minden, Louisiana, had already responded to Noland's

124. *Ibid.,* Feb. 13, 1858.
125. *Ibid.,* Oct. 10, 1857.
126. *Spirit of the Times,* Dec. 15, 22, 29, 1849; Jan. 12, 26, 1850.
127. *Gazette,* Oct. 24, 1857.
128. *Ibid.,* Nov. 28, Dec. 5, 12, 19, 1857; Jan. 2, 9, 23, Feb. 20, Mar. 20, 27, 1858.
129. *Ibid.,* Dec. 12, 19, 1857; Feb. 13, May 1, 1858.
130. *Ibid.,* Jan. 2, 1858.
131. *Ibid.,* Apr. 17, 1858; Worley and Nolte, *Pete Whetstone,* xxx.
132. *Gazette,* June 26, 1858.
133. *Ibid.,* July 24, 1858.

sketches with one article. The *Gazette* had reprinted it,[134] but no others came from him. A year and a half after Noland's death, the gifted William Quesenbury took up the project, but wrote only three articles, none of which was as worthwhile as Noland's.[135]

Danley's attendance at the Democratic district convention at Camden in May, 1858 was not taken as a sign that he wanted to return to his old party, it being well understood that he was there as a spectator. His report of the proceedings was laced with ridicule, and he professed complete indifference to the outcome of the struggle between the two Democratic factions.[136]

Shortly after the two Democratic district conventions, a few Know Nothings began to announce their candidacies for the legislature and county offices. Apparently the remnant of the old American party organization was behind them, but its name was now recognized as a liability, and was not used during the campaign except for an occasional inadvertent reference. These candidates had no party label in the beginning except that of "the Opposition" to the Democratic party, but near the end of the campaign they called themselves "the People's party," [137] possibly to distinguish themselves from dissatisfied Democrats running under the Independent label.

In the spring, Noland had predicted in a facetious vein that Danley and Dick Johnson would vie for the Pulaski-Prairie seat in the state Senate. Danley was one of the first Opposition candidates in the field, but his opponent was not Johnson but another Dynasty Democrat, Col. Francis Augustus Robinson Terry. Danley retired temporarily from the *Gazette* to devote his full attention to the canvass, leaving Holtzman to do double duty as editor and publisher. Holtzman had never written a newspaper article, but he conducted the *Gazette* through the campaign ably.[138]

A standing feature called "Home News," consisting of news items taken from other Arkansas newspapers, had been started with the issue of April 24. Besides increasing the scope of Arkansas news coverage, it greatly reduced Holtzman's unfamiliar task of producing original material.

From the beginning of the canvass at Brownsville on May 25, Danley campaigned against the Dynasty's policies. He made a special point of the rottenness of the caucus system by which Democratic candidates were chosen on the county level, contending that these candidates were "willing instruments of a party despotism," not the choice of a majority of party members, but of a small clique. He never said how his own ticket was made up, except that it was in accordance with "the known wishes of a large number of the voters." [139] The Pulaski County slate consisted of Danley for the Senate and William Q. Pennington and Joseph Stillwell for the House. The Democratic

134. *Ibid.*, May 1, 1858.
135. *Ibid.*, Dec. 10, 1859; Jan. 28, 1860; Feb. 4, 1860.
136. *Ibid.*, May 22, 1858.
137. *Ibid.*, July 24, 1858.
138. *Ibid.*, Apr. 17, May 29, Aug. 14, 1858.
139. *Ibid.*, May 29, July 24, 1858.

Pictorial nameplate used by the *Arkansas Gazette*
between 1850 and the fire of 1854.

candidates for the House were James B. Johnson, brother of Bob and Dick Johnson, and Sandford C. Faulkner, "the Arkansaw Traveler," personally popular but politically unimportant.

As Danley, Pennington, and Stillwell lashed out against the current state administration, the *True Democrat* as zealously defended it, and made effective counter-attacks. The Opposition candidates were accused of trying to conceal their contempt for foreign-born citizens while trying to get their votes. Terry contrasted his affluence, as shown by his ownership of a large plantation and many slaves, with Danley's modest success in business to prove that he was a man of substance and therefore better qualified than Danley to take a hand in the management of the state's business. The *Gazette* made an issue of this, saying Terry implied that the poor man should be disfranchised and the government placed in the hands of the rich. In the last issue before the election, the mechanics of Little Rock were reminded that Terry was the owner of Negro mechanics who competed with them for jobs. This issue also played up Danley's military service in the Mexican War, Terry having brought his government pension into the discussion.[140]

Danley had every reason to hope for success, for Pulaski County had traditionally voted against Democratic candidates, but only Pennington on the Opposition ticket was victorious, and he by a small majority. The *Gazette* acknowledged defeat with the announcement, "We have met the enemy and —we are theirs." The *Gazette* did not report the vote, but said Danley received 25 more votes locally than Lorenzo Gibson had received in the 1856 election, and that at least 35 Know Nothings were absent from the city and 50 or more from the rest of the district. Danley's defeat was attributed to an extraordinary exertion against him, including large sums of money spent

140. *Ibid.,* July 24, 1858.

on the campaign and illegal voting, and the treachery of some who still gave lip service to Know Nothingism but voted Democratic.[141]

The regular Democratic nominees for Congress, Thomas C. Hindman in the First District and the incumbent Albert Rust in the Second District, won easy victories over Independent candidates.

Danley was back in the editor's chair for the issue of August 14, and had yet one more matter to settle with his victorious opponent. Danley alleged that Terry had based his campaign on "shameless humbuggery and willful lies." Danley claimed to have publicly proved him a liar in eleven townships in Pulaski County and at Clear Lake in Prairie County, by the testimony of men of unassailable integrity. Although it was their word against Terry's, Danley said Terry had reacted meekly to exposure of his falsehoods. Dr. Lorenzo Gibson had provided this "proof" at Little Rock on July 3, and had delivered one of his most eloquent denunciations. The point on which he testified was a seemingly trivial one, but it was the one that caused the most trouble. Terry was said to have stated before the Pulaski County canvass began that he had told Gibson before the 1856 election that he knew Gibson would be defeated in his race for Congress. Gibson testified on the stump that Terry had told him no such thing, but had repeatedly predicted his election. Gibson added that Terry habitually denied his own previous statements.

As the canvass moved into Prairie County, Danley was advised to arm himself, because it was rumored that Terry would be backed up by "armed bullies" who would attempt physical intimidation, but Danley went forth unarmed. Terry appeared at Clear Lake accompanied by what Danley called his body guard, but when Danley again denounced him from the stump as a liar, Terry said his opponent's lameness protected him from vengeance. Danley replied that he was Terry's physical equal and was ready to fight him on the spot, but Terry declined, saying he would demand satisfaction after the election. Danley then said duelling was illegal, immoral, and barbarous, and that in any case, Terry was no gentleman and would therefore be disqualified from challenging him under the Code of Honor.[142]

Terry was in a quandary. Danley's lameness gave him immunity from both a fist fight and a challenge, on the ground of physical inequality, although Terry suddenly remembered his own crippled left shoulder, which he said should protect him from attack. Besides, Danley had publicly expressed his disdain for duelling and had indicated that he did not consider Terry a gentleman, which would give him grounds to decline a challenge. Terry's only recourse seemed to be to seek satisfaction from Dr. Gibson, who he understood was also opposed to duelling.

Terry published a card in the *True Democrat* shortly after the election, calling upon Gibson to challenge him to a duel. He said he had given Gibson

141. *Ibid.*, Aug. 7, 1858.
142. *Ibid.*, Aug. 14, 21, 1858.

"the lie direct," which was valid ground for a challenge under the Code of Honor. Both Danley and Gibson responded that they had delivered the same insult to Terry more than a month before he called Gibson a liar. Gibson refused to retract his earlier insulting statements, and said it was true that he detested duels but that he would not refuse to participate in one under proper circumstances. He would not challenge Terry, but he dared Terry to challenge him and said he would not decline the challenge. He proposed such far-fetched terms as pistols at two feet, or with their left arms lashed together to make them equal in every respect. It was much ado about nothing, for nobody concerned had any real intention of fighting a duel. Terry's departure late in August for Mississippi brought the discussion to an end.[143]

As the 1858–1859 session of the legislature approached, the *Gazette* again offered its issues containing the proceedings for 50 cents, a rate that had by now become standard. Danley had spent the last three weeks in September at Hot Springs and two weeks in October visiting county fairs in White and Prairie counties,[144] and was ready to get down to business.

During the summer, citizens' committees had been drumming up support for two measures that were to come before the legislature. An effort to move the seat of government from Little Rock to a point on White River had begun in the previous legislature, and was taken seriously by the people of Des Arc, but came to nothing.[145] Of far more general interest was the long debated legislation to exclude free Negroes from the state. Most of the *Gazette's* editors had advocated this from time to time, but there had never been a regular editorial campaign in its favor. An 1843 law prohibited further migrations of free Negroes into the state, and its constitutionality had been upheld by the Arkansas Supreme Court.[146] An act expelling all free Negroes had failed to pass the 1856–1857 legislature because many thought it was unconstitutional, but the famous Dred Scott decision handed down by the United States Supreme Court in March of 1857 and the enactment of a similar law in Mississippi encouraged a renewal of effort.

In his message to the legislature in November, Governor Conway called for legislation to expel free Negroes from Arkansas, and for once, Conway and the *Gazette* were in complete agreement.[147] The act was passed in February, 1859, and gave free Negroes until January 1, 1860 to leave the state, their only alternative being to become slaves.[148]

William K. Sebastian was re-elected to the Senate in this session. In the election for public printer on November 13, only the firm of Johnson and Yerkes was nominated, and received all but one of the votes cast.[149]

143. *Ibid.,* Aug. 14, 21, 28, 1858.
144. *Ibid.,* Sept. 11, 25, Oct. 2, 16, 1858.
145. *Ibid.,* Aug. 28, Oct. 9, Dec. 11, 1858.
146. Pendleton v. the State, Jan. Term adjourned to April, 1846, 6 *Ark.* 509.
147. *Gazette,* Nov. 13, 1858.
148. *Ibid.,* Feb. 19, Mar. 5, 1859.
149. *Ibid.,* Nov. 20, 1858.

The bickering between the *Gazette* and the *True Democrat* became increasingly personal, and the *Gazette* said Conway's writing style could be recognized in some of the *True Democrat's* editorials.[150] John W. Woodward, who worked in the state auditor's office, was doing much of the *True Democrat's* editorial work about that time, but it was not until the middle of February that the *True Democrat* announced that he was its new associate editor. He was a well educated deaf mute, nicknamed "Dummy," who handled his disabilities so well that sometimes his friends momentarily forgot that he could neither hear nor speak. He had come to Little Rock from Clarksville, where he had conducted the state's first school for deaf children. In his salutatory he said he had been writing for newspapers and other periodicals for 16 years but had never considered his articles worth preserving, to which the *State Rights Eagle* of Camden replied, "We imagine there is a great unanimity of opinion upon that point."

Some of those articles had been contributed to the *Gazette,* for Woodward was a former Know Nothing, and Danley considered that he prostituted his principles to work for the *True Democrat.* Danley's appraisal of him was, "He is a sprightly writer, of facile antecedents, uncertain status, elastic conscience, and marketable principles." He surmised that Woodward's employment was the first step in Dick Johnson's rumored plans to run for governor at the end of Conway's term, and predicted that the next step would be to make Woodward editor-in-chief, leaving Johnson free for the campaign.[151]

Danley and Woodward exchanged harsh words on many subjects, among them the public printing. On February 5, 1859, the *Gazette* revealed that the *True Democrat's* publishers had been paid on their own certification $39,021.47 since the publication of the biennial reports of 1856, of which $7,887.52 was for printing the governor's message and accompanying documents. This discussion was still going strong when Danley left for New Orleans on March 9.

Danley returned early in April, having obtained several New Orleans advertisements or received them through Thomas Shields, who had become the *Gazette's* New Orleans agent on March 5. J. S. Post and Company acted as the *Gazette's* St. Louis agent at this time.[152]

Another attack of what he called rheumatism in the eyes began late in May, and Danley went again to Hot Springs, returning on the evening of July 9.[153] The name of the temporary editor of the *Gazette* during these two periods was not announced.

John W. Woodward's connection with the *True Democrat* was severed early in August, 1859. Danley's eyes were bothering him again, and he

150. *Ibid.,* Jan. 15, 1859.

151. *Ibid.,* Feb. 19, 26, Mar. 5, 12, 1859; Bess Michaels Riggs, *A Brief History of the Education of the Deaf in the State of Arkansas* (Little Rock: Arkansas School for the Deaf, 1934), 7; *Washington Telegraph,* Feb. 22, 1865; *National Democrat,* Feb. 11, 1865.

152. *Gazette,* Jan. 29, Mar. 5, 12, Apr. 9, 1859.

153. *Ibid.,* May 28, June 4, 18, July 9, 1859.

was unable to write much for the paper, but he held out long enough to write a short article for each of three consecutive issues about the "marketable commodity" who was "nauseous enough to turn the stomach even of the *True Democrat*." After the second article, Woodward published a card saying he would not condescend to notice anything Danley might say about him in the future.[154]

Danley's problem with his eyes was eliminated soon afterwards. He later said that none of the prescriptions or other remedies he had tried had helped him in the least, but a bottle of the eye water invented by Gabriel McCowan of Little Rock had completely and permanently cured his affliction within a few days.[155] McCowan was an old friend, and the announcement in the *Gazette* of May 25, 1855 of the birth of his son had been the *Gazette's* first birth announcement, and also its last until well after the Civil War.

Danley's attitude towards Woodward, who had many admirable qualities and had once been a valued friend, is indicative of the depth of his emotions regarding the American party. The party had reached its peak with the 1856 presidential election, and its organization without its name had carried its members through county elections in 1858. The results of that election had put an end to the incongruity of a party based on national issues but having only local strength and influence. Danley and his *Gazette* were among those who thus became political orphans, for no party they could call their own emerged from the rubble. They were forced into a somewhat negative position, having more to be against than for, and having no organization to give them cohesion.

154. *Ibid.*, Aug. 6, 13, 20, 1859.
155. *Ibid.*, Apr. 5, 1871. This is a testimonial written July 29 and August 7, 1863, when McCowan was contemplating putting his invention on the market. This evidently was prevented by the federal occupation of Little Rock soon afterwards, and was finally accomplished by McCowan's heirs in 1871.

16

THE ROAD TO SECESSION

C. C. Danley, William F. Holtzman

1859-1861 THE PAPER THAT CAME from the *Gazette's* press on July 9, 1859 began a new volume, and had a new title, again the *Arkansas State Gazette*. The nameplate was in Roman type, and was still six columns wide, with the heads of columns one and eight flush with the tops of the letters in the nameplate.

The change was made on the day of Danley's return from New Orleans, and his explanation for dropping the word *Democrat* was deferred until the issue of July 16. He had retained it when he joined the American party in 1855 because he had considered that this party was founded on principles basic to the old Democratic party as he had known it in earlier years. He still clung to the policies of Democracy as advanced by Jackson, Calhoun, and Polk, but the present Democratic party under Buchanan's leadership had abandoned them and had embraced most of the principles of its former opponents, the Federalists and the Whigs. The endorsement of Buchanan's administration by a majority of the party was the equivalent of endorsement of his recommendations favoring issuing paper money without specie in the treasury for its redemption, federal financing of such internal improvements as a Pacific railroad, and a bankruptcy law for banks only. Buchanan also had deserted his party's time honored stand against a protective tariff, showed flagrant disregard for the United States Constitution, and held other positions in violation of state rights and the sanctity of state constitutions, all for the purpose of aiding the abolitionists. These had been considered dead issues in 1855, and Danley had not then seen any good reason for him to change his paper's name. But now they were again before the country, and the majority of Democrats were going along with Buchanan on them. The national party was also corrupt in many ways, and was saturated with abolitionism in the north. Danley had simply decided he would stand on his old principles, and let the Democrats enjoy their monopoly of a once revered name. "It is evident," he said, "that if they are democrats, we are not."

Possibly it was an oversight that the volume and issue numbers of both the *Gazette* and the *Democrat* continued in use until August 27, when the paper adopted the volume number of the *Gazette* because it was the older of the two and the issue number of the *Democrat* because it corresponded with the paper's fiscal year. At the same time, the volume number was changed from Roman to Arabic numerals. Apparently nobody in authority paid much attention to the volume numbering, for the issue of September 10, 1859 was numbered Volume 41, Number 10, when it should have been Volume 40, Number 10. The error was continued thereafter, and the *Gazette* inadvertently "gained" a year in age.

Also on August 27, the *Gazette* appeared in a complete new dress, its brevier and minion fonts having been selected from the stock of Scotch-cut faces offered by two leading Eastern foundries.

The old motto, "ERROR ceases to be dangerous, when REASON is free to combat it," continued in use until the issue of May 5, 1860, when it was dropped without editorial comment, and "Established 1819" took its place in the center of the front page dateline under the nameplate. This should have called attention to the error in volume numbering, but it went unnoticed.

Danley had overcome his aversion to subscription clubs, and was offering the *Gazette* to clubs of five or more for $2 a year in advance, renewable at the same rates only by the formation of another club.[1] This was changed on January 14, 1860 to reduce the advance subscription price from $2.50 to $2 for all subscribers.

In spite of the extra bookkeeping involved and the inefficiency of the postal system, *Gazette* subscribers were told that if they planned to spend the summer of 1859 away from home, the *Gazette* could follow them anywhere in the country if they would notify the office.[2]

One of the circulation problems that summer was a law passed by the last legislature prohibiting circulation of $5 bank bills and imposing heavy penalties for violations. Danley had been encouraging subscribers to send $5 bank bills to cover two subscriptions, and he joined many other business men in ignoring the new law and planning to resist it to the highest tribunal if necessary. Admitting that gold and silver coin were the only legal currency recognized by the Constitution, he argued that the legislature could not take away the citizen's right to attach value to anything he pleased, and to sell his goods or services for chips, whetstones, bank notes, or anything else he valued.[3]

As sectionalism increased, Danley repeatedly made it clear that the South's welfare was his first concern in national politics and government, but he did not carry it so far as to exclude Northern advertisements from his paper. The *True Democrat* took exception to an ad for the New York *Tribune* in the *Gazette* of August 7, 1859, on the ground that it promoted a Northern propa-

1. *Gazette,* Feb. 5, 1859.
2. *Ibid.,* July 2, 1859.
3. *Ibid.,* July 16, 1859.

ganda sheet. Danley replied that he regarded advertising as a business and would publish any "proper" ad for which the *Gazette's* rates were paid. He could not consider the *Tribune's* ad offensive, and pointed out that many of his best Southern exchanges had also published it. He called attention to the garishly illustrated patent medicine ads that often appeared in the *True Democrat,* and said the *Gazette* refused them because the "quack proprietors" of the medicine firms would not pay the *Gazette's* rates.[4]

About this time, Danley resorted to his advertising policies to attempt to solve an editorial problem. Except in the case of public figures having news value, obituaries were usually no more than two or three sentences long, and some were disposed of with one sentence. In most cases, an obituary could be considered complete if it gave the person's name and the date and place of his death. But grieving friends and relatives often sent long, sentimental eulogies testifying to the worth of the departed, and sometimes ending with a memorial poem, original or copied. Since they were of interest only to the small circle of friends and relatives of the deceased, they were not worth as much space as they took in a four-page newspaper, but the day had not arrived when editors felt free to edit such contributions. With the issue of August 27, 1859, the *Gazette* added to its schedule of advertising rates a notice that obituaries that went beyond a simple announcement of death would be charged the usual advertising rates of $1 per square. Many other newspapers were adopting a similar policy, but it was not found to be the ideal solution, for contributors tended to ignore it and soft-hearted editors published their eulogies anyhow.

Danley wrote his editorial for the issue of September 3 before leaving on August 31 for a month at Hot Springs, and sent weekly letters from Hot Springs to take the place of his usual lead editorial. In these letters, he advocated the nomination as independent anti-caucus candidates Sam Houston of Texas for president and Edward Everett of Massachusetts for vice president.[5] Upon his return, he gave a mild editorial blessing to the candidacy of Charles A. Carroll for the legislature, frankly admitting he was motivated by personal friendship and not admiration for Carroll's Democratic politics.[6]

Danley was so proud of the 1860 Carrier's Address that he said he had a strong notion to enter it for a premium in the next United States fair. It was two columns of unsigned poetry with many references to local people, and was indeed the best Carrier's Address published in the *Gazette* so far.[7]

Danley spent the month of February at St. Louis, again sending the *Gazette* weekly letters to take the place of his editorials, though the month was half gone before the first one could be published. Like the New Orleans trip, this trip obviously was made to promote his policy that the South should cut off its trade with the North, giving all its domestic trade to Southern states

4. *Ibid.,* Aug. 13, 1859.
5. *Ibid.,* Sept. 17, 24, 1859.
6. *Ibid.,* Oct. 8, 1859.
7. *Ibid.,* Dec. 24, 31, 1859; Jan. 7, 1860.

and handling its trade with Europe directly instead of through Northern importers and exporters.[8]

These trips brought the *Gazette* many St. Louis and New Orleans ads. Most of the time all of pages three and four and about half of page one were solid advertisements, and the ads spilled over to page two often in the spring of 1860. Each new ad received a free paragraph in the editorial columns, sharply reducing the space for news, and the *Gazette* did not cover the news as well as some of its contemporaries. In spite of Danley's proclaimed preference for Southern businesses, the *Gazette's* largest ad during this period was for A. M. Biniger and Company, wine importers at New York. It was three columns wide and more than half a page deep and ran for one year, beginning March 24, 1860. Other ads from New York and other Eastern cities occasionally appeared up to the beginning of the Civil War.

Danley left Little Rock for the Eastern cities by stagecoach on the morning of April 18, 1860. Perhaps because it was inconsistent with his current policy, he did not announce that he was going to New York to buy a new press, but the same issue that told of his departure had an ad for R. Hoe and Company of New York and Boston, manufacturers of the finest printing presses available.[9] This meant nothing to the average reader, but any printer knew it meant he was about to purchase some new equipment.

He had borrowed $2,000 from his brother, Benjamin F. Danley, for which he gave his note dated April 1, 1860, agreeing to pay 10 per cent interest per annum. This debt was not paid in his lifetime.[10] Most of the money un-

8. *Ibid.,* Dec. 17, 1859.
9. *Ibid.,* Apr. 21, 1860.
10. C. C. Danley Estate Papers, Folder 137, Pulaski County Probate Files. These are papers filed by the administrator, most of which are not entered in the ledgers known as the Probate Records.

doubtedly was used to buy the press. His partner, William F. Holtzman, did not sign the note.

The trip was timed to coincide with the Democratic national convention at Charleston, South Carolina and the Constitutional Union national convention at Baltimore, Maryland. Danley was present for only a part of the Democratic convention,[11] but was not surprised when the slavery question split it into two irreconcilable groups. The result was the nomination in June of Stephen A. Douglas of Illinois and Herschel V. Johnson of Georgia by the Northern wing, and of John C. Breckinridge of Kentucky and Joseph Lane of Oregon by the Southern wing.

From Charleston, Danley went to New York, where he took care of the *Gazette's* business in a few days and then proceeded to Washington. Here he saw an excursion party made up of editors from the Western, Southwestern and Northwestern states. His invitation apparently had been lost in the mail, and he declared his disapproval of such free trips and held himself aloof from the group most of the time, though he was persuaded to accept a free side trip to Wheeling. He disdained to accompany the editors to pay their respects to President Buchanan, saying he owed Buchanan no respect.[12]

He was present when the Constitutional Union convention assembled at Baltimore on May 9, and had official status as a delegate. This new party was composed largely of the remnants of the Whig and American parties, and was so little known in Arkansas that the small gathering at Helena on April 30 that purported to be its state convention was called the Opposition State Convention.

The Baltimore convention adopted as its platform "The Constitution of the Country, The Union of the States, and The Enforcement of the Laws," which meant preservation of the union by adherence to statutory and organic laws protecting slavery. John Bell and Edward Everett were nominated for president and vice president, and the convention adjourned on May 10. Danley still preferred Sam Houston for president, but was willing to accept Bell's nomination.[13]

The *Gazette* raised the Bell and Everett banner on May 19, and Danley arrived at Little Rock ten days later.[14] The Union party's electoral slate took its place under the editorial head with the issue of June 16. Danley addressed the Union ratification meeting at Little Rock on June 16,[15] and was one of Pulaski County's delegates to another state convention at Hot Springs on June 21. Unlike the earlier convention, this one was well attended, and here the real organization of the party was effected. Danley was made a member of the business and resolutions committees and chairman of the executive committee. A large number of "assistant electors" were appointed, their duty

11. *Gazette,* May 5, 12, 1860.
12. *Ibid.,* June 16, 1860.
13. *Ibid.,* May 12, 19, 1860.
14. *Ibid.,* June 2, 1860.
15. *Ibid.,* June 23, 1860.

being to canvass their neighborhoods for the party's nominees. Because time was short, no nominations were made for the August state election, and it was decided to delay the all-out effort for Bell and Everett until it was over. But since Danley and many others were not involving themselves in the state election, they proceeded immediately with the presidential campaign.[16]

The state political situation was hopelessly confused, because the two Democratic factions were the equivalent of two rival parties in some races, yet maintained a grudging unity in others. Robert Ward Johnson was not a candidate for re-election to the Senate, and it was understood that Elias Conway would run for that office at the legislature's next session. Richard Henry Johnson's ambition to succeed Conway as governor had been generally known for a long time. It was predictable that their greatest opposition would come from the anti-Dynasty wing of their own party, which now had a formidable leader and which made some surprising proselytes from the Dynasty's ranks.

Thomas Carmichael Hindman had thrown himself into local political activity soon after his move to Helena from Mississippi in 1854, and had canvassed his district against the Know Nothings with remarkable effectiveness in 1856. This had made Danley his bitter enemy, but had endeared him to the Dynasty. His alliance with the Dynasty was of short duration, because there was no room for him at the top of its organization, and in the words of one of his closest friends, "he regarded Arkansas as an empire of which he should be emperor." [17] He was elected to Congress on the Democratic ticket in 1858, but the rift between him and the Dynasty had begun.

During the 1858 campaign, a rumor was circulated that a second Democratic newspaper would be started at Little Rock, as the organ of the anti-Dynasty wing,[18] and Hindman was said to be behind it. When the *Old Line Democrat's* prospectus appeared in Memphis newspapers in July of 1859, the Dynasty charged that it was fostered by Know Nothings, and insinuated that Danley and the *Gazette* were somehow connected with it. Danley denied any involvement, and said he had no more information about the proposed paper than street gossip provided, and did not even know who its editor would be. "Not being on speaking terms with the chief founder of this new paper," he said, "we, of course, know nothing of his plans." [19] He so thoroughly despised Hindman that·he preferred even Bob Johnson to him, because "Senator Johnson has never harmed the American party; whereas, the whole stock in trade of the Congressman in the Northern district was made in an unjust and unfair war upon that party." [20]

Danley predicted a lively battle between the two Democratic papers,

16. *Ibid.,* June 30, 1860.
17. Dr. Charles Edward Nash, *Biographical Sketches of Gen. Pat Cleburne and Gen. T. C. Hindman together with Humorous Anecdotes and Reminiscences of the Late Civil War* (Little Rock, Ark.: Tunnah & Pittard, Printers, 1898), 57, 62, 76.
18. *Gazette,* July 3, 1858.
19. *Ibid.,* July 16, 1859.
20. *Ibid.,* Mar. 10, 1860.

with offices and not principles as the stakes. He also predicted that the *Old Line Democrat* would fail unless it had at least $10,000 cash capital and sound business and editorial management. When the *True Democrat* persisted in accusing him of having something to do with it, he replied that the *True Democrat* was afflicted with "the Mange of Meanness and the Leprosy of Lying." [21]

The first issue of the *Old Line Democrat* appeared on September 15, 1859, published by the firm of Peek, Butler, and Doolittle. Danley was at Hot Springs, and his substitute at the *Gazette* praised the salutatory of its editor, Thomas C. Peek, recently of Virginia, and the typographical work of James D. Butler. [22]

The Democratic state convention met at Little Rock on April 2, 1860, and on the second ballot nominated Richard Henry Johnson for governor, by as irregular a procedure as any Arkansas convention had ever indulged in, even in the Dynasty's palmiest days. On April 14, he retired as editor of the *True Democrat* to begin work on the canvass, and announced that his partner, Rueben S. Yerkes, was now sole owner. [23] In June, Elias C. Boudinot, late editor of the Fayetteville *Arkansian,* became senior editor of the *True Democrat,* and J. H. Black, late of the Washington *South Arkansas Democrat,* became its junior editor. [24]

Three minor candidates entered the race against Johnson, but did not conduct aggressive campaigns. The cards of Robert E. Waters and Simeon Kirkpatrick, both of Yell County, were in the *Gazette* from May 5 until June 24, when they withdrew from the race. Thomas Hubbard of Washington was known as a candidate, but had no card in the *Gazette*. Both Hubbard and Waters were identified as "Opposition" candidates, and were members of the Constitutional Union party. Hubbard remained in the contest to the end but was a weak candidate, having held no office higher than the county level, and not being well known outside southwest Arkansas. His stepson, Augustus Hill Garland, was a candidate for elector on the Constitutional Union ticket.

In spite of strong opposition by the *True Democrat,* the northern district convention made Hindman the Democratic party's regular nominee for Congress. This made it necessary for the *True Democrat* to give him nominal endorsement, but the editors made it clear that they would be pleased if he were defeated. Hindman in turn was prevented from giving open opposition to Johnson's candidacy for governor, but his preference for another candidate was generally known. The southern district convention made a dual nomination whereby both Charles B. Mitchel and Edward W. Gantt were allowed to campaign as the party's regular nominee for Congress, each with the backing of his faction.

Henry Massie Rector's break with the Dynasty had been repeatedly threat-

21. *Ibid.,* July 16, 23, 1859.
22. *Ibid.,* Sept. 17, 1859.
23. *Ibid.,* Apr. 14, 1860.
24. *Gazette,* June 9, 16, 1860.

Henry Massie Rector.

ened and occasionally accomplished, only to be temporarily healed by a political favor. The most recent effort to pacify hm had been his election by the Dynasty-controlled legislature to the position of associate justice of the Arkansas Supreme Court, following the death on January 20, 1859 of Judge Christopher C. Scott. Probably it had been the plan for him to be the Hindman wing's candidate for governor, but Hindman's nomination made it impossible for him to help Rector openly. On May 10, Rector resigned from the Supreme Court and entered the race for governor as an Independent Democrat.

A set of candidates less worthy of a level headed editor's support could hardly have been found in Arkansas. The contest was altogether between Johnson and Rector, and the voters could only try to decide which was the lesser evil. As for Danley, there was no decision to be made. He congratulated himself that he was no longer a Democrat, and settled down to sit this one out. Whatever the result of the election, Arkansas would pass through the most crucial period in her history without sound, dependable leadership. At one point during the campaign, a Democratic editor in south Arkansas claimed to have seen a letter in which Danley committed himself to support Rector. Danley said, with caustic embellishments, that he was taking no sides in either the gubernatorial or the congressional campaign, and did not "care a cent" who won.[25]

25. *Ibid.*, July 14, 1860.

William Quesenbury felt much the same way. A memorable campaign document from his pen was reproduced from his paper, the Fayetteville *Arkansian,* in the *Gazette* of June 16. It was an editorial satirizing the "Tom, Dick, and Harry" campaign, with one-column cartoons of each candidate.

Another renegade from the Dynasty's ranks appeared late in May, when Albert Rust declared himself a candidate for the Senate. Like his distant relative, Henry Rector, he had previously shown signs of apostasy, and had been placated by the usual trade-outs. He had been promised the Dynasty's support in the Senate race, but had lately heard that Conway would be the Dynasty's candidate. He published a long circular in which he charged that the Dynasty had been planted and perpetuated by patronage, and denied that he owed his seat in Congress to the machine. He made a withering attack on Conway's eight-year administration of the state government, and the *Gazette* gave his circular hearty approval.[26] John Selden Roane chimed in to say that he had been allowed to serve as governor only because no available Johnson had been old enough and "the Conways don't breed," but had been shoved aside after one term to make way for Elias Conway.[27]

The *True Democrat* became the first Arkansas newspaper to publish oftener than once a week on July 4, 1860, when the first issue of the *Tri-Weekly True Democrat* appeared. Danley was not to be goaded into following the *True Democrat's* example, although the new press he had ordered would have made it mechanically possible. He said the *Gazette* would publish only the usual weekly edition until the railroad and telegraph were completed to Memphis, when he would publish a daily. Peek could not match the *True Democrat's* effort, but decided to make the *Old Line Democrat* a semi-weekly until after the election.[28]

Danley's insistence upon railroad and telegraph service made good sense, for without daily news bulletins by telegraph there would not be enough important news to justify publication of a daily paper, and its circulation outside the Little Rock area would not be efficient without railroad transportation. For a long time there had been trouble with mail carried by stagecoaches, for the bulky newspapers were often left behind to accommodate additional passengers, and sometimes postmasters caused this kind of mail to be left behind. The Overland Mail company had volunteered to bring the Memphis exchanges all winter, but the Memphis postmaster had not put them into the mail bags. In April, the problem was temporarily solved when the stagecoach firm of Chidester, Rapley and Company volunteered to carry the exchanges both ways, outside of the mails.[29]

Dick Johnson was an able writer, but was such a boring speaker that he lost votes with every speech. Rector was a far better orator, though prone to use too many big words and take too long to say too little. He kept John-

26. *Ibid.,* June 2, 9, 1860.
27. *Ibid.,* July 21, 1860.
28. *Ibid.,* Mar. 12, 1859; Mar. 31, July 7, 14, 1860.
29. *Ibid.,* Aug. 21, 1859; Apr. 14, 1860.

son on the defensive all summer. He made the long reign of the Dynasty a major issue, and it won him more votes than any other, in spite of the fact that he was himself a relative of "the Family" and had received his share of its patronage. He used the irregularities of the nominating convention as evidence of the Dynasty's corruption and his justification for opposing his party's nominee. The public debt incurred by the State and Real Estate banks was another warmly debated issue. Johnson favored a continuance of Conway's policy of liquidating the banks' assets to make them pay the debt. Rector was unalterably opposed to repudiation, and promised to work out some other practical plan before the campaign ended, but the closest he came to a solution was a plan to establsh a sinking fund that would shift the burden of the debt to future generations.[30]

The *Gazette* commented freely on all phases of the campaign, but the newspaper controversy was chiefly between the *True Democrat* and the *Old Line Democrat*. The *True Democrat* blamed Hindman for Rector's candidacy, and said Rector was merely Hindman's tool. Hindman was said to have promised to campaign for Rector, but illness in his family kept him off the stump even in behalf of his own candidacy, and he said in his circulars that he would take no stand against Johnson. Peek's marriage on June 18 to Laura L. Rapley, a niece of Rector's deceased first wife, brought forth caustic comment by the *True Democrat* about his eligibility for a part of the spoils as a member of the Rector family, and lists of Rector's and Hindman's relatives on the public payroll were published to counter the attacks on the Dynasty.[31]

The *True Democrat* accused Peek of selling his principles, and backed it up with quotations from his salutatory as editor of the Bloomington, Illinois *Statesman,* dated June 9, 1858, in which he endorsed Stephen A. Douglas and the doctrine of popular sovereignty and non-intervention on the slavery question in the territories, in sharp contrast with his current position against both. Peek's allusions to Boudinot as a "mongrel Indian," Boudinot being a half-breed Cherokee, were equally resented. At one point it was rumored that Peek and Black would settle their differences on the duelling ground after the election.[32]

At the election on August 6, Rector won with 30,577 votes to Johnson's 28,618 and Hubbard's 274. In the congressional election, Hindman won an easy victory in the First District over his Independent opponent, Jesse N. Cypert, by a vote of 20,051 to 9,699. In the Second District, Edward W. Gantt won with 16,569 votes to Charles B. Mitchel's 13,007, while an Independent candidate, James A. Jones, received 891.[33]

According to local gossip, Rector intended to take full advantage of his victory and replace Dynasty men with his own supporters in all state jobs and offices he could control. Most of the long list of people to whom he was

30. *Ibid.,* June 16, 23, July 21, 28, 1860; *True Democrat,* June 2, July 20, 1860.
31. *True Democrat,* June 30, July 7, 20, Aug. 4, 1860.
32. *Ibid.,* July 14, 1860; *Gazette,* July 14, 1860.
33. *True Democrat,* Sept. 1, 1860.

expected to give preferment were his relatives, and it was said that even the Negro servant who waited on the various offices in the state house would be replaced by one of Rector's slaves. Many of these changes could not be made unless the legislature had a majority of Rector supporters, which Rector thought was the case. Johnson's friends thought a majority of the legislators had campaigned as Johnson supporters but they had evidence that Rector supporters had been advised to take any position that would get them elected, and they could not know how many would vote contrary to their campaign promises.[34]

Many of the 3,727 residents of Little Rock read the election returns by gas light. The Slaughter gas works began operations on the evening of July 31, 1860, illuminating most of the town's business houses and many of its residences. The streets remained dark temporarily because the low stage of the river had delayed shipment of the iron lamp posts.[35]

As the presidential campaign gathered momentum after the state election, the people could no longer be guided by familiar party ties, but placed themselves in the ranks of the candidate who best expressed their own sentiments on the slavery issue. No set of candidates advocated immediate abolition, but the Republican nominees, Abraham Lincoln and Hannibal Hamlin, wanted to prohibit slavery in the territories and thereby prevent further admissions of slave states to the union. Southerners recognized this as a scheme for eventual abolition, and believed it had to be resisted before the slave states were in the minority. The Republican party had no organization and no electoral ticket in Arkansas, and did not campaign here.

The Douglas and Johnson platform favored popular sovereignty, by which residents of each territory made their own decision about slavery. This was unpopular in Arkansas, because zealous abolitionists swarmed into the territories and outvoted the slaveholders. However, there were at least three Douglas newspapers in Arkansas by the end of July, and on August 21, Dr. Cincinnatus V. Meador started the leading organ of this party at Little Rock. He called his paper the *National Democrat,* and had it printed at the *True Democrat* office.[36]

The *True Democrat* was the principal spokesman for the Breckinridge and Lane ticket, although many other Arkansas newspapers were on its side, including the *Old Line Democrat.* These candidates represented the most extreme segment of the pro-slavery forces, and a vote for them was interpreted as an indication of secession sympathies. They approved secession only as a last resort, but calm observers disagreed with them as to what constituted that last resort. This strong emotional issue brought old enemies together, as Rector, Hindman, Peek, and others of their wing of the Democratic party fought for Breckinridge and Lane shoulder to shoulder with the

34. J. W. Woodward to David Walker, Little Rock, Aug. 19, 1860, Ms. in *Arkansas Gazette* Foundation Library.

35. *Gazette,* Aug. 4, 1860; *True Democrat,* Aug. 4, 1860.

36. *Gazette,* July 28, Aug. 25, 1860.

Johnsons, Conway, and others of the Dynasty. However, this agreement on national issues did not restore harmony to the local party.

The *Gazette* was the leading organ in Arkansas for Bell and Everett, the conservative candidates who argued that the Constitution gave slavery ample protection, and pledged strict adherence to its provisions. Among the other Bell and Everett newspapers were the Washington *Telegraph,* the *Ouachita Herald* of Camden, the *Southern Shield* of Helena, and the *Independent Balance* of Batesville, all of which were old and respected journals.[37]

The *Gazette* had no agents at this time, and got good response from an invitation to any responsible person who felt an interest to organize subscription clubs, the usual campaign rate of three months for 50 cents being in effect.[38]

The new Hoe drum cylinder press Danley had ordered in New York was put into service about the middle of September, and considerably lightened the mechanical task of producing a campaign newspaper. When it had been in use five weeks, Danley pronounced it a machine of many virtues and no faults, and "a beauty to look upon." Its form measured 31 by 43 inches, and the floor space it occupied was less than 7 by 13 feet. It could be operated by steam power, but Danley had not bought the necessary equipment for steam operation. Steam power would have made 900 impressions an hour possible, but one man could operate it manually at the rate of 750 an hour. Already it had been used at almost peak capacity on one job, when it ran off 5,000 impressions in less than seven consecutive hours.[39]

In addition to his editorial duties, Danley made speeches for Bell and Everett, and sent election tickets to every county that could not provide them locally.[40] He was due much of the credit for the good showing his candidates made in the election on November 6, but it was not good enough. Arkansas gave her electoral votes to Breckinridge and Lane by a popular vote of 28,732 to 20,094 for the Bell and Everett ticket. Douglas and Johnson received 5,227, and Lincoln and Hamlin received none, not being on the ballot.

When it became certain that Lincoln had been elected, Southern fire-eaters clamored for immediate secession. It was loudest in South Carolina, where secessionism was virtually unanimous, and was almost as loud in the Gulf states. Public opinion in Arkansas fell into two main categories. The Secessionists were the most vocal, because they knew exactly what they wanted to do: secede without delay, because they believed the Lincoln administration would ignore organic and statutory laws protecting slavery. The Conditional Unionists wanted to remain in the union until the last possible means of compromise had been attempted, and were willing to secede only

37. *Ibid.,* Sept. 1, 1860.
38. *Ibid.,* Aug. 25, Sept. 1, 15, 1860.
39. *Ibid.,* Oct. 20, 1860; Oct. 5, 1870; Apr. 27, 1874; Mar. 16, Apr. 21, 1875; *National Democrat,* Feb. 27, 1864.
40. *Gazette,* Oct. 20, 27, 1860.

when they were convinced that slave states would not be guaranteed equal rights with free states. Because their judgment of the best course depended upon what happened next, each new development caused them to modify their opinions. This made them appear to be too elastic to take a stand and stick to it, but it was only because one by one the straws they clutched vanished. There were a few Unconditional Unionists, who wanted to stay in the union regardless of the fate of slavery, but most of them kept their opinions to themselves, since their neighbors were in no mood to tolerate such sentiments.

Danley's finest hour as an editor came during this period of mass indecision. Previously he had not particularly distinguished himself, for his paper had suffered by his frequent and prolonged absences, and his observations of politics and government had become too hit-and-miss and too much based on personalities to give him great stature. But when logic seemed likely to yield to hysteria during this transition period, he kept a cool head and took a calm, objective approach to the crisis. Unfortunately, he could not offer a practical solution, for there was none. He tried to drown out the rabid cries for immediate secession with reports of meetings favoring unionism and with editorials pointing out that nothing had happened yet to change the situation and that it was senseless to dissolve the union because of fear of what might happen.

When the legislature met in November, there was great pressure by the Secessionists for it to authorize a convention to take Arkansas out of the union. The *Old Line Democrat,* which favored secession, began the publication of a daily paper to extend through the session, with the promise that it would continue thereafter if it received enough encouragement. The *True Democrat,* also on the side of secession, started a daily issue a few days later. Its tri-weekly had not been profitable and had been discontinued after the August election, but its owners considered it worthwhile in molding public opinion.[41]

Rector's inaugural address on November 15 placed him on the side of immediate secession, and a dispatch sent from Washington late in December by Senator Johnson and Congressman Hindman took the same position.[42] Because many people believed Arkansas would soon secede, the legislature toyed with the idea of not electing a senator, but finally elected Charles B. Mitchel.

Governor Rector told the legislature on December 12 that the union no longer existed, and said Arkansas should call a convention "to prepare for coming events." The Secessionists heartily endorsed the convention, but the Conditional Unionists opposed it and managed to stave off legislative action temporarily. Danley opposed it at first, but felt sure the "fanatics and fools" in the legislature would authorize it. So he made sure by private corre-

41. *Ibid.,* Nov. 3, 10, 17, 1860.
42. *Ibid.,* Dec. 29, 1860.

spondence that strong union candidates would run for positions as delegates if the bill should pass.[43]

Danley's facility with words was remarkable for one of limited formal education. When he was searching for words, it was his habit to chew absentmindedly on scraps of paper torn from the margin of exchange newspapers.[44] He must have chewed many such scraps during this period, but his editorials remained conversational in tone, and the flow of words did not seem to be labored.

He did not believe that the states had a constitutional right to secede, but he held that revolution against an oppressive government was an inherent right of the people. He could see nothing in the present situation to warrant such a drastic measure, but he favored revolution over secession if violent action should become necessary. He repeatedly asked his fellow Southerners to await further developments, to consider the possibilities of a peaceable settlement through the various conferences proposed, and to pin their hopes on a "returning sense of justice" in the free states.

He was not so naive as to suppose that all his subscribers agreed with him, but as late as Christmas Eve, only one had canceled his subscription for this reason or expressed dissatisfaction with his editorial policies. He told the irate subscriber that he felt no obligation to pander to the prejudices of his readers or to take an editorial stand according to popular opinion, but rather had to advocate what he thought was right.[45]

The secession of South Carolina on December 20 and the certainty that

43. W. J. Lemke (ed.), *Judge David Walker, His Life and Letters* (Fayetteville: Washington County Historical Society, 1957), 100.

44. Dickison Brugman, "The Life Story of a Newspaper Veteran," *Gazette,* Nov. 7, 1931.

45. *Gazette,* Dec. 29, 1860.

other states would follow suit moved Danley to prophesy that the South could be united only by the shedding of blood. Admitting now that a dissolution of the union was inevitable, he spoke of the wide variations of opinion on what course the Southern states should take after their secession, and said that only an attempt by the North to coerce them into returning to the union would cement them together.[46]

The legislature passed an act on January 14 referring the convention question to the people, and the governor approved it the next day. An election was to be held on February 18 to decide the question, and also to elect delegates in case the decision was in favor of a convention. Its powers were not clearly enough defined to prevent its going far beyond a decision between secession and the alternative cooperation with other slave states towards a compromise. Worse yet, it failed to provide for its ordinances to be ratified by the people, which gave it almost unlimited power. Many opposed it for this reason alone.

By this time, Danley was in favor of a convention. Four states had seceded and three others were almost sure to do so, and at least five more were expected to hold conventions to make the decision. Danley thought Arkansas had to be largely guided by the action of adjoining states, especially Tennessee and Louisiana, for their interests overlapped too much for them to take opposite positions safely.[47]

Among the many indications that Rector's supporters in the legislature were in the minority was the controversy over the public printing. The *Old Line Democrat,* having been his organ from the beginning of his campaign, had high hopes of getting the contract. This office had been awarded the premiums for the best ornamental job printing and the best printed newspaper at the first Pulaski County Fair early in November, but there had been no other entries in the ornamental job printing division. The *Gazette* had won the premium for the best plain job printing, but Danley had freely admitted that most of the judges were not qualified to judge printing. When the two Democratic papers began arguing over the public printing, Danley suggested that the best remedy would be to elect him public printer.[48] But the *True Democrat* got the job, and a few days later, Richard H. Johnson resumed his old position as its senior editor. The *Old Line Democrat* about the same time suspended publication,[49] undoubtedly because it could not continue without the subsidy of the public printing.

By an act approved January 21, 1861, the legislature appropriated $100,-000 to purchase arms and munitions for the state and appointed Danley and Thomas J. Churchill as commissioners to make the purchase, working "in connection with the governor."[50]

46. *Ibid.,* Jan. 5, 1861.
47. *Ibid.,* Jan. 19, 1861.
48. *Ibid.,* Nov. 17, 1860; Jan. 5, 1861.
49. *Ibid.,* Feb. 2, 1861.
50. *Ibid.,* Jan. 26, 1861.

Ironically, the arms and munitions could not be bought in the South, so Danley and Churchill set out on an overland trip to New York about the first of February. Holtzman was left in charge of the *Gazette,* and Danley sent a long letter every week to take the place of his usual lead editorial. Soon after their arrival at New York, Danley came down with a fever. The arms and munitions had already been purchased and the earliest possible delivery promised. Churchill stayed with Danley until he was sure his illness was not dangerous, and left for Little Rock on February 16. Danley remained in his New York hotel room for a few days, and then started home alone.[51]

A telegraph line had been built from St. Louis to Fayetteville during the summer of 1860, and it had been extended subsequently to Fort Smith. Another line was in operation between Memphis and Helena, and others were being built or planned. A line from Memphis to Little Rock was completed late in January, and the Little Rock office opened for business on January 28. Danley and Solon Borland, now editor of the Memphis *Enquirer,* exchanged congratulatory messages, and Danley issued a prospectus for a daily edition of the *Gazette.* It was to be published at $8 a year if enough subscribers wanted it,[52] but it was quietly laid aside in the weeks that followed.

The new telegraph service became the means of giving wide circulation to unfounded rumors, and played an important part in the seizure of the United States arsenal at Little Rock in the name of the state. The arsenal had long been used only as an arms and munitions depot, and when Capt. James Totten's artillery company arrived in November of 1860 from Fort Leavenworth to garrison the arsenal, the excitable Secessionists viewed it as part of the federal government's preparations against the threat of secession. Most of the people of Little Rock, where Conditional Unionists predominated, did not worry about this, for Totten had grown up at Little Rock, and besides, his 60 men could hardly be considered an effective force either for defensive or offensive action.

The first message sent by telegraph from Little Rock, before the office opened, was written by John M. Harrell. It consisted of an assortment of local news items, including a rumor that troops had been ordered from Fort Gibson to reinforce the arsenal. The message was relayed from Memphis to Helena, a hotbed of secessionism. The next morning Governor Rector received a telegram from Helena, notifying him that resolutions had been passed at a mass meeting there stating that it was his duty to seize the arsenal and expel the troops, and offering him the services of 500 volunteers.

Rector instructed Edmund Burgevin, his brother-in-law and adjutant general, to reply that state authorities had no right to take possession of the arsenal as long as Arkansas remained in the union, but that the governor would consider its reinforcement the equivalent of a declaration of war, and that volunteer troops would not be needed unless either reinforcement or secession occurred. Burgevin changed the wording of the message so as to

51. *Ibid.,* Feb. 16, 23, Mar. 2, 1861.
52. *Ibid.,* Feb. 2, 1861.

imply that the governor could not initiate a move to seize the arsenal, but would support spontaneous action by the people for that purpose. Four volunteer companies from Phillips County immediately prepared to go to Little Rock, and the word spread to other counties.

Rector notified Totten on January 29 that he would not be allowed to hold possession of the arsenal in the event of secession, reinforcement, or any attempt to remove or destroy the arms and munitions stored there. A few days later, there was a rumor that 300 or 400 federal soldiers were on their way up the Arkansas River on the steamboat S. H. Tucker to reinforce the arsenal. The rumor was false, but it stirred up the people of Pine Bluff, and two companies of volunteers started for Little Rock to help the governor seize the arsenal.

The Pine Bluff soldiers reached Little Rock on February 5, and the next day between 800 and 1,000 volunteers from at least nine counties were in town, and the governor also called out Pulaski County's two militia companies. The volunteers believed that Rector had called for their services, and that the people of Little Rock were in favor of the seizure of the arsenal. But Rector denied any knowledge of such an order, and the local people were highly indignant about the whole affair. To prevent disorderly attempts at seizure that might cause serious trouble, the City Council and certain responsible citizens urged Rector to seize the arsenal in the name of the state. After an exchange of correspondence between Rector and Totten, the troops evacuated the arsenal and the property was turned over to the governor on February 8. Totten's command left for St. Louis four days later.

So far as the people of Little Rock were concerned, Totten was the hero of the hour, for he had handled a difficult situation admirably and had avoided bloodshed. Rector and his friends were extremely unpopular locally. Many people believed that Rector had engineered the incident to precipitate secession. Others believed he was less responsible for it than some of his close associates who had promoted the gathering of troops without informing him of all the details.[53]

While Jefferson Davis was being inaugurated as president of the Confederate States of America on February 18, Arkansas voters straggled to the polls and voted 27,412 to 15,826 in favor of holding a convention.[54] Dan-

---

53. *Ibid.*, Feb. 9, 16, 1861; *National Democrat*, June 11, 1864; *The War of the Rebellion: A Compilation of the Official Records of the Union and Confederate Armies* (128 vols., Washington: Government Printing Office, 1880–1901), Series I, Vol. I, 638–646, 681–683; LIII, 617, 483–484; John M. Harrell, "Arkansas," in Clement A. Evans (ed.), *Confederate Military History* (12 vols., Atlanta, Ga.: Confederate Publishing Company, 1899), X, 6–10; *Message of Henry M. Rector, Governor of Arkansas, to the State Convention; March 4th, 1861* (Little Rock: True Democrat Book and Job Office Print, 1861), 6–7; *Journal of Both Sessions of the Convention of the State of Arkansas, which were begun and held in the capitol, in the city of Little Rock; Published by Authority* (Little Rock: Johnson & Yerkes, State Printers, 1861), Appendix, 477–485.

54. *Gazette*, Mar. 9, 1861.

ley's brother, Benjamin, was a candidate for the convention on a secession platform in Pulaski County, but the *Gazette* endorsed his unionist opponents, and he and his running mate were defeated.

Abraham Lincoln was inaugurated on March 4, and the Convention assembled at Little Rock on the same day. David Walker, a Conditional Unionist from Washington County, was elected president by a majority of five votes, and the Unionists held control of the Convention by this slender margin day after day, steadfastly resisting the pressure applied by Secessionists and the rabid tirades of the *True Democrat* and other Secessionist newspapers. Lincoln's inaugural address foretold coercion, and the Secessionists considered this reason enough to leave the union, but the Conditional Unionists still insisted upon waiting for a tangible act of coercion while continuing to seek a basis for compromise.

When it became apparent that the convention's small union majority would block all efforts towards secession, the Secessionists clamored to refer the question to the people, believing that a majority of the voters wanted to secede. The Conditional Unionists thought they still had a small but safe majority, and believed it would increase as the current excitement subsided. By a compromise reached outside the Convention hall, the Convention voted to submit the question of secession to the people, but set the date of the election at August 5, four and a half months away. The Convention then adjourned on March 21, to reassemble on August 19 to take whatever action was indicated by popular vote. It could not legally reconvene sooner unless its president called it into session.

Speakers on both sides began a canvass of the state, and the newspapers devoted most of their space to the secession issue. Danley appeared confident that the popular vote would be unfavorable to secession, and in the *Gazette* of April 13, he pleaded with the losers to accept the will of the majority as shown by the August election, to make Arkansas a solid unit one way or the other.

Arkansas became virtually a solid unit in favor of secession during the following week. News of the siege and surrender of Fort Sumter that ended on April 13 was closely followed by news of Lincoln's proclamation of April 15, calling for 75,000 volunteers to retake the forts and arsenals that had been seized by the seceded states. The quota set for Arkansas was one regiment of 780 men. Here at last was not only the first real act of coercion, but an ultimatum to the Southern states that remained in the union. Most Arkansans reached a decision in a matter of seconds: if they had to fight, it would be on the side of the Southern states whose interests were identical with theirs.

Danley changed with the rest, but he did not like the idea of plunging headlong into disaster as an emotional reaction. He still preferred revolution to secession, but he realized that the tide of public sentiment was overwhelmingly in favor of immediate secession. Collectively and individually, the people called upon David Walker to reconvene the Convention, because only this

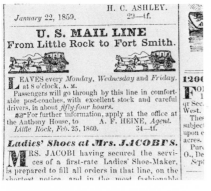

body had legal authority to take Arkansas out of the union. Danley also urged Walker to do this, to prevent a state of anarchy.[55]

On Saturday, April 20, public meetings were held in every crossroads community in the state, and with fiery oratory and formal resolutions, the people made known their eagerness to secede. In some instances, the American flag was dramatically ripped from its honored place and the Confederate flag raised. All eyes were upon Walker, and on this day he at last issued a proclamation calling the Convention to reassemble on Monday, May 6.[56]

Freight shipped from Northern ports to the South already had been a matter of much concern, with Southerners hoping to prevent army garrisons from receiving supplies and munitions, and Northerners hoping to prevent potential enemies in the South from being supplied. Ordnance stores and other supplies sent to the garrison at Fort Smith had been seized on the Arkansas River early in February. Materials of war that commissioners Danley and Churchill had ordered at St. Louis were received before the fall of Fort Sumter, and warrants for $36,954 were drawn on the governor's contingency fund to pay for them. Those ordered at Cincinnati, New York, and other points were seized by the Home Guard at Cincinnati immediately after Lincoln's proclamation appeared, as were arms and munitions ordered privately by Arkansans, and there was an unofficial embargo on non-military shipments to the South. In retaliation, steamboats owned by Cincinnati people were seized at Helena, Napoleon, and Memphis, and two steamboats carrying army supplies to Fort Smith were seized at Pine Bluff.[57]

55. C. C. Danley to David Walker, Little Rock, Apr. 15, 1861, Ms. in *Arkansas Gazette* Foundation Library.
56. *Gazette,* Apr. 27, 1861.
57. *Ibid.,* Apr. 20, 27, May 2, 11, 1861; *True Democrat,* Apr. 25, May 2, 1861; A. Clark Denson, *Westmoreland: or, Secession Ferocity at the Breaking Out of the Rebellion* (St. Louis: P. M. Pinckard, Printer, 1865), 16–23; J. Wm. Demby, *The War in Arkansas, or, A Treatise on the Great Rebellion of 1861; Its Progress, and Ultimate*

Governor Rector had been behaving as if Arkansas had already seceded for some time. As early as January, he had opened negotiations with the Indian tribes to the west on the premise that Arkansas would secede, and had sent arms and munitions to the western border about the same time.[58] He had also sent Gen. James Yell with state militia troops to take up a defensive position on the Mississippi opposite Memphis.[59] Now he gave permission for a Confederate battery to be planted at or near Helena,[60] and sent five companies of state troops to demand the surrender of Fort Smith.

Solon Borland, who had recently sold the Memphis *Enquirer* and moved back to Little Rock, was made an aid-de-camp to Governor Rector with the rank of colonel, and was placed in command of the Fort Smith expedition. The troops left Little Rock on April 21 on two steamboats, and reached Fort Smith on the night of April 23. The two cavalry companies garrisoned there evacuated the fort about an hour before the state troops arrived, leaving the quartermaster behind to surrender the fort. Both Little Rock editors were on this expedition, Dick Johnson as a private in Churchill's company, and the disabled Danley as a spectator.[61]

When the troops returned to Little Rock on April 30, they learned that the governor had received a requisition for troops from Lincoln's secretary of war and had indignantly refused to honor it. He had also received a request for one regiment from the Confederate secretary of war for service in Virginia, and had replied that only the Convention had authority to comply with it. However, men who had ambitions to be the staff officers of such a regiment offered to raise the regiment as private citizens, and it was immediately accepted for Confederate service.[62]

The Convention assembled on the morning of May 6, and the ordinance of secession was introduced that afternoon. An attempt to make it subject to ratification by the people was voted down 55 to 15. There could be little doubt that it would be ratified by a large majority, but most people wanted the matter settled without the delay of an election. The vote on the ordinance was 65 to 5 in favor of it, but four of the dissenters changed their votes to the affirmative, and only Isaac Murphy of Madison County recorded a final vote against secession. The ordinance was passed at 4:10 that afternoon, and Arkansas was officially no longer a part of the United States of America.[63]

Results upon the Destinies of the State (Little Rock, Ark., 1864), 60–64; *Journal 1861 Convention,* 151, 165.

58. *Journal 1861 Convention,* 156; *Official Records,* Ser. I, Vol. XIII, 490–491.

59. *Journal 1861 Convention,* 152–153.

60. *Official Records,* Ser. I, Vol. I, 685–686, 689.

61. *Ibid.,* 650–652; *Journal 1861 Convention,* 151; *Gazette,* Apr. 27, May 4, 18, 25, 1861; *True Democrat,* Apr. 25, May 2, 1861; *New York Herald,* Apr. 26, 1861; W. E. Woodruff, [Jr.], *With the Light Guns in '61–'65* (Little Rock: Central Printing Company, 1903), 13–17.

62. *Official Records,* Ser. I, Vol. I, 687–689; LIII, 674–675; *Gazette,* Apr. 27, 1861; *True Democrat,* Apr. 25, May 2, 1861.

63. *Journal 1861 Convention,* 120–124.

17

THE CIVIL WAR

1861-1865 THE BIRTH OF THE Confederate States of America and the organization of its army brought about a great show of patriotism, but did not subdue the instincts of some for self preservation or personal glory. The rivalry for high military rank began with the first regiment Arkansas sent to the Confederate army, and there was similar competition for non-combat positions. As Danley saw it, those who had clamored for secession earliest and loudest were the worst offenders; as they saw it, they were the ones most entitled to the favors of the new government.

The disposition was now to catalog a man's politics according to the date he began to favor secession, those who had wanted to secede before the fall of Fort Sumter being called Original Secessionists and the others Original Unionists. The Original Secessionists still were divided between the Dynasty and Rector factions.

Those who viewed Henry Rector's election as the final overthrow of the Dynasty were mistaken. The Dynasty had weathered worse disasters, and all its major setbacks had come from within, led by men who had once stood high in its favor. Arkansas had not rid herself of the nepotism and corruption that had characterized the Dynasty, but had simply swapped governors.

The Dynasty's majority in the legislature had given Rector a bad time. Its strength in the Convention was slightly less than that of the Conditional Unionists, and it was unable to control the first session. But in the second session, as the Convention elected some of its own members to other positions of responsibility, the slender margin of power held by the Original Unionists dwindled and the Dynasty gained at least equal power. Rector had no influence in the Convention, and both the other factions were determined to deprive him of as much power as possible.

The Dynasty's rising influence became evident with the election of delegates to the Confederate Provisional Congress on May 10. Robert Ward Johnson was elected on the first ballot, along with two Original Unionists,

Augustus Hill Garland and Hugh F. Thomasson. It took two more ballots to elect Albert Rust and W. W. Watkins.[1]

The *Gazette* described Rector's management of the state's military organization as "so extravagant and so pompously unmilitary, as to render the pronunciamentos and home wars of Mexico almost respectable," and said it was the Convention's duty to take it out of the governor's hands.[2] And that was precisely what the Convention set out to do.

Rector had assigned brigadier generals to command troops on the eastern and western borders, and on May 11, the Convention made new appointments for both positions. Two days later, the Confederacy ordered Brig. Gen. Ben McCulloch to assume command on the western frontier.[3] Almost immediately there was conflict between McCulloch and the state general in the west, and the troops in the east revolted and deposed their state general.

Under ordinary circumstances, administration of the state's military organization would have been the responsibility of the governor, as commander-in-chief of the state militia. But the Convention, meeting now behind closed doors, had no intention of permitting this. There was talk of deposing Rector, but it was decided instead to create a board of three men to take charge of military affairs.[4]

At the request of some members of the Convention, the ordinance creating the Military Board was written by Thomas C. Hindman, who was back in the Dynasty's good graces.[5] It was introduced by James Yell, chairman of the military affairs committee, and was adopted after modification on May 15. The board consisted of the governor and two advisers, thus granting Rector a voice in a function that previously had been entirely his, yet providing for restraint. The next day the Convention elected C. C. Danley and Benjamin C. Totten to serve with Rector on the board.[6]

Rector chafed at the many encroachments on his authority, and was particularly incensed by the creation of the Military Board, which he and his friends said was done by the friends of the *Gazette* and the *True Democrat* to fetter and discredit him.[7] He sent the public printer a proclamation calling a special session of the legislature for June 1. The Convention learned of the proclamation on the morning of May 22, and asked Rector to withdraw it. He complied, possibly because of the threat of deposing him, and the Military Board held its first meeting later in the day. On the same day, the Con-

1. *Journal of Both Sessions of the Convention of the State of Arkansas, which were begun and held in the capitol, in the city of Little Rock*. Published by Authority. (Little Rock: Johnson & Yerkes, State Printers, 1861), 184–187.

2. *Gazette*, May 18, 1861.

3. *Ibid.; True Democrat*, May 16, 1861; *Convention Journal*, 209; *The War of the Rebellion: A Compilation of the Official Records of the Union and Confederate Armies* (128 vols., Washington: Government Printing Office, 1880–1901), Series I, Vol. III, 575–576.

4. *True Democrat*, July 25, 1861.

5. *Ibid.*, Dec. 19, 1861.

6. *Convention Journal*, 250, 254; *Gazette*, May 18, 1861.

7. Little Rock *Daily State Journal*, Dec. 5, 1861.

vention elected a major general to coordinate the state military organization. James Yell was elected over Solon Borland by a vote of 43 to 20, with six votes cast for men not in nomination.[8] The Convention adjourned June 3.[9]

Danley's service on the Military Board was almost a full time job for two weeks. Danley and his friends wanted to turn over the entire control of military affairs in Arkansas to the Confederacy, including the state's troops, arms, and equipment, to avoid ruinous expense and conflicting authority. The Rector faction wanted a strong state military organization at any cost. Danley, Johnson, and others thought Rector was primarily interested in the patronage appointments it afforded, but there were other reasons, chiefly the fear that the Confederacy would send the troops and arms to battlefields east of the Mississippi, leaving Arkansas undefended.

The board's policies followed Danley's reasoning for two weeks, and he went to Richmond to arrange the transfer of troops and equipment to the Confederacy. He resigned from the board on June 5, just before he left for Richmond, saying that his official duties conflicted with his private interests. He was expected to obtain assurance that the Confederacy would not merely accept nominal control, but would provide effective defense for Arkansas. He presented his proposition to President Davis on June 13,[10] and on June 25, Brig. Gen. William J. Hardee was ordered to take command in northeast Arkansas, attached to a department commanded by Brig. Gen. Leonidas Polk.[11]

No sooner was Danley out of the way than Rector dominated the Military Board, and the Arkansas press agreed almost unanimously that he intended to use it to retain control of state troops, working at cross purposes with the Confederacy. Besides competing with General McCulloch for volunteers, the board called General Yell to active duty in northeast Arkansas, and he began his service by trying to persuade his troops not to agree to transfer to Confederate service.[12]

At Little Rock on July 15, the Military Board and General Hardee drew up a new agreement for the transfer of state troops, and on July 22, Hardee established his headquarters at Pitman's Ferry, and the state generals were recalled from service.[13]

All the state's newspapers condemned the conduct of the Military Board, and the *Gazette* and the *True Democrat* led the protest. It was difficult to get used to the harmony that now existed between these two ancient enemies, for they now agreed on everything of importance. Because the other side had no newspaper to argue its case, the *Gazette* published a pseudonymous defense of the Military Board on July 20, attributing the *True Democrat's*

8. *Convention Journal*, 298, 303; *True Democrat*, May 23, 1861; *Gazette*, May 25, July 25, 1861.
9. *Convention Journal*, 473; *Gazette*, June 6, 1861.
10. *Gazette*, June 8, 29, 1861; *Official Records*, LIII, 698–699.
11. *Official Records*, III, 598; IV, 362; *True Democrat*, July 4, 11, 1861.
12. *True Democrat*, July 4, 11, 18, Dec. 2, 1861; *Gazette*, July 20, 1861.
13. *Official Records*, III, 608–610, 612; *Gazette*, July 20, 1861.

criticism to its editor's defeat by Rector in the race for governor in 1860. The *True Democrat* on July 25 published an unsigned reply to the *Gazette's* attack on General Yell, suggesting that the real reasons for Danley's opposition might have been Yell's denunciation of him as an abolitionist and his defeat of Borland in the contest for major general. Both editors made it clear that they disagreed with the writers, and thought their remarks about the other editor should not have been made.

About this time, Danley and Johnson began a voluntary censorship of military news. All the newspapers were filled with information about the organization of military units, troop movements, and other such material. On June 27, the *True Democrat* said it would suppress such publications to prevent giving information to the enemy, and appealed to other editors to adopt the same policy. The *Gazette* concurred on July 20, having previously withheld much of this kind of information without comment. Later the *True Democrat* implied that it had followed the lead of the *Gazette* in this matter.[14]

Notwithstanding the arguments that state troops could not be taken out of Arkansas, those in northwest Arkansas crossed the state line to fight with McCulloch's Confederates and Maj. Gen. Sterling Price's Missouri state troops in the battle of Oak Hills or Wilson's Creek, Missouri on August 10, 1861. The battle was a victory for McCulloch, although his enemy also halfheartedly claimed it.

At no time during the Civil War did either army have a system whereby official notification was given to families of soldiers who were killed, wounded, captured, or missing in action. Casualty lists and accounts of battles were sent to home town newspapers unofficially, and many a family learned the fate of its relative through newspaper casualty lists or letters from other soldiers.

The *Gazette's* first accounts of the battle of Oak Hills, with casualty lists, were published in its regular issue of August 24, and the *True Democrat* had the story on August 29. An "extra" was issued from the *Gazette* office earlier, containing the first reports received. It was sold on the streets by young Dickison Brugman, who spent his spare time at the *Gazette* office and soon began his apprenticeship there. His profit was $13.25, the first money he ever earned.[15]

As the Confederacy made the transition from provisional to permanent government and held its first presidential election, there was unity such as only war can bring. The election on November 6 for president, vice president, and members of Congress was announced by Rector's proclamation on August 24. Since the old political parties no longer existed, candidates

14. *True Democrat,* Oct. 31, 1861.

15. Fred W. Allsopp, *Twenty Years in a Newspaper Office* (Little Rock: Central Printing Company, 1907), 106–107. We are handicapped in writing about this period by a gap in available *Gazette* files. Between July 6, 1861 and March 1, 1862, only the issues dated July 20, August 24, and December 14, 1861 have been located.

could not be selected by the usual methods. Richard Johnson promised his readers on August 29 that he would find a way to make up a slate without holding a state political convention. During the next week he met with Danley and John R. Eakin, editor of the Washington *Telegraph,* and made up a slate of six candidates for electors. They recognized former party lines by choosing three who had been Democrats and three who had been Constitutional Unionists, but said no opposition to Jefferson Davis for president and Alexander H. Stephens for vice president was anticipated or would be tolerated from the candidates they supported.[16]

Believing it was unpatriotic to revive old animosites or create new ones that would divide the people in time of war, Danley and Johnson agreed that their papers would not participate editorially in the canvass for Congress.[17] When Johnson's cousin, Jilson P. Johnson, entered the race in the Third District on October 10, the *True Democrat* could help him only by publication of letters to the editor.

There was an unusually large number of candidates in all four districts, but most of them decided against a vigorous canvass. The winners, as certified by the governor, were Augustus H. Garland, Grandison D. Royston, Felix I. Batson, and Thomas B. Hanly. Garland was credited with 2,156 votes to Jilson Johnson's 2,125, but on the day Rector signed his certificate of election, an error in Arkansas County's returns was corrected to give Johnson the office by eight votes. The *True Democrat* protested the issuance of the certificate to Garland, but Rector said he had only unofficial information about the error until after the legal deadline, and had to base his action on the official vote as certified by the secretary of state.[18] Johnson contested the election, but Congress decided in Garland's favor in the fall of 1862, with a minority report in Johnson's favor. Johnson did not drop the contest until January of 1863.

The Convention had not provided for the election of Confederate senators, and a special session of the legislature convened on November 4 with this as one of its most important duties. The *True Democrat* explained that Robert Ward Johnson's decision to retire from the United States Senate in 1860 was because he was tired of public life, and that only a sense of duty could induce him to serve again. For more than two months before the election, the *True Democrat* attempted to draft Johnson, using letters, reprinted articles, and occasional restrained editorial support. Johnson and Charles B. Mitchel were easily elected on the first ballot on November 9.[19]

The new rapport between the *Gazette* and the *True Democrat* was tested early in September. The *True Democrat* was the public printer, but Rector sent two proclamations to the *Gazette* for publication, probably hoping to revive the old feud between the two editors and get one of them off his back.

16. *True Democrat,* Sept. 5, 1861.
17. *Ibid.,* Dec. 19, 1861.
18. *Ibid.,* Dec. 19, 26, 1861; Mar. 13, 1862; *Daily State Journal, Dec. 29, 1861.*
19. *True Democrat,* Sept. 12, Nov. 14, 1861.

The *True Democrat* copied the proclamations in its next issue, and quoted the law requiring the public printer to do "all book, pamphlet, and job printing, work of every kind and description, for which the State shall be liable to pay." Danley did not reply editorially, but published an answer by an anonymous spokesman for the governor. Misquoting the law by omitting the word "work," this writer said proclamations were not book, pamphlet, or job printing, and therefore did not come under this law. Johnson called attention to the distortion,[20] and that ended the discussion.

The *Gazette* and the *True Democrat* carped at the Military Board from the time Danley resigned. The Arkansas press followed their lead, and Rector's side of the story had no newspaper outlet until October 31, when the first issue of the *Daily State Journal* appeared. Its editor was Thomas C. Peek, who had been provided for with several appointments of minor importance since the suspension of the *Old Line Democrat*.[21] The only paper available was the small size ordinarily used for daily editions, so the *Journal* began without a weekly edition, and was never able to add it. Peek said his paper started with a city circulation larger than the *Gazette's* and the *True Democrat's* combined,[22] which possibly was true, but no newspaper could live on Little Rock circulation alone. The *Journal* was an all-out defender of Rector, and was soon justly accused of trying to revive old enmities, particularly animosities against the Johnson faction.[23]

Gen. Albert Sidney Johnston had succeeded Polk as department commander in September, and had requisitioned Rector for more volunteers. When Johnston canceled the call in November and instructed Rector to disband these troops unless they were fully armed and equipped, Rector asked the special session of the legislature to authorize organizing them into a brigade of state troops for duty on the northern border, and to authorize two additional regiments made up of German and Irish volunteers. But the legislature refused to provide for a state army.

Danley's editorial of November 30 was a particularly harsh criticism of the Military Board. He said it had hampered the transfer of troops by its invention of the soldier voting policy, by sending officers to influence soldiers against voting to transfer, by calling for ten regiments when McCulloch was also calling for volunteers before the battle of Oak Hills, and by calling for five regiments for one year when McCulloch calling for five regiments

20. *Ibid.*, Sept. 5, 12, 1861.

21. Peek was appointed inspector of the penitentiary on Jan. 18, 1861, and the governor placed him in charge of the property and military stores at the Little Rock arsenal when the state assumed control of it in May. On Sept. 12, he was appointed aid-de-camp to Brig. Gen. George M. Holt, commander of the Second Brigade of Arkansas Militia, with the rank of major, and was called "Major Peek" the rest of his life. See *Message of Gov. Henry M. Rector, to the General Assembly of Arkansas, In Extra Session, Nov. 6, 1861* (Little Rock: Johnson & Yerkes, State Printers, 1861), 27; *Convention Journal*, 297; *True Democrat*, Sept. 26, 1861.

22. *Daily State Journal*, Nov. 2, 14, 1861.

23. *Ibid.*, Nov. 6, 1861.

for three years or the duration of the war. He also accused the board of send-ing Col. Francis A. Terry's battalion to Kentucky instead of leaving it in Ar-kansas. Actually, Rector had sent the battalion to northeast Arkansas because of a rumored invasion there, though his instructions from Richmond were to send it to McCulloch. This had made it part of Hardee's brigade, which General Johnston had ordered to Kentucky, leaving only a small force un-der Col. Solon Borland to defend northeast Arkansas.

The *Journal* replied that the soldier voting policy had been adopted on Hardee's recommendation, that the board's agents had done nothing more than read the order and conditions of transfer to the soldiers, and that the board's calls for troops had been made according to accepted procedure, while McCulloch's had not.[24]

Edmund Burgevin, adjutant general of the Arkansas Militia, was one of the officers the Military Board had sent to make the transfer, and he took exception to Danley's accusation that these officers had influenced the volun-teers against entering the service of the Confederacy. He published a card in the *Journal* on December 1, pronouncing Danley's editorial "villainously false from beginning to end."

Danley replied in the *Gazette* of December 7, this time making specific reference to Burgevin's activities in opposition to the transfer. Danley saw Burgevin twice on the morning this editorial was published, and both times Burgevin was extremely cordial. But at two o'clock that afternoon, Governor Rector brought Danley this note, signed by Burgevin:

"Sir: In your paper of this morning, you have attempted to cast reflections upon my honor, *and as you are not my equal in physical ability,* warranting on my part an assault, I demand a retraction of your avowals, or that you render that satisfaction which is due to a gentleman upon the field of honor. Governor Rector, the bearer of this, acting for me, will arrange the necessary preliminaries for the adjustment of our difficulties."

Few editors, said Danley, had received a challenge from as low a vaga-bond, borne by as high a public functionary. He made no written reply, but sent word to Burgevin that he was his physical equal.

Burgevin and Danley chanced to meet again about dark, and Burgevin seemed satisfied with Danley's explanation that the offensive editorial was not a personal attack but assailed only his public acts. But the *Journal* the next morning contained a card addressed by Burgevin to the public, de-nouncing Danley as a gross calumniator, an impostor in the ranks of honor, and a coward.

Danley had suggested that Burgevin should serve as a common soldier until his military ability was discovered and rewarded with rank. Burgevin's card in the *Journal* was accompanied by an advertisement calling for payment of debts due to the firm of Burgevin and Field. It was headed "Pronuncia-mento," and began: "Whereas, the undersigned having been reduced to the ranks, ordered to shoulder his gun and repair to the army by an edict of old

24. *Ibid.,* Dec. 4, 1861.

Jack Falstaff of the *Gazette,* finds it necessary in the absence of his partner in business, now a private in the 6th Reg't. Ark. Volunteers, to put their house in order as quickly as possible, that he may render prompt obedience to the said edict."

Danley blamed Rector for the challenge, since Burgevin had not been disturbed by the editorial until he had discussed it with Rector. Danley accused Rector of trying to stifle a free expression of opinion of his administration, and said this was another case of a challenger who never intended to go beyond the paper work of a duel.[25]

Several Arkansas editors marveled at the continuation of the truce between Danley and Johnson, and some said it was a coalition for political purposes. The *True Democrat* said on December 19 that the motivation was pure patriotism, a desire to lay aside old feuds to prevent divisions of public sentiment that could harm the war effort. Some may have accepted this explanation, but Rector and Peek did not believe a word of it. Peek called it "glimmerings of the Millineum," and said it foretold the approach of "that happy period when the lion shall lie down with the lamb."

The two editors reprinted each other's editorials with introductions that fairly glowed with approval, and extravagant mutual admiration was evident in almost every issue. Danley even reprinted an editorial by John W. Woodward, who was back on the *True Democrat's* staff, and called it "a volume of truth, well and piquantly told." This editorial complained of Rector's habit of wangling positions for his youthful favorites as aids-de-camp and others carrying rank as high as major or colonel, and advised them to demonstrate their patriotism by serving in the ranks. This was too much for Peek, who called attention to the same situation among the Dynasty's leaders and their relatives.[26]

On January 18 and 19, Peek reprinted excerpts from the *Gazette* of March, 1859, in which Danley reviled the editor of the *True Democrat* for selling his principles to write the convictions of others. This had been published before Peek's time at Little Rock, and he did not know that the editor Danley had assailed had been Woodward, not Johnson. Somebody set Peek straight on this point, and kept him from repeating his misidentification in the second batch of reprints.

Having failed to put a brigade of state troops into the field, the governor ordered the militia to fill its vacancies and hold company drills and battalion musters more frequently. Danley saw this as another attempt to establish a standing state army.[27] Peek's work as aid-de-camp to Brig. Gen. George M. Holt took him out of the *Journal* office from November 18 until December 9, and Dr. Cincinnatus V. Meador edited the paper in his absence, assisted by the local and news editor, Sam Raymond.[28]

25. *Ibid.,* Dec. 8, 1861; *Gazette,* Dec. 14, 1861; *True Democrat,* Dec. 19, 1861.
26. *Daily State Journal,* Jan. 5, 7, 1862.
27. *Ibid.,* Dec. 15, 1861.
28. *Ibid.,* Nov. 20, 21, Dec. 5, 6, 8, 10, 1861.

Solon Borland was the center of controversy about that time. First there was a dispute with Lt. Col. James M. Gee of Camden, which had been brewing all summer and came to a head with a false rumor of invasion early in November.[29] It was soon over, because the *Gazette* and the *True Democrat* could not spare the space for long letters. On its heels came Borland's order of November 29, intended to control speculation and extortion in his district by placing an embargo on produce, munitions of war, and medicines.[30] The *Gazette* and the *True Democrat* commended him, but other papers in Arkansas and at Memphis called the embargo an unwarranted interference with trade and a dangerous extension of military power. Governor Rector set aside Borland's order by a proclamation issued on December 20, but Borland did not recognize his right to annul a Confederate military order. His subordinates continued to enforce the embargo, and it looked as if a test of authority was shaping up between civil officers of the state and military officers of the Confederacy. The Confederate secretary of war intervened late in January, revoking Borland's order and ordering him to report in person to General Johnston.[31]

It was later said that Borland was relieved of his command, and it was even rumored that he was tried for the offense offered by the embargo order.[32] The public was told only that he was physically unable to continue as a military commander, and that his offer to serve in the army's medical department was not accepted. He resumed the practice of medicine at Little Rock on June 19.[33] Gee may have been correct in supposing that he had had an ambition to be a brigadier general, but his health would not permit active field duty, and the controversy over the embargo may have hastened his resignation.

Although 75 per cent of the *Journal's* space was filled with ads, it opened the new year with complaints of inadequate advertising patronage. The staff saw the handwriting on the wall and found other employment, and on February 7, the *Journal* suspended publication.[34]

The excitement and anguish of war had created a new demand for newspapers, but the difficulties of producing them were sharply increased by the loss of editors and printers to the army and the acute shortage of paper. By the middle of the summer of 1861, an estimated 400 newspapers on both sides of the conflict had suspended, and about 1,200 others had reduced the size of their sheets.[35]

For the first time, Arkansas newspapers had more subscribers and adver-

29. *Ibid.,* Nov. 10, 15, Dec. 29, 1861; *Gazette,* Dec. 14, 1861; *True Democrat,* Nov. 14, Dec. 26, 1861.

30. *Gazette,* Dec. 14, 1861; *True Democrat,* Dec. 12, 1861; *Daily State Journal,* Dec. 10, 1861.

31. *True Democrat,* Dec. 26, 1861; *Daily State Journal,* Jan. 11, 14, 23, 1862.

32. Washington *Telegraph,* Sept. 17, 1862.

33. *Gazette,* Mar. 15, 1862; *True Democrat,* June 19, 1862.

34. *Daily State Journal,* Jan. 1, 18, Feb. 6, 7, 1862.

35. *True Democrat,* Aug. 1, 1861.

tisers than they could serve indefinitely, and publishers were reluctant to waste precious paper on customers who did not pay. In the summer of 1861, Danley dropped all subscribers who owed for two or more years, saying, "The idea of furnishing a paper for nothing, has at last exploded." [36] He continued this policy when he announced on December 14 that the *Gazette's* subscription rates were advanced to $2 a year in specie or $2.50 in paper money. He could purchase supplies only with gold, and had to have it or suspend. "Our receipts from Job work and advertising having long since almost entirely ceased," he said, "we have to rely solely upon the subscriptions to the paper to keep it going."

The *True Democrat* said on September 26 that it had been apparent for six or eight months that it must adopt the cash system or suspend. It announced the same rates as the *Gazette* on November 14, and discontinued subscriptions as they expired unless payment for the next period had been received. Late in September more than 1,000 of its subscriptions were discontinued, and four months later another 947 were dropped.[37] The *True Democrat* reduced its sheet from eight to seven columns with the issue of August 8, 1861, but announced on September 19 that it was issuing a daily bulletin containing all the telegraphic news, distributed only by mail.

A printer's union at Little Rock was proposed in the fall of 1861 for "trade protection and contributary benefits," and to allow local printers to send a delegate to the convention of the Confederate National Union at Atlanta, Georgia the next spring.[38] The convention, scheduled for March 13, 1862, probably was canceled by the spring military campaigns. It was to be more like a press association than a labor union, for its membership was to consist of editors and proprietors of Southern newspapers. It was expected to organize a Southern Telegraphic Associated Press, to provide regular, reliable news dispatches at reasonable rates.[39]

No evidence is found that the local union was organized, possibly because of the organization on December 3, 1861 of the Mechanics Association, which included workers in all mechanical fields and had greater bargaining power than the printers alone. Their main concern was to establish a fair scale for evaluation of the depreciated paper currency with which their salaries were paid.[40]

The western section of the Memphis and Little Rock Railroad was completed with a ceremony on January 26, 1862. William E. Woodruff, a director of the railroad company and the oldest representative of the press in Arkansas, drove the last spike, and Danley made a short speech. The railroad had been chartered by an act of the legislature approved on January 10, 1853. Because of the difficulty and expense of bridging the Mississippi and

36. *Gazette,* May 11, June 8, 1861.
37. *True Democrat,* Oct. 3, 1861; Feb. 6, 1862.
38. *Daily State Journal,* Nov. 14, 1861.
39. *Ibid.,* Jan. 30, 1862.
40. *Ibid.,* Nov. 29, Dec. 5, 8, 19, 20, 26, 1861.

Arkansas rivers, the railroad stopped short of both its projected terminal points, the eastern terminus being at Hopefield opposite Memphis and the western terminus at the depot called Huntersville, opposite Little Rock. Its construction was planned in three divisions, only two of which were in operation at this time. The eastern division, from Hopefield to Madison, on the St. Francis River, had been in operation since 1858. The western division just completed ran from Huntersville to DeValls Bluff, on White River. The 45-mile middle division, between the White and St. Francis rivers, was not built for want of funds, though preliminary work was done and efforts were made to get money from the state and the Confederacy to complete the project.[41]

The winter of 1861–1862 was a time of preparation for spring military campaigns. Changes would be necessary in the Confederate military organization west of the Mississippi, and it was the general hope that it would be made a separate department, so its commander could concentrate on reclaiming Missouri without the constant transfer of his troops to battlegrounds east of the Mississippi. Maj. Gen. Sterling Price, the popular commander of the Missouri State Guard, had high hopes of being made a Confederate major general and assigned to command the new department. He had the enthusiastic support of the press and the people throughout the Mississippi Valley. Ben McCulloch, who was considered Price's only important rival for the new command, had few outspoken critics or defenders in Arkansas. But the area west of the Mississippi was not yet to be a separate department, and on January 10, 1862, it became the Trans-Mississippi District of Department No. 2. Jefferson Davis was determined that his department and district commanders should be West Point graduates, and besides, he would not lay aside an old personal grudge against Price that dated back to the Mexican War. He gave the command to Maj. Gen. Earl Van Dorn, who arrived at Little Rock on January 28, and then went to his headquarters at Pocahontas and planned a spring campaign he hoped would take him all the way to St. Louis.

To fill Van Dorn's requisition for ten regiments, Governor Rector divided the state into four recruiting districts, and threatened to draft men in counties that did not meet their quotas. The *True Democrat,* asked to condemn the draft, said it would sustain Rector and the Military Board if a draft should become necessary. Both the *Gazette* and the *True Democrat* began to modify their criticism of the Military Board in January, and often approved the course of its majority, which now consisted of Col. C. W. Board and Dr. Levin D. Hill.[42]

Brig. Gen. Samuel Ryan Curtis, commander of the federal Southwestern District of Missouri, planned a campaign to drive Price out of Missouri, clear Arkansas of all Confederate commands, and occupy Little Rock. A more

41. *Ibid.,* Dec. 6, 10, 1861; Jan. 28, 1862; *Telegraph,* Feb. 5, 1862; *Gazette,* Dec. 14, 1861; *True Democrat,* Sept. 26, Oct, 3, 1861.

42. *Official Records,* LIII, 776–779; *Daily State Journal,* Feb. 2, 1862; *True Democrat,* Jan. 2, 16, Feb. 6, 13, 1862; *Telegraph,* Feb. 12, 1862.

important Union campaign began about the same time. As Brig. Gen. Ulysses S. Grant swept victoriously down the Mississippi River, Forts Henry and Donelson in Tennessee fell on February 6 and 16. Arkansas people began making frantic preparations against invasion from the Mississippi, and Van Dorn took steps to concentrate most of his force near Pocahontas.

On February 10, Curtis marched from Lebanon against Price at Springfield, and Price fell back to make a junction with McCulloch. The combined armies of Price and McCulloch retreated to the Boston Mountains in Arkansas. Van Dorn went to their camp, assumed command of the Confederate forces, and moved forward to attack Curtis in the Sugar Creek valley near Elkhorn Tavern. The result was the hard-fought battle of Pea Ridge on March 6–8, in which McCulloch was killed. The Confederates retreated to Van Buren and Fort Smith, and Curtis was left in possession of the battlefield, but it was too far from his base of supply and of too little strategic importance to be worth holding.

The telegraph line, intended to connect Little Rock and Fort Smith, had been built only as far westward as Clarksville, and news of the battle was sent by courier over the 50-mile stretch between Van Buren and Clarksville. Moreover, a storm a few days after the battle interrupted telegraphic service for several days, and high waters delayed the mails during the same period.[43]

Meanwhile, the legislature met in special session on March 5, reached a quorum on March 17, and adjourned after five working days. Impatient with the constant hassle over a state army, the legislature passed an act unanimously, to abolish the militia and to provide for a registration as a basis for a future draft system. The registration was funded by a separate act that appropriated $575,000 to implement "the present military law of the state," meaning the new law. Just before adjournment, the legislators realized they had not made this sufficiently specific, and had unwittingly made it possible for the governor to accomplish by trickery what he had been unable to do any other way. They tried to prevent this by passing a supplemental act prohibiting the use of the money for paying militia officers under the old system, but it was too late.

Rector pocketed the act abolishing the militia and authorizing the registration, and also the act limiting the use of the appropriation, allowing them to die for want of his signature. But he signed the appropriation act, and thus not only kept his militia but gained $575,000 for it. Some of the indignant legislators wanted to start a grass-roots movement to call for Rector's resignation, but the *True Democrat* advised them instead to put their faith in the two advisory members of the Military Board, who had the power to prevent unnecessary active duty for the militia and to control use of the money. At the same time, Johnson denounced Rector for his willingness to ruin the state simply to get his state army. John R. Eakin of the *Telegraph* regarded the whole thing as a great joke Rector had pulled on the legislature.[44]

43. *True Democrat,* Mar. 13, 20, 1862.
44. *Ibid.,* Mar. 27, 1862; *Telegraph,* Mar. 26, Apr. 2, 1862.

Danley took a dim view of the attempts of Col. Edward W. Gantt, commander of the Twelfth Arkansas Infantry Regiment, to get an appointment as a Confederate brigadier general. Danley's editorial attacks on Gantt during the first three months of 1862 brought down on him the wrath of Gantt's regiment and much of the population of southwest Arkansas. Danley said Gantt was not qualified to be a colonel, much less a general, and that his regiment had behaved as a drunken, undisciplined mob when it passed through Little Rock. The regiment's officers passed resolutions expressing indignation and calling on their friends at home to withdraw patronage from the *Gazette* in protest. The Washington *Telegraph* and some of its correspondents vigorously defended Gantt and his regiment, as did the *Daily State Journal* in its final issue.[45]

The fort at New Madrid, Missouri fell on March 14, and Island No. 10 on April 7. Gantt, who was promoted to brigadier general during the siege of New Madrid, but whose commission was never confirmed by the Confederate Congress, surrendered and became a prisoner of war along with most of the other Confederates engaged at Island No. 10. He was severely criticized for his conduct both at New Madrid and at Island No. 10, and the *Gazette* was among those censuring him, but he still had his defenders.[46]

Van Dorn had intended to march to Jacksonport after the battle of Pea Ridge and proceed with his expedition against St. Louis. With this in mind, he stripped Arkansas of all government provisions and materials of war, including much of the telegraph line between Fort Smith and Little Rock.[47] He was still crossing Arkansas when the Union army won another victory at Shiloh or Pittsburg Landing in Tennessee on April 6–7. His troops were ordered to Corinth, Mississippi, where a large Confederate force was assembling. Price went with him, as a Confederate major general.[48] Van Dorn also took all available troops, and left Brig. Gen. Albert Rust at Little Rock to continue organizing and forwarding recruits to him. Brig. Gen. John Selden Roane was left in charge of military affairs in Arkansas, and was ordered on April 11 to establish his headquarters at Little Rock. Congress had just passed a conscription law, to go into effect on May 15, but it could hardly be expected to provide for the immediate defense of Arkansas.[49]

With one of the most exciting periods of Arkansas history ahead, and with reliable news desperately needed for public morale, the *Gazette* ran out of paper. For a long time the *Gazette* had purchased paper from the wholesaler Otis Goodman of St. Louis, whose salesman was still calling on customers at Little Rock as late as June of 1861.[50] Federal occupation of St. Louis had cut off this source of supply, and there was not a paper mill west of the Missis-

45. *Gazette,* Mar. 1, 13, 1862; *Daily State Journal,* Feb. 7, 1862; *Telegraph,* Feb. 12, Mar. 5, 1862; *True Democrat,* Feb. 27, Mar. 13, 1862.

46. *Telegraph,* Mar. 26, Apr. 2, Aug. 13, 1862; *True Democrat,* May 1, 1862.

47. *True Democrat,* Mar. 27, Apr. 3, 10, 1862; *Official Records,* XIII, 815.

48. *True Democrat,* May 1, 1862.

49. *Ibid.,* Mar. 13, 20, 1862; *Telegraph,* May 21, 1862.

50. *Gazette,* Apr. 20, June 22, 1861.

sippi in Southern territory.[51] Southern towns where paper mills were located fell into enemy hands in the spring of 1862, and Arkansas publishers knew that the paper on hand might be their last. They began to reduce the size of their sheets, while frantically looking for a new source of supply.

Sometime between December 14, 1861 and March 1, 1862, the *Gazette* reduced its sheet from eight to seven columns, and on March 8, 1862 began publication on a half-sheet. A year's supply of paper had been ordered from a mill at Huntsville, Alabama, but Huntsville had since been taken by the federals.[52] The seven-column half-sheet had the same format that pages two and three had formerly had. By retiring the nameplate for the duration of the paper shortage, the *Gazette* gained a few extra inches for news. Volume numbering and the statement of proprietorship, formerly a part of the front page dateline, were discontinued temporarily, and the *Gazette* now had only its one-column editorial head to identify and date it.

The Washington *Telegraph* began half-sheet publication on March 19, but kept its nameplate. The *True Democrat* discarded its nameplate when it began half-sheet publication on April 3. Advertising was limited now to legal ads, proclamations, and others considered necessary for the good of the public. Many communications from readers were left out because they were too long or not of general interest, and Johnson called for shorter obituary notices and proceedings of meetings.[53]

Danley went to Hot Springs with Borland to rest and recuperate on March 8, and soon afterwards made a trip to Richmond. The main purpose of this trip probably was to urge a course of action for the defense of Arkansas, but it was also partly to scout for paper. He was back home before May 3.[54] The last of the *Gazette's* paper was used to print the issue of May 10, and its suspension was announced. The *True Democrat's* editor expected to continue publishing for at least a year, and said he would move his press further south if Little Rock should be occupied by the federals, which he doubted.[55]

The *Gazette* missed only three issues, and Danley spent part of that time with Borland at Jester's Sulphur Springs near Hot Springs. He resumed half-sheet publication on June 7, having unexpectedly received enough paper to last "until times are better or worse." [56] He had bought this inferior wrapping paper at Augusta, Georgia for $8 a ream, and the expense of its transportation to Little Rock was greater than the cost of the paper and transportation combined would have been from Louisville, St. Louis, or Cincinnati.[57] The *Gazette* now followed the *True Democrat's* example and placed its volume number and statement of proprietorship under the editorial

51. *Telegraph,* Feb. 26, 1862.
52. *True Democrat,* May 10, 1862.
53. *Ibid.,* May 15, 1862; *Telegraph,* May 21, 1862.
54. *Gazette,* Mar. 15, Apr. 12, May 3, 1862.
55. *True Democrat,* May 15, 1862; *Telegraph,* May 21, 1862.
56. *Gazette,* June 7, 1862; *True Democrat,* June 12, 1862; *Telegraph,* June 11, 1862.
57. *Gazette,* Nov. 29, 1862.

head, but the accuracy of the volume numbering was still so uncertain that it cannot be used as an indication of missing issues. With the revival of the *Gazette,* Arkansas had only eight newspapers, not counting those of temporary publication by soldiers, as compared with 30 or 40 before the war started.[58]

News from the east side of the Mississippi was scarce and unreliable. Telegraph lines in that area were in the hands of the federal army, and the United States secretary of war imposed strict censorship regulations on telegraphic dispatches. After March 24, newspaper editors were forbidden to publish information that had been excluded from the telegraph under penalty of having their papers excluded from the mails.[59] The Confederacy had no censorship regulations except those imposed in specific areas by military commanders. In the spring of 1862, Confederate editors were requested not to publish news that might give military information to the enemy. They could publish this kind of information if they saw it in Northern newspapers, provided they did not give it additional authenticity.[60]

By the spring of 1862, the *Gazette* was receiving no subscriptions for a shorter period than six months, and was automatically discontinuing those at the end of that time. The *True Democrat* took nothing less than six months beginning September 19, 1861. The *Gazette's* rate for six months was $1.50. Advertising rates were $2 for ten lines on the first insertion, and 50 cents for each additional insertion.[61]

While General Curtis was marching from Pea Ridge through southern Missouri and northern Arkansas, hoping to capture Little Rock, another federal column under Brig. Gen. Frederick Steele was marching from southeast Missouri with orders to take Pitman's Ferry, Pocahontas, Jacksonport, Batesville, and Helena.[62] There could hardly have been a situation better calculated to vindicate Governor Rector's repeated attempts to maintain a separate state army, for it looked now as if Arkansas would be defended mostly by a citizens' army.

When news came on May 4 that Curtis' advance was at Grand Glaize and apparently was headed for Little Rock, Rector sent word to General Roane at Pine Bluff that he must do something in the way of military defense, and telegraphed Beauregard and Van Dorn for permission to stop some Texas regiments en route for Corinth. Roane stopped them before he had this authority, and also stopped sending recruits to Van Dorn.[63]

Rector issued a proclamation dated May 5, calling for volunteers for state service and promising they would not be transferred to the Confederacy without their individual consent. He gave vent to his bitterness against the Confederacy for abandoning Arkansas, threatened that Arkansas might secede

58. *True Democrat,* June 12, 19, 1862.
59. Frank Moore (ed.), *The Rebellion Record: A Diary of American Events, 1860–'62* (New York: G. P. Putnam, 1862), Part XXI, 67.
60. *True Democrat,* Mar. 6, 27, 1862.
61. *Gazette,* Mar. 1, June 7, 28, 1862.
62. *Official Records,* VIII, 578–580.
63. *Ibid.,* XIII, 933–934; *True Democrat,* May 29, 1862.

from the Confederacy, and implied an invitation to other states west of the Mississippi to join Arkansas in forming a new government. Confederate editors saw it as treason, and Northern editors as evidence that the South was sick of its bargain, while Arkansas editors could only say that the governor spoke for nobody but himself.[64]

About the same time, Rector ordered the removal of the seat of government from Little Rock, to prevent its capture. The clumsily managed move had all the elements of a slapstick comic opera, and showed that the governor was literally frightened out of his wits. The Supreme Court did not receive the order and ignored its unofficial information, and never left Little Rock. The other state departments and agencies, with their records hastily packed in boxes, went to Hot Springs, where the seat of government was established without public announcement. People having business with the various state offices could not be sure where they were, and some of Rector's antagonists contended that legally the seat of government was still at Little Rock.[65]

The forces of Steele and Curtis united at Batesville about the middle of May, and paused to reorganize. Curtis did not show signs of giving up his march to Little Rock until the latter part of May, and in the meantime his advance guard came as close as Searcy, 49 miles from Little Rock.[66]

On May 14, Van Dorn wired Roane orders to assume command of all forces in Arkansas and defend the state. In the next few days, Roane gathered supplies for an army, took the first steps to put the conscription law into operation, and threw a few troops forward to harass Curtis' advance. On May 19, he declared martial law over a 20-mile area surrounding Little Rock, and strict regulations were announced by George C. Watkins as provost marshal. The *True Democrat* heartily approved, and suggested that Roane should extend Watkins' authority over the entire state. Said Johnson, "The flight of the Executive from Little Rock has left the State without any government whatever, at a time when it was most needed, and we should like to see Gen. Roane supply the want as far as it lies in his power." [67]

Johnson knew that Rector had returned to Little Rock on May 16, and Rector said his remarks were a deliberate misrepresentation. On May 21, he sent Johnson a note demanding a retraction and asking whether the editorial was intended to advocate overthrow of the civil government in favor of a military government. Johnson refused to make a retraction, and named Capt. Charles A. Carroll as his friend who would handle further correspondence on the subject. Rector then demanded satisfaction, sending the challenge by Edmund Burgevin.

64. Henry M. Rector, *Governor's Message,* Nov. 3, 1862, 9–15; New York *Herald,* May 22, 1862; *True Democrat,* May 8, June 12, 19, 1862; *Telegraph,* May 28, 1862; *Gazette,* June 14, 1862.

65. *True Democrat,* May 22, July 3, 1862; *Gazette,* June 28, Sept. 6, 1862; William R. Miller, *Auditor's Report,* Nov. 5, 1862, 2, 6.

66. *Official Records,* XIII, 378, 369–371, 375–376, 384, 397–398.

67. *True Democrat,* May 15, 22, 29, 1862.

Burgevin found several points on which he could disagree with Carroll, and Carroll modified all but one to suit Burgevin. Carroll would not concede that both duellists should have a voice in choosing the time and place and Burgevin made this his excuse for backing out of the duel. Johnson published the correspondence in the *True Democrat* on May 29. When the *Gazette* resumed publication on June 7, Danley said the point of disagreement was trivial, that Rector had come off second best in the correspondence, and that it was another case of a challenge without any intention of actually fighting a duel.

This unpleasant episode did not stop the *True Democrat's* criticism of the move of the seat of government, but Johnson had little room to ridicule Rector for this. It was said that he moved most of his stock of paper out of town when Little Rock was threatened, and that he arranged for a Little Rock man to occupy his home about that time, as he expected to be absent.[68]

Senator Robert Ward Johnson arrived at Little Rock a few days after the archives left, and went to Corinth about the middle of May to try to persuade Beauregard to send Van Dorn's army back to Arkansas to repel Curtis. Beauregard refused, but agreed to allow the Texas troops to stop in Arkansas and sent Roane orders to assume authority and defend the state. Shortly afterwards, he created the Trans-Mississippi District as a subdivision of his department, and at Johnson's request, assigned Maj. Gen. Thomas C. Hindman as its commander. At the same time, pressure was applied in Richmond for the defense of Arkansas, and the secretary of war responded by creating the Trans-Mississippi Department. Coincidentally, the orders creating the district and the department were both issued on May 26.[69] The secretary of war's orders eventually would supersede Beauregard's, but meanwhile there was a 70-day reign of terror in Arkansas under Hindman's rule.

With almost no army, no materials of war, no supplies, and a population that had not yet come to grips with all-out war on home ground, no faint-hearted man could have saved Arkansas. This was Hindman's explanation for the ruthlessness that made him the most despised man in Arkansas. "I have come here to drive out the invader, or perish in the attempt," he declared as he assumed command at Little Rock on May 31.[70]

Memphis was being evacuated by the Confederates when Hindman passed through on his way to Arkansas, and fell to the Union on June 6. Because he was practically cut off from the rest of the Confederacy, he tried to make his district self-supporting by establishing factories and otherwise arranging to supply his own needs.

Faced with the necessity of raising an army mostly by conscription, Hindman's first step was to eliminate Rector's volunteer state army. He informed Rector that he would conscript his volunteers and impress his stores. Rector knew it was no idle threat, and he promptly transferred his troops and mili-

68. Little Rock *Arkansas Patriot,* Oct. 2, 1862.
69. *Official Records,* XIII, 28, 814–816, 829; IX, 713; X, Part II, 547.
70. *Ibid.,* XIII, 830; *True Democrat,* June 5, 1862; *Telegraph,* June 11, 1862.

tary property to the Confederacy.[71] Hindman began rigid enforcement of the conscription law, dragging into service every man eligible for conscription and many who were legally exempt. He had guerrilla companies organized as home guard units, composed of men unable to perform regular military duty. He sent to Texas for some regiments, and made Brig. Gen. Albert Pike send more from the Indian country. He impressed domestic arms and ammunition, and even used public documents in the state library for cartridge paper.[72]

An act of the Confederate Congress authorized military commanders to order cotton burned if it was in danger of falling into the hands of the enemy. Hindman destroyed vast quantities of cotton in Arkansas, and established depositories for storage of cotton preparatory to burning if necessary. Many people felt that this should not be done until the last possible moment before the arrival of enemy troops having a reasonable prospect of victory, but they were slow to speak their minds because Hindman ordered the arrest as traitors of all who resisted the order.[73]

Hindman extended martial law to cover all of Pulaski County on June 10, to apply also to a five-mile area around Fort Smith and Van Buren on June 17, and to cover the entire Trans-Mississippi District on June 30. Few aspects of civilian life escaped minute regulation, and there was a long list of offenses that would cause the offender to be arrested for treason and dealt with accordingly. Col. Benjamin F. Danley, who had returned to Arkansas with Hindman, was the provost marshal, charged with the execution of martial law.[74]

Under Hindman's tyrannical rule, the people suffered more hardships and loss of freedom than they ever experienced at the hands of an enemy, but few dared to protest. The *True Democrat* sustained Hindman every step of the way, probably because Senator Johnson had specifically requested him as the district's commander. Johnson also sustained Hindman in the Senate, when the protests against his course came before Congress.[75]

When Curtis halted his march at Batesville, throwing his advance guard out to Searcy, he planned to continue to Little Rock. But with his army reduced by the transfer of his infantry to the east side of the Mississippi, with his supply line from Missouri cut, and believing Hindman's army was larger than it was, he decided to march to Clarendon to meet a supply boat. He withdrew his advance on June 5, and marched out of Batesville on June 24, reaching Clarendon on July 8. Learning that the supply boat had not waited for him, he headed for Helena. About the middle of July his nearly starving

71. *Official Records,* XIII, 31, 829–830; *True Democrat,* June 5, 1862; *Gazette,* June 7, 1862; *Telegraph,* June 11, 1862.
72. *Official Records,* XIII, 30–34, 934.
73. *Ibid.,* 33–34; *True Democrat,* May 15, June 12 ,1862; *Telegraph,* May 21, 1862.
74. *Official Records,* XIII, 835–836; *True Democrat,* June 12, July 3, 1862.
75. *Patriot,* Nov. 6, 13, 1862.

army reached Helena, where he established his headquarters in Hindman's home.[76]

While Curtis was marching across Arkansas, a commander for the Confederate Trans-Mississippi Department was being selected at Richmond, and Sterling Price was again the favorite of a large circle of admirers. Christopher Danley was not among them, having witnessed some of the demonstrations in Price's favor on his trip to Richmond. On June 14, the *Gazette* chided Price for his "overweening vanity" that led him to arrange a public show of admiration for himself. Price had no particular military ability, said Danley, but would do very well so long as he had a superior officer to restrain him.

Maj. Gen. Theophilus Hunter Holmes was assigned to command the department, and reached Little Rock on August 12. He placed Hindman in command of the District of Arkansas, composed of Arkansas, Missouri, and the Indian country,[77] and busied himself with administrative details. Holmes was under instructions from President Davis to end some of the policies Hindman had adopted that were the basis for many complaints.[78] However, it was soon apparent that Hindman had the stronger will, and that Holmes would make no important changes. The people slowly came to realize that the man who should have been their deliverer was completely under Hindman's spell.

One who was not afraid to buck Hindman was Brig. Gen. Albert Pike, who had fumed over the liberties Van Dorn had taken with his command and who had found his lot infinitely worse under Hindman's command. Beginning about June 24, Pike wrote long letters of protest to everybody he thought could change the situation, sending copies of most of them to the newspapers. Finally on July 12, he resigned his commission in the Confederate army.[79] Acceptance of his resignation was withheld at Hindman's request, to keep him subject to court martial for circulars he had distributed among the Indians. Holmes backed Hindman up in this, but granted Pike a leave of absence. With a wagon load of books from his personal library, Pike went to Grayson, Texas to await action on his resignation.

He reported to Holmes on October 23 that he had decided to resume his command, his leave of absence having expired. The next day he began another long series of complaining letters. On October 27, the secretary of war notified Holmes that Pike's resignation had been accepted.[80] Pike was arrested on November 14 on Hindman's order for commanding without authority. He had preferred charges against Hindman in August, and on November 19 he also preferred charges against Holmes. Both were ignored in Richmond. Pike was brought to Little Rock and released. In December,

76. New York *Tribune,* Aug. 6, 1862.
77. *Official Records,* IX, 731; XIII, 855, 860, 876–877; *True Democrat,* Aug. 13, 1862.
78. *Official Records,* XIII, 874, 886–887; *Telegraph,* Oct. 8, 1862.
79. *Official Records,* XIII, 841–844, 846–851, 856–858, 936–943, 948–950, 954–962; *Telegraph,* Sept. 17, 1862.
80. *Official Records,* XIII, 906–907.

1862, he wrote an open letter to Holmes, and published it as a pamphlet in February, 1863. He went to Richmond to press the matter, but could stir up no interest in it, and retired to civilian life in southwest Arkansas.

Among the serious offenses Pike charged against Hindman was muzzling the press. Edward W. Gantt, who was released from military prison and returned to his home at Washington early in November,[81] saw it as a coalition between Hindman and the Johnsons for their mutual benefit, each making the other his tool from time to time. It was his theory that both Little Rock newspapers were subservient to Hindman, and that their silence on the subject of his oppression was bought by his appointments of the close relatives of the editors to positions of influence.

The editors did indeed withhold much information about Hindman's activities. About August, a weekly newspaper called the *Army Bulletin,* by Gould and Briley, began publication from Hindman's headquarters, and contained the military information that Hindman was willing to have published.[82] At no time did Johnson and Danley indicate that they were not free to ignore Hindman's requests that they withhold certain information, but Hindman made it clear that all his requests were orders.

On July 31, the state archives left Hot Springs in wagons, and reached Little Rock on August 2. This removed Hindman's best excuse for martial law. Probably Rector's decision to return the seat of government to Little Rock was influenced by his precarious political position. It was apparent that Johnson and Danley intended to force a gubernatorial election that would put him out of office, though he had served only half of the four-year term for which he had been elected.

The new Constitution provided for most constitutional officers to complete the terms for which they had been elected, but this clause did not specifically mention the governor and several others, and set the date for the first election as the first Monday in October. Rector did not believe the Convention had deliberately omitted his office from the list of those entitled to complete the current term. But since there had been a threat of deposing him, it seems likely that it was indeed intentional, and that it may have been planned not to call attention to it unless it should be necessary for the good of the state to get him out of office. Rector's friends said George C. Watkins wrote the clause, but Johnson denied it and said he himself had had no agency in it and no knowledge of it at the time.[83]

As early as February 20, 1862, Johnson had commented in the *True Democrat* that June or July would be soon enough to start a canvass, and had casually remarked that "a Governor, members of the Military Board and all State officers" would be elected in October.

No candidates had announced for any office on June 2, when somebody at Little Rock wrote a letter to the *Telegraph* over the signature "Vindex."

81. *Telegraph,* Nov. 5, 26, 1862.
82. *True Democrat* Aug. 20, 1862.
83. *Ibid.,* Aug. 6, 20, 1862.

He quoted the Constitution on the subject of the election, concluded that it applied to the office of governor, and mentioned Watkins and Harris Flanagin as possible candidates. The *Telegraph* published the letter on June 11, and the *True Democrat* reprinted it on June 19, and the *Gazette* on June 21, both Little Rock papers endorsing it fully. "Vindex" wrote again on June 25, pointing out the necessity of electing two new advisory members of the Military Board.[84]

Rector's election proclamation early in July did not include the offices of governor and the Military Board. Danley, in the *Gazette* of July 12, argued that the sheriffs should be compelled to include those offices, and "Vindex" wrote on July 17 of the dangers of allowing a governor and a Military Board to serve without constitutional authority.[85]

Danley and Johnson called upon Pulaski County Sheriff Thomas Fletcher to include the questionable offices in his election proclamation, and Fletcher refused, unless compelled by legal authority. Danley and Johnson then submitted a petition for mandamus to Judge John J. Clendenin of the Pulaski Circuit Court, which Clendenin refused to grant. They then took it to the Supreme Court. The opinion, written by Justice H. F. Fairchild, was handed down between August 13 and 16. The court held that the Constitution did indeed cut short the governor's term of office, as well as three others then filled by the legislature, those of secretary of state, auditor, and treasurer.[86]

Rector considered the court's opinion advisory and not mandatory upon the executive, but he issued a new election proclamation on August 16, and included in it the offices of governor and two advisory members of the Military Board.[87] He declared himself a candidate for re-election in a circular issued on August 22, in which he defended his proclamation of May 5, his move of the seat of government, and his pocket veto of the act abolishing the militia. He also presented some arguments against the Supreme Court's decision, all of which Johnson and Eakin ably refuted.[88]

A recommendation of Harris Flanagin for governor, dated August 21, was circulated at Little Rock and gathered 20 signatures of men from Pulaski and several other counties, with eight others added later. Elias Conway's name led the list, but neither Little Rock editor signed it.[89] The *Gazette* placed Flanagin's name under its editorial head on August 23,[90] and the *True Democrat* did the same on August 27, with further endorsements.

John S. H. Rainey of Camden announced his candidacy on August 28, backed by a card signed by 56 Camden men calling upon him to run. He published a circular, but said he could not canvass the state.[91]

84. *Telegraph,* July 2, 1862.
85. *Ibid.,* July 23, 1862.
86. Danley and Johnson, *Ex Parte,* June Term 1862, 24 *Ark.* 1–6; *Gazette,* Aug. 16, 1862; *True Democrat,* Aug. 20, 1862.
87. *True Democrat,* Aug. 20, 1862.
88. *Ibid.,* Sept. 3, 10, 1862; *Telegraph,* Sept. 10, 1862.
89. *True Democrat,* Aug. 27, Sept. 3, 1862.
90. *Telegraph,* Sept. 10, 1862.
91. *Ibid.,* Sept. 3, 17, 1862; *True Democrat,* Sept. 10, 17, 1862.

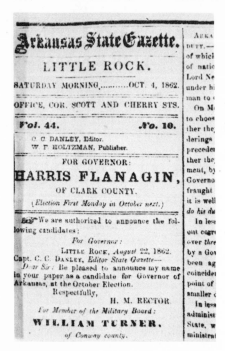

When the True Democrat received two letters and several verbal recommendations of Danley for state senator from Pulaski and Prairie counties, Johnson said the best way was to draft him. Danley said he would serve if elected, but would not exert himself to get the office.[92]

The *Gazette* and the *True Democrat* waged an aggressive campaign for Flanagin, with the help of several other papers, including the Pine Bluff *True Southron* and the Fort Smith *Bulletin*. It was more a campaign against Rector than for Flanagin, relying heavily upon a recital of the incumbent's blunders. Flanagin was then serving as colonel of the Second Arkansas Mounted Rifles in Tennessee and later in Kentucky, and was not heard from on the subject of his candidacy. It has been said that he did not even know he was a candidate, but when it was murmured that he would not accept the office if elected, the *Gazette* and the *True Democrat* emphatically assured the people that he would.[93]

Rector's most persuasive campaign argument was that he had been persecuted by the old Dynasty machine, now strengthened by its alliance with Danley. He was supported by the *Ouachita Herald* of Camden and the *War Bulletin* of Pine Bluff.[94] On September 25, James D. Butler started the

92. *True Democrat*, Aug. 27, 1862; *Gazette*, Aug. 30, Sept. 3, 1862.
93. *Gazette*, Sept. 27, 1862; *True Democrat*, Oct. 1, 1862.
94. *Gazette*, Sept. 13, 1862; *True Democrat*, Sept. 17, 1862.

Arkansas Patriot at Little Rock and gave Rector enthusiastic support, but published only two issues before election day.

The friends of both Flanagin and Rector saw Rainey's candidacy as nothing more than a vote splitter, each contending it would be an advantage to the other, and urging him to withdraw.[95]

The election was held October 6, and some of the Arkansas regiments serving outside the state were allowed to vote. Flanagin's regiment voted unanimously for their commander, who also received most of the votes of the other regiments stationed in the vicinity. The official vote was not certified until the middle of November. Flanagin received 18,189, Rector 7,419, and Rainey 708. Five counties in eastern Arkansas made no returns, probably because they were occupied by Curtis' army.[96]

Danley lost the election for the state Senate, receiving only 164 votes in Pulaski County out of 741 votes cast.[97] The Prairie County vote in this race was not published.

Danley set out for Richmond on the morning of October 29, 1862, on government business, the nature of which was not disclosed. Two miles from Little Rock, he was thrown from his buggy and dashed against the rocks at the side of the road. He was brought back to Little Rock in an ambulance, and it was found that he had a compound fracture of the right arm, a broken right thigh bone, and a fractured patella. The arm was so badly crushed that an immediate amputation above the elbow was necessary. His physicians, Dr. Philo O. Hooper and Dr. Craven Peyton, reported that he came safely through the operation and was on the road to recovery.[98] Since he lived at the *Gazette* building, he was soon able to resume some of his duties, but he never fully recovered from this accident, and was an invalid the rest of his life.

The high price of paper and other supplies forced another rise in subscription rates on October 4, 1862, to $3 a year or $2 for six months. The *Telegraph* doubled its rates on November 12, making it $5 a year or $3 for six months, with the explanation that the price of paper had increased fivefold, and in addition there were the risk and expense of its transportation. The *True Democrat* reduced its sheet from seven to four columns and refused to accept new subscribers on October 22, because its paper supply was almost exhausted. By December 3, it had been replenished and the sheet was again seven columns on December 10, but the rates were raised to match the *Telegraph's*. The *Gazette* reduced its sheet to four columns with the

95. *Gazette,* Sept. 3, 1862; *True Democrat,* Sept. 10, 1862.
96. *True Democrat,* Nov. 12, 1862; *Telegraph,* Nov. 12, 1862.
97. *Patriot,* Oct. 9, 1862.
98. *Gazette,* Nov. 1, 1862; *Telegraph,* Nov. 5, 1862; *True Democrat,* Nov. 5, 1862; C. C. Danley Estate Papers, Folder No. 137, Pulaski County Probate Files. No part of the doctors' bills had been paid when Danley died in 1865. Dr. Hooper presented a bill for $771, covering the period from Oct. 29, 1862 through Sept. 25, 1865. Dr. Peyton evidently was called in to assist with the surgery and set the broken leg, and his bill was $200.

issue of November 1 and did not return to the larger sheet, but raised its rates to $5 a year or $3 for six months on December 6.

Besides the cost of the paper itself, the expense of its transportation had skyrocketed, since Southern railroads were busy carrying troops and munitions of war, and river transportation had become impossible. Paper was brought to Vicksburg and thence to Monroe, from which point it could be brought to Arkansas only by wagon, at enormous prices.[99]

During this period Danley was issuing shinplasters, or change tickets, for making change in the absence of small bills. It was illegal, but many business men ignored the law and the penalty of $50 to $300 fine and imprisonment of up to twelve months was rarely if ever imposed. Shinplasters had become a nuisance because many who issued them could not or would not redeem them.

Danley's were considered sound, and were among the few that were generally accepted by merchants. They were difficult to counterfeit, but one spurious one turned up at Pine Bluff in December, and several others in Pike County in April. Those in Pike County did not even follow the form used by Danley.[100]

When the legislature convened on November 5, Rector delivered a long farewell address that ended with his resignation. Thomas Fletcher, president of the Senate, served as acting governor until Flanagin's inauguration on November 15.[101]

Since the two Confederate senators had been elected at a special session and the Confederate Constitution stipulated that they should be elected at a regular session, the legislature confirmed the earlier election. This was for the benefit of Charles B. Mitchel, who had drawn the long term. Robert Ward Johnson had drawn the short term and was up for re-election at this session. The anti-Johnson forces concentrated on Augustus Hill Garland, and it took twelve ballots to elect Johnson, 46 to 42, with two votes cast for Felix I. Batson, who was not in nomination.[102]

The *Patriot* made Johnson's support of Hindman an issue against him, and Johnson made a long speech to the legislature defending his action in bringing Hindman back to Arkansas and his subsequent support of him in the Senate.[103]

Martial law had become a problem in other parts of the Confederacy too, and Grandison D. Royston had had help from other members of the Arkansas delegation and some from other states in his attempt to end it in Arkansas by congressional action. The House had passed a resolution stating that only the president had constitutional authority to declare martial law, but the Senate had failed to act upon it, and many people believed Hindman

99. *Gazette,* Nov. 29, 1862.
100. *True Democrat,* Dec. 31, 1862; Apr. 29, 1863; *Patriot,* Dec. 18, 1862.
101. *True Democrat,* Nov. 5, 1862; *Telegraph,* Dec. 3, 1862.
102. *True Democrat,* Nov. 12, 1862; *Telegraph,* Nov. 26, 1862.
103. *Patriot,* Oct. 30, Nov. 6, 13, 1862; *Official Records,* XIII, 913.

was protected by Senator Johnson and President Davis.[104] On October 11, the secretary of war had directed Holmes to rescind martial law. He issued no order revoking it, but did issue one on November 13 saying that since the legislature was in session, it was no longer necessary for military authorities to take action on any matter pertaining to the well being of the people.[105] He later said he "quietly dispensed" with martial law, but Hindman's critics said many of its objectionable features remained in effect.

During Rector's administration, some of the most profitable printing jobs had been given to James D. Butler, who operated a job press after the *Old Line Democrat* suspended and before the *Arkansas Patriot* began. Richard H. Johnson and Reuben S. Yerkes, as official public printers, contended that the auditor had no legal authority to draw warrants for public printing payable to anybody except the public printer. There was considerable wrangling over this about the time the legislature convened, and it was impossible to determine how many of the accusations made by the two editors were entitled to credence or on which side justice lay.[106]

Danley and Holtzman showed no interest in the public printing, and it looked as if the contest would be entirely between the *True Democrat* and the *Patriot*. But the legislature avoided taking sides in their current dispute by electing William H. Etter and John R. Eakin, publisher and editor of the Washington *Telegraph,* as public printers on November 26. It would be an unprofitable job, because the legislature's prices for printing failed to allow for the high cost of materials. Johnson said he could sell the paper for the price paid for the printing.[107]

One of the two counties created by this General Assembly was Woodruff County, named in honor of William E. Woodruff, founder of the *Gazette*. It was taken from the lower part of Jackson County and the western end of St. Francis County.[108]

Holmes was notified on October 17 of his promotion to lieutenant general.[109] He more or less agreed with his superiors that his first goal should be to regain Helena, but Hindman had managed to get his tentative approval of his plan to lead an expedition to reclaim Missouri through northwest Arkansas. His corps was at the western end of the line near Fort Smith.

Holmes ordered Hindman on November 15 to bring most of his corps to Little Rock to prepare to march on Helena. But Hindman tarried long enough to fight the Missouri-based forces of Brig. Gen. James G. Blunt and Brig. Gen. Francis J. Herron at Prairie Grove on December 7. There was no clear-cut victor when darkness closed the battle for the day, but Hindman had outfought the federals most of the day.

104. *Telegraph,* Sept. 24, Oct. 8, Nov. 12, 1862.

105. *Official Records,* XIII, 886–887, 915.

106. *Patriot,* Oct. 9, Nov. 13, 27, 1862; *True Democrat,* Nov. 26, Dec. 3, 1862.

107. *Gazette,* Nov. 29, 1862; *Telegraph,* Dec. 3, 17, 1862; *True Democrat,* Dec. 3, 1862.

108. *True Democrat,* Nov. 26, 1862.

109. *Official Records,* XIII, 906–907.

Meanwhile, the federal expedition against Vicksburg had failed, and the federal forces doubled back to capture the weak and insignificant Confederate garrison at Arkansas Post on January 11, mostly as a morale booster. Hindman was ten miles below Lewisburg when he learned of this, and his ragged, half-starved, demoralized army reached Little Rock on January 14.

Rumors that the federals were following up their victory at Arkansas Post and the advantages they had gained in western Arkansas by a march on Little Rock from two directions caused many to believe that federal occupation of the capital city was imminent. Dick Johnson decided that his office was too large and transportation facilities too limited to allow him to move the *True Democrat* for refugee publication. But he vowed he would never publish a paper under federal control or sufferance, and informed his readers that any newspaper that might come to them under those circumstances should not be attributed to him, even if it should bear his paper's title.[110] The *Gazette* office would have been equally difficult to move, and had the added disadvantage of an invalid editor, physically unable to endure the hardships of displacement.

Changes in the command of the Trans-Mississippi Confederate army were made soon after this, in response to the demands of the Arkansas congressional delegation and Governor Flanagin, reflecting the dissatisfaction of everybody concerned. Lt. Gen. Edmund Kirby Smith assumed command of the department on March 7, moving its headquarters first to Alexandria and on April 24 to Shreveport. Holmes was retained as Smith's subordinate, commanding the District of Arkansas, with headquarters at Little Rock. Hindman, as eager to leave Holmes' command as the people were to get rid of him, was transferred east of the Mississippi, and Sterling Price was sent from Mississippi to take his place.

As Grant's siege of Vicksburg and Port Hudson continued, the optimistic predictions of the previous spring that the federal blockade of the Mississippi River would soon be lifted were no longer heard in Arkansas. Supplies of all kinds from east of the Mississippi became more and more difficult to obtain, and nothing was scarcer than paper. The *Gazette* used the last of its supply with the issue of February 28, 1863, and announced a temporary suspension.[111]

It was not easy to convince the people that newspaper space should be saved for items having general interest. They continued to submit obituary notices that sometimes covered five or six pages of foolscap, and were more sentimental than informative. Dick Johnson said they showed "a selfishness in their grief that is not commendable," and on April 15, he limited free obituaries to five lines for civilians and ten lines for soldiers, and said he would charge 20 cents for every line in excess of that. By the end of the year, the *Telegraph* announced that it would no longer publish obituaries,

110. *True Democrat,* Jan. 21, 1863.
111. *Ibid.,* Mar. 4, 1863; *Telegraph,* Mar. 11, 1863.

and also declined advertisements that were not important to the general public.[112] But the people continued to send obituaries, and the soft-hearted Eakin continued to publish them.

Reuben Yerkes, publisher of the *True Democrat,* left for Georgia in April to buy paper, and the *True Democrat's* sheet was reduced from seven to four columns with the issue of May 6, in an effort to keep it in business until his return. While Yerkes waited at Natchez for a chance to cross the river with the paper he had obtained, the supply at home was exhausted. Johnson had a small quantity left, but not enough to print one regular issue of 10,000 copies, and he decided to use it instead for bulletins. On July 8, he printed the last issue of the *True Democrat* on coarse brown wrapping paper. The fall of Vicksburg on July 4 cut off all hope of replenishing the paper supply, and the *True Democrat* never resumed publication.

Meanwhile, Danley had received some paper and the *Gazette* had resumed on May 30.[113] No Arkansas paper is known to have been printed on wall paper during the Civil War, but Danley advertised in the *Gazette* of July 11 for yellow straw or Manilla wrapping paper, not less than 19 by 25 inches, and presumably planned to use it for the *Gazette* when his current supply of paper was gone. He had used a similar grade of paper during much of 1862. Advertising rates were now up to $2 for every insertion for a square of ten lines or less.[114]

The imperfections of Confederate military records at Richmond had long caused much concern, because they did not credit Arkansas with the full number of soldiers she had sent to the Confederate army. This weakened arguments that Arkansas had sent too many men to the army to have so few troops on her own soil, and that she had not had her fair share of general officers. All efforts to correct the records had failed.

John F. Wheeler, a veteran Fort Smith editor, suggested the organization of a statewide historical society, having collection and preservation of military records and other wartime documents as one of its principal objectives, but soliciting other types of historical material as well. On June 20, 1863, the State Historical Society was organized at the *Gazette* office. The press was well represented in its officers, and several had served the *Gazette* as editor. Danley was elected president, and John E. Knight corresponding secretary. The vice presidents were William E. Woodruff, Harris Flanagin, William Read Miller, William Quesenbury, John R. Eakin, David Walker, John S. Horner, George C. Watkins, and John W. Woodward. They were expected to write papers relating to Arkansas history, and at least one secretary in each county was to be appointed to gather source material. Several contributions were made to the collection,[115] but the organization did not survive the war.

112. *Telegraph,* Dec. 2, 1863.
113. *Ibid.,* June 3, 1863; *True Democrat,* May 27, 1863.
114. *Gazette,* June 13, 1863.
115. *Ibid.,* July 4, 1863; Little Rock *National Democrat,* Jan. 16, 1864.

After months of indecision, Holmes attacked Helena on July 4. He commanded the expedition, his first field duty since his arrival in Arkansas, and was badly defeated.

The defeat of Gen. Robert E. Lee's Army of Northern Virginia at Gettysburg on July 3 was a far greater disaster, and the surrender of Vicksburg on July 4 and of Port Hudson on July 8 gave the federals complete control of the Mississippi River, dividing the Confederacy into two parts that must operate independently of each other.

The campaign for the Confederate Congress was just getting under way when the battle of Helena was fought. The *Gazette's* price for announcing a candidate for this race was $25 in advance.[116] The *Gazette,* the *Telegraph,* and the Camden *Herald* wanted all four incumbents re-elected without opposition, because of the disunifying effect of a hard-fought campaign. The *True Democrat* supported incumbents Felix I. Batson in the First District and Grandison D. Royston in the Second, but said it would support any well qualified opponent of Augustus H. Garland in the Third District and Thomas B. Hanly in the Fourth. [117] But neither the *Gazette* nor the *True Democrat* remained in business during the crucial weeks of the campaign. When the election was held on November 4, most of the First and Fourth Districts were occupied by federal troops, and a regular election was held only in the Second and Third Districts. As late as January of 1864, only Garland and his brother, Rufus King Garland, who had defeated Royston, were sure they had won.

The fall of Vicksburg made possible the execution of long delayed plans for other operations. By the middle of July, a new federal offensive was beginning in Arkansas, with an army commanded by Maj. Gen. James G. Blunt marching from Fort Scott, Kansas through the Indian country to capture Fort Smith, and another army commanded by Maj. Gen. Frederick Steele preparing to march from Helena to capture Little Rock. Steele had the support of Brig. Gen. John W. Davidson's cavalry from southeast Missouri, which took the field more than three weeks before the main body left Helena.

On July 23, Holmes temporarily relinquished the command of his district to Price, saying he was ill. Price knew he could not save Little Rock, but for the sake of morale, he went through the motions of preparing to defend the city. He concentrated his infantry near Little Rock and threw his cavalry forward to retard the federal advance, while he hastily built fortifications and quietly evacuated the public stores to southwest Arkansas.[118] Governor Flanagin also moved the state offices and archives to safety, and the seat of government finally came to rest at Washington.

Many civilians left their homes at Little Rock to live as refugees in southwest Arkansas or Texas. The able bodied men who remained, regardless of

116. *Gazette,* July 11, 1863.
117. *True Democrat,* June 24, 1863.
118. *Official Records,* XXII, Part I, 520.

age, were expected to help defend the city. There was strong civilian opposition to calling out the militia, even in this emergency. William E. Woodruff, now almost 68, was said to be in the trenches every day from eight in the morning until eight at night, and Henry M. Rector and his old enemy, Robert Ward Johnson, were reported to be "fighting side by side in the intrenchments." [119]

When Davidson's cavalry dislodged the Confederate cavalry from Brownsville on August 25, the Confederates fell back to Price's first line of defense, the fortifications on the south side of Bayou Meto, about 12 miles east of Little Rock. Too late, Price realized that this position was untenable, and that he would have to concentrate on his last line of defense, a line of rifle pits and other defensive works on the north side of the Arkansas River and extending about two and a half miles in front of Little Rock. The cavalry fought Davidson at Reed's Bridge over Bayou Meto on August 27, and then fell back nearer Little Rock.

Early in the morning of September 10, while Steele's infantry marched up the north side of the river to attack the fortifications, Davidson's cavalry crossed to the south side near Terry's Ferry, about eight miles below the city, with a diversionary move at nearby Buck's Ford. Their crossing was contested in both places by the Confederate cavalry, which fell back about five miles to Fourche Bayou to make another stand. The firing at Buck's Ford and Terry's Ferry told Price that his fortifications would be useless, and he quickly began an orderly evacuation, sending Marmaduke's cavalry and part of the infantry to Fourche Bayou to delay the federal cavalry and cover the Confederate retreat southward.

It was almost dark when a part of Davidson's cavalry rode into the city on Cherry Street, now East Second. Later in the evening, Steele crossed the river on one of the partially burned pontoon bridges.

Meanwhile, Brig. Gen. William L. Cabell had directed the removal of Confederate government property from Fort Smith, and had fought the final engagement in resistance of Blunt's advance on August 31 at Backbone Mountain, 16 miles southeast of Fort Smith. Blunt had taken possession of Fort Smith on September 1.

The first steps to re-establish civil government under federal authority began soon after the United States flag was raised at Little Rock and Fort Smith. The differences of opinion that divided the nation on the subject of reconstruction were present in Arkansas, as two distinct political factions emerged, but there was at first no sharp line of distinction. Members of the more extreme faction in Arkansas first called themselves Unconditional Unionists, then Radical Unionists, and finally Radical Republicans. They wanted a total destruction of the South's economic and political power, and believed it could be accomplished only by fighting the war until the last rebel was crushed in defeat, by adoption of punitive policies towards the rebellious states after their surrender, and by permanent, nationwide aboli-

119. *Telegraph,* Sept. 9, 1863.

tion of slavery without delay. The opposing faction was known nationally as the Peace Democrats and was derisively nicknamed the Copperheads, but applied no official name to itself locally. It was more conservative, its members favoring a negotiated peace, a policy of kindness and conciliation that would make it easier for rebels to return to their old loyalty, and a system of gradual emancipation in the loyal states that would make the transition easier for both races. Steele was a Conservative and Davidson was a Radical.

Mass meetings were held and union clubs were organized, with military personnel prominently involved. The civilians who voluntarily took the oath of allegiance to the United States and participated in this movement were at first few in number, but they were important as a means of giving it the appearance of a spontaneous popular movement back to the union.

Danley and Holtzman had published the last issue of the *Gazette* on September 5, and had most of the issue for September 12 in type when the federal army entered the city, but it was never printed.[120] Holtzman took the oath early in the occupation and was active in the union club, for he was one of ten whose signatures were on an invitation for Col. C. C. Andrews to address the club, dated November 9.[121]

According to local gossip, Davidson sent a message to Danley, asking him to continue publication of the *Gazette* as a union newspaper, but Danley declined, saying he would make a better federal prisoner than a federal editor. Davidson then issued his Special Order No. 1, dated September 12: "J. W. Demby is hereby authorized to take possession of the office of the Little Rock *Gazette,* and enter upon the duties of editor and proprietor of the same." Within a few days, Demby had published the first issue of *The National Union* from the *Gazette* office. Its tone was more in line with Steele's conciliatory policies than with Davidson's Radical views,[122] which probably explains why no reference is found to a second issue.

Little Rock's second federal newspaper was even stronger in its conservatism, and Davidson gave Steele's headquarters full credit for its establishment and protection. This paper was the *National Democrat,* edited and published by Dr. Cincinnatus V. Meador at the office of the *True Democrat.* Meador made arrangements with Reuben Yerkes to rent the office, and hired Yerkes as a printer.[123] Its first issue probably appeared on Tuesday, September 19, 1863.[124]

On October 8, Valentine Dell began publication of the *Fort Smith New*

120. *Gazette,* Nov. 20, 1869.

121. C. C. Andrews, *Early Steps in Reconstruction; Speeches by General C. C. Andrews, of Minnesota, In Texas and Arkansas* (Washington, D. C.: Union Republican Congressional Committee, n.d.), 4.

122. *Telegraph,* Sept. 30, 1863.

123. Papers in the case of Yerkes v. Meador, assumpsit, Pulaski Circuit Court, May Term 1865, in the library of Margaret Ross.

124. Date figured from the earliest available issue, Vol. I, No. 4, dated Oct. 20, 1863. The issue of Oct. 6 is mentioned in the *Telegraph,* Oct. 14, 1863.

Era, which was also dependent upon army headquarters for paper and telegraphic dispatches,[125] and was strongly Radical in policy.

The Radicals at Little Rock sent a delegation to Washington in November to request permission and instructions for reorganization of the state government, but those at Fort Smith about the same time simply usurped the authority to put the machinery in motion. They called a Constitutional Convention and held an election in Sebastian and Crawford counties on November 23, electing delegates to the Convention and electing Col. James M. Johnson of Madison County to Congress.

The Little Rock group went along with the Fort Smith movement, and delegates purporting to represent some 24 counties assembled at Little Rock on January 4, 1864 as a Constitutional Convention. Its members were elected by highly unorthodox methods, some by the vote of a few men on the streets of Little Rock.

William Meade Fishback, a Fort Smith lawyer who had fled to St. Louis in 1862 and had come to Little Rock with Steele's army, led the Radicals at Little Rock. Another who was briefly prominent was Edward W. Gantt, the former rabid rebel, who had switched to the union side in June after failing to get confirmation as a Confederate brigadier general.

Before the Convention met, Lincoln's plan for reconstruction was announced. His amnesty proclamation of December 8 outlined the plan and gave the text of the amnesty oath to be taken by all participants. It offered full pardon to all who had participated in the rebellion except those in certain categories, and even those could be individually pardoned by the president and have their citizenship rights restored. In the ten seceded states in which no loyal state government had been maintained, ten per cent of the number that had voted in the 1860 presidential election had to take the amnesty oath before reorganization of the government could begin.

Lincoln's plan was popular with the Copperheads but not with the Radicals, because it placed former Confederates on an equal footing with those who had remained loyal, and because it meant endorsement of the administration's policy of gradual emancipation in the loyal states. A mass meeting at Little Rock on Christmas Eve brought out the strong conflict between the two factions.

The Radicals were annoyed by the *National Democrat's* Copperhead policies and by its editor's refusal to print some of their communications, which Meador later said promoted Gantt.[126] A letter written by Fishback under a pseudonym in the St. Louis *Missouri Democrat* of December 12 gave Meador the first news that arrangements were being made for a Radical newspaper at Little Rock, with Fishback as editor.[127] The first issue of the *Unconditional Union* was published at the *Gazette* office on January 23, 1864, and the masthead listed Fishback and T. D. W. Yonley as editors and

125. Fort Smith *New Era,* Nov. 10, 28, Dec. 26, 1863.
126. *National Democrat,* Mar. 25, 1865.
127. *Ibid.,* Dec. 26, 1863; *Telegraph,* Jan. 13, 1864.

publishers. The Convention adjourned on the same day, and the first issue contained the text of the new Constitution.

The Convention had modified the 1836 Constitution to provide for immediate emancipation of slaves, and had also created a few offices, made changes in election laws, and made the offices of secretary of state, auditor, treasurer, and Supreme Court judges elective by popular vote instead of by the legislature.

The Convention also had elected and inaugurated a set of provisional state officials on January 20. The provisional government was to remain in effect until the general election on March 14, when the voters would ratify or reject the Constitution and elect permanent officials. Isaac Murphy of Madison County was the provisional governor, chosen by the Radical faction mostly because he had been the only member of the 1861 Convention whose final vote had been against secession. Calvin C. Bliss of Independence County filled the new office of lieutenant governor, and Robert J. T. White was secretary of state.

The conflict between Steele and Davidson came out in the open in January, 1864, when Steele saw in the *Missouri Democrat* a letter Davidson had written to Senator S. H. Boyd, making harsh criticisms of Steele's administration of his command and his conciliatory policy.[128] On January 30, at Steele's request, Davidson was relieved of his command and transferred. Davidson was furious, and increased his efforts to undermine Steele in Washington.

Lincoln chose to accept the reorganization of the state government, though it had not been done according to his plan.[129] A campaign began immediately to register the 5,406 amnesty oaths required to validate it. An effective weapon in this program was the beginning of the operation of the federal Confiscation Act, by which all property owned by rebels or sold by rebels since July, 1862 was classified as abandoned property and placed under the control of the United States Treasury Department. It could be leased by loyal citizens upon application to the local treasury agent. Loyal Case, agent for the Little Rock District, arrived at Little Rock on January 22, and appointed Enoch Howard as local agent.[130]

On February 19, Howard informed the people of Little Rock that they could not purchase goods of any kind without exhibiting their oaths or permits from his office.[131] A similar order had been issued by military authorities several months earlier, but many people had been able to evade it because its enforcement was lax. This time, they had to take the amnesty oath to keep from starving or losing their property.

The offices of the *Gazette* and the *True Democrat* were among the first property confiscated, and Case advertised the rebel interest in both for sale

128. *Telegraph,* Feb. 24, 1864.
129. *National Democrat,* Feb. 6, 1864; *New Era,* Feb. 6, 1864.
130. Little Rock *Unconditional Union,* Jan. 23, 1864.
131. *National Democrat,* Feb. 27, 1864.

on February 27. Holtzman's one-third interest in the *Gazette* was safe, because he had taken the oath of allegiance soon after the beginning of federal occupation, and evidently also the amnesty oath. Only Danley's two-thirds interest was confiscated and exposed to sale at a public auction to be held on the premises on April 5. The real estate, owned solely by Danley, was not included.

The *Gazette's* equipment advertised for sale included one new drum cylinder press, size 31 by 40; one Lawyer jobber, size 14 by 15; one Superior Royal Hoe Washington press; one standing paper press, with boards; one Ruggles paper cutter; three marble imposing stones; and a large quantity of news, book, and job type of every quality. The *True Democrat's* equipment was more impressive, including four steam presses with a good engine and six other presses of various types. Only Johnson's half interest was confiscated, Yerkes having taken the oath.[132] Danley saved his interest in the *Gazette* by taking the amnesty oath at the last minute, along with many others who now felt they had no reasonable alternative, and the advertised sale was not held.

William E. Woodruff was one of the first casualties of the Confiscation Act at Little Rock. He took the amnesty oath on February 27, and wrote a long explanatory letter to a friend at Washington. In obedience to regulations requiring approval of letters to be sent through the lines, he took his letter to the office of the Radical provost marshal. To Woodruff's amazement, there were objections to his professions of continued loyalty to the Confederacy in spite of his oath to the contrary, and to his account of the community's adverse reaction to the elopement of a Yankee lieutenant with a young lady who had boarded in Woodruff's home.

A few days later, Steele ordered Woodruff and his family banished beyond the federal lines before March 10, and his property seized and held for military uses. His family still in the home at that time consisted of his wife, four unmarried daughters, and a 14-year-old son. The Washington *Telegraph* implied that his daughters came to Washington with him, but actually only 23-year-old Evelina shared his exile. They lived in the home of Daniel T. Witter until about the time the war ended, and then went to Louisville, Kentucky to live with his daughter Harriet, wife of John Jabine. They were absent from their home at Little Rock for more than 16 months.[133]

The election lasted three days, March 14, 15, and 16, and resulted in the election of those who had served as provisional officers, and the ratification of the Constitution by a vote of 12,177 to 226. T. M. Jacks, A. A. C.

132. *Ibid.; Telegraph,* Mar. 16, 1864. The size of the *Gazette's* press probably was 31 by 43, and the measurement given here must have been a typographical or clerical error.

133. *Telegraph,* Mar. 16, 1864; Ted R. Worley (ed.), *At Home in Confederate Arkansas* (Little Rock: Pulaski County Historical Society, 1955), 51; William E. Woodruff to J. M. Tebbetts, Little Rock, Dec. 29, 1865, photostat of Ms. in *Arkansas Gazette* Foundation Library; Frances Woodruff Martin, "William E. Woodruff, as Remembered by His Three Daughters," *Gazette Supplement,* Nov. 20, 1919, p. 30.

Rogers, and James M. Johnson were elected to Congress, and other state and county officers were elected. Jacks and Rogers joined Johnson in Washington to apply for admission to the House, without success.

Ten days after the election, editor Meador began a belated discussion of the defects of the new Constitution and the irregularities of the election. When it became known that Fishback wanted to be elected to the United States Senate, Meador used every conceivable argument against him.

Steele's army marched out of Little Rock on March 23 and 24 for an expedition to Camden, uniting on the march with a force from Fort Smith. This was in cooperation with Maj. Gen. Nathaniel P. Banks' disastrous Red River Expedition, intended to capture Shreveport, then the headquarters of the Trans-Mississippi Department. Camden was heavily fortified, and was the headquarters of the District of Arkansas, now temporarily commanded by Sterling Price, who had superseded Holmes.

Steele occupied Camden on the night of April 15. Price went into camp at nearby Woodlawn, where he could control the approaches to Camden. It was only a matter of time for Price to starve Steele out of Camden. Steele's first disaster was the battle of Poison Spring on April 18, when a large foraging party was attacked and chased back to Camden with heavy losses. The Red River Expedition had failed, and Kirby Smith came to Price's headquarters on April 19 and assumed command of the Confederate forces. A large supply train returning to Pine Bluff was attacked by the Confederates at Marks' Mill on April 25, and the bloody battle ended with another victory for the Confederates. Steele began his retreat to Little Rock the next night, and Smith pursued him to Jenkins' Ferry, where a major battle was fought on April 30. Steele's starving, demoralized army reached Little Rock during the next three days.

After the Camden Expedition, most of the military activity in Arkansas was of a guerrilla nature, though often fought by regular troops. The only noteworthy attempt at regular warfare was a raid into Missouri by Price that began on August 27 and ended on December 2, 1864.

There was considerable excitement in the Little Rock newspaper offices during Steele's absence on the Camden Expedition. When Danley took the amnesty oath about April 1st and regained control of his property, he ordered the *Unconditional Union* to vacate the *Gazette* office. The new secretary of state, Calvin C. Bliss, became editor and proprietor of the *Unconditional Union* and found it a new home. Bliss bought Yerkes' half interest in the office and real estate of the *True Democrat,* leased Johnson's half from the Treasury Department's special agent, and made arrangements for the military authorities to put him in possession of the office without the formality of serving notice on Meador.

Meador had no inkling of any of this, and was not at the *True Democrat* office when Bliss took possession of it on April 9. Meador was furious at being done out of the best equipped printing office south of St. Louis, though he had paid none of the rent he had agreed to pay Yerkes, nor had he paid Yerkes the salary as printer he had promised him. Unable to get his office back, Meador rented the *Gazette* office and published the *National Democrat* there, beginning with the daily issue of April 11 and the weekly issue of April 16. Neither Fishback and Yerkes nor Bliss had paid Danley any rent.[134]

The legislature convened on April 11, and Isaac Murphy was inaugurated on April 18. Fishback and Elisha Baxter were elected to the Senate, but did not win the election easily by any means. Meador's opposition to Fishback's election caused the House to withdraw his privilege of covering the proceedings of the House.[135]

Rivalry between the *National Democrat* and the *Unconditional Union* had been keen from the beginning, mostly because of political differences, but after Bliss became proprietor of the *Unconditional Union,* it became a grim battle for survival. The newspaper business at Little Rock had never been less profitable, and probably neither paper was self sustaining.

When the legislature met on November 7, 1864, its greatest problem was financing the state government, but it was able to function only by juggling the rules governing the quorum. The legislators were incensed by Governor Murphy's veto of two acts that attempted to provide the necessary funds by unwise means, and not only passed them over his veto, but considered calling for his resignation. The rift between Murphy and the Radical leaders had been revealed in a similar instance in the spring session, after his refusal to negotiate a loan authorized by the Convention.[136]

Murphy worked in harmony with General Steele, and Steele's friends excluded Murphy from the condemnation they heaped on Fishback, Yonley, Bliss, and other Radical leaders for trying to get rid of Steele. He was relieved of his command by order of Maj. Gen. Edward R. S. Canby, issued on November 25, 1864 under instructions from the Headquarters of the Army, and confirmed two days later by order of the secretary of war, who acted under the direction of the president. Steele made his farewell speech on December 17, and Maj. Gen. Joseph J. Reynolds assumed command on December 22.[137]

As the 1864 presidential campaign got under way, it became obvious that Lincoln's opposition in Congress did not intend to concede to the president the right to decide when and how the seceded states should be restored to the union, and would not recognize state governments reorganized under the amnesty proclamation. The Peace Democrats, favoring a negotiated peace, nominated George Brinton McClellan for president. The opposing part of the Democratic party joined with the Republicans under the label of the National Union party, and nominated Lincoln and Andrew Johnson,

134. *National Democrat,* Apr. 16, 1864; *Unconditional Union,* Apr. 16, 1864; Papers in case of Yerkes v. Meador.
135. *National Democrat,* May 14, 1864.
136. *Ibid.,* Dec. 24, 31, 1864; Jan. 7, 21, 1865.
137. *Ibid.,* Dec. 24, 1864.

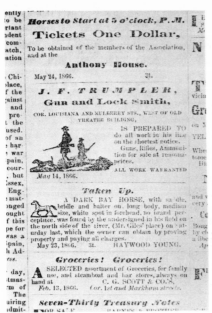

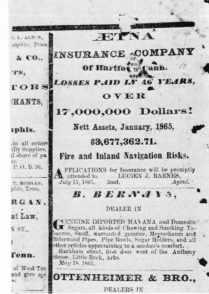

General style and make-up of Ads in the
Gazette, 1865–1866

Terms of subscription and advertising rates,
October 1865

THE GAZETTE

IS PUBLISHED DAILY AND WEEKLY BY
W. F. HOLTZMAN.

Terms of Subscription to the Gazette.

For the Weekly.............. $4 00 a year.
For the Daily, 30 cents a Week, payable to the Carriers.
Single copies 10 cents. All subscriptions to be paid in advance.

Terms of Advertising.

One Square of ten lines Minion, one insertion..$1 50
Each subsequent insertion 75
One square, *renewable,* $12 a month—standing advertisements $10 a month a square. A liberal deduction will be made to those who advertise largely.
☞ All transient advertisements must be paid for at the time of their insertion.
The bills for monthly advertisements will be called for on the Saturday after the first insertion.
☞ To insure their insertion advertisements must be handed in by *half-past five o'clock* in the evening.

SPECIAL NOT

NOTICES INSERTED IN THIS G
USUAL RATES.

BATCHELOR'S HA

The Original and Best in the V
true and perfect Hair Dye. Harml
Instantaneous. Produces immed
Black or Natural Brown, with out in
skin. Remedies the ill effects of ba
all Druggists. The genuine is si
Batchelor. Also,
REGENERATING EXTRACT OF
for Restoring and Beautifyir
CHARLES BATCHELO
Aug. 21, 1865.

L. M. FILKINS.

FOWLER   &

but refused to include the conciliatory policy in its platform, thereby bringing the Radical element to Lincoln's support.

Not having been readmitted to the union, Arkansas and the other states in the process of reconstruction could not participate in the election on November 8, 1864, in which Lincoln defeated McClellan by an electoral vote of 212 to 21.

On December 30, 1864, the legislature elected William D. Snow of Pine Bluff to the Senate in place of Fishback, because many thought Fishback's vote for secession in the 1861 Convention was the state's main stumbling block in its fight for readmission, as well as prejudicial to the interests of other states seeking readmission. There was a question as to whether a quorum was present at the time of Snow's election, and a further argument against his eligibility was that he had moved North in the late spring of 1864, and therefore was no longer a resident of Arkansas.[138]

By a joint resolution approved on February 1, 1865, Congress proposed to the state legislatures the Thirteenth Amendment to the Constitution, abolishing slavery. Ratification by the Arkansas legislature was requested even though the state had not been readmitted, and Governor Murphy called a special session for its consideration. The legislature convened on April 3, voted unanimously for ratification, and Murphy signed the joint resolution to that effect on April 20. Most authorities agree that a legal quorum was not present during most of the session.[139]

The Thirteenth Amendment brought into sharp focus the question of citizenship rights for Negroes. Negro suffrage was the greatest question, and some hoped to allow Negroes to vote and enjoy all other rights and privileges of full citizenship on the same basis white people had always enjoyed them. Others hoped to make literacy a qualification for voting, and some hoped to establish an all Negro colony outside the United States or a Negro state in the union. There was similar disagreement about the political status of repatriated rebels. Some thought they should not be allowed to vote or hold office, and argued that they could out-vote loyal men in their own localities.

The legislature had passed an act, approved May 31, 1864, authorizing collection of real estate taxes only from people who had not taken the amnesty oath. Since most of the people liable to this tax were not then living in their old homes, it was a thinly disguised way to place their property liable to forfeiture for delinquent taxes. Collections began in Pulaski County on September 19 and 20, 1864.[140]

An even more formidable threat to Confederate owned property in the spring of 1865 was the operation of the federal Confiscation Act of July 17, 1862 and the acts authorizing collection of direct taxes, approved on August

138. *Ibid.,* Dec. 31, 1864.
139. *Unconditional Union,* Apr. 20, 1865; *New Era,* Apr. 29, 1865.
140. *Unconditional Union,* Sept. 1, 1864.

5, 1861 and June 7, 1862. All were later set aside as unconstitutional, but meanwhile they gave rebel property owners a great deal of trouble. The confiscation and sale was valid only for the life of the rebel owner, and title would revert to his heirs after his death.[141]

Gen. Robert E. Lee's Army of Northern Virginia evacuated Richmond during the night of April 2, and federal troops occupied the city the next morning. With Lee's surrender on April 9, it was certain that all the other Confederate armies in the field would have to surrender, but this was not actually accomplished until late in May and early in June.

At sunrise on April 17, the people of Little Rock were awakened by the booming of cannons at Fort Steele. They thought at first that it was announcing the final victory, but they learned that President Lincoln had been assassinated by John Wilkes Booth at Ford's Theatre in Washington on the night of April 14, and had died the next morning.[142]

As the first post-war political campaign shaped up, Cincinnatus V. Meador decided to run for Congress, and on May 9, he announced his retirement from the *National Democrat* to become a candidate in the Second District, to fill the unexpired term of A. A. C. Rogers.[143] The next day, the *Gazette* was back in business, with a daily and a weekly edition.

141. *Ibid.,* Apr. 6, 27, May 11, 1865; *National Democrat,* Feb. 4, Apr. 22, 1865.
142. *Unconditional Union,* Apr. 20, 1865; *National Democrat,* Apr. 22, 1865.
143. *National Democrat,* May 9, 1865; *New Era,* May 27, 1865; *Telegraph,* May 24, 1865.

18

DANLEY AND HOLTZMAN

1865-1866 WHEN C. C. DANLEY and William F. Holtzman revived the *Arkansas Gazette* on May 10, 1865, the war was over except for a few formalities, and the work ahead was the repatriation of former Confederates. Danley's first editorial outlined the *Gazette's* major objectives: to sustain the civil and military authorities; to labor for confidence, faith, and security among the people, promoting love and trust instead of hatred, distrust, and animosity; and to persuade absent citizens to return to their homes, resume their allegiance to the union, and do all they could for the country and themselves.[1]

The daily edition began on Wednesday morning, May 10, and was published Mondays through Fridays. The weekly edition was published on Saturdays, beginning on May 13. All editions were printed the day before the date of issuance. Newspaper proprietors had not yet adopted the practice of staggering work schedules to publish seven days a week, including holidays. When holidays fell on working days, the daily edition for the next day was not published, because the entire staff had a day off. This did not affect regular publication of the weekly, which could be worked off a day early or a day late. Sunday was the staff's only regular day off, so the Monday paper was printed on Saturday. One issue of the daily, August 14, 1865, was not published because a shaft on the cylinder press broke, and the next issue had to be worked off on the hand press.[2]

Nameplates for both editions were the same, *Arkansas State Gazette,* until July 6, when the daily appeared in a new dress with the title *Little Rock Daily Gazette*. Materials probably were purchased from the printers' and binders' warehouse of R. Hoe & Company of New York and Boston.[3] By the spring of 1866, the *Gazette* was purchasing paper from Chatfield &

1. *Gazette* (daily), May 10, 1865; (weekly), May 13, 1865.
2. *Ibid.* (daily), Aug. 16, (weekly) Aug. 19, 1865.
3. *Ibid.* (weekly), July 22, 1865.

Woods of Cincinnati, a firm that had supplied the *Gazette* at one period before the war.[4]

Both editions still had only four pages, the daily being four columns wide and the weekly six. Volume numbering had long ago fallen into error, and the last issue before federal occupation in 1863 had been numbered Volume 43, Number 45. The weekly resumed with Volume 44, Number 46, but the new daily started with Volume I, Number 1. The second weekly issue had "Established 1819" in its old place under the nameplate.

Apparently the *Gazette* inherited the advertising contracts of the *National Democrat,* including the ads for unclaimed letters in the post office. Cash rates for the weekly were $2 a square for the first insertion and $1 thereafter.[5] In the daily, one square cost $1.50 for the first insertion and 75 cents thereafter. One square renewable was $12 a month, and standing ads were $10 a month per square, payable on the Saturday after the first insertion. A square was figured at ten lines minion. Liberal discounts were offered to "those who advertise largely." [6] On July 12, it was announced that death notices not exceeding five lines would be published free, but longer obituaries and tributes of respect by organizations would be charged as advertisements.

Subscription rates for the daily were 30 cents a week, payable to the carrier, and for the weekly $4 a year. Single copies were ten cents. News depots were given a discount, and early in June, Charles Haight's news depot and stationery store on Markham Street began keeping the *Gazette* for sale to non-subscribers. This helped alleviate the problem of friends who thought they could get a paper free by calling at the office.[7] There was no out-of-state agent until December, when S. H. Parvin of Cincinnati took it up again.[8]

Prices Current, the local markets report, began in the daily on May 16 and in the weekly on June 10. It was prepared by the firm of Kramer & Miller, and was corrected every day. River news was not collected under one head during the first nine months, but soon after the general steamboat agency of Ashley & Robards opened for business, its proprietors contracted to prepare a feature for the daily edition. It gave the stage of the river at four o'clock every afternoon, and listed arrivals, departures, and boats in port. It began on February 2, 1866, but did not appear in the weekly until June 23, 1866. Beginning on May 11, it was prepared by Ashley & Brown, successors to Ashley & Robards.

Most newspapers having daily editions hired a reporter to write the local news, but Danley and Holtzman did all the editorial work themselves,[9] and

4. *Ibid.,* Mar. 3, 1866.
5. *Ibid.,* May 13, 1865.
6. *Ibid.* (daily), May 10, 1865.
7. *Ibid.,* May 26, June 7, July 12; (weekly), May 27, June 10, 1865.
8. *Ibid.* (weekly), Dec. 30, 1865.
9. *Ibid.,* Oct. 14; (daily), Oct. 9, 1865.

both local and state news were inadequately reported. Page three of the daily was the "local page," but there was never a full column of news. However, some local news items were often found on page two, the editorial and state news page. All the articles in the daily were usually repeated in the weekly under "daily heads," captions indicating the date of publication in the daily.

The advent of the telegraph had brought about a new method of reporting news from outside Arkansas. There was as yet no national press association or other agency to disseminate news by wire, but regional organizations were beginning to function. The *Gazette* was the only Little Rock newspaper that subscribed to the telegraphic news service. The contract was for news via St. Louis, which was also the route by which Little Rock was in telegraphic communication with Memphis and New Orleans.[10]

The proximity of the *Gazette* office to the Town Branch was still a source of annoyance. A heavy rain on the night of July 15, 1865 caused the branch to overflow the next morning, damaging or destroying its bridges and the nearby buildings and streets. The street and sidewalks in front of the *Gazette* building were torn up, and water stood six inches deep in the printing office. Municipal government had not been resumed, and the post provost marshal had the responsibility of maintaining public property. He sent work crews to repair the damage within the next two weeks.[11] Early in November, Holtzman called attention to the dilapidated condition of the old wooden bridge across the branch at the corner of Cherry and Scott, but the necessary repairs were not made.[12]

The two office rooms in the *Gazette* building that had always been rented to others were vacant early in the summer of 1865, but a restaurant opened there about the middle of August.[13] By October, the rooms were occupied as an office by Dr. Charles Minor Taylor.[14] William E. Woodruff, Jr. and Luther H. Pike formed a law partnership later that month, and occupied these rooms until December.[15]

Both Danley and Holtzman were very ill when the *Gazette* resumed publication, and neither could give as much attention to the paper as it needed. They would have found it difficult to attend to the routine business of the weekly edition alone, but it was now necessary to publish a daily edition too, to meet competition. Danley had never recovered from the injuries received in his 1862 buggy accident, and new complications made his condition grave shortly after the *Gazette* resumed. It took the combined skill of Dr. J. J. McAlmont and two high ranking army doctors to save his life. Holtzman did the editor's work from about the first week in June until

10. *Ibid.* (daily), June 6, 8, 16, July 12; (weekly), June 17, 1865.
11. *Ibid.* (daily), July 18, 31; (weekly), July 22, Aug. 5, 1865.
12. *Ibid.* (weekly), Nov. 4, 25, 1865.
13. *Ibid.,* June 10, Aug. 19; (daily), June 5, Aug. 15, 1865.
14. *Ibid.* (daily), Oct. 10; (weekly), Oct. 14, 1865.
15. *Ibid.* (weekly), Oct. 28, Nov. 11, Dec. 30, 1865.

THE DAILY GAZETTE.

LITTLE ROCK.

THURSDAY MORNING.........OCT. 5, 1865.

☞ Dr. LORENZO GIBSON is a candidate for Congress from the Second Congressional Di-trict of Arkansas, composed of the counties of Pulaski, Saline, Hot Spring, Jefferson, Dallas, Bradley, Drew, Desha, Chicot, Ashley, Calhoun, Union, Ouachita, Columbia, Hempstead and Lafayette.

☞ We are authorized to announce JOHN H. ASKEW, a candidate for Congress in the Second Congressional District of Arkansas, composed of the counties of Pulaski, Saline, Hot Spring, Jefferson, Dallas, Bradley, Drew, Desha, Chicot, Ashley, Calhoun, Union, Ouachita, Columbia, Hempstead and Lafayette.

DEATH OF CAPT. C. C. DANLEY.—Capt. C. C. DANLEY for a long series of years, the editor of this paper, died at his rooms in the Gazette building, on the morning of Tuesday last, the 3d October (inst.)

CHRISTOPHER COLUMBUS DANLEY was born in Missouri, on the 5th of June, 1818, and was consequently in the 48th year of his age when he died. His parents emigrating to this State, when he was yet quite young, and the country a wilderness, he only received the rudiments of an English education, and a very brief acquaintance with the classics.

About the year 1836, when he was yet a boy, his soul was stirred by the achievements of the brave men who were fighting for the independence of Texas, and he volunteered and marched

July 6, when Danley was able to work again, though still very weak.[16] He had not left his room since the accident, but by the end of July, he was able to tour the city in the commercial hacks of Isaac Huyck and a former Ashley slave, Bill Archie Rector.[17] Holtzman was in the last stages of consumption, and was confined to his room much of the time, but somehow managed to do his work and much of Danley's.[18]

Probably it was Danley's illness and his dependence upon Holtzman to put the paper out that caused him to deed to Holtzman all his interest in the *Gazette,* including the real estate. The stated consideration was a one-sixth interest in 200 bales of cotton, valued at an estimated $4,000. This was done on May 20, 1865,[19] about the time Danley's health took a serious turn for the worse, and he may have considered it a "survivor take all" end to the partnership.

The state archives and the records of Pulaski County were returned to Little Rock on June 20, 1865.[20] Refugee civilians and former Confederate soldiers flocked back to their homes to take the amnesty oath and salvage what they could of their property. The work of administering the amnesty oath began on July 3,[21] and those ineligible for amnesty found a friend in Governor Murphy, who made recommendations for presidential pardons in cases he considered worthy until the big Fourth of July celebration. Participation by the Masonic Lodge, the hook and ladder company, and even

16. *Ibid.;* July 8, Oct. 7; (daily), July 6, Oct. 5, 1865.
17. *Ibid.* (daily), July 27; (weekly), July 29, 1865.
18. *Ibid.* (daily), Oct. 9, 1865; (weekly), Oct. 14, 1865; June 30, Aug. 18, Sept. 8, 1866.
19. Pulaski County Deed Book A (new series), 328.
20. *Gazette* (daily), June 20, 1865.
21. *Ibid.,* July 3; (weekly), July 8, 1865.

the band that had gone to war with the Capital Guards made it appear that the former rebels joined in the celebration. But aside from a few who were on the program, the old citizens were conspicuously absent. Murphy was so disillusioned by "the ingratitude and rebellious spirit" of some of the prominent returned rebels that he notified the president he would make no more recommendations for pardons.[22]

William E. Woodruff came home about the middle of May, but was allowed to stay only two weeks. He then went to live with his daughter in Kentucky, and received permission near the end of July to return to Little Rock. His home was restored to him more than a month later, but its furnishings had been used by army officers in other parts of town, and not all of them were recovered. Jonas M. Tebbetts of Fayetteville was then in Washington and obtained Woodruff's presidential pardon, apparently for a fee.[23] In anticipation of his return to Little Rock, his son, Alden, had reopened the Arkansas General Land Agency on July 7, and acted as his father's agent in conducting the business until his return.[24]

Danley died on the morning of October 3, 1865, at his rooms in the *Gazette* building. Judge Liberty Bartlett adjourned Pulaski Circuit Court to allow members of the bar to attend the funeral, and Pike Lodge No. 12 of the IOOF paid tribute to the order's past grand master by wearing a badge of mourning for 30 days. The next daily and weekly editions of the *Gazette* were draped in mourning, and Holtzman announced that he would continue the paper alone. He advertised for a compositor, but expected to get along without editorial assistance.[25] Danley died intestate, and his estate was administered first by his brother, William, and later by another brother, Benjamin.[26]

Following the policies Danley had laid out, Holtzman made the *Gazette* a non-partisan journal. He felt that the country had suffered too much from party strife, and that the need now was for harmony.[27] He endorsed only one candidate. In the campaign for Congress that started about the time the *Gazette* resumed publication, the paper supported Dr. Lorenzo Gibson, but did not oppose his opponents, Dr. Meador, G. H. Kyle, and J. H. Askew. Paid political announcements were under the editorial head as usual, but the usual list of endorsed candidates was not there. At the election in October, Gibson carried Little Rock by 91 votes, but lost the election to Kyle.[28]

22. *Ibid.* (daily), July 5; (weekly), July 8, 1865; Fort Smith *New Era,* Aug. 5, 1865; *Unconditional Union,* July 6, 1865.

23. *Gazette* (weekly), Aug. 5, 1865; William E. Woodruff to J. M. Tebbetts, Little Rock, Dec. 29, 1865, photostat of Ms. in *Arkansas Gazette* Foundation Library.

24. *Gazette* (weekly), July 8, 1865.

25. *Ibid.,* Oct. 7, 14; (daily), Oct. 5, 1865.

26. *Ibid.* (weekly), Nov. 11, 1865; C. C. Danley Estate Papers, Folder 137, Pulaski County Probate Files.

27. *Gazette* (daily), Sept. 11; (weekly), Sept. 16, 1865.

28. *Ibid.* (weekly), Oct. 14, 21, Nov. 18, 1865.

Governor Murphy had been at odds with the Radicals for some time, mostly because he would not go along with their methods of financing the state government. During the summer of 1865, a rift developed between him and the Conservatives, largely because of his election proclamation. It included the oath that voters were required to take, swearing they had not voluntarily borne arms against the United States or aided Confederate authorities in any way since April 18, 1865. This oath, required by an act of the legislature, ruled out many recently amnestied rebels, and it was argued that the legislature had no constitutional authority to decide qualifications of voters. Murphy said it was the law of the land until declared unconstitutional in court, and that the governor had no choice but to enforce it. His critics contended that he was sworn to uphold the Constitution, not the legislature.[29]

The *Gazette's* first direct criticism of Murphy was based on this argument, and did not come until October, after he had requested a larger military force in Arkansas. It had been rumored for some time that the state government would be set aside and replaced by a provisional government, with a provisional governor appointed by President Johnson. Some thought General Reynolds would receive the appointment. The *Gazette* had supported the state government, and had said it should be recognized by Congress, but now Holtzman gave full approval to the rumored provisional government. He also approved the choice of Reynolds for provisional governor, but a week later he thought Jesse Turner of Van Buren would be right for the job.[30]

Municipal government was reinstated at Little Rock with an election on January 1, 1866, in which nearly 600 votes were cast. The mayor, Dr. J. J. McAlmont, the eight aldermen, two justices of the peace, city recorder, and constable were all old residents of Little Rock. The board of aldermen organized on January 8, and selected the *Gazette* as the medium for publication of its ordinances and resolutions.[31]

As the political season approached, the *Gazette* set its rates for political announcements at $10 for county judges, clerks, and sheriffs, $7.50 for other county offices, and $5 for township offices.[32]

By a deed dated April 6, 1866, Holtzman relinquished to Danley's estate all his claim to the *Gazette's* real estate and the two-thirds interest in the business originally owned by Danley, thus annulling Danley's conveyance to him of the previous May 20, which he had not filed for record until the day after Danley's death. In return, William Danley conveyed to Holtzman the machinery, materials, and other appurtenances of the printing office,

29. *Ibid.,* Sept. 9, 1865.
30. *Ibid.,* Oct. 21, 28, 1865.
31. *Ibid.,* Jan. 6, 13; (daily), Jan. 3, 11, 1865.
32. *Ibid.* (weekly), Apr. 14, 1866.

In his old age, William E. Woodruff's interest in the newspaper he had founded was increased when his son and namesake became its editor and proprietor.

and gave him a two-year lease on the part of the building occupied by the *Gazette,* setting the rent at $400 a year.[33]

These instruments undoubtedly were part of Holtzman's preparations to retire from the *Gazette,* because of his steadily failing health. On June 29, he announced the sale of the *Gazette* to Major William E. Woodruff, Jr., the son of its founder.[34]

Thirteen days later, at 12:30 on the morning of August 12, 1866, Holtzman died at the age of 41 of consumption, or phthisis as it was entered in the mortuary report. The inside pages of the *Gazette* were draped in mourning, and Pike Lodge No. 12 of IOOF wore the badge of mourning for 30 days.[35] He was buried at Mount Holly cemetery.

Danley and Holtzman had made a valiant effort to keep the *Gazette* abreast of the times. They had revived it on short notice, with obsolete equipment, no editorial assistance, and no subscribers or advertisers except those inherited from the *National Democrat.* Their financial resources, never very impressive, had been wiped out by the war, and they had not been able to convert the old press to steam power or buy other machinery they needed, or to employ more than the minimum crew. Worst of all, they had both been

33. Pulaski County Deed Book G-2, 364, 365.
34. *Gazette* (daily), June 29; (weekly), June 30, 1865.
35. *Ibid.* (weekly), Aug. 18, 25, Sept. 8, 1866.

desperately ill. Yet they had managed to publish a reasonably good daily and weekly newspaper and to hold their own in advertising competition.

The political situation during the last months of their lives had not required much of their lagging energy, but the years ahead would be hard ones for the defeated South. There would be many battles for the *Gazette* to fight, and they would require more physical stamina and more ingenuity than Danley and Holtzman had had in recent years. If the *Gazette* was to maintain a position of leadership, or even to survive, it would need a vigorous, aggressive, bold, and self-sacrificing manager.

The new proprietor was such a man. He was abundantly endowed with what his father had called "enterprise," and he was willing to pour all the *Gazette's* profits back into the business. A new era in American journalism was just beginning, and the changes would be particularly drastic west of the Mississippi, where some of the pre-war innovations were not yet established. His problems would be quite different from those his father had encountered.

Only a few people were still living in Arkansas who had read the first issue of the *Gazette,* but there were many who had been subscribers before William E. Woodruff's retirement. Those who knew the Woodruff family well must have felt that the *Gazette's* future was secure when they saw the daily of July 2 and the weekly of July 7, 1866, with the statement of proprietorship, "By W. E. Woodruff, Jr.," under the nameplate.

Bibliography

I. PRIMARY SOURCES

MANUSCRIPTS

Elliot H. Fletcher Papers. Arkansas History Commission.
Luther C. Gulley Collection. Arkansas History Commission.
John E. Knight Collection. Arkansas History Commission.
Manuscript collection of *Arkansas Gazette* Foundation Library.
Robert W. Trimble Papers. Arkansas History Commission.
Maria Toncray Watkins, diary, 1821-1829. Arkansas History Commission.
Wheeler Family Papers. Owned by George H. Stone, North Stonington,
    Connecticut in 1959.
Samuel W. Williams Collection. Arkansas History Commission.
Hannah Clarke Woodruff, family Bible record. Arkansas History Commission.
Jane Eliza Woodruff, family Bible record. Arkansas History Commission.
William E. Woodruff Papers. Arkansas History Commission.

PUBLIC RECORDS

United States Census, 1850 (Hot Spring, Lafayette, and Pulaski counties, Ar-
    kansas), and 1860 (Dallas County, Arkansas.)
Arkansas. Auditor's Register of Warrants A, 1820-1838. *Arkansas Gazette*
    Foundation Library.
Arkansas Territory. Record of Commissions, 1819-1836. Original in office of
    Arkansas Secretary of State; photocopy in *Arkansas Gazette* Foundation
    Library.
Arkansas County, Arkansas. Deed Book C. Circuit clerk's office, Arkansas
    County court house, DeWitt, Arkansas.
Pulaski County, Arkansas. Deed Books B, C, D, E, F, G, H, I, K, L, M, Q, T,
    U, W, X, A (New Series), G-2. Circuit clerk's office, Pulaski County court
    house, Little Rock, Arkansas.
————Probate Court Records, Books B and C. County and probate clerk's
    office, Pulaski County court house, Little Rock, Arkansas.
————Probate Court Files. County and probate clerk's office, Pulaski County
    court house, Little Rock, Arkansas. These are papers filed by administrators
    or executors of estates, and the probate clerk was not required to keep them
    after the probate court had reviewed them. They have survived by accident.
    Some of them are recorded or summarized in the Probate Court Records.
————Transcript of trial of M. Cunningham vs. Chester Ashley and Roswell

Beebe in Pulaski Circuit Court in Chancery, certified September 29, 1848 by Gordon N. Peay, clerk. Arkansas Supreme Court library.

Davidson County, Tennessee. Deed Books O and P. Microfilm at the Tennessee State Library and Archives, Nashville, Tennessee.

Williamson County, Tennessee. Deed Books J, K, M, N. Circuit clerk's office, Williamson County court house, Franklin, Tennessee.

NEWSPAPERS

Arkansas Advocate, Little Rock, Arkansas, Apr. 10, 1835-Apr. 27, 1837, and scattered issues earlier.

Arkansas Banner, Little Rock, Arkansas, Sept. 16, 1843-May 19, 1846.

Arkansas Gazette (title varies), Arkansas and Little Rock, Arkansas, Nov. 20, 1819-Sept. 8, 1866, and scattered issues and supplements thereafter.

Arkansas Patriot, Little Rock, Arkansas, Oct. 2, 1862-Sept. 1, 1863.

Arkansas State Democrat (title varies), Little Rock, Arkansas, May 21, 1846-Feb. 1, 1850.

Arkansas Times and Advocate, Little Rock, Arkansas, July 11, 1838.

Arkansas True Democrat, Little Rock, Arkansas, Feb. 2, 1860-July 8, 1863, and scattered issues earlier.

The Clarion, and Tennessee State Gazette, Nashville, Tennessee, Sept. 1818-Apr. 1820, and scattered issues thereafter.

The Clipper, Little Rock, Arkansas, Feb. 19, 1887.

Commercial Appeal, Memphis, Tennessee, Aug. 7, 1927.

Courrier de la Louisiane, New Orleans, Louisiana, Sept. 21, 28, Oct. 4, 1824.

Daily State Journal, Little Rock, Arkansas, Nov. 2, 1861-Feb. 7, 1862.

Fort Smith New Era, Fort Smith, Arkansas, Oct. 8, 1863-Aug. 19, 1865.

Memphis Appeal, Memphis, Tennessee, Dec. 27, 1844.

National Democrat, Little Rock, Arkansas, Oct. 20, 1863-May 6, 1865.

New York Herald, New York, New York, Apr. 26, 1861; May 22, 1862.

New York Tribune, New York, New York, Aug. 6, 1862.

North Little Rock Times, Argenta, Arkansas, Mar. 10, 1906.

The Press, Van Buren, Arkansas, Apr. 21, 1888.

Republican Banner and Nashville Whig, Nashville, Tennessee, Apr. 28, 1851.

Spirit of the Times, New York, New York, Dec. 15, 22, 29, 1849; Jan. 12, 26, 1850.

The Times, Little Rock, Arkansas, Jan. 30, 1835-Aug. 1, 1836.

Unconditional Union, Little Rock, Arkansas, Jan. 23, 1864-Dec. 21, 1865.

Washington Telegraph, Washington, Arkansas, Jan. 15, 1862-Dec. 20, 1865.

OFFICIAL PRINTED MATERIALS

Arkansas Constitutional Convention. *Journal of the Proceedings of the Convention met to form a Constitution and System of State Government for the People of Arkansas at the Session of the said Convention held at Little Rock, in the Territory of Arkansas, which commenced on the fourth day of January, and ended on the thirtieth day of January, one thousand eight hundred and thirty-six.* Published by Authority. Little Rock, Ark.: Printed by Albert Pike, 1836.

————*Journal of Both Sessions of the Convention of the State of Arkansas, which were begun and held at the capitol, in the city of Little Rock;* Published by Authority. Little Rock: Johnson & Yerkes, State Printers, 1861.

Arkansas General Assembly. *Acts Passed by the General Assembly of the Territory of Arkansas, at the Session in October, 1823.* Published by Authority. Little Rock: Printed by William E. Woodruff, Printer to the Territory, 1824.

————*House Journals* (titles vary) for the sessions of 1831, 1837, 1838, 1842, 1850, 1852, 1854, 1856.

————*Senate Journals* (titles vary) for the sessions of 1831, 1837, 1838, 1848, 1850, 1854. (Note: Other *Acts* and *Journals* were seen as needed in the files of the *Gazette* and other newspapers.)

Arkansas Supreme Court. *Reports of Cases* (titles vary; cited by number of volume and *Ark.*), Vols. 1, 2, 3, 4, 5, 6, 7, 8, 10, 11, 12, 14, 20, 22, 24.

Ball, William McK. and Sam. C. Roane (comp.), *Revised Statutes of the State of Arkansas, Adopted at the October Session of the General Assembly of Said State, A. D. 1837.* Notes and index by Albert Pike. Boston: Weeks, Jordan and Company, Publishers, 1838.

Carter, Clarence Edwin (ed.), *The Territorial Papers of the United States.* Vol. XV, *The Territory of Louisiana-Missouri, 1815-1821.* Washington: United States Government Printing Office, 1951.

————Vol. XIX, *The Territory of Arkansas, 1819-1825* (1953.)

————Vol. XX, *The Territory of Arkansas, 1825-1829* (1954.)

————Vol. XXI, *The Territory of Arkansas, 1829-1836* (1954.)

Heitman, Francis B. *Historical Register and Dictionary of the United States Army, from its organization, September 29, 1789, to March 2, 1903.* Washington: Government Printing Office, 1903; Urbana: University of Illinois Press, 1965. 2 vols.

Hempstead, Samuel H. *Reports of Cases Argued and Determined in the United States Superior Court for the Territory of Arkansas, from 1820 to 1836; and in the United States District Court for the District of Arkansas, from 1836 to 1849; and in the United States Circuit Court for the District of Arkansas, in the Ninth Circuit, from 1839 to 1856. With Notes and References and Rules of Court.* Boston: Little, Brown and Company, 1856.

Herndon, Dallas T. (comp.) *The Arkansas History Commission, Bulletin of Information No. 6.* Little Rock, June, 1913.

Miller, William R. *Auditor's Report.* Little Rock, Nov. 5, 1862.

Rector, Henry M. *Message of Henry M. Rector, Governor of Arkansas, to the State Convention; March 4th, 1861.* Little Rock: True Democrat Book and Job Office Print, 1861.

————*Message of Gov. Henry M. Rector, to the General Assembly of Arkansas, In Extra Session, Nov. 6, 1861.* Little Rock: Johnson & Yerkes, State Printers, 1861.

————*Governor's Message, Nov. 3, 1862.*

United States Department of Commerce, Bureau of the Census. *Thirteenth Census of the United States Taken in the Year 1910. Statistics for Arkansas Containing Statistics of Population, Agriculture, Manufacturers, and Mining for the State, Counties, Cities, and Other Divisions.* Washington: Government Printing Office, 1914.

United States Senate. *Extra Session [216]. In the Senate of the United States. Report of Mr. Grundy of the Committee on the Judiciary, to whom were referred the credentials of the honorable Ambrose H. Sevier, March 7, 1837.*

The War of the Rebellion: A Compilation of the Official Records of the Union and Confederate Armies. 128 vols. Washington: Government Printing Office, 1880-1901.

OTHER PUBLISHED MATERIALS

Allsopp, Fred W. *Twenty Years in a Newspaper Office. Consisting Principally of Random Sketches of Things Seen, Heard and Experienced on the "Arkansas Gazette."* Little Rock, Arkansas: Central Printing Company, 1907.

Andrews, C. C. *Early Steps in Reconstruction; Speeches by General C. C. Andrews, of Minnesota, In Texas and Arkansas.* Washington, D.C.; Union Republican Congressional Committee, undated.

Arkansas Star. Prospectus of the Arkansas Star, A new paper, to be established at the City of Little Rock, in the State of Arkansas. Little Rock, Arkansas, April, 1839. (Broadside.)

Barker, Eugene C. (ed.) *The Austin Papers,* Vol. II of *Annual Report of the American Historical Association for the Year 1919.* In 2 parts. Washington: Government Printing Office, 1924.

Beebe, Roswell. *Memorial of Roswell Beebe, addressed to the General Assembly of the State of Arkansas: With an Appendix.* Little Rock: Printed by G. H. Burnett, 1840.

Demby, J. Wm. *The War In Arkansas, or, A Treatise on the Great Rebellion of 1861; Its Progress, and Ultimate Results upon the Destinies of the State. A Defense of the Loyalty of the People, Their Wretched Condition Considered; A Review of the Policy of the Government Towards Union People and the Rebels.* Little Rock, Ark., 1864.

Denson, A. Clark. *Westmoreland: or, Secession Ferocity at the Breaking Out of the Rebellion.* St. Louis: P. M. Pinckard, Printer, 1865.

Douglas, Walter B. (ed.) *Three Years Among the Indians and Mexicans,* by General Thomas James. St. Louis: Missouri Historical Society, 1916.

Flint, Timothy. *Recollections of the Last Ten Years, Passed in Occasional Residences and Journeyings in the Valley of the Mississippi, from Pittsburgh and the Missouri to the Gulf of Mexico, and from Florida to the Spanish Frontier; in a Series of Letters to the Rev. James Flint, of Salem, Massachusetts.* Boston: Cummings, Hilliard, and Company, 1826.

Foote, Henry S. *The Bench and Bar of the South and Southwest.* St. Louis: Soule, Thomas, & Wentworth, 1876.

Fulton, Maurice Garland (ed.) *Diary & Letters of Josiah Gregg, Southwestern Enterprises, 1840-1847.* Norman: University of Oklahoma Press, 1941.

———*Diary & Letters of Josiah Gregg, Excursions in Mexico & California 1847-1850.* Norman: University of Oklahoma Press, 1944.

Harrell, John M. "Arkansas," Vol. X in Clement A. Evans (ed.), *Confederate Military History.* 12 vols. Atlanta, Ga.: Confederate Publishing Company, 1899.

"Official Correspondence of Governor Izard 1825-1826," in John Hugh Reynolds (ed.), *Publications of the Arkansas Historical Association,* Vol. I. Fayetteville, 1906.

Jones, George W. "Eyewitness Account of Newton-Sevier Duel," *Pulaski County Historical Review,* Vol. I. Little Rock, June, 1953.

Knight, Mrs. Hannah Donnell. "Hospitality of Early Days," *The Arkansas*

Pioneers, Vol. I. Little Rock: Arkansas Pioneers Association, Sept., 1912.

Lemke, W. J. (ed.) *Judge David Walker, His Life and Letters.* Fayetteville: Washington County Historical Society, 1957.

Lucke, Jessie Ryon. "Correspondence Concerning the Establishment of the First Arkansas Press," *Arkansas Historical Quarterly,* XIV (1955.)

Nash, Dr. Charles Edward. *Biographical Sketches of Gen. Pat Cleburne and Gen. T. C. Hindman together with Humorous Anecdotes and Reminiscences of the Late Civil War.* Little Rock, Ark.: Tunnah & Pittard, Printers, 1898.

Nuttall, Thomas. *A Journal of Travels into the Arkansa Territory, During the Year 1819, with Occasional Observations on the Manners of the Aborigines.* Philadelphia: Printed and published by Thos. H. Palmer, 1821.

Parmelee, T. N. "Recollections of an Old Stager," *Harper's New Monthly Magazine,* XLVI. January, 1873.

[Pike, Albert.] *To the American Party South.* [1856.]

Pope, William F. *Early Days in Arkansas, Being for the Most Part the Personal Recollections of an Old Settler.* Little Rock: Frederick W. Allsopp, 1895.

Poultney, Evan. *An Appeal to the Creditors of the Bank of Maryland, and the Public Generally.* Baltimore: Printed by John D. Toy, 1835.

Read, Opie. *I Remember.* New York: Richard R. Smith, Inc., 1930.

Rogers, John. *The Autobiography of Elder J. T. Johnson.* Cincinnati, 1861.

Ross, Margaret Smith (ed.) *Letters of Hiram Abiff Whittington 1827-1834.* Little Rock: Pulaski County Historical Society, 1956.

Scott, Rev. Allen M. *Chronicles of the Great Rebellion from the Beginning of the Same until the Fall of Vicksburg.* Cincinnati: C.F. Vent & Co., 1863.

Underwood, Quincy K. "Address of Judge Q. K. Underwood, Before the Old Folks, April 2, 1872," in Leon Trousdale and others (eds.), *Old Folks' Historical Record,* Vol. I, No. 12. Memphis: R. C. Hite, 1875.

White, Lonnie J. (ed.) "A Letter from Robert Crittenden to John J. Crittenden," *Arkansas Historical Quarterly,* XXI (1962.)

Woodruff, Jane Georgine. "William E. Woodruff," *Arkansas Pioneers,* Vol. I, No. 5. Little Rock: Arkansas Pioneers Association, October, 1913.

Woodruff, W. E. [Jr.] *With the Light Guns in '61-'65.* Little Rock: Central Printing Company, 1903.

Worley, Ted R. (ed.) *At Home in Confederate Arkansas.* Little Rock: Pulaski County Historical Society, 1955.

————"A Letter of Governor Miller to His Wife," *Arkansas Historical Quarterly,* XIII (1954.)

II. SECONDARY WORKS

Biographical and Historical Memoirs of Southern Arkansas, Comprising a Condensed History of the State, a number of Biographies of its Distinguished Citizens, a brief Descriptive History of each of the Counties mentioned, and numerous Biographical Sketches of the Citizens of such County. Chicago, Nashville and St. Louis: The Goodspeed Publishing Co., 1890.

Allen, Albert H. (ed.) *Arkansas Imprints 1821-1876.* New York: Published for The Bibliographical Society of America by R. R. Bowker Company, 1947.

Allen, John E. *Newspaper Designing.* New York and London: Harper & Brothers Publishers, 1947.

Baylor, Orval W. *John Pope, Kentuckian, His Life and Times 1770-1845.* Cynthiana, Ky.: The Hobson Press, 1943.

Brigham, Clarence S. *History and Bibliography of American Newspapers 1690-1820.* Worcester, Massachusetts: American Antiquarian Society, 1947, 2 vols.

Browne, Junius Henri. "George D. Prentice," *Harper's New Monthly Magazine,* L (1874-1875.)

Duncan, Robert Lipscomb. *Reluctant General. The Life and Times of Albert Pike.* New York: E. P. Dutton & Co., 1961.

Hallum, John. *Biographical and Pictorial History of Arkansas.* Albany: Weed, Parsons and Company, Printers, 1887.

Hempstead, Fay. *A Pictorial History of Arkansas.* St. Louis and New York: N. D. Thompson Publishing Company, 1890.

Houck, Louis. *A History of Missouri from the Earliest Explorations and Settlements until the Admission of the State into the Union.* Chicago: R. R. Donnelley & Sons Company, 1908. 3 vols.

Hudson, John A. and Robert L. Peterson. "Arkansas Newspapers in the University of Texas Newspaper Collection," *Arkansas Historical Quarterly,* XIV (1955.)

Jacoway, Peggy. *First Ladies of Arkansas.* Kingsport, Tenn.: Southern Publishers, Inc., 1941.

Johnson, Allen (ed.) *Dictionary of American Biography.* New York: Published under the auspices of American Council of Learned Societies by Charles Scribner's Sons, 1943. 22 vols.

McMurtrie, Douglas C. *Early Printing in Tennessee.* Chicago, 1933.

Meek, Melinda. "The Life of Archibald Yell," *Arkansas Historical Quarterly,* XXVI (1967).

Moore, Frank (ed.) *The Rebellion Record: A Diary of American Events, 1860-'62.* New York: G. P. Putnam, 1862.

Morris, Robert L. "Three Arkansas Travelers," *Arkansas Historical Quarterly,* IV (1945.)

Overdyke, W. Darrell. *The Know-Nothing Party in the South.* [Baton Rouge:] Louisiana State University Press, 1950.

Reynolds, John Hugh and David Yancey Thomas. *History of the University of Arkansas.* Fayetteville: University of Arkansas, 1910.

Riggs, Bess Michaels. *A Brief History of the Education of the Deaf in the State of Arkansas.* Little Rock: Arkansas School for the Deaf, 1934.

Scully, Francis J. "The High-Lights of the Early Days of Western Star Lodge No. 2," *Arkansas Research Lodge No. 739, Free & Accepted Masons,* Vol. I [Little Rock, 1947.]

Speer, William S. and John Henry Brown (eds.) *The Encyclopedia of the New West.* Marshall, Texas: The United States Biographical Publishing Company, 1881.

Stokes, D. A., Jr. "The First State Elections in 1836," *Arkansas Historical Quarterly,* XX, (1961.)

Taft, William H. (comp.) *Missouri Newspapers: When and Where 1808-1963.* Columbia, Missouri: The State Historical Society of Missouri, 1964.

Talley, Robert. *One Hundred Years of the Commercial Appeal.* Memphis, Tenn.: The Commercial Appeal, 1940.

Webb, Walter Prescott and H. Bailey Carroll (eds.) *The Handbook of Texas.* Austin: The Texas State Historical Association, 1952. 2 vols.

The National Cyclopaedia of American Biography, being the History of the United States as illustrated in the lives of the Founders, Builders, and Defenders of the Republic, and of the Men and Women who are doing the Work and Moulding the Thought of the Present Time. New York: James T. White & Company, 1893.

White, Lonnie J. *Politics on the Southwestern Frontier: Arkansas Territory, 1819-1836.* Memphis: Memphis State University Press, 1964.

Williams, Samuel C. "George Roulstone: Father of the Tennessee Press," *The East Tennessee Historical Society's Publications,* No. 17. Knoxville, 1945.

Wold, Ansel (comp.) *Biographical Directory of the American Congress 1774-1927,* 69th Cong., 2d Sess., House Doc. No. 783. Washington: Government Printing Office, 1928.

Worley, Ted R. and Eugene A. Nolte (eds.) *Pete Whetstone of Devil's Fork.* Van Buren, Ark.: The Press-Argus, 1957.

UNPUBLISHED WORKS

Key, Howard Cresap. "The *Arkansas Gazette,* 1819-1843: Its Literary Trends," unpublished M. A. Thesis, University of Texas, 1935.

Truesdell, Karl. *Descendants of John Trousdale of Orange County, North Carolina.* Chevy Chase, Md., 1952. (Typescript, Tennessee State Library and Archives, Nashville, Tenn.)

III. MISCELLANEOUS

Quertermous, F. M. (comp.) Map of Post of Arkansas, Territory of Arkansas, 1829. Little Rock: Arkansas Publicity and Parks Commission, undated.

Tombstone inscriptions, Mount Holly Cemetery, Little Rock, Arkansas.

Index

Adams, John D.: 249
Adams, John Quincy: 10, 45, 61, 70, 87, 88, 91, 222
Adams, Louisa Katherine Johnson: 89 n.
Adams, Samuel: 204, 210, 217
Adams, W. W.: 305, 312
Agricultural society: 179
Alexander Military Institute: 244
Alexandria, La.: 135, 145
Alexandria *Louisiana Herald:* 9 n.
Alexandria *Louisiana Planter:* 9 n.
Alexandria, La. *Red-River Herald:* 9 n.
Alhambra building: 272 n., 305–306
Allen, William O.: 24, 25–26
Almanacs: 34, 243
American Party: 209, 314–316, 317, 320 ff., 331 ff., 336, 337, 341, 342
American Party South: 320
Amnesty: 387 ff., 398–399
Andrews, C. C.: 386
Annear, William: 245 n.
Anthony House: 214, 259, 260 n., 283, 284, 307, 314
Anthony, J. J.: 151, 156
Anthony, Philip Lee: 193, 243
Anti-Gambling Assn.: 124
Arcade Saloon: 214
Arkansas: territorial capitol building, 36, 38, 39; state house, 98, 106, 110, 164
District of, C.S.A., 375, 382
geological survey of, 196
history of, 298, 330
orthography of, 17
population, required for statehood, 109; in 1833, 109; in 1835, 126; in 1840, 179
secession of, 356
(see also Statehood)
Arkansas Advocate: 90, 91, 99–100, 102 f., 106, 108 f., 118 ff., 132, 136, 138, 139, 144, 145, 149, 190, 307

Arkansas Banner: established, 195 f., 197 ff., 203, 210, 212, 213; and Ashley, 206; proprietors and staff, 210, 213, 223, 225, 230, 255, 260, 288, 293–294; and public printing, 210, 281 ff.; and Pike-Roane dispute, 238; and politics of 1846, 216 ff., 230, 231, 233; of 1848, of 1848, 241, 251 ff., 260, 262 ff., 266; of 1852, 290; press of, 197, 230; Mexican War maps, 228; title changes, 293–294; mention, 276 f., 280, 317, 318, 319
Arkansas Democrat: 216, 218, 220, 223, 224, 229, 230, 235, 238, 241, 250, 273, 277, 338; circulation, 235, 266; offices, 231, 265, 272; and politics of 1848, 241 f., 248, 250, 251 f., 254, 256 f., 260, 262, 264; merged with *Gazette,* 270
Arkansas Form Book: 190
Arkansas Gazette: advertising, 19, 20 f., 34, 44 ff., 53, 104, 113, 116, 128, 146, 149, 166 ff., 177, 180 f., 206–207, 244, 267, 286, 306, 308, 319, 338 ff., 366, 370 f., 396
agents, 32–33, 46, 266, 267, 286, 299, 324, 348, 396
birth announcements, 336
book publication, first in Arkansas, 39
circulation and subscription rates, 19 ff., 33, 45 f., 63, 87, 98, 104, 107, 113, 120, 125, 128, 138, 143 f., 149, 161, 166, 177 f., 181, 196 f., 221, 234 f., 243 f., 265 f., 270 f., 277 ff., 295, 299, 301, 305 f., 319, 322 ff., 334, 338, 345, 348, 350, 352, 362, 366, 369, 371, 379, 396
collections of accounts, 33, 113, 120, 161, 165 f., 176 ff., 181, 221, 166 f., 269, 272, 277, 299 f., 306, 338
contest, 287

continuity interruptions, 41, 43, 44 f., 264 f., 269, 306, 308, 370, 373, 382 f., 393, 395
daily edition, 352, 393, 395, 397
exchanges, 20, 32, 45, 100, 138, 179, 265
extra editions, 30, 32, 45, 96, 132 ff., 137, 139, 156, 172, 207, 360
features, agricultural articles, 168, 179
   calendar, 46, 125 f., 267
   carrier's addresses, 46, 234, 267, 287, 304, 319, 330, 339
   fashion articles, 286 f.
   historical articles, 330
   legal news, 181
   markets, 29 ff., 46, 144, 303 f., 396
   poetry, 20, 46 f., 104, 125, 144, 168, 318, 319 f.
   religion, 236
   river news, 396
   weather, 29, 30, 46, 47, 104, 308
foreign languages in, 26 f.
format, 19, 44 f., 53, 63, 87, 105, 112 f., 120, 143 f., 178 f., 246, 271 f., 299, 308, 319, 325, 370, 379 f., 396, 397
illustrations, 31, 44, 208, 226 ff., 267, 286, 291, 295 f., 303, 319, 320, 328, 345
job printing, 21, 53, 104, 155, 176, 243, 285, 351, 366
marriage notices, 20
materials, 163, 267, 271, 306 f., 389
   type, 12 f., 27, 63, 105, 106, 113, 120, 143 f., 172, 243 f., 286, 307, 319, 338, 395
   paper, 31 f., 43 ff., 63, 99 f., 151, 173, 178 f., 188, 189, 286, 325, 362, 366, 369 f., 379 f., 382 f., 395 f.
motto, 195, 227, 271, 299, 308, 319, 338
nameplates, 20, 63, 87, 120, 144, 244, 271, 272, 299, 308, 319, 337, 370, 395
news coverage, 20, 31 f., 62, 168, 187, 235, 323, 331, 340, 371, 396 f.
obituaries, 20, 339, 396
offices, at Arkansas Post, 8, 17, 34, 39; move to Little Rock, 36, 37, 41; map of Little Rock locations, 12; 1821 to 1824, 37, 43, 55; 1824 to 1827, 53, 54–55, 308; 1827 to 1840, 72 f., 74, 78, 81, 84, 100 f., 104, 118, 163; 1840 to 1845, 163,
   164 f., 172 f., 174; 1845 to 1848, 214, 231, 261, 313; 1848 to 1850, 264 f.; 1850 to 1854, 272, 299, 305 f.; 1854 to 1866, 307 f., 312, 328, 388 f., 390, 379, 386, 397, 398, 400 f.
oldest newspaper west of the Mississippi River, 8–9 n.
presses, 11 f., 113, 120, 163, 271, 307, 340 f., 345, 348, 389, 395, 401
proprietorship, Woodruff-Briggs partnership, 25, 33 f.; Steele's effort to buy, 111 f.; Woodruff-Pew partnership, 134 ff., 138, 144; Woodruff to Cole, 160, 163, 192, 194; Cole to Burnett, 172 ff.; sold back to Woodruff, 180, 181; Woodruff to Borden, 191–194, 195, 197, 199, 206, 218 ff., 252 f., 255, 260, 262; Borden to Hayden, 244 ff., 269; Hayden to Webb, 269; Webb to Woodruff, 269 f.; Woodruff to Danley, 297; Danley-Borland partnership, 314, 321; Danley-Holtzman partnership, 325; to Holtzman, 398, 399, 400; Holtzman to Woodruff, Jr., 401, 402
sidelines sold at office, 35, 57 f., 72, 103, 164, 176
staff, apprentices and journeymen, 21, 22, 33, 43, 56, 74, 77, 90, 105 f., 167, 173, 190, 360, 395, 396, 399
   editors not proprietors, Tucker, 178; Weller, 183 f.; Logan, 190; unidentified substitutes for Borden, 207, 210–211; John B. Borden, 224, 225; Fowler, 229; Knight, 273, 276; Trousdale, 278–280; Alden Woodruff, 284 f., 301, 302; William E. Woodruff, 301, 302; Knight, 302, 303; unidentified substitutes for Danley, 323 f., 335, 343; Noland, 327–329; Holtzman for Danley, 352, 397 f.
title, 17–18, 20, 63, 87, 120, 144, 270, 271, 292, 293 f., 299, 317, 319, 337, 395
value, 180
volume numbering, 272, 299, 308, 338, 370 f., 396
Arkansas Herald (Arkansas Post): 9 f., 34
Arkansas Herald (Davidsonville): 35
Arkansas Industrial University: 244

Arkansas Intelligencer (Van Buren): 186, 207 f., 211, 216, 246, 251 f., 253 ff., 260, 287

Arkansas militia: Cole and Thorn, 164; alerted, 223; Tucker, 225; Hayden, 245 n.; in 1860–1861 crisis, 353, 356; in Civil War, 358 ff., 362 ff., 368, 371, 373, 377, 385

Arkansas Post, Ark.: 9 f., 13 f., 32, 41 f., 46, 382

Arkansas River: 227, 253, 272, 304, 367

Arkansas State Fair: 305, 329

Arkansas State Temperance Society: 183, 208

Arkansas Supreme Court: 78, 123, 141, 159, 168, 169, 172, 181, 190, 234, 243, 282, 288 f., 292, 334, 344, 372, 377, 388

Arkansas Territorial Capitol Restoration: 54, 55 n., 328

Arkansas Territory: creation of, 8, 15; newspaper opportunities in, 8–11; appointments in 1819, 15; seat of government, 35–37

Arkansas Times and Advocate: 149, 153, 156, 159, 168 f., 171, 177 ff., 186, 188 ff., 203 f., 208, 223, 273 n.

"Arkansas Traveller" painting: 296

Army Bulletin: 376

Arrington, Alfred W.: 205

Ashley and Brown: 396

Ashley and Robards: 396

Ashley, Chester: 43, 85, 111, 121, 151, 169, 194, 203 f., 236, 239, 241, 242, 246, 247, 256, 258, 272–273 n., 273, 280; arrival in Arkansas, 22; Little Rock title dispute, 36, 37, 41; marriage, 40; Little Rock lot sales, 54, 55 n., 72, 73, 79 n., 104; and political factions, 59, 64 f., 130 ff; 1827 campaign, 73 f., 76, 81 f.; partnership with Crittenden, 60, 67, 69; land speculation, 89; said to control *Gazette,* 102, 103; "Jaw Bone" letters, 93, 103; home of, 72, 98; and death of Garrett, 83–84; and statehood, 110; and construction of State House, 110; power in party, 139 ff., 215; suboration of perjury charge, 141; director State Bank, 141, 142; Drew's analysis of, 230; candidate for elector, 204 ff.; rivalry with Yell and election to Senate, 205 f., 210, 211, 215 ff., 229, 230; and Lawrence Land District

controversy, 239 f.; death of, 250–251, 252

Ashley, Mary W. W. Elliott: 40, 43, 55 n., 63, 89, 104, 157, 204, 251

Askew, J. H.: 399

Austin, Stephen Fuller: 24

Backbone Mountain: 385

Badgett, Noah H.: 214

Baldwin, D. J.: 193

Ball, William McK.: 98, 152 ff.

Bank of Maryland: 103, 113

Bank scandals: 187 f., 194, 196, 206, 211, 241, 254

Barkeloo, William: 307

Barnes, A. S. and Co.: 307

Barnet, Martin M.: 120

Bartlett, Liberty: 399

Bates, Catherine E. Pankey: 55 n.

Bates, Frederick: 23 f.

Bates, James Woodson: 22 ff., 25, 27 f., 29, 34, 45, 48 f., 49 ff., 58, 62 f., 70 f., 95 f.

Bates, Mary Clarissa: 55 n.

Bates, William: 55 n.

Batesville, Ark.: 371, 372, 374

Batesville *Commercial Standard:* 300

Batesville *Eagle:* 253, 260

Batesville *Independent Balance:* 348

Batesville *News:* 169, 196, 197

Batson, Felix I.: 361, 380, 384

Baxter, Elisha: 391

Bayly, John W.: 234

Beall, Asa, Sr.: 176

Beall, Samuel T.: 248 n.

Bean, Jonathan L.: 62

Bedell, Charlotte: 106 n.

Beebe, Roswell: 55 n., 173, 286, 273 n., 299

Beirne, A., Jr.: 273 n.

Bell, John: 341, 348

Bender, David and Co.: 273 n., 305

Bennett, Peter H.: 33

Benton, Ark.: 156

Bertrand, Charles Pierre: 145, 212, 288, 309, 330; picture, 74; *Gazette* apprentice, 56, 74; and death of Garrett, 91 ff.; editor *Advocate,* 90, 91 ff., 94 f., 97, 99 f., 102 f., 106, 108, 120

Bindery: 121, 122

Biniger, A. M. and Co.: 340

Binney and Ronaldson Type Foundry: 12

Biscoe, Henry L.: 100

Black, J. H.: 343, 346
Black, William: 230 n.
Blackburn, William Jasper: 330
Bliss, Calvin C.: 214 n., 388, 390 f.
Bloomington, Ill. *Statesman:* 346
Blunt, James G.: 381, 384
Board, C. W.: 367
Boardman, Norman: 173
Bonneville, B. L. E.: 4
Borden, Benjamin J.: 207, 209, 246, 266, 269 f., 313; purchase of *Gazette,* 192; family and background, 195; marriage, 209; duel with Borland, 200–203; education and religion, 236; as editor of *Gazette,* 196 f., 203, 206 f., 210, 211, 212, 218, 219, 223, 226, 227 f., 229, 233, 235 f.; refused to sell to Woodruff, 221 f.
Borden, Charlotte Beck: 195
Borden, John B.: 224, 225, 236
Borden, Levi: 195
Borden, Sarah Yeiser: 209
Borden, William B.: 193, 208, 229
Borland, Eliza Hart: 198 n.
Borland, Euclid: 198 n., 318
Borland, Fannie: 318
Borland, George Godwin: 321 n.
Borland, Harold: 198 n., 321 n.
Borland, Huldah Wright: 198 n.
Borland, Mary Isabel Milbourne: 213, 321 n.
Borland, Mary M.: 321 n.
Borland, Solon: 209, 215, 264, 300, 302, 309, 313, 352; editor *Banner,* 197 ff., 217, 223, 228, 255; family and background, 197 f., 200 f., 268, 275, 277, 301 f.; duel with Borden, 200 ff.; illnesses and absences, 207, 214, 268, 297, 315; law practice, 210; medical practice, 217; adjutant general and elector, 213; d'Estimauville scandal, 205, 212 f., 226, 318; marriage, 213; in Mexican War, 224 ff., 234 f., 238 f., 241; rift with Yell faction, 230 f., 234 f., 241; political career, 241 f., 246 ff., 249 f., 253 ff., 275, 277, 280 f., 292 f., 296 f., and subornation of perjury accusation against Woodruff, 255; dispute with Clay, 250, 251, 254; declines appointment in Spain, 248 f., 257, 268; street argument with Johnson, 268; avoided duel with Flournoy, 251 f., 256 f.; avoided duel with Foote, 274 f.; and Danley-Whiteley fight, 283 f., 287 f.; fight

with Kennedy, 289; home at Little Rock, 311 f.; mission to Central America, 300 f., 310 ff.; picture, 301; considered Memphis paper, 314; partnership in *Gazette,* 314, 315 ff., 321; seizure of Fort Smith garrison, 356; in Civil War, 359, 363, 365, 370
Borland, Thomas (Dr.): 197–198 n.
Borland, Thomas: 198 n., 321 n.
Boudinot, Elias C.: 343, 346
Boyd, S. H.: 388
Bradford, Benjamin J.: 11 n.
Bradford, Thomas G.: 7, 8, 35
Bradford, William: 29, 49, 52, 53, 65
Brand, William: 255
Brearley, Colonel: 39
Brearley, David: 61
Breckinridge, John C.: 323, 341, 347, 348
Brickmakers at Little Rock, 53–54
Briggs, Robert: 25, 33 f.
Briley, —: 376
Brindley, Jacob: 149
Brisbin, J. and Co.: 305
Brookhaven, N. Y.: 4
Brookin, Henry: 306
Brooklyn, N. Y.: 4, 163
Brooks-Baxter War: 298 n.
Brower, Capt.: 6
Brown, Jacob: 163, 172, 173
Brown, Richard Conway Sevier: 101 n.
Brownsville, Ark.: 331, 385
Bruce, David: 4 n.
Bruce, George: 6, 120, 172, 286, 307
Brugman, Dickison: 308, 360
Brumback, Christian: 53–54, 55 n.
Bryan, James: 35, 37
Buchanan, James: 323, 328, 337, 341
Buckner, Simeon: 160
Budd, John J.: 149, 267, 281
Buena Vista, battle of: 235, 237 f., 279 n.
Burgevin and Field: 363
Burgevin, Edmund: 352, 363 f., 372 f.
Burke, —: 306
Burnett, George H.: 172 ff., 175 f., 178, 179, 180, 186
Burnett, Susan W. Beall: 176
Burnside, J.: 273 n.
Burrow, N. B.: 329
Butler, James D.: 316, 343, 378 f., 381
Butler, John Milton: 221 n., 295, 316
Butler, William O.: 252 f.
Byrd, Richard C.: 199 f., 203, 208, 258, 262, 272 n., 273 n., 281
Byrne, James W.: 72 f.

Cabell, William L.: 385
Cadron, Ark.: 36
Cairo and Fulton Railroad: 296 f., 300
Calhoun, John C.: 274, 276, 337
California: gold rush, 267 f., 284; and
    Compromise of 1850, 273 f.
Camden, Ark.: 390
Camden *Arkansaw Traveler:* 313
Camden *Ouachita Herald:* 348, 378, 384
Camden *South Stamp:* 315
Camden *State Rights Eagle:* 335
Cameron, Ewen: 259 n.
Canby, Edward R. S.: 391
Cane Hill, Ark.: 114, 115
Capital Guards: 399
Carroll, Charles A.: 339, 373 f.
Carrollton, Miss. *Weekly Democrat:* 279
    n.
"Casca" letters: 139 ff.
Case, Loyal: 388
Cass, Lewis: 252
Cassidy, Henry: 24
Catholics: 209, 235 f., 285, 314, 316, 317
Censorship of news: 360, 371, 376
Census of 1850: 289
Central America: 300 f., 310 f.
Cerro Gordo, Battle of: 228, 235
Chapman, Daniel J.: 182, 185, 200, 201,
    204, 216
Chapman, W. D.: 199
Chapultepec, battle of: 180
Charless, Joseph: 8 n.
Chase and Lincoln: 122
Chase, Luther: 122, 193
Chatfield and Woods: 395 f.
Chattanooga, Tenn. *Rebel:* 285 n.
Cherokee Indians: 20, 94
Chicot County, Ark.: 46, 114, 119, 183,
    269
Chidester, Rapley and Co.: 345
Chism, Stephen H.: 260
Choctaw Treaty of 1820: 27 f., 48
Christian Church: 212, 236
"Chronicles": 137 f.
Churchill, Thomas J.: 351 f., 355
Cincinnati, Ohio: 150, 267, 355
Cincinnati Type Foundry: 243, 286
Civil War: 268, 285 n., 298 n., 357 ff.
Claiborne, J. C.: 300
Clarendon, Ark.: 374
Clarke, George W.: 207 f., 246, 251 f.,
    280 f.
Clarke, W. P.: 236
Clarksville, Ark.: 279, 335, 368
Clarksville *Standard:* 251

Clay, Cassius M.: 250, 251, 254
Clay, Henry: 66 f., 87, 88, 103, 200, 201,
    239, 250
Clemens, Benjamin: 54
Clemens, Jere: 321 n.
Clendenin, John J.: 180, 377
Cleveland, Grover: 285 n.
Clifford, Nathan: 249, 254
Cockcroft and Overend: 244
Cocke, John H.: 95
Colby, Eli: 149, 168 f., 169 f., 171, 177,
    182 f., 186, 188 f., 191, 203, 273 n.
Colby, John: 203, 210, 273 n.
Cole, Edward: 106, 159, 160–164, 168,
    169–174, 177, 186, 194, 214
Columbia, Mo. *Herald-Statesman:* 9 n.
Compromise of 1850: 275 ff., 279 f.
Conditional Unionists: 348 f., 352, 353,
    357
Confederate Army: 357 ff., 362 f., 365,
    367 ff., 371 ff., 379, 381 ff., 390, 393;
    1st Ark. Inf. Regt., 356; 2d Ark. Mtd.
    Rifles, 378; 12th Ark. Inf. Regt., 369
Confederate National Union: 366
Confederate States of America: 353, 356
    f., 367, 371
Confiscation Act: 388 f., 390 f., 392 f.
Conner and Cooke: 143 f., 172
Conservatives: 386, 400
Constitution (Arkansas): of 1836, 130,
    132 ff., 136, 388; of 1861, 376 f.;
    of 1864, 388, 390
Constitutional Convention: of 1836, 109
    f., 126 ff., 130, 132, 141 f.; proposed
    in 1854, 309; of 1861, 349 ff., 353
    ff., 356, 357, 358 f., 361, 376, 392;
    of 1864, 387, 388
Constitutional Union Party: 341 ff., 347
    f., 361
Contreras, battle of: 239
Conventions, nominating: (state), caucus
    of 1836, 131 f., 141, 199; in 1842,
    182 f.; in 1843, 199 f., 204; in 1846,
    217; in 1848, 240, 242; in 1851, 280
    f.; in 1852, 289 f.; in 1853, 301; in
    1854, 308 f.; in 1856, 321, 322; in
    1858, 331; in 1860, 341, 343, 346,
    361
Conventions, nominating (national): in
    1836, 135, 145; in 1844, 200; in 1848,
    242, 252; in 1852, 289; policy, in
    1854, 315; in 1856, 320; in 1860,
    341
Conventions, ratification (state): 317
Conway, Elias Nelson: 130, 136, 151,

154, 196, 201, 210, 224, 240, 241, 249, 255, 317, 335, 342, 345, 377; and sale of *Gazette* to Whigs, 191, 193, 194; candidate for governor, 199 f., 204; defeated for auditor, 259 ff., 278; elected governor in 1852, 290 ff., 302 f., 310, 313; re-elected in 1856, 322 f., 326 f., 328, 334

Conway, Henry Wharton: 37, 129, 130; background, 27; election to Congress in 1823, 49–53, 60; picture, 56; and appointments to Superior Court, 58; 1825 campaign, 62 f.; borrowed Quapaw money, 60 f., 65; and events preceding 1827 campaign, 59, 62, 64, 66 f., 70 ff.; 1827 campaign, 65, 72–80; duel with Crittenden, 80 ff., 85, 107

Conway, James Sevier: 62, 130, 137, 139, 141, 146, 147, 168, 197, 240

Conway, William (B.): 50, 281, 290

Copp, William: 123

Copperheads: 386, 387

Counterfeiting: 186 f., 380

Crittenden, Ann Innis Morris: 49, 67, 78, 81

Crittenden, John: 67

Crittenden, John Jordan: 48, 50, 88

Crittenden, Morris: 67

Crittenden, Robert: 34, 37, 91, 93, 97, 100, 102, 127, 137; picture, 23; secretary Arkansas Territory, 15 f.; reappointment, 70; removal, 89; political machine of, 22 f., 59; rift with Woodruff, 22 f., 28 f., 35, 39 ff., 59 f.; attempts to start rival paper, 35, 87; and control of *Advocate*, 92, 93, 102; and 1819 election, 24; and 1821 election, 29; and elections of 1821 and 1823, 48–51, 52; friend of Oden and Allen, 25 f., and Choctaw treaty, 48; marriage, 49; partnership with Ashley, 60, 67, 69; recommended for governor, 61; applied for appointment as governor, 87 f.; and Conway's borrowing from Quapaw funds, 60 f., 65, 73, 80; rift with Izard, 62, 63–68; negotiation of Quapaw treaty, 67; 1827 campaign and preceding controversy, 69–80; and title to Woodruff's lots, 73; duel with Conway, 80 ff., 85, 107; and death of Garrett, 84, 92 f.; reconciled with Bates, 96; and 1831 campaign, 96 f.; home of, 72, 98; candidate for Congress in 1833, 106 f.; and attempted impeachment of Johnson, 106; challenged Eskridge, 107; and Pike, 108; rejected union with Pope, 112; death, 120

Crittenden, Thomas: 82

Cross, Edward: 157 f., 168, 176, 182 f., 184 f., 230, 255, 239

Crutchfield, Peter T.: 173

Cummins, Ebenezer: 245

Cummins, William: 106, 107, 127, 137, 139, 142, 157 f., 169, 182, 185, 245

Cunningham, Eliza: 43

Cunningham, Matthew: 40, 43, 56, 74 f., 83, 84, 90, 91 ff., 93, 100, 103

Cunningham, Robert: 74

Curran, James M.: 302

Currency: 57, 166, 181, 186 f., 337, 338, 366, 380

Curtis, Samuel Ryan: 367 f., 371 f., 374 f., 379

Cypert, Jesse N.: 346

Dallas, George M.: 209

Dallas County, Ark.: 212 f., 244

Danley, Benjamin F.: 283 f., 302, 307, 340, 353, 374, 399

Danley, Christopher Columbus: 236, 257, 383; picture, 301; family and background, 259 n.; in Mexican War, 226, 235, 238 f., 241, 247, 259, 260; mentioned for governor, 241; home from war, 251; state auditor, 259 ff., 278, 302 f., 310; and 1851 election, 280; controversy with Whiteley, 281–284, 287 ff.; bought *Gazette*, 297; as *Gazette's* editor-proprietor, 299 f., 301–336, 337–356, 357–384, 386; and American party, 312–316, 320 f.; home of, 307, 308; illnesses, 323, 327, 329, 335, 336, 352, 379, 397 f.; candidate for state Senate in 1858, 331 ff.; in 1862, 378, 379; avoids duel with Terry, 333 f.; with Burgevin, 362 ff.; commissioner to buy arms, 351 f., 355; on Military Board, 358, 359, 362; in Federal occupation, 386, 390; revived *Gazette*, 393, 396, 401 f.; death and estate, 399

Danley, Eleanor: 259 n.

Danley, James: 259 n.

Danley, James M.: 259 n., 302, 307

Danley, Mary Ann Fenton: 259 n.

Danley, William: 283 f., 399, 400

Davidson, John W.: 384 f., 386, 388
Davidsonville, Ark.: 35
Davis, Jefferson: 289, 353, 359, 361, 367, 375, 381
Dayton, William L.: 323
DeBaun, James: 272–273 n.
Defiance Hook and Ladder Co.: 306 f.
Dell, Valentine: 386
Demby, James William: 386
Democratic Central Committee: 195 f., 197, 199, 213, 217, 230
Democratic party: 161, 175, 196 ff., 215 ff., 229 ff., 231, 233 f., 274, 299, 315 f., 337, 361, 386; and *Gazette* in 1819, 20, 25; Pike's analysis of party leadership, 139 f.; in legislature, 152, 187 ff., 191, 257–261; campaign paper of 1840, 171; and sale of *Gazette* to Whigs, 192 ff.; and 1850 sale of *Gazette,* 269; established *Banner,* 195 f.; organs of, 293 f.; and *Gazette's* switch to American party, 317 (see also Elections.)
DeMun, Auguste: 10 n.
Des Arc, Ark.: 334
Desha, Benjamin: 96
d'Estimauville, Ark.: 212, 213, 318
d'Estimauville de Beau Mouchel, Madame: 205, 212 f., 226, 318
Dibrell, James A.: 203
Dickinson, Samuel S.: 113
Dickinson, Townsend: 37, 141
Digest of laws: of 1834, 115 ff., 121, 152; of 1837–1838, 152–155
Dodge, Roderick L.: 328 n.
Donelson, Andrew Jackson: 320
Doolittle, —: 343
Douglas, Stephen A.: 289, 341, 346 ff.
Dover, Ark.: 279, 322
Drew, Thomas Stevenson: 204 f., 206, 208, 211, 216, 223, 224, 230, 232, 233, 240 f., 242 f., 246 f., 248, 249, 250, 252, 258 f., 261, 262
Dudderidge, James E.: 324
Dudley and Nelson: 173
Duels: 82 f., 86, 94 f., 102, 106, 261, 262; McArthur-DeMun, declined, 10 n.; Allen-Oden, 25 f.; Scott-Selden, 58, 71; Pope-Cocke, 95; Pope-Noland, 95 f., 107; Sevier-Newton, 80, 197; Sevier-Cummins, declined, 107, 257; Crittenden-Conway, 80 ff., 85, 107; Crittenden-Eskridge, declined, 107; Foote-Prentiss, 107; Borland-Borden, 200–203; Borland-Flournoy, de-
clined, 251 f., 256 f.; Borland-Foote, avoided, 274 f.; Borland-Kennedy, avoided, 289; Scott-Pew, avoided, 138; Logan-Clarke, 207 f.; Pike-Roane, 236 ff., 261; Hayden-Whiteley, declined, 263 f.; Danley-Terry, avoided, 333 f.; Danley-Burgevin, avoided, 362 ff.; Peek-Black, avoided, 346; Johnson-Rector, avoided, 372 f.
Dyer, William H.: 56
Dynasty: 196, 199 f., 201, 205, 210, 288, 294, 302, 309 f., 313, 322, 329, 331 f.; background, 27; summary 1823 to 1836, 129–132; beginning of nickname, 197; in 1848 politics, 240, 248, 249 n., 251, 252, 254, 255, 259, 261; in 1860 election, 342, 343–347, 348; in Civil War: 357, 358, 364, 378

Eakin, John R.: 361, 368, 377, 381, 383
Eastin, Thomas: 9 n.
Eastman, M. H.: 177
Ecklin, S. and Co.: 120
Edington, Haley S.: 262
El Dorado saloon: 305
El Mexicano: 9 n.
Elections: in 1819, 17, 19, 20, 22–25; 1820, 25 ff.; 1821, 29, 45, 49; 1823, 49–53, 58, 60; 1825, 62 f.; summary prior to 1827, 58 f.; 1827, 59 f., 73–80, 86; 1828, 87; 1829, 89; 1831, 96 f.; 1832, 100; 1833, 106 f.; 1835, 126 f.; 1836, 128–132, 135 f., 139, 140 f., 142 f., 146 f., 219; 1838, 157 f.; 1840, 167 f., 170, 171, 175, 176; 1842, 182 f., 184 f.; 1844, 199 f., 203–207, 208 f.; 1846, 206, 210, 215, 217, 226, 229, 230 f., 232, 242; 1848, 239–243, 246 ff., 250 ff., 253–259, 309; 1849, 261 ff., 345; 1851, 280 f.; 1852, 289 ff., 292 f., 345; 1853, 301 f.; 1854, 308 ff.; 1856, 320–323, 342; 1858, 331 ff., 342; 1860, 335, 339, 341–346, 347 f., 360; 1861, 351, 353 f., 354, 360 f.; 1862, 376 ff.; 1863, 384; 1864, 387, 388, 389 f., 391 f.; 1865, 393, 399, 400
Elkhorn Tavern, battle of: 368
Eller, David G.: 55 n.
Elliott, Clarissa: 55 n.
Elliott, Elias Austin: 37
Elliott, Eliza Ann: 63
Elliott, Henry: 37
Elliott, L. M. and Co.: 324

Encarnacion prisoners: 235, 238 f., 242, 247, 250, 253 f.
English, Elbert H.: 210, 213, 234, 288, 293, 309
Eskridge, Thomas P.: 51, 58, 107
Etter, William H.: 381
Evans, Lemuel D.: 78 n., 182, 185
Everett, Edward: 339, 341, 348

Fairchild, H. F.: 377
Far West Course: 180
Farley, John W.: 173, 213, 221 n.
Farrelly, Robert C.: 295
Farrelly, Terrence: 330
Faulkner, Sandford C.: 332
Fayetteville, Ark.: 137, 322, 352
Fayetteville *Arkansian:* 343, 345
Fayetteville *South-West Independent:* 305, 319
Fenton, E. J.: 259 n.
Ferguson, Robert: 11 n.
Ferguson, William D.: 157
Ficklin, J. S.: 232
Field, William: 55 n., 100, 101, 111, 114 f., 124 f., 203, 210, 250
Fillmore, Millard: 252, 253, 320
Finn, John: 168
Fire Place, Long Island, N.Y.: 4
Fishback, William Meade: 387, 390, 391, 392
Fisher, Charles: 196
Flanagin, Harris: 377 ff., 380, 382 ff.
Fletcher, Thomas: 377, 380
Florida: 110
Flournoy, Thompson B.: 256 f., 258, 278
Foote, Henry S.: 107, 274 f.
Fort Smith, Ark.: 203, 208, 238, 352, 355, 356, 384, 385, 368, 369, 381
Fort Smith *Bulletin:* 378
Fort Smith *New Era:* 386
Fort Sumter, S.C.: 354, 357
Fourche Bayou: 227, 385
Fowler, Absalom: 99, 127, 137, 139, 152– 155, 169, 176, 229, 232, 322
Fowler, Milton: 229
Frankfort, Ky.: 138
Franklin *Missouri Intelligencer, and Boon's Lick Advertiser:* 9 n.
Franklin, Tenn.: 4 n., 11
Franklin, Tenn. *Independent Gazette:* 11 n.
Franklin, Tenn. *Monitor:* 4 n., 11
Franklin, Tenn. *Western Balance:* 4 n.
Free Negroes: 126, 184, 269, 278, 325, 326, 334

Free Soil party: 268, 323
Fremont, John C.: 320, 323
Fugitive Slave bill: 279
Fulton, Ark.: 24
Fulton, David: 103, 142
Fulton, John T.: 100 f., 125
Fulton, William Savin: 89, 91, 93, 101, 102, 103, 110 f., 119 f., 121, 122, 126 f., 130, 139, 140, 141, 146, 202, 205, 206, 230, 255

Gaceta de Texas: 9 n.
Gaines, Edmund P.: 139
Gaines, John P.: 235
Gaines, William H.: 192
Gallatin, Tenn. *Tenth Legion:* 279 n.
Gallatin, Tenn. *Union:* 110 f.
Gambling: 124
Gantt, Edward W.: 343, 346, 369, 376, 387
Garland, Augustus Hill: 343, 358, 361, 380, 384
Garland, Rufus King: 384
Garner, C. J.: 228
Garrett, John T.: 83 f., 91 ff.
Garritt, Fred S.: 281
Gee, James M.: 365
Gibson, Lorenzo: 158, 188, 203, 208, 258, 325 f., 328, 332, 333 f., 399
Giles, Josiah: 221 n.
Gish, Jacob: 208, 210
Goodman, Otis: 369
Goodrich, Lemuel H.: 173
Gould, —: 376
Green, Joshua F.: 285
Greenwood, Alfred B.: 301, 308 f., 322
Greer, David B.: 233, 281 f., 288
Greer, Henry: 311
Greytown, Nicaragua: 310 f., 317
Gutiérrez-Magee Expedition: 9 n.

Haight, Charles: 396
Hall, Sergeant: 9 n.
Hamlin, Hannibal: 347, 348
Hammond, Andrew: 207
Hampton, John R.: 282, 328
Hanly, Thomas B.: 361
Haralson, Herndon: 232
Hardee, William J.: 298 n., 359, 363
Hardin, Joseph: 37
Harper and Brothers: 4
Harper, James: 4
Harper, John: 4
Harrell, John M.: 352

Harris, Carey Allen: 11 n.
Harris, Isham G.: 285 n.
Harrison, William Henry: 170, 176, 178, 245
Hawkins, Richard C.: 134
Hayden, George B.: 244, 245 f., 249, 250, 253, 255, 260, 261, 262 f., 263 f., 264–270
Hayden, Ella Corinne: 245 n.
Hayden, James: 245 n.
Hayden, Louisa: 245 n.
Helena, Ark.: 111, 114, 123, 136, 166, 279 n., 341, 342, 352, 355, 356, 371, 374 f., 381, 384
Helena *Arkansas Journal:* 207, 217
Helena *Herald:* 111, 112, 126
Helena *Southern Shield:* 233, 348
Hempstead, Elizabeth Rebecca Beall: 248 n.
Hempstead, Sally Rector: 248 n.
Hempstead, Samuel H.: 193, 196, 203, 224, 240, 248–252, 329
Henderson, Joseph: 63 n.
Henry, Isaac N.: 9 n.
Herron, Francis J.: 381
Hicks, J. C. M.: 221 n.
Higbee, J. O.: 177
Hill, Levin D.: 367
Hindman, Thomas Carmichael: 333, 342 ff., 346 f., 349, 358, 373–376, 380 ff.
Hoe, Richard and Co.: 307, 340, 395
Hogan, Edmund: 29, 86
Holliday, Benjamin: 9 n.
Hollins, George N.: 311
Holman, ——: 138, 139
Holmes, Theophilus Hunter: 375 f., 381, 382, 384
Holt, George M.: 362 n., 364
Holtzman, Jenetta Brookin: 325 n.
Holtzman, William Frederick: 325, 329, 331, 341, 352, 381, 386, 389, 395, 396, 397, 401 f.
Hooper, Philo O.: 379
Hopefield, Ark.: 367
Horner, John S.: 383
Horner, William B. R.: 24
Hot Springs, Ark.: 105, 125, 214, 241, 251, 253, 256, 268, 275, 277, 300, 301, 322, 323, 327, 329, 334, 335, 339, 341, 342, 370, 372
Houston, John S.: 217
Houston, Samuel: 93 f., 339, 341
Howard, Enoch: 388
Hubbard, Thomas: 343, 346
Hughes, Simon P.: 300

Hummell, ——: 306
Hunt, Andrew Jackson: 121, 123 f., 127
Hunter, Edward: 236
Huntersville, Ark.: 367
Huntsville, Ala.: 149, 370
Huntsville, Ala. *Democrat:* 113 n.
Hutt, John: 284
Huyck, Isaac: 398

Illinois Intelligencer: 9
Independent Order of Odd Fellows: 265, 306, 317, 399, 401
Indian Affairs: 67 (see also Choctaw Treaty of 1820, Cherokee Indians, Quapaw Indians)
Indian Territory: 203, 208, 238
Indians: 94, 103, 356, 375
Internal Improvements: 285, 290 f., 299, 337
Irving, Washington: 103
Island No. 10: 369
Izard, George: 59, 61 f., 63–68, 74, 76, 82, 83, 87
Izard, Mark W.: 204

Jabine, Hallie: 298 n.
Jabine, John Nicholas: 298 n., 389
Jacks, T. M.: 389 f.
Jackson, Andrew: 28, 60, 87 f., 89, 90, 91, 103, 121, 122, 129, 131, 137, 138, 226, 337
Jackson County, Ark.: 381
Jackson, Mo. *Independent Patriot:* 9 n.
Jackson *Missouri Herald:* 9 n.
Jacksonport, Ark.: 369, 371
Jefferson County, Ark.: 234, 253, 323
Jefferson, Thomas: 121, 184, 271, 319, 338
Jenkins' Ferry, battle of: 390
Jester, Joseph: 247
Jester's Sulphur Springs: 370
Johnson, Andrew: 391, 400
Johnson, Benjamin: 37, 48, 61, 106, 107, 115 f., 119, 129, 130, 261
Johnson, Euclid L.: 182, 185, 196
Johnson, Herschel V.: 341, 347, 348
Johnson, James B.: 249, 332
Johnson, James M.: 387, 390
Johnson, Jilson P.: 361
Johnson, John T.: 61
Johnson, Joshua: 89 n.
Johnson, L. and Co.: 307

Johnson, Richard Henry: 214 n, 288, 293, 294, 313, 314 f., 317, 323, 326 f., 332, 334, 335, 342, 343–347, 348, 351, 355, 359, 360, 361, 362, 364, 372 f., 376, 377, 378, 381, 382, 383, 389, 390
Johnson, Richard Mentor: 48, 110, 129, 130, 131, 134, 143, 167 f.
Johnson, Robert Ward: 196, 240, 248, 249, 258, 282, 288, 329, 332, 342, 348, 349, 385; picture, 216; and sale of *Gazette* to Borden, 193, 194, 224; election to Congess in 1846, 199, 215, 217, 229; party faction leader, 239 ff.; 1848 campaign, 241, 242, 246, 252; in Congress, 247, 280, 281, 296 f.; said to own interest in *Banner,* 255; conflict with Borland, 268, 300; and Compromise of 1850, 274, 276 f., 280; re-elected to Congress in 1851, 280 f.; and 1852 Senate election, 292 f., 294; not candidate for Congress in 1853, 301; appointed to Senate in 1853, 302; elected to Senate in 1854, 313; and *True Democrat,* 313; in C.S.A. Provisional Congress, 357; in C.S.A. Senate, 361, 373, 374, 376, 380, 381
Johnson, Thomas: 262
Johnston, Albert Sidney: 362, 363, 365
Johnston, Thomas Wyatt: 82
Johnston, William F.: 320
Jones, George W.: 81 n.
Jones, James A.: 346
Joselyn, A. H.: 307
Jouett, Charles: 15
Joy, Levi: 285 n.
Joy, Martha Johnson: 285 n.

Keatts, James B.: 95, 203, 328
Keith, William S.: 326
Kendall, Amos: 145
Kennedy, Joseph Camp Griffith: 289
Kimber, T. H.: 266
King, John F.: 132
King, William R.: 290
Kirkpatrick, Simeon: 343
Knight, Hannah Donnell: 273 n., 274
Knight, John Elliot: 231, 235, 238, 268, 273, 274, 275 f., 302, 303, 383
Knight, Lizzie: 273 n.
Know-Nothing party: see American party

Knoxville (Tenn.) *Gazette:* 11 n.
Kramer and Miller: 396
Kyle, G. H.: 399

Labor Unions: 313, 324 f., 366
Lacy, Thomas J.: 141
Lafflin, Stevens and Co.: 173
Lamb, S. H.: 299
Lambert, David: 169 ff.
Land speculation: 60, 89, 205, 206
Lane, Joseph: 341, 347, 348
Laurie, Shepherd: 245, 269
Lawrence County, Ark.: 24, 143
Lawrence Land District: 239 f.
Lawson, James: 193
Lawson, James, Sr.: 195
Leadbetter, Burrell: 186 f.
Lee, Robert E.: 384, 393
Legislature: 136; Sevier's control of, 140, 141; apportionment dispute, 29; changes advocated, 309; secretary-judges session of 1819, 15; session of 1820, 27, 35, 36 f.; of 1821, 39, 41; of 1827, 82, 83; of 1831, 97 ff., 101; of 1833, 108, 110; of 1835, 126, 127, 130; of 1836, 139, 141 f., 143, 150 f.; of 1837, 151–155; of 1838, 158 f.; of 1842–1843, 182 f., 184, 187 ff., 191, 196, 197, 210, 219; of 1844, 206, 210 ff., 241; of 1846, 229, 231 ff., 254; of 1848, 257–261, 254, 255; of 1850, 277 ff.; of 1852, 294 f.; demand for 1853 special session, 302, 310; session of 1854, 313; of 1856, 325 ff., 328; of 1858, 334; of 1860, 357; of 1861, 347, 349, 351; 1861 special sessions, 358, 361, 362; 1862 special session, 368; session of 1862, 380 f.; of 1864, 391, 392
Lemmon, James: 84
Letcher, Robert P.: 15
Levy, Jonas: 180
Levy's Dry Goods Store: 306
Lewis and Thomas: 21
Lewis, Eli J.: 20 f., 42
Lewisburg, Ark.: 382
Lewisville, Ark.: 236
Lexington, Ky.: 7, 135, 170
Lexington *Kentucky Gazette:* 135, 145
Libel suits: Hogan v. Russell, 29; Crittenden v. Woodruff, 75 f., 77, 83, 85; Ashley v. grand jury, 141; Finn v. Obaugh, 168
Liggin, James Madison: 173

Lincoln, Abraham: 347, 348, 354, 355, 356, 387, 388, 389, 391 f., 393
Lincoln, Lemuel R.: 121, 122, 234
Lindsley, Darwin: 164, 172, 307 n.
Linebaugh, Benjamin: 305
Linebaugh, Henry W.: 305
Linn, Lewis F.: 10 n.
Little Rock and California Assn.: 268
Little Rock, Ark.: title dispute and fight for seat of government, 22, 24, 35–39, 41, 72; Pulaski County seat, 41; progress of, 53; description in 1821, 43; in 1841, 180; view of, in *Gazette's* nameplate, 272; and cholera epidemic, 103; and anti-gambling movement, 124; and counterfeiting ring, 186; fires, 134, 165, 214, 305 f.; tornado of 1840, 170; drainage problem, 227; Elm Street, 214, 273 n.; ferry at, 125, 159 f.; Town Branch, 265 f., 307 n., 397; almanac for, 243; gas lights, 347; telegraph, 352; market, 144, 304; population in 1833 and 1835, 377; in election of 1836, 143; of 1865, 399; municipal government, 100, 134, 320, 397, 400; post office, 100 f., 114 f., 125 f., 322 f., 396; efforts to remove seat of government, 334; removal of seat of government in Civil War, 372, 373, 376, 377, 398; seizure of arsenal, 353; military campaigns against, 367, 371–375, 382; capture of, 384 f.
Little Rock *Arkansas Patriot:* 379, 380, 381
Little Rock *Arkansas Star:* 169 ff., 177, 178, 186
Little Rock *Arkansas Whig:* 304, 306, 312
Little Rock Association of Regular Baptists: 48
Little Rock *Chronicle:* 276 n.
Little Rock *Daily State Journal:* 362, 363, 364, 365, 369
Little Rock Debating Society: 120
Little Rock *Arkansas Farmer:* 208
Little Rock Foundry and Smithery: 286
Little Rock Guards (of 1835): 124
Little Rock Guards (of 1846–1847): 224 f., 237 f., 263 f.
Little Rock *Independent Democrat:* 199
Little Rock *Medical Reporter:* 312
Little Rock *National Democrat:* 214 n., 347, 386, 387, 390 f., 393, 396, 401
Little Rock *National Union:* 386

Little Rock *Old Line Democrat:* 342, 343, 345, 347 f., 349, 351, 362, 381
Little Rock *Political Intelligencer:* 111 f., 114, 115, 116 ff., 121
Little Rock *Spirit of the Age:* 208
Little Rock *Staats Zeitung:* 214 n.
Little Rock *Times:* 121, 123 f., 126, 127 f., 130, 132, 134, 136, 137 f., 142, 145, 149
Little Rock *True Democrat:* 214 n., 296, 303 f., 314, 315, 316 f., 322, 323, 324, 327, 332, 333, 335 f., 338 f., 349, 351, 354, 358–379, 382–384, 386, 388 f.; title of, 293; and 1852 public printing, 294 f.; office burned, 305 f.; office after fire, 313; office of, in federal occupation, 389; and Woodward, 335 f.; in 1860 election, 343–348
Little Rock Typographical Union: 324 f.
Little Rock *Unconditional Union:* 214 n., 387 f., 390 f.
Logan, John D.: 190, 192, 207 f.
Logan, Sarah: 190
Logan, S. F.: 210
London *Punch:* 286
Long and Scantland Hotel: 31
Long-Island Star: 4, 6, 7, 106, 163
Long, James: 9 n.
Louisiana: 9 n., 351
Louisville, Ky.: 3, 7, 150, 170, 190, 198, 250, 267, 389
Louisville, Ky. *Courier:* 286
Louisville, Ky. *Journal:* 135, 145, 156, 201, 263, 319
Louisville Medical Institute: 198 n.
Lucas, James H.: 22
Lyon, Matthew: 29
Lynching: 122 f., 305

Madison, Ark.: 367
Mail service: in 1820, 32; in 1821–1826, 45 f.; in 1823, 51, 52; in 1829, 104; in 1838, 157; disrupted by rain, 264; importance to *Gazette,* 32, 45 f., 178, 267, 345; and Woodruff-Field dispute, 114 f., 124 f.; and abolition tracts, 126; nominated for Constitution messenger, 132; regulations, 46, 126, 177, 207, 244, 267, 286; complaints against Woodruff's management of, 223; Danleys as carriers, 259-260 n.; Danley's complaints against, 322 f.; in Civil War, 368, 371

Maps: 227 ff.
Marcus, Edward: 316
Marks' Mill, battle of: 390
Mars, Allen: 53–54 n.
Martial law: 372, 374, 376, 380 f.
Martin, Jared C.: 196, 255, 309
Martin, J. M.: 166, 178, 186
Mason, Dudley D.: 123
Masonic Lodge: 243, 265, 306, 398
Mathers, Thomas: 79
Maumelle Mountains: 272
Maury, Evarist: 9 n.
May, John: 237
Mayers, A. G.: 188
Meador, Cincinnatus V.: 347, 364, 386, 387, 390 f., 393, 399
Mears, Gaston: 226
Mechanics Assn.: 366
Mechanics Institute: 325
Memphis and Little Rock Railroad: 329, 366 f.
Memphis, Tenn.: 4 n., 137 n., 213, 266, 345, 352, 355, 356, 373, 397
Memphis, Tenn. *Appeal:* 4, 198 n., 285 n., 314
Memphis, Tenn. *Commercial:* 285 n.
Memphis, Tenn. *Enquirer:* 321 n., 352, 355
Memphis, Tenn. *Gazette:* 198 n.
Memphis, Tenn. *Western World and Memphis Banner of the Constitution:* 198 n.
Memphis University: 225
Menefee, Nimrod: 98 f., 132, 158
Methodist Church: 317
Mexican War: 180, 223, 224 ff., 227 ff., 230 f., 232, 234 f., 236 ff., 241, 246, 247 f., 249, 254, 263 f., 268, 273, 279, 282, 283, 367
Mexico: 139, 209, 213, 266; treaty with, 247 ff., 253, 254, 257
Mexico City, Mexico: 238 f., 241, 247
Michigan: 110, 126, 179
Mier Expedition: 259 n.
Milbourne, George: 213, 302, 313
Military Board: 298 n., 358, 359, 362 f., 367, 368, 376, 377
Military bounty lands: 57
Miller County, Ark.: 116
Miller, Isaac: 4
Miller, James: 15, 20, 22, 37, 40, 41, 47, 48, 60, 61, 70
Miller, John: 188, 239 f., 257, 258
Miller, William Read: 383
Mills, Daniel R.: 113, 125, 159 f.

Mississippi River: 329, 366, 368, 382, 384
Missouri: 8–9 n., 367, 381
Missouri Compromise: 273
Missouri State Guard: 360, 367
Mitchel, Charles B.: 343, 346, 349, 361, 380
Moffett, —: 307 n.
Monroe, James: 58, 61
Monterey, battle of: 232, 235, 279 n.
Montgomery, William: 82
Montgomery's Point, Ark.: 13
Moon, James A.: 261 f.
Mooney, Daniel: 42
Moore, James Wilson: 235, 259 n.
Moore, Thomas: 6 n.
Moores, James C.: 318 n.
Morison, William: 164, 172
Morris, James T.: 309
Morton, Elijah: 25 f., 35
Murphy, Benjamin: 36, 37
Murphy, Isaac: 356, 388, 391, 392, 398 f., 400
Murrell, John A.: 122
Myrtle, W. C.: 309

McAlmont, J. J.: 312, 397, 400
McArthur, John: 9 f., 34
McCampbell, James: 116, 123, 152
McClellan, George B.: 391 f.
McCowan, Gabriel: 336
McCulloch, Ben: 358, 359, 360, 362, 363, 367, 368
McCurdy, Samuel: 170, 177, 178
McKee, William F.: 144
McKeen, Thomas H.: 35
McKenney, Thomas L.: 61
McLain, John: 103, 214
McQuaid, John: 196

Nacogdoches *Texas Republican:* 9 n.
Napoleon, Ark.: 355
Napoleon *Journal:* 166, 178, 186
Napoleon *Messenger:* 178
Nashville, Tenn.: 7–13, 149
Nashville, Tenn. *Clarion, and Tennessee State Gazette:* 7 f., 11 n., 18, 35
Nashville *Tennessee Gazette:* 11 n.
Nashville, Tenn. *Rights of Man, or, Nashville Intelligencer:* 11 n.
Nashville, Tenn. *Union and American:* 285 n.
Natchez, Miss.: 150 f.
National bank: 163, 184

National Union party: 391
Nativism: 209, 314, 316, 320, 332
Negroes: 392 (see also Slavery and Free Negroes)
Neill, Henry: 239 f.
New Madrid, Mo., battle of, 369
New Mexico Territory: 300
New Orleans, La.: 135, 150, 156, 181, 325, 335, 337, 339 f., 397
New Orleans *Louisiana Advertiser:* 31
New Orleans *Delta:* 228, 238
New Orleans *Courier:* 228
New Orleans Prices Current: 46
New Orleans *Tropic:* 237
New York *Courier and Enquirer:* 113 n.
New York *Musical World and Times:* 305
New York *Spirit of the Times:* 330
New York *Tribune:* 338 f.
Newton, Thomas Willoughby: 59, 64 f., 75, 80, 192, 197, 202, 206, 207, 208 f., 232, 242, 246, 252
Nicaragua: 310 f.
Nixon and Co.: 286
Noland, Charles Fenton Mercer: 49 n., 95 f., 107, 130, 132 ff., 141, 152, 205, 232, 257 f., 260, 292, 327 ff., 330 f.
Norman, B. M.: 227
Norman, J. P.: 227
North Carolina Chronicle, or Fayetteville Gazette: 11 n.
Norvell, Joshua: 9 n.

Oak Hills, Mo., battle of: 360, 362
Oakley, Allen M.: 83
Obaugh, James H.: 168
Obituaries: 382 f.
Oden, Robert C.: 25 f., 37, 58, 59, 60, 65, 71 f., 72 f., 78, 80, 82
O'Dowd, James: 106
O'Hara, William M.: 35
Oldham, Williamson S.: 204, 212, 217, 250, 258
Opposition party: 331
Overland Mail Co.: 345
Owen, Ezra M.: 99

Palmer, V. B.: 286
Palo Alto, battle of: 228, 235
Parrott, William H.: 92
Parvin, S. H.: 286, 324, 396
Paschal, George W.: 232
Patten, Nathaniel: 9 n.

Paul, Frank M.: 285 n.
Pea Ridge, Ark., battle of: 368, 371
Peace Democrats: 386, 391
Peach, William: 173
Pearce, James A.: 289
Peay, Gordon N.: 283
Peay, Nicholas: 84
Peay's and Pope's Hotel: 163
Peek, Laura L. Rapley: 346
Peek, Thomas C.: 343, 345, 346, 347, 362, 364
Peeler, Richmond: 17, 34
Pegues, Robert L.: 295
Pelham, William: 118, 130
Pennington, William Q.: 331 f.
People's Anti-Caucus Party: 134, 137, 139
Pettengill, S. M.: 286, 324
Pew, Thomas Jefferson: 134, 135, 136, 137, 138, 142, 145 f., 149, 152, 156, 168
Peyton, Craven: 312, 379
Phillips County, Ark.: 353
Phillips, Sylvanus: 82
Pierce, Franklin O.: 295 f., 300, 302, 311
Pike, Albert: 108, 120 f., 123 f., 127 f., 135 f., 138, 142, 145, 149, 245, 263, 264, 269, 318 n., 374, 375 f.; "Casca" letters, 139 ff.; and digest of laws, 153; candidate for Senate, 188; and sale of *Gazette* to Borden, 192; and 1844 campaign, 206 f.; control of *Gazette* charged, 206, 207; and printing jobs, 190, 243; in Mexican War, 224 f.; dispute and duel with Roane, 236 ff., 261; and American party, 317, 320
Pike County, Ark.: 380
Pike, Luther H.: 397
Pike, Mary Ann Hamilton: 120
Pillow, Gideon J.: 289
Pine Bluff, Ark.: 146, 314, 353, 355, 380, 390
Pine Bluff Female Academy: 146
Pine Bluff *Native American:* 322
Pine Bluff *Republican:* 310
Pine Bluff *True Southron:* 378
Pine Bluff *War Bulletin:* 378
Pitman's Ferry, Ark.: 359, 371
Pittsburg Landing, Tenn.: 369
Pizerinctums: 322
Pocahontas, Ark.: 180, 367, 368, 371
Poison Spring, battle of: 390
Polk, James Knox: 168, 197 f., 209, 210, 218 f., 248, 337
Polk, Leonidas: 359, 362

Pope County, Ark.: 108
Pope, Elizabeth Dorcas Janet Johnson: 89 n.
Pope, Frances Watkins Walton: 89 n.
Pope, John: 93, 97, 100, 101, 102, 112, 132; appointed governor, 88; and public printing, 91; and Pope-Cocke duel, 95; vetoed acceptance of Crittenden's home, 98; and 1833 campaign, 106; rift with Woodruff, 108 f., 111, 113 f., 114–119; rift with Fulton, 110 f.; and *Political Intelligencer,* 111 f., 113 f.; end of service as governor, 121 f.
Pope, John W.: 283
Pope, William F.: 103, 171, 322
Pope, William Fontaine: 95 f., 107
Post, J. S. and Co.: 335
Powell, William Byrd: 196, 227
Prairie County, Ark.: 255
Prairie Grove, Ark., battle of: 381
Prentice, George D.: 135, 145 f., 156, 319
Prentiss, S. S.: 107
Presbyterian Church: 265, 285
Press Association: 313, 366
Preston, John, Jr.: 281
Price, Sterling: 360, 367, 368, 369, 375, 382, 384 f., 390
Princeton, Ark.: 308
Protection Insurance Co.: 180
Pseudonyms: 20, 24 f.
Public printing: federal, 10, 34 f., 47, 91, 178; territorial, 39, 47 f., 57, 69 f., 83, 91, 97 f., 99 f., 102, 108, 127 f.; state, 142, 151 f., 152 f., 156, 158 f., 176, 188 f., 190, 191, 210, 233 f., 267, 281–284, 287 ff., 294 f., 326 f., 334, 335, 351, 358, 361 f., 381; Constitutional Convention, 128, 132 f.; city, 100, 400
Pulaski Circuit Court: 190, 284, 288, 310, 377, 399
Pulaski County, Ark.: county seat of, 41; in election of 1838, 158; of 1840, 176; of 1844, 208; of 1852, 291; of 1856, 323; of 1858, 332; martial law, 374; real estate tax, 392; records of, 398
Pulaski County Fair: 351
Pulaski Lyceum: 144

Quapaw Indians: 38, 60 f., 65, 67, 73, 80
Quesenbury, William: 305, 319, 320, 326, 331, 345, 383
Quitman, Gen.: 239

Radical Unionists: 385
Radicals: 385, 386, 387, 391, 400
Railroads: 303, 310, 329, 337, 345 (see also Cairo and Fulton Railroad)
Rainey, John S. H.: 377, 379
Ramage, Adam: 11 n.
Randolph, Lewis: 121
Randolph, Tenn. *Recorder:* 135
Rapley, Charles: 202
Rapley Building: 306
Raymond, Sam: 364
Real Estate Bank: 142, 155 f., 164, 169, 182, 187 f., 192 f., 197, 243, 246, 269 f., 346
Reardon, John E.: 305, 322 f.
Reardon, Lambert, Sr.: 229, 238
Reardon, Lambert Jeffrey: 203, 230, 238, 248, 252, 255, 260, 263, 277, 283 f., 293
Reardon, Mrs. Lambert: 305
Recess Building: 214, 313
Reconstruction: 385–393, 400, 402
Rector, Bill Archie: 398
Rector, Elizabeth Conner: 248 n.
Rector, Frederick: 248 n.
Rector, Henry Massie: 240, 260 n., 385; picture, 344; U. S. marshal, 197; and Borland-Borden duel, 197; in legislature in 1848, 255, 257 f.; in 1854, 309 f.; surveyor general, 313; elected governor in 1860, 343–346, 360; as governor, 346 f., 349, 351, 352 f., 356, 357, 358, 359 f., 361, 362, 364, 365, 367, 368, 371–374, 380, 381; and Burgevin-Danley duel, 363 f.; 1862 campaign, 376-379
Rector, Stephen: 62
Rector, W.: 62
Rector, Wharton: 141, 205
Rector, William: 27
Red River Expedition: 390
Redditt and Pullen: 146
Reed, John H.: 127, 134, 136, 138 f., 142, 149, 190
Reider, Jacob: 305
Religious controversies: 90, 212, 235 f., 285
Remington, Stephen: 9 n.
Repatriation: 395, 398 f., 400 (see also Amnesty)
Republican Party: 323, 347, 385, 391, 392 (see also Radicals)
Repudiation: 346
Resaca de la Palma, battle of: 228, 235
Reyburn, William P.: 77, 91

Reynolds, Joseph J.: 391, 400
Richmond, Va.: 359, 370, 379, 393
Ringgold, John: 147, 329
Ringo, Daniel: 141
Rives, John C.: 230
Roane, Ewing H.: 229
Roane, John Selden: 226, 229, 235, 236
    ff., 261 ff., 290, 319, 345, 369, 371,
    372, 373
Roane, Mary Kimbrough Smith: 319
Roane, Samuel Calhoun: 20, 21, 50, 52,
    152–155, 229
Robins, John: 164, 172, 307
Rogers, A. A. C.: 389 f., 393
Rome, Ark.: 13
Rorer, David: 125
Ross, John M.: 261
Ross, Nathan: 325
Roulstone, George: 11 n.
Rouse, Lewis: 53–54 n.
Royston, Grandison D.: 55 n., 154, 258,
    361, 380, 384
Russell, William: 29, 36–39, 41, 42
Russellville, Ky.: 7
Rust, Albert: 188, 210, 212, 232, 308 f.,
    322, 329, 333, 345, 358, 369
Rutherford, Archibald Hamilton: 217,
    219 f., 221, 222, 223
Rutherford, Eloise Maria Beall: 176
Rutherford, Samuel Morton: 21, 111, 118,
    176, 180

Sag Harbor, N. Y.: 4
Sag Harbor, N. Y. *Suffolk Gazette:* 4, 18
Sag Nichts: 315
Sage of Monticello: 138 n.
St. Francis County, Ark.: 381
St. Francis River: 329, 367
St. Louis, Mo.: 339 f., 353, 355, 367, 369,
    397
St. Louis *Emigrant and General Adver-
    tiser:* 9 n.
St. Louis *Enquirer:* 9 n.
St. Louis *Globe-Democrat:* 9 n.
St. Louis *Missouri Democrat:* 387, 388
St. Louis *Missouri Gazette:* 8–9 n.
St. Louis *Republic:* 9 n.
St. Louis *Western Journal:* 9 n.
Scott, Allen M.: 137 f., 144
Scott, Andrew: 15, 37, 58, 59, 71, 86, 87,
    102 n.
Scott, Beauford P.: 144
Scott, Christopher C.: 344
Scott, George W.: 26, 59

Scott, John Rice Homer: 25
Scott, S. M.: 313
Scott, Winfield: 247 f., 295
Searcy, Ark.: 372, 374
Searcy, Richard: 33, 65, 86, 89
Sebastian, William King: 231, 250, 258,
    292, 297, 329, 334
Secession: sentiments in 1850, 274, 275,
    276, 279 f., 281; in 1860–1861, 348–
    351, 352 f.; secessionists in Conven-
    tion, 353, 357; from Confederacy,
    threatened, 373 f.
Selden, Joseph: 58, 71
Sevier, Ambrose Hundley: 59, 88, 89, 95,
    96, 98, 100, 101, 137, 138 n., 206,
    213, 229, 230, 231, 239 f., 247, 253
    f., 256 f., 273, 292; picture, 74; ar-
    rival in Arkansas, 27; Izard's friend,
    64; partnership with Oden, 60, 71 f.;
    and 1827 campaign, 71–79; duel with
    Newton, 80; elected to Congress in
    1827, 86; in 1829, 89; in 1831, 96;
    in 1833, 106 f.; in 1835, 127; said to
    control *Gazette,* 103; defended John-
    son, 106 f.; declined challenge from
    Cummins, 107; and statehood, 109 f.,
    114, 126, 133; and Pope-Woodruff
    rift, 114–119, 121 f.; and mail service,
    124 f.; and Dynasty, 129–132, 246;
    position in party, 140; elected to
    Senate in 1836, 141; appointed, 146;
    Weller's support of, 183, 185; bank
    scandals, 187 f., 206, 211; and sale of
    Gazette, 194; *Gazette* opposed, 196
    f.; and *Banner,* 196, 197, 230, 255;
    wife's death, 212 f.; and 1846 Senate
    election, 215 f., 222; in 1848 cam-
    paign, 240 f.; Senate election of 1848,
    248, 251 f., 253–259, 309, 317; and
    treaty with Mexico, 247 ff., 253, 254,
    257; death of, 261, 263
Sevier, Valentine: 278
Shaler, William: 9 n.
Shanks, Lewis: 225
Shaw, Henry F.: 307
Shaw, John M.: 299
Shields, Thomas: 335
Shiloh, Tenn.: 369
Shreveport, La.: 390
Simpson, —: 87
Slaughter gas works: 347
Slaughter, S.: 104
Slave Henry: 260 n.
Slaves: thefts of, 122 f.; as job competi-
    tion, 325; in nameplate, 272

Slavery: as political issue, 110, 126, 161 ff., 209, 268 f., 273, 276, 315, 316, 320, 321, 323, 337, 341, 346, 347, 348 f., 385 f., 387 f., 392; and free Negroes, 184, 278; and Knight, 273, 274

Sleight, Henry C.: 7

Smith, Bernard: 67

Smith, Edmund Kirby: 382, 390

Smith, Jefferson: 126, 134

Smith, Jefferson C.: 190

Smith, John: 83

Smith, Nathan D.: 69 n.

Smith, Samuel S.: 112

Smith, William Steuber: 89 n.

Smithson, Bryan H.: 176, 261 ff., 290 ff.

Snow, William D.: 392

South Carolina: 317, 351

Southern Literary and Advertising Agency: 286

Southern Telegraphic Associated Press: 366

Southwestern Journal of Education: 285 n.

Speer, John: 149

Spittal, —: 272

Spooner, Alden: 4, 56, 106

Spooner, George W.: 105 f.

Sprague, Alden: 265

State Bank: 141, 142, 150, 155 f., 167, 172, 173, 182, 187 f., 288 n., 346

State Historical Society: 383

Statehood: 109 f., 114, 126 f., 130, 132 ff., 136 f., 140, 141, 146, 215

Steamboat Arkansas: 327

Steamboat Big Rock: 298 n.

Steamboat Comet: 31

Steamboat Cotton Plant: 250

Steamboat Eagle: 44

Steamboat Fox: 318

Steamboat General Jackson: 7 n.

Steamboat Hallie: 298 n.

Steamboat Little Rock: 160

Steamboat Medium: 261

Steamboat Maumelle: 298 n.

Steamboat Neosho: 133

Steamboat S. H. Tucker, 353

Steck, Michael J.: 149

Steele and Lincoln: 121

Steele, Frederick: 371, 372, 384 f., 386, 387, 388, 389, 390, 391

Steele, John: 111 f., 113, 114, 115–118, 121, 122 f., 125, 152

Steele, Mary: 111, 115

Stephens, Alexander H.: 361

Sterne, Thomas: 186

Stevenson, William W.: 134, 193

Stillwell, Joseph: 26 f., 34

Stillwell, Joseph (II): 309, 331 f.

Stokes, Benjamin M.: 9 n.

Stone, Cornelius: 170, 177, 178

Strange, Tubal E.: 9 n.

Strong, William: 157, 330

Sullivan, C. L.: 164, 172

Superior Court: 15, 25, 27, 36, 37 f., 48, 50, 58, 71, 85, 98, 100, 114, 120

Surplus revenue, 1837: 150 f.

Sutton, William H.: 276 f.

Swamp Lands legislation: 253, 293, 326

Swords, T. and J.: 6

Swymmer, W. S.: 324

Tacabaya, battle of: 239, 241

Taylor, Charles Minor: 397

Taylor, John: 156 f.

Taylor, Zachary: 223, 239, 242, 245, 252, 253

Tebbetts, Jonas M.: 399

Telegraph: 266, 345, 352, 368, 369, 371, 397

Temperance reform: 304

Tennery, George F.: 9 n.

Tennessee: 11 n., 351

Terry, Francis Augustus Robinson: 331 ff., 333 f.

Terry's Ferry: 385

Texas: 9 n., 139, 201, 209, 213

Thirteenth Amendment: 392

Thomasson, Hugh F.: 322, 358

Thompson, Davis: 232

Thorn, Thomas: 164, 172, 272 n.

Thornhill, Joseph: 37, 55

Thornton, Abner E.: 267

"Tincartiana": 145

Toledo, José Alvarez de: 9 n.

Tollison, J. C. P.: 207

Tornado, The: 171

Totten, Benjamin C.: 309, 358

Totten, James: 352 f.

Towers, Lem: 289

Trans-Mississippi District and Department, C.S.A.: 367, 373 ff., 382, 390

Trapnall, Frederick W.: 202, 256, 301 f.

Trimble, William: 37, 50 ff., 58, 59

Trist, Nicholas P.: 247 f.

Trousdale, Bryson Blackburn: 279 n.

Trousdale, Cincinnatus: 280

Trousdale, Leonidas: 278 ff., 281, 284, 285

Trousdale, Susan Hicks Harrington: 279 n.
Trousdale, Virginia Frances Joy: 285 n.
Trowbridge, Samuel G.: 186
Truslow, J. F.: 236
Tucker, Stephen S.: 178 ff., 180, 187, 195, 225, 228, 239
Tucker, Sterling Hartwell: 74, 304, 307
Tulip, Ark.: 213, 244
Tulip Female Seminary: 244
Tully, Lewis B.: 157 f., 203, 208
Turner, Jesse: 400
Tyler, John: 134, 170, 176, 178, 197

Unconditional Unionists: 349, 385
Underwood, Quincy K.: 233
United States Army: 367 f., 382, 384 f.
United States Arsenal (Little Rock): 251, 352 f., 362 n.
United States Court, Western District of Arkansas: 253 f.
University of North Carolina: 195, 198 n.

Van Buren, Ark.: 178, 322, 368
Van Buren, Martin: 71, 129, 130, 134, 143, 167 f., 176, 203
Van Buren *Western Frontier Whig:* 207 f.
Van Dorn, Earl: 367, 368, 369, 371, 372, 373, 375
Van Horne, Francis M.: 173, 186
Van Pelt, Henry: 3 f., 7, 11, 198 n.
Versailles, Ky.: 135, 145 f.
Vicksburg, Miss.: 380, 382, 384
Von Seckendorff, H.: 221 n.

Wait, William B.: 214, 273 n., 306
Walker, Alexander S.: 86, 139
Walker, David: 203, 205, 208, 257, 354, 355, 383
Walker, E. G.: 309
Walker, J. G.: 217
Wallace, Alfred: 212
Walton, Matt: 89 n.
Walworth, H. F.: 141
War of 1812: 6, 15
Warren, Edward A.: 301 f.
Washburn, Edward Payson: 296
Washington, Ark.: 143, 225, 226, 244, 384
Washington, D. C. *National Intelligencer:* 45, 136, 274, 276
Washington *South Arkansas Democrat:* 343

Washington *Telegraph:* 348, 361, 368, 369, 370, 376, 377, 379, 381, 382 f., 384, 389
Waters, Robert E.: 343
Watkins, George C.: 180, 294, 372, 376, 377, 383
Watkins, Henry: 89 n.
Watkins, Isaac: 37, 83
Watkins, Maria: 83
Watkins, W. W.: 358
Weaver, Samuel M.: 196
Webb, Albert W.: 245, 269
Webb, Samuel H.: 146
Weller, Cyrus W.: 183 f., 187, 190, 194, 195 f., 199 f., 203 f., 208, 223
Wells, O. and H.: 105
Wheeler, Amos: 35, 36, 37
Wheeler, John F.: 383
Wheeling, Va. *Times:* 325 n.
Whig party: 129, 130, 135, 137, 142, 143, 147, 151, 152–155, 157 f., 168–171, 178, 182 f., 185, 187 ff., 190–194, 195, 200, 203–209, 210, 221, 229, 232, 239, 242, 243, 246, 252 f., 256, 257 ff., 262 f., 266, 269, 281, 295, 296, 301 f., 309 f., 316, 317, 320, 337, 341
White County, Ark.: 242, 246, 247
White, Hager and Co.: 104, 144
White, Hugh Lawson: 134, 143
White, John T.: 307
White River: 123, 334
White River, Mouth of: 13, 63, 70, 81
White, Robert J. T.: 388
Whiteley, Lambert A.: 263 f., 281–284, 287 ff.
Whitmore, Ira B.: 186
Whittington, Hiram Abiff: 56, 71, 79, 105 f.
Wiley, E. W.: 286
Wilkins, John H.: 35
Williams, Barnett: 215, 219
Williamson, T. T.: 188
Wilson, Cyrus W.: 262 f.
Wilson, John: 151, 156
Wilson's Creek, Mo., battle of: 360
Wisconsin: 110
Witter, Daniel T.: 389
Woodlawn, Ark.: 390
Woodruff, Alden Mills: 225, 268, 284 f., 287, 298, 301, 399
Woodruff, Chester Ashley: 284 n.
Woodruff, Clementine Clay Sparks: 298 n.
Woodruff County, Ark.: 381
Woodruff, Eliza Sizer: 298 n.

Woodruff, Evelina Walton: 285 n., 389
Woodruff, George: 298 n.
Woodruff, George Brown: 4 n.
Woodruff, George Watkins: 285 n.
Woodruff, Hannah Clarke: 4
Woodruff, Harriet Maria: 285 n., 298 n., 389, 399
Woodruff, Jane Eliza Mills: 37, 83, 285 n.
Woodruff, Jane Georgine: 285 n.
Woodruff, Janie: 298 n.
Woodruff, Jehiel Hildreth: 4 n.
Woodruff, Lizzie Ashley: 285 n.
Woodruff, Maria Jane: 285 n.
Woodruff, Mary Eliza: 285 n.
Woodruff, Matthew Edmund: 4 n.
Woodruff, Nathaniel: 4
Woodruff, Nathaniel Milton: 4 n., 160
Woodruff, William: 298 n.
Woodruff, William Edward: 64, 83, 104, 105 n., 108, 118, 127, 137, 141 f., 163 f., 190, 197, 198, 202, 203 f., 225, 256, 301, 302, 307, 313, 314, 330, 366, 383, 402; pictures of, frontispiece, 10, 401; family, 4, 285 n.; marriage, 83; apprenticeship, 3, 4, 5, 6 f.; move westward, 3, 7–13; founding of Gazette, 8–13, 17 f., 19; rift with Crittenden, 22 f., 28 f., 35, 39 ff., 59 f.; partnership with Briggs, 25, 33 f.; other business interests, 35, 57 f., 72, 100, 103, 125, 158 ff., 297, 399; land speculation, 60, 89; move to Little Rock, 41 f.; engagement, 63; home at Arkansas Post, 17; at Little Rock, 43, 55 n., 72, 163, 214, 231; 1827 campaign and preceding controversy, 69 f., 71, 73–79; and Crittenden-Conway duel, 82; and Pope-Cocke duel, 95; and Pope-Noland duel, 96; and anti-gambling movement, 123 f.; postmaster, 100 f., 215, 218, 219, 223, 229; and municipal government, 100, 134; dispute with Menefee, 98 f.; and death of Garrett, 84, 91 f.; breach with Pope, 108 f., 114–119; and Pope-Fulton rift, 110 f.; and statehood, 109 f., 126; and digest of laws, 115–118; advocated lynching, 122 f.; dispute with Field, 114 f., 124 f.; and 1831 campaign, 97; and 1836 campaign, 128 f.; and Dynasty, 131 f.; partnership with Pew, 134; as "retired editor" (business manager), 135, 136, 139, 149; as state treasurer, and 1837 default, 132, 141 f., 149 ff., 154, 155, 159, 191, 192, 211 f., 218, 219, 233, 241; director Real Estate Bank, 155; retirement from Gazette in 1838, 159, 160, 161; and Cole's departure, 172 ff.; returned to Gazette in 1841, 180, 181; power in party, 140, 215; and 1842 campaign, 182 f., 185; hostility against, for sale of Gazette to Borden, 196, 218, 219 f.; and 1844 campaign, 206; and Ashley's political career, 217–223, 230; and Democrat, 220 f., 223, 225 f., 228 f., 230, 266; and 1848 campaign, 239–243; and death of Ashley, 250; and Borland-Sevier rivalry, 246 ff., 249, 250, 251 f., 254, 255, 256 f., 259, 261; and Danley's election as auditor, 259 ff.; bought Gazette in 1850, 269 f.; and 1851 campaign, 280 f.; and 1852 campaign, 290 f.; and Danley-Whiteley dispute, 281 f.; as proprietor Gazette and Democrat, 271, 274, 275 f., 278 f., 280, 281, 285 f., 287, 295; and True Democrat's name, 292, 293 f.; final retirement from Gazette, 297 f.; county named for, 381; in Civil War, 385, 389, 399
Woodruff, William Edward, Jr.: 284, 397, 401, 402
Woodruff, Willie: 298 n.
Woodward, John W.: 335 f., 364, 383
Wright, Silas: 138
Wyatt, Isham W.: 299

Yeiser, Daniel: 209
Yell, Archibald: 193, 196 f., 197, 210, 225, 240, 321; ambition to be governor, 130; elected to Congress in 1836, 137, 139, 141; re-election, 146 f.; not candidate in 1838, 157, 158; position in party, 140; elected governor, 167, 168, 176; elected to Congress in 1844, 204 f., 208; resigned, 232; rivalry with Ashley, 205 f., 215–223, 231 f.; in Mexican War, 226, 232, 234 f.; rift with Borland, 230 f., 234 f., 241; death, 235
Yell, James: 321, 323, 356, 358, 359, 360
Yerkes, Reuben S.: 313, 326 f., 334, 343, 381, 383, 386, 389, 390 f.
Yonley, T. D. W.: 387, 391